GLOBAL PREDATOR

U.S. Wars for Empire

Stewart Halsey Ross

2011

GLOBAL PREDATOR

U.S. WARS FOR EMPIRE

Copyright 2009-2010 © by Stewart Halsey Ross - All Rights Reserved

Published by Progressive Press,

PO Box 126, Joshua Tree, Calif. 92252,

www.ProgressivePress.com

Release Sept. 11, 2011

ISBN 1-61577-461-0, EAN 978-1-61577-461-6

355 pages, with index and illustrations.

BISAC Subject Area Codes

HIS027110 HISTORY / Military / United States

POL031000 POLITICAL SCIENCE / Political Ideologies / Nationalism

POL045000 POLITICAL SCIENCE / Colonialism & Post-Colonialism

Global Predator is a damning account of the atrocities committed by invading US armed forces, from the 1846 war on Mexico to the recent wars on Iraq. In between are chapters on the Spanish and Philippines War, the World Wars, Korea, and Vietnam, plus appendices on other incursions. As he marshals the facts for a contrarian view of US history, author Stewart Halsey Ross is angered by a persistent pattern of brutality, jingoism and hypocrisy which he finds behind America's mask of "Manifest Destiny" — yet he notes the great reluctance of the American people to enter into five of these eight wars. Ross (d. 2010) was an expert on military affairs. His earlier book published by Progressive Press, *Propaganda for War*, tells how Woodrow Wilson and the British twisted the truth to get the US into the Great War.

Table of Contents

Chapter I: Preface 5
Chapter II: Introduction 9
Chapter III: The Mexican War 19
Chapter IV: The Spanish and Philippines Wars 31
Chapter V: The Great War 70
Chapter VI: World War II 105
Chapter VII: The Korean War 152
Chapter VIII: The Vietnam War 178
Chapter IX: The First Iraqi War 218
Chapter X: The Second Iraqi War 237
Chapter XI: 9/11 249
Chapter XII: Epilogue 288
Appendices 292
   1. A History of Interventions by U.S. Armed Forces in the Western Hemisphere, 1806-1933 292
   2. America's First Red Scare, 1917-1921 298
   3. Woodrow Wilson's *Aide-Memoire* to Allied Ambassadors Regarding U.S. Intervention in Russia, July 17, 1918 300
   4. Wake Island, 1895-1945 302
   5. The Military-Industrial Complex, January 17, 1961 303
   6. The U-2 Incident, May 1, 1960 304
   7. The Potsdam Declaration, July 26, 1945 306
   9. The Saga of the Banana, United Fruit Company, and U.S. Interventions in Latin America, 1890-1970 310
   10. Nuclear Weapons, 1945 On 313
   11. The B-2 Stealth Bomber, 1990 to Present 314
Bibliography 316
Acronyms and Abbreviations 344
Author Biography 347
Index 348

VOL. XLIX. No. 1257. PUCK BUILDING, New York, April 6th, 1901. PRICE TEN CENTS.

Puck

Entered at N. Y. P. O. as Second-class Mail Matter.

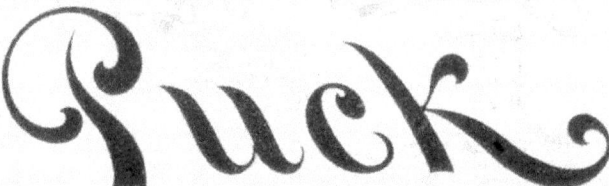

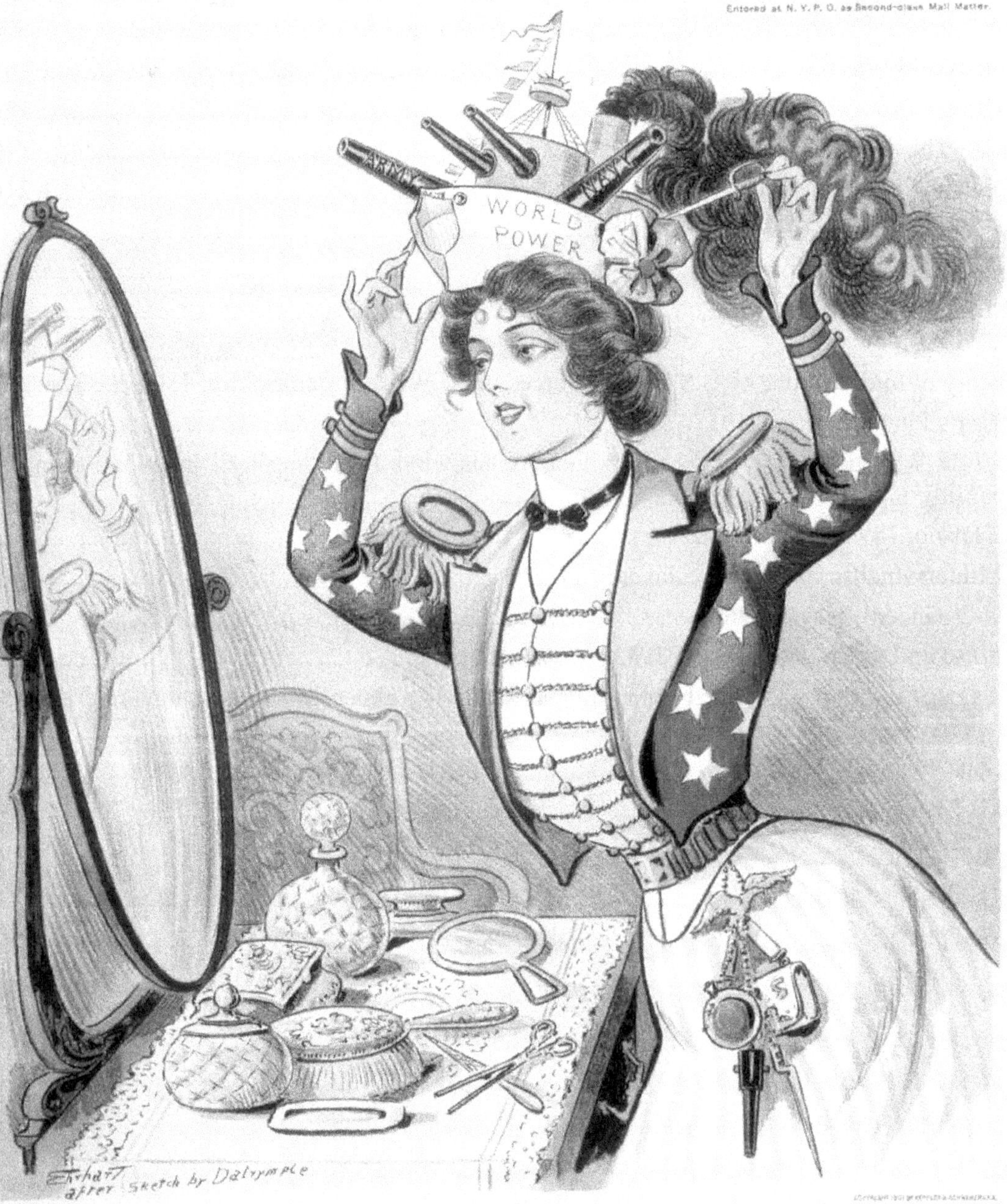

COLUMBIA'S EASTER BONNET.

Chapter I:
Preface

In 1817, America's minister in London, John Quincy Adams, reported that "the universal feeling of Europe in witnessing the gigantic growth of our population and power is that we shall, if united, become a very dangerous member of the society of nations. They therefore hoped what they confidentially expect, that we shall not long remain united."[1]

IN APRIL 2006, during an interview by a *Norwalk Hour* staff writer for my new book, *How Roosevelt Failed America in World War II*, he asked me to name those wars in the history of the United States in which America "justifiably sent soldiers abroad." After a brief pause, I told him I could not think of one. The Pearl Harbor strike in December 1941 by the Japanese, although permanently entrenched in U.S. folklore as a "sneak attack" by "treacherous Japs," comes closest but doesn't quite qualify. It was engineered by President Franklin D. Roosevelt to bring the United States into war with Nazi Germany through the "back door."[2] It was then that I decided to write this book.

When President George W. Bush announced the start of bombing in Afghanistan following the attacks of 9/11, he declaimed piously that "we are a peaceful nation." The record is not ambiguous: there is no evidence that we are peace-loving or ever have been.

> We shoved the Indians off their lands without a how-do-you-do; drove out the Dutch, British, French, and Spanish; fought Mexico and seized California with as little ceremony as the Russians grabbing the Baltic states; engaged in a savage civil war; fought in Cuba and the Philippines; staged our own 'revolution' in Hawaii against the native Queen; kept gunboats in China; and invented and used the great horror weapon, the nuclear bomb, in World War II [and in later wars, used such diabolical anti-personnel weapons as napalm, cluster bombs, and crop-destroying chemicals]. Through it all we have maintained a righteous air, contending that we have committed mayhem and felony with purest motives... Our violent spirit is evident to the tourist. Our parks are crammed with statues of men on horseback with upraised swords. Our newspapers are full of accounts of violence. Our television dramas—the popular culture of America—are filled with a fascinating ferocity. Our children play with toy soldiers, toy bombs, and toy guns...We worship our war heroes and elect them to the Presidency.[3]

Historian Glenn W. Price has written wryly:

> This is not a record which indicates a disinclination to resort to mass violence. Perhaps some nations of Western Christendom have been more aggressive, some less so; but it is quite impossible to make out the American experience as uniquely restrained in the use of force, or as resorting to force for defensive purposes only.[4]

"There were many [people] around the world who admired and celebrated the birth of a republic based on the principles of human equality and natural rights. But most of the world's governments were apprehensive. 'This federal republic is born a pigmy,' the Spanish minister in Paris remarked, but 'a day will come when it will be a giant, even a colossus.'"[5]

IF ONE SHOULD suggest that the United States, in its relentless drive for empire and global dominion, has continually waged preemptive and aggressive wars, particularly in the Western Hemisphere [see Appendix]; that the government's relentless propaganda apparatus has obfuscated and covered-up these wars in the guise of bringing "freedom" and "democracy" to supposedly subjugated peoples; that its military has waged unrestricted warfare against civilian populations, with all of the diabolical weapons at its command that have led to ghastly war crimes and to repeated and flagrant violations of international law and norms—you'd be labeled as a dangerous "peacenik," almost certainly a Socialist, or perhaps only as a self-delusional ignoramus. Don't dare mock the fear mongers' twin mantras, one going as far back as the Great War: "if we don't fight them over there, we'll have to fight them over here," and Lyndon Johnson's infamous "falling dominos" theory to justify his expansion of the war in Indochina. Further, your listeners likely wouldn't agree that America is an empire; however they might define the term. If you sum up and dare declare the United States a predator state—an outlaw country—you risk being snarled at: "If you don't like the United States, why don't you live elsewhere?"

America has increasingly flexed its muscles—military and economic, and less frequently, diplomatic—octopus-like around the globe. A culture of militarism and flag-waving patriotism has been foisted upon American society that paints all such U.S. "adventures" in bright red, white, and blue Day-Glo colors.

> *"I.F. Stone was one of the great journalists of our time. He would be invited to speak to students in journalism schools who were going to be reporters. 'Among all the things I'm going to tell you today about being a journalist, all you have to remember is two words: governments lie.' It's very important to know that. Otherwise we are victims of whatever the authorities say."*[6]

THE PICTURE at the start of the 21st century is a gloomy one. The United States is in the seventh year of a winless guerilla- and civil-war in Iraq, whose infrastructure the U.S. Air Force bombed into rubble in the First Iraq War of 1991, and ravaged again in 2003 at the start of the Second Iraq War. The number of Iraqi civilian deaths, to date and counting, is variously estimated at over 200,000 and the wounded in excess of 500,000. By contrast, less than 4,300 uniformed Americans have died there; some 140,000 still remain on duty there.

The despised occupiers lose their legs and arms and eyes, when they are not blown to smithereens by roadside bombs. The war in Afghanistan is no longer being touted by the Pentagon as a "mission accomplished." New President Barack Obama has told Americans that Afghanistan is now the country's "war of choice" and in February 2009, told the American people he was sending 17,000 additional U.S. troops to that troubled country. The phony "war on terror," the conflict that George W. Bush initiated as a pretext to keep his neoconservative agenda alive and well, and his party the majority in Congress, also promises to go on far into the future. The "terror" attacks on September 11, 2001—so useful to the Bush administration—are gradually being subjected to a rigorous critique. There is much evidence already that points to a monstrous conspiracy,[7] the biggest since Pearl Harbor.

Then there is the host of manufactured "enemies" to be countered and their leaders demonized. In the near background stands the Communist People's Republic of China, the most powerful adversary of all—certain to challenge the U.S. for its rightful share of the world's oil—and likely to be supported by Russia if push comes to shove. As dangerous to the health of the United States over the short- and intermediate-run is the nearly universal hatred of the United States all over the world, by Muslims in particular, engendered by the arrogant actions of George W. Bush and his henchmen during the

Republican Party's eight-year control of the Congress. President Obama, elected in 2009 with majorities in both houses of the Congress, is earnestly trying to repair America's image in the world.

> *When New Yorker magazine correspondent Jonathan Schell was touring Quang Ngai Province [Vietnam] in the summer of 1967, a GI who was driving him around in a jeep suddenly turned to him and said: "You wouldn't believe the things that go on in this war." "What things?" Schell asked. "You wouldn't believe it." "What kind of things, then?" "You wouldn't believe it, so I'm not going to tell you," the GI said, shaking his head "No. No one's ever going to find out about some things, and after this war is over, and we've all gone home, no one is ever going to know."*[8]

Casting its shadow over the nation like a monstrous flying raptor from pre-history is an all-powerful military-industrial complex that dictates its insatiable needs to a subservient Congress, and a compliant media that falls into lock-step whenever the White House announces a new war.

Lastly, there is another monster that intrudes on the nation's psyche: all-pervasive government propaganda that continuously taints and obfuscates the truth.[9] One can only wonder what a sweet world it would be if government leaders told the truth.

"Patriotism is the last refuge of a scoundrel."

—James Boswell, 1775

I MAKE NO PRETENSE TO IMPARTIALITY, as the reader likely has already concluded. I have been strongly influenced by the against-the-grain views of the giants of revisionist scholarship of the recent past: Harry Elmer Barnes, Sidney Bradshaw Fay, Charles Callan Tansill, C. Hartley Grattan, and Charles Austin Beard, among others. I walk proudly to their cadence. My selection of supporting information, my emphases, and my analyses are colored by my skepticism, even cynicism, regarding government "information." I feel strongly that the writer of history owes his or her readers a frank point of view, rather than a concealed bias in the guise of unattainable objectivity.

In an increasingly dangerous world, it is more than ever a necessity for candid analyses of America's aggressive foreign policies, and of the government's deceitful explanations of the costly wars that have followed. Those who share the author's reasoned hostility to U.S. militarism and misguided foreign policies will find this book a needed compilation and a frank overview.

Stewart Halsey Ross

Norwalk, Connecticut

May 2009

Notes

[1] Robert Kagan, *Dangerous Nation* (Alfred A. Knopf, New York, 2006), p. 3.
[2] Robert B. Stinnett, *Day of Deceit: The Truth About FDR and Pearl Harbor* (Simon & Schuster, New York, 2000); Stewart Halsey Ross, *How Roosevelt Failed America in World War II* (McFarland & Company, Inc., Publishers, Jefferson NC, 2006), Charles Callan Tansill, *Back Door to War: The Roosevelt Foreign Policy—1933-1941* (Henry Regnery Company, Chicago, 1952).
[3] Tristram Coffin, The Passion of the Hawks: Militarism in Modern America (Macmillan Co., New York, 1964).

[4] Glenn W. Price, *Origins of the War with Mexico: The Polk-Stockton Intrigue* (University of Texas Press, Austin TX, 1967), p. 8.

[5] Kagan, p. 4.

[6] Howard Zinn, *Terrorism and War* (Seven Stories Press, New York, 2002), p. 63.

[7] See Chapter X.

[8] Seymour M. Hersh, *My Lai 4: A Report on the Massacre and Its Aftermath* (Random House, New York, 1970), p. 14-15.

[9] Sidney Rogerson has written in *Propaganda in the Next War* (Garland Publishing, Inc., New York, 1972), p. 8-9, that until the Great War of 1914, "propaganda had no other significance than that perpetuated in the Society for the Propagation of the Gospel, nor were there any self-styled propagandists other than the missionaries of the Church... the word was dragged from its academic obscurity and invested with a new meaning."

Chapter II:

Introduction

"We don't seek empires. We're not imperialistic. We never have been. I can't imagine why you'd even ask the question."

—Defense Secretary Donald Rumsfeld on April 28, 2003, when asked by an al-Jazeera correspondent if the Bush administration was "empire-building."

"By any historical definition, the United States is an empire. From the birth of the Republic in 1776 to the outbreak of World War II, the area under the domain of the United States increased from 400,000 square miles to 3,738,393 square miles, expanding to a continental domain of about 3,026,789 square miles and overseas possessions and territories of 711,604 square miles."[1]

ALMOST FROM ITS BIRTH, the United States has sought out other lands to add to its domain or to covertly control, whether by purchase, above-board diplomacy, or—most often—by skullduggery and preemptive war. As early as 1786 Thomas Jefferson declared:

> "Our confederacy must be viewed as the nest, from which all America, North and South, is to be peopled."[2]

As far as Jefferson was concerned, there were no boundaries to the colonizing capacity of the United States or to the will of the American people to extend the boundaries. In 1801, as president, he projected his long-range views:

> "...our present interests may restrain us within our limits; it is impossible not to look forward to distant times, when our rapid multiplication will expand it beyond those limits, and cover the whole northern if not the southern continent, with people speaking English."[3]

Jefferson supported his words with action. In 1803, he purchased the 820,000-square-mile Louisiana Territory from Napoleon, doubling the size of the thirteen colonies overnight. The cost of what has been called the Louisiana Purchase ever since was $15,000,000, or about 4 cents per acre. The giant territory contains all of present-day Arkansas, Iowa, Kansas, Missouri, Nebraska, and Oklahoma. It also includes most of South and North Dakota, part of Minnesota south of the Mississippi River, northeastern New Mexico, and portions of Texas, Montana, Wyoming, Louisiana, Colorado, plus the city of New Orleans.

Looking southward to the Spanish territory of the Floridas, James Madison, the next president, brazenly took part of West Florida in 1810 and swallowed up the remainder in 1812. That same year, Madison took America to war against Great Britain—the War of 1812—ostensibly in defense of neutral rights. His pretext was the Royal Navy's impressments of American sailors. Rather, his intent was to drive the British out of North America and the Spanish out of the rest of Florida. Historians generally agree today that the fundamental reasons for Madison's declaration of war against England were the southern states' desire for the Floridas, the northern and western states' land hunger, frontier anger against British support of the Indians from Canada, and Spain's inability to stop Indian raids out of the Floridas.

The war ended in a stalemate: the United States had been singularly unsuccessful in invading Canada, while Britain's retaliatory raids on U.S. soil, except for the burning of Washington, were also notable failures. Public opinion in the United States strongly favored peace, and British citizens at home remained oblivious to the war, being more concerned with the happenings in Europe. The peace Treaty of Ghent was signed on December 24, 1814. Only one of America's land-grabbing adventures in years to come would end up *status quo ante bellum*. On March 1, 1815, Napoleon escaped from exile in Elba, rekindling the wars in Europe and forcing the British to withdraw their troops from North America.

In 1819, President James Monroe completed the takeover of East Florida, the present-day state of Florida, and five years later, in his annual message to Congress, he warned the European colonial powers to stay out of the Caribbean region and Central America. The edict erected virtual "no trespassing" and "private property" signs all across Latin America. Monroe's caveat was later transformed into one of the cardinal principles of U.S. foreign policy, the Monroe Doctrine.[4]

Texas, formerly part of Mexico, was annexed in 1845, the same year President James K. Polk's transparently preemptive war with Mexico was begun. It ended two years later with a "victor's" treaty in which the United States extended U.S. territory to the Pacific coast by gobbling up nearly half of Mexico's lands to its north. While Americans have forgotten the Mexican War, present-day Mexicans have not.

To the south, ninety miles off the tip of Florida, lay the island of Cuba. Jefferson had considered appropriating it as early as 1808, and John Quincy Adams had later on likened it to an apple tree whose fruit would ultimately ripen and fall. By mid-century, Cuba had "ripened," but had not as yet dropped to the ground. U.S. envoys to Europe decided to "shake the tree" to speed up the process by offering to buy it from Spain. When Spain refused, the unabashed Ostend Manifesto was announced which proclaimed the right of the United States to seize the island. Such a high-handed expansionist project was never realized at that time because it was advocated by southern slaveholders looking for further lands in which to plant their "peculiar institution." The schism between the North and the South was already taking shape, and would come to full flower in 1861.

In 1846, J. B. D. DeBow, a native of South Carolina moved to New Orleans and founded a monthly paper that bore his name. Modesty was not one of his virtues and in 1850, after the United States had annexed nearly all of the northern territories of Mexico, he declared famously:

> We have a destiny to perform, a 'manifest destiny' over all Mexico, over South America, over the West Indies and Canada. The Sandwich Islands [Hawaii] are as necessary to our western commerce as the isles of the gulf are to our eastern commerce. The gates of the Chinese empire must be thrown down by the men from the Sacramento and the Oregon, and the haughty Japanese tramplers upon the cross be enlightened in the doctrines of republicanism and the ballot box. The eagle of the republic shall poise itself over the field of Waterloo, after tracing its flight among the gorges of the Himalaya or the Ural mountains, and a successor of Washington ascend the chair of universal empire![5]

The "War Between the States" had barely ended before America resumed its southward push into the Caribbean.[6] General Nathan Banks, chairman of the House Committee on Foreign Affairs, worked diligently for annexations of the Danish West Indies, Haiti, and Santo Domingo. He declared that he wanted to identify his name with the acquisition of the Gulf of Mexico as "a Sea of the United States." When in 1868 an insurrection broke out in Cuba, Banks tried unsuccessfully to arouse popular passions as the ideal excuse for a war like Polk's.

II. Introduction

The French engineer Ferdinand de Lesseps, who built the Suez Canal, had plans to construct an isthmian canal in Central America using private capital. But President Rutherford Hayes took the position that any such canal would be "virtually a part of the coastline of the United States," and for that reason it must be owned and controlled by the United States. In the event, de Lesseps failed mightily, not only to gain the support of American private capital but to build the canal. The U.S. took over and completed the job; and the Panama Canal opened for traffic in 1914.

Following the War Between the States and the start of the Spanish-Philippines War in 1898, U.S. productivity—both agricultural and industrial—grew at a stunning pace, matching the nation's ravenous appetite for lands to conquer.

> American wheat production increased by 256 percent, corn by 22 percent, refined sugar by 460 percent, coal by 800 percent, steel rails by 523 percent, and the miles of railway track in operation by 567 percent. Production of crude petroleum rose from about 3,000,000 barrels in 1865 to over 55,000,000 barrels in 1898 and that of steel ingots and castings from less than 20,000 tons to 9,000,000 tons.[8]

Secretary of State William H. Seward was called by historian Richard W. Van Alstyne,

> …the central figure of nineteenth-century American imperialism. He understood the nature and the directions which American expansion historically strove to follow—the effort to absorb British North America... the drive southward into the Caribbean; and the trans-Pacific thrust into northeast Asia. With the suppression of the Southern rebellion in 1865, Seward acted adroitly to set these forces again in motion.[7]

In 1867, Seward took advantage of Russia's offer to sell Alaska. Russia had previously offered to sell Alaska in 1859, believing the expanded presence of the U.S. would counter the designs of Russia's greatest rival in the Pacific: Great Britain.

While the $7.2 million purchase price was derided by many as "Seward's Folly," a major gold deposit was discovered in the Yukon in 1896 and Alaska became the gateway to the Klondike gold fields. This silenced all detractors. For three decades after its purchase, the United States paid little attention to Alaska, which was governed under military, naval, or Treasury Department rule; at times it was under no visible rule at all. The strategic importance of Alaska was finally recognized in World War II and Alaska at last became a state—the 49th—on January 3, 1959. Alaska's 63,000 square miles made it by far the largest in the Union.

Seward lost no time in turning his attention toward Asia, seeking to annex Hawaii, which had been "Americanized" for years by U.S. whalers and missionaries. He had to settle for second best, temporarily—Midway Island. With the signing of a reciprocity treaty in 1875, Hawaii at last came under U.S. suzerainty and in 1887 the Hawaiian government agreed to hand over Pearl Harbor to the U.S. as a naval base and coaling station.

The rest of the Hawaiian Islands fell to the United States in 1893, with the overthrow of Hawaii's monarchy through a revolution fomented by American sugar planters and the deposition of Queen Liliuokalani. This was the same "revolution" model used by the Americans in the 1846 coup over California. By making the islands part of the United States, the growers would be able to ship their sugar to markets on the mainland without paying import duties. President William McKinley would state that annexing Hawaii was "the inevitable consequence" of 75 years of American expansion into the Pacific. This first "military adventure," Stephen Kinzer wrote:

"... was a tentative, awkward piece of work, a *cultural* tragedy staged as comic opera. It was not a military operation, but without the landing of American troops, it probably would not have succeeded."[9]

In 1895, Richard Olney, President Grover Cleveland's pugnacious Secretary of State, took a belligerent stand against the English over a dispute on Venezuela boundaries with British Guiana. Olney insisted that the United States was sovereign on the continent, and "its fiat is law upon the subjects to which it confines its interposition." In plain English, Olney was asserting the right of unlimited intervention by the United States in any issues that even remotely impacted the U.S. The crisis ended amicably a year later. But the near-clash was a clear reminder to those European powers which had discounted the Monroe Doctrine that meddling in Latin America henceforth would be at their peril.

Henry Cabot Lodge, the powerful chairman of the Senate Foreign Relations Committee and another articulate voice of U.S. imperialism, was not to be outdone. He declared that the United States should annex Canada, and the Isthmus Canal, too, when it was built. As for Cuba and territories east, Lodge was not reticent:

> We should have among those islands at least one strong naval station, and when the Nicaraguan canal is built, the island of Cuba... will become to us a necessity. Almighty God has marked us as His chosen people, henceforth to lead in the regeneration of the world... Our largest trade henceforth must be with Asia... The Pacific is our ocean... China is our natural customer... The power that rules the Pacific is the power that rules the world. And that power is and will forever be the American Republic.[10]

In 1898, a small American naval squadron squared off against warships of Kaiser Wilhelm II's *Hochseeflotte* in the tiny group of Samoan Islands of the far South Pacific. No cannons were fired, but bold headlines in jingo U.S. newspapers hinted at war. Cooler heads prevailed, however, and at a follow-on Congress of Berlin to ease tensions; the United States, Germany, and Great Britain divided up the imperialist spoils, each annexing one of the main islands.

The nation's next imperial stride took place that same year. The Spanish and Philippines Wars showed the world a new face of America—a globally ambitious one—willing and able to flaunt its powerful navy and send its troops in large numbers halfway around the world. It ushered in a long era during which the United States greedily intervened militarily in foreign governments, not merely by influencing or intimidating them, but by overthrowing them. These intrusions were euphemistically labeled "regime change." Each time the U.S. intervened, the Defense Department's monstrous propaganda apparatus shifted into high gear, defending its aggressive actions to its own citizens with the rhetoric of "national security"—and promising "freedom" and "democracy" for those who had been invaded.

WHEN PRESIDENT WILLIAM MCKINLEY took the United States to war against Spain in 1898, his actions were supported by a jingo press in New York City whose day-after-day propaganda convinced Americans that the intervention was on humanitarian grounds. The subsequent 100-day war in Cuba, with few American battle casualties (but many deaths from yellow fever, never reported by the press) was extremely popular at home. America's navy quickly won two well-publicized naval battles with overmatched Spanish fleets. The follow-on war in the Philippines—not an *insurrection* as the newspapers called it—was less popular. It lasted more than three years with Filipino civilian and insurgent deaths later estimated at over 200,000.

Racial fears of dark-skinned populations in the Philippines and Caribbean becoming U.S. citizens tamped down enthusiasm for further outright annexations. Senator Carl Schurz spoke for many when he pointed out that if more former colonies were acquired it meant statehood that would contaminate America:

> Imagine what that would mean... fancy the Senators and Representatives of ten or twelve millions of tropical people, people of the Latin race mixed with Indian and African blood... fancy them sitting in the Halls of Congress, throwing the weight of their intelligence, their morality, their political notions and habits, their prejudices and passions, into the scale of the destinies of this Republic... Tell me, does not your imagination recoil from the picture?[11]

> *"So much of the American tradition of war—savage, total, racist—was inherited from the Indian Wars, then given ideological meaning through Manifest Destiny and the Monroe Doctrine. It was a tradition that generally allowed for merciless attacks on civilian populations. The legacy was continued during wars with Mexico and Spain, turning outward with colonial expansion in the twentieth century. Not surprisingly, the U.S. has consistently rejected international treaties and protocols for protecting civilians against the horrors of war."*[12]

In the years following, "banana imperialism" [See Appendix] under the administrations of Woodrow Wilson, Warren Harding, and Calvin Coolidge, corralled nearly the whole Caribbean area, though none of the countries was formally annexed. By then, America had built a modest-sized empire, not nearly on a par with those of Great Britain or even France. World War II would change all that.

FOLLOWING THE SPANISH WAR, America granted self-government to the Cubans—up to a point. An amendment to the new Cuba constitution in 1903 by Senator Orville Hitchcock Platt—the Platt Amendment—pompously gave the United States:

> "The right to intervene for the preservation of Cuban independence, and the maintenance of a government adequate for the protection of life, property and individual liberty."[13]

The United States also expropriated a tiny sliver of land at Guantanamo Bay on Cuba's southeastern coast, ostensibly to "guard" the Panama Canal. "Gitmo" a hundred years later was converted into an extra-territorial prison to house so-called "detainees" from the Iraqi and Afghanistani wars. As "detainees" rather than "prisoners-of-war" they had no protection under the Geneva protocols. Indeed, these detainees were subjected to torture, including the dread "water torture," ostensibly to pry out useful information. In the 2008 presidential election, the subject of American torture became a campaign issue.

When Vice President Theodore Roosevelt was sworn in as president following the assassination of McKinley in September 1901, he ushered in seven years of a bold imperialistic U.S. foreign policy. In his State of the Union message to Congress in 1904, he introduced what came to be called "the Roosevelt Corollary" to the Monroe Doctrine. It was an arrogant declaration to the world, albeit a confusing one, of a new colossus on the march to empire and world dominion:

> Chronic wrongdoing, or an impotence which results in a general loosening of the ties of civilized society, may in America as, elsewhere, ultimately require intervention by some civilized nation, and in the Western Hemisphere the adherence of the United States to the Monroe Doctrine may force the United States, however reluctantly, in flagrant cases of such wrongdoing or impotence, to the exercise of an international police power.[14]

In 1903, the U.S. fomented a revolution in the Panama Department of Colombia that led to the establishment of a new nation that would be an American doormat: the Republic of Panama. The U.S. sent a gunboat to prevent Colombia from sending military forces to put down the artificial insurgency and immediately recognized the new government by sending in troops to protect its "new interests." At the end of the year, Phillipe Bunau-Varilla, a French citizen not authorized to sign treaties without approval of the Panamanians, nevertheless signed the Hay-Bunai-Varilla Treaty which granted the U.S. rights to a ten-mile-wide strip of land running from the Atlantic to the Pacific coast. It also gave the U.S. the right to build and administer—in perpetuity—the Panama Canal. T.R. was not bashful. To anyone who asked him, he said: "I took the Canal and let Congress debate."

The Panama Canal takeover was the first of some sixty armed interventions in the first thirty years of the 20th century. Here is a sampling: Cuba, 1898-1902; Cuba turned into a "protectorate" under the Platt Amendment, 1901; Dominican Republic, 1905-1941, financial supervision, with troops sent in 1913 and 1917-1924; Haiti, 1914-1941, military occupation to "restore order," with Marines shooting over 2,000 Haitians who resisted "pacification"; Nicaragua, 1909-1910 and 1911-1925, financial supervision and large-scale military operations in 1927—plus Coolidge's "private war" and occupation until 1933; Mexico, 1914, bombardment and capture of Veracruz.[15]

The model for American empire-builders was Great Britain. The British Empire was the largest the world had ever seen, bigger even than the Roman Empire of antiquity. It consisted of some 12,000,000 square miles of territory and close to a quarter of the population of the earth. Indeed, "the sun never set" on the British Empire as the globe rotated. At a time when navies were the primary war weapon, its Royal Navy was equal in numbers to the next two largest fleets combined. Britain had a network of naval bases for coaling and cable stations for rapid communications that girdled the globe; its merchant marine was the world's largest by far, and the financial services of the City of London made Britain the biggest investor, banker, insurer, and commodity broker. The roaring multitudes in London during Queen Victoria's Diamond Jubilee celebration in 1897 had much reason to cheer their empress.

In April 1917, Woodrow Wilson took a mostly disinterested nation, but one that had been brainwashed by Great Britain's flood of anti-German propaganda, into the first European war in a century. America emerged one of the victors, but the Congress refused to sign the peace treaty and rejected the League of Nations championed by its own president.

While it would take World War II to finally topple the British off their pedestal as principal global empire and imperialist, the slaughter of 700,000 (plus nearly 2,000,000 wounded) of their youth in the trenches of France was disastrous. Writing candidly in his 1920 epic *Now It Can Be Told*, Philip Gibbs—the noted British journalist later knighted for his contributions to the British Empire—foresaw "ruin, immense, engulfing, annihilating to our strength as a nation and as an empire:"

> The nation is in great peril after this war, and that peril will not pass in our lifetime except by heroic remedies. We won victory in the field at the cost of our own ruin. We smashed Germany and Austria and Turkey, but the structure of our own wealth and industry was shattered, and the very foundations of our power were shaken and sapped.[17]

In fact, Gibbs, for all his perspicacity, did not realize the full extent of the terrible losses of British soldiers—that their wanton deaths spelled the beginning of the end of the British Empire. The generals in France did not know this, nor did the diplomats in London.

Right up to the Japanese attack on Pearl Harbor in December 1941, Americans remained overwhelmingly noninterventionist. It took that attack to give a conniving Franklin D. Roosevelt the war he sought with Nazi Germany. Part of FDR's package was cruel combat with Japan in the Pacific, ending with the "unleashing of the atom", an act that has threatened global Armageddon ever since.

Were these two wars truly "the war to end wars" and the "good war", as proclaimed in the United States? Or were they geopolitical conflicts among empires and would-be-empires, as more and more historians postulate? Wasn't it strange that the "bad guys" both times were the Germans?

> *... The United States in the course of their short but highly imperialistic history had constantly proclaimed the highest virtue while as constantly violating their professions and resorting to the grossest materialism. They observed that all Americans like to feel in terms of Thomas Jefferson but to act in terms of Alexander Hamilton. They observed that such principles as the equality of man were not applied to the yellow man or to the black or brown-skinned. They observed that the doctrine of self-determination had not been extended either to the Red Indians or even to the Southern States. They were apt to examine "American principles and American tendencies" not in terms of the Philadelphia declaration but in terms of the Mexican War, of Louisiana, of those innumerable treaties with the Indians which had been violated shamelessly before the ink was dry. They observed that, almost within living memory, the great American Empire had been won by ruthless force.*[18]

In 1934, well-publicized congressional hearings probed the role of American arms manufacturers in consort with their European brethren to bring on the Great War. Had these rich and influential companies been involved in an arms race that was a root cause of the Great War? Readers of the best-seller *Merchants of Death* had no doubts. In fact, most modern historians, not only revisionists, have concluded that it was a colossal mistake for the United States to have joined the Allied powers in 1917, even as an "associate power" as Woodrow Wilson insisted. If America had stayed genuinely neutral, Germany, as almost certainly the victor, would have forced an early end to the war. Further, that outcome—according to these same historians—would not necessarily have been bad. Germany would have become middle-Europe's acknowledged hegemon, a position she regained by the early 1930s and the 1950s, respectively, despite being on the losing side of both World Wars. Not inconsequently, Adolf Hitler, who rose to power because of the inequities of the Versailles Treaty, would have remained an unimportant painter of buildings and scenery.

AMERICA'S GRASP for global dominance finally matched its reach in 1945. The United States emerged, alone among the great wartime powers, unscathed by destruction of its cities and industries—by default a true empire.

Subsequently, America tightened its hold on its acquisitions and engaged in a savage war in Korea (1950-1953) and an even-more-brutal conflict in Indochina (1965-1975). The Korean War ended in an unsatisfactory stalemate for the United States, and the "10,000 day" war in Vietnam saw America's expensive and vaunted military withdraw from Indochina with its tail between its legs.

During this period, oil emerged as the world's most important mineral. The United States, until then a net exporter able to rely on its own sources, became a net importer and sought to control oil reserves under lands in the Middle East. During those same postwar years, America jousted with the Soviet Union in what was called the "cold war." In the 1980s, driven by a mature and increasingly influential military-industrial complex—and with the slick vocal leadership of a handsome but not-too-bright movie-actor-president—America became the world's self-proclaimed policeman. When the Soviet Union dissolved in 1991, the coast was clear for the United States, backed by the most powerful armed forces the world had yet seen, to tighten its hold on its new empire and to round up more oil resources.

That same year, America peremptorily attacked Iraq, which sat atop the world's second-largest reserves of oil, destroying its infrastructure and killing ten of thousands of civilians in six weeks of round-the-clock bombings. Again, in 2003, the nation made preemptive war with Iraq. The second time around, America invaded—and remains in—Iraq as a hated occupier, seven years and counting.

> *"Almost every American overthrow of a foreign government has left in its wake a bitter residue of pain and anger. Some have led to the slaughter of innocents. Others have turned whole nations, and even whole regions of the world, into violent cauldrons of anti-American passion."*[19]

To hold together its far-flung empire, the United States has been increasingly willing to flirt with global Armageddon. As one example, in March of 1956, President Dwight D. Eisenhower gave the go-ahead to USAF overflights of the Soviet Arctic region with small squadrons of RB-47 reconnaissance bombers. These RB-47s could just as well have been carrying armed nuclear bombs as camera equipment as far as the Russians were concerned. Fortunately for mankind, the Soviet radar screen did not, at that time, extend into the Arctic. According to historian James Bamford, these provocative overflights, code-named *Homerun*, were "perhaps the most serious and risky espionage operations ever undertaken by the United States…Details are still [2000] wrapped in secrecy."[20]

One is entitled to ask: How many other such secret provocations have taken place in the last fifty years, which have brought America to the brink?

LIKE EVERYTHING ELSE ABOUT AMERICA, to Americans, her undoubted empire remains exceptional. Americans have been conditioned by incessant propaganda to think that these attitudes originate from the purest motives. But most political figures elsewhere in the world nearly unanimously ascribe this national self-portrait not to America's unique idealism but rather to its ongoing hubris and callous economic expansionism.

Noted British Historian Arnold J. Toynbee offered this cold-blooded assessment of the United States *more than thirty years ago:*

> To most Europeans, I guess, America now looks like the most dangerous country in the world. Since America is unquestionably the most powerful country, the transformation of America's image within the last thirty years is very frightening for Europeans. It is probably still more frightening for the great majority of the human race who are neither Europeans nor North Americans, but are Latin Americans, Asians and Africans. They, I imagine, feel more insecure than we feel. They feel, at any moment, America may intervene in their internal affairs, with the same appalling consequences as have followed from the American intervention in Southeast Asia.
>
> In today's climate, wherever there is trouble, violence, suffering, tragedy, the rest of us are now quick to suspect that the CIA—the new bogey man—had a hand in it. Our phobia about the CIA is, no doubt, as fantastically excessive as America's phobia about world communism used to be; but in this case, too, there is just enough convincing evidence to make the phobia genuine. In fact, the roles of the United States and Russia have been reversed in the eyes of much of the world. Today, America has become the nightmare.[21]

Under the cloak of national security, America's top elected officials and their appointees have embraced all of the trappings of a fascist state—a government answerable to no one, operating in secrecy, untrammeled by congressional oversight, and above the law. Atop this security-obsessed hierarchy reigns the president of the United States, put into office by free elections, but a dictator by any rational definition. Today, it is possible that the entire nation can be destroyed and most of its citizens killed by the unilateral action of a single individual and his cabal of elected or appointed ideologically like-minded associates.

> *Empires and civilizations rise and fall and they go through a series of stages in the process. We were already in our twilight phase when Ronald Reagan, with all the insight of an ostrich, declared it to be 'Morning in America'. Twenty-odd years later, under the 'boy emperor' George W. Bush... we have entered the Dark Ages in earnest, pursuing a short-sighted path that can only accelerate our decline.*[22]

Notes

[1] Richard J. Barnet, *Roots of War* (Penguin Books, Inc., Baltimore MD, 1973), p. 17.

[2] Richard W. Van Alstyne, *The Rising American Empire* (Blackwell and Mott, Ltd., New York, 1960), p. 81.

[3] Ibid. p. 87.

[4] The famous message of December 2, 1823, contained two widely separated passages that came to be known as the Monroe Doctrine. The first, aimed at Russia: "... the American continents, by the free and independent condition which they have assumed and maintain, are henceforth not to be considered as subjects for future colonization by any European power." The second referred to the Spanish colonies: "We owe it, therefore, in candor, and to the amicable relations existing between the United States and those powers, to declare that we should consider any attempt on their part to extend their political system to any portion of this hemisphere as dangerous to our peace and safety. With the existing colonies and dependencies of any European power we have not interfered and shall not interfere. But with the governments who have declared their independence and maintained it, and whose independence we have, on great consideration and just principles acknowledged, we could not view any interposition for the purpose of oppressing them, or controlling in any other manner their destiny, by any European power in any other light than saw the manifestation of an unfriendly disposition towards the United States." Dexter Perkins, *Hands Off: A History of the Monroe Doctrine* (Little Brown and Company, Boston, 1945), p. 28.

[5] Robert H. Ferrell, *American Diplomacy: A History* (W.W. Norton & Company, Inc. New York, 1969), p. 61. The phrase "Manifest Destiny" was also used by John L. O'Sullivan in an article he had written dealing with the annexation of Texas for the July-August 1845 edition of the *United States Magazine and Democratic Review*. It was adopted by those anxious to acquire the Oregon Territory, California, Mexican land in the Southwest, and the island of Cuba. By the start of the 20th century, those who had embraced Manifest Destiny were using Darwinist reasoning that it was the duty of the "fittest" to rule over the "less fit"; this included nations beyond the continental boundaries, beyond the Caribbean and into the far Pacific.

[6] For die-hard Southerners, it was "The War of Northern Aggression". Others have called it "The War for Southern Independence". For nearly every American today, it remains the Civil War.

[7] Van Alstyne, p. 152.

[8] Ibid. p. 163.

[9] Stephen Kinzer, *Overthrow: America's Century of Regime Change from Hawaii to Iraq* (Henry Holt and Company, LLC, New York, 2006), p. 2.

[10] Paul Kennedy, *The Rise and Fall of the Great Powers: Economic Change and Military from 1500 to 2000* (Random House, New York, 1987), p. 22.

[11] Ibid. p. 36.

[12] Van Alstyne, p. 165.

[13] Ibid. p. 187.

[14] George Black, *The Good Neighbor: How the United States Wrote the History of Central America and the Caribbean* (Pantheon Books, New York, 1988), p. 17.

[15] Ibid. p. 22.

[16] Carl Boggs, *Masters of War: Militarism and Blowback in the Era of American Empire* (Rutledge, New York, 2003), p. 207.

[17] Phillip Gibbs, *Now It Can Be Told*, 1920, *p.* 554.

[18] Michael Parenti, *The Anti-Communist Impulse* (Random House, New York, 1969), p. 114-115.

[19] Kinzer, p. 302.

[20] James Bamford, *Body of Secrets: Anatomy of the Ultra-Secret National Security Agency From the Cold War Through the Dawn of a New Century* (Doubleday, New York, 2001), p. 35.

[21] Arnold J. Toynbee, *Experiences* (Oxford University Press, London, 1985), p. 275.

[22] Morris Berman, *Dark Ages America: The Final Phase of Empire* (W.W. Norton & Company, New York, 2006), p..

Chapter III:

The Mexican War

South of the Rio Grande River, what to U.S. Americans is the Mexican War is known as the War of the Northern Invasion. Mexicans also call it:
La Intervencion Norteamericana (The North American Intervention),
La Invasion Estadounidense (The United States Invasion),
La Guerra de Defensa (The Defensive War), or
La Guerra del 47 (The War of 1847).

ON MAY 11, 1846, President James K. Polk sent a message to Congress stating arrogantly that Mexico had "invaded our territory and shed American blood upon the American soil" and asked for a declaration of war. Two days later, a joint session of Congress approved the declaration. Southern Democrats were strongly supportive because they expected "spoils" from the annexation of Mexican land which would permit the expansion of slavery.

The United States and Mexico were then, as today, sister republics in name only.[1] English was spoken in one country, Spanish in the other; one was Protestant, the other Roman Catholic. More importantly, one was structured by a strong central government and its population was vigorous and growing. The other, which had been colonized by a decaying empire:

> "...was torpid… and weakened by an oppressive clergy and upper class and by the immemorial Latin custom of celebrating today's revolution by toasting tomorrow's."[2]

The origins of the conflict could be dated earlier: to 1819, when the United States reluctantly conceded that the Louisiana Purchase did not extend to the Rio Grande, as France had claimed; or to 1821, when Mexico gained independence from Spain and took title to the lands of the Southwest; or to 1836, when the United States supported the Texas revolution.

It was a border dispute that finally triggered the provocation that Polk sought. Mexico maintained that the Nueces River, about 150 miles north of the Rio Grande, was its border with Texas. The United States maintained that the Rio Grande was the border, citing an 1836 treaty that Mexico had never ratified.

In 1845, Polk invoked the Monroe Doctrine in his first message to Congress. The president, with his eyes on Mexico's Oregon and California territories—and concerned that Great Britain also was interested in acquiring one or both of the same regions to add to its gigantic empire—announced that the principles applied "with greatly increased force" to the establishment of any new colony in North America.

THE FEAR THAT GREAT BRITAIN also coveted the western Mexican territories was a view commonly held by U.S. expansionists. This attitude was rooted in the actions of the British going back to Francis Drake. In 1579, on his famous circumnavigation of the world, Drake symbolically seized the California province from the Spanish, renaming it *Nova Albion*.

Other European monarchs also eyed the Spanish holdings in the new world. By 1819, the Czars and Empresses of Russia had moved their territories across the Bering Strait and had set up operations at Bodega Bay at the mouth of the Columbia River, where they took advantage of the benign climate and fertile soil to grow food for their northernmost outposts. It was said in some quarters that Czar Alexander I had offered the King of Spain a squadron of ships-of-the-line plus 20,000 soldiers to use in regaining territories that had revolted in South America, "solely to obtain in return, Upper and Lower California... Its object was not merely California but all America's Northwest Coast."[3]

There was also the unresolved question of title to the Oregon territory which had been a long standing dispute with Britain.

(Map from *The American Republic: Through Reconstruction* by Hofstadter et al, 1970)

President Polk had more to announce in his inaugural address than a simple reiteration of Monroe's warning to Europeans. The Democratic Party's platform of 1844 had committed Polk to acquire both Texas and Oregon territories, but Polk was determined to extend the United States even further: to the Pacific coast. Once president, he boldly declared to the world that the United States had a clear title to the Oregon territory and that Americans would soon establish it by settlement. As for the California territory and other Mexican lands, Polk thought it a better idea not to show his hand prematurely. He would start a preemptive war with Mexico at a time of his choosing.

Polk tried first to intimidate the Mexicans by a show of American military power along the disputed Texas-Mexican border. Then he tried bullying Mexico into selling California. He intrigued with exiled Mexican president Santa Anna to restore him to power in return for his help in gaining California. When these "diplomatic" dealings failed, Polk resorted to war.

In mid-January, 1846, he ordered General Zachary Taylor to march his army to Corpus Christi on the Rio Grande River, just across from the Mexican town of Matamoros. Taylor parked his troops there, built a makeshift fort, and waited for developments. As provocations, he drilled his soldiers in full view of the Mexicans and trained his easily visible cannons on the public square. Taylor sent cavalry patrols splashing up and down the north bank of the narrow and shallow river as further irritants.

On April 24, a more-than-1,000-strong Mexican cavalry detachment crossed paths with a much smaller U.S. cavalry unit. In the skirmish that followed, eleven American soldiers were killed. It later became known as the Thornton Affair after the slain U.S. officer who had been in command.

On May 3, Mexican artillery at Matamoros opened fire on Taylor's fort and U.S. cannons replied in kind. Over the next week, Mexican forces surrounded the fort and General Taylor responded with reinforcements to relieve the garrison. In turn, the Mexicans countered with their own reinforcements and the battle was joined. The American forces easily routed the overmatched Mexican forces. President Polk had his shooting war with Mexico.

To judge by the documents that survive, it was a popular war. Eager for the nation to grow, chauvinistic Americans looked upon negotiation as a sign of weakness, and they considered war an appropriate solution to conflict over territorial rights. When the call came for volunteers, recruiting officers had no trouble meeting their quotas.

There was also opposition to the war, particularly among the Whigs and abolitionists. Among the principal dissenters were former President John Quincy Adams and Congressman from Illinois Abraham Lincoln. "Show me the spot," Lincoln skeptically demanded in the House, "where the battle had taken place." American blood undeniably had been shed, but had it spilled on American soil? Lincoln further challenged Polk's conduct.

> ...it is a singular fact that if any one should declare the President sent the army into the midst of a settlement of Mexican people who had never submitted, by consent or force, to the authority of Texas or of the United States, and that there and thereby the first blood of war was shed, there is not one word in all the President has said which would either admit or deny the declaration. This strange omission it does seem to me could not have occurred but by design.[4]

Northern abolitionists attacked the war as an effort by slave-owners to expand slavery and thus ensure their ongoing influence in the federal government. As late as 1880 a Republican Congressional Committee referred to the war as:

> ...feculent, reeking corruption—one of the darkest scenes in our history, a war forced upon our and the Mexican people by the high-handed usurpations of President Polk in pursuit of territorial aggrandizement of the slave oligarchy.[5]

Five years later, former President Ulysses S. Grant, who had served as an army officer in Mexico, published his *Memoirs*.

> Generally, the officers of the army were indifferent whether the annexation was consummated or not; but not so all of them. For myself, I was bitterly opposed, and to this day regard the war as one of the most unjust ever waged by a stronger against a weaker nation. It was an instance of a republic following the bad example of European monarchies, in not considering justice in their desire to acquire additional territory.[6]

Grant also wrote that the war against Mexico had brought God's punishment on America in the shape of the nation's War Between the States:

> "The Southern rebellion was largely the outgrowth of the Mexican war. Nations, like individuals, are punished for their transgressions. We got our punishment in the most sanguinary and expensive war of modern times."[7]

> *Polk "was a man without wide culture or knowledge, wholly devoid of imagination, untraveled, unacquainted with either the Spanish or the Mexican character, and with little experience in the conduct of foreign affairs. He was not Polk the Mendacious [as called by some], but simply Polk the Mediocre."*[8]

Polk intended to make the most of his war and his aims were reflected in his initial moves. At the same time, he insisted on absolute authority over military affairs as commander-in-chief. He made no attempt to further strengthen Taylor's small army along the Rio Grande. Instead, he sent troops west to capture Santa Fe and the rest of the New Mexican territory and repeated his orders to the Pacific naval squadron to seize San Diego and San Francisco on the Pacific coast. The cunning president wanted the United States to have military control of both territories when Mexico sued for peace. He could then demand New Mexico and California as indemnity for American costs of the war. In the event, the Mexicans did not agree to Polk's outrageous peace terms until early 1848.

> *"No sooner had the war begun than it received a name indicating its alleged origin—President Polk's War. It was the dishonored successor of President Madison's War, unhonored predecessor of Mr. Lincoln's War, forerunner of the wars of Mr. McKinley, Mr. Wilson, Mr. Roosevelt, and Mr. Truman."*[9]

MEXICO, OUTNUMBERED 20 MILLION TO 7 MILLION, entered the war with a standing army of some 30,000 men. These troops were distributed throughout the country to preserve order and, in the larger cities, to act as bulwarks against revolutions that took place frequently. The British Ambassador to Mexico candidly said of the Mexican army in 1846:

> "It was perhaps the worst to be found in any part of the world: ignorant, incapable, and insubordinate... The ranks were filled chiefly by Indians and poor laborers who were marched along, handcuffed or roped in pairs, by press gangs, and who deserted at every opportunity."[10]

Prisoners convicted of minor offenses were added to this mélange when the need arose, effectively acting as a reserve force, albeit an unreliable one. Mexican cavalry, most of them lancers caparisoned in handsome uniforms, were mounted on their small Mexican horses which stood little chance against the more heavily mounted U.S. cavalry. Mexican artillery was also feeble; their French cannons were obsolete and the gunners had little technical training. Remarkably, Mexican soldiers usually fired their muskets from the hip to avoid the recoil to their shoulders, sacrificing whatever minimal accuracy their blunderbusses could achieve. A military attaché attending a review in 1842 noted that the white uniforms were well scrubbed and the muskets shone brightly. He also praised the regimental bands, which he said were generally the best parts of their organizations.

BATTLE OF CHURUBUSCO.

Historian Alfred Hoyt Bill wrote that the ability of these ragged and ill-equipped soldiers led by incompetent officers:

> "...to defeat any army that the United States could send against them, people in Mexico and people elsewhere ought to have known better... In an outburst of Latin enthusiasm the Spanish Minister at Washington said that there were no finer troops in the world than the Mexican."[11]

There was one bright hope that contributed to the Mexicans' fragile sense of security in the face of certain attack from the north: the misplaced belief that England and France would promptly intervene on Mexico's behalf because of concern over their own holdings in the region.[12] In the event, neither European power elected to intervene. Mexico was left on its own.

NORTH OF THE RIO GRANDE there was also a sense of military superiority, based more on fact than fancy. In this first American war of outright aggression, U.S. troops and their officers stereotyped the Mexicans as shiftless and lacking the will to fight; when hard-pressed, so the tale went, the Mexican soldiers would drop their obsolete muskets, raise both arms high, and yell *"amigo"* in unison. Many U.S. Army officers came from the ranks of the U.S. Military Academy at West Point, an unequalled training ground for professional soldiers then as now. As for weapons, the

United States boasted such manufacturers of high-quality firearms as Colt, Springfield, Winchester, and Remington. U.S. munitions-makers, headed by gunpowder-maker Du Pont, would easily meet the demands of even a prolonged war.

In Europe, however, the fighting qualities of Americans in their most recent war (War of 1812) were remembered as "frequently disgraceful." The London *Morning Herald* wildly prophesized that, in lieu of a navy, swift Mexican slave ships would become privateers and disrupt U.S. commerce. The *London Times* scoffed:

> "The invasion and conquest of a vast region by a state which is without an army and without credit is a novelty in the history of nations."[13]

Overlooked in the rosy glow of American overconfidence were significant realities. Waging an offensive war against Mexico involved the movement of troops over great distances, across barren mountains and wide-open prairies. Furthermore, there was the specter of yellow fever, considered by level-headed critics as "the most deadly and dependable of Mexican allies".[14]

FROM A MILITARY PERSPECTIVE, the war would prove to be a dazzling success for the United States. U.S. forces won a succession of battles in northern Mexico that fixed the southern border in America's favor once-and-for-all, occupied the essentially undefended Mexican provinces of New Mexico and California to the west, and boldly landed an army on the beaches at Vera Cruz on its way to capture the enemy's capital, Mexico City, to end the war.

The Mexican War spawned four presidents, three from the field and one from Polk's cabinet: General Zachary Taylor; Brigadier General Franklin Pierce who had served under Winfield Scott in Mexico; and James Buchanan, Secretary of State, who succeeded Pierce in 1856. Jefferson Davis was later president of the short-lived Confederate States of America.

Of all the military achievements in the conflict, none matched the remarkable amphibious landings by General Winfield Scott's troops on the beaches of Vera Cruz on their way to capture Mexico City. It was the first such joint Army/Navy action and set a pattern for future U.S. wars of conquest. This last campaign of the war required transporting some 10,000 troops by ship and landing them on beaches held by the enemy. The logistics were daunting.

The landings were not haphazard.[15] The Army built special "surf boats" to ferry troops onto the beaches from the big transports standing offshore. These landing craft came in three sizes, nested inside one other like Chinese boxes for convenient transport.

> "The largest were forty feet long, twelve feet wide, four feet deep... All were double-ended and almost flat bottomed, and they would take between fifty and eighty soldiers each, besides eight oarsmen."[16]

Naval gunfire covered the landings in to-be-classic amphibious-landing doctrine of the Pacific War a hundred years in the future. The heavy cannons later bombarded the city in support of the attackers moving inland from their beachheads, and during the siege.

III. The Mexican War

On March 9, 1847, the invading U.S. fleet moved to close off the beaches and the assault troops clambered down rope ladders from their transports into their bobbing landing craft. There was little opposition and by nightfall U.S. troops had established a defensible beachhead. It took a week to build up reserves of supplies before the troops moved onto the city of the True Cross and lay siege to the well-defended city. By noon of the 29th, the siege was over and General Scott at the head of his troops galloped in to ceremoniously plant the American flag over the city. Mexican resistance had been a token act and the invaders suffered less than a hundred casualties.

The westward route that Scott used on his way to the Mexican capitol was the same one used by Hernando Cortez and his *conquistadores* three centuries earlier. After marching only a few miles inland, the Americans were surprised to discover they were tramping on Mexico's National Highway, a paved and graded road in excellent condition built by Cortez and used every day since.

In mid-August, the U.S. Army arrived at the outskirts of Mexico City, a city of some 200,000 at the time. Located at an altitude of about 7,500 feet in the center of a huge ancient volcanic crater—surrounded by large lakes and craggy mountains—the city was an ideal defensive bastion. It took a month of sometimes-intense fighting before the American flag flew over the city. On September 14, a delegation from the city approached Scott's headquarters and under a flag of truce surrendered the city.

IN TERMS OF ACQUISITION OF TERRITORY, the one-sided conflict was an even more spectacular triumph. In the Treaty of Guadalupe Hidalgo that ended the war, signed by both parties on February 2, 1848, the intent was to reestablish "amity between the two countries," and to insure "concord, harmony and mutual confidence." Nevertheless, by any objective standard, it was a cruel victor's peace: Mexico was forced to cede enormous territories to the United States. It was called the Mexican Cession in the United States in which the Mexican territories of *Alta California* and *Santa Fe de Nuevo Mexico* were surrendered to the U.S.

The United States gained about 40% of Mexico's territory: New Mexico (which later became the states of New Mexico, Nevada, Utah, and Arizona plus a small corner of present-day Wyoming and the western and southern portions of Colorado) and Upper California (which later became the state of California). By these acquisitions and with the earlier annexation of the Texas Republic, the United States could claim that it had grown by more than one million square miles of territory; in total its borders enclosed an expanse of no less than ten degrees of latitude. The country had gained an unbroken coast-to-coast vista, overnight making the United States into a Pacific power, with important implications for the international community. The fact that the U.S. paid Mexico $15 million dollars after it was all over—'conscience money', some called it—

> "...seemed to confirm the ugliest charges of those who had denounced the war as a cynical, calculated despoiling of the Mexican state, a greedy land-grab from a neighbor too weak to defend itself."[17]

Five thousand U.S. soldiers—one in every five—died during the seventeen months of armed conflict, most from disease. The Mexican toll was far higher: some 25,000 died and many times that number were wounded and maimed.

> *The editor of Scientific American at the time lauded the expansion into Mexico as a triumph of American "mechanical genius": "We hold the keys of the Atlantic on the east and the Pacific on the far distant west. Our navies sweep the Gulf of Mexico and our armies occupy the land of the ancient Aztecs...Every American must feel a flow of enthusiasm in his heart as he thinks of his country's greatness, her might and her power."*[18]

IN HIS SECOND ANNUAL ADDRESS to the Congress on December 7, 1847, in the midst of the war, President Polk employed much of the same disingenuous rhetoric that that would find favor among speechwriters and their presidents in the future.

> Though the United States were [sic] the aggrieved nation, Mexico commenced the war, and we were compelled in self-defense to repel the invader and to vindicate the national honor and interests by prosecuting it with vigor until we could obtain a just and honorable peace.[19]

If there remained any Americans who were still uncertain of their nation's destiny, Polk set their minds at ease. He ended his address by stating that the U.S. government was "the most admirable and wisest system of well-organized self-government among men ever devised by human minds."[20] This transparent chauvinism bordering on racism would become the nation's stock-in-trade in all its future wars.

> *A French minister wrote in 1846 of American foreign policy that of the four great powers of the world at the time—France, Great Britain, Russia and the United States—only the U.S. was aggressively expanding. What the Frenchman and his fellow Europeans couldn't abide was the newly minted Monroe Doctrine that covered territory encompassing a hemisphere.*

Historian Robert H. Ferrell wrote that after Mexico had ratified the peace treaty on March 10, 1848, showman Polk waited four months before proclaiming the treaty "in effect"–on the anniversary of American independence, July 4, 1848:

> By this stroke of war, following upon the stroke of diplomacy which had gained Texas in 1845, the United States had added altogether—including Texas—1,200,000 square miles to its domain, an increase of more than sixty-six percent.[21]

Ferrell pointed out the obvious:

No American today [1959] would like to give up the territories secured from Mexico. Those expanses so varied in their riches gave us first gold, then oil, now uranium, and have increased enormously the power of the United States... If the nation had stopped at the Sabine River, the American people might today find their personal and public circumstances altogether unenviable.[22]

Ferrell closed his introspection:

Americans may as well admit that in 1846-1848 they fought a war of aggression against Mexico. Such a confession is discomfiting to make in the middle of the aggression-ridden twentieth [and 21st] century, but the facts of the case substantiate it.[23]

ONE HUNDRED FIFTY YEARS LATER, at raucous demonstrations in cities across the United States, particularly in the southwest where their numbers have become significant, Mexican-Americans—the newest American hyphenates—loudly call for better treatment of their kind, for "amnesty" for the millions of illegal Mexicans in the United States, and for "open borders." They proudly fly the flag of Mexico when they parade. They speak Spanish at home, to their numerous trailing toddlers in supermarkets, and to their compatriots everywhere. They have their own Spanish-speaking television and radio stations, their own newspapers, their own restaurants, their own food markets, *and their own culture.* In the presidential election of 2008, their votes are credited with electing Barrack Obama president.

A Zogby Poll in June 2002 asked Mexicans in the United States:

"Do you agree or disagree that the territory of the U.S. Southwest belongs to Mexico?"

Nearly 60 percent agreed.

"Only 28 percent disagreed, while 14 percent... were unsure whether California, Texas, New Mexico, and Arizona rightfully belonged to Mexico or the United States."[25]

A key element in Mexico's demand for an open border is "regime survival." It is incumbent on the United States, Mexican officials say brazenly, to continue to accept the millions of Mexican poor, uneducated, and jobless lest they foment revolution that would have serious implications north of the border. Let them go north, they say, and let the wealthy *gringos* take care of them.

Mexico's history since 1848 has not been a happy one: brutal suppression by emperor Maximilian; stern dictatorship under Porfiorio Diaz; one bloody revolution after another from 1900 on; a historically single-party government and all that it implies. Mexico has a terrible history of autocracy, a corrupt legal system, tribalism, endemic racism, poor education, an absence of family planning, and lack of religious diversity. All the while, pervasive poverty and ongoing corruption prevail.

Even more ominously, the United States has become a sort of safety valve for Mexico's exploding population, millions of whom are unable to find jobs inside Mexico. Mexican workers in the United States, furthermore, send billions of dollars back to their destitute relations in Mexico. The figure has been estimated at $16 billion a year, the second highest source, after oil, of Mexico's hard currency.[26]

"Mexico is one nation of 123 million—100 million who live in Mexico and 23 million who live in the United States."

—Mexican President Vincente Fox, July 16, 2002

THE NEW YORK TIMES, in a three-chapter series titled "Three Sisters," at the end of December 2006, traced the lives of three Mexican women. One had legally entered the United States; one had moved illegally to San Antonio, Texas with a husband and three young children; and the last one moved back to Mexico because she had constantly worried about being apprehended by U.S. Border Patrol agents.

The story of Veronica, 31, the mother of three who has lived illegally in the United States for six years, is revealing. When she drives, she said she uses side streets and conscientiously stops when a yellow traffic light flashes; as far as she is concerned, running a yellow light and being stopped by a police officer is not an option. Border Patrol agents routinely monitor the main streets in San Antonio, so Veronica and her friends and relatives have set up informal alert networks. Spanish-language radio also does its part in warning of the presence of *limones verdes*, or green limes, "are sprouting" near the highway, using shorthand for the agents' green uniforms.

Veronica says, "We're careful." She admits she had much to lose if she and her family were to be deported. Her list of accomplishments would be the envy of nearly everyone still living in the decrepit Mexican neighborhood where she grew up. Her family now lives in a tiny stone and stucco house, with a rusting trampoline on a neglected lawn, and they own two old but serviceable cars. Her common-law husband earns $15 an hour, without benefits, but his boss is otherwise generous: giving a refrigerator, a washing machine and other presents. She says her children speak to each other in English and claims they get A's and B's in school. Their prized possession is a big-screen TV, which naturally offers Spanish-speaking channels. Veronica told the *Times* reporter that when she was growing up in Monterrey, Mexico, her bed was a single box spring, which she shared with eight siblings, and coffee cans to catch the rain from a leaking roof.

She admits she works "off the book" and so does not pay taxes on the wages she makes from working weekends cleaning her husband's boss's offices. Her sister, who is a legal resident, bought Veronica a cell phone, as it requires a Social Security number, which she doesn't have. Veronica insists she knows she should learn English. She can't check her children's homework and she can't understand what they say to each other when they speak English, which she says makes her both nervous and proud. "I went to some free classes and learned a bit," she said, smiling. "I can say hello, order some hamburgers."

> "With 100,000 whites leaving California each year, the Asian population soaring 42 percent in a decade, and 43 percent of all Californians under eighteen Hispanic, California is becoming—indeed, has become—a Third World state."[24]

ONE OF CRITIC PATRICK BUCHANAN'S dire conclusions, as he peers into his crystal ball, is that in 2050 America will be "...a multiracial, multiethnic, multilingual, multicultural conglomerate... a Tower of Babel, a replica of the Roman Empire after the Goths and Vandals had passed over."[27]

He declares that it is suicidal for Americans not to understand that Mexicans harbor an ingrained hatred for America, claiming that Mexicans have been taught that the whites of the north have robbed them of half their country.

Some four million illegal immigrants— mostly Mexican, but no one is sure about the number, , have crossed America's porous southern borders in the past five years, and there are thousands more pouring in every day. There are already some ten to fifteen million illegal Mexicans in the U.S., although no one is sure of this number either.

A comparison between these present-day numbers and previous periods of heavy immigration is startling. There are in the United States today, according to Buchanan, "...as many illegal aliens as all the German and Italian immigrants who ever came [legally], the two largest immigrant groups in our history."[28]

Arizona Congressman J.D. Hayworth adds: "At a minimum, almost 4,500 people cross into Arizona illegally *each day* without getting caught..." He estimated that "1.6 million [illegal immigrants] come through Arizona alone, every year."[29]

Quoting a January 2005 Bear Stearns study, Buchanan suggests: "The number of illegal immigrants in the United States may be as high as 20 million people."

If so, he concludes, "We have millions more illegal aliens in America today than the sum total of all the Germans, Italians, Irish, and Jews who ever came to America [legally] in the four hundred years of our history on this continent."[30]

He also projects that unless the United States gets control of its borders [northern as well as southern]; by 2050, Americans of European descent will be a minority in the country of their forebears, and that "...no nation has ever undergone so radical a demographic transformation and survived."[31]

At the same benchmark year, the Hispanic population will have tripled to 102 million, or 24 percent of the nation. Most will be Mexicans and concentrated in the southwest, a part of the United States separated from the remainder by language, ethnicity, history, and culture. Some Mexican chauvinists have not so quietly made clear their intent is to reclaim through demography and culture what their ancestors lost through force of arms.

> *[Mexico] "is a society sitting on a demographic time bomb of almost 100 million with a population growth rate of 2 percent per annum—and no feasible way of providing jobs, health care, social justice or personal safety to a nation, half of which will soon be under the age of twenty five. Without the promised land to the north, there might well loom either political revolution or African-style famine and plague."*[32]

Lastly, there remains the controversial U.S. policy of granting instantaneous citizenship to the newborn of illegal aliens. One observer wrote:

> We see pregnant women with no cash, no husband, no English and no papers who rush to the local hospital at the last minute to bring forth a United States citizen. The birth is a miraculous event indeed, for in theory the infant spontaneously can anchor a new American existence for a full array of parents and assorted relatives of illegal status. How surreal![33]

Notes

[1] Mexico revolted against Spain in 1810 and gained its independence in 1821. In 1824, the Mexicans established a federal constitution based on the U.S. model. Five years later a military leader, Bustamante, subverted the new constitution and took office for three years. He was displaced by Antonio Lopez de Santa Anna, who was in and out of power several times in the next 20 years. There was constant political turmoil in Mexico until 1877 when General Porfirio Diaz seized power. He held it with absolute authority until 1911, when the United States first stepped in to tailor the government to its—and Woodrow Wilson's—liking.

[2] Robert Leckie, *The Wars of America* (Harper & Row, Publishers, New York, 1968), p. 320.

[3] Glenn W. Price, *Origins of the War with Mexico: The Polk-Stockton Intrigue* (University of Texas Press, Austin TX, 1967), p. 9.

[4] Robert H. Ferrell, *American Diplomacy: A History* (W.W. Norton & Company, Inc., New York, 1959), p. 85.

[5] Price, p. 95.

[6] Ulysses S. Grant, *The Personal Memoirs of Ulysses S. Grant* (Charles L. Webster & Company, New York, 1885), p. 64.

[7] Ibid., p. 65.

[8] Price, p. 100.

[9] Warren I. Cohen, *The American Revisionists: The Lessons of Intervention in World War I* (The University of Chicago Press, Chicago, 1967), vol. 1, 4.

[10] Ferrell, p. 94.

[11] Alfred Hoyt Bill, *Rehearsal for Conflict: The War with Mexico 1846-1848* (Alfred A. Knopf, New York, 1947), p. 81.

[12] Ibid., p. 82.

[13] Otis A. Singletary, *The Mexican War* (University of Chicago Press, Chicago, 1963).

[14] The U.S. generals' fear of Yellow Fever decimating their armies was well founded. The disease that occurs in tropical regions is spread by mosquitoes in the hot months of late spring and summer. It kills or disables its victims quickly. Symptoms on the first day are headache, sensitive skin, and drowsiness. Next the victim gets severe stomach pains and vomits a black liquid, the reason the Mexicans called it *el vomito negro*. Within three days, the victim's skin turns greenish and the eyes become yellow (hence the name of the disease) and the gums and nose bleed. The individual either dies on the fifth or sixth day, or endures a slow and painful recovery. For an army in the field, either outcome can be disastrous. In the decade leading up to 1803, Yellow Fever killed over forty thousand British and French soldiers who had been dispatched to quell uprisings in Saint-Domingue (later Haiti). Don Nardo, *The Mexican-American War* (Lucent Books, Inc., San Diego CA, 1999), p. 68.

[15] Not so a half-century later at the start of the Spanish War, when General William Shafter's disorganized army took almost a week to disembark in Cuba from their transports—noisily and in disarray. Fortunately for the Americans, the Spanish defenders were even more incompetent.

[16] Singletary, p. 160-161.

[17] Ibid.

[18] Noam Chomsky, *Turning the Tide: The U.S. and Latin America* (Black Rose Books, New York, 1987), p. 88.

[19] Price, p. 91.

[20] Ibid., p. 89.

[21] Ferrell, p. 50.

[22] Ibid.

[23] Ibid, p. 61.

[24] Donald Barr Chidsey, *The War with Mexico* (Crown Publishers, Inc., New York, 1968), p. 122.

[25] Ferrell, p. 106.

[26] Ibid, p. 107-108.

[27] Patrick J. Buchanan, State of Emergency: The Third World Invasion and Conquest of America (Thomas Dunne Books, New York, 2006), p. 49.

[28] Ibid., p. 105.

[29] Ibid., p. 130.

[30] Ibid., p. 246.

[31] Ibid., p. 10.

[32] Victor Davis Hanson, *Mexifornia: A State of Becoming* (Encounter Books, San Francisco, 2003), p. 28.

[33] Ibid.

Chapter IV:
The Spanish and Philippines Wars

"It was a war entered without misgivings and in the noblest frame of mind. Seldom can history have recorded a plainer case of military aggression, yet seldom has a war been started in so profound a conviction of its righteousness."[1]

TO THE CITIZENS OF A WARRIOR NATION,[2] it was a restless time. Few were still alive who could remember the war with Mexico; it was, after all, 50 years in the past. But it was only 30 years since Robert E. Lee handed his sword to Ulysses S. Grant at Appomattox; most Americans alive had vivid memories of that brutal conflict, particularly Southerners on whose land the battles raged and its society raped.

The celebrated generals of the War Between the States were passing into obscurity; soon only their equestrian statues and cannons in carefully manicured battlegrounds and in town squares would be visible reminders. The war's passions had lost much of their luster and its agonies were mostly forgotten, although Southerners—with much good reason—continued to spit streams of brown tobacco juice when despised Union General William Tecumseh Sherman's name was mentioned. The bloody Indian genocide had ended in 1890 with the butchery of Big Foot and his decimated Sioux tribe at Wounded Knee Creek by the U.S. cavalry. The enormous buffalo herds that sustained the Plains Indians had been wiped out nearly to the last bison. The Census Bureau had announced there was no longer a land frontier, and U.S. Navy Captain Alfred Thayer Mahan, the articulate voice for the nation's expansionists, prophesized: "Whether they will or no, Americans must now begin to look outward."[3]

The Cuban insurrection that began in February 1895, thus came at an opportune time for the rebels. Cuba, a Spanish colony near the southern tip of Florida, had long been looked at with more than passing interest by America's business and political leaders. U.S. foreign policy concerning the strategic island had been undeviating: it was to keep the British and French out even if that meant accepting, grudgingly, Spanish rule. There were profitable American commercial and business interests on the island and Spain's heavy-handed treatment of the rebels was an emotional and moral issue that drew many Americans into sympathy with the revolutionaries. Had not Americans themselves revolted against tyranny and oppression in their own War for Independence?

"It has been a splendid little war, begun with the highest motives, carried on with magnificent intelligence and spirit, favored by that fortune which loves the brave. It is now to be concluded, I hope, with that fine good nature which is after all, the distinguishing trait of our American character."[4]

It was the second time that Cubans had sought to overthrow their Spanish masters. In 1868, a band of sugar plantation workers in eastern Cuba "launched the shout" that became what was called the Ten Years' War. That conflict of guerrilla fighting in the jungles, never moved to the rich and populous western end of the island and its capital, Havana. Its main support had been a *junta* with offices in New York City and Key West, Florida. The *junta's* principal activities were anti-Spanish propaganda in the United States, raising money for the cause, and gun-running to the rebels. In 1878, the insurgents had been persuaded to lay down their arms by the Spanish with the promise of an amnesty and the Pact of Zanjón was signed, formally ending the insurrection.

The new conflict's council consisted of the earlier war's expatriates, with the same two headquarters:

> The insurrection of 1895 was made in the United States, the work of *émigrés* who had no real stake in the island, who had dissociated themselves from its life, and many of whom had scarcely even set foot upon its soil during the whole period in which they were laboring to involve it again in a civil war. It was these men—the unemployed generals of the Ten Years' War... who kept the passions of the earlier struggle alive, and abroad perfected the technique of insurrection until conditions made it possible for them to import it once more into Cuba.[5]

Contributing in a major way to the uprising had been the ill-conceived U.S. tariff of 1894 which imposed a duty of up to forty percent on sugar imports, knocking the bottom out of the market. The price of sugar, which had been eight cents a pound, dropped to two cents. As a result, Cuban plantations were forced to close and workers, losing their jobs, readily joined the rebellion.

> *"Theodore Roosevelt called the Spanish War 'the most absolutely righteous war of the century' and labeled as 'impertinent' any European leader, 'whether Pope, Kaiser, Czar, or President' who offered any other interpretation."*

STRATEGICALLY the island of Cuba dominates the approaches to the Gulf of Mexico. Mahan's widely read *The Influence of Sea Power on History*,[6] published in 1890, added credence to those who saw the need for Cuba as a naval base. At the same time, America began to modernize its navy. Like all the navies of the world at that time, steel was replacing wood and steam-power was taking the place of wind and sail. For ultra-chauvinist Mahan, "sea power" meant everything that made water-borne commerce vital and secure for an international trader like the United States. It meant a large merchant fleet to ensure that American goods would not have to ship on foreign bottoms or be dependent on foreign interests. Above all, it meant a powerful navy to protect its merchant ships as well as keep open critical water routes in time of war; and, importantly, colonies for bases and coaling stations to give the navy wide-ranging flexibility. Mahan and his supporters in the Congress, in particular the Senate's then reigning jingo,[7] Henry Cabot Lodge of Massachusetts, looked to the nearby Caribbean and saw the proposed canal across Central America—whether in Nicaragua with a sea-level canal or with a "locked" canal across the Panama Department of Colombia—as indispensable to the creation of an "American lake."

Lodge had published an article in March 1895 unambiguously titled "Our Blundering Foreign Policy." He wrote:

> England has studded the West Indies with strong places which are a standing menace to our Atlantic seaboard. We should have among those islands at least one strong naval station, and when the Nicaragua Canal is built, the island of Cuba...will become to us a necessity.... Cuba was required both 'for future expansion and present defense.'[8]

As early as 1854, Cuba had been a nagging foreign-policy issue. President Franklin Pierce at that time ordered U.S. ministers to Spain, Great Britain, and France to meet and discuss actions to be taken against Spain over alleged interference in U.S. commerce with Cuba. The meeting took place in neutral Ostend, Belgium. What came to be called the Ostend Manifesto was a document that recommended that America offer to purchase Cuba from Spain for $120 million. If Spain refused the offer, the United States would be free to go to war. Secretary of State W. L. Marcy disavowed the document. War awaited a new administration.

HENRY WATTERSON, editor of the Louisville *Courier-Journal,* decades ahead of the 1930's Senate Munitions Hearings that focused on the political influence of arms-manufacturers, called the rising clamor for war with Spain "counterfeit patriotism," writing perceptively that there were incentives for:

> "...men to make money from contracts to erect coast defenses, build ships, and sell supplies and equipment to an enlarged army and navy."[9]

The term Manifest Destiny had more recently been resurrected as a rallying cry for expansionists. The uprising in Cuba was seen as another opportunity for America to fulfill its divine sanction.

In the White House, Grover Cleveland, in the middle of his second term, remained steadfast. When he had first taken office in 1885, concerned with the hallowed issue of George Washington's "entangling alliances," he had revoked a treaty with Nicaragua dealing with an isthmian canal. He then withdrew from the Senate "for further study" a treaty that would have annexed Hawaii, saying it would be interference in the internal affairs of the far-away Pacific islands. A group of interventionists, encouraged by the Benjamin Harrison administration, overthrew the Hawaiian government in January 1893. A month later Harrison signed a treaty of annexation with the coup leaders, and the Senate Foreign Relations Committee approved it two days later.

THE 1895 REVOLT was orchestrated by the same single-minded revolutionary chieftain of the earlier Ten Years' War: Máximo Gómez. He knew Cuba and the Cubans and he understood the Spanish. Gómez efficiently directed his fast-moving bands of rebel horsemen who harassed the Spanish regulars in classic guerrilla hit-and-run fashion. The insurgents would gallop in swiftly, set fire to a sugar cane field, derail a train, or slaughter livestock, and disappear as quickly. Like all guerrillas before and since, Gómez had no illusions of achieving a military victory over his well-equipped enemy, and he studiously avoided pitched battles which he knew he could not win. His was a brutal campaign of terrorism and he hoped, over time, thereby to squeeze the life out of the Cuban economy.

Gómez's tactics bedeviled the Spanish commander-in-chief, Governor-General Arsenio Martinez de Campos and his army of 140,000 regulars. Campos, who had brought the Ten Years' War to a successful end seventeen years earlier, was unable to cope with the deteriorating situation this time. By the end of 1895, the guerrilla forces had advanced so far west that the smoke from torched sugar cane fields could be seen from Havana. Sensibly, the discouraged and worn-out Campos cabled Madrid with his resignation: a younger, more vigorous commander was needed. Cuba was in chaos. He recommended as his successor General Valeriano Weyler y Nicolau, who arrived in Cuba in February 1896.

Weyler was a logical choice to step in and restore order. He had a long record of military successes and he had also served as a subordinate general during the Ten Years' War in Cuba. As a young officer, he had been military attaché at the Spanish legation in Washington during America's War Between the States, and had accompanied Union General Sherman as an observer during his punitive march through Georgia at the end of that war. Like most Spaniards familiar with the Cuban revolt, Weyler believed that the insurgents would have long since been defeated but for the continuous incitement by the "yellow press" in New York City and the clandestine arms and supplies furnished them by the filibuster ships from the United States that regularly slipped into Cuba.[10]

As America would later do in every one of its overt wars in the twentieth century and beyond, government propagandists promptly sought out an individual in the enemy camp, *or prospective enemy,* to demonize. General Weyler was an easy pick as the contemporary fiend, and his arrival in Cuba was greeted by an avalanche of vindictive press propaganda in the United States. He was:

> ...noted for extreme cruelty; is well known for his bloodthirstiness; his appointment leaves little hope for any decent treatment for anyone who may be slightly suspected of lack of active sympathy with Spain; barbaric war is expected on the coming of General Weyler.[11]

Inside Cuba there was near-hysteria, according to exaggerated American press reports, which grew more extravagant as the months passed. Cubans were said to be leaving the country in droves, and outbound steamers were supposedly crammed full to the rails.

To restore order, which was his first job, Weyler resorted to extreme measures. In October 1896, Weyler issued his infamous decree, establishing *zonas de reconcentración* close to fortified cities and towns. Troublesome rural populations were forcibly uprooted from their homes and land and resettled in these pacified zones, exactly like the South Vietnamese in an American war sixty years in the future. Spanish forces then scoured the immediate areas of food to starve the rebels. Weyler recruited Cuban mercenaries, *guerrilleros*, to do the dirty work of driving peasants off their land. These cruel relocation measures proved effective and for a time dealt a setback to the revolutionaries.

> The mother country was desperately trying to save Cuba. At the time of Weyler's arrival on the scene, an estimated 150,000 Spanish soldiers had seen service in Cuba's jungles. By 1898, some 50,000 were dead, and another 50,000 disabled by disease and wounds.[12]

THE UNITED STATES in the last decade of the nineteenth century was a nation of newspaper readers and people in all walks of life depended on them—nearly all only a penny or two—not only for current affairs but also for entertainment. Broadcast radio would not become a reality, much less a commonplace, until the 1920s. There were some 1,900 dailies and 14,000 weeklies nationwide, and they were read by a surprisingly literate population, estimated at 88 percent nationwide, an astonishing figure by twentieth-century American standards. In New York City, for example, with a population then of about 2,800,000, including tens of thousands of non-English-speaking immigrants who had their own newspapers, the combined circulation of the dailies was almost two million. New York City had eight morning and seven evening dailies and some thirty weeklies; and those with large circulations had national influence far beyond their narrow geographical limits. Railroads efficiently delivered papers overnight to distant cities and syndication ensured that what was printed in New York was reprinted elsewhere.

At the outbreak of the insurrection in Cuba, the most influential and widely read paper in New York was Joseph Pulitzer's *World*. Pulitzer had been born in Hungary and came to the United States at the start of the War Between the States for the $500 bounty offered substitutes for men avoiding the North's draft. After the war he settled in St. Louis where he became a reporter for the German-language *Westliche Post*. His first newspaper acquisition was the St. Louis *Evening Post* which he renamed the *Post-Dispatch,* promptly making it a financial success.

Pulitzer came to New York City in 1883, bought the rundown *World* and almost overnight transformed it into a new kind of newspaper. His paper, he announced, would be:

not only cheap but bright, not only bright but large, not only large but truly democratic—
dedicated to the cause of the people rather than that of purse-potentates—devoted more to the
news of the New than the Old World—that will expose all fraud and sham, fight all public evils
and abuses—that will serve and battle for the people with earnest sincerity.[13]

To the contrary, scandal, gossip, and innuendo were the *World's* stock-in-trade at that period in
American history, and would remain so for years to come. Pulitzer directed his reporters and editors
to embellish the news and his make-up staff and artists to use provocative banner headlines and
garish illustrations. One of the chroniclers of the period observed that the reckless headlines and
sensational appeals to the masses had profound implications for the entire nation and helped shape a
new school of journalism. On the newsstands side by side with its staid competitors, the *World* stood
out boldly; circulation and advertising revenues skyrocketed. The year Pulitzer bought the *World*, it
was an eight-pager with a daily circulation of about 5,000. By 1895, it had grown to a sixteen-pager,
sold for the same two cents, and had a daily circulation of over 555,000. Continuing its meteoric rise,
three years later the *World's* circulation reached over five million copies per week, the largest of any
newspaper printed in any language in any country.

PULITZER'S RADICAL JOURNALISM attracted mimickers from as far away as San Francisco,
where William Randolph Hearst, in 1887, had been given control of the *Examiner* by his wealthy
father, who had acquired it for a bad debt. Hearst, who would later build his own even more powerful
media empire, gradually turned the dull *Examiner* into a financial success. In 1895, looking eastward
for new conquests, he bought the moribund New York *Morning Journal* and shortened it to the
Journal.

A year earlier, the *World* had printed its first Sunday comic in color, using a clown and a wolfhound
as its two main characters. Created by artist Richard Felton Outcault, the comic was the predecessor
of the famous "yellow kid of Hogan's Alley" which was intended to portray life in New York City's
tenements. Outcault drew his ragamuffin bald and toothless, and dressed him in an oversized yellow
nightshirt. The "kid" had indistinct Asian features and a manic expression on his face, to lampoon the
"yellow peril" frenzy that had gripped the nation following the Sino-Japanese War in 1895. The
comic was a roaring success for the *World,* and it became a key prize in the coming circulation battle
between newcomer Hearst and veteran Pulitzer. Not incidentally, the term "yellow journalism" had
its origin in Outcault's popular comic.

Hearst's ambition was clear-cut: he intended that his *Journal* surpass the *World* in readership and
influence—and he left no stones unturned in his single-minded quest. He reduced his paper's
newsstand price from two cents to one. He transferred the best staffers from his *Examiner* to New
York and then began a methodical pirating of the top reporters, correspondents, and illustrators from
the *World*. He even managed to lure away cartoonist Outcault and his "yellow kid." He added a daily
magazine that focused on popular science, included news in capsule form for busy readers, and
printed a once-weekly 24-page women's supplement. Hearst was also a relentless promoter, hiring
bands and plastering the city with colored posters announcing the features of upcoming editions.

Hearst's penny newspaper was an irresistible buy and its circulation growth was extraordinary. He
was losing money on every newspaper sold, but he had deep pockets thanks to his widowed mother's
inherited fortune, and she freely financed his East Coast venture. During 1896, Hearst claimed an
astonishing average daily increase of 1,500 readers. In 1898, the day following William McKinley's
election as president, the *Journal* printed over 950,000 copies.

He would do better—and would finally win his personal circulation war with Pulitzer. On the day that the *Journal* printed illustrations of a wholly fictitious "infernal machine" that destroyed the battleship *Maine,* its circulation passed that of the *World,* with an unprecedented 1,026,624 copies. Following Commodore Dewey's annihilation of the Spanish fleet in Manila Bay on May 1, 1898, *Journal* circulation exceeded 1,600,000 copies.[14]

THE INSURRECTION in Cuba was a fine opportunity for publishers to sell newspapers by printing exciting stories of Spanish violence—real, imagined, and contrived. Many of the country's leading newspapers had correspondents in Havana and these men, in the delightful climate and inside the cool bars where rum flowed freely and wonderful local cigars were cheap, were particularly creative. Far from the action, these reporters nevertheless wrote "eye-witness" stories that were based on hearsay and lies from the rebel propagandists. Hearst's famous alleged rejoinder to artist Frederic Remington's complaint from Cuba that he could not find a war there:

"You furnish the pictures; I'll furnish the war"—

...typified the relationship of the journalist in the field and his editors back in the home office. Collectively, the reporters fabricated a fearful and wholly misleading picture of Cuba as a tortured land, where a corrupt foreign autocracy, unable to extinguish the heroic aspirations of a courageous people, was drowning them in a sea of blood. It made for stirring headlines, nearly all hyperbole—and wonderful reading!

There was another, more convenient source of "information." It came from the New York City headquarters of the Cuban *junta*. Every afternoon, reporters looking for a story for the next day's papers, would gather at what became known as the "peanut club" on lower Broadway in Manhattan. There they found an unending supply of mouth-watering roasted peanuts in-the-shell along with the current news from the rebels: always victories—and the most bloodcurdling Spanish brutalities. The Cuban rebels were masters of atrocity propaganda; their goal was to convince Americans that Weyler's troops in Cuba were rapists, murderers, and worse, in Victorian America, defilers of womanhood.

Hearst's *Journal* led the way right from the start of the revolt, regularly reporting from Havana that

"the Spaniards stabbed to death all Cuban rebels who came under their power; that it was everyday practice for Spanish jailers to select at random several prisoners from the forts and shoot them; that the Spaniards routinely bayoneted insurgent hospital patients."[15]

Feeding prisoners to the ravenous sharks that supposedly frequented Cuban inshore waters and watching their frenzied attacks was a common pastime of Spanish jailers, according to news reports by American correspondents. In a December 1896 editorial:

"Credible witnesses have testified that all prisoners captured by Weyler's forces are killed on the spot... and that Weyler's intention seems to be to murder all the *pacificos* in the country."[16]

SALACIOUS TALES were big attractions. There was Hearst's imaginary incident involving three Cuban women passengers on the American steamer *Olivette*. According to a dispatch from well-known newspaperman Richard Harding Davis, Havana correspondent for the *Journal*, Spanish police had boarded the ship before it left the harbor to search the women, one of whom was suspected of carrying rebel dispatches. Frederic Remington's famous drawing of a naked lady surrounded by three policemen took up a half-page in the February 12 issue. The pencil sketch, titled "Spaniards Search Women on American Steamer," has since become legendary and can be found in American-history books of the period as an example of the behavior of the yellow press. The *Journal* declared piously:

> "War is a dreadful thing, but there are things more dreadful than even war, and one of them is dishonor."[17]

The news story was hokum and so was Remington's artwork, the *World* promptly announced, exhibiting in person in New York one of the ladies in question who denied indignantly that any such incident had occurred. Under the spotlight's glare, Davis was forced to recant his yarn. He claimed that he had been misquoted, that, in fact, the women had been examined by a police matron in the privacy of a stateroom while the police officers waited outside. Score one for the *World* in its ongoing competition with the *Journal*.

Then began the even more renowned case of imprisoned Senorita Evangelina Cossio y Cisneros and her dauntless escapade, worthy of the best pulp writers of the period. Senorita Cisneros was a niece of the Cuban president who headed the civil government of the rebels. Her saga began when she supposedly voluntarily accompanied her father into exile on the Isle of Pines for his complicity with the rebels. There she was involved in an abortive attempt to free him and she was arrested and imprisoned, awaiting trial in Havana. According to the *junta* propagandists, Senorita Cisneros' only crime had been to resist the lustful advances of a Spanish officer.

Hearst immediately recognized the sensational story that could be developed. It triggered the start of a *Journal* crusade to "enlist the women of America" on her behalf—a campaign that Historian Walter Millis wrote in 1931,

> "...is still famous in American newspaper history."[18]

Madrid was alarmed at all the adverse publicity, but Spanish officials in Cuba stubbornly refused to release the prisoner. Hearst then came up with a clever scheme. In August, he dispatched one of his trusted underlings to Havana to organize a jailbreak and rescue Senorita Cisneros. It was cloak-and-dagger stuff, and made sensational copy. On October 10, the *Journal* bellowed its success:

> "Evangelina Cossio y Cisneros is at last at liberty, and the *Journal* can place to its credit the greatest journalistic coup of this age."[19]

According to the *Journal* the jailbreak had gone smoothly: the paper's second-story man himself had crawled across the roof of an adjoining building in the dark of night, hack-sawed his way through a barred window, and chivalrously lifted out the prisoner. He smuggled her out of Cuba disguised as a sailor on a tramp steamer to New York. There, Hearst arranged for a big reception in Madison Square Garden to welcome the heroine. She then visited Washington for another orchestrated pageant, where Senorita Cisneros, by this time referred to as the Cuban Joan of Arc, was introduced to the president. McKinley was reported to have said blandly of her rescue to the *Journal's* escort that:

> "It was a most heroic deed."[20]

MANEUVERING SKILLFULLY BETWEEN the country's interventionists and the peace factions, McKinley made two important appointments after coming into office. He picked Theodore Roosevelt to be the new Assistant Secretary of the Navy. Roosevelt was known to his detractors as a loudmouthed warmonger and would need little encouragement from the president to influence Secretary John D. Long,

> "...a weak, stuffy hole in the air."[21]

His appointment of Fitzhugh Lee to continue as consul general in Havana, on the other hand, gave the appearance if not the substance that the McKinley administration was continuing Cleveland's nonintervention policy. McKinley had been informed privately that Lee, too, was a jingo,

> "...of the most mendacious sort, a man who, as Cleveland himself put it, had 'fallen into the style of rolling intervention like a sweet morsel under his tongue.'"[21]

Both appointments would soon bear fruit.

At that time, in the fall of 1897, public sentiment over the plight of the Cuban rebels had waned at the same time as General Weyler's counterinsurgency actions were proving successful. McKinley waited until spring of the following year to advance his hidden agenda. On May 17, 1898, he sent Congress a message announcing that Consul Lee had just confirmed that

> "...large numbers of American citizens on the island were starving to death for want of provisions and supplies."[22]

According to Lee, these unfortunates were innocent victims of Weyler's indiscriminate *reconcentrado* policies. McKinley asked the Congress for a $50,000 appropriation to ease their plight. Cuban peasants being rounded up by Spanish soldiers and put into concentration camps was one thing, American citizens being subjected to such atrocious behavior by a foreign army was quite another.

Lee's exaggerated message was an overnight sensation. Newspapers hailed the note and intervention fever swept over the country. Hearst's *Journal* led the outcry:

> "The relief-bearer is but the American camel intruding its head in the Spanish tent in Cuba."[23]

Unlike his cautious communications with his countrymen, McKinley dealt firmly with Spain over its conduct in Cuba. From the beginning, he arrogated to his office the right to dictate Spanish conduct in Cuba and to intervene by force if Spanish actions ran counter to American interests in that country. On May 26 he sent a bellicose note to Spain's ambassador, for the first time exposing his cards. Spain would have to achieve peace in Cuba or the United States would send in troops, he wrote. Peace alone would not be sufficient to prevent U.S. intervention, McKinley warned. Spain would have to meet two further conditions: revoke Weyler's *reconcentración* order and enact reforms on the island that would persuade the rebels to lay down their arms.

Three weeks later, the president applied additional diplomatic pressure on Spain. He instructed his new ambassador to Spain, Stewart Woodford, to add a third condition to his demands: Spain had only "a reasonable time" to comply with U.S. demands. He also directed Woodford to sound out European governments to find out if they would come to the aid of Spain in what would obviously be a preemptive war by the United States [they would not].

While Woodford was testing the waters in Europe, McKinley was covertly erecting the foundation for another imperialistic stroke, this time in the Pacific. On June 16, he submitted to the Senate for their approval a new treaty of annexation with the Hawaiian government, publicly assuring the foes of expansion that this acquisition would be his last. He later confided to his private secretary, invoking the magic words:

> "We need Hawaii just as much and a good deal more than we did California.
> It is Manifest Destiny." -- President McKinley

The president was about to have his war with Spain.

President Grover Cleveland had originally appointed Fitzhugh Lee as consul general in 1896 for reasons other than his fitness to handle the job: he neither spoke Spanish nor understood it and knew little about Cuba. His credentials otherwise were excellent: he was a nephew of Confederate General Robert E. Lee, and had been a cavalry general in that war. More recently he had been governor of Virginia. Lee believed Spain was incapable of changing her brutal colonial ways and that the rebels were equally unfit to establish and run a viable government. He was also convinced that the Spanish empire's control over Cuba was shaky, and that a modest show of force by the United States might be sufficient to topple the Spanish regime. In December 1897, there were street riots in Havana with what Lee interpreted as anti-American overtones. He cabled the State Department suggesting that "one or two" U.S. Navy men-of-war be sent to Havana as a precautionary measure.

Dispatching a warship on a "courtesy call" to Havana had often been talked about in McKinley's cabinet. Cleveland had earlier ended such visits out of concern that they might trigger a serious incident, which could escalate into a full-blown diplomatic crisis. McKinley, privately seeking just such a crisis and happy to comply with Lee's suggestion, decided as a first step to detach a battleship from the North Atlantic Squadron and station it close to Cuba, but not too close as to be transparently provocative to the Spaniards. It was a fateful decision.

THE BATTLESHIP was the *Maine*,[24] and on October 8 she steamed to Port Royal, South Carolina, to await further orders. In mid-November she was ordered to the naval base in Norfolk, Virginia and was dry-docked. There her hull was scraped of barnacles and given a new coat of anti-fouling paint. Hull and topsides, *Maine* was freshly painted white, as was traditional at the time for U.S. Navy warships in peacetime. On December 10, the battleship departed for Key West, Florida to await a summons from Consul General Lee. Earlier, the *Maine's* Captain, Charles D. Sigsbee, had received a secret cable from Navy Secretary Long that upon receipt of a coded message from Lee, he should immediately weigh anchor and proceed to Havana.

Sigsbee's sailing orders arrived on January 24—not from Lee but in the form of a telegraph from Long to the Commander of the North Atlantic Squadron, delivered by torpedo boat at the *Maine's* anchorage in the Dry Tortugas. It read in part:

> "Order the Maine to proceed to Havana, Cuba, and make friendly call—pay his respects to the authorities there—particular attention must be paid to usual interchange of civility..."

Late morning on January 25, 1898, the *Maine* stood off Morro Castle at the entrance to Havana Harbor, awaiting a harbor pilot. The 319-foot man-of-war with twin stacks amidships, towering basket-weave masts fore and aft, and a main battery of four ten-inch cannons mounted in twin turrets, was an impressive sight. Big crowds had gathered to watch its arrival. The *Maine* was the largest ship in the port of Havana and an impressive platform for "showing the flag"—then and ever since one of the most important diplomatic protocols for projecting a nation's military might.

When the Cuban pilot came aboard, he showed Captain Sigsbee a chart of the harbor and pointed to an open mooring in the man-of-war section. Sigsbee had no reason to question the pilot's recommendation and said it was satisfactory. He recalled later that the Cuban pilot had skillfully maneuvered the ponderous warship snugly up to its mooring buoy.

FOR THREE WEEKS the *Maine* remained at her mooring under a burning tropical sun. Sigsbee, rightfully concerned that his crew might run afoul of the local constabulary for raucous behavior which could lead to an "incident," had cancelled liberty for his enlisted sailors. The monotony of shipboard routine combined with the heat had drained the sailors; most turned in when the bugler sounded taps. On the evening of February 15, taps was at 9:10. All was quiet aboard ship, except for a group of officers on an upper deck, catching whatever breeze there was and enjoying the flavor of their marvelous Cuban cigars, partaking of the local rum, and comparing their latest exploits with the all-too-willing ladies in Havana.

In his stateroom below decks, Sigsbee later recalled that the bugler's notes were beautiful in the oppressive stillness of the night. He had been writing a letter to his wife and had just sealed the envelope, when he was thrown out of his chair by a powerful blast and deafened by a crashing roar. On the stern deck of a steamer berthed nearby, passengers were startled by what they later reported was a "shot" that turned them toward the *Maine* in time to see the bow rise up and the center of the vessel explode in a blinding flash of fire that lit up the whole harbor.

Witnesses on shore said later they saw bodies propelled high into the air. Another observer recounted that it had looked like the entire upper works of the ship had blown outward and that the explosion appeared to have been centered forward on the port side of the ship. Whatever triggered the detonation, there was no doubt that the *Maine's* ammunition magazines had erupted.

Two hundred sixty of the ship's company of 354, nearly all enlisted men who had berths forward, were killed outright from the explosion or were drowned when the ship went down. Sigsbee was unhurt as were most of the commissioned officers who were quartered aft. He was the last man to leave the crippled ship, which ponderously settled into the muck of shallow Havana Harbor, rumbling and shuddering all the while with muffled explosions of ammunition deep inside her.

Was the cause of the tragedy an accident, sabotage by disgruntled crew members, or a premeditated act by unknown parties?

TWO DAYS after the disaster, the Navy's most prominent explosives authority publicly refuted the idea of sabotage in an interview with the *Washington Evening Star*. He stated:

> "No torpedo such as is known to modern warfare, can of itself cause an explosion as powerful as that which destroyed the *Maine*. We know of no instances where the explosion of a torpedo or mine under a ship's bottom has exploded the magazine within."[25]

Experts from the Navy's Bureau of Ordnance suspected that the cause might have been a fire in a coal-bunker that had spread to an adjoining ammunition magazine, separated by only a single steel un-insulated bulkhead, igniting gunpowder and triggering the massive explosion. The Navy's coal-fired warships, particularly the earliest-generation models like the *Maine*, were prone to the development of slow-burning fires in their coal bunkers caused by spontaneous combustion.[26] While U.S. Navy ship builders recognized the potential hazard of coal bunkers adjacent to magazines, the tradeoff was considered acceptable because such designs theoretically "buffered" the magazines and thus provided additional protection from incoming enemy shells. Temperature sensors in the bunkers connected to alarms on the bridge were intended to warn ships' crews of incipient spontaneous combustion; these sensors, however, were notoriously unreliable.

Theodore Roosevelt immediately declared that the sinking was "an act of dirty [Spanish] treachery." He gave no reason why Spain would benefit from the destruction of a U.S. Navy battleship in its principal harbor. The conservative Navy Department remained neutral, issuing a statement that the cause of the disaster was unknown.

AS FAR AS the *World* and the *Journal* were concerned there was no doubt: the *Maine's* destruction was no accident; it had been the work of "perfidious" Spaniards. Historian W.A. Swanberg wrote elegantly in 1961 that:

> "Hearst's coverage of the *Maine* disaster still stands as the orgasmic acme of ruthless, truth less newspaper jingoism."[27]

Swanberg supported his unambiguous view by listing the main headlines in the *Journal* in the week immediately following the ship's destruction.

February 16: "CRUISER MAINE BLOWN UP IN HAVANA HARBOR"—the last honest front-page headline for almost two weeks.

February 17: "WARSHIP MAINE WAS SPLIT IN TWO BY AN ENEMY'S INFERNAL MACHINE"—the issue included a full-page illustration of the ship anchored over mines, with wires leading from the mines to a Spanish fortress on shore.

February 18: "THE WHOLE COUNTRY THRILLS WITH THE WAR FEVER"

February 20: "HOW THE MAINE ACTUALLY LOOKS AS IT LIES WRECKED BY SPANISH TREACHERY IN HAVANA BAY"

February 21: "HAVANA POPULACE INSULTS THE MEMORY OF THE MAINE VICTIMS"

February 23: "THE MAINE WAS DESTROYED BY TREACHERY"

Hearst quickly offered a $50,000 reward for details of the plot, initiated a drive for a memorial to the *Maine*, created a "War with Spain" card game, and collected a group of headline-seeking

Congressmen to travel to Cuba on one of his yachts to serve as "*Journal* commissioners." In fact, two years earlier, Hearst had begun his campaign for a war with Spain. In December, 1896, his *Journal* brazenly mailed questionnaires to the governors of every state, asking for their views on American intervention in Cuba and how many volunteers each of the states could be expected to supply in the event of war. Better late than never, as far as Hearst was concerned; finally he, too, would have his war with Spain.

Not to be outdone, the *World's* headline on February 17 also left no doubt as to the cause:

> "Maine Explosion Caused by Bomb or Torpedo."

Subsidiary heads announced that the *World* had sent a

> "Special Tug, with Submarine Divers, to Havana to Find Out."

Then came the paper's stock-in-trade, unsubstantiated "plots" and "expert reports":

> Dr. F. C. Pendleton, Just Arrived from Havana, Says He Overheard Talk There of a Plot to Blow Up the Ship; Capt. Zalinski, the Dynamite Expert, and Other Experts Report to The *World* that the Wreck Was Not Accidental.

In the upper corners of the front page was the number "863,956", captioned "*World's* Circulation Yesterday."

TO ESTABLISH THE OFFICIAL cause of the disaster, the Navy Department appointed a three-member Naval Court of Inquiry whose qualifications would be beyond dispute. The Court's fourth member and presiding officer was Captain William T. Sampson, commander of the new battleship *Iowa* and an acknowledged expert on ordnance—who shortly would become a hero in the battle of Santiago Bay. The Court first went to Havana to interrogate surviving crewmen and eye-witnesses and otherwise gather evidence. Navy divers were also sent down to the wreck. The Court next moved to Key West to hear accounts of the disaster from surviving crewmen. Then it was back to Havana to interview the divers about what they had observed underwater that might reveal the origin of the explosion. The last session in Havana was held on March 15 and Sigsbee wrote to his wife that while he did not know what the findings of the court would be, he was not concerned about anything which would reflect unfavorably on his command.

On March 11, preempting the Court's official findings, the *Journal* unequivocally claimed that the "Spanish government blew up the *Maine*." Two days later, pounding the war drums louder, the *Journal* declaimed on the front page that it:

> "...can stake its reputation as a war prophet on this assertion: There will be a war with Spain as certain as the sun shines unless Spain abases herself in the dust and voluntarily consents to the freedom of Cuba."

E. L. GOTKIN, editor of the New York *Evening Post* and one of the city's few voices of press moderation, on March 17 commented caustically:

> Every one who knows anything about yellow journals knows that everything they say and do is intended to promote sales... No one, absolutely no one—supposes a yellow journal cares five

cents about the Cubans, the *Maine* victims, or any one else. A yellow journal is probably the nearest approach to hell existing in any Christian state.

Earlier Gotkin had taken aim squarely at both the *Journal* and the *World*:

> Nothing as disgraceful as the behavior of these two newspapers in the past week has ever been known in the history of journalism. Gross misrepresentation of facts, deliberate invention of tales calculated to excite the public, and wanton recklessness in the construction of headlines which outdid even those inventions have combined to make the issues of the most widely circulated newspapers firebrands scattered broadcast throughout the community.[28]

The *Evening* Post, however, had a circulation of only 25,000!

The members of the Court completed their deliberations and signed off on their findings on May 21. A week later their formal report was delivered to Congress.

> The court finds that the loss of the *Maine*... was not in any respect due to the fault or negligence on the part of any of the officers or members of the crew of said vessel.

> In the opinion of the court the *Maine* was destroyed by the explosion of a submarine mine, which caused the partial explosion of two or more of the forward magazines.

> The court has been unable to obtain evidence fixing the responsibility for the destruction of the *Maine* upon any person or persons.[29]

That was all there was to it. Three months of work. Three sentences. And so many questions unanswered.

On April 2, the Spanish belatedly sent the results of their parallel inquiry to the State Department. Their report, with its rational findings, pointed out that at the time of the explosion, there was no wind or waves. Since the *Maine* was motionless, secured to its buoy, a mine under the ship would have had to have been exploded by electricity rather than the hull bumping detonating knobs—and no wires or a shore-based control station were found. Further, the report continued, an exploding mine would almost certainly have produced a geyser of water, and none had been observed—and no dead fish were found floating on the surface alongside the wreck, which would normally be found after a powerful underwater explosion. The Spanish analysis noted in its conclusion that responsible naval officers throughout the world knew the potential dangers from spontaneous combustion of bunkered coal and that

> "...it was astonishing that magazines should still be placed adjacent to coal bunkers,"

This was a calculated poke in the eye to the U.S. Navy's warship designers. General Weyler in Madrid added his own acerbic comment that would, three-quarters of a century later, prove to be nearly on-target, that the explosion had been due

> "to the indolence of the vessel's crew."

The contrary Spanish report, as might be anticipated, was ignored by the McKinley administration, the U.S. Navy, and, most importantly, by America's newspapers.

CONTRIBUTING TO THE FRENZIED patriotism stoked by the newspapers was a private letter written several months before by the Spanish minister in Washington, Enrique Dupuy de Lome, criticizing McKinley as:

> "...weak and a bidder for the admiration of the crowd."

and

> "a would-be politician who tries to leave a door open behind himself while keeping on good terms with the jingoes of his own party."

A pro-rebel Cuban secretary had leaked the contents of the letter to the *junta* who in turn relayed it to Hearst. Under a fat headline on February 9 in his *Journal*, he declared:

> "Worst Insult to the United States in its History."

Hearst made the most of the indiscretion. The story was a page-one feature in other newspapers throughout the country as well. In fact, these comments were, as the *Raleigh News and Observer* noted, "only in line with what the newspapers of this country say of Mr. McKinley every day."[30] For the Spanish government, de Lome's indiscretion came at a particularly inopportune time. The letter's impact paralleled the infamous Zimmermann Telegram of 1917 that helped propel America into the Great War.

On February 25, Navy Secretary Long was gone for the afternoon. History records that Assistant Secretary of the Navy Roosevelt made remarkable use of that short period without supervision. The next morning when Long reached his office, he discovered:

> ... an appalling state of affairs... Roosevelt, in his precipitate way, has come very near causing more of an explosion than happened to the *Maine*... He seems to be thoroughly loyal, but the very devil seemed to possess him yesterday afternoon... Mr. Roosevelt had begun to 'launch peremptory orders,' distributing ships, ordering ammunition, summoning experts, providing guns for a still nonexistent auxiliary fleet, and even 'sending messages to Congress for immediate legislation authorizing the enlistment of an unlimited number of seamen'... He has gone at things like a bull in a China shop.[31]

Long's journal omitted mention of a Roosevelt telegram, put on the wire that fateful afternoon, which subsequently became famous:

> Dewey, Hong Kong
>
> Secret and Confidential.
>
> Order the squadron, except *Monocacy*, to Hong Kong. Keep full of coal. In the event of declaration of war with Spain, your duty will be to see that the Spanish squadron does not leave the Asiatic coast, and then offensive operations in Philippine Islands. Keep *Olympia* until further notice.
>
> Roosevelt[32]

"Dewey" was Commodore George Dewey and "Hong Kong" was where Dewey had gathered his Asiatic Fleet from their anchorages in and around the Japanese port city of Nagasaki. By early March, he had dry-docked his vessels, had their bottoms scraped of barnacles and a fresh coat of bottom paint applied, and had their hulls and upperworks repainted from peacetime white to drab gray—the color of war.

On April 18, with scarcely any debate, Congress passed a joint resolution authorizing the president to demand that Spain give Cuba its independence. The next day McKinley signed the resolution and the United States broke off diplomatic relations with Spain. To secure congressional support for intervention in Cuba, McKinley agreed to accept an extraordinary amendment offered by Senator Henry Teller of Colorado. It began by declaring that "the people of the island of Cuba are, and of right ought to be, free and independent."

It ended with this solemn pledge:

> "The United States hereby disclaims any disposition or intention to exercise sovereignty, jurisdiction, or control over said island [Cuba], except for the pacification thereof, and asserts its determination when that is accomplished to leave the government and control of the island to its people."

The Senate approved the amendment unanimously, which became known as the Teller Amendment. Two days later, the U.S. Navy took up blockade stations off Havana Harbor and other Cuban ports. On the 25th of April, 1898, America formally declared war on Spain. On that day, Long wired Dewey another portentous message:

> "War has commenced between the United States and Cuba. Proceed at once to the Philippine Islands. Commence operations at once, particularly against the Spanish fleet. You must capture vessels or destroy. Use utmost endeavors."[33]

According to Historian Brian McAllister Linn, the declaration of war with Spain and the call-up of volunteers,

> …was greeted in most communities with an enthusiasm that appears almost unbelievable almost a century later. A decade of economic convulsion and social turmoil had left many eager for any noble cause that would take the nation's mind off internal problems. The Yellow Press portrayed Spain as fanatical, merciless, wicked, and corrupt, and it reinforced American views of their nation's role as the great liberator, destined to bring freedom and civilization to the oppressed peoples of the world.[34]

The War Department, totally unprepared for war, increased the Regular Army from 28,000 to 60,000 and went about organizing and training these recruits as well as 200,000 volunteers who flocked to the colors. The U.S. Navy, by contrast, was ready and immediately went into action.

Five days after McKinley happily signed on to the new war, Americans had a smashing naval victory to celebrate and a new hero to lionize, handsomely mustachioed George Dewey. The naval battle had taken place in the Philippines, halfway around the world. There was the persistent myth that when the president learned about Dewey's success, he had confessed that he could not have told within two thousand miles where the islands were; that he had to look them up on a globe. In fact, McKinley almost certainly knew where the Philippine Islands were, and may have also been told that in Manila Bay was a rusting, effectively immobile Spanish fleet, a juicy target for an American naval attack. Most Americans, however, had never heard of the giant archipelago, its approximately seven thousand islands strung out from north to south over one thousand miles of the Pacific. Its strategic location north of the Dutch East Indies (today's Indonesia) and east of China, was not lost on U.S. Navy war planners.

What became known as the battle of Manila Bay was less a battle than target-practice for Dewey's gunners. It began on the night of April 30, 1898, as Dewey's nine-ship squadron slid past the island of Corregidor, which guarded the entrance to the bay. For some inexplicable reason, the indolent Spanish failed to fire their big shore-based cannons as the U.S. fleet passed within easy range of the island's batteries. At daybreak, however, Spanish shore batteries along the coast finally opened fire on the U.S. men-of-war. Dewey gave no reply, resolutely leading his squadron in single-column formation toward the tip of Cavite where the Spanish fleet of twelve ships rode at anchor. The Spanish ships fired first, their shells falling far short. Still Dewey held his fire. Finally, at 5:45 am on

May 1, when his ships had closed the range to two-and-a-half miles, Commodore Dewey cryptically issued the command to Captain Charles V. Gridley of the flagship *Olympia* that was to make him eternally famous:

> "You may fire when you are ready, Gridley."

Seven hours later, the battle was over. Only one Spanish ship remained afloat and its guns had long been silenced. Not a single American ship had been damaged and only U.S. one sailor had died, a coal stoker—of heat exhaustion. By contrast eleven Spanish ships had been sunk and some two-hundred Spaniards had been killed. It had been an overwhelming victory for Dewey—and the United States. A Chicago *Times-Herald* editorial spoke for most Americans:

> Our jubilation over Dewey's unparalleled naval achievement was weighted with apprehension as to our responsibilities and with fear as to possible complications with other powers. The belief was general that we had acquired through the unavoidable exigencies of war something we did not want. But all this has changed. We find we want the Philippines. We also want Puerto Rico.... We want Hawaii now.... We may want the Carolines, the Ladrones, the Pelew, and the Mariana groups. If we do we will take them... Much as we may deplore the necessity for territorial acquisition, the people now believe the United States owes it to civilization to accept the responsibilities imposed upon it by the fortunes of war.[35]

IN THE INTERIM, Americans were treated to what was called "the remarkable voyage of the battleship *Oregon*." The record-setting voyage delighted the public and inspired a corny popular song, "The Race of the *Oregon*."

> Lights out! And a prow turned toward the South.
> And a canvas hiding each cannon's mouth
> And a ship like a silent ghost released
> Is seeking her sister ships in the East.
> When your boys shall ask what the guns are for
> Then tell the tale of the Spanish war.
> And the breathless millions that looked upon
> The matchless race of the *Oregon*.

After commissioning in 1896, *Oregon* had been assigned to what was then called the Pacific Station (later the Asiatic Fleet). Following the sinking of the *Maine* and as tensions with Spain grew, the Navy ordered *Oregon* to San Francisco to coal and provision for what became the most historic voyage ever undertaken by a U.S. Navy warship.

Oregon hoisted her anchor on March 19, headed for Callao, Peru, the first leg of her voyage south along the west coast of South America, around Cape Horn into the Atlantic Ocean, and north up the east coast of South America into the Caribbean. *Oregon* was a ghost ship as far as Americans were concerned; once she cleared San Francisco Bay, she was incommunicado except for brief periods when she steamed into a port to resupply. U.S. newspapers followed the passage with breathless accounts, most based on speculation. Fourteen thousand miles and sixty-six days later, *Oregon* arrived at Key West on May 26, to the relief and joy of the nation. She then joined Admiral Sampson's fleet off Santiago harbor, in time for the one-sided battle. Equally as important, *Oregon's* Pacific-to-Atlantic dash underscored the need for completion of the Panama Canal.

Meanwhile, in the Atlantic, Rear Admiral Pascual Cervera y Topete with the best of the Spanish Navy under his command—four modern armored cruisers and three destroyers—had sailed from the Cape Verde islands off the coast of West Africa, their destination the Caribbean. His orders were vague: to attack the far more formidable American battleships in the blockade off Cuba would be suicidal; to defend Puerto Rico was scarcely a better option. On paper, this Spanish fleet was more powerful than the decrepit fleet Dewey had annihilated in Manila Bay. In actuality, Cervera's warships were hardly battle-ready, nor, amazingly, did he have up-to-date navigation charts of the waters in the Caribbean.

It was not until May 20 that Admiral Sampson learned the whereabouts of Cervera's Fleet, which had been wandering around the Caribbean looking for coal. It ended up in Cuba, more by happenstance than intent, and was safely anchored in the harbor of Santiago. Cervera had luckily slipped through the U.S. Navy's blockading battleships on his way into the well-defended harbor. Spanish authorities, both in Madrid and Havana, insisted that national honor was at stake, and only a face-saving attempt to run the blockade was acceptable. Cervera was ordered to attempt his "withdrawal" when Santiago surrendered. The coming battle with the U.S. Navy's modern battleships that were closely guarding the mouth of Santiago Harbor would be akin to a suicide mission, and Cervera knew it.

Orders were orders, and on July 3, the Spanish fleet came charging resolutely out of the harbor led by Cervera's flagship, the *Infanta Maria Teresa*, her huge red and gold battleflags stiff in the wind, black smoke cascading from her funnels, her stokers feverishly feeding the boilers. She was followed by the *Vizcaya, Cristóbal Colón,* and *Almirante Oquendo.* Behind the cruisers were the *Furor* and *Plutón,* the Spaniard's highly touted torpedo-boat destroyers.

The initial momentum carried the Spanish ships past the American blockading battleships, and the engagement quickly became a chase westward along the coast with the heavy guns of the U.S. fleet battering the Spanish cruisers and setting afire their wooden decks. One by one, the blazing enemy ships were driven ashore, except for one destroyer which blew up and sank. Spanish losses: 474 casualties and 1,750 prisoners of war. U.S. losses: 1 killed, 1 wounded.[36] The Battle of Santiago Bay was another lopsided victory for the U.S. Navy—and a July 4th "present" to America as Sampson proclaimed the encounter.

In September 1899, Admiral Dewey came home to a hero's welcome and the biggest crowds ever recorded along the parade route on Manhattan's Fifth Avenue. His fleet was anchored close by in the Hudson River and a special Victory Arch was built in his honor. It was not until Charles A. Lindbergh had "his" parade up Fifth Avenue after his memorable flight to France in 1927 that Dewey's welcome was surpassed.

A stanza of juvenile newspaper poetry summed up the nation's euphoria:

Oh, dewey was the morning,

Upon the first of May,

And Dewey was the admiral,

Down in Manila Bay.

And dewey were the Spaniards' eyes.

Them orbs of black and blue,

And dew we feel discouraged?

I dew not think we dew!

> *"We will not repudiate our duty... We will not renounce our part in the mission of our race, trustee under God, of the civilization of the world... We will move forward to our work... with gratitude... and thanksgiving to Almighty God that He has marked us as His Chosen People henceforth to lead in the regeneration of the world...The Pacific is our ocean... Where shall we turn for consumers of our surplus? ...China is our natural customer... The power that rules the Pacific...is the power that rules the world. And, with the Philippines, that power is and will forever be the American Republic."*[37]

THE STAGE HAD BEEN SET for the costly, long, and bloody Philippines War, euphemistically referred to even today as the Philippine Insurrection in American history textbooks. The intent of this subterfuge was to convey the impression that American forces were subduing a rebellion against lawful authority. A further propaganda ploy was to refer to the U.S. Army's enemies in the Philippines as *ladrones*, or bandits. In fact, the rebels were nationalists and America had sent an occupying army to put down a legitimate independence movement—shades of the numerous interventions in Latin America in decades to come. Few then could imagine it would involve some 100,000 American soldiers over a three-year period and cost the lives of an estimated 200,000 Filipinos, civilians and the so-called *ladrones*.

Almost from the beginning, the war became a racist conflict, its barbarities little different from those of the Indian Wars so recently concluded—and so similar to the Vietnam War two generations later. Search-and-destroy missions, the hallmark of American infantry wars in the Philippines and later in

Vietnam, Laos, and Cambodia, were first practiced by the U.S. Cavalry during the Indian Wars. Mounted soldiers had made a practice of riding through Indian encampments—when the braves had been drawn off by subterfuge—shooting through wigwams and killing squaws and children, driving off or shooting their horses, and pillaging and setting fire to what remained. High-ranking officers in the Philippines were former cavalry lieutenants from the Indian Wars; "Indian hunting" was a term used by U.S. soldiers when they moved through the jungles of the Philippines seeking out the "niggers."

Unlike in Vietnam, however, the United States did prevail in the Philippines, even though fighting continued in parts of the archipelago years after July 1902, when President Theodore Roosevelt formally declared the war was won against the "insurrection".

BACK IN THE UNITED STATES, the Army decided by June 1898 that it had gathered together enough soldiers—some 17,000—and was prepared to embark for Cuba. Some of the top brass, however, wanted to wait until fall for cooler weather and more training for the green volunteers. McKinley would likely have agreed, but the public—driven by the baying and yelping press—was rabid for military action, the sooner the better.

Finally on June 14, General William Shafter and his army departed Tampa, Florida, under naval escort, destination Cuba. The expeditionary force, aboard thirty-seven troop transports, included most of the available Regular Army plus three regiments of volunteers—including the First Volunteer Cavalry, Lt. Colonel Theodore Roosevelt's soon-to-be-made-famous "Rough Riders."

A week later, the U.S. invasion flotilla arrived off Cuba and Shafter landed his troops at Daiquiri, an open roadstead near Santiago. Although there were some 200,000 Spanish troops on the island, fewer than 35,000 were in the Santiago area, and the garrison of Santiago totaled only 13,000. Surprisingly, there was no opposition, and for about a week troops and equipment came noisily ashore in near-total disorder. A coordinated attack by the somnolent Spanish during the landing operations would almost certainly have resulted in heavy American casualties and the destruction of the beachhead. It never came.

"Take up the White Man's Burden—

Send forth the best ye breed—

Go bind your sons to exile

To serve your captives' need;

To wait in heavy harness

On fluttered folk and wild—

Your new-caught, sullen peoples,

Half devil and half child." [38]

FOR TWO WEEKS, General Shafter, his huge frame drooping atop a mule, blundered into the dense jungle, heading his troops in the general direction of Santiago. Running short of provisions and confronted by a surprisingly well-coordinated defense in strongly fortified positions, Shafter's forces faced imminent surrender or annihilation. That he managed to avoid both contingencies was not due to his superior leadership but rather to the inept generalship of Captain-General Ramon Blanco y Erenas, the Spanish commander.

The burned locomotives at Daiquiri, Cuba, 1898.

By the end of the month, the army had managed to arrive within sight of Santiago. Barring the road to the city was San Juan Ridge, with well-defended Kettle Hill in front. Northeast of the city was another strong point, El Caney. On July 1, 1898, Shafter attacked both defensive positions simultaneously. Roosevelt, clad in a custom-fit uniform from Brooks Brothers in Manhattan, supposedly led the charge of his Rough Riders up Kettle Hill and San Juan Ridge—and overnight galloped into American folklore. He was also to be catapulted into the vice presidency as McKinley's running mate in 1900.

At the end of the day's fighting, U.S. forces held the ridge and had overrun El Caney, sealing the fate of Santiago. American casualties were about 1,500, with estimated Spanish losses of 850. After two weeks of negotiations, with the Spanish as reluctant as the Americans to fight a pitched battle or to undergo a long siege, the Spanish formally surrendered on July 17. The 100-day war in Cuba was over. On July 25, a U.S. force of 5,000 soldiers landed on the nearby Spanish island colony of Puerto Rico and quickly overwhelmed the Spanish defenders, with little bloodshed on either side.

IV. The Spanish and Philippines Wars

ON AUGUST 12, diplomats representing Spain and the United States met in the White House and signed a "protocol of peace" that ended the war. With victory won, the time had come for the withdrawal of American troops from Cuba and Puerto Rico and, as codified in the Teller Amendment, "leave the government and control of the island to its people." It would not happen!

Within days, U.S. officials started telling the Cubans to forget about independence.

First was President McKinley, who declared that the United States would rule Cuba under "the law of belligerent right over conquered territory."

Attorney General John Griggs was even more blunt:

> "... the U.S. Army in Havana is an 'invading army that would carry with it American sovereignty wherever it went.'"

Teddy Roosevelt and his Colts atop San Juan Hill

At the same time apologists for the flip-flop turned to the Teller Amendment. The publisher of the *New York Tribune* and a confidant of the president rejected the Amendment as "a self-denying ordnance possible only in a moment of national hysteria." *The New York Times* claimed that Americans had a "higher obligation" than merely conforming to hastily made promises, and must become: "permanent possessors of Cuba if the Cubans prove to be altogether incapable of self-government."

Jingo Senator Beveridge stated the Amendment was not binding because it had been approved by the Congress "in a moment of impulsive but mistaken generosity".

> *"In foreign policy McKinley was neither conservative nor radical but a mainstream Republican. Foreign policy was not his principal interest. He had never served on a foreign affairs or military affairs committee in Congress.... Early in his presidency he assured New York Senator Carl Schurz there would be 'no jingo nonsense' in his administration... He regarded Roosevelt as a loose cannon. (Roosevelt returned the compliment, suggesting that McKinley had all the backbone of a 'chocolate éclair'.)"*[39]

Wreck of the Reina Mercedes, Santiago, Cuba, 1898

IN THE PEACE TREATY, signed in Paris on December 10, 1898,[40] Spain ceded to the United States the islands of Cuba, the Philippines, tiny Guam in the distant Marianas,[41] and Puerto Rico in the nearby Caribbean. It was further agreed that the United States would pay $20 million within three months of treaty ratification on both sides. There was no explanation given in the treaty for the payment, but it was considered a gesture of good will. Cuba was granted its independence from Spain, and the United States Army undertook a program of rehabilitation intended to make the island a showcase of American capitalism and democracy for all of Latin America to emulate. That was not to happen.

No representative of Cuba, the Philippines, or Puerto Rico was present in Paris during the negotiations that determined their countries' fates. As far as most Americans were concerned, the very idea that the victors should listen to the views of the defeated was absurd. Latin Americans and Asians, in the eyes of racist Americans, were incapable of self-government, among their various other deficiencies.

Yet there were racial fears of American annexation of dark-skinned Cubans and Filipinos. Senator Schurz pointed out that if the two former colonies were acquired, it meant statehood that would contaminate America. Imagine what that would mean, he declared:

> ...fancy the Senators and Representatives of ten or twelve millions of tropical people, people of the Latin race mixed with Indian and African blood...fancy them sitting in the Halls of Congress, throwing the weight of their intelligence, their morality, their political notions and habits, their prejudices and passions, into the scale of the destinies of this Republic.... Tell me, does not your imagination recoil from the picture?[42]

Midway Island, acquired by the United States in 1867, and newly-possessed Guam became strategic Pacific stepping-stones to the Far East. Postage-stamp-sized Wake Island, formally annexed by the United States on January 17, 1899, filled the broad ocean gap between Midway and Guam; these three islands would play a prominent role in a later war with Japan. Also falling to America in 1899 was the island of Tutuila in the Samoan group, the country's share in the partitioning by the big European powers. The Hawaiian Islands, with one of the best large-warship anchorages in the Pacific—Pearl Harbor—had been formally annexed on June 15, 1898 after a carefully arranged *coup d'etat* by U.S. businessmen. It would become the fulcrum of a growing and aggressive naval United States presence in the Pacific.

In January, Senator Beveridge, only a half step behind his war-mongering colleague, Cabot Lodge, in his indefatigable pursuit of American empire, addressed the Senate by suggesting that the times called for forthrightness. He pulled out all of the stops.

> The Philippines are ours forever... and just beyond the Philippines are China's illimitable markets. We will not retreat from either.... We will not renounce our part in the mission of our race, trustee, under God, of the civilization of the world.... The Pacific is our ocean.... China is our natural customer.... No land in America surpasses in fertility the plains and valleys of Luzon. Rice and coffee, sugar and cocoanuts, hemp and tobacco... the wood of the Philippines can supply the furniture of the world for a century to come. At Cebu the best informed man on the island told me that 40 miles of Cebu's mountain chain are practically mountains of coal.... It has been charged that our conduct of the war has been cruel. Senators, it has been the reverse... you must remember that we are not dealing with Americans or Europeans. We are dealing with Orientals.[43]

THE SPANISH WAR, far-reaching in its consequences, had, indeed, been "splendid." Of a total of 274,000 officers and men who served in the army during the war and the period of demobilization (to the end of 1898), the total number of deaths in the American Army at all camps in the United States and in all theaters of war, was 5,462; these latter figures were never announced by the government. The U.S. Navy, in two memorable battles, albeit against a third-rate naval power, had distinguished itself. A corollary: the North and the South, for the first time since 1861, were united, sending an unmistakable message to the world that America henceforth would be a nation to be reckoned with in international affairs.

In 1901, Secretary of State Elihu Root and Senator Orville Hitchcock Platt of Connecticut, chairman of the Senate Committee on Relations with Cuba, jointly wrote the law that would control the destiny of Cuba for decades to come. America granted limited self-government to the Cubans and an amendment to the new Cuban constitution—the Platt Amendment—specifically gave the United States,

> "…the right to intervene for the preservation of Cuban independence, and the maintenance of a government adequate for the protection of life, property and individual liberty."[44]

Santiago — the dead line at the arsenal, 1899

It became a vital document in the history of U.S. foreign policy, and Washington would later apply the Platt Amendment's restrictive provisions in many parts of Latin America, where it is known to this day as *plattismo*.

In 1902, in an election the Americans supervised, Tomas Estrada Palma, who had lived for years in the town of Central Valley, New York, was chosen as the first president of the Republic of Cuba. General Wood, the military governor, wrote in a private letter what every informed Cuban and American already knew:

> "There is, of course, little or no independence left Cuba under the Platt Amendment."[45]

Whenever the United States felt the Cuban people needed to be saved from internal, or later *external Communist* chaos, they sent in the Marines: in 1906, when a civil war supposedly threatened; in 1912, to quash a rebellion of ex-slaves and protect the cane fields of the Cuban-American Sugar Company; and in 1917 when Woodrow Wilson sought to ensure sugar supplies as he took the United States into the Great War. Each time, the government pronounced its intentions as benign and the presence of Marines as temporary.

THE TELLER AMENDMENT to the war resolution prohibited outright annexation of Cuba. What about the other spoils of the war? In particular, what should America do about the Philippines, the biggest prize of all? Swallow up the entire archipelago, as the imperialists demanded; keep only the city of Manila on the island of Luzon and Cavite naval base on Manila Bay, as Admiral Dewey advised; or return all the islands to the Filipinos, as the anti-imperialists insisted? The lines were sharply drawn.

Opposition to annexation ranged across a broad spectrum—from idealists with noble humanitarian concerns to out-and-out racists. Those who felt that the war had been in the name of freedom for Spain's vassals opposed takeover of any kind. In their view, the United States was on the verge of becoming a new colonial power, and the idea did not sit well with them. There were also concerns about the nation absorbing additional colored populations. The War Between the States had been over slavery, and the South still smarted from that conflict's legacies. Senator John McLaurin of South Carolina spoke for his racist constituents—and the entire South as well—when he warned that the Filipinos were a heterogeneous compound of inefficient humanity, and that attempting to assimilate them into American society could mean disaster for the nation. Other anti-imperialists contended that it was ridiculous to talk about bringing self-government to a people genetically unfit to govern themselves.

On the opposite side were the vocal interventionists who considered the acquisition of the Philippines fundamentally America's Manifest Destiny. They issued declarations appealing to national chauvinism:

"Where the flag goes up it must never come down."

There were also many Americans who believed fervently that it was their nation's duty to bring Christianity as well as civilization to the "savages" who lived in the Philippines, not caring to learn that most Filipinos had been Roman Catholics for generations. In addition, many invoked the deity as "the unseen hand of divine destiny" that mandated America to acquire the islands.

Then there remained the question: would the natives benignly accept American occupation and be content to be wards of the liberators? The first military commanders on the scene thought so—and were blindly confident that the Filipinos would welcome United States rule if it promised peace and prosperity.

Filipino leader Emilio Aguinaldo and his followers were considered only a noisy minority, commanding no significant allegiance from the general population. On January 5, 1899, when Aguinaldo proclaimed himself head of the Philippine Republic, the Americans scoffed: his hand-made republic was a house of cards and could easily be overwhelmed. Aguinaldo himself was considered an opportunist readily managed, or a "Chinese half-breed adventurer" with no legitimate authority to head a Philippine government. Nor could he presume to speak for the hundreds of diverse tribes scattered among the archipelago's hundreds of habitable islands. The arrogant occupiers were wrong on all counts! In fact, Aguinaldo had shown his mettle when he helped Dewey take over Manila. If the Spanish War had been "splendid," the coming Philippines War would be anything but.

> *"Finally, it should be the earnest and paramount aim of the military administration to win the confidence, respect, and affection of the inhabitants of the Philippines by assuring them in every way possible that full measure of individual rights and liberties which is the heritage of a free people, and by providing to them that the mission of the United States is one of benevolent assimilation, substituting the mild sway of justice and right for arbitrary rule."*

—Excerpt from President William McKinley's "Benevolent Assimilation" Proclamation, December 21, 1898

WHAT TO DO with the Philippines was the president's call, and as always he held his cards close to his vest. Initially the taciturn McKinley appeared to favor take-over of only a port, Manila perhaps? But as the debate in the Congress heated up over the vote for or against annexation of Hawaii, McKinley changed his mind. A year after he sent U.S. troops to "benevolently assimilate" the Filipinos, McKinley allegedly told a visiting Methodist Missionary group how he had arrived at his final decision.

> I didn't want the Philippines, and when they came to us as a gift from the gods, I did not know what to do with them. I thought first we would only take Manila; then Luzon; then other islands, perhaps, also. I walked the floor of the White House night after night until midnight; and I am not ashamed to tell you gentlemen, that I went down on my knees and prayed Almighty God for light and guidance... And one night it came to me this way... One—that we could not give them back to Spain—that would be cowardly and dishonorable; Two—that we could not turn them over to France or Germany—our commercial rivals in the Orient—that would have been bad business and discreditable; Three—that we could not leave them to themselves—they were unfit for self-government—and they would soon have anarchy and misrule over there worse than Spain's was; and Four—that there was nothing left for us to do but to take them all, and to educate the Filipinos, and uplift and civilize and Christianize them, and by God's grace do the very best we could by them... And then I went to bed.[46]

> *"The most ultimately righteous of all wars... is a war with savages which establishes the foundations for the future greatness of a mighty people... of incalculable importance for the dominant races."* To fervent racist Theodore Roosevelt, the Filipinos were *"Chinese halfbreeds, Malay bandits, savages, barbarians, a wild and ignorant people, Apaches, Sioux, Chinese boxers."*[47]

THE PHILIPPINES WAR began in earnest in February 1899 when a Filipino patrol supposedly intruded on territory marked as American outside Manila;[48] rifle fire was exchanged and reinforcements were called in. American casualties during the first week totaled 268. It was going to be a vicious counterinsurgency war in the jungles of the Philippines, remarkably similar to America's undeclared guerrilla wars in the jungles of Indochina and the mountains of Afghanistan sixty and a hundred years in the future.

To bigoted U.S. soldiers and their officers, the Filipinos were demeaned as "niggers" and "gugus," to be "civilized" with the Americans' powerful .30/.40 Krag-Jorgensen five-shot, bolt-action repeating rifle that was standard issue. The Army's search-and-destroy missions in the Philippines were not labeled as such; they were euphemistically called "patrols"—as American soldiers routinely burned down villages and gunned down the villagers: men, women, and children. The carabao, a species of buffalo upon which the natives depended for agriculture, transportation, and meat, were purposefully decimated by the marauding American troops. Without carabao, the Filipinos could not cultivate rice, their staple food, leading to mass starvation.

Reprisals against the guerrillas, who set ambushes and booby-traps behind them as they melted away in the thick jungles, became increasingly cruel and dehumanized, particularly when the Americans suffered casualties. To cite an example, Captain Matthew Batson initially deplored the actions of his troops as they looted and destroyed villages. In a letter to his family, Batson wrote first that "We come as a Christian people..." He wrote later:

> The time has now come, when it is necessary to conduct this warfare with utmost rigor"—this after he had lost a comrade in a guerrilla ambush, when he ordered the next town they came upon would be razed to the ground.[49]

It wasn't long before troops on patrol marched to such xenophobic songs as:

> Damn, damn, damn the Filipinos!
>
> Cut-throat Khakiac *ladrones!*
>
> Underneath the starry flag,
>
> Civilize them with a Krag.
>
> And return us to our beloved home.[50]

To extract information from recalcitrant Filipino prisoners—when they weren't immediately bayoneted or shot—U.S. soldiers used was called the "water cure." Today it is called "water boarding." During a Congressional committee hearing following the war, a witness described its use.

> The prisoner was tied and placed on his back under a water tank holding probably 100 gallons. The faucet was opened and a stream of water was forced down or allowed to run down his throat. His throat was held so he could not prevent swallowing the water.... When he was filled with water it was forced out of him by pressing a foot on his stomach... and this continued from five to fifteen minutes. A native interpreter stood immediately over this man as he lay on the floor and kept saying some word which I should judge meant 'confess' or 'answer.' If the prisoner did not respond, the process was repeated, this time with a syringe from a five-gallon can. If the prisoner still held out, the doctor [Dr. Palmer Lyons, an Army contract surgeon] ordered a second one. This second syringe was inserted into the prisoner's nose and the doctor ordered some salt thrown into the water.[51]

AT THE BEGINNING of the war, correspondents and their editors handled the subject of U.S. atrocities with kid gloves, reluctant initially—as in every U.S. war since—to appear unpatriotic. But gradually the press began to take the issue seriously; besides, such stories were popular with readers. U.S. news reporters in the Philippines were expected to avoid gruesome details that put the American soldiers in a bad light. Those who focused on atrocities were sent back to the United States; Philippine newsmen, for the same violation, were exiled to far-away Guam. However, letters home were not censored, and many of these found their way into newspapers.

A letter that was published in a small California newspaper before it was picked up by the big eastern newspapers illustrated how at least some soldiers acted toward the Filipinos.

"We only tell a man once. If he refuses, we shoot him. We killed over 300 natives the first night... If they fire a shot from a house, we burn the house down and every house near it, and shoot the natives, so they are pretty quiet now."[52]

Prayer Before the Surrender. Philippine Insurgents., ca. 1900

Another letter home from an artilleryman described what followed the shelling of a village.

"We went in and killed every native we met, men, women, and children. It was a dreadful sight, the killing of the poor creatures."[53]

The U.S. soldiers of 1899 to 1903 had gotten orders to "spare no one" because several Americans had been captured and "hacked to pieces." The same regiment was involved in "the slaughter of one thousand men, women, and children." During the destruction of Titatia, according to another supposed eye-witness:

I am in my glory when I can sight my gun on some dark-skin and pull the trigger," wrote another soldier. And from yet another, of the killing frenzy that had developed in his regiment: "Our fighting blood was up, and we all wanted to kill 'niggers.' This shooting human beings is a 'hot game' and beats rabbit hunting all to pieces... such a slaughter you never saw. We killed them like rabbits, hundreds, yes, thousands of them.[54]

A *Philadelphia Ledger* correspondent filed a story that was chilling in its candor and a convincing indictment of the American Army's loose discipline:

The present war is no bloodless, fake, *opera bouffe* engagement. Our men have been relentless; have killed... men, women, children, prisoners and captives, active insurgents and suspected people, from lads of ten and up, an idea prevailing that the Filipino is little better than a dog, a noisome reptile in some instances, whose best disposition is the rubbish heap. Our soldiers have pumped salt water into men to 'make them talk,' have taken prisoner people who held up their hands and peacefully surrendered, and an hour later, without an atom of evidence to show that they were even *insurrectos*, stood them on a bridge and shot them down one by one, to drop into the water below and float down as an example to those who found their bullet-ridden corpses.[55]

A former U.S. Army contract surgeon came up with an expedient rationalization of American atrocities: it was the climate! According to his idiotic view, such "transgressions" were a result of

> "the tropical and vertical sun, impairing the judgment of men from cooler climates."

Furthermore, according to that apologist's skewed reasoning, because of the intense heat,

> "it does not take the American soldier, from private to general, long to conceive of the *insurrectos* as vermin, only to be ridded by extermination."[56]

One general told reporters that "it might be necessary to kill half the native population in order to bring 'perfect justice' to the surviving half", which recalls the infamous declaration of a U.S. Army officer in Vietnam that he was

> "forced to destroy a native village in order to save it."

Underlying the atrocities was the unconcealed bigotry of the American troops who looked upon the Filipinos as inferior beings to justify their genocide.

> Our 'little brown brother'... is without doubt unreliable, untrustworthy, ignorant, vicious, immoral and lazy... and, as a race, more dishonest than any known race on the face of the earth," wrote an Associated Press reporter in a book on the war, which was so full of details of atrocities—and his own bigotry—that he had it originally published under a *nom de plume*.[57]

> *"In 1899, we were compelled to defend ourselves against the Filipinos, who 'assailed our sovereignty' as President McKinley announced angrily to Congress: 'there will be no useless parley, no pause, until the insurrection is suppressed and American authority acknowledged and established,' the pretext of rescuing the Philippines from Spanish rule having been abandoned."*[58]

IN THE VILLAGE of Balangiga on the island of Samar, at the end of September, near the end of the third year of the undeclared war, some fifty U.S. soldiers were killed at breakfast. Bolo-knife-wielding Filipino laborers attacked the unarmed Americans and chopped up their bodies. Historian Miller wrote that,

> "No single event in the Philippines so shocked the American people.... It was... the worst disaster for the United States Army since Custer's fate at Little Big Horn."[59]

Severe retaliatory measures were called for and President Roosevelt set the tenor for retaliation-in-kind. As commander-in-chief, he gave a direct order to General Adna Chaffee, the top officer in the Philippines at the time, to do whatever was necessary to "pacify" Samar.

Chaffee was a hard-bitten soldier's soldier, and as a former cavalryman was more at home seated on a galloping horse than behind a desk. Like nearly all the high-ranking officers in the Philippines, he had spent his early career chasing Indian braves on the plains of the American West and demolishing their villages. Chaffee, in turn, gave the job of pacification to Brigadier General Jacob Smith, an old reliable Indian fighter himself and a veteran of the Wounded Knee massacre in 1890. He knew what had to be done and Chaffee assigned a brigade of Marines to help him do it. Smith reportedly told the Marines:

> "I want no prisoners. I wish you to kill and burn.... I want all persons killed who are capable of bearing arms in actual hostilities against the United States."[60]

The lower age limit of those to be killed was set at *ten years*. He also ordered his men to turn the entire island of Samar into what he graphically called "a howling wilderness." Smith was later court-martialed and convicted of "conduct to the prejudice of good order and military discipline," but received lenient treatment and was merely forced to take an early retirement.

U.S. ARMY AND ROOSEVELT administration officials covered up the ruthlessness of the conflict, and emphasized that most of the natives welcomed U.S. sovereignty. Cruelties were the work of only a tiny minority of the soldiers, it was implied. Those atrocity reports that newspapermen managed to pry loose were watered-down versions of the truth. As a result, few Americans then or now know that tens of thousands of American soldiers and sailors were sent to the Philippines to put down a popular insurrection.

The insurgents were finally subjugated, more or less, not by bayoneting prisoners or shooting everyone over the age of ten or turning the islands into howling wildernesses. The "victory" was accomplished by taking a page out of "Butcher" Weyler's playbook for which he had been so resoundingly condemned six years before: concentration camps. Typical of orders from headquarters to station commanders was the following, dated December 1, 1901:

> To put an end to enforced contributions now levied by insurgents upon the inhabitants of sparsely settled and outlying barrios and districts by means of intimidation and assassination, commanding officers... will immediately specify and establish plainly marked limits surrounding each town bounding a zone within which it may be practicable... to exercise efficient supervision over and furnish protection to inhabitants (who desire to be peaceful) against the depredations of armed insurgents.[61]

Inhabitants were to be informed of the danger of noncompliance:

> ...unless they move by December 25...with all their movable food supplies, including rice, chicken, livestock, etc., to within the limits of the zone established at their own or nearest town, their property (found outside of said zone at said date) will become liable to confiscation or destruction.[62]

The final costs of the war to the U.S. Army were 4,243 killed and 2,818 wounded in action. Filipino losses were estimated to be between 16,000 and 20,000 insurgents killed. Filipino noncombatants who were killed by U.S. troops and died of disease and famine were more difficult to estimate; the figure lay between 100,000 and 200,000.[63]

DOMESTICALLY, ONE OF THE MAJOR political consequences of the war with Spain was the meteoric rise of Rough Rider Theodore Roosevelt to national prominence. He was elected governor of New York State in 1899, then ran successfully as vice president with McKinley in 1900. He succeeded to the presidency on September 12, 1901 when McKinley died of his wounds following an assassination attempt in Buffalo, New York a week earlier. Roosevelt had dramatically buckboarded his way from his remote hunting lodge in New York's Adirondack Mountains to the North Creek station of the single-track Delaware and Hudson Railroad to get to Washington for his swearing in. After filling out the unexpired term of office of McKinley, Roosevelt was easily elected president in 1904.

Roosevelt had his eye trained on the presidency again in 1919. Most political analysts of the period agreed that he almost certainly would have won the Republican Party's nomination, going on to defeat the inept James Cox-Franklin D. Roosevelt ticket in 1920. However, his untimely death in 1919 prevented him from becoming America's first three-term president.

Historian Miller concluded his *Benevolent Assimilation* by writing that the lessons of Batanga and Samar seem:

> To have been lost even on well-educated Americans. In 1970, a Harvard professor decided that one hundred years ago, or even as recently as World War II, 'nobody would have raised an issue such as the Song My [My Lai 4] massacre. Americans *had* raised such issues before, during the war in the Philippines, after Wounded Knee, and as early as the eighteenth century when friendly Indians were slaughtered in a wave of hysteria at Paxton, Pennsylvania... Lieutenant William Calley, Jr. helped revive memories of earlier and very similar atrocities in the Philippines.'[64]

IN THE DECADE after the end of the Spanish and Philippines Wars, the U.S. Navy and Cuban authorities agreed that something should be done about the wreck of the *Maine* in Havana Harbor, its two masts sticking up incongruously out of the water. From the Cubans' perspective, it was an eyesore taking up valuable harbor space; a shoal was also building up, increasingly a hazard to shipping in the confines of the harbor. Patriotic organizations in the United States and next of kin also had an agenda: the remains of the estimated seventy bodies of the battleship's crew interred inside the hull should be identified if possible and given heroes' rites. Congress finally appropriated $650,000 to recover the remains of the crew and tow the hulk offshore for final burial. The plan called for building a cofferdam around the ship, pumping out the water to expose as much of the wreck as feasible, and then patching and refloating the derelict.

At the time, Congress did not call for a new investigation of the tragedy. But once the project was underway, it seemed a sensible idea to examine the wreck more closely when more of it was above water and accessible. A new Court of Inquiry was appointed with Rear Admiral Charles E. Vreeland as its head. The new team acknowledged that an ammunition magazine explosion triggered by a coal bunker fire could have caused the major damage uncovered in a far-forward structural frame, but it also concluded that an exploding magazine could not have ripped up hull plating farther aft as was discovered as the hull rose out of the water. After due deliberation, the Vreeland Court concurred with the first Court: the destruction of the *Maine* had been caused by an external mine.

On February 13, 1912, the cofferdam was flooded and the *Maine* refloated. Four days later, escorted by a small flotilla of U.S. Navy warships and gunboats of the Republic of Cuba, the hulk was towed offshore, cast off, and with proper military ceremony allowed to sink in waters estimated to be 3,600 feet deep.

DESPITE THE TWO Naval Courts' consistent findings, nagging questions remained well into the 20th century. Had politics influenced the judgments of the members of the 1898 inquiry? The yellow press had been clamoring for a war with Spain. All eyes had been on the Court; were the members immune to such pressures? The first Court faced an urgency to complete its assigned task, a "rush to judgment" that may have precluded the calling of expert witnesses to testify. The second Court, acknowledged to be more technically competent and under no time constraints, had also conducted its investigation without bringing in any forensic specialists—of which the Navy had many. Could the Vreeland Court dare to broach the issue that the United States had gone to war thirteen years before, "Remember the *Maine*" its battle cry, without justification?

Admiral Hyman George Rickover was a serious student of American history: he published a book in 1972 entitled *Eminent Americans: Namesakes of the Polaris Submarine Fleet*.[63] During early tours of duty in Panama and the Philippines, Rickover came to regard the Spanish War as pivotal in American history. In 1974, he recalled, when he read an article in a Washington newspaper, "Returning to the Riddle of the Explosion that Sank the *Maine*," he was intrigued. Was it, in fact, an external explosion that had sunk the ship? One point raised by the author of the newspaper story that particularly irked Rickover was the statement by the Chief of the Navy's Bureau of Steam Engineering in 1898 that the cause was an internal explosion, yet he had not been asked to testify at the Court of Inquiry.

Rickover threw down his gauntlet. He intended to unravel the mystery and he would do it with his characteristic verve, his technical brilliance, and attention to detail that marked his successful management of the Navy's nuclear-propulsion and *Polaris* missile programs. As a four-star Admiral, he had a big staff to help and plenty of bureaucratic clout. Rickover's research was thoroughgoing. He first asked the naval attachés of the Spanish, British and French embassies to dig out related documents from their nations' archives, and then had the office of the Director of Naval Intelligence translate those from Spain and France.

Rickover recruited two technical specialists, one an expert on interpretation of underwater photography, the other an authority on warship battle damage. The two sifted through all of the technical material from both the 1898 and 1911 investigations. Their sober conclusions:

> We have found no technical evidence in the records examined that an external explosion initiated the destruction of the *Maine*. The available evidence is consistent with an internal explosion alone. We therefore conclude that an internal source was the cause of the explosion. The most likely source was heat from a fire in a coal bunker adjacent to the 6-inch reserve magazine.

However, as conservative engineers, they hedged their bets:

> "... since there is no way of proving this, other internal causes cannot be eliminated as possibilities."[64]

Indeed, the standard Cuban view holds that the *Maine* was intentionally blown up by the U.S. itself.

Captain Sigsbee had been a principal witness during the first inquiry. Based on his testimony of seventy-seven years before, Rickover first judged him mildly "an individual who was unfamiliar with his ship." Later in his book, *How the Battleship Maine was Destroyed*, Rickover was more severe, broaching the idea that Sigsbee must share in the blame for not putting into practice stricter measures to safeguard his command. In particular, in Rickover's unforgiving view, Sigsbee certainly knew about the dangers of spontaneous combustion and should also have been aware that bunker temperature alarms were notoriously inaccurate. Rickover's research also established that two of Sigsbee's earlier commands, the *Kearsarge* and the *Texas*, were found to be dirty upon inspection.

RICKOVER further pilloried Sigsbee with a series of "might-have-beens":

> He might have been a good seaman and a brave man, but perhaps also the victim of the new technology which was transforming the Navy. He might not have understood the complexities of the ship he commanded. He might have suffered from the division in the Navy which separated line officers from shipboard engineers.... The vagueness and uncertainty in his testimony might stem from a belief that giving an order was tantamount to its execution. Whatever the reasons, he appears to have been isolated from the day-to-day routine.[65]

Finally, to buttress their conclusion that the explosion was almost certainly caused by spontaneous combustion in a coal bunker, Rickover's team explored Navy records that documented coal-bunker fires in American men-of-war in the three-year period preceding the *Maine* explosion. There were three such fires in the *Olympia*; four in the *Wilmington;* and at least one in the *Petrel*, the *Lancaster*, and the *Indiana;* several in the *Brooklyn;* and hazardous ones on the *Cincinnati*, the *New York*, and the *Oregon* "that almost caused the magazines to explode."

WHOSE WAR HAD IT BEEN, AFTER ALL? Was it William Randolph Hearst and Joseph Pulitzer and their "yellow newspapers?" Hearst all along had claimed it was his *Journal's* war, and nearly every newspaper publisher in the United States—"yellow" or plain black-and-white—had willingly collaborated in hoodwinking the public. In 1934, in a landmark study of the New York press from 1895 to 1898, historian John L. Offner opined that

> The Spanish-American War would not have occurred had not the appearance of Hearst in New York newspaper publishing precipitated a bitter battle for newspaper circulation. The Cuban insurrection and its attendant horrors furnished a unique opportunity to the proprietors of the sensational press to prove their enterprise and provide the types of news that sold papers.[66]

What about American business? Wall Street has always been a sensitive barometer of U.S. business and financial interests. Rumors of increased strain in U.S.-Spanish relations were generally accompanied by declines in stock prices and editorial demands from the financial press for easing of tensions. Reports of peace overtures rallied prices. The leading voice of business in the United States at that time, the *Journal of Commerce*, consistently opposed a war with Spain. The Spanish government, for its part, particularly in the final months before America went to war, worked diligently to protect U.S. property and to amicably settle claims for damages.

What role had the *junta* played? Comfortably ensconced in New York City, the group served more than delicious peanuts to American reporters. Their loud and effective anti-Spanish propaganda undoubtedly contributed to a public opinion that greased the way for McKinley's declaration of war.

Offner straddled the fence, spreading the blame and concluding,

> Hearst's drive to dominate New York City journalism caused the public hysteria that galvanized the nation to intervene. But sensational journalism had only a marginal impact. Hearst played on American prejudices, but did not create them. Hearst charged that Spaniards had sunk the Maine, yet he did not write the naval report [erroneous as it turned out] that propelled the nation toward war.[67]

There was as yet in the United States no full-blown military-industrial complex, that combination of purchasers and manufacturers of weapons that would later grow to dominate decisions of war and peace. There were, however, the glimmerings of such a cabal: the formation of the Navy League in 1904 to promote a bigger Navy. This organization consisted of naval officers, active and retired, so-called "patriots," and representatives of companies—particularly steelmakers—that stood to benefit by increases in Naval expenditures.

FINALLY, WAS IT WILLIAM MCKINLEY'S WAR? On the surface, McKinley and his entire cabinet–with the exception of Russell A. Alger, Secretary of War–were anxious to avoid war. So were the Republican leaders in Congress, despite the drumbeats from Henry Cabot Lodge and indefatigable warrior Theodore Roosevelt. To most of his contemporaries, McKinley was an enigma. No one could say for certain what his political intentions were. His public statements were purposefully vague, and he never disclosed his aims, if he had any. His actions, too, were ambiguous.

> Those who visited him at the White House came away impressed with his sweetness of temper, his soothing disposition, his willingness to please, to placate, to agree, but they saw few signs of personal force or deeply held conviction... men thought him amiably weak... not only weak, but supine.[68]

If McKinley had been required to submit his design for a remodeled republic in a referendum to the electorate, few would have approved it. Instead, he gained national support for his modest revolution by taking the "back door," armed intervention in Cuba—the same unsavory entrance FDR employed in 1941 against Nazi Germany.

WHILE MOST AMERICANS had been conditioned by the flood of propaganda to believe they had gone to war out of highest motives, in Europe it was another story. The combination of U.S. belligerence in the Venezuelan dispute followed by the transparent aggression against Spain created downright hostility—and a "to hell with Manifest Destiny" attitude. Across Europe there was unanimous condemnation of U.S. actions. Leading the charge was Kaiser Wilhelm II, whose

> "...first romantic impulse was to fly to the aid of Maria Cristina [of Spain] in defense of monarchical principles."

Czar Nicholas II also sympathized with Spain, as did Queen Victoria, who apparently was outraged at U.S. demands for Cuban independence:

> "They might just as soon declare Ireland independent."[69]

Understandably, the Spanish press flagellated the United States as:

> "...a nation of immigrant outcasts and avaricious shopkeepers, without culture, without honor, without a soul... hegemonic, materialistic hypocrites."[70]

Closer to home, many American historians have also condemned McKinley's decision for war when no vital U.S. interests were involved; these critics have described the war as "unnecessary" and "totally unnecessary." Others took a different tack: that American professions of moral outrage against the Spanish were simply cover for selfish economic interests. Maybe the business community, after all, had quietly pushed the country to war to acquire new markets. Nevertheless, it is difficult to avoid the conclusion that seems obvious in hindsight: that it was a deliberate war of aggression for the purpose of territorial expansion, similar to Polk's war on Mexico. Indeed, it was a giant leap forward for the United States on its path to empire.

THE SPANISH AND PHILIPPINES WARS were pivotal in American history for other reasons, too. For the first time, U.S. soldiers fought overseas. For the first time, America acquired lands far beyond its shores, the former colony becoming colonialist. The acquisition of the Philippines also sharply polarized America between interventionists and isolationists. In different guises and involving diverse theaters, Americans would debate essentially the same issue to this day.

The most brazen imperialistic legacy of the war remained the continued American presence in a 45-square-mile sliver of territory on Guantánamo Bay on Cuba's southeastern cost. The last lease, signed in 1934—coinciding with President Franklin D. Roosevelt's "good neighbor" policy—ceded perpetual use of this tiny wedge of land to the United States in return for an annual rent of $4,085. Cuban President Fidel Castro, who called the foreign base a dagger plunged into the heart of Cuban soil, has always refused to cash the checks. At this writing, it is home to Camp Delta, the controversial detention-and-interrogation operation run by the U.S. Defense Department which incarcerates incommunicado, contrary to the Geneva Convention, suspected *jihadists* and terrorists, most captured in Afghanistan. They are called "enemy combatants" rather than "prisoners of war," to allow their torture. *The New York Times* of January 13, 2004, reported that senior Pentagon officials have stated shamelessly that:

> "They were planning to keep a large portion of the detainees at Guantanamo Bay for many years, perhaps indefinitely."[71]

Notes

[1] Walter Millis, *The Martial Spirit: A Study of Our War with Spain* (The Literary Guild of America, Cambridge MA, 1931), p. 160.

[2] Starting with the War for American Independence in 1775, the United States has engaged in almost continuous war and armed interventions up to the present day: Shay's Rebellion, 1786-1787; Little Turtle's War, 1786-1795; Whiskey Rebellion, 1794; American–French Quasi War, 1798-1800; Tripolitan War, 1801-1805; War of 1812, 1812-1814; Creek War, 1812-1814; Algerine War, 1815; First Seminole War, 1817-1818; Fredonian Rebellion, 1826-1827; Black Hawk War, 1832; Second Seminole War, 1835-1840; Texas War of Independence, 1835; Aroostook War, 1838-1839; Bear Flag Rebellion, 1846; U.S.-Mexican War, 1846-1848; Mariposa War, 1850-1851; Yuma and Mojave Uprising, 1851-1852; "Bleeding Kansas" Guerrilla War, 1854-1861; Rogue River War, 1855-1856; Third Seminole War, 1855-1858; Yakima War, 1855; Spokane War, 1858; Pyramid Lake War, 1858; Apache and Navajo War, 1860-1868; Civil War, 1861-1865; Minnesota Santee Sioux Uprising, 1862; Cheyenne and Arapaho War, 1864-1865; War for the Bozeman Trail, 1866-1868; Hancock's War, 1867; Snake War, 1866-1868; Sheridan's Campaign, 1868-1869; Modoc War, 1872-1873; Kiowa War, 1874-1875; Apache War, 1876-1886; Sioux War for the Black Hills, 1876-1877; Nez Perce War, 1877; Bannock War, 1878; Sheepeater War, 1879; Ute War, 1879; Sioux War, 1890-1891; Walker's Invasion of Mexico, 1853-1854; Walker's Invasion of Nicaragua, 1855-1857; Spanish War, 1898; Philippines War, 1899-1902; Boxer Rebellion, 1899-1901; Moro War, 1901-1913; Panamanian Revolution, 1903; Nicaraguan Civil War, 1909-1912; Villa's Raids and the Pershing Punitive Expedition, 1916-1917; The Great War, 1917-1918; Nicaraguan Civil War, 1925-1933; World War II, 1941-1945; Korean War, 1950-1953; Vietnam War, 1954-1975; Lebanese Civil War, 1958/1975-1992; Nicaraguan Civil War, 1978-1979/1982-1990; Honduran Civil War, 1981-1990; Grenada Intervention, 1983; U.S. invasion of Panama, 1989; Persian Gulf War, 1991, Bosnian War, 1992-1995; Somalian Civil War, 1988; Kosovo Crisis, 1996-1999;

Afghanistan War, 2000-present; Iraqi War, 2002-present. There were also "undeclared" wars in Korea, Laos, Thailand, Cambodia, and Vietnam in the 1950s and 1960s.

In *Perpetual War for Perpetual Peace: How We Got to Be So Hated*, published in 2002, Gore Vidal stated that the Federation of American Scientists had catalogued nearly 200 military incursions since 1945 in which the United States has been the aggressor. The title is taken from historian Charles Beard. Cited at http://findnsave.sacbee.com/Product/564785

See also Appendix 1, A History of Interventions by U.S. Armed Forces in the Western Hemisphere, 1806-1933.

[3] *Atlantic Monthly*, December, 1900.

[4] U.S. Ambassador to England and soon-to-be Secretary of State John Hay to Colonel Theodore Roosevelt of the Rough Riders, July 27, 1898. Millis, p. 348.

[5] Millis, p. 16.

[6] Kaiser Wilhelm II, Germany's emperor, thought Mahan's book so important that he ordered that every ship in his *Reichmarine* be issued a copy.

[7] The term jingo, or an extreme nationalist, was first used in Great Britain during the Russo-Turkish War of 1877-1878 by those who wanted England to join in the fight with Russia. It had appeared earlier in a popular London music-hall performance in which the chorus sang: "We don't want to fight, but, by jingo, if we do, we've got the ships, we've got the men, we've got the money, too."

[8] Jack Cameron Dierks, *A Leap to Arms: The Cuban Campaign of 1898* (J.B. Lippincott Company, New York, 1970), p. 7.

[9] Charles H. Brown, *The Correspondents' War: Journalists in the Spanish-American* War (Charles Scribner's Sons, New York, 1967), p. 5.

[10] The term filibuster was derived from the Spanish *filibustero* or freebooter, who in the mid-1800s were involved in revolutions in Latin-America. It has since come into more common usage as a political delaying tactic used in the Congress.

[11] Joseph E. Wisan, *The Cuban Crisis as Reflected in the New York Press, 1895-1898* (Columbia University Press, New York, 1938), p. 88-89.

[12] Howard Wayne Morgan, *America's Road to Empire: The War With Spain and Overseas Expansion* (Wiley, New York, 1965), p. 6.

[13] Joyce Milton, *The Yellow Kids: Foreign Correspondents in the Heyday of Yellow Journalism* (Harper & Row, Publishers, New York, 1989), p. 83.

[14] Brown, p. 11.

[15] Ibid., p. 12.

[16] Wisan, p. 21.

[17] Millis, p. 67.

[18] Ibid., p. 83. "Mrs. Jefferson Davis... was induced to sign an appeal to the Queen Regent of Spain, asking that she... save her from a fate worse than death... Mrs. Julia Ward Howe signed an appeal to Pope Leo XIII. The *Journal* then prepared a petition for general signature... and the names of 20,000 women were collected. Among them [were]... Mrs. Mark Hanna, Mrs. Nancy McKinley, the mother of the President, and Mrs. John Sherman, the wife of the Secretary of State.... In England... petitions went from London with the signatures of officers of organizations representing 200,000 women."

[19] Ibid., p. 84.

[20] Ibid.

[21] Both quotes from Walter Karp, *The Politics of War: The Story of Two Wars Which Altered Forever the Political Life of the American Republic 1890-1920* (Harper & Row, Publishers, New York, 1979), p. 78.

[22] Ibid., p. 71.

[23] Ibid., p. 84.

[24] *Maine* was one of the first two modern steel battleships built for the U.S. Navy. Her keel had been laid in the Brooklyn Navy Yard in 1888 as an armored cruiser, her original design an awkward hybrid: sails and coal-fired steam engines. During the years of her construction, the pace of military naval

architecture quickened, and when she joined the fleet in 1895 she no longer had masts and yardarms. In the same period, newer and more powerful battleships had been commissioned and built, and the *Maine* was downgraded to a second-class battleship.

[25] The term torpedo at the time was used interchangeably with the term mine, referring to a fixed marine munition, not a self-propelled, guided underwater missile with an explosive warhead.

[26] Spontaneous combustion is the ignition of combustible material as a result of internal heat generation usually caused by rapid oxidation. Bituminous (soft) coal which was used in Navy ships at the time was known to be more susceptible to spontaneous combustion than anthracite (hard) coal because of its superior burning characteristics. Fires ignited by spontaneous combustion often smoldered deep below the exposed surface of coal piles and emitted no visible smoke or flames. U.S. Navy shipboard regulations required that every day before 10AM the ship's engineering officer inspect the coal bunkers for excessive rise in temperature.

[27] W. A. Swanberg, *Citizen Hearst—A Biography of William Randolph Hearst* (Charles Scribners' Sons, New York, 1961), p. 91.

[28] Millis, p. 127

[29] Ibid., p. 98.

[30] Ibid., p. 127.

[31] Robert Kagan, *Dangerous Nation* (Alfred A. Knopf, New York, 2006), p. 397.

[32] Donald W. Mitchell, *A History of the Modern American Navy: From 1883 Through Pearl Harbor* (Alfred A. Knopf, New York, 1946), p. 57.

[33] Millis, p. 149.

[34] Brian McAllister Linn, *The Philippine War 1899-1902* (University Press of Kansas, Lawrence KS, 2000), p. 11.

[35] Millis, p. 317.

[36] Linn, p. 15-16. The Philippine archipelago covers an area of 500,000 square miles. Three principal groups of islands run north to south. Luzon is the largest and most populous and the site of Manila, the capital. The Visayas Islands group is next in size and includes Cebu, Layte, Negros, Panay, and Samar. Mindanao Island and the Sulu archipelago and a string of small islands extend to Borneo. Mountains, dense jungles, and swamps further separate the inhabitants.

[37] R. Ernest Dupuy and Trevor N. Dupuy, *The Encyclopedia of Military History* (Harper & Row, Publishers, New York, 1970), p. 908.

[38] Rudyard Kipling addressed "The White Man's Burden" to Americans and sent the poem directly to President Theodore Roosevelt, urging the United States to take advantage of its recent conquest of the Philippines. Roosevelt's response: "It was rather poor poetry, but good sense from the expansionist viewpoint."

[39] Stephen Kinzer, *Overthrow: America's Century of Regime Change From Hawaii to Iraq* (Henry Holt and Company, New York, 2006), p. 41.

[40] Ibid, p. 300. A gloomy painting, *The Signing of the Protocol of Peace Between the United States and Spain on August 12, 1898,* by French artist Theobald Chartran, gives the Treaty Room in the White House its name. It is the first thing visitors see as they enter. It depicts President William McKinley—the first American practitioner of "regime change"—observing diplomats signing the treaty that turned Cuba into an American protectorate and Puerto Rico into a colony. The so-called "protocol of peace" signed that day in Paris was not a pact between equal states; it was a victor's peace the United States forced on Spain after defeating its army in Cuba.

[41] During the Pacific War in 1945, Guam, along with Tinian and Saipan, served as an air base for the B-29 city firebombing campaign against Japan. During the Christmas, 1972, bombing of North Vietnam, more than 150 B-52's flew from Guam. The 209-square-mile island subsequently lost its strategic importance until 2004 when the wars in Afghanistan and Iraq renewed interest in Guam as a forward base. *The New York Times* of April 7, 2004, reported that facilities were under construction for the basing of the Air Force's B-52 and B-1 bombers and one nuclear-powered attack submarine; in addition to "a huge new

war reserve material warehouse... new underground pipes for delivering aviation fuel directly to parking pads for jets, and the first of 60 munitions storage 'igloos.' The article quoted Admiral Thomas B. Fargo, the senior military officer in the Pacific as declaring, "Guam's geo-strategic importance cannot be overstated."

[42] Frank Friedel, *The Splendid Little War* (Little Brown and Company, Boston, 1958), p. 13.

[43] George Black, *The Good Neighbor: How the United States Wrote the History of Central America and the Caribbean* (Pantheon Books, New York, 1988), p. 17.

[44] Howard Zinn, *The People's History of the United* States (Harper & Rowe, New York, 1980), p. 313-314.

[45] Black, p. 22.

[46] Millis, p. 384.

[47] Ibid., p. 86.

[48] America's war of conquest and its attendant atrocities in the Philippines is a subject rarely covered in history texts. When it is, the sordid episode is reduced to a bare mention of an "insurrection against American rule." Six decades later, Secretary of State Christian Herter maintained this myth when he denied a request from his good friend, Ambassador Carlos Rumulo, to recognize officially, as a final act of the Eisenhower Administration, that the "insurrection" was, in fact, the "Philippine-American War". Stuart Creighton Miller, *Benevolent Assimilation: The American Conquest of the Philippines, 1899-1903* (Yale University Press, New Haven CT, 1982), p. 266.

[49] Stanley Karnow, *In Our Image: America's Empire in the Philippines* (Ballantine Books, New York, 1990), p. 154.

[51] Ibid., p. 155.

[52] G. J. A. O'Toole, *The Spanish War: An American Epic, 1898* (W.W. Norton, New York, 1984), p. 389.

[53] Ibid., p. 396.

[54] Ibid., p. 397.

[55] Ibid., p. 398.

[56] Ibid., p. 399

[57] Ibid.

[58] Ibid., p. 400.

[59] Stuart Creighton Miller, *Benevolent Assimilation: The American Conquest of the Philippines 1899-1903* (Yale University Press, New Haven CT, 1982), p. 145..

[60] Noam Chomsky, *Turning the Tide: U.S. Intervention in Central America and the Struggle for Peace* (South End Press, Boston, 1985), p. 86.

[61] As the Navy's driving force behind the development and deployment of nuclear-powered submarines, and acquiring the sobriquet "Father of the Atomic Submarine," Rickover was well-positioned to write authoritatively on the subject. It had been former U.S. Navy practice to name submarines after fish and other marine life, but the new missile-launching submarines were huge capital ships in their own right, larger than some cruisers. It was decided to name them after distinguished figures in American history, well known and obscure, ranging from George Washington and Patrick Henry to Daniel Boone, Will Rogers, Tecumseh, chief of the Shawnees, and Kamehameha, king of the Hawaiians. The Navy's first nuclear-powered submarine, the *Nautilus*, on the other hand, was named after Captain Nemo's submarine in Jules Verne's prophetic science-fiction novel, *20,000 Leagues Under the Sea*. These submarines carried sixteen *Polaris* nuclear-tipped missiles that were launched underwater through vertical tubes, much like a torpedo. Once above the water's surface the solid-fuel rocket ignited, propelling the missile which would be guided to targets thousands of miles away.

[62] Theodore Rockwell, *The Rickover Effect: How One Man Made a Difference* (Naval Institute Press, Annapolis MD, 1992), p. 345.

[63] Norman Polmar and Thomas B. Allen, *Rickover* (Simon and Schuster, New York, 1982), p. 525-526.

[64] Hyman G. Rickover, *How the Battleship Maine was Destroyed*, (Naval History Div., Dept. of the Navy, Washington, 1976), p. 127-128.

[65] Ibid., p. 94.
[66] John L. Offner, *An Unwanted War—The Diplomacy of the United States and Spain Over Cuba, 1895-1898* (The University of North Carolina Press, Chapel Hill NC, 1992), p. 229.
[67] Ibid., p. 260.
[68] Walter Karp, *The Politics of War: The Story of Two Wars Which Altered Forever the Political Life of the American Republic 1890-1920* (Harper & Row, Publishers, New York, 1979), p. 71.
[69] Wisan, p. 460.
[70] Karp, p. 75.
[71] While the Bush administration insisted that the detainees be imprisoned indefinitely, that position flies in the face of both international law and morality. The detainees sought the three most basic elements of due process which they were denied: to be informed of the charges against them; to meet with their attorneys and family, and to have the opportunity to contest their incarceration. Alexander Hamilton wrote in Federalist No. 84: "The practice of arbitrary imprisonments has been in all ages one of the favorite and most formidable instruments of tyranny."

Chapter V:
The Great War

"I have always detested Germany. I have never gone there. I have read many German books on law. They are so far from our views that they have inspired in me a feeling of aversion."
—Woodrow Wilson, June 14, 1919.

AMERICAN HISTORY BOOKS closely tie Woodrow Wilson's presidency to the Great War. This is as it should be. It was clearly Wilson's intervention and his war. It was he who had sanctimoniously asked a joint session of the Congress on April 2, 1917, which he had called back to Washington from recess, for a war declaration against Germany:

> We are glad, now that we see the facts with no veil of false pretense about them, to fight thus for the ultimate peace of the world and for the liberation of its peoples, the German people included; for the rights of nations great and small and the privilege of men everywhere to choose their way of life and obedience. The world must be made safe for democracy.... To such a task we dedicate our lives and fortunes, everything that we are and everything that we have, with the pride of those who know that the day shall come when America is privileged to spend her blood and her might for the principles which gave her and the peace she has treasured. God helping her, she can do no other.[1]

The Congress stood, clapped, and vigorously cheered Wilson's words. By that date, relentless British propaganda had convinced most Americans that it was Germans who started the war, it was Germans who cut off the hands of little boys and the breasts of young women in Belgium, it was Germans in submarines who drowned innocent women and children on the high seas. It was also Germans who shot brave British nurse Edith Cavell for being a spy, and it was Germans who shot prisoners and used poison gas in the trenches. Most Americans were ready to follow their president in his quest to "make the world safe for democracy," whatever that vague slogan meant.

At the same time as the president spoke that fateful night, U.S. cavalry patrolled Pennsylvania Avenue from the White House to the Capitol in response to rumors of bombings. Instead of the national consensus Wilson sought, there was still ambivalence. While most Americans hissed when the thoroughly demonized German Kaiser's picture flashed on movie screens, not all did, and not all wanted their country to go to war. Once the nation was into the war, however, nearly every recalcitrant patriotically swung into line, or was vigorously pressed into line by repressive edicts that Wilson enthusiastically and hypocritically supported.

Wilson picked up another catch phrase that he used in later speeches, plagiarized from British science-fiction writer H.G. Wells in a pamphlet printed in 1914: "The war to end war."

To understand the entire 20th century it is necessary to understand Europe during the Great War. It was Europe's first major war in 100 years, since the time all of Europe had combined to defeat Napoleon. Out of the war grew myths and legends that still haunt nations: supposedly, Germany was solely guilty of starting the war, Germany waged war contrary to the laws of humanity, German people were genetically cruel, the German Emperor himself was mad, and Germany was out to conquer the world. Woodrow Wilson urged on the American people to total victory, much as a prophet in a white cape leading his flock into the Promised Land, his staff raised in triumph. In a spring, 1918, speech opening the campaign for a Third Liberty Loan he proclaimed quasi-religiously:

> There is but one response possible for us: Force, force, to the utmost, force without stint or limit, the righteous and triumphant force which shall make right the law of the world, and cast every selfish dominion down into the dust.[14]

In fact, the war in Europe had nothing to do with lawlessness and everything to do with selfish national interests and balance-of-power politics.

Earlier in his career, Wilson had rejected the use of military force for imperialistic purposes. In *Division and Reunion,* published in 1893, he pilloried President James Polk's preemptive war with Mexico as "ruthless aggrandizement." Yet Wilson was a firm believer in the righteousness of the even more aggressive Spanish and Philippines Wars, and exulted in the way they helped heal the wounds of the War Between the States. As president of Princeton University, in 1902, writing about the Filipinos, he took the low road, reflecting his fundamental racism: it was America's "peculiar duty" to teach the peoples of the new colonial frontiers "order and self-control" and to "impart to them if it be possible... the drill and habit of law and obedience."

> *"Woodrow Wilson, the revered apostle of self-determination, invaded Mexico and sent his warriors to Haiti and the Dominican Republic, where they blocked constitutional government, reinstated virtual slavery, tortured, murdered and destroyed, leaving a legacy of misery that remains until today. Evidently, there could be no Bolshevik threat at the time, so we claimed we were defending ourselves against the Hun."*[2]

In the nearly five years before he drew America into the war across the Atlantic, Wilson regularly used the powers of his presidency to quash what he determined was "instability" or "political turmoil" in Central America. In his two terms as the nation's chief executive he outdid his two predecessors combined, Theodore Roosevelt of "the big stick" and William Howard Taft of "dollar diplomacy," in the number and duration of U.S. armed interventions in the region. Yet it was not his frequent armed incursions there that most marked Wilson's presidency [See Appendix]. It was the Great War and his wholly inept performance at the Paris Peace Conference that remains his legacy.

> *Before the American declaration of war, the Germans released a propaganda document, "The Archives of Reason," suggesting that Americans who contemplated joining the fighting should first "dig a trench shoulder-high in your garden; fill it half-full of water and get into it. Remain there for two or three days on an empty stomach. Furthermore, hire a lunatic to shoot at you with revolvers and machine guns at close range."*[3]

A COMFORTABLE MYTH that some Americans embrace even today is that their government was neutral from August, 1914, to April, 1917, and only when an aggressive Germany became a clear threat to U.S. security did their sorely pressed president take an unenthusiastic country to war. According to this view, belligerency had been thrust on a peace-loving nation. Not so!

From the beginning of the war, Woodrow Wilson sided with the Allies—but quietly. On August 30, 1914, he confided to his principal adviser, Colonel Edward M. House, that the Germans must not be allowed to win the war:

> "If Germany won, it would change the course of our civilization and make the United States a military nation."[4]

Colonel House and Woodrow Wilson

Hypocritically, he had declared publicly twelve days earlier:

> "The United States must be neutral in fact as well as in name during these days that try men's souls. We must be impartial in thought as well as in action, must put a curb upon our sentiments as well as upon every transaction that might be construed as a preference of one part of the struggle before another."[5]

> *"Mr. Wilson's one passion is English political history.... Whenever he had a chance he has spent a vacation in England, whose scenery he delights in, enshrining as it does all the literary and historical associations which furnish and adorn his mind, and whose people he sincerely admires.... When unable to go to England he has retreated to Bermuda, the nearest point at which glimpses of English life can be enjoyed. This is natural and laudable in one whose mother was born in England and all four of whose grandparents were British subjects."*[6]

There were also other powerful pro-Allied influences diligently at work. From August 1914 the great international banking houses in the U.S. took a distinctly non-neutral attitude, favoring investment in the bonds of the Allies, while discouraging and even refusing investment in the paper of the Central Powers. This immediately gave the United States a strong financial interest in the cause of the Entente, and this stake loomed ever larger as the war progressed. American industry also became robustly pro-Ally. This was due simply to the Royal Navy blockade, which cut off sales of armaments to the Central Powers and at the same time made enormous war profits dependent on purchases by Britain, France, Russia, and Italy. By late 1915, following the sinking of the *Lusitania* in November,[7] the American press had become conspicuously pro-Ally. Woodrow Wilson's hidden agenda was also influenced by his egotistical conviction that he could not lead world policy through pacific methods only—but that he might assume world leadership if he pulled America into the war and could thereby dominate the peace conference.

OVERARCHING IN ITS IMPACT on American public opinion was the avalanche of propaganda from Great Britain.[8] It began early in the morning on August 5, when England was officially at war with Germany. The Royal Navy's specialized cable-layer *Telconia* sailed into the North Sea off the German city of Emden, anchored over a precise location, then grappled to the surface and hauled to the deck the five submarine cables that linked Germany with the United States. The cables were cut and the ends dropped back into the ocean. The next day *The New York Times* appraised the cable-cutting mission by pointing out that:

> "Until direct cable service is restored [it never was], all word of happenings in Germany must pass through hostile countries—Russia on the east, France on the west, and England on the north."

At the same as British propaganda worked diligently to involve the United States as an active belligerent on its side, Germany sought vainly to maintain a precarious neutrality by the U.S. Both sides flooded America with war "news": pamphlets, books, speakers, movies, all presenting one-sided versions of the origins of the war and the righteousness of their cause. This struggle was unequal from the start, for most Americans were bound to Great Britain by language and unspoken tradition.

One month into the war, nearly every English-language newspaper in the United States was parroting England's propaganda line, with emphasis on the atrocities allegedly committed by the godless "Huns" in Belgium,[9] the country that had been overrun by German troops. Tainted news stories of imaginary battlefield successes by the Entente—and exaggerated German losses—filled the front pages of U.S. newspapers. Anti-German books and pamphlets written by Great Britain's familiar novelists and poets were rushed to printers and shipped across the Atlantic without delay. These same authors followed their books into America as popular lecturers. Personal letters signed by well-known Englishmen were mailed to America's opinion-makers. Celebrities and near-Royalty figures crossed the Atlantic to meet personally with America's elite—to balance bone-china teacups and saucers on their laps and declaim against alleged historic German militarism.

Quincy Howe, no Anglophile, wrote sarcastically:

> "British propagandists did not forget even the great unwashed."

In the fall of 1914, U.S. labor leader Samuel Gompers met with two of his peers from England who had been sent to the American Federation of Labor Convention

> "...to do spadework in the American trade unions."[10]

Revisionist historian Harry Elmer Barnes wrote at the time:

The favorable attitude of the American press toward the Entente Powers was an enormous advantage to the latter. We were made to feel that the Entente was fighting the cause of the small and weak nations against the ruthlessness of a great bully. We were inevitability led to believe that the War had been started through the deliberate determination of Germany to initiate her alleged long-cherished plan to dominate the planet, while the Entente had proposed diplomatic settlement from the beginning and had only taken up arms in self-defense with the utmost reluctance. This theory of the German provocation of the War and the German lust for world dominion was played up in the newspapers... until the danger from Germany struck terror into the hearts of Americans.[11]

Not only was a barrage of falsehoods used to hoodwink Americans, but rigid censorship concealed the very real desire inside Germany from 1916 on for a peace settlement, and the reasonable nature of German peace proposals. The few peace feelers that managed to slip through the British web to the Americans were condemned by the English as sinister German propaganda intended to divide the Allies.

It was the persistent British, too, who were responsible for putting the secret Zimmermann Telegram of January 17, 1917,[12] into the hands of the Americans. British cryptanalysts had intercepted and decoded the message almost immediately, yet it was not until February 23 that it was given to Ambassador Walter Hines Page in London for transmittal to Washington. Germany had announced resumption of unrestricted submarine warfare effective February 1. The five-week delay was purposefully calculated by the British to coincide with an anticipated rise in Allied ship sinkings [which did occur] and thus provide enhanced leverage for Britain's propaganda efforts.

> "I never pass the statue in Trafalgar Square to Nurse Cavell without reflecting that after the inscription "Patriotism is not Enough" should be added "Propaganda is also Necessary"... The Germans were guilty of no act of injustice in shooting her, but merely of a gross error of judgment.... Yet it is a matter of history that not long after she was executed the French authorities shot two German nurses for similar offenses!"[13]

WHILE THE BRITISH were busily lying to Americans through every medium available, a second propaganda onslaught was directed at Americans by order of their president, once America was into the war. Wilson established the euphemistically titled Committee on Public Information, the first overt government propaganda agency in the nation's history. Headed by indefatigable George Creel, CPI totally managed the news and intimidated dissenters. The many historians recruited by CPI rewrote modern world history in dozens of booklets printed by the tens of millions. Well-dressed and well-spoken speakers lectured movie patrons nightly. Hate-filled posters and advertisements were everywhere. Extreme patriotism and loyalty were the order of the day: German-Americans, war protesters, and pacifists were to be distrusted, despised, jailed, and deported. They were!

Charlie Chaplin, comedy star of the "movies," making his first speech for the third Liberty Loan in front of the State, War and Navy Building, Washington, D.C., on first anniversary of U.S. entry into war, 04/06/1918

With America safely in the war, albeit as an "associate power" as Wilson demanded, the British Foreign Office set about undermining one of the pillars of U.S. foreign policy that had first been enunciated by George Washington: freedom from entangling alliances. The idea of a League of Nations, almost universally credited to Woodrow Wilson, in fact did not originate with him. According to Eugene J. Young, cable editor of *The New York Times:*

> It was born deep in the recesses of the British Imperial Defense Council, and was afterward passed on to the American President. Under Article X of the Covenant, all nations were bound to defend indefinitely the boundaries and possessions of members as they existed at the time it was adopted. This, in effect, recognized the British Empire as a permanent institution to be upheld by the whole world.[15]

IT IS FAIR TO ASK: DID WOODROW WILSON have any noble principles at all? Or was his exalted rhetoric, with its contradictions, fabrications, and circumlocutions, a convenient substitute for them? In asking the Congress for a declaration of war, he declared that it was not the German people who were America's enemy, but their leaders. Yet, at the peace conference two years later he approved Article 231—*Kriegschuldfrage*—the infamous sole-war-guilt clause that damned all Germans:

> The Allies and Associated governments affirm and Germany accepts the responsibility of Germany and her Allies for causing all the loss and damage to which the Allied and Associated governments and their nationals have been subjected as a consequence of the war imposed upon them by the aggression of Germany and her Allies.

Wilson told the world he was for freedom of the seas. Yet he gave a stamp of approval to the Royal Navy to blockade U.S. commerce with Europe and abandoned freedom of the seas together with the remaining thirteen of his Fourteen Points at the peace conference.

The principle of self-determination was supposedly a bedrock tenet of Wilson's psyche, but at the peace conference he readily agreed to the carving-up of German-speaking Europe and the distribution of these lands to Czechoslovakia, Poland, Italy, and France. He knew that Austria was in favor of a union with Germany after the peace treaty took away her empire. Yet, Wilson approved an article that prohibited such a merger, even if a later plebiscite would represent a democratic solution.

DID WOODROW WILSON know the *new kind of war* young Americans would face in Europe? Did he know that terrible poison gases were being used, and how the cream of American youth was being suffocated, some quickly, some agonizingly over days? He couldn't know! War correspondents were kept away from the front lines, away from the puddles of mustard gas and from the smell of the putrefaction of the tens of thousands of unburied or partly-buried dead or their parts, in the trenches and mud of no man's land. Replacement troops could tell they were approaching the front lines by the nauseating smell that grew more intense the closer they got.

The British inaugurated a system of "embedment" for a selected group of only *six* of their newspapermen, ensuring that news bulletins from the battlefields hewed to restrictive regulations. Rigid censorship demanded victories and never a hint of defeats. Royal Navy hospital ships always docked at night, and their cargoes of the hideously maimed were quickly offloaded, out of sight of curious bystanders. The dead were buried in France, so there was no need to hide stacks of coffins. Like the Americans, the British at home never learned of the horrors of trench warfare and the particular terrors of poison gas. Neither did the French, the Russians, the Germans, nor the Austro-Hungarians.

It was the soldiers on the Western Front in France who first learned all about poison gas, starting on April 22, 1915. Ypres that day was a place of unique terror on a long-ago spring afternoon. Towards evening, a breeze sprang up, coming from the north behind the German lines, and across the barbed wire of no man's land, into the faces of French and Algerian troops in their trenches. Almost at the same time, German artillery which had been intermittently shelling the French lines all day, suddenly stopped. An unaccustomed silence descended over the front. Then at 5PM the Germans launched red rockets into the sky, which signaled the resumption of a German artillery barrage. The horrors of chemical warfare in the form of poison gas were about to be introduced to mankind.

The *poilus*, crouching low in their trenches, watched with fascination first, then with apprehension, and finally with horror as a huge cloud of greenish-yellow gas billowed out behind the enemy's trenches, moving slowly downwind toward them. The mist clung to the earth, filling every shell crater and hollow as it moved forward at the speed of the wind. Then as the first fringes of the cloud enveloped their trenches, the victims found themselves choking in unimaginable agony as they fought desperately for breath. Those able to move and still lucid, ran panic-stricken to the rear, trying to outstrip the cloud of poison that followed on their heels. As the onrushing toxic tide washed over the struggling men, their faces turned blue as they strained to breathe, some coughing so violently they ruptured their lungs, fluid frothing from their mouths and noses. Any exertion resulted in deeper breaths and more acute poisoning.

Out of sight behind their front lines in special dugouts, German troops had opened the valves of some 6,000 steel cylinders spaced out across a four-mile front. The cylinders were filled with liquid chlorine and the instant the pressure was released and the liquid came in contact with the air, it vaporized, hissing out to form a dense cloud. The Germans had released 160 tons of the poison into the air, resulting in fatal concentrations of the gas. Chlorine gas does not suffocate *per se*; it strips the lining of the bronchial tubes and lungs, rapidly producing severe inflammation that in turn generates a massive quantity of fluid that blocks the windpipe and fills the lungs, literally drowning its victims.

As German infantry followed gingerly behind the chlorine cloud, they wore rudimentary gas masks of moist gauze and cotton tied around their faces. As they advanced slowly, they stepped through a surreal landscape of the dead and the dying. The dead lay where they had fallen, faces contorted in agony. The dying lay sprawled, gasping for air, their destroyed lungs expelling mouthfuls of yellow fluid. The Germans were surprised to find that all metal objects were tarnished by the powerful oxidizing effect of the gas; watches, coins, steel buttons had turned a dull green. Rifles and machine guns were rusted, as if they had been unattended for weeks.

Had the Germans developed a weapon for which there was no defense? Initially that was so. The Germans, however, were unprepared to exploit the breakthrough and the Ypres salient quickly reverted to yet another month of stalemate and butchery—and over 100,000 more Allied and German casualties—in what became to be known as the Second Battle of Ypres. The decision to retaliate in kind was made in less than a month, and the first English gas attack using chlorine was launched on September 25, at the battle of Loos.

PHOSGENE ARRIVED ON THE BATTLEFRONTS in December, 1915, again introduced by the Germans, whose bio-chemists found they could improve the effectiveness of pure chlorine by combining it with other elements to form this new killing agent. Phosgene was some twenty times as powerful as chlorine, and being practically colorless and odorless, was much more difficult to detect. It disabled or killed in hideous fashion following a delay of one or two days. The victim who inhaled a lethal dose of phosgene initially felt only a mild irritation of the throat and eyes; these first symptoms then disappeared. Meanwhile the lungs of the victim were filling with fluid and collapse followed. Victims coughed up large quantities of a yellowish watery fluid, up to four pints per hour; some victims took forty-eight hours to die—in agony.

On July 12, 1917, at 10PM, German front-line forces introduced a third new and improved gas, with horrific maiming characteristics, dichlorethylsulphide or mustard. Prior to the development of nerve gases by the Germans in 1936, mustard was called the "king of the battle gases."

The Ypres front was again the target, and again the Germans achieved surprise, this time by projecting artillery shells filled with mustard gas into enemy trenches. What the shells delivered was not gas in the sense the Allied soldiers were used to. It was a brown liquid, similar in color to sherry, and gave off a smell that was described as "like garlic" and "like mustard."

Aside from slightly irritated eyes and throat for those afflicted, there were no initial effects. Most of the soldiers went back to sleep.

> But in the early hours of the morning, they began to wake up with 'intolerable pain in the eyes'.... Then they began to vomit uncontrollably. As the night wore on, the pain in the eyes became so intense that many had to be given morphine. The following day the sun rose over an army that looked as if it had been stricken by some biblical plague.[16]

The field hospitals were flooded with casualties. It was quickly learned that the new gas was a vesicant or blistering agent. Two days after the attack, the first deaths occurred. Death was a lingering and excruciating process. Some victims took a week or more to die. It wasn't necessarily the severe burns on the skin and outer extremities that killed, but rather the destruction that mustard produced in the throat and lungs that slowly suffocated the casualties.

Mustard was a persistent agent and retained its deadly properties for several weeks. The liquid formed pools in shell craters and in trenches, ready to contaminate the careless. In cold weather it froze like water and remained in the soil. Mustard spread in the winter of 1917 poisoned men in the spring of 1918 when the ground thawed. A conventional gas mask that protected the wearer against chlorine and phosgene was useless against mustard.

The Germans had stockpiled huge reserves of mustard-filled shells and were prepared to drench Allied trenches on a giant scale.

> In ten days Allied positions were pounded with more than a million shells containing 2,500 tons of gas. Within three weeks of introducing Yellow Cross shells,[17] the Germans had caused as many gas casualties as had resulted from the entire gas shelling of the previous year. By the end of the first week, the number of gassed men admitted to British medical units was 2,934; by the end of the second week, a further 6,476; by the end of the third week, another 4,886.[18]

It had taken Germany's eight giant chemical cartels gathered together in the Ruhr known as the *Interessen-Gemeinschaft*—the IG—six months to gear up production of the highly complex and dangerous chemical compound. It took the French until June 1918, and the laggard British until September, to produce quantities of mustard for the battlefields.

By the spring of 1918, Americans had developed a gas of their own, Lewisite, a fast-acting disabling agent. It caused immediate excruciating pain upon striking the eyes, almost uncontrollable sneezing and coughing, tightness and severe pain in the chest upon inhalation, and often nausea and vomiting. The first lot of 150 tons of Lewisite was still at sea when the Armistice was signed.[19]

On October 14, a barrage of mustard shells fell on the rubble-filled Belgian village of Werwick, causing heavy casualties among the exhausted grenadiers of Germany's 16th Bavarian Reserve Infantry. In three weeks, just days before the Armistice, a trainload of the wounded survivors of the Werwick attack headed home to Germany. Among them was a twenty-nine-year-old corporal, blinded and hardly able to contain his anger. He would recover his sight completely—and was determined to avenge Germany's defeat. During World War II, he announced that Germany would not be the first to use poison gas. The *Third Reich* never did, although the Germans might have used their potent nerve gases to cause a terrible effect on the beaches of Normandy in 1944. The corporal was Adolf Hitler.

All the belligerents used chemical agents to the limits of their productive capabilities. By war's end,

At least 1.3 million men had been wounded by gas [including 70,000 U.S. casualties by mustard alone]; 91,000 of them had died. Germany, France and Britain had all suffered about 200,000 gas casualties; Russia, more than double that figure. An estimated 113,000 tons of chemicals had been used."[20]

Wilfred Owen's celebrated poem, perhaps the best-remembered poem of the Great War in English, graphically described the hideous last few moments of a soldier fitting on his gas mask too late.

Dulce et Decorum Est
[It is sweet and fitting]

Bent double, like old beggars under sacks,
Knock-kneed, coughing like hags, we cursed through sludge,
Till on the haunting flares we turned our backs
And toward our distant rest began to trudge.
Men marched asleep. Many had lost their boots
But limped on, blood-shod. All went lame; all blind;
Drunk with fatigue; deaf even to the hoots
Of tired, outstripped Five-Nines that dropped behind.

Gas! Gas! Quick boys!—An ecstasy of fumbling,
Fitting the clumsy helmets just in time;
But someone still was yelling out and stumbling,
And flound'ring like a man in fire or lime...
Dim, through the misty panes and thick green light,
As under a green sea, I saw him drowning.

In all my dreams, before my helpless sight,
He plunged at me, guttering, choking, drowning.

If in some smothering dreams you too could pace
Behind the wagon that we flung him in,
And watch the white eyes writhing in his face,
His hanging face, like a devil's sick of sin.
If you could hear, at every jolt, the blood
Come gargling from the froth-corrupted lungs,
Obscene as cancer, bitter as the cud
Of vile incurable sores on innocent tongues,
My friend, you would not with such high zest
To children ardent for some desperate glory,
The old Lie: Dulce et decorum est
Pro patria mori."[21]

[It is sweet and fitting to die for your country.]

AT 11AM ON November 11, 1918—a time and a date still hallowed in Europe as the 11th hour of the 11th day of the 11th month, but far less revered or even remembered in the United States—German commanders signed the Armistice, which brought to a close four years of slaughter—nearly. News spread rapidly on both sides of no-man's land that the war would officially end that morning. However, celebrations in many parts of the Allied lines gave way to disbelief and then despair as it became clear that, Armistice or no Armistice, the attacks already scheduled for that morning were to proceed as planned.

While some front-line commanders called an immediate cease-fire as a common-sense decision, the commanders of nine of the sixteen U.S. divisions on the Western Front ordered their men forward in one final, futile [and bloody, as always!] assault.

> Some did so simply because the previous orders to attack had not been rescinded... some because, as career officers, they saw it as their last chance for glory, medals before the peacetime ossification of their ranks; and some—reflecting the belief of their supreme commander, General Pershing, whose 'thin, crescent-shaped mouth... turns down like a bulldog's and makes him look as if he had never smiled in his life'—from a desire to inflict the maximum possible punishment on German troops.... By the time the guns finally fell silent, 11,000 more casualties were strewn across no-man's-land. The day's total was greater than the number who fell on D-Day in Normandy in 1944.[22]

Earlier, when U.S. troops engaged the German infantry at Chateau-Thierry and Belleau Wood in ferocious fighting, enormous U.S. casualties had shocked the top brass. John J. Pershing and his generals had followed doggedly—insanely, some would later say—in the footsteps of their French and British counterparts, in particular Britain's General Sir Douglas Haig who was notorious for squandering the lives of his men. Haig's tactics were simple: after preliminary heavy artillery bombardment of enemy positions which was intended to cut the wire in no man's land and destroy dug-in German machine gun nests, it was up and over the top of trenches for the Tommies (British soldiers). Incredibly, they were ordered to walk in orderly formation—straight into still-standing barbed wire that would snare them, making easy targets for the astonished machine gunners who would spring out of their trenches after the artillery barrage ceased and quickly set up their machine guns.

> "Just like the British on the first day of the Somme almost two years before, the American dead at Belleau Wood 'lay in beautifully ordered lines where the traversing machine guns had caught them.'"[23]

> *"Never was any previous war so widely proclaimed to have been necessary in its origins, holy in its nature, and just, moderate and constructive in its aims. Never was a conflict further removed in the actualities of the case from such pretensions.... The World War was unquestionably the greatest crime against humanity and decency since the missing link accomplished the feat of launching homosapiens upon his career."*[24]

WOODROW WILSON REQUIRED A CHAIR at the peace table if he was to properly act the role of a prophet leading his flock into the Promised Land. He got his chair but at a stunning human cost. "Black Jack" Pershing's doughboys had been in combat only about 200 days; during that time more than 50,000 were supposedly killed in action; nearly 200,000 were wounded, many maimed for life; over 62,000 died of disease, most from influenza, astonishingly over half of them in training camps in the United States.[25] It has long been an article of faith in official U.S. military publications that the army had lost 50,510 men in France, and that the Marines lost another 2,457 dead. Historian John Mosier wrote that, to the contrary,

> "…these figures are disingenuous to the point of dishonesty. In the eight military cemeteries in European, 85,252 American remains were buried (including memorials for 4,452 whose remains were 'never recovered or identified') so 85,000 seems the most accurate figure."

These casualty numbers were nowhere near those of the War Between the States, which have been estimated at 620,000, total, for the Yankees and the Rebels, but on a *per diem* rate they were nearly the same.

> *"Wilson discovered too late that the crimes of two thousand years of European diplomatic and military chicanery could not be effaced in a few weeks by the therapeutic influence of fourteen moral principles. Then Wilson tried his hand at diplomacy, with the results that would normally attend the entrance of a rural clergyman into a poker game on a trans-Atlantic liner."*[26]

Wilson was surprised at the almost universal opposition to his plan when he announced that he intended to go the Peace Conference—within his cabinet, the Congress, the press, and among ordinary citizens. He learned from Colonel House, then in Paris, that Allied leaders told him they would be happier if Wilson remained in Washington. House also advised Wilson to select someone other than himself to be chief American potentate at the conference. While he could not say so to Wilson, House rightfully felt he should be the one. In fact, most diplomats and historians retrospectively agreed that House was the most qualified American to represent the United States during the sometimes-harsh give-and-take bargaining that took place, for which the former college professor with his formal *pince-nez* balanced on his nose was monumentally ill-equipped to handle.

Wilson had burned his bridges behind him, stubbornly playing partisan party politics from which he could not be budged. He arrogantly chose only one Republican to accompany him to Paris as a peace commissioner: Henry White, a long-retired diplomat with little residual clout in the GOP. Wilson rejected all those recommended to him, obstinately naming as commissioners, Secretary of State Robert Lansing, nonentity General Tasker H. Bliss, and Colonel House. Senate Republicans were so enraged by the choice of White, which they rightly considered a sop casually tossed to them, that they discussed sending a committee to Paris to independently report on the conference. They never did, but swallowed their bile and bided their time. When Wilson returned with copies of the Versailles Peace Treaty and his League of Nations seeking Congressional ratification, it would be payback time for the Republicans.

On December 2, 1918, Wilson delivered his state-of-the-union message to Congress. At its end, the out-of-touch president specifically asked Congress to support him on his mission. Congress' response was frigid. Applause was minimal and confined entirely to a handful of Democrats. This was an obvious sign that Congress as a whole was affronted by Wilson's failure to select one of them as a peace commissioner. The president showed no emotion as he left the House of Representatives.

The next morning Wilson—accompanied by his second wife, Edith, his daughter, Margaret, his trusty physician and jack-of-all-trades, Admiral Cary Grayson, his propaganda czar George Creel, and a tiny White House staff—boarded the *USS George Washington* for Brest, France. Short-sightedly—many would later say naively—Wilson left behind Joseph Tumulty, his loyal and people-wise secretary, whose absence in Paris would prove to be more costly than he ever imagined.

THE EMINENT BRITISH ECONOMIST John Maynard Keynes was in Paris as an observer. In his analyses of the conference, *The Economic Consequences of the Peace*, he condemned Wilson as the most inept of the major diplomats in Paris, and clearly ignorant of European power politics. According to Keynes, he was no match for Britain's agile-footed Prime Minister, David Lloyd George. He was,

> A blind and deaf Don Quixote entering a cavern where the swift and glittering blade was in the hands of the adversary. Not only was he ill-informed—but his mind was slow and inadaptable. The president's slowness among the Europeans was noteworthy. He could not, all in a minute, take in what the rest were saying, size up the situation with a glance, frame a reply, and meet the case by a slight change of ground.[27]

Was Wilson's "slowness" a result of a series of minor strokes in Paris that kept him bedridden on several occasions, precursors of his nearly totally debilitating stroke in October 1919? Or had a single bout with influenza caused the rapid decline in his cognitive powers and his subsequent strange behavior in Paris? Even after these many years, historians are not of one mind.

John M. Barry, author of *The Great Influenza: The Epic Story of the Deadliest Plague in History*, published in 2004, is convinced that it was influenza, and presents compelling evidence to support his view. He wrote that the killing disease struck down Wilson on April 3, 1919. At 3PM that day, Wilson seemed to be in fine health.

> "Then, very suddenly at six o'clock, Grayson saw Wilson seized with violent paroxysms of coughing, which were so severe and frequent that it [sic] interfered with his breathing." [28]

At first, Wilson's physician Dr. Grayson suspected poisoning in an assassination attempt. That night, the ever-present physician later recalled, was one of the worst nights the president had ever passed through. Barry notes that a young aide on the U.S. peace delegation came down with influenza on the same day, and died four days later.[29]

Wilson lay in bed for several days, scarcely able to move. Just before his illness, Wilson had childishly threatened to return to the United States without a treaty rather than give in on his principles. From his sickbed he repeated that threat again, ordering chief-cook-and-bottle-washer Grayson to ready the *George Washington* to sail. On April 8, Wilson changed his mind and decided to rejoin the negotiations. Georges Clemenceau and Lloyd George came to his bedroom, but the discussions went poorly. Clemenceau had been infuriated by Wilson's public warning that he would leave the conference if the French remained obstinate, judging it a bluff and privately calling him "a cook who keeps her trunk ready in the hallway."

Members of the U.S. delegation who interacted soon after with Wilson found his actions bizarre, his reactions hesitant, and his appearance ghastly. Herbert Hoover recalled that Wilson's mind had lost "resiliency." Edmund Starling, the head of the Secret Service contingent responsible for Wilson's safety, noticed that Wilson lacked "his old quickness of grasp." Journalist Ray Stannard Baker was shocked at Wilson's sunken eyes, at his weariness, at his pale and haggard look. Chief Usher Erwin "Ike" Hoover remembered Wilson's sudden obsession with who had used the delegation's official automobiles and his concern that French spies were surreptitiously shadowing his every move.

Then, strangest of all, still in bed and without consultation with anyone, Wilson suddenly abandoned principles he had previously insisted were non-negotiable.

> He approved a formula written by Clemenceau demanding German reparations and that Germany accept all responsibility for starting the war. The Rhineland would be demilitarized;

Germany would not be allowed to have troops within thirty miles of the east bank of the Rhine. The rich coal fields of the Saar region would be mined by France and the region would be administered by the new League of Nations for fifteen years, and then a plebiscite would determine whether the region would belong to France or Germany. The provinces of Alsace and Lorraine, which Germany had seized after the Franco-Prussian War, were moved from Germany back to France. West Prussia and Posen were given to Poland—creating the 'Polish Corridor' that separated two parts of Germany. The German air force was eliminated; its army limited to 100,000 men; its colonies stripped away—but not freed, simply redistributed to other powers.[30]

Wilson's most egregious legacy was his kow-towing to the outrageous reparations demands of the French and British. Lloyd George insisted that in the treaty of peace the Allies should "assert their claim" and Germany should recognize "her obligations for all the costs of the war." When Colonel House declared that this was contrary to the pre-Armistice agreement, Clemenceau reassured him that it was largely "a question of drafting." In fact, this experiment in drafting turned out to be the infamous Article 231.

Interior of the Palais des Glaces during the signing of the Peace Terms. Versailles, France, 06/28/1919

BACK IN THE UNITED STATES, on September 25, 1919, returning to Washington after an arduous [for him] series of whistle-stop speeches across the West promoting his League of Nations to the American people, Wilson collapsed. The breakdown was the precursor of the massive stroke—a cerebral thrombosis—that a week later paralyzed half his body. From that day forward and for the next eighteen months of his presidency—and for the rest of his life—Wilson's cognitive powers were sharply reduced, and he could no longer perform such ordinary tasks as writing his signature. "Ike" Hoover admitted later that when it came to important matters of state requiring his signature, such letters—composed by Tumulty and others in the confines of the White House, including Edith's brother, John Randolph Bolling—would be slowly read to him. A pencil would then be placed in his trembling hand, and his hand steadied and guided into some crude facsimile of his original signature. Hoover recalled:

> If there was ever a man in bad shape, he was.... He could not talk plain[ly], mumbled more than he articulated, was helpless and looked awful...The stories in the newspapers from day to day may have been true in their way but never was deception so universally practiced in the White House as it was in those statements being given out from time to time. And the strange part to me was that the President in his feeble way entered into the scheme.[31]

Woodrow Wilson's illness was successfully covered up by Edith Wilson, who covertly play-acted his role as president, aided by Cary Grayson and Joseph Tumulty in a monumental three-person conspiracy to hide his paralysis from the American people. Historian Thomas Fleming calls the conspiracy "the greatest deception in the history of American politics."[32]

SOON AFTER THE WAR, a wave of disillusionment began to wash across America, prompted by the high death toll of America's soldiers in France; the tens of thousands who returned with missing limbs and worse; the obvious inequities of the Versailles Treaty; England and France's unwillingness to repay their war debts to the United States; and, as one historian cynically noted:

> "Perhaps it was the prospect of being faced with a choice between Cox and Harding in November."[33]

Historians began questioning what had previously been conventional wisdom surrounding America's entry into the war. A band of courageous American historians who had at first been uncomfortable with Woodrow Wilson's declaration of war against Germany saw the issues more clearly as the fog of war lifted. Harry Elmer Barnes, Sidney Bradshaw Fay, C. Hartley Grattan, John Kenneth Turner, and Charles Callan Tansill: these revisionists were taking a close look at what the Great War had wrought, and asked pointed questions. What about Germany's alleged war guilt and other malicious articles that had been written into the Treaty of Versailles, particularly by the *revanche*-seeking premier of France, Georges Clemenceau? If Germany didn't start the war, who did? Was Kaiser Wilhelm II the ogre he was portrayed? Were the atrocities purportedly committed by German soldiers in Belgium just lies by the *Entente*? What about the Committee on Public Information, its stacks of booklets and teams of smooth-talking speechmakers, the "Four-Minute Men"—were those American lies? Had American intervention been "to make the world safe for democracy," or was it straightforward imperialism as the Bolsheviks said, when they left the war and signed a separate peace at Brest-Litovsk with the Germans?

C. Hartley Grattan wrote presciently—and elegantly:

> The World War is on all fours with every other war in having an economic foundation. Every reputable historian who has dealt with it, no matter how great his preoccupation with the diplomacy of its precipitation, regards the diplomacy, the propaganda, the alleged aims and objects for fighting, as mere secondary structures reared on the foundation of money and trade.

The flag follows trade, the politicians follow the flag, the propagandists follow the politicians, and the people follow the propagandists.[34]

In 1920, Barnes added:

If we honestly face the facts we shall probably have to agree that the entry of the United States into the World War was an almost unmitigated disaster, not only to us but to Europe.[35]

WHO WERE OTHER KEY PLAYERS involved in behind-the-scenes dealings with the British, besides the quiet, nearly-always-invisible Colonel House? According to Harry Elmer Barnes and others, the principal ringleader for dragging America into the war, apart from Woodrow Wilson himself, was Walter Hines Page, the former editor of *The World's Work* and the near-fanatical anglophile U.S. Ambassador to the Court of St. James's in London. In this indictment, Barnes, over the years, consistently assigned fulsome blame to Page:

Had Mr. Wilson dismissed Mr. Page early in the war and replaced him by an honest, courageous, far-sighted and well-informed Ambassador, there seems little doubt that the War would have come to an end by December of 1916, and would have been settled by a treaty of peace infinitely superior in every way to that which was worked out in 1918-1919 and imposed by the victors at Versailles. The desolation and despair brought about in Europe by the prolongation of the War is what established Lenin in Russia and Mussolini in Italy.[36]

Hartley Grattan, with a few sarcastic twists of the screw, was even more severe in his lengthy condemnation of Page:

Walter Hines Page [was] universally recognized as the greatest Englishman America ever produced. His ardent partisanship of the British position has become the wonder of every student of the period. Today his collected letters are a full arsenal of British propaganda. So rank did his partisanship become that he forfeited the respect of his chief, Woodrow Wilson.... According to the old saw, a diplomat is a man sent abroad to lie for the benefit of his country. Page reversed the maxim to read, a diplomat is sent abroad to lie for the benefit of the country to which he is accredited.... Page was ever ready to admit the validity of an English argument. As each American defeat was recorded he sent up a whoop. He could see nothing more in the American protests than an attempt to bring about trouble between the two countries. That America might have some rights entered his head but infrequently.... Sir Edward Grey tells us that Page was chief advisor to the Foreign Office on American affairs: 'Page's advice and suggestions were of the greatest value in warning us when to be careful or encouraging us when we could safely be firm.' Grey then cited an example of Page's technique: 'One incident in particular remains in my memory. Page came to see me at the Foreign Office one day and produced a long dispatch from Washington contesting our claim to act as were doing in stopping contraband going to neutral ports. 'I am instructed,' he said, 'to read this dispatch to you.' He read, and I listened. He then said: 'I have now read this dispatch, but I do not agree with it; let us consider how it should be answered!'[37]

Barnes also refuted a principal myth about Wilson, that he was strongly pacifist up to February 1917, two months before he declared war, and was only won over to the Allied cause when he learned that the Germans had decided to resume unrestricted submarine warfare. To the contrary, Barnes claimed he possessed:

Direct and reliable information that Mr. Wilson had been converted...to intervene on the side of the Allies by the early spring of 1916. Sir Edward Grey tells us in his memoirs that Colonel

House brought him Wilson's assurances in February 1916, that he would do his best to bring the United States into the war on the Allied side.[38]

Only the possibility of a split in the Democratic Party over the issue caused Wilson to wait until his reelection in 1916 before showing his true interventionist colors. Wilson's idealistic pronouncements, when no longer obscured by the miasma of war propaganda, were seen as the pretensions they had been. and American historians, novelists, and old congressional foes alike took turns skewering him. Robert La Follette—one of the two Senators who had voted against the war resolution and the man Wilson had unsuccessfully tried to silence for his antiwar views—reacted acidly to Wilson's baldly false claim that his Fourteen Points had been incorporated into the treaty: La Follett lashed out:

> "I sometimes think the man had no sense of things that penetrate below the surface. With him the rhetoric of a thing is the thing itself. He was either wanting in understanding or convictions or both. *Words—phrases, felicity of expression and blind egotism have been his stock in trade* [author's emphasis]."[39]

[Note: Also see Wilson's *Aide Memoire* in the Appendix to Allied Ambassadors regarding U.S. intervention in Russia.]

IN 1922, JOHN KENNETH TURNER, a revisionist historian early out of the lists, published his caustic *Shall It Be Again?*. He addressed perhaps the most significant question of all: had Imperial Germany been a military threat to the United States? The idea of such an invasion across the Atlantic Ocean was a "gigantic hoax,"[40] he wrote, one that was promoted by interventionists to frighten Americans. The navies of the two nations had sparred in the Samoan Islands and in Manila Bay before the turn of the century, but these were minor skirmishes and no cannons had been fired. Propaganda, notably from Britain's Wellington House but also from America's interventionists, had focused on the to-become-infamous mantra with its incredibly long life:

> "If we don't fight them over there, we'll have to fight them here."

As for Germany's High Sea Fleet crossing the Atlantic, according to Turner, the idea of escorting troopships and supply vessels for amphibious landings on America's East Coast would have been laughable, even if Germany had not been burdened by war with other enemies.

> "This was the judgment of the highest experts in the service of America, sworn to before Congressional committees while the country was at peace."[41]

Strengthening Turner's argument many years later was an article in the April 24, 2007, issue of *The New York Times*. "A Footnote: Kaiser's Plan to Invade U.S." outlined a supposed plan "to attack and invade the United States at least 14 years before the United States entered World War I."

According to Holger H. Herwig, the *Times'* source for the story, the scheme involved sending the German High Sea Fleet into the Caribbean, trailed by troop ships and supply vessels. From a base there, amphibious landings would be made on major cities along the east coast. For the invasion to succeed, however, the war planners depended on complete surprise, according to Herwig. On that point, the plan was deemed unrealistic and abandoned; how could a large invasion fleet steam across the Atlantic Ocean without being detected?[42]

Herwig told the *Times* that his evidence was contained in some 1,500 handwritten pages that he discovered in German military archives. He claimed that the handwriting was of German military leaders, such as Admiral von Tirpitz, Admiral von Diederichs, Count von Schlieffen, and Major Ludendorff.

IN 1928, SIDNEY BRADSHAW FAY wrote, in his monumental two-volume work, *Origins of the First World War,* that if one nation had to be selected for "starting the war," it certainly was not Kaiser Wilhelm's Germany. He wrote unambiguously:

> Germany did not plot a European War, did not want one, and made genuine, though too belated, efforts, to avert one.... It was the hasty Russian general mobilization—assented to on July 29 and ordered on July 30—while Germany was still trying to bring Austria to accept mediation proposals, which finally rendered the European War inevitable.[43]

Fay focused on Russia's secret preparatory military measures which alarmed Austria and Germany during the diplomatic negotiations. He concluded that it was primarily Russia's mobilization "which precipitated the final catastrophe," causing Germany to mobilize in turn and declare war.[44] In 1914, mobilization meant war.

Fay concluded:

> The verdict of the Versailles Treaty that Germany and her allies were responsible for the War, in view of the evidence now available, is historically unsound. It should therefore be revised.[45]

By the mid-1930s, historians Walter Millis (*Road To War: America 1914-1917*), Charles Callan Tansill (*America Goes to War),* and others were publishing books that no longer were considered revisionist but mainstream. They all assailed Wilson's decision to take the United States into the war as misguided, at a minimum. All contributed to America's isolationism as many Americans declared "never again." Millis's easy-reading book was an immediate success and became a fixture on the *New York Times* bestseller lists.

MODERN HISTORIAN THOMAS FLEMING took his turn pummeling Wilson. He wrote scathingly:

> Wilson regularly applied his rhetoric of principles after the fact or in blithe indifference to the facts... He took political positions, then cooked up principles to justify them. One might almost call it a bad habit which caused him immense trouble all his life.[46]

Fleming went on, with a bludgeon:

> Wilson was not a very profound thinker or a good historian. Unlike Theodore Roosevelt's books on the War of 1812 and the history of the western movement, Wilson's biography of Washington and his other books on American history are virtually unreadable today.[47]

Woodrow Wilson must also be brought to account for his ruthless crushing of dissent once America was into the war. In his Flag Day speech on June 14, 1917, he had cautioned:

> Woe to the man or group of men who seeks [sic] to stand in our way in this day of high resolution.

The next day, almost as a reprise, Wilson signed the bitterly repressive Espionage Act.[48] Only once before in the nation's history had the Congress dared enact such a despotic law: the 1798 Alien and Sedition Act, which gave the president the power to deport aliens he considered dangerous to the nation's "peace and safety," or who were suspected of committing "treasonable activities" against the government. Those who committed "false, scandalous, and malicious writings" were also subject to punishment. When Thomas Jefferson took office as president in 1801, he pardoned all those imprisoned by the act and the Congress eventually repaid the fines. The 1917 law, which reflected a growing national phobia against "enemies from within," was much harsher, and a unanimous Supreme Court decision in 1919 upheld the Espionage Act as constitutional.

On September 5, 1917, operatives from the Department of Justice descended on the offices of the anti-war and anti-draft Industrial Workers of the World, also known as the Wobblies, in fifteen cities across the country. These official vigilantes smashed furniture and files, seized literature and records, and otherwise applied strong-armed methods in threatening the occupants of the offices, all of whom were arrested. A few days later, the national headquarters of the Socialist Party, also opposed to the war and the draft, were raided. Such harsh arrests, indictments, and convictions continued almost until the Armistice. Federal judges obediently meted out harsh sentences, broadly interpreting the freshly minted Espionage Act and imposing prison terms of five, ten, and even twenty years on over a thousand defendants. However, only the shortest of the sentences were served to completion. President Warren Harding sensibly pardoned most of those jailed, and successor Calvin Coolidge released the last of the political prisoners as a Christmas gesture in 1923.

On October 6, 1917, the Congress passed the Trading-with-the-Enemy Act, which authorized censorship of messages between the U.S. and foreign countries. Then on May 16, 1918, using as a subterfuge a number of gruesome examples of mob violence against antiwar activists, the Senate Judiciary Committee amended the Espionage Act by adding nine new offenses. The revised law became known as the Sedition Act and gave Postmaster General Albert Sydney Burleson extraordinary powers of censorship, allowing him, upon "satisfactory evidence," to return mail to those he personally deemed violators of the law.

George Creel, chairman of The Committee on Public Information (CPI), was the nation's principal propagandist and censor, but Burleson was a far more malevolent force for reaction. Burleson wielded his power capriciously and ruthlessly. He cracked down on radical publications, although he "didn't know socialism from rheumatism," according to the prominent socialist Norman Thomas. For example, he cut off mailing privileges from a single issue of *The Masses,* a radical publication, because it contained what he decided were anti-government cartoons, and then refused to reinstate the magazine's mailing permit because it missed one issue—the one banned—and hence was not a *bona fide* periodical.

A second cabinet officer sharing Burleson's reactionary views—and who was positioned to implement them—was Attorney General Thomas A. Gregory. At first opposed to surveillance of German aliens, he soon came around to the popular view that German-Americans posed security threats to America. To watch over what he considered the dangerous followers of an evil foreign power, Gregory integrated into his department an organization of volunteer vigilantes unique in the country's history—the American Protective League. Gregory and his minions fingered those who they determined "casually or impulsively uttered disloyal statements."

Once before in the nation's history, in 1798, President John Adams, under pressure from an undeclared war with France, pushed through Congress the Sedition Act, which made it unlawful to "print, utter, or publish... false, scandalous, or malicious writing" directed against the government. The second time around, the new Sedition Act was far stricter. Those who were found to "utter, print, write, or publish any disloyal, profane, scurrilous, or abusive language" aimed at the U.S. government were in violation of the new law and subject to severe punishment by Old-West-type hangin' judges.

Wilson's personal vindictiveness reached its peak with the arrest and imprisonment of Socialist leader and frequent presidential candidate Eugene V. Debs in June 1918, when he declared in a speech:

> "The master class has always declared the war, the subject class has always fought the battles. The master class had all to gain and nothing to lose, while the subject class has had nothing to gain and all to lose—especially their lives."[49]

The day he left office, a crippled and bitter Woodrow Wilson, to his eternal discredit, purposefully and spitefully refused to grant a pardon to Debs, who was also seriously ill.

> "It [the American war with Russia] was not a war at all. It was a free-booter's excursion, depraved and lawless. A felonious undertaking without the sanction of the American people. During the winter of 1919, American soldiers, in the uniform of their country, killed Russians and were killed by Russians.... Our war was with Germany, but no German prisoners were ever taken...."[50]

IN EARLY 1917, a remarkable series of fast-paced events began that quickly changed the entire political landscape—in Europe as well as in the United States. On February 1, the Germans resumed unrestricted submarine warfare, which together with the Zimmermann Telegram gave Woodrow Wilson all he needed to pull America into the war. America entered the War on April 6.

A month later there was another bombshell. A revolution in Russia swept away the Romanov dynasty, which had ruled the country for 304 years, and a provisional government headed by Alexander Kerensky was established. This new government affirmed to the world that Russia would stay in the war, and for the short term it honored its commitment. This continued support of the Allied cause, however, led to its undoing. The Russians suffered enormous casualties, more than all the other Allies put together.[51]

Later, in October, came a second revolution—and the birth of the Union of Soviet Socialist Republics. On the 7th of November, a date that Russians were to embrace for nearly 90 years as their key anniversary, the Bolsheviks (from the Russian *bolshinstvol*, the majority) seized power and Kerensky fled. They were headed by V. I. Lenin (real name Zederblum) and L. D. Trotsky (real name Bronstein). Lenin immediately announced a Decree of Peace for all the warring powers that would be based on "no annexations and no indemnities." The first act of the new government was to open peace talks with Germany, which began in mid-December in the city of Brest-Litovsk. The subsequent treaty was a spiteful victor's peace, with harsh terms for Russia, and was signed on March 3, 1918.[52]

The Brest-Litovsk accord meant reneging on the Treaty of London, which had bound the Allies together and forbade separate peace negotiations. Another Russian government had signed that pact, so the Bolsheviks were unconcerned with what was considered a small issue, a decision that understandably did not sit well with the Allies. Furthermore, the Bolshevik regime correctly regarded the war as an "imperialist" and "capitalist" conflict, and, certain to inflame its former Allies, defiantly urged the "oppressed peoples of the world" to follow their lead and overthrow their despotic rulers, repudiate foreign loans, and nationalize foreign assets.

That the Allies had never declared their war aims was a further reason for the Bolsheviks' distrust and for their unilateral action. Adding fuel to the fire was the Soviets' publication and wide dissemination of the Allied governments' secret treaties that divided the spoils of the war even before it ended.[53] Coinciding with these political sea changes, the spring offensive by the Allies in France had stalled after enormous casualties. Among French troops in particular, morale was low, and there were widespread mutinies punished by ruthless drum-head firing squads.

THEN IN THE SUMMER OF 1918, without declarations of war, the armed forces of 13 Allied states invaded the new Soviet Russia: the United States, Great Britain, France, Japan, Italy, Czechoslovakia, Serbia, China, Finland, Greece, Poland, Rumania, and Greece—in almost certainly the most flagrant double-cross in modern history. The Allies sent in thousands of troops when they were sorely needed on the Western Front, to subvert the new government and help put down a counter-revolution in the fledgling Soviet Union.[54]

What was it about the October 7th People's Revolution in 1917, understandable to anyone with a sense of history and a knowledge of the corrupt, pitiless Czarist regimes, that so alarmed the most powerful nations in the world? What impelled them to form a coalition and invade a country that had fought loyally on their side for three years? This, while the butchery in the trenches in France continued unabated! Britain's Minister of War, Winston Churchill, early on in his long and commanding diplomatic career and as a master of the English language, graphically called for "strangling this monster at birth".

Author William Blum put his finger on the fundamental cause: it was not to punish the Bolsheviks because they had broken a treaty and bailed out of the war, leaving a dangerous military vacuum; nor was it their call for subjugated peoples of the world to depose their rulers, renounce foreign loans, and nationalize foreign properties.

> ...the Bolsheviks had displayed the far greater audacity of overthrowing a capitalist-feudal system and proclaiming the first socialist state in the history of the world. This was uppityness writ incredibly large. This was the crime the Allies had to punish, the virus which had to be eradicated lest it spread to their own people.[55]

The invasion did not result in the "eradication of the virus," but its consequences, in fact, were portentous, and they persist to this day. Professor D.F. Fleming, Vanderbilt University historian of the cold war, treated the U.S. intrusion in the Soviet Union in stark terms.

> For the American people the cosmic tragedy of the interventions in Russia does not exist, or it was an unimportant incident long forgotten. But for the Soviet peoples and their leaders the period was a time of endless killing, of looting and rapine, of plague and famine, of measureless suffering for scores of millions—an experience burned into the very soul of a nation, not to be forgotten for many generations.[56]

Wilson at first was opposed to U.S. military intervention in Russia. But the British government, so effective with their propaganda in bringing America into the war in the first place, kept the pressure on and finally got Wilson to agree to join the coalition. Wilson's only proviso was that U.S. doughboys could be used only "to guard military stores which may subsequently be needed by Russian forces in the organization of their self-defense"; and U.S. military forces would not "take part in organized intervention in adequate force from either Vladivostok or Murmansk and Archangel".

His *Aide Memoire* [see Appendix] laboriously spelled out the restrictions. This 1,600-word tome was representative of Wilson's writing that put meaningless rhetoric ahead of substance. When the president finally agreed to send troops into Russia, he avoided calling the measure "intervention" in their internal affairs: rather, he said absurdly that American soldiers would be helping restore self-government to a deserving people.

It was, in fact, the president's "personal hostility" toward the Bolsheviks that led to the American intervention, according to historian William Appleman Williams. Williams wrote that Wilson "in the last hours of his administration approved a plan calculated to maneuver Lenin out of power."[57]

Historian G. J. A. O'Toole labeled the U.S. armed intervention in the Soviet Union "The Russian Muddle." He called it a:

> …strange two-year escapade... an episode all but forgotten by Americans yet remembered and cherished as an anti-American grievance by the authors of Soviet history books. Indeed, the immensely complex sequence of events that led to the adventure still defies comprehension even in the light of historical investigation.[58]

Historian Benjamin D. Rhodes called the war a "diplomatic and military tragicomedy" on the front cover of his book.[59] Major General William S. Graves, who was directly involved in the invasion, termed it a fiasco:

> "I was in command of the United States troops sent to Siberia and I must admit, I do not know what the United States was trying to accomplish by military intervention."[60]

THE AMERICAN WAR with Soviet Russia was actually two separate wars.[61] One took place in Archangel Province, with the center of activity in the port of Archangel (Archangelsk) on the Barents Sea. During the winter months, Archangel freezes and to give the Allies access to Russia; an ice-free port, Murmansk, had been built. The second war was some 6,000 miles to the east in Siberia around Vladivostok, a port on the Sea of Japan directly opposite the Japanese city of Sapporo and near the Chinese border.

In August of 1918, the *U.S.S. Olympia*, Admiral Dewey's flagship at the Battle of Manila Bay twenty years earlier, docked in Archangel. Fifty bluejackets went ashore, half joining British and counter-revolutionary White Russian troops in driving the Bolsheviks out of the city. At the same time, the Americans discovered that the storerooms were empty. The Bolsheviks had earlier cleaned out everything of value. If the object of the Archangel Expedition had been to safeguard the vast munitions and stores there, it had failed right at the beginning.

Also in August, 1,400 infantry officers and men departed from Manila, where they had been garrisoned, for Vladivostok, Siberia, by way of Japan. At the same time, 1,900 officers and men, plus support units, embarked from Fort Mason, San Francisco for their 4,750-mile voyage to Vladivostok. The first American troops arrived in Siberia on August 15.[62]

In September, a contingent of 4,500 U.S. Army reinforcements landed at Archangel. Two-thirds of this force was immediately sent south to fight on the front lines against the Red Army, some 200 miles inside Russia. This bold deployment of U.S. troops was a transparent breach of Wilson's *Aide Memoire,* but there is no record of this information being sent to the president at that time. In late November, however, it was pointed out to Wilson that American troops both in Northern Russia and Siberia were being used for purposes other than those originally agreed. Instead of standing up for the principles he had so excruciatingly enunciated in his *Aide Memoire,* he lamely remarked that he found it "harder to get out than it was to get in."[63]

THE BEST EXAMPLE OF AMERICA'S UNTIDY ENTRY into the equally messy Soviet civil war was the narrative of Edgar Sisson, whom Wilson appointed as a committee-of-one to set up a propaganda office in Petrograd. Sisson was an associate chairman of the Committee of Public Information and a former editor of *Cosmopolitan Magazine*. He understood what propaganda was and knew how to implement it. However, he did not speak, read, nor understand Russian, nor did he profess any background knowledge of the country or its history. In his book, *One Hundred Red Days: A Personal Chronicle of the Bolshevik Revolution,* Sisson gave no reason for his appointment.

Earlier, during the brief period of the Provisional Government's honeymoon with the United States, Wilson, with apparent good intentions, sent a fact-finding and goodwill team headed by Elihu Root to Russia. Root was a distinguished lawyer and elder statesman, and a former Secretary of State and Secretary of War. The reasons for Root's appointment were "not entirely clear," according to George F. Kennan.

> "As Root himself sourly observed, 'Wilson would never have sent me if I had not been 73 years of age.'"[64]

The president had also dispatched to Russia an Advisory Commission of Railway Experts and an American Red Cross Commission. Neither of these two Commissions had any positive impact on the fast-moving course of events. The Root mission returned from Russia having accomplished nothing.

A day after his first and only meeting with Wilson, who outlined the principles that would guide him, Sisson received a personal note from the president with specific instructions:

> We want nothing for ourselves and this very unselfishness carries with it an obligation of open dealing. Wherever the fundamental principles of Russian freedom are at stake we stand ready to render such aid as lies in our power, but I want this helpfulness based on request and not upon offer. Guard particularly against any effect of officious intrusion or meddling and try to express the disinterested friendship that is our sole impulse.[65]

The tenor of this note indicates that Wilson was apparently still sincere about helping the Soviets. This attitude was almost certainly a carryover of the deposed regime of Alexander Kerensky, a former fellow college professor. Wilson's view of the new regime rapidly underwent a sea change. For example, in September 1919 during his whistle-stop speaking tour across the country, to sell the League of Nations to a recalcitrant nation, Wilson railed against the "poison of disorder, the poison of revolt, and the poison of chaos" that had gotten into the veins of the Russian people.

Sisson's brief contact with Woodrow Wilson

> "convinced him that he was going abroad as a personal representative of the President, endowed with the latter's very special confidence; that great things depended, in the President's view, on the completion of his mission..."[66]

Once in Russia, Sisson's correspondence reveals him as quickly becoming antagonistic to the Bolshevik regime. , Sisson's views hardened after a meeting with Lenin on January 11. He was convinced that the Soviet government's policies represented a long-term threat to U.S. security, and decided to brand Lenin and Trotsky as dangerous and conniving German spies.

IN EARLY FEBRUARY, Raymond Robins, one of the principal members of the U.S. Red Cross Commission, brought Sisson a stack of documents he claimed he had gotten from a source that he was unwilling to reveal. They were English translations of what were alleged to be reports of the

German General Staff, the German Ministry of Finance, the *Reichsbank*, and other German ministries, dating from the outbreak of the war. The essence of the material was that Kaiser Wilhelm II's government had developed plans for sabotage and subversion in the Allied countries—by themselves unremarkable and quite understandable findings—and that the Bolshevik leaders had conspired with the Germans in the implementation of the plans. This latter finding flew in the face of conventional wisdom. The documents also obliquely hinted that not only had Germany materially assisted the Bolsheviks in their October revolution but that the top Bolshevik leaders, Lenin and Trotsky included, were paid agents of the German General Staff.

Sisson understandably was infatuated with the documents; they supported his own contentions of an evil-empire-in-the-making and he spent the remainder of his time in the Soviet Union, not involved in propaganda as he had been tasked to do, but investigating the origins of the papers. Sisson had convinced himself that he possessed material of crucial importance to the Allied war effort.

In May, 1918 he returned to the United States triumphantly with the sixty-eight supposedly incriminating documents he had smuggled out of Russia. By that time, they had already been published in Europe and were recognized in England and the U.S. State Department as clumsy forgeries. One can question why Sisson was unaware of these facts. Or, as Kennan wrote acidly, was it Sisson's:

> Enthusiasm...which tapped to the deepest roots not only of his unquestionable and fiery patriotism, but also his anti-German feelings (violent to the point of blindness), his innate suspiciousness, and his congenital eagerness, as a good professional journalist, to unearth and bring to public knowledge an important and sensational story?[67]

There is no evidence that Wilson knew the documents were counterfeit, or perhaps even cared to know. However, uncertain about the diplomatic fallout, Wilson withheld public disclosure of the documents for four months. House recorded in his diary that he had told the president that their public disclosure was tantamount to "a virtual declaration of war upon the Bolshevik Government" and that Wilson acknowledged he understood their foreign-policy import. In the event, they were released to the press as if they were fresh discoveries and genuine. Newspapers began printing "the Sisson Papers," as they became known, on September 15th, for seven installments. Creel reprinted them in the form of a CPI propaganda booklet, *The German-Bolshevik Conspiracy* to give the papers even wider circulation.

BEFORE, DURING, AND AFTER the Versailles Peace conference, Winston Churchill, unrequited warrior and unceasing defender of the British Empire, aggressively promoted his virulent anti-Bolshevik views. He wrote unabashedly:

> Of all the tyrannies in history, the Bolshevist tyranny is the worst, the most destructive and the most degrading and unless it was destroyed, there would be a union between German militarism and Russian Bolshevism which would be unspeakably unfriendly to Britain and to the United States and France.[68]

On March 3, 1919, addressing the House of Commons, Churchill defended the coalition's invasion of the USSR and put on it his own spin.

> There is no use people raising prejudice against this expedition. Everyone knows why it was sent. It was sent as part of our operations against Germany. It was vitally necessary to take every measure in regard to Russia during the war which would keep as many German troops as

possible on the Russian front, and reduce that formidable movement of the German armies which carried more than a million men to the Western Front, and which culminated in that immense series of battles which began on the 21st March last year.[69]

At the same time as Sisson delivered his cache of documents that ostensibly tied Germany to the birth of Bolshevism, two American foreign diplomat returnees were publishing eye-witness accounts of supposed German perfidy. The hottest property as far as publishers were concerned was James W. Gerard, former U.S. ambassador to Germany. He had been in Germany since 1913 and he had so much to relate that it took two books to tell it all.

In his first book, *My Four Years in Germany*, Gerard had no doubts about the origin of the war. He wrote:

> It is because in the dark, cold Northern plains of Germany there exists an autocracy, deceiving a great people, poisoning their minds... and preaching the virtue and necessity of war; and until that autocracy is either wiped out or made powerless, there can be no peace on earth.[70]

As for a negotiated settlement of the conflict, Gerard was unequivocal:

> There must be no German peace. The old regime, left in control of Germany, of Bulgaria, of Turkey, would seek only a favorable moment to renew the war, to strive again for the mastery of the world.[71]

According to Gerard, it was the heavy eating and drinking habits of Germans that made them aggressive and irritable, and therefore ready for war. Nevertheless, Gerard's *My Four Years* was more an informative travelogue than virulent anti-German propaganda.

In the second book, *Face to Face With Kaiserism*, the mild and mannerly Dr. Jekyll became the predatory Mr. Hyde. This book was as savage and sustained an indictment of Germans and Germany as any made by a high American official during the war and after. In such provocatively titled chapters as "When the Kaiser Thought We Were Bluffing," "Germany's Plan to Attack America," "Home Life and 'Brutality' of the People," the former ambassador and his team of ghostwriters spewed forth gobs of hate-filled nonsense. Reflecting the frenzied efforts to put it together quickly while the war was still on, *Face to Face* ended up with a hodgepodge of so-called diary entries, warped history, and anecdotal polemics.

Who had been responsible for the sinking of the *Lusitania*? Gerard had no doubts.

> All evidence points to the Emperor himself... who ordered or permitted this form of murder... I have heard that in parts of Germany school children were given a holiday to celebrate the sinking of the *Lusitania*.[72]

Gerard wrote that he did not believe all the atrocity stories, but noted that that while he was in Berlin:

> One of our servants... came back from the East and said the orders were to kill all Cossacks. Our washerwoman reports that her son was ordered to shoot a woman in Belgium and I myself heard an officer calmly describe the shooting of a seven-year-old Belgian girl child.[73]

Talk about hearsay evidence! Gerard's researchers dug back more than 300 years into European history to establish a congenital Teutonic thirst for war and conquest. *Face to Face* observed:

> There is no more horrible event in all history than that of the sack of Rome by the German mercenaries in 1527.... Prelates were tortured. Altars were defiled, sacred images broken. In fact conditions in Belgium today had their counterparts centuries ago in Rome.[74]

Preposterously, Gerard's ghostwriters maintained that in Germany:

Military training is always in view and the use of the knapsack on walking tours is universal, even school children carry their books to school in knapsacks and so become accustomed, at an early age, to carry this part of the soldier's burden.[75]

THE SECOND RETURNEE was Henry Morgenthau, Ambassador to Turkey. He had been appointed to the "Jewish" diplomatic post as payback for his fund-raising work and large financial contributions to Wilson's first campaign for the presidency. He had expected a cabinet post as his reward and only grudgingly accepted the minor ambassadorship.

Nevertheless, he made the most of his short tour of duty in Constantinople, putting his name on a book, *Ambassador Morgenthau's Story;* that had consequences far beyond his wildest dreams. His ghost-writer was a well-known journalist, Burton J. Hendrick. *Story* sold widely in the United States and was printed abroad as *Secrets of the Bosphorus.*

Morgenthau quit his post in Constantinople early in 1916,

> For a leave of absence so that I might pay a visit to the United States, which I had not seen for more than two years. I had begun to feel the effects of the nervous strain of my labors to avert the terrible fate of the Armenians and Jews.[76]

As events unwound, this statement was the first of a whopping web of lies. In fact, it was not a "leave of absence" that had brought Morgenthau home because he never returned to Constantinople, resigning soon after.[77] Perhaps he had yearned for New York City's lights, but more likely he still coveted the post of Secretary of the Treasury and saw an opportunity to enhance his chances by working for Wilson's reelection. And in the back of his mind was a book that would convince readers, once and for all, that it was the Germans who started the war. Henry Morgenthau, born in Germany, hated Germans.

Like Gerard, Morgenthau protested that it had taken a herd of oxen, figuratively, to draw the "true story" from his supposedly discreet lips:

> By this time [October 1918] the American people have become convinced that the Germans deliberately planned the conquest of the world. Yet they hesitate to convict on circumstantial evidence and for this reason all eye witnesses to this, the greatest crime in history, should volunteer their testimony. I have therefore laid aside any scruples I had as to the propriety of disclosing to my fellow countrymen the facts which I learned while representing them in Turkey.[78]

Morgenthau's "true story" was the wholly fictitious tale of the Potsdam Crown Conference of July 5, 1914, a happening and a date that American and Allied propagandists would fix as the ultimate proof that Germany had started the Great War. This highest-level war-planning conference that never took place was cited by the Commission of Reparations at the Paris peace conference, chaired by U.S. Commissioner Robert Lansing, as one justification for the notorious "sole war guilt" Article 231 of the treaty.

Morgenthau claimed in his book that he based his account on what he called his "private conversations" with Germany's ambassador to Turkey, Baron Hans von Wangenheim. It was because von Wangenheim "was sometimes led into indiscretions," especially when the German Army scored military successes in the early fall of 1914, that Morgenthau learned certain facts which he thought would have great historical value.

According to Morgenthau, Wangenheim left for Berlin shortly after the Sarajevo assassinations. The reason: the Kaiser had summoned him to an imperial conference on July 5th. When he returned to Constantinople, Wangenheim described the conference and told Morgenthau, using no names, who had attended: the top military officers, the great bankers, important diplomats, and the captains of German industry—all of whom were as necessary to Germany's war preparations as the army itself. According to Wangenheim's account, Wilhelm had solemnly asked each attendee in turn:

> Are you ready for war?" All replied 'yes', except the financiers. They said they needed two weeks to sell their foreign securities and make loans.... This conference... took all precautions that no suspicions would be aroused. It decided to give the bankers time to readjust their finances for the coming war, and then the members went quietly back to their work or started on vacation.[79]

Morgenthau, the author, and Hendrick, his skillful ghost writer and a Germanophobe himself, concluded their intricate fable of German war guilt this way:

> This indiscretion certainly had the effect of showing me who were really…the guilty party in this monstrous crime.... For my conclusions as to the responsibility are not based on suspicious belief or the study of circumstantial data. I do not have to reason to argue about the matter. I know. The conspiracy that has caused this greatest of human tragedies was hatched by the Kaiser and his imperial crew.... Whenever I hear people arguing about the responsibility for this war or read the clumsy and lying excuses put forth by Germany, I simply recall the burly figure of Wangenheim puffing away at a huge black cigar, giving me his account of this historic meeting. Why waste any time discussing the matter after that?[80]

Why, indeed?—Except that Wangenheim was never able to rebut the accusations; he died in August 1915. It took a decade after the end of the war for historians to learn details of Morgenthau's despicable perfidy. By then, of course, the war was long over and Article 231 was indelibly marked on Germany's psyche.

Historian Sidney Fay wrote damningly in 1930 that the contemporary documents available to him proved conclusively that there was hardly a word of truth in Morgenthau's entire narrative. He summed up his extensive research tellingly.

> It is clear that the 'Potsdam Council' was a myth. It is an interesting example of the way a legend will grow up, flourish, and receive the widest currency in an atmosphere of war propaganda and readiness to believe anything about an enemy.... Is it not extraordinary that Baron Wangenheim should have given to Mr. Morgenthau so many picturesque details which are in flat contradiction with the facts? How could he have dared make such an important revelation so prejudicial to the interests of his government? Germany at this time, in the early weeks of the war, was trying hard to win the good will of the United States and make the world believe she was fighting in self-defense in a war forced upon her.[81]

Fay put the clincher on the Morganthau/Hendrick string of lies this way:

> And is it not difficult to understand why the American Ambassador did not report to Washington what was perhaps the most important thing he ever heard at Constantinople? Yet a careful search through the files of the State Department at Washington shows that there is no dispatch or telegram recounting this interesting conversation with Baron Wangenheim; nor does Mr. Morgenthau in his book say anything about having made a report on the subject to Washington.[82]

AS FOR THE U.S. INVASION of Russia in 1918, more and more American historians began to roundly condemn Woodrow Wilson's final war. One author concluded, for example, that under the pretext of showing the Russian people the path to peace, democracy, and freedom:

> An attempt had been made to overthrow the Soviet Republic under the appearance of guarding railways and extending economic assistance.... Russia had been invaded, blockaded and disrupted with subsidized civil strife that wrought ruin and destruction to her cities and farms and carried suffering and death to thousands of her people.[83]

Another author, John Cudahy, chose to remain anonymous when his book was first published, using the name "A Chronicler" as the author of *Archangel: The American War With Russia.* In it he pointedly refuted the idea that it had been a "friendly intervention," even at the beginning.

> All too vividly comes to mind a picture during the Allied occupation of Archangel Province while the statesmen at Paris pondered and deliberated in a futile attempt to find dignified escapement from this shameful illegitimate war.... Why had we come and why did we remain, invading Russia and destroying Russian homes?[84]

Cudahy concluded his book with a paragraph whose ending struck a remarkable parallel with the dilemmas of the Vietnam War and the Second Iraqi War.

> We had waged war upon Russia. Whether willfully or unwillingly, our country had engaged in an unprovoked intensive, inglorious, little armed conflict which had ended in disaster and disgrace. Perhaps this was a laudable thing to do. Perhaps it is always idealistic and praiseworthy to intervene for self-conceived righteousness in the internal affairs of another nation, as England might have done in the case of the American Confederacy, and as we did in the case of this civil war among the Russians. *It is easy enough to enter the battle lists, but, once in it, it is not so easy to withdraw from the fight with self-respect unsullied and honor undefiled* [author's emphasis].[85]

The Japanese, although a full-fledged Ally from August of 1914 on, had scrupulously avoided combat on the Western Front. Their territorial interests lay elsewhere. They had joined the coalition for fear of a German victory that would make the Russians dominant in the Far East. But close-by Manchuria and parts of Siberia in the east also were tantalizing tid-bits to the expansionist Japanese. Japan also wanted to safeguard the huge Russian naval base at Vladivostok in eastern Siberia, right across the Sea of Japan, against any occupation from a then or later hostile power. Within a month, there were over 70,000 Japanese soldiers stationed in Siberia and Manchuria where they would remain as occupiers until the end of World War II.

Following the Armistice, Wilson at first resisted War Department pressure to bring U.S. forces home from Russia. He also obstinately refused to release a statement explaining U.S. policy toward the Bolsheviks—in fact; he did not have a policy, cogent or otherwise. The morale among U.S. troops was bad and getting worse. The Allied forces seemed to be strengthening the resolve of the Bolshevik regime rather than weakening it. It was time to admit defeat and pull out. The last contingent of U.S. troops left Vladivostok on April 1, 1920. U.S. soldiers in Russia had suffered over 500 casualties.

The Literary *Digest* had already summed up the intervention, remarking facetiously that:

> "some might have liked us more if we had intervened less, some might have disliked us less if we had intervened more, but that, having concluded that we intended to intervene no more nor no less than we actually did, nobody had any use for us at all."

IN SEPTEMBER 1959 SOVIET PREMIER NIKITA KHRUSCHEV, on his first and only visit to the United States, was invited to a luncheon in his honor by Spyros P. Skouras, president of the Twentieth Century-Fox Film Corporation in Los Angeles. During a rambling address that was billed by the media as "a debate" with Skouras, Khruschev responded to Skouras' reference to U.S. aid rendered to the Soviet Union in 1922. He said,

> "That was by the American Relief Administration headed by Herbert Hoover. We know all about that and we are grateful for it. There is one 'but'."

Khruschev then described unabashed American imperialist acts that few in the big audience had ever heard of—the invasion of the new Soviet Union by U.S. armed forces 40 years before.

> The Russian people remember how the American Relief Administration saved thousands of Russian children in the Volga region from starvation. But we also remember the grim days when immediately after the great October Revolution, American soldiers went to our soil headed by their generals to help our White Guard combat the revolution. And not only the Americans: the Japanese landed on the shores of our country; the French, the Germans, advanced right up to the northern Caucasus; the Poles marched against Kiev; the British, all the capitalist countries of Europe and of America marched upon our country to strangle the new revolution.

The Soviet premier then asked his audience to imagine "what the situation then was" in his battered country.

> The mines were not working; the factories were destroyed; we had nothing to eat; nothing to wear. And, yet, I remember that time—I served in the army—and yet, we routed those that attacked us and threw them into the sea. If you had not landed upon our shores, then we would not have had a civil war. Our industry would have remained intact. We would not have starved.

He ended his brief overview of Soviet history by declaring that despite these circumstances, the Soviet people were grateful for the help from America that was rendered.

> And that was the greatest unpleasantness that there was between our two countries because never until then had we any quarrels with the United States.... Never have any of our soldiers been on American soil, but your soldiers were on Russian soil. These are the facts.

In May 1972, when President Richard M. Nixon was in Moscow on an official visit, he stated that there were no reasons for Americans and Soviets to be foes,

> "Especially because they had never fought one another in war."[86]

Pravda omitted that statement when it printed Nixon's speech. In 1984, with the Cold War on high-burner, President Ronald Reagan, in a speech directed at the Soviet Union, asserted,

> "It's true that our governments have had serious differences. But our sons and daughters have never fought each other in war. And if we Americans have our way, they never will."[87]

One wonders if *Pravda* picked up on that second example of American presidential speech-writers' and their researchers' ignorance of American history. The writers were not alone; a 1985 *New York Times* poll found that only fourteen percent of those surveyed were aware that in 1918 the United States landed troops in Russia in an attempt to destroy the fledgling Soviet Union.

A most remarkable post-war incident was the washing up on the rocks at Falmouth, England, of two German U-boats. They were cast up but a few feet apart; both had been sunk during the war.
International News Photos., 1921

Notes

[1] The final vote in the Senate was 82 to 6 in favor of going to war. The House vote was 373 in favor to 50 against, including the "nay" vote by Miss Jeanette Rankin, the first woman in the nation's history to play a part in a declaration of war by the Congress. Twenty-four years later, on December 8, 1941, Rankin would cast the House's only vote against war with Japan.

[2] Noam Chomsky, *Turning the Tide: U.S. Intervention in Central America and the Struggle for Peace* (Black Rose Books, New York, 1987), p. 86.

[3] Neil Hanson, *Unknown Soldiers: The Story of the Missing of the First World War* (Alfred A. Knopf, New York, 2006), p. 192.

[4] Stewart Halsey Ross, *Propaganda for War: How the United States Was Conditioned to Fight the Great War of 1914-1918* (McFarland Publishing Company, Inc, Jefferson NC, 1995), p. 145; reprinted by Progressive Press, 2009.

[5] Ibid.

[6] Stephen S. Ivor, *Neutrality* (The Neutrality Press, Chicago, 1916), p. 103.

[7] Was the sinking of the British passenger liner by a German submarine a random act of war, drowning 128 American passengers and more than 1,000 others, or was it an example of jingo Winston Churchill purposefully putting the ship in harm's way? Revisionist historians continue to point their fingers at the First Lord of the Admiralty. A week before the disaster, he had written to Walter Runciman, president of

the Board of Trade, pointing out that it was "most important to attract neutral shipping to our shores, in the hopes especially of embroiling the United States with Germany."

[8] Ross, p. 27-90.

[9] The origin of the term "Hun" originated with Kaiser Wilhelm II. When giving a sendoff to his troops embarking for China to help quell the Boxer Rebellion, Wilhelm exhorted them on July 3, 1900 to: "Give no quarter, spare nobody, take no prisoners. Use your weapons so that for a thousand years hence no Chinaman will dare look askance at any German... Be terrible as Attila's Huns." Charles Callan Tansill, *America Goes to War* (Little, Brown and Company, Boston, 1938), p. 15.

[10] Quincy Howe, *England Expects Every American To Do His Duty* (Simon and Schuster, New York, 1937), p. 16.

[11] Harry Elmer Barnes, *The Genesis of The World War: An Introduction to The Problem of War Guilt* (Alfred A. Knopf, New York, 1926), p. 609-610.

[12] Barbara W. Tuchman, *The Zimmerman Telegram* (The Viking Press, New York, 1958), p. 146. The telegram (from German Foreign Minister Arthur Zimmermann to Herr von Eckhardt, the German minister in Mexico) read: "We intend to begin unrestricted submarine warfare on the first of February. We shall endeavor in spite of this to keep the United States neutral. In the event of this not succeeding, we make Mexico a proposal of alliance on the following basis: make war together, make peace together, generous financial support, and understanding on our part that Mexico is to reconquer the lost territories in Texas, New Mexico, and Arizona. The settlement in detail is left to you. You will inform the president [of Mexico] of the above most secretly as soon as the outbreak of war with the United States is certain and add the suggestion that he should, on his own initiative, invite Japan to immediate adherence and at the same time mediate between Japan and ourselves. Please call the president's attention to the fact that unrestricted employment of our submarines now offers the prospect of compelling England to make peace within a few months. Acknowledge receipt."

[13] Sidney Rogerson, *Propaganda in the Next War* (Garland Publishing, Inc., New York, 1938), p. 28.

[14] Thomas Fleming, *The Illusion of Victory: America in World War I* (Basic Books, NewYork, 2003), Frontispiece.

[15] Ibid., p. 270.

[16] Harry Elmer Barnes, *The Christian Century*, November 19, 1925), p. 14.

[16] Ibid., p. 17.

[17] Robert Harris and Jeremy Paxman, *A Higher Form of Killing: The Secret History of Chemical and Biological Warfare* (Random House Trade Paperbacks, New York), p. 26.

[18] The Germans named their gases after the markings on the shell cases: Green Cross for phosgene and chlorine, Yellow Cross for mustard, and White Cross for tear gas. Americans followed suit in the Vietnam War 50 years in the future, naming their poison defoliants by the colored stripes painted on the drums, Orange the most common.

[19] Ibid., p. 28.

[20] Ibid., p. 34

[21] Ibid, p. 36.

[22] Hanson, p. 221.

[23] Ibid., p. 221-222.

[24] Fleming, p. 307. According to a report of the National Disabled Soldiers' League, at the beginning of 1921, there were over 640,000 former American soldiers mutilated for life. The War Between the States began on April 12, 1861, when the Rebels shelled Fort Sumter and ended April 9, 1865, when Lee surrendered to Grant at Appomattox—1,460 days, or about seven times as long. Including deaths from disease, U.S. losses in the Great War were 112,000 compared to 620,000 in the War Between the States. The *per diem* death rate is thus comparable.

[25] John Kenneth Turner, *Shall It Be Again*? (B.W. Huebsch. Inc., New York, 1922), p. 133.

[26] John M. Barry, *The Great Influenza: The Epic Story of the Deadliest Plague in History* (Viking, New York, 2004), p. 383.

[27] Fleming, p. 313.
[28] John Maynard Keynes, *The Economic Consequences of the Peace* (Macmillan and Co., Limited, London, 1920), p. 44.
[29] Barry, p. 384.
[30] Ibid., p. 385-386.
[31] C. Hartley Grattan, *The Deadly Parallel* (Stackpole Sons, New York, 1939), p. 127.
[32] Turner, p. 147. For a detailed overview of what this author has called "Conspiracy in President Woodrow Wilson's White House, 1919-1920," please see Appendix E in the author's *How Roosevelt Failed America in World War II*.
[33] Fleming, p. 419.
[34] Warren I. Cohen, *The American Revisionists: The Lessons of Intervention in World War I* ((The University of Chicago Press, Chicago, 1967), p. 34. James A. Cox was the Democratic candidate for president with Franklin D. Roosevelt as his running mate, and Warren G. Harding was the Republican; neither of the two candidates was given high marks by political analysts. As president, Harding and his corrupt administration surprised few.
[35] Grattan, p. 222.
[36] Harry Elmer Barnes, *The Genesis of The World War: An Introduction to The Problem of War Guilt* (Alfred A. Knopf, New York, 1926), p. 639.
[37] Harry Elmer Barnes, "Why America Entered the War," *The Christian Century,* November 1925, 1443. Page managed to snare B. J. Hendrick, a Pulitzer Prize winner, to be his biographer and ghost-writer. The first volume of the hagiographic *The Life and Letters of Walter Hines Page* was published in 1922. One measure of Hendrick's lack of integrity was his willingness in 1918 to ghost-write the purposefully deceiving memoir of Henry Morgenthau, which had political consequences far beyond what Hendrick could have imagined and what Morgenthau hoped for. Sidney Bradshaw Fay demolished *Ambassador Morgenthau's Story* in *The Origins of the World War.* In particular, see also Appendix D, Ross, *How Roosevelt Failed America in World War II*: "The Portentous Lie of Ambassador Henry Morgenthau, Sr., 1918." The British, to show their appreciation of Page's assistance, embedded a small marble tablet into a wall in a remote corridor in Westminster Abbey: "Walter Hines Page—The friend of Britain in her sorest need." The unveiling drew a large crowd of dignitaries. Only two other Americans had been so honored: Henry Wadsworth Longfellow and James Russell Lowell.
[38] Barnes, The Genesis of The World War, p. 639.
[39] Barnes, "Why America...," 1443.
[40] Fleming, p. 307.
[41] When the German High Sea Fleet fell into the hands of the British at the end of the war—and before it was scuttled in Scapa Flow by its mutinous crews—it was discovered that the coal-bunker capacities of the German battleships was small, giving them short range and clearly demonstrating that they had been designed for close in-shore cruising. Any sustained or extended operations in distant waters were thus ruled out: proof, if any was needed, that the German government had never entertained any ideas of crossing the Atlantic and attacking the United States. The idea of a foreign power attacking the continental United States, since the Great War, has remained a "gigantic hoax," used as fear propaganda by the U.S. government as a pretext in every major American war since, idiotic as the concept may appear when looked at rationally. The mantra—"we had best fight them over there before we have to fight them over here"—is humbug, yet there is strong evidence that it always works to frighten Americans. One is tempted to ask, are Americans gullible—or merely stupid?
[42] Turner, p. 147.
[43] The Japanese First Air Fleet, consisting of six aircraft carriers, some 400 aircraft including the as yet unmatched Mitsubishi *Zero*, two fast battleships plus cruisers, destroyers, and oil tankers, with submarines in the van, managed to cross the North Pacific in late November and early December 1941 unobserved, on their way to strike Pearl Harbor. Their radio communications gave away their positions., The United States, Great Britain, the Netherlands and China then tracked their positions and decoded

their messages. Robert B. Stinnett, *Day of Deceit: The Truth About FDR and Pearl Harbor* (Simon & Schuster, New York, 2000).

[44] Sidney Bradshaw Fay, *The Origins of The World War* (The Macmillan Company, New York, 1928), p. 554.

[45] Ibid., p. 555.

[46] Ibid., p. 558.

[47] Fleming, p. 476.

[48] Ibid., p. 477.

[49] The Espionage Act: Whomsoever shall make or convey false reports or false statements with intent to interfere with the operation or success of the military or naval forces of the United States or to promote the success of its enemies and whoever, when the United States is at war, shall willfully cause or attempt to cause insubordination, disloyalty, mutiny, or refusal of duty, in the military or naval forces of the United States, or shall willfully obstruct the recruiting or enlistment service of the United States, to the injury of the service or of the United States, shall be punished by a fine of not more than $10,000 or imprisonment for not more than twenty years, or both.

[50] Sidney Lens, *Permanent War: The Militarization of America* (Scoken Books, New York, 1987), p. 109.

[51] John Cudahy, *Archangel: The American War With Russia* (A.C. McClurg & Co., Chicago, 1924), p. 30. Cudahy was a skeptic concerning Woodrow Wilson's vague reasoning for intervention, as he reported in the book, and perhaps felt more comfortable remaining anonymous, at least in the short term.

[52] In the first ten months of combat, Russia lost 3,800,000 soldiers. By the end of 1916, total Russian casualties were a staggering 5,250,000. In World War II, the Russians again suffered enormous casualties. Including the millions of civilians killed during the *Wehrmacht's* initial advance into Russia and the *Gestapo's* organized genocide, estimates of Russian dead numbered 20 million. Miles Hudson, *Intervention in Russia 1918-1920, A Cautionary Tale* (Leo Cooper, Barnsley, South Yorkshire, England, 2004), p. 27-28.

[53] The Treaty of Brest-Litovsk: Lenin agreed to the loss of the Ukraine, Finland, and all the Baltic provinces. The USSR lost over 1 million square miles of territory, one-third of its population, one-third of its cultivated land, and half its industry. Turkey, an ally of Germany, would get back all territory in Asia Minor occupied since the start of the war. Hudson, p. 33.

[54] The Secret Treaties: France would regain its lost provinces of Alsace-Lorrain and acquire a large section of Germany's Ruhr basin with its valuable coal and iron-ore mines. The French would also divide with England Turkey's Mediterranean empire and Germany's African colonies. Japan would acquire Germany's Far East colonies and gain control of China's strategic Shantung peninsula. Italy, a latecomer to the Allied cause, entering the war in 1915, would acquire the Austrian South Tyrol and Trieste regions, gain control of the Dalmatian coast on the Adriatic Sea, and get those German colonies in Africa not already spoken for.

[55] Michael Sayers and Albert E. Kahn, *The Great Conspiracy: The Secret War Against Soviet Russia* (Little Brown and Company, Boston, 1946), p. 79.

[56] William Blum, Killing Hope: U.S. Military and CIA Interventions Since World War II (Common Courage Press, Monroe ME, 1995), p. 9.

[57] D.F. Fleming, *The Cold War and Its Origins, 1917-1960* (Doubleday, Garden City NY, 1995), p. 840.

[58] William Appleman Williams, *American Russian Relations, 1781-1947* (Rinehart, New York, 1952), p. 170.

[59] G. J. A. O'Toole, *Honorable Treachery: A History of U.S. Intelligence, Espionage, and Covert Action From The American Revolution to the CIA* (The Atlantic Monthly Press, New York, 1991), p. 291.

[60] Benjamin D. Rhodes, *The Anglo-American Winter War with Russia, 1918-1919: A Diplomatic and Military Tragicomedy* (Greenwood Press, Westport CT, 1988), p. 99.

[61] There had been friendly ties between Russia and the United States going back as far as America's War for Independence. Russia had "intervened" on America's behalf in the form of its Declaration of Armed Neutrality of 1780. The previous Napoleonic Wars had also involved both countries, and America's War

of 1812 had begun almost at the same time as the Napoleonic invasion of Russia. During the Crimean War in the 1850s, both countries stood aloof together. Russia had sided with the Union during the War Between the States, partly out of gratitude for America's neutrality and partly out of self-interest. On March 30, 1867, the Czar agreed to cede "all the territory and dominion now possessed by his Majesty on the continent of America and in the adjacent islands." That was Alaska. The price: $7,200,000 in gold. Frederick Lewis Schuman, *American Policy Toward Russia Since 1917: A Study of Diplomatic History, International Law & Public Opinion* (International Publishers, New York, 1928), p. 20-21. It would prove to be a colossal bargain. During the Russo-Japanese War, American sympathies were initially with Japan.

[62] Carol K.W. Melton, *Between War and Peace: Woodrow Wilson and The American Expeditionary Force in Siberia*, 1918-21 (Mercer University Press, Macon GA, 2001), p. 48-49.

[63] George F. Kennan, *Russia Leaves The War: Soviet-American Relations 1917-1920* (W.W. Norton & Company, New York, 1958), p. 20.

[64] Ibid., p. 50-51.

[65] Edgar Sisson, *One Hundred Red Days: A Personal Chronicle of The Bolshevik Revolution* (Yale University Press, New Haven CT, 1931), p. 101.

[66] Kennan, p. 414-415.

[67] Ibid., p. 418-419

[68] Ibid., p. 419.

[69] Ibid.

[70] James W. Gerard, *My Four Years in Germany* (George H. Doran Company, New York, 1917), p. 432.

[71] Ibid., p. 433.

[72] James W. Gerard, *Face to Face With Kaiserism* (George H. Doran Company, New York, 1918), p. 43.

[73] Ibid., p. 58.

[74] Ibid., p. 130-131.

[75] Ibid., p. 169.

[76] Ross, p. 255.

[77] Ibid. Morgenthau's sudden return to the United States did not go unnoticed. The author discovered a fascinating letter dated March 20, 1916, in Morgenthau's file in the Manuscript Division, Library of Congress. It was addressed to Morgenthau at his apartment at 30 West 72 Street in New York City;

"Dear Mr. Morgenthau:

Does it appear to you proper that during critical times which we have at present for you to leave your post as Ambassador to Turkey and come to the United States to make propaganda, or in other words to practice self-advertising?

We have had a great number of Ambassadors returning to their country, but all came back with modesty, not one showed eagerness to appear before the public as you are doing. There is quite some talk in the different Clubs about you, and I thought there would be no harm in calling your attention to it.

The object of your return at this time seems rather mysterious. Pardon the information, but accept it with good grace. It can do you no harm.

Respectfully yours,

Robt. Williams" (signed)

Some might suggest Williams' letter was a case of anti-Semitism, as Morgenthau was a wealthy Jew. Or had Morgenthau's "self-advertising" been so blatant as to be obvious to his wealthy peers in Manhattan?

[78] Ibid., p. 256.

[79] Ibid.

[80] Ibid., p. 257

[81] Fay, p. 278.

[82] Ibid. In *The Origins of the World War* Fay placed the blame for the Great War on the system of secret alliances embodied in The Triple Entente.

[83] Frederick Lewis Schuman, *American Policy Toward Russia Since 1917: A Study of Diplomatic History; International Law and Public Opinion* (International Publishers, New York, 1956), p. 176.
[84] Cudahy, p. 200.
[85] Ibid., p. 85-86.
[86] The New York Times, May 16, 1972.
[87] Ibid., September 15, 1959.

Chapter VI:
World War II

"By early October [1941] we had also broken many of the Japanese military codes, specifically parts of the Kaigun Ango: the twenty-nine separate naval codes which gave us a good idea of what their fleet was up to during the entire year before Pearl Harbor.... On Saturday, November 15, 1941, General Marshall, the U.S. Army Chief of Staff, called in various Washington newspaper bureau chiefs. After swearing them to secrecy, he told them that we had broken Japan's naval codes, and that war with Japan would start sometime during the first ten days of December."[1]

"By the autumn of 1939, GCSS had reconstituted the JN-25 codebook. As with all Japanese codes, JN-25 started off very simply and only later did the Japanese try to make it more complicated. So by the end of 1939, GCSS and FEBC could read JN-25, used between Navy headquarters in Tokyo and all their ships and shore stations."[2]

THE BELIEF that there was American foreknowledge of the Japanese Navy's air attack on Pearl Harbor in 1941 is difficult to accept for those who still cling to the conventional wisdom that it was as, President Franklin D. Roosevelt declared, a "dastardly" deed on a day that would endure in "infamy." These die-hard Americans base their views on two allegations that U.S. propaganda has chiseled into granite: that U.S. cryptographers had failed to solve JN-25, the Japanese naval code, prior to December 7 (but had finally solved the code in time for the battle of Midway on June 4-6, 1942), and that American intelligence could not possibly have known where and when the assault would come because the attacking Japanese carrier force was steaming under radio silence. New studies show *both presumptions to be patently false*.

We also now know with certainty that the British, Dutch, and Nationalist Chinese radio intercept and decoding stations were also reading the messages between the task force heading to Hawaii and Imperial Japanese Navy Headquarters in Tokyo. *Some in Washington also knew the Japanese First Air Fleet was steaming toward Pearl Harbor—but Navy and Army commanders in Hawaii were purposely kept in the dark.*

In 1939, the U.S. had terminated its 1911 commercial treaty with Japan, an action intended to serve as a warning to Japan to end its war with China. Japan continued the war unfazed, and drew further apart from the United States by signing the Anti-Comintern Pact with Nazi Germany. In 1940, Japan signed a Tripartite Pact with Germany and Italy, forming the Axis Powers.

Roosevelt, also undeterred, kept ratcheting up the pressure, quietly negotiating a "destroyers-for-leases"[4] arrangement with Churchill and pushing through Congress an even more provocative Lend-Lease program. While Lend-Lease was being vigorously debated in the Congress, Churchill swung his not-inconsiderable weight behind the legislation. In a radio broadcast in England on February 9, 1941—aimed rifle-barrel-straight at American citizens—Churchill's speechwriters were at their alliterative best.

... President Roosevelt: Put your confidence in us. Give us your faith and your blessing, and, under Providence, all will be well. We shall not fail or falter; and we shall not weaken or tire.

> Neither the sudden shock of battle, nor the long-drawn-out trials of vigilance and exertion will wear us down. Give us the tools, we will finish the job.[5]

By that time, nationwide public-opinion polls had begun to swing FDR's way as isolationism began to wane: 72 percent of Americans had come to regard "defeating Nazism" as "the biggest job facing their country," and 70 percent preferred American belligerency to an Allied defeat. British and American propaganda had begun to work their magic!

> The first thing to know when reading public-opinion polls commonly cited from 1939 to 1941 is that none of them was produced by disinterested seekers of truth. The most prominently published polls were all under the influence of British intelligence, its friends, employees, and agents.[6]

Both the "destroyers deal" and Lend-Lease were in clear violation of international law, but the president showed no concern. Adolf Hitler, too, disregarded such obvious acts of war; he wanted no part of a war with the United States when he was planning to invade the USSR.[7] However, Franklin Roosevelt wanted a war with Germany, the sooner the better. In the event, Lend-Lease was voted into law on March 11, 1941. The scheming president also took the country three giant steps closer to war in Europe: he sent a bill for the nation's first peacetime conscription to the Congress (it was passed by a margin of *one vote* in the Senate), he called up the National Guard to active duty, and he signed legislation creating a two-ocean navy.

But none of these war-mongering ploys by the president appeared to be working. Roosevelt's chief speechwriter, Robert E. Sherwood, wrote:

> "He had no more tricks left. The hat from which he had pulled so many rabbits was empty. The front door to war in Europe seemed to be closed and barred."[8]

THERE WAS A BACK DOOR AS WELL—in Asia—and FDR, ever the consummate juggler, knew how to pry it open. In October of 1940, Lt. Commander Arthur H. McCollum, head of the Far East desk of the Office of Naval Intelligence, completed a secret assignment. McCollum's "eight-action memorandum" was a graduated response intended to incite a Japanese attack not only on the principal holdings of the U.S. in the Pacific (Hawaii and the Philippines) but also against the British (Singapore and Malaya) and Dutch (Dutch East Indies) colonial assets. He prefaced his list by reciting the fashionably old and disreputable saw that a British defeat would mean the Royal Navy would fall intact into the hands of enemy powers.[9]

These eight actions were:

1. Arrange with Britain for the use of British bases in the Pacific, particularly Singapore.
2. Arrange with Holland for the use of base facilities and acquisition of supplies in the Dutch East Indies.
3. Give all possible aid to the Chinese government of Chiang Kai-shek.
4. Send a division of long-range heavy cruisers to the Orient, Philippines, or Singapore.
5. Send two divisions of submarines to the Orient.
6. Keep the main strength of the U.S. Pacific Fleet in the vicinity of the Hawaiian Islands.
7. Insist that the Dutch refuse to grant Japanese demands for undue economic concessions, particularly oil.

8. Completely embargo all trade with Japan, in collaboration with a similar embargo imposed by the British Empire.¹⁰

Would an America at war with Japan automatically trigger declarations of war from Germany and Italy, which his commander-in-chief sought? McCollum thought so. FDR hoped so.

FDR and his handful of military and civilian advisers, with little fanfare, then clamped an economic stranglehold—McCollum's Number 8—on Japan. This embargo—of scrap metal, oil, and machine tools—was intended to back the Japanese into a corner. The United States also closed the Panama Canal to Japanese shipping. On July 28, the Dutch followed the U.S. and Great Britain in embargoing oil to Japan.

The Japanese, nevertheless, appeared to seek a diplomatic solution and were working in Washington with Cordell Hull to negotiate a settlement literally up to the last hours of peace. But FDR did not want a *modus vivendi* with Japan. He wanted a war with Germany. A Roosevelt-hater in 1941—and their number was legend—could point out that Roosevelt gladly took any war he could get!

German Submarine of the UB Class in Rough Seas

Earlier, under the cloak of bogus neutrality, the president had been waging a *de facto* war in the Atlantic with Admiral Karl Doenitz's submarine forces. U.S. Navy destroyers were under orders to track and depth-charge German submarines, and to radio their locations to Royal Navy/Royal Air Force hunter-killer teams, even to serve as convoy escorts alongside British naval forces. This warlike convoy policy first bore fruit for the conniving president on October 16, 1940, when the destroyer USS *Kearny* was torpedoed, but not sunk, killing eleven sailors. Within 24 hours the Congress voted by a margin of two-to-one to mount cannons on American merchant ships, ending any semblance of neutrality.

On October 30, 1941, 115 American sailors went down with the torpedoed *USS Reuben James*. The destroyer *James* was not the battleship *Maine*, but it would do just fine as a symbol of Nazi aggression, as far as FDR and his interventionist supporters were concerned. Two weeks later, the House passed revised neutrality laws that loosened restraints. Roosevelt then sent U.S. troops into Greenland as occupiers and relieved British troops, garrisoning Iceland with American soldiers—all flagrant acts of war.

FDR also inaugurated what he called "pop-up" cruisers as incitements to war. He had been sending pairs of heavy cruisers into Japanese home waters to "pop-up here and there". In one instance, the two warships had to make smoke to cover their rapid withdrawal and avoid confrontation with the Japanese Navy.

On July 18, FDR announced his decision to freeze Japanese assets—another step toward war. Japanese nationals were allowed to withdraw up to $500 a month from their frozen bank accounts. One week later came even more drastic measures. All Japanese ships in U.S. ports were prevented from sailing; all Japanese balances in U.S. banks were impounded; and all Japanese business transactions were suspended.

On the eve of war, December 1, FDR had the gall to direct that "three small vessels" from the Asiatic Fleet in the Philippines be sailed on one-way suicide missions as "bait" to lure the Japanese Navy in striking the first blow.[11] This latter directive is puzzling, since overwhelming evidence now proves that FDR and his top advisers knew *that a Japanese fleet with six aircraft carriers and over 400 aircraft was bearing down on Pearl Harbor.*

IN MID-AUGUST, Roosevelt met in secret with Prime Minister Winston Churchill for five days in Argentia Bay off the coast of Newfoundland, in what was loftily called the Atlantic Conference. The communiqué that summarized the meeting's agreements was appropriately called the Atlantic Charter. Read critically, the Charter was merely a laundry-list of platitudes, yet it later was used as the basis for the Charter of the United Nations. The document was also splendid propaganda and a copy of it was put on display in the National Museum in Washington. It was exquisitely framed and illuminated like an ancient manuscript. Visitors could gawk at what was presumed to be one of history's most important documents.

At a press conference following the Teheran Conference in 1943, FDR was asked about the Atlantic Charter. Had the agreements reached with Stalin had any impact on it? The newsmen could scarcely believe what the president then proceeded to tell them. There had never been a complete Atlantic Charter, Roosevelt said without hesitation, and went on to the further amazement of all in attendance:

> "It was just a press release. It was scribbled on a piece of paper and just handed to the radio operators aboard the American and British warships to be put on the air as a presidential news release."[12]

It was later learned that Stephen Early, FDR's press spokesman, had distributed it on his own with the facsimile signatures of Churchill and Roosevelt affixed. What about the document hanging in the National Museum? An inquisitive reporter asked the curator that question, who told him that it had been loaned to the Museum by the Office of War Information (OWI), but not before that propaganda agency had printed about a quarter of a million copies and distributed them nationally and internationally. The exhibit was quietly removed.

When the prime minister returned to London following the meeting, he told his Cabinet what had been agreed to.[13] The British documents were finally released thirty years later. *The New York Times*, January 2, 1972, reported the disclosure:

> "Formerly top secret British Government papers made public today said that President Franklin D. Roosevelt told Prime Minister Winston Churchill in August 1941 that he was looking for an incident to justify opening hostilities against Nazi Germany.... He [FDR] obviously was determined that they should come in.... The president had said he would wage war but not

VI. World War II

declare it and that he would become more and more provocative. If the Germans did not like it, they could attack American forces.... Everything was to be done to force an incident."

"I do not care so much for the principles I advocate as for the impression which my words produce and the reputation they give me."[14]

—Sir Winston Churchill

But while Winston had no principles, there was one constant in his life: he loved war. As a child he had a huge collection of toy soldiers, 1,500 of them, and he played with them for many years after most boys turned to other things.[15]

On August 5, 1940, the British Chiefs of Staff sent to Churchill's War Cabinet a report that updated the planned defense of the Far East—Singapore, Hong Kong, Malaya, and the Dutch East Indies. In 1937, the Chiefs had estimated that the longest period the defenders of Singapore could be expected to hold out against an attack by Japan, including the time required for a Royal Navy fleet to sail around the Cape of Good Hope, was 70 days. That calculation optimistically assumed that:

Britain would not be at war with Germany and thus could spare ten battleships and two battle cruisers, which with their attendant escorts plus the Royal Navy's China Station ships would be more than a match for Japan's fleet of only nine battleships.[16]

One could suggest that the British war planners' assumptions remained fixed in Vice Admiral Horatio Nelson's era, when having superiority in numbers of ships-of-the-line and good seamanship was all that it took to win a war. Not so, emphatically, 140 years later! In fact, the big-gun battleship, so long the symbol of maritime power had already given way to the aircraft carrier with its complement of relatively cheap airplanes—but few knew that yet.

The report from August of 1940 made depressing reading for all concerned. It stated that England was not prepared to resort to war if Japan attacked Britain's Far East holdings and the only course was to try to buy time with a deliberate policy of appeasement. In particular, the Royal Navy could not assemble a Far East fleet. Churchill judged the report so pessimistic that he allowed no discussion of it in his War Cabinet—and sent no copies to the Australian or New Zealand governments.

Later that year, the *Atlantis*, a big merchant ship converted by the German Navy into a "Q" ship, one that could assume many disguises, began its cruise, sinking and capturing when feasible unsuspecting Allied merchantmen. On November 11, 1940, *Atlantis,* with some of the crew on deck masquerading as women passengers hanging out wash to dry in the sun, closed on the British merchantman *Automedon.* Aboard was a merchant navy master acting as an Admiralty courier in charge of *Automedon's* secret mail. He was under orders, at the first sign of danger, to throw overboard certain mail that was packed in special weighted bags.

Atlantis identified herself in English by megaphone, fired a round from her previously hidden 5.9-inch cannon across *Automedon's* bow, and ordered her to heave to immediately. Instead, *Automedon* began transmitting a "Raider sighted" distress signal. *Atlantis* responded by opening fire again, this time for effect, aimed at the bridge, to silence the transmission. The courier who had been on the bridge was knocked unconscious. By the time he recovered, so the dramatic story went, the German boarding party had blown open the master's safe and the ship's strongroom.

The haul was an incredible treasure trove of secrets... First of all there were all the usual ship's confidential papers. Then there was $6 million worth of new Straits currency fresh from the printers in England. Next, the entire secret mail for the Far Eastern Command, Singapore, which included sets of new Royal Navy fleet codes. Some of the other sixty sealed packages contained secret mail from MI6 to their stations in Singapore, Hong Kong, Shanghai, and Tokyo, which included summaries of the latest intelligence reports of Japanese military and political activities. In one green Foreign Service canvas bag, heavily weighted, sealed, and marked "Safe Hand— British Master Only," was an envelope addressed to the C-in-C Far East, Singapore. Inside was the secret Chiefs of Staff report of August 5.[17]

Authors James Rusbridger and Eric Nave concluded that the captured Chiefs of Staff report was the catalyst that put the Japanese on the path to their attack on Pearl Harbor. They also wrote,

> "By any standard, the [*Automedon*] incident remains one of the worst intelligence disasters in history."[18]

Coincident with the German capture of the *Automedon* documents was the Royal Navy's successful nighttime air attack against the Italian Navy at anchor at Taranto. This first-ever torpedo strike from an aircraft carrier (HMS *Illustrious*) used the best torpedo bombers in the Royal Navy's inventory— Fairey *Swordfish* fabric-covered biplanes with open cockpits and a top speed of 138 miles per hour. Nevertheless, 21 planes that came in two waves sank one Italian battleship and heavily damaged two others plus a heavy cruiser. As a result of the strike, the Italians withdrew the rest of their fleet farther north to Naples.

Prior to Taranto, it was dogma in all navies that aerial torpedoes could not be used successfully against ships in shallow water anchorages, less than 100 feet deep. The British had modified their torpedoes so they would run shallow, and the *Swordfish* torpedo planes released them from just above wave tops so they would not dive deep. Japanese Navy officials studied all aspects of the raid they could obtain and gained confidence that their modified torpedoes would work in their tentatively planned raid against anchored warships in the 40-foot depths of Pearl Harbor.

> *"Faced with the growing prospect of war with Germany, the British government mounted in 1939 a massive secret political campaign in the United States (including the use of front groups, agents, collaborators, manipulation of polling data, involvement in election campaigns) to weaken the isolationists, bring the United States into the war, and influence U.S. war policy in England's favor."*[19]

THERE WAS GLOOM in the Exchequer in the late 1930s, as the British government secretly girded itself for a likely war with Germany. Britain did not have enough money to wage the expensive conflict that was anticipated by her strategic planners. In 1936, for example, when the Admiralty proposed a ship building program to up-grade the Royal Navy's capabilities, the Cabinet responded that the modernization "lay beyond the bounds of financial possibility."[20] Nor could they freely borrow from the United States as they had done during the Great War. The Johnson Act of 1934 prohibited loans to any government in default on its debts to the United States—and that meant Great Britain, in particular.[21]

Compounding Britain's monetary problems at home was isolationism in the United States. Public-opinion polls all showed Americans determined to stay out of a new European war. In a national poll taken in February 1937, those responding were asked:

> "If another war like the World War develops in Europe, should America take part again?"

A nearly unanimous 95 percent said "no." In April of 1939 another national poll posed a slightly different question:

> "If England and France should go to war with Germany, should this country declare war on Germany?"

Again, 95 percent answered "no." In June 1940, people were asked:

> "If the question of the United States going to war against Germany and Italy came up for a national vote within the next two or three weeks, would you vote to go into the war?"

This time 86 percent responded with a "no." As late as November 1941, a Gallup Poll listed 88 percent of the respondents still indicating they wanted no part of a European war. No poll asked recipients about a war with Japan.

STARTING WITH ENGLISHMAN John Maynard Keynes' devastating attack on the inequities of the Versailles Treaty in his 1920 landmark book, *The Economic Consequences of the Peace,* there were books from respected American historians, including a new breed of American revisionists—Harry Elmer Barnes, Walter Millis, Sidney Bradshaw Fay, Charles Austin Beard, and Charles Callan Tansill, for example—who went further, exposing Britain's sinister role in maneuvering the U.S. into the Great War. There were also the disquieting disclosures of Senator Gerald Nye's well-publicized Munitions Committee Hearings in the mid-1930s that tied U.S. arms and munitions makers and their American bankers to America's entry into the war. A best-selling book, *Merchants of Death,* described the behind-the-scenes power of armaments makers.

> "During testimony at the Munitions Hearings, Chairman Nye was asked how one might distinguish between arms for national defense—and for mass murder? His famous response was another question: 'Does national defense mean that people should go to all corners of the earth to wage war?'"[22]

Merchants of Death introduced its readers to Irénée Du Pont who, in 1802, opened the first big American gunpowder factory, which became today's giant conglomerate: E.I. Du Pont de Nemours and Company. During the War Between the States, Irénée sided with the North, and by the end of the conflict there was a virtual partnership between the powder-maker and the U.S. government.

In 1974, biographer Gerard Colby Zilg's thoroughgoing *Du Pont: Behind the Nylon Curtain* revealed much more about the *Du Ponts.*

> They happen to be the richest family on earth. The Du Ponts of Delaware own more personal wealth and control more multimillion dollar corporations than any one family in the world. They employ more servants than Britain's royal family, own more yachts, cars, swimming pools, planes, and estates than any family in recorded history.[23]

More than their yachts and swimming pools, the Du Ponts wielded breathtaking power. Of the almost fifty families that constituted the "inner core," these Du Ponts controlled more assets than the GNP of most nations.

> The Du Ponts own the state of Delaware. They control its state and local governments, its major newspapers, radio, and TV stations, university and colleges, and its largest banks and industries.... The Du Pont Company employs more than 11 percent of Delaware's labor force, and when the family's other holdings are included, the percentage rises to over 75 percent.... Predictably, the long arm of Du Pont can also be found in Washington. Du Pont family members represent Delaware in both houses of Congress. In the last 25 years [since 1949] Du Pont lieutenants have served as representatives, senators, U.S. Attorney General, secretaries of defense, directors of the CIA, and even Supreme Court justices.[24]

Zilg wrote that the self-named "Armorers of the Republic" had helped put America into two world wars, covertly sabotaged global disarmament conferences, consorted surreptitiously with the Nazis before World War II, and once were implicated in an attempt to overthrow the U.S. government, according to charges brought before a Congressional committee. The family's ambition, once limited to a U.S. monopoly in gunpowder manufacture, had expanded to the entire world.

AT THE START OF the second World War, the British no longer had the services of Sir William Wiseman, Sir Gilbert Parker and Charles F.G. Masterman, with their team of more than fifty expert propagandists at Wellington House aiming their missives at the United States. They no longer had such famous English authors as H.G. Wells, Arnold Bennett, Sir Arthur Conan Doyle, John Galsworthy, Rudyard Kipling, and Thomas Hardy journeying to America to tell bold lies before enthralled audiences and write slanted books. They no longer had the flagrantly anti-German Dutch newspaper cartoonist Louis Raemaekers and his obscene anti-German works. They no longer had as their standard bearer Viscount James Bryce, internationally respected British scholar, historian, and former ambassador to the United States, to catalog German atrocities in Belgium that had never occurred. There was no longer a wildly Anglophilic, conniving ambassador in the U.S. Embassy in London, of the likes of Walter Hines Page.

The 81,000-ton *Queen Mary*, launched in 1936 and somewhat larger and swifter than the *Lusitania*, could be filled with passengers and munitions and purposefully steamed into harm's way. German submarines would again patrol off the British west coast. However, the British Admiralty realized that they wouldn't be able to get away with that tragic but successful stratagem a second time.

WHAT THE ENGLISH STILL HAD WAS THEIR LANGUAGE and novelists, poets, playwrights, biographers, and screenwriters who could be harnessed to play a role in Britain's coming propaganda war in the United States. The only problem was the difficulty of conveying British virility with English accents which to critical American ears sounded effete. Above all, the Brits were careful that the words "British" and "Empire" never appeared side-by-side; to Americans this conjured up the mountains of lies that crossed the Atlantic east to west from 1914 to 1918.[25]

There was also a new and enormously powerful medium of mass communications—broadcast radio—the most effective propaganda instrument yet developed. The British took advantage of its novelty and its presence in nearly every American household to amplify their war-mongering messages. By 1938, for example, the United States housed half of the world's radio receivers, and more homes had radios than telephones, vacuum cleaners or electric irons.

> *"I went up to father's bedroom [Winston Churchill's].... 'Sit down, dear boy... I think I see my way through." He resumed his shaving. I was astonished, and said: 'Do you mean that we can avoid defeat?' —which seemed credible— 'or beat the bastards'—which seemed incredible. He... swung around, and said: — 'Of course I mean we can beat them.' Me: 'Well, I'm all for it, but I don't see how you can do it.' By this time he had dried and sponged his face and turning round to me said with great intensity: — 'I shall drag the United States in.' "*[26]

Just how powerful radio could be in influencing behavior had been graphically illustrated on Halloween night, October 30, 1938 in a studio of the Columbia Broadcasting System in New York City. Orson Wells on his popular weekly drama, *Mercury Theater on the Air*, broadcast a creative version of H. G. Wells' science-fiction fantasy, *War of the Worlds*. The producers and actors had planned to entertain their listeners for an hour with Wells' scary story. Much to the surprise of everyone in the studio, their broadcast—which described an invasion by Martians—was so realistic that tens of thousands of people across the country panicked. With a creative soundtrack and enthusiastic readers of the script, listeners pictured hideous monsters moving around in giant vehicles with long legs, armed with death rays, spewing poison gas, destroying everything in their paths. More of them were landing every hour. There appeared to be no escape. Was it the end of the world?

> "Long before the broadcast had ended, people all over the United States hurried to inform neighbors, sought information from radio stations, summoned ambulances and police cars. At least six million people heard the broadcast. At least a million of them were frightened or disturbed."[27]

The New York Times the next day ran the story of the gigantic hoax on the front page, headlined: "Radio Listeners in Panic, Taking War Drama as Fact – Many Flee Homes to Escape 'Gas Raid from Mars'—Phone Calls Swamp Police at Broadcast of Wells' Fantasy." Other newspapers told the story of a "tidal wave of terror that swept the nation." It was obvious that a panic of national proportions had occurred. The chairman of the FCC the next day called the program "regrettable." From Berlin, Chancellor Hitler cited the panic in the United State as "evidence of the decadence and corrupt condition of democracy."

As well as being exciting science-fiction thrillers, Wells' novels were notable for their prophetic ideas and concepts. *The War in the Air*, published in 1908, envisioned the use of the airplane for the purpose of warfare and the coming of World War I. Wells' young British hero witnessed the Battle of the North Atlantic and the bombing of New York as well as aerial battles between German and American forces. In Europe, Great Britain, France, and Italy fought the German and Swiss forces, leading to the destruction of London, Paris, Hamburg, and Berlin. The story advanced a few years into the future to find global humanity resembling barbarians in a brutal feudal society after the war's carnage.

The force of Wells' message and its impact on readers came from his insight that the rapid development of heavier-than-air machines would soon erase the distinction between combatants and civilians. Wells believed that once aerial navigation was mastered, it was inevitable that the world's great cities would be destroyed.

HITLER ALSO UNDERSTOOD propaganda; *Mein Kampf* devoted two chapters to the subject. In the Great War, he had been powerfully influenced by expert British propaganda; as well he might have, as the British at that time had no peers.

> The fact that a world empire the size of the British could not be put together by mere subterfuge and swindling was unfortunately something that had never even occurred to our exalted professors of academic science. The few who raised a voice of warning were ignored or killed by silence. I remember well my comrades' look of astonishment when we faced the Tommies in person in Flanders. After the very first days of battle the conviction dawned on each and every one of them that these Scotsmen did not exactly jibe with the pictures they had seen fit to give us in the comic magazines and press dispatches.[27]

Hitler also knew how to create effective propaganda and he harped upon this element throughout his book:

> All propaganda must be popular and its intellectual level must be adjusted to the most limited intelligence among those it is addressed to.... The more modest its intellectual ballast, the more

exclusively it takes into consideration the emotions of the masses, the more effective it will be....
The receptivity of the great masses is very limited, their intelligence is small, but their power of
forgetting is enormous.[28]

In 1928, he named his comrade Dr. Paul Josef Goebbels *Reichspropagandaleiter*—Head of State Propaganda. When he became Chancellor in January 1933, Hitler established a *Ministerium für Volksaufklärung und Propaganda*—Ministry of Public Enlightenment and Propaganda—and named Goebbels to head it. Goebbels was a graduate of Heidelberg University and an avid student of the late 19th century sociologist Gustav Le Bon, whose seminal work *The Crowd,* greatly influenced him. Le Bon was an elitist with contempt for the masses, which appealed to Goebbels, who was intrigued by how people could be manipulated.

Goebbels embraced radio as a vital adjunct to his propaganda work. Writing in *Das Reich,* the Nazi Party's weekly newspaper in 1933, he considered "radio to be the most modern and most crucial instrument for influencing the masses." He saw to it that radio manufacturers received grants from the government to make what were called "Little Black Boxes" affordable to everyone—*Deutscher Kleinempfänger*—much like the "People's Car," the *Volkswagen*. In a diary entry of May 22, 1941, he wrote

> Relaxation of radio scheduling to take effect immediately. Our people and our soldiers want light music. Otherwise they will listen to English stations. I do not intend to listen to the killjoys any more. Better light music than foreign propaganda.[29]

In a March 1, 1942 *Das Reich* newspaper article titled *The Good Companion* he showed his understanding of the wartime role of Nazi radio as well as his own knowledge and appreciation of classical music. Goebbels wrote that broadcasting light music was "not an injustice to Beethoven or Bruckner, who can be injured only if one attends to their music carelessly." As for jazz music, however, Goebbels was unequivocal:

> We can flatly reject jazz, if by it one understands a kind of music that entirely ignores or mocks melody and depends only on rhythm, and in which the rhythm is carried primarily by unpleasant sounding instrumental squawks that pain the ear. This so-called music is despicable, because it is not really music at all, but only an untalented, random playing with tones.[30]

He then modulated his criticisms of jazz by suggesting that the waltz of our grandfathers and grandmothers:

> ...is the pinnacle of musical development... We no longer live in the Biedermeier era but rather in a century whose melodies are governed by the hum of machines and the sound of motors. Our war songs today are different than those of the World War. The radio must take account of this if it is not to run the risk of being stuck in frock coats. The German radio cannot satisfy everyone. It should do as much as it can, paying most attention to those with the greatest need. They are our soldiers and all those who must work hard in the service of the fatherland. They are thankful for pleasant and entertaining hours. The radio brings them pleasure; it is a good friend and comrade in these difficult times; it cheers them up; it urges them on; it is a constant comrade through the events of the war. It should educate and clarify the great questions of the day. When necessary, it should raise the hearts and touch the conscience. It should attack the enemy wherever he may be. It should defend the interests of the fatherland when that is necessary... The German radio should be a good companion.[31]

Apparently, not all Nazis were boors.

An intriguing side-bar to the issue of radio broadcasting in Germany was Hitler's refusal to deliver his major speeches over the radio because he felt they lost impact. Only by delivering his speeches in person, such as at the giant outdoor Nuremberg Rallies, Hitler felt, could his listeners appreciate his special skills as an orator. Indeed, the *Führer* was a remarkable speaker, almost certainly the most compelling among the world's leading public figures. For Chancellor Hitler and the Third *Reich*, television arrived some fifteen years too late!

FRANKLIN ROOSEVELT also was a big user of broadcast radio. Early in his first term he began his famous "fireside chats," his speechwriters selecting newsworthy topics of broad general interest to the American people. He delivered thirty of these evening speeches from 1933 to 1944, attracting more regular listeners than the most popular radio shows of the period.

FDR's speechwriters took particular care in making his chats understandable to ordinary Americans.

Specifically, eighty percent of the words used were among the 1,000 most commonly used in American vocabulary. The chats were brief, ranging from fifteen to forty-five minutes long. They were broadcast strategically on all national networks around 10PM Eastern time—early enough that Easterners were still up but late enough that those on the West Coast were home from work. The successes of FDR's chats were evidenced by the millions of letters that arrived at the White House in the days following each speech. The writers typically expressed confidence in their president, and many told of listening to the speeches with a group of family members and friends.

Roosevelt also delivered his propaganda messages through regular press conferences and frequent speeches. For example, on October 27, 1941, Roosevelt, in the middle of his annual Navy Day speech, paused and waved a piece of paper in front of his audience and made a sensational claim.

> "I have in my possession a secret map, made in Germany by Hitler's government, by planners of the new world order. It is a map of South America and part of Central America as Hitler proposes to organize it."

He said the map showed the reorganization of the fourteen countries of the region into five vassal states under the rule of Hitler. The map made clear, FDR declared,

> "…the Nazi design, not only against South America but against the United States itself."

Skillfully, almost as an afterthought, he added details of what he called Nazi plans to abolish the Christian religion inside the *Reich*. It was all lies, but coming from the nation's president it commanded a modicum of respect by most Americans. *After all, in 1941, presidents didn't lie!* Germany's Foreign Minister Joachim von Ribbentrop spoke for all of his countrymen and for perhaps for some skeptical Americans the next day when he said that FDR's accusations were "ludicrous" and the map a "forgery of the crudest and most brazen kind." The American press clamored for further details, but the furtive president refused to release the map. According to FDR, the map contained handwritten annotations that could not be published without exposing the source. That, too, was a fabrication. Franklin D. Roosevelt was a leader:

"...deeply untroubled by his own deceptions and frequently appeared to prefer them to the truth.... Roosevelt's first instinct was always to lie, but halfway through an answer, the president realized he could tell the truth and get away with it, so he would shift gears and sometimes truth would trickle out."[32]

Like the publication of the Zimmermann Telegram in 1917, FDR's phony map was fear-mongering taken to a high plateau. The map made its final "appearance" on December 11, 1941, when Hitler revived the incident in the text for his declaration of war—as obvious evidence of American deceit.

IN 1939, FACED WITH THE GROWING LIKELIHOOD of an imminent war with Nazi Germany, the British government organized a massive secret political campaign inside the United States to weaken the isolationists, influence American war policy in England's favor, and ultimately bring the United States into the war. This campaign included the use of front groups, secret agents, collaborators, manipulation of polling data, and indirect involvement in national and state elections.

> Susan A. Brewer wrote in 1997 that the British propaganda campaign was 'a highly plotted, well orchestrated endeavor with concrete goals... Propagandists studied American opinion, set up discreet organizations, identified target audiences, defined themes, and chose methods of dissemination.'[33]

For example, with considerable foresight, the British also expanded their American propaganda coverage by increasing the number of consulates from seventeen before the war to thirty-three in 1942.

> Before the 'war to win the peace' the only British consulates between the Mississippi River and the Pacific states were in St. Louis and Galveston. The new consulates, staffed with information officers, filled in the middle of the country in Cincinnati, Houston, St. Paul, Kansas City, and Denver.[34]

SCARCELY BLUSHING FOR HIS HYPERBOLE, British historian Thomas E. Mahl wrote in *Desperate Deception: British Covert Operations in the United States, 1939-44*:

> Britain's World War II influence-shaping campaign in the United States was one of the most important and successful covert operations of history. In a time of great national crises... covert operations were the tool that ultimately was responsible for saving England. As history knows now, England's saving was the world's.[35]

A book by another patriotic Englishman, Nicholas John Cull, covered *overt* propaganda in the United States.

> During the period of Britain's campaign, American public opinion clearly changed. American foreign policy on the eve of Pearl Harbor stood in radical contrast to the knee-jerk isolationism of the 1930's.[36]

THE BRITISH CHOSE WISELY when they selected Lord Lothian (Philip Kerr) to replace Sir Ronald Lindsey as Ambassador to Washington in 1939. Cull's book gave deservedly highest marks to Lothian as the single most significant figure in the development of British propaganda in the United States.

For almost two years, Lothian skillfully wooed and won the respect of the U.S. press corps, and made friends with such leading columnists and publishers as Walter Lippmann, Arthur Hays Sulzberger, and Helen Ogden Reid. However, it was his role as principal spokesman for his native land that Lothian shone particularly brightly. He spoke often and extremely well, his cultured "limey" accent the proper blend of British upper-class pronunciations Americans so dearly loved sprinkled with American idioms inserted by the American speech-writers on his team. On December 12, 1940, he died suddenly of uremic poisoning. Lothian was a devout Christian Scientist, which forbade conventional medical treatment. In retrospect, Lothian's rigid adherence to his religion proved a serious but temporary liability for his nation.[37]

British operatives in New York City and Washington and their American accomplices saw to it that every Lothian speech was delivered to an important and friendly audience, carried in its entirety in *The New York Times* and in other important big-city newspapers—and was broadcast live on the major networks. His speechwriters expertly constructed talks that both pandered to and flattered his American audiences, at the same time striking sparks for the British Empire, as the following excerpts show. Lothian treated the subject of propaganda gingerly.

He led off on October 25, 1939 in a speech to the "Pilgrims of the United States."

> I have been told that if I talk on so dangerous a subject as the war, I shall be accused of propaganda. But may I say this about propaganda. There is all the difference in the world between the publicity characteristics of the democracies and the propaganda of totalitarian states. As a fellow democrat, therefore, I feel that we have the right, indeed the duty, to tell you our story.... But having done that, we feel that it is for you and for you alone to form your own judgment about ourselves and about the war. That is, of course, your inalienable right and that is what we mean when we say that the British Government conducts no propaganda in this country.[38]

In a speech celebrating the fiftieth anniversary of all-women's Barnard College on November 14, Lothian compared British higher education with that in the United States. He told his audience what they came to hear:

> You realized long before we did in England that an adequate education for all citizens was absolutely vital to democracy. You have by far the largest educational equipment in the world—more primary schools, more high schools, more universities than almost the rest of the world put together. That has been a job magnificently done. We have been much slower.... The last twenty years have seen an immense change in the position of women in England.... Women now have the entry into all the professions and the Civil Service.[39]

Lothian's next address was to the Chicago Council of Foreign Relations, on January 4, 1940. It was by far his longest speech to an American audience, some 6,800 words long, and it gave Lothian an opportunity to weave in carefully the issue of British propaganda into his address.

> The genius of democracy depends upon freedom of speech. That means that every true democracy wants to hear all sides of every great question. It must do so if it is to arrive at sound judgments... so I am going to take my courage in my hands and talk to you about the war.... I do not see how we can arrive at any sane programme for peace unless we talk frankly to one another. Propaganda is the deliberate attempt to influence your own countrymen, or other nations to a particular course of action, by lies or half truths or tendentious innuendos. The truth is never propaganda.

His speechwriters wisely gave Lothian a loose rein:

> The first attempt to establish a true world peace system was badly bungled.... The Versailles Treaty was not a good treaty. But it was nothing as bad as, under Dr. Goebbels' inspiration, is now generally supposed... I often wish honest historians, three American, three French, and three British, and, if you like, three German historians, would get together and publish a joint statement of the facts about the post-war era. The British Government is not trying to drag you into this war. It knows that no democracy will accept the hideous consequences of war unless it is convinced that its own vital interests, which include its ideals, are at stake.

And then this pronouncement, eerily prescient:

> If ever you are driven to action it will not be because of propaganda but because of the relentless march of events.[40]

On April 19, in a speech to the St. Louis Chamber of Commerce, Lothian reiterated why a peace at that time would only play into the hands of despotism:

> It would be no more than a truce—a short interval between two world wars.... There are two sayings which each contain the proverbial half-truth which I cannot forbear to quote tonight, because they tend to put the question in a humorous perspective. 'England expects every American to do his duty'—that is, come to the assistance of the British Empire when it is in trouble. The other is the British gag about the attitude of the United States, 'America expects the British Navy to defend her right to be neutral.'[41]

To the English-Speaking Union, in New York City on May 14, 1940, Lothian piled on as many famous Americans as his ghostwriters could unearth and that Lothian could manage without cracking a smile. Halfway through, he remarked that it was not possible for him to sit down without talking about the war.

> In the last few weeks the Allies have been going through a bad time. Some of our defects in prescience, promptness in action, and preparedness have been exposed. And now the decisive battle has begun in the West. Whether Hitler is confident that he can win or whether he realizes that he must win this summer or not at all, I cannot pretend to know... The issue is nakedly clear. On the one side are those ideals of individual freedom, national self-government and democracy which have slowly evolved under Christian influence and for which the English-speaking world unflinchingly stands. On the other side is a system which respects none of those spiritual values and has subordinated everything else to prepare for aggressive war, and which uses violence to the limit and utterly regardless of any moral restraint in order to establish its pagan domination over mankind.[42]

On June 4, in New York City, Lothian finally got to talk about the Royal Navy, a subject he had previously side-stepped.

> What Hitler is now after, of course, is the British fleet. For if he can seize that, he steps from the domination of Europe to the domination of the world.

That was sheer hyperbole and Lothian should have known better if his writers had not.

> It is not for us to offer you any advice as to what you should do about this grave problem, any more than it is for you to offer us any advice as to what we should do with our Navy, if and when that tragic crisis comes.[Author's emphasis][43]

Lothian's next address, before Yale University Alumni in New Haven, Connecticut, on June 19, focused again on the Royal Navy and challenged America's "illusions" about the fleet. He had finally run out of patience and it showed.

> No preamble, just straight talk. France has fallen and England is in great peril. We [and he meant both the United States and Great Britain] have all been far too much bemused by illusion in recent times. For more than a century the primary line of defence both of the British Commonwealth and the United States has been the command of the seas.... That sea system of security is now under challenge—mainly because of the development of air power.... It is now only a question of days, or at most a few weeks, before he [Hitler] seems likely to attempt to do to Britain what he has already done to France.... He will attempt to overrun Great Britain and capture our fleet. The outcome of this grim struggle will affect you almost as much as it will affect us. For if Hitler gets our fleet, or destroys it, the whole foundation on which the security of both our countries has rested for 120 years will have disappeared.... These are grave facts—very grave. They may thrust themselves into the foreground of decisions in a few weeks. It is essential that neither we nor you should entertain illusions about them.[44]

Lothian cautioned his listeners that it was clear to him that many in the United States mistakenly believed that if Britain were invaded and overrun, the Royal Navy would cross the Atlantic to Canada and still be available to the U.S. as part of its own defense system. "I hope you are not building on that expectation. If you are, I think you are likely to find your hopes mistaken, that you have been building on an illusion."[45]

On December 9, 1941, the British learned first-hand just how much "that sea system of security" was "challenged," when its new battleship, *The Prince of Wales*, declared "unsinkable" by the Admiralty, and the WWI battlecruiser, *Repulse*, were sunk by Japanese bombers off the coast of Malaya. So early in the war, the Japanese Navy magnanimously allowed the Royal Navy destroyers that were part of the task force to pick up survivors. One Japanese aviator overflew the floating wreckage the next day to drop flowers. In his memoirs, Churchill described the sinkings as his greatest shock of the war.

Sinking of British aircraft carrier HMS Hermes in the Indian Ocean by Japanese warplanes, April 9, 1942.

Lothian's last speech on December 11, his first full-length address in five months, was delivered by Neville Butler, his deputy. The speech closed on an almost plaintive note, as if Lothian knew he was dying.

> We are, I believe, doing all we can. Since May there is no challenge we have evaded, no challenge we have refused. If you back us you won't be backing a quitter. The issue now depends largely on what you decide to do. Nobody can share that responsibility with you. It is the great strength of democracy that it brings responsibility down squarely on every citizen and every nation. And before the judgment seat of God each must answer for his own actions.[46]

Many Americans doubtless saw through the veil of Lothian's slick rhetoric and those who understood Great War history recognized that "perfidious Albion" was once again up to her old tricks. According to their lights, the Brits were dangling the Royal Navy as bait to blackmail the United States into fighting the second of Great Britain's wars to hold together the British Empire.

In June 1941 Sir Gerald Campbell of the British Minister of *Information* (like the U.S. Office of War *Information*—and unlike the Third Reich's straightforward Ministry of *Public Enlightenment and Propaganda*) sent to his propaganda operatives in New York and Washington the following directive, not leaving out a single instrument in the modern propaganda orchestra:

> It is... essential that our machinery should be able to bring into play all the instruments of modern propaganda... Action must be taken through news... the film, the radio, the sermon, the photograph, the whispered rumour, the Ambassador's press conference, the special interview, the declaration at home, the repercussion of articles in the English press, the voices of our Allies—all these must be used and harmonized in our orchestra. Though the score may be written at home, it must be interpreted by the conductor in this country [the U.S.]. And the orchestras must be numerous, disciplined and efficient.[47]

At the same time, the BMI also laid down three ground rules that were "explicitly dedicated to bringing the United States into the war":

> 1. Never say that we do not want America to come into the war.
>
> 2. Never say officially we want an American expeditionary force, but do not discourage Americans from preparing public opinion for the idea that this may become necessary.
>
> 3. Stress that this is America's war as much as ours and that it would be impossible for her to come to terms with Hitler in the event of a British defeat.[48]

MOVIES WERE EXCELLENT PROPAGANDA, and well before Britain went to war with Germany, its studios were cranking out anti-German movies, all aimed at both British and American moviegoers. At the same time, Hollywood also found it was profitable to produce anti-German and anti-Japanese motion pictures. Gore Vidal, progressive American essayist, novelist, and playwright wrote tellingly:

> We served neither Lincoln nor Jefferson Davis: we served the Crown. For those who find disagreeable today's Zionist propaganda, I can only say that gallant little Israel of today must have learned a great deal from the gallant little Englanders of the 1930s. The English kept up a propaganda barrage that was to permeate our entire culture.[49]

Noted World War I Historian Sidney Rogerson added these perspicacious comments in 1938:

> In modern times by far the most successful, if not the greatest, propaganda force that the world has ever witnessed is the American film industry. Although this is uncontrolled and dictated solely for commercial profit, it has had a greater effect on the outlook, habits, and morals of wide sections of mankind of all races in a short time than any other movement—sociological or religious.[50]

The author recalls vividly how thrilled he was as a teenager in the 1940s by the British-made movie *In Which We Serve*. It told the story of a Royal Navy destroyer, HMS *Torrin*, assigned to Mediterranean Sea convoy duty—and her brave and resolute crew, including famous actor Noel Coward as the captain. *Torrin* was first bombed, then towed to Crete for repairs, went to sea again, was torpedoed again and finally sunk. There was the mandatory footage of the survivors, oil-covered [invariably!] and gallantly clinging to a Carley raft [inevitably!] awaiting rescue [in the dark of night nearly always] as one by one the wounded and less capable dropped off.

In between, *Torrin* had been ordered to Dunkirk to pick up British troops and ferry them back across the English Channel. Britain's screenwriters saw to it that there was much good inter-service banter on *Torrin's* bridge. A memorable scene, particularly heart-warming for British viewers—the propaganda highlight of the film—showed battered and bandaged Tommies slowly debarking *Torrin*. They lined up raggedly on the dock, only a few carrying rifles, purposefully, until a high-strutting sergeant-major strode onto the dock. He curtly ordered the walking wounded into a tight formation, and marched them off in two columns, lock-step, with appropriate martial music on the soundtrack– extremely good patriotic stuff for those at home. These soldiers would live to fight another day! For American viewers, there were the gallant wives and mothers at home, "stiff upper lips" and all that.

THEN THERE WAS FAMOUS *Mrs. Miniver*, the fictional upper-middle-class Englishwoman created in 1937 by Jan Struther, a weekly columnist for the London *Times*. *Mrs. Miniver* lived in a house in exclusive Chelsea, had a cottage in the country, and was happily married to a successful architect. She had two children at home, a son at Eton, a live-in housekeeper/cook, and a gardener. Originally a series of brief columns depicting lighthearted domestic scenes to entertain readers of the newspaper, *Mrs. Miniver's* everyday trials were *English* right down to the core. These sketches were published in book form in 1939 after the start of the war, becoming a huge success in the United States.

The gusseted-up wartime tribulations of the Miniver family surprisingly struck a sympathetic nerve in many Americans. Read sixty years later, Struther's novel came across to this critic as not particularly well-written, filled with snooty dialog and incomprehensible British clichés, and most of all with a corny plot. The film adaptation was produced in 1942 in the United States, with British stars Greer Garson and Walter Pidgeon, both well-known to American moviegoers. The OWI and Hollywood screenwriters saw to it that any traces of snobbery and social privilege that had appeared everywhere in the book were eliminated in favor of more "democratic" images, a "people's war," so to speak. The too-syrupy movie with the same inane plot of the book deserved only one-star. Nevertheless, the film grossed $5.4 million in North America, the highest for any MGM motion picture at the time, and $3.5 million abroad. In England *Mrs. Miniver* was named the top box-office attraction of 1942; and U.S. film critics overwhelmingly named it the best film of 1942.

PEARL HARBOR

Pearl Harbor was not an accident, a mere failure of American intelligence, or a brilliant Japanese military coup. It was the result of a carefully orchestrated design, initiated at the highest levels of our government.... Pearl Harbor was the only way, leading officials felt, to galvanize the reluctant American public into action."[51]

At the end of November 1941, Chief of Naval Operations Admiral Harold "Betty" Stark ordered Admiral Husband Kimmel, commander of the Pacific Fleet in Pearl Harbor, to ferry pursuit planes to Wake and Midway Islands, using the Pacific Fleet's two remaining aircraft carriers in Pearl Harbor, the *Enterprise* and *Lexington*,. The third carrier assigned to the Pacific Fleet, *Saratoga*, was in California undergoing refit. The twelve Marine Corps F-4F3 *Wildcats* that were flown off from the *Enterprise* to Wake made a welcome addition to the soon-to-be-beleaguered island's defenses, although ten were destroyed on the ground during the first Japanese air attack on December 8th. Sycophant Stark rarely did anything on his own; *the order to get the carriers and their modern cruiser and destroyer escorts out of Pearl and harm's way, in the nick of time as it turned out, almost certainly had originated with Franklin Roosevelt.*

ON DECEMBER 4, a glaring headline in the Chicago Tribune announced Rainbow Five, the government's Top Secret plan to initiate a war with Germany. The story disclosed what FDR had been denying for so many months. Indeed, announcement of Rainbow Five at last made a transparent liar out of the slippery president. Included in the article were a word-for-word copy of the document, and a copy of FDR's authorization letter for the preparation of the war plan. Army, Navy, and War Department officials were beside themselves with rage by its publication.

The New York Times got the story second-hand and, surprisingly, ran it on page three the next morning. It included the comments of Stephen T. Early, who would neither confirm nor deny the revelation, but pointed out that even during times of peace it was the duty of the Army and Navy to plan for emergencies.

Rainbow Five made fascinating reading for some; others felt deep foreboding:

> Forces deemed necessary to defeat the Axis forces in the field would include five field armies including 215 divisions (infantry, armored, motorized, airborne, mountain and cavalry) with appropriate supporting elements. It is estimated that the transportation of this number of men [five million] over a period of one year, would require 7,000,000 tons of shipping, or 1,000 ships, and that to maintain such a force in the theatres of operations would require about 10,000,000 tons, or 1,500 ships. If our European enemies are to be defeated it will be necessary for the United States to enter the war, and to employ a part of its armed forces offensively in the Eastern Atlantic and in Europe and Africa.

Who was the leaker? The definitive answer has eluded historians to this day. Major Albert C. Wedemeyer, who wrote the document, was a prime suspect, but the FBI was unable to pin it on him. Franklin Roosevelt? He had a genuine motive and had much to gain—*his war with Germany*—by infuriating Hitler. Three days after the leak, the issue and the identity of the culprit became academic. There was a war to win.

Was the United States clandestinely becoming a martial nation? Yes, it was! But it was not until war's end—with the British Empire in tatters, French colonial holdings in disarray, and Soviet Russia severely battered—that America had its first blueprint for global dominion. It was George Kennan's famous 1947 "long telegram" from Moscow to the State Department outlining a new policy of "containment."

> *Speaking in New York City on January 31, 1944, Arthur Hays Sulzberger, president and publisher of The News York Times, said: "I happen to be among those who believe that we did not go to war because we were attacked at Pearl Harbor. I hold rather that we were attacked at Pearl Harbor because we had gone to war."*

ON THE EVENING OF DECEMBER 6, the president, playing a deceitful role as peacemaker, initialed a last-minute cable to Emperor Hirohito. He appealed to the Emperor.

For the sake of humanity... to give thought in this definite emergency to the ways of dispelling the dark clouds... to restore traditional amity and prevent death and destruction in the world.[52]

The trite message was a bluff! Roosevelt received no reply, nor had he expected one. Instead, the next day it was the Japanese First Air Fleet's bombers, torpedo planes, and fighters that replied—with a devastating attack on the remaining elements of the Pacific Fleet then berthed in Pearl Harbor, including all the old battleships, most of the Army and Navy aircraft, and shore installations.[53] The Japanese did not attack the fuel tank farms nor the submarine base with its submarines, which were important tactical mistakes. Without fuel, the Pacific Fleet would have had to "retreat" to California; destruction of the submarines would have materially stalled their attacks on Japanese shipping.

Nine hours after the attack had begun in Hawaii, General Douglas MacArthur's powerful air force in the Philippines was caught on the ground on Luzon and wiped out by Japanese bombers. His reaction to the news of the attack on Pearl Harbor was strange; he locked himself in his office all morning, refusing to meet with or take phone calls from his air commander. Stranger still had been his refusal to allow his B-17s to strike Japanese forces on Formosa even under direct orders to do so from the War Department. Either MacArthur had committed an enormous blunder—or had been ordered to sacrifice his B-17s for some perceived greater good. If, in fact, it was a gaffe, it is amazing how he escaped reprimand, kept his command, and got his fourth star to boot along with a Congressional Medal of Honor. No historian has yet been able to account for MacArthur's lack of action on that first day of war.

> *Sixty years after that "day of infamy," the attack on Pearl Harbor remains controversial among revisionist historians; every few years a new telling of the story stokes the fire. In 1982, historian John Toland wrote: "The comedy of errors on the sixth and seventh [of December] appears incredible. It only makes sense if it was a charade, and Roosevelt and the inner circle had known about the attack." A massive cover-up began a few days later, according to an officer close to [General George C.] Marshall, when the Chief of Staff ordered that a lid be put on the affair. "Gentlemen," he told half a dozen officers, "this goes to the grave with us."*[54]

Sinking of the USS Arizona

On December 8, Roosevelt went before a joint session of the Congress in the House and, to tumultuous applause and cheering, declared the United States was at war with Japan.

The next day FDR delivered a radio address to the nation that is rarely touched on in history books and that few Americans remember. He accused Hitler of being behind the Japanese attack on Pearl Harbor. That accusation was another of FDR's crude lies. He was trying to bait Hitler into declaring war or, failing that, to persuade Americans to support a preemptive U.S. declaration of war on Germany and Italy. The president then pulled out the remaining stops. He recited what he called a pattern of aggression by Japan, Italy, and Germany, going back as far as 1931:

> Your government knows Germany has been telling Japan that if Japan would attack the United States, Japan would share the spoils when peace came. She was promised by Germany that if she came in she would receive control of the whole of the Pacific area and that means not only the Far East but all the islands of the Pacific and also a stranglehold on the west coast of North and Central and South America.[55]

That rhetoric was also cut out of whole cloth. Germany and Japan did not have a joint naval plan leading up to Pearl Harbor. In fact, the air attack came as a surprise to Hitler. Japan had no interest in attacking the west coast of the United States. Nippon's goal was to create a new order in the Far East—the Great East Asia Co-Prosperity Sphere—displacing the British, the French, the Dutch, and the Americans. Germany was not interested in the Pacific; Hitler's goal was to dominate middle Europe and gain *Lebensraum* at the expense of the Soviet Union.

On December 11, Hitler went before an expectant *Reichstag* in Berlin and announced that Germany and Italy had been provoked to declare war on the United States. His decision, he said, had been forced on him by stories in American newspapers which had revealed "a plan by President Roosevelt... to attack Germany in 1943 with all the resources of the United States. Thus our patience has come to a breaking point." A roaring, foot-stamping *Reichstag* drowned out their *Fuhrer's* last words. Foreign Minister Joachim von Ribbentrop said later:

> "A great power does not allow itself to be declared war upon. It declares war on others."[56]

Franklin D. Roosevelt finally got his war with Nazi Germany—and one with Imperial Japan and Mussolini's Fascist Italy in the bargain. Immutable warrior Winston Spencer Churchill had the last say:

> No American will think it wrong of me if I proclaim that to have the United States on our side was to be the greatest joy.... England would live; Britain would live; the Commonwealth of Nations and the Empire would live. How long the war would last or in what fashion it would end no man could tell, nor I at this moment care. Once again in our long island history we would emerge... safe and victorious.... Being saturated and satiated with emotion and sensation, I went to bed and slept the sleep of he saved and thankful.[57]

ONE OF THE GREAT MYTHS in the long, legend-filled history of the British Empire is the tale of the evacuation of some 220,000 British and half that many French troops from the beaches and harbor of Dunkirk, France, at the end of May 1940. It has become enshrined as the "miracle of Dunkirk" in British folklore, and has just as firmly become entrenched in American history. The May 31 issue of the *New York Herald Tribune* declared majestically:

> There have been trapped armies before, terrible retreats, perilous embarkations, and heroic rearguard actions in the past, but no combination of them on a scale like this. Defeat sustained

with such fortitude is no disaster.... These are soldiers of civilization, enrolling themselves imperishably among those who will save, by suffering, all that makes civilized life of value.

A *New York Times* editorial of the same date nearly got mired in its own glutinous eloquence:

> So long as the English tongue survives, the word Dunkirk will be spoken with reverence. For in that harbor, in such a hell as never blazed on earth before, at the end of a lost battle, the rages and blemishes that have hidden the soul of democracy fell away. There, beaten but unconquered, in shining splendor she faced the enemy.

If Hitler had had these editorials read to him in German, he might well have doubled over in laughter. He knew better and so did his generals, many of whom lived long enough "to show and tell" in their postwar interviews and memoirs. There is ample evidence today that Hitler purposefully allowed the British and French to retreat across the Channel almost intact, except for their military equipment. His "Fuhrer order" of May 22 stopped the *Panzers'* headlong advance in their tracks for three days.[58]

General Ewald von Kleist recalled that when he got the order it made no sense to him.

> "My armoured cars actually entered Hazebrouck, and cut along the British lines of retreat.... But then came a more emphatic order that I was to withdraw behind the canal. My tanks were kept halted there for three days."[59]

Meanwhile, the British forces and remnants of the French Army streamed back toward Dunkirk, and built a strong defensive position to cover their reembarkation. The German *Panzer* commanders sat on their hands and watched the defeated British army slipping away under their very noses. On May 24, two days after German forces were halted in full stride, Hitler met with his staff at their headquarters in Charlesville, France, According to General Gunther Blumentritt,

> "Hitler was in very good humour, acknowledging that the course of the campaign had been 'a decided miracle.' He would conclude a reasonable peace with France and then the way would be open for a similar agreement with Britain."[60]

Hitler then apparently astonished his commanders by speaking with admiration of the British Empire and the necessity of its continued existence and comparing it with the Catholic Church, saying both were essential elements of stability in the world. He insisted that all he wanted from England was her acknowledgement of Germany's primacy on the continent. The return of Germany's lost colonies was desirable but not essential and he said, amazingly, he would even offer to support Britain with the *Wehrmacht* and *Luftwaffe* if Britain should become involved in any international difficulties. General Gerd von Runstedt, who had always sought agreement with France and Britain, was satisfied. After Hitler left, he commented:

> "Well, if he wants nothing else, then we shall have peace at last."[61]

The British, banking on America's almost-inevitable entry into the war, then proceeded to reject out of hand all of Hitler's subsequent peace initiatives. Hitler's three-day gamble had not paid off! Instead, as General Heinz Guderian wrote in his memoir of Hitler's intervention on May 24,

> "...for the left wing to halt on the river Aa [in France, was] to have a most disastrous influence on the whole future course of the war."[62]

On June 4, in an address to Parliament, Churchill effortlessly turned the disastrous defeat in Dunkirk into a British victory and an inspiring boost for British morale. Eloquently, the prime minister and his ghost-writers closed with a dramatic passage aimed at influencing U.S. public opinion as much as that of the English and their Dominions. In sonorous cadence he vowed that Great Britain would never surrender:

> We shall defend our island, whatever the cost may be. We shall fight on the beaches, we shall fight on the landing-grounds, we shall fight in the fields and in the streets, we shall fight in the hills; we shall never surrender, and even if, which I do not for a moment believe, this island or a large part of it were subjugated and starving, then our Empire will... carry on the struggle, until, in God's good time, the New World [a.k.a., the United States] with all its power and might, steps forth to the rescue and liberation of the Old.[63]

In a radio address two weeks later, Churchill followed up with another elegantly phrased propaganda thrust aimed squarely at the Americans. As always *The New York Times* carried the speech in its entirety.

> The battle of France is over. I expect the battle of Britain is about to begin... Hitler knows he will have to break us in this island or lose the war. If we can stand up to him, all Europe may be free and the life of the world may move forward into broad, sunlit uplands, but if we fail, then the whole world, including the United States, and all that we have known and cared for, will sink into the abyss of a new Dark Age made more sinister, and perhaps more protracted, by the lights of a perverted science. Let us therefore brace ourselves to our duty and so bear ourselves that if the British Empire and its Commonwealth last for a thousand years men will still say, 'This was their finest hour.'[64]

> *Gagged by this idiotic slogan [unconditional surrender], the Western Allies could offer no terms, however severe. Conversely, their enemy could ask for none, however submissive. So it came about that, like Samson, Hitler was left to pull the edifice of Europe down upon himself, his people and their enemies.*[65]

FDR'S UNCONDITIONAL SURRENDER EDICT on January 24, 1943, at the end of the meeting between Roosevelt and Churchill in Casablanca, Morocco, must be given the attention it merits. Despite its mammoth impacts on the war in Europe and in the Pacific, the declaration has been given too short shrift by many historians.

Smiling broadly with his long cigarette holder at a jaunty angle, a self-confident FDR was seated next to the prime minister in front of the newsmen who had been flown in especially for the occasion. Standing behind was a line of high-ranking military officers from both nations to pose in the picture-taking ceremonies. The president announced first that the United States and Great Britain had reached total agreement on the future conduct of the war and that any differences had been ironed out to everyone's satisfaction. That was a bold lie. While the two leaders themselves apparently had argued cordially, their staffs had been at loggerheads on most of the issues. In fact, the negotiations were considered the most contentious ever to take place between the Western Allies during the war.

After the two leaders finished answering the correspondents' questions, Roosevelt loosed what can only be called a bolt from the blue. Casually, he announced that he and the prime minister had agreed,

> "...to accept nothing less than the unconditional surrender of Germany, Japan, and Italy."

Churchill had agreed to nothing of the kind. In fact, the subject never came up during the deliberations. But Churchill reportedly assented by muttering "hear, hear." Roosevelt continued enthusiastically that the just-concluded conference should be called the "Unconditional Surrender meeting." However, the final communiqué of the meeting never mentioned those two fateful words.

U.S. officers in attendance were quietly ferocious in their criticisms of the new edict. General Dwight D. Eisenhower, for one, considered that the slogan would achieve nothing but American lives lost. In February 1945, as Supreme Allied Commander, he gave his homespun views on the military impact of FDR's foolhardy credo:

> "If you were given two choices—one to mount the scaffold and the other to charge twenty bayonets, you might as well charge twenty bayonets."[68]

A more severe critic was Albert Wedemeyer, by now a General, who had spent two years in Berlin at the German War College in the 1930s. He knew many of the *Wehrmacht's* generals personally, and felt strongly that the new catchphrase would:

> "...unquestionably compel the Germans to fight to the very last."

Later, Wedemeyer concluded that a combination of errors in strategic planning by the Allies together with Unconditional Surrender:

> "…certainly lengthened the war by a full year."[69]

U.S. Air Force General Ira Eaker, commander of the Eighth Air Force, recalled that when he returned to England to tell his staff about Unconditional Surrender, they all mocked the term.

> "Everybody that I knew at that time when they heard this said: 'How stupid can you be?' All the soldiers and the airmen who were fighting this war wanted the Germans to quit tomorrow... A child knew that once you said this to the Germans, they were going to fight to the last man."[70]

British Air Marshal Sir John Slessor wrote after the war:

> "...as far as I remember the use of the words... made no particular impact on our minds at the time... It is difficult to believe that any subsequent explanations putting its meaning in a less unpalatable form had any effect in countering its value to Goebbels in stiffening German resistance— to which was added... the preposterous Morgenthau Plan for the deindustrialization of Germany."[71]

Sir Maurice D. Hankey, also a member of the British delegation, was equally disparaging in his retrospective, writing that:

> "...the communiqué itself was a bit thin—not very substantial Pablum for press-men who had come so far and were in a state of high expectancy. The work of the Conference had been of major military importance... and not much could be said about the plans.... Unconditional surrender, therefore, provided a useful make-weight to the colourless communiqué. Yet…, how many human lives, how much destruction and what misery would have been saved... if it had never been accepted as a worthy war aim."[72]

Hankey then reviewed the effect of FDR's edict on Germany and Japan:

> "It was not surprising that the Germans held out to the last possible moment. They intended to hold out longer still behind the mountain barriers of Bavaria, Austria, and North Italy... the object of this desperate expedient was to try and secure better terms than Unconditional Surrender."

As for Japan, she held out:

> "With equal, if not greater tenacity.... In these circumstances, to secure Unconditional Surrender without excessive prolongation of the war, the allies decided at Potsdam to use the atomic bomb."[73]

In Berlin, Josef Goebbels was delighted when he learned of FDR's decree, which was splendid grist for his propaganda mills. Creatively calling it "world historical tomfoolery of the first order," he told his staff:

> "I should never have been able to think up so rousing a slogan. If our Western enemies tell us, we won't deal with you, our only aim is to destroy you... how can any German, whether he likes it or not, do anything but fight on with all his strength?"[74]

German generals were also uniformly cynical of the decree as they wrote in their memoirs. To a man, they all agreed that Unconditional Surrender materially lengthened the war, resulted in the unnecessary destruction of Germany, and resulted in the deaths of tens of thousands if not hundreds of thousands more Germans, Americans, Englishman, and Russians, civilians and military personnel alike.

In a hate-filled speech on September 21, 1943, before the House of Commons, Churchill picked up the thread of Unconditional Surrender. He first charged that Prussia was the source of "the pestilence," and that "Nazi tyranny and Prussian militarism are the two main elements in German life which must be absolutely destroyed." The prime minister then accused the German people:

> "twice within our lifetime, and three times counting that of our fathers, of plunging the world into their wars of expansion and aggression. They combine in the most deadly manner the qualities of the warrior and the slave. They do not value freedom themselves, and the spectacle of it in others is hateful to them."[75]

These arrows were no-holds-barred wartime propaganda and ridiculous as well: that an inherently warlike Prusso-German spirit—a genetic trait, perhaps, from Churchill's bigoted perspective?—was responsible for the two previous European wars. By that time, European historians were in general agreement that Prussia in 1879 and Wilhelmine Germany in 1914 were innocent of starting both wars.[76]

"Just strip it. I don't care what happens to the population. I would take every mine, every mill and factory and wreck it... Steel, coal, everything. Just close it down... Make the Ruhr look like some of the silver mines in Nevada."—Henry Morgenthau, Jr., to his staff, 1944.[77]

BY THE MIDDLE OF THE SUMMER OF 1944, war news from Europe was uniformly upbeat for the Allies. U.S. forces had broken through stubborn *Wehrmacht* defenses at Avaranches and General George Patton's Third Army was coiled to strike east. The U.S. Fifth Army, leaving the open city of Rome in its wake, was poised to capture Florence in its drive north and east. The Red Army had regrouped and refitted and begun its massive offensive to drive the Germans out of the Ukraine. The British army was about to take Brussels at the same time as token French forces marched ceremoniously into Paris.

Dwindling numbers of German submarines in the Atlantic were no longer a threat to Britain's lifeline; and the *Luftwaffe,* which had fought so tenaciously defending its homeland for so many months, was finally being shot out of the sky by overwhelming numbers of long-range P-51 *Mustangs* with Rolls-Royce *Merlin* engines. The war was being brought home to ordinary Germans, whose cities and towns were being bombed to rubble by thousand-plane USAAF and RAF air raids.

The end of the war in Europe was on the near horizon, and Allied strategists were focusing on plans for a peace treaty with Germany.

The most controversial of the schemes was put forth by Treasury Secretary Henry Morgenthau, Jr.[78] It was a "scorched-earth" plan of extraordinary vindictiveness, which called for the "pastoralization" of the mightiest industrial power in Europe. Like his father, Morgenthau had a visceral hatred of the Germans, and what became known as the Morgenthau Plan was his personal vendetta. Coming on the heels of the declaration of Unconditional Surrender it redoubled the Germans' resolve to fight to the very end. In Roosevelt, Morgenthau had a fellow Germanophobe of equal intensity.

> "We have got to be tough with Germany and I mean the German people not just the Nazis. We either have to castrate the German people or you have to treat them in such a manner so they can't keep on reproducing..."

—Franklin D. Roosevelt to Henry Morgenthau, Jr., August 19, 1944[79]

Morgenthau wrote in his diary that on August 6, 1944, he had read a draft of the War Department's proposed plan for administering postwar Germany. It came as a shock and then and there he decided that he would fight for his own plan. Among all the cabinet officers, Morgenthau was closest to Roosevelt and he would use his special relationship as a club to beat down opposition in the cabinet, just as he had done on other issues in the past.[80] His peers loathed him for it.

In an August 26 memorandum to War Secretary Henry L. Stimson, the president showed where he stood on what had rapidly become a controversial issue—the postwar treatment of the vanquished enemy—with hawks and doves in Washington staking out their territories. Roosevelt used the draft of the *Handbook for Military Government in Germany*, intended as a guide to the military for their occupation of Germany, to express his views.

> This so-called *Handbook* is pretty bad.... It gives me the impression that Germany is to be restored just as much as the Netherlands or Belgium, and the people of Germany be brought back as quickly as possible to their prewar state.... I do not want them to starve to death, but... if they need food to keep body and soul together... they should be fed three times a day from Army soup kitchens. They will remember that experience all their lives.[81]

At the Treasury Department, Morgenthau goaded his staff to work up drafts of his proposal to demand that the Ruhr and Saar valleys, the center of Germany's vital coal and steel industries, be turned into a huge ghost town. According to Morgenthau, if that region were stripped of its machinery and its mines flooded, dynamited, and wrecked, Germany would be "impotent to wage more wars." Assistant Secretary Harry Dexter White warned correctly that shutting down the Ruhr would impoverish millions of German workers at the same time it would impact much of the rest of Europe, which needed the coal and steel from that region to rebuild its devastated infrastructure. Stubbornly, Morgenthau refused to bend:

> "I am for destroying it first and we will worry about the population second. I am not going to budge an inch."[82]

There was another cabinet member with Morgenthau's same obstinate character but with a far deeper understanding of global imperatives. He was Henry L. Stimson, a self-assured Republican whom FDR had chosen for a cabinet post because of his years of experience in military and foreign affairs. Intent on forestalling what he considered Morgenthau's ill-advised initiatives, Stimson met with the president and suggested he appoint a Cabinet Committee to thrash out the differences. Roosevelt amiably agreed and named five to the new committee: Morgenthau and Stimson along with Cordell

Hull and Frank Knox.[83] FDR later added Harry Hopkins, his closest confidant, to the committee. Stimson made a record of his own divergent views:

> "…for history—to show future generations that not every high official under Roosevelt had run 'amuck' at this vital period."[84]

He followed with a brief European history lesson for his four "students," outlining the role of Germany as a source of vital raw materials for all of Europe, as a producer of high quality manufactured goods, and finally as an important customer for the foodstuffs of many European nations. Like a good history professor, Stimson showed his mettle by bringing his four readers into the present:

> I cannot treat as realistic the suggestion that such an area in the present economic condition of the world can be turned into a nonproductive 'ghost territory' when it has become the center of one of the most industrialized continents in the world, populated by people of energy, vigor, and progressiveness.[85]

In the event, the irascible Morgenthau was unable to convince his fellow Cabinet Committee members of the wisdom of his severe approach to a defeated Germany. Further, Roosevelt, coming under fire from many directions, decided to back out quietly from his original commitment to Morgenthau and his plan. While he never formally renounced Morgenthau's proposed program, he henceforth avoided discussing the issue.

But the word had gotten out: the United States was planning to destroy Germany. Serious damage to the Allied cause had been done and could not be undone. The price that had to be paid was in blood—in the desperate resistance by German troops which was reflected by the continuing high number of Allied casualties up to the last weeks of the war. For example, the Soviets took 100,000 casualties while capturing Berlin in the spring of 1945.

Goebbels' propaganda ministry had a field day, jubilantly blaring that the Morgenthau Plan intended to turn Germany into a vast turnip and potato patch. At that time, the U.S. Army was fighting ferocious German resistance to capture Aachen, their first important city inside Germany. Goebbels exhorted the people of Aachen that "every house should resemble a fortress" to avoid the horrible fate awaiting them from the Morgenthau Plan.

Until his death in 1967, Morgenthau stuck by his conviction that his plan had been the right one. Yale historian John Morton Blum, who produced a three-volume work based on Morgenthau's diaries, contended that the plan had serious flaws. Still confrontational in his declining years, feisty Henry Jr. figuratively gave his biographer a slap on the wrist:

> "You're too young to know whether the Morgenthau Plan was a mistake. And I'll bet you—though I won't be around to collect—that you're going to have to fight Germany again before you die."[86]

EVEN BEFORE IT BECAME OBVIOUS to war planners in Washington that the war was coming to an end in Europe, in addition to the need for guidelines for managing postwar Germany, the government wanted answers to questions about the role played by the USAAF in winning the war. Had the results of the bombings, tangible and otherwise, been commensurate with the enormous costs in highly trained aircrews and airplanes?[87] A nation bent on global dominance beyond the end of the war and deep into the future needed honest answers. The United States Strategic Bombing Survey, newly minted in June 1944, intended to provide the answers.

All throughout the war, USAAF generals thirsted for parity with the Army and the Navy, to become an untrammeled separate service. The U.S. Army Air Corps became the U.S. Army Air Forces in 1942 and finally, in 1947, the U.S. Air Force. The generals created heroes and glorified them, glamorized their airplanes, exaggerated their accomplishments, and assiduously covered up their failures.

The facts were these. The B-17 was less a "flying fortress" than a "flying coffin" to *Luftwaffe* pilots; it could not defend itself from the cannon-firing Messerschmitt Bf-109s and 110s or the more capable Focke-Wulf Fw-190s, and stood no chance against the even more dangerous Messerschmitt Me-262. The planes managed to survive—just!—by flying in tight formations. Only when defended by swarms of friendly fighters were the B-17s able to hold their own. The B-24 was a dangerous airplane to fly in tight formations because its advanced-design wing was subject to high-speed stall. The B-29 had engines that were prone to catch fire when heavily loaded, particularly at takeoff and initial climb. The skeletons of charred *Superfortresses* on Tinian, Saipan, and Guam offered mute testimony to the scores of B-29s—and their crews—that never made it beyond the end of the runway. The tirelessly publicized Norden bombsight was nearly useless over a cloud-covered Europe—and totally useless over Tokyo with its extremely high winds at altitude. As for the Norden dropping bombs into pickle-barrels from four miles up, that was plain hokum. Americans back home could be told none of this, of course.

But the USAAF would not be denied. Three days after the Pearl Harbor attack, it collaborated with MacArthur's public information staff in the Philippines to create from whole cloth the nation's first war hero. He was Captain Colin P. Kelly, Jr. As a headline in *The New York Times* jubilantly reported, he:

> "…helped even the score that the Japanese ran up at Pearl Harbor when he planted three bombs on the Japanese battleship *Haruna*."

According to the news story, Kelly paid for his heroic deed with his life.

Kelly was made into Sergeant York and ace flyer Eddie Rickenbacker, both of Great War fame, rolled into one. According to an AAF communiqué, Kelly had bravely attacked the *Haruna*:

> With utter disregard of murderous antiaircraft fire and swarms of enemy fighters—alone and unprotected—he and his crew traded their B-17 and their lives for the destruction of a powerful, modern and heavily armed Japanese battleship. His feat will live in the history of the Army Air Forces. (in *US Air Services*, vol. 27, 1942)

Garishly illustrated tabloids described in detail a mortally wounded Kelly in his last minutes, courageously fighting the controls of his damaged bomber. Penny bubble-gum war cards in lurid colors showed Kelly's flaming airplane crashing into the deck of a battleship.

There was just one problem with the propaganda narrative: it never happened. Postwar Japanese Navy records clearly establish that there had been no Nippon battleships in Philippine waters in early December: only one light cruiser, six destroyers, and four transports. No bombs had fallen near the cruiser on December 10th.

Four months later came another opportunity for the Air Force to showcase its capabilities. On April 18, sixteen B-25 medium bombers flew off the aircraft carrier *Hornet* in the North Pacific, destination Tokyo, in a publicity stunt that put a sixteen-ship task force in harm's way for essentially no military payoff. The twin-engine B-25 *Mitchell* was a land-based aircraft, but tests showed it could take off successfully from a carrier, although it could not return to a carrier. Each plane would carry four 500-

pound bombs, three conventional demolition bombs and a single incendiary cluster bomb, plus its ordinary five-man aircrew.

The mission became known, likely in perpetuity, as the "Doolittle Raid" named after its originator and commander Lt. Colonel James Doolittle, who came to his Air Force commission as a famous daredevil flyer. He had written to General "Hap" Arnold extravagantly that it was his intent "to bomb and fire the industrial center of Japan." With 16 tons of bombs? There was more to come from Doolittle's fertile imagination: the raid would cause confusion and disrupt war production throughout all of Japan. That, too, was an exaggeration.

The purpose of the raid was to buoy the spirits of Americans still smarting from the attack on Pearl Harbor, as well as to show the Japanese how vulnerable their cities were to air attack. For these purposes, the raid was an unmitigated success, despite the loss of eleven aircrew and all the aircraft.

Plans called for the planes to drop their bombs on Tokyo and other large cities in the area, head for China, and find their way–at dusk–to airstrips in China under control of Chiang-Kai-shek's forces. The planes would land if possible, or the aircrews would bail out and be rescued by friendly Chinese. Not all the flyers managed to parachute over Chinese territory, and three aircrews were captured by the Japanese. After a prompt show trial that convicted three of the captive airmen for war crimes, they were executed by firing squad. One plane crash-landed in Russia and the American flyers were interned for a year. The entire crews of fourteen B-25s eventually returned to the United States or to Allied control.

IN NOVEMBER, the *United States Strategic Bombing Survey (*USSBS) TEAM was ready to go to work.[88] However, it waited until Germany's surrender in May 1945, and the surrender of Japan, three months later. The USSBS was *two separate surveys:* one covering the B-17/B-24 *strategic air war over Europe* and one for the B-29's *strategic air war over Japan*. These Surveys also included the results of the thousands of *tactical* sorties flown by B-25 and B-26 medium bombers, and fighter-bombers like the P-47s, P-38s, and P-51s over European targets, and the thousands of sorties by carrier-based Navy fighter-bombers hitting Japan.

Prominent civilians were named directors rather than military officers in an attempt to achieve objectivity. John Kenneth Galbraith, the renowned economist and author, was named civilian director of the organization's "Effects and Area Bombing" department.[89] Galbraith would prove to be the most vocal and insistent critic of the Survey's work as well as one of its most cogent contributors. The final table of organization included 300 civilians, 350 military officers, and 500 enlisted men.

The Survey was conducted on a huge scale. In addition to the unearthing of German and Japanese wartime records, over 8,000 questionnaires were distributed to industry managers, and hundreds of government officials and military personnel were individually interviewed. Over 300 summary reports were written and a huge trove of statistical data compiled for researchers to digest and synthesize later on.

Short-term, the information gleaned from the bombing of Germany was helpful for the strategic bombing campaign then being planned for Japan. The size, scope, and mission of a future independent Air Force would also be shaped by the Survey's findings.

Many of the Survey's published conclusions were more advocacy than impartial assessment; individuals with their personal agendas, hidden or otherwise, could be expected to grind their own axes. Collectively the reports were contradictory and individually often ambiguous. Four glaring examples of such contradictory conclusions that found their way into the Survey's final reports are these:

> ...it would appear that the air attacks which laid waste to [these] cities must have substantially eliminated the industrial capacity of Germany. Yet this was not the case. The attacks did not reduce the German war production as to have a decisive effect on the outcome of the war.[90]
>
> Allied air power was decisive in the war in Western Europe.[91]
>
> The mental reaction of the German people to air attack was significant. Their morale, their belief in ultimate victory or satisfactory compromise and in their leaders declined, but they continued to work efficiently as long as the physical means of production remained.[92]
>
> Bombing appreciably affected the German will to resist. Its main psychological effects were defeatism, fear, hopelessness, fatalism, and apathy.[93]

The most vocal critic of the Eighth Air Force's strategic bombing offensive was latter-day muckraker Galbraith. Not only had strategic bombing not won the war in Europe as Air Force generals insisted, but it was a "disastrous failure" according to his department's "patiently gathered data."

> At most, it had eased somewhat the task of the ground troops.... The aircraft, manpower, and bombs used in the campaign had cost the American economy far more in output than they had cost Germany. However, our economy being much larger, we could afford it.[94]

In the event, there were many significant facts uncovered that were neither contradictory nor ambiguous. For example, Survey reports showed time and again that American intelligence had totally misread the German economy. Nazi Germany had been simplistically considered an armed camp, dedicated solely to making war. What Allied planners did not know—but a significant point that intelligence should have known—was that while Adolf Hitler was the driving force behind the Nazi military machine, he considered war an instrument of short-term policy. He had hoped to employ only minimum economic resources to meet these short-term military needs. Concerned as well about maintaining domestic political support, Hitler was also intent on preserving high standards of living for the German people. As long as he could, until well into 1943, Chancellor Hitler provided "butter" to go along with "guns."

When Survey interrogator Guido R. Perera talked with Kurt Tank, president of the Focke-Wulf Aircraft Company, he was told a startling story. It was sharply at odds with the American (and British) intelligence view that Germany had gone to war with its war industries going full tilt. Such a tightly bound economy—it was reasoned logically [but erroneously]—would be susceptible to unraveling by bombing. Tank shocked his interviewer when he told him that not once during the entire war did his company's production of Focke-Wulf Fw-190s, the *Luftwaffe's* best propeller-driven fighter, suffer from lack of plant capacity, labor, raw materials or components.[95]

The Survey also highlighted the resourcefulness and patriotism of civilian German workers in repairing bomb-damaged factories and infrastructure, and dispersing critical industries, such as ball-bearing plants. Underground assembly lines that were impervious to bomb damage were built for such vital weapons as the V-1 missile, V-2 rocket, and the Me-262 jet fighter, although such construction was labor-intensive and costly.

Of the total tonnage of bombs dropped on German targets by the USAAF, almost one-quarter had been aimed at the centers of large cities, nearly twice the amount released over all industrial targets combined. The Air Force never acknowledged that city centers were targets, nor did they admit to "area bombing" which was RAF Bomber Command's stock-in-trade, but when dense cloud-cover hid the primary targets, squadron leaders were under orders to unload their bombs on adjacent broad-area city centers. While the purpose of the city attacks was to erode the morale of the civilian population, particularly skilled workers, the USSBS discovered that the effects of bombing on the behavior of the workers and their productivity, was small. German factory workers, though angry and discouraged, kept on working. FDR's Unconditional Surrender declaration and the threat to the very nature of their society posed by the Morgenthau Plan were undoubtedly motivating factors. For example, right up to the final weeks of the war, workers in Berlin were repairing rail yards even as they came under long-range artillery fire from the advancing Red Army.

Dresden Destroyed

U.S. investigators were surprised to discover that even in Hamburg, Germany's second largest city, which had suffered the most destructive Allied air raids—and the first ever man-made fire storm—weapons production resumed near-normal levels within several weeks.[96]

It was also learned that by far the most effective of the bombing offensives over Germany were on rail transport and synthetic oil plants—neither of which could be put underground. Small and ineffective air attacks had been made on the synthetic oil facilities in May, 1943, by the Eighth Air Force, but it was not until after the Normandy landings that the tempo picked up. These plants were sprawling, easily identifiable targets and while they were heavily defended, persistent—and costly—attacks significantly reduced their outputs. In May 1944, as a benchmark, the plants produced 316,000 tons; in June, output dropped to 107,000 tons. At the start of 1945, Germany's oil production began a precipitate decline—from 660,000 tons per month, to 420,000 tons in mid-year, to 260,000 tons in December, and to 80,000 tons in March 1946.

The Survey found that the impact on supplies of aviation-grade fuel had been dramatic, which contributed significantly to the decline of the *Luftwaffe*. The shortage of fuel meant inadequate training of new pilots who flew in combat against USAAF pilots, who had many more hours of flying time in their logs. Limited fuel also meant that the final run-in time for new piston engines was cut from two hours to half an hour, significantly reducing engine life and reliability.

THE HANDWRITING ON THE WALL was clear to Albert Speer, Nazi Minister of Armaments, who viewed the fall in oil production as "catastrophic." When the *Wehrmacht* launched its desperate Christmas Offensive—commonly referred to as the *Battle of the Bulge* in the United States—in the Ardennes on December 16, its fuel reserves for the attack were known to be insufficient. Plans called for capturing Allied fuel dumps early in the offensive but when *Panzer* units were unable to do so, many sputtered to a stop in the heat of battle.

USSBS Vice-Chairman Henry Clay Alexander, the author of both the Summary Report and the Overall Report on the European War, presented upbeat conclusions. He reported at a Pentagon press conference in October 1945 that:

> It was the judgment... that Allied air power was decisive in the war in Western Europe.... In the air its victory was complete. At sea, its contribution combined with naval power, brought an end to the U-boat; on land it helped turn the tide overwhelmingly in favor of Allied ground forces. Its power and superiority made possible the success of the invasion. It brought the economy which sustained the enemy's armed forces to virtual collapse.... It brought home to the German people the full impact of modern war with all its horror and suffering. Its imprint on the German nation will be lasting.[97]

Historian David MacIsaac wrote that Alexander's heavily biased encomium,

> "…albeit exaggerated and chauvinistic, was the most-quoted paragraph from the Survey's findings in Europe."[98]

A critic can point out that there was not even a hint by Alexander that the Red Army had existed, much less played a role in the defeat of Nazi Germany. Historians generally agree today that the defeat of the celebrated German Sixth Army at Stalingrad, the greatest military reversal in Prussian/German history, meant the ultimate defeat of Germany. Far fewer observers go so far, however, as to agree with the author that the Red Army's contributions were almost certainly *the most decisive factor* in the war in Europe; in fact, the Anglo-American landings in Normandy would not have been possible without the Russians on the Eastern Front drawing off hundreds of thousands of Germany's veteran combat troops. Overall, Soviet Russia's combat-troop losses were far greater than combined U.S. and British losses; their total has been estimated at 20 million, including civilians.

THE WAR IN THE PACIFIC was a far different conflict than that waged by U.S. ground forces in North Africa, Sicily, Italy, France and Germany. There, battles ranged across the broad expanse of the largest ocean on the planet, involving the largest navies in the world—Japanese, American, and to a lesser extent, British–Fleets for the first time fought each other "over the horizon," and aircraft carriers quickly replaced battleships as the principal naval weapons. By early in 1945, the U.S. Navy could boast it had "about 100 aircraft carriers." U.S. Navy submarines destroyed almost all of Japan's merchant shipping, bringing the country to the verge of starvation by August 1945. The USAAF's long-range heavy hauler, the B-29, fire-bombed 62 of Japan's largest cities into rubble even before the two atomic bombs were dropped.

The most effective firebomb used over Japan was the ingenious 6.2-pound M-69. Externally the M-69 was deceptively innocent looking, disguising its sophisticated destructive capabilities inside a 3-inch-diameter plain steel cylinder. There were no stabilizing fins that made it look like a bomb; instead it contained a 3-foot-long strip of cloth, like a kite's tail, that popped out when it deployed to prevent tumbling. As the sturdy unit punched its way through the thin roof of a house, a time-delay fuse triggered which, after 3 to 5 seconds, detonated an ejection-ignition charge. By this time the bomblet was on its side or its nose embedded in a floor. The exploding charge in turn ignited a small quantity of white phosphorous powder which instantly set fire to the napalm main charge and blew a fiercely burning glob of napalm out the tail as far out as 100 feet. Whatever the burning glob landed on, it adhered to and the fire was difficult to extinguish.

What distinguished the Pacific War was the barbarous, take-no-prisoners fighting between invading Marines and tenaciously defending Japanese soldiers, intent on dying for their Emperor on one tiny atoll after another in the Central and South Pacific "island-hopping" campaigns. As the American invaders swept closer to the Japanese home islands, fighting became increasingly ferocious and atrocities were commonplace on both sides.

The U.S. and U.K. war in Europe, on the other hand, was marked by adherence to the generally accepted Rules of War and the Geneva Protocols. It was a different picture between Red Army and the *Wehrmacht* on the eastern front. It has been estimated that the Germans took as many as 5.5 million Soviet prisoners-of-war, at least 3.5 million of whom were dead by mid-1944. Of the 235,473 U.S. and U.K. prisoners reported captured by German and Italy together, only 4 percent (9,348) died in the hands of their captors, whereas 27 percent of Japan's Anglo-American POWs (35,756) did not survive.[99]

The war in the Pacific was strictly an American "show" and the United States initially sought no military help from any of its allies. America intended that it alone would reap the spoils of the war that soaked up so much American blood. There would be no more "mandated" territories as after The Great War that shared out former German colonies among the victors. There would be only *one victor* this time: the United States of America. It would have the Pacific territories all to itself, vital for the nation's imminent role as global hegemon.

The enormous casualties on Iwo Jima and Okinawa, however, and the certainty that the projected U.S. invasions of Kyushu and Honshu, Japan's principal islands, would be a bloodbath, led to Truman's "invitation" at Yalta for Russia to break its nonaggression pact with Japan. Stalin agreed and promised that the Red Army would attack Japan three months after the war in Europe ended. He was as good as his word but by that time, America had successfully tested its prototype uranium bomb at Alamagordo—and all bets were off.

ONE OF THE NAGGING QUESTIONS about the Pacific War which has dogged thoughtful Americans and continues to be asked today: Why was a second atomic bomb dropped on Japan? The correct answer is not among such conventional-wisdom responses as these: that there had been an immutable bombing schedule; or that the Japanese had not responded to the Potsdam Declaration [See Appendix]; or that a second target would provide further useful information for subsequent bomb design; or that the U.S. sought to show the Soviets it had built more than one bomb.

This was Hiroshima.

The right answer is the different nature of the two bombs and where each was assembled. The Hiroshima bomb (*Little Boy*) was a uranium bomb and was assembled at the Oak Ridge, Tennessee facility. The Nagasaki bomb (*Fat Man*) was a plutonium bomb and was assembled at Hanford, Washington.

> From the moment [Leslie] Groves learned that there would have to be two different types of bombs, whenever anyone suggested that the use of the atomic bomb would end the war, Groves would reply, 'Not until we drop two bombs on Japan.' The implication is clear. One bomb justified Oak Ridge, the second justified Hanford.[100]

This was Nagasaki.

In fact, there was genuine concern among some top scientists of the Manhattan Project that the Japanese might try to surrender before both types of bombs could be used. Galbraith rigorously insisted initially and for years after that the bombs had not been decisive, despite the almost unanimous view to the contrary among every level of American society. He wrote that it was a myth that their use made an invasion of the Japanese home islands unnecessary, supposedly saving the lives of thousands if not hundreds of thousands on both sides. "These are the facts," Galbraith steadfastly maintained:

> The bombs fell after the decision had been made by the Japanese government to surrender. That the war had to be ended was agreed at a meeting of key members of the Supreme War Direction Council with the Emperor on June 20, 1945, a full six weeks before the devastation of Hiroshima. The next steps took time. The Japanese had the usual bureaucratic lags between decision and action. The means for approaching the Allies had also to be agreed upon. And there was the need to ensure the acquiescence or neutralization of recalcitrant and suicidal officers and their military units. The atomic bombs only advanced the decision.[101]

SURVEY TEAMS WERE REDEPLOYED to the Pacific immediately after the Japanese surrendered. There the researchers faced a simpler task. The scale of air attacks, while formidable, had been smaller as had been the duration compared to the bombing of Germany.

General Curtis LeMay's frequent statements that Japan's war production relied mainly on so-called "cottage industries," linking the civilian population directly to the country's war machine and thus making them legitimate targets for his B-29s, were found to be self-serving rationalizations as well as propaganda tuned to Americans at home.

Conversely, USSBS analysts learned that the firebomb raids on Japan had a far greater impact on both civilian morale and war production than had similar attacks on German cities. It was also discovered that many of the factories razed had already been put out of operation by the naval blockade, which had cut off supplies of raw materials. Those plants still working at war's end were faced with the breakdown of the country's transportation networks that the factories depended upon for moving parts and finished goods.

The figures the Survey came up with regarding Japanese merchant shipping losses highlighted the significant and generally unsung role of the U.S. Navy's submarine fleet and its carrier-based bombers in defeating Japan. In December 1941, Japan's merchant fleet had totaled about six million tons. One year later, this fleet had been reduced to five million tons, to about three million tons by 1944, and by war's end to two million tons. By April 1945, oil imports had been eliminated and by July steel and coal had become virtually unobtainable.

The Survey also tracked the decline in Japanese civilian morale from June 1944, when only about two percent of the population believed that Japan faced likely defeat; to December, when about 10 percent believed victory was no longer possible after Japanese armies had been defeated in the Philippines; to March 1945 after the firebombing had begun and the food ration was cut drastically, with 19 percent believing that the war was lost; to June, 46 percent; and in August on the eve of surrender, 68 percent.[102]

Even the apparent total destruction of Hiroshima was not what it initially appeared to be. Most of the city's industrial production came from factories in the suburbs, with about half coming from only five companies. In this regard, the USSBS report maintained:

> Of these larger companies, only one suffered more than superficial damage. Of their working force, 94 percent were uninjured... plants ordinarily responsible for three-fourths of Hiroshima's industrial production could have resume normal production within 30 days of the attack had the war continued.[103]

Galbraith summed up his against-the-grain views of the air wars over Germany and Japan by writing that future American foreign policy would have been served better if the USSBS findings had been interpreted more critically,

> "…for this would have better prepared us for the costly ineffectiveness of the bombers in Korea and Vietnam."[104]

> *"It seems clear that even without the atomic bomb attacks, air supremacy over Japan could have exerted sufficient pressure to bring unconditional surrender and obviate the need for invasion.... Based on a detailed investigation of all the facts, and supported by the testimony of the surviving Japanese leaders involved, it is the Survey's opinion that certainly prior to December 31, 1945, Japan would have surrendered even if the atomic bombs had not been dropped, even if Russia had not entered the war, and even if no invasion had been planned or contemplated."*

—USSBS 4, Summary Report on the Pacific War, 1945.

OF THE MANY BOOKS WRITTEN about the Pacific War in "I was there" genre, one stands out for its graphic story-telling, its obvious integrity, and its mature insights. It is Eugene B. Sledge's *With the Old Breed at Peleliu and Okinawa*. In fact, Sledge's sensitive chronicle serves properly as a microcosm of the terrible life-and-death struggles between young Americans and young Japanese—over which country would temporarily possess a tiny atoll in the middle of the Pacific Ocean of no intrinsic value at the time. Sledge takes his reader into his foxholes in Okinawa, a new one every night, into the knee-deep mud mixed with putrefying corpses and fat maggots feasting on body parts.

He described the particular terrors of the night: not being able to distinguish infiltrating foe from friend. He recorded that one night he came to the realization that he and his fellow Marines were expendable and that such understanding was difficult for him to accept—and a humbling experience.

Sledge related the first time he killed a Japanese soldier up close.

> ... I saw a Japanese soldier appear at the blasted opening [of a pillbox]. He was grim determination personified as he drew back his arm to throw a grenade at us. My carbine was already up. When he appeared, I lined up my sights on his chest and began squeezing off shots. As the first bullet hit him, he face contorted in agony. His knees buckled. The grenade slipped from his grasp... and went off at his feet. Even in the midst of these fast-moving events, I looked down at my carbine with sober reflection. I had just killed a man at close range. That I had seen clearly the pain on his face when my bullets hit him came as a jolt. It suddenly made the war a very personal affair. The expression on that man's face filled me with shame and then disgust for the war and all the misery it was causing.[105]

Sledge described such grisly details as these:

> The situation was bad enough, but when enemy artillery shells exploded in the area, the eruptions of soil and mud uncovered previously buried Japanese dead and scattered chunks of corpses... If a Marine slipped and slid down the back slopes of the muddy ridge, he was apt to reach the bottom vomiting. I saw more than one man lose his footing and slip and slide all the way to the bottom only to stand up in horror—stricken as he watched in disbelief while fat maggots tumbled out his muddy dungaree pockets, cartridge belt, legging lacings. We didn't talk about such things. They were too horrible and obscene even for hardened veterans... Nor do authors normally write about such vileness; unless they have seen it with their own eyes, it is too preposterous to think that men could actually live and fight for days and nights on end under

such terrible conditions... But I saw much of it there on Okinawa and to me the war was insanity.[106]

Sledge wrote about watching with macabre fascination as U.S. graves registration teams identified and collected the American dead. Each of these men wore extra-large rubber gloves and carried a long pole with a stiff flap attached to the end, like a huge spatula. They would lay a poncho next to a corpse, then place two or more poles under the body, and then roll it onto the poncho. Often a corpse fell apart and the limbs and head were separately pushed onto the poncho

> "like bits of garbage. With the corpses being moved, the stench of rotting flesh became worse (if possible) than ever before."[107]

Six decades after the United States dropped two nuclear bombs on Japan, many Americans have grown skeptical of President Harry Truman's postwar claim, now embedded in popular lore, that these two bombs saved 500,000 GI lives. In his memoir, Truman wrote that he hadn't lost any sleep over his decision to hit the Japanese with the bombs. Declassified files now reveal that military planners before Hiroshima had estimated between 20,000 and 46,000 U.S. lives would have been lost in the invasion and conquest of the Japanese home islands. Winston Churchill came up with far bigger guesses: he declared after Nagasaki that the two bombs had saved over 1,200,000 Allied lives, including about 1,000,000 American lives.

Barton J. Bernstein, noted nuclear-energy scholar, wrote in the June/July 1986 issue of the *Bulletin of the Atomic Scientists:*

> Perhaps in the aftermath of Hiroshima and Nagasaki, Truman developed a need to exaggerate the number of U.S. lives that the bombs might have saved by possibly helping render the invasion unnecessary. It is probably true... that he never lost any sleep over his decision. Believing ultimately in the myth of 500,000 lives saved may been a way of concealing ambivalence, even from himself. The myth also helped deter Americans from asking troubling questions about the use of atomic bombs. The destruction of this myth should reopen these questions.

ONE OF THE GREAT FRAUDS of World War II was the ballyhooed "precision bombing" by B-17 and B-24 bombers over Germany. Over Japan it was city destruction from the get-go by B-29s; the Air Force's public relations officers forgot about the famed Norden bombsight that supposedly could put bombs into a pickle barrel from 20,000 feet.

The Norden was a complex mechanical assembly of tiny motors, even tinier gear trains, and close-tolerance optical elements—more than 2,000 separate parts in all. It could be likened to a 50-pound Swiss watch. When bolted into the nose of a pitching, yawing, and rolling airplane, buffeted by radical temperature changes and air pressures from the ground to bombing altitudes, subjected to severe shock loads during hard landings, assaulted by the vibrations of four big reciprocating engines and nearby .50 caliber machine guns, and generally banged around in an inhospitable environment, one can only question how reliably the Norden could be expected to perform.

The Bombing Tables developed at test ranges in the U.S. used by the bombardiers were based on wind velocities—speeds and directions—from the bombers' altitude and at the instant of release of the bombs all the way to the ground. Of these last data, the bombardier scarcely had a clue. Finally, because the bombardier had to see his target before he could attempt to hit it, the persistent cloud cover over central Europe, particularly during winter months, precluded even a semblance of precision. Eighth Air Force heavy bombers more often pockmarked the countryside, sometimes bombed the wrong city, and on three occasions bombed the wrong country, Switzerland. In February 1944, the Swiss border town of Schaffhausen was hit. A year later nine B-24s bombed Basel and six B-24s struck Zurich. Their target had been Freiburg, Germany, *25 miles from Basel and 45 miles from Zurich.* By war's end, many B-17 and B-24 bombardiers routinely became "toggeliers," ordered to release their bombs at the same time as the squadron leader's plane, whose navigator and bombardier were supposedly the best in the squadron.

The USAAF was losing scores of heavy bombers with their aircrews of ten every month; folks back home could not be told this. Instead, Americans were told bold lies by their military leaders, like General H. H. Arnold, who stated in a press conference:

> Fiction: We did it in daylight and we did it with precision, aiming our explosives with the care and accuracy of a marksman firing a rifle at a bullseye. We moved in on a city of 50,000 [Schweinfurt] and destroyed that part of it that contributes to the enemy's ability to wage war on us. When that part was a heap of twisted girders, smoking ruin and pulverized machinery, we handed it back, completely useless to the Germans.[108]

> Fact: On October 14, 1943, 16 bomb groups flew over 500 miles into Germany, target: Schweinfurt, without escorting fighters... The cost was high—60 out of 229 B-17s bombing that day were lost. Overall, one bomb out of ten hit within 500 feet of the targets and there were 63 direct hits. Three bearing plants lost 10 percent of their machines damaged or destroyed.[109]

It would be months after VJ-Day before Americans began to learn details of the horrors of the fire-bombing war in Japan. Even before the two nuclear bombs were released over Hiroshima and Nagasaki, more than 60 of Japan's biggest cities had been firebombed to rubble. Aerial photographs showed almost barren landscapes where once were teeming cities. To this day, photographs of the terribly disfigured survivors of the two nuclear bomb blasts are kept under government lock-and-key.

Books about the bloody infantry battles on the tiny atolls defended to the death by the Japanese, on the other hand, began to appear almost immediately. Were the stories honest depictions? How far was the truth stretched? Hard to tell! As a reader with his or her own agenda, one could accept or reject the stories as partly fiction or entirely fiction.

ONE UNIQUE OVERVIEW of the battles waged on these tiny Pacific-island battlegrounds was by Charles A. Lindbergh. In his autobiography, *The Wartime Journals of Charles A. Lindbergh*, he described the informal discussions he had with officers on atrocities that took place on the islands where he touched down. He was then a civilian test pilot for Chance Vought, manufacturer of the gull-winged F-4U *Corsair.*

In 1927, when he returned to the United States after his solo flight across the Atlantic he was given a hero's welcome unmatched in American history to that time. In the intervening years, Lindbergh became disenchanted with and a severe critic of American society. He came to despise crowds and avoided the press. To Lindbergh,

> "the masses, and by extension the democratic system, represented a descent into mediocrity, a universe... whose only standard and measure of achievement was the ability to entertain, titillate, gratify low and trivial desires."[110]

Above all, he was permanently embittered when his infant son, Charles, Jr., was kidnapped and murdered. The trial of the killer turned into a hideous circus. Charles, Sr. and his small family were hounded by early versions of the *paparazzi*. He and his wife were fed up with guards at their gate, obscene newspaper headlines, even the omnipresent mother-in-law. In December 1935, the Lindberghs with toddler son Jon secretly boarded a U.S. passenger-freighter, destination Liverpool. They spent the next three years in England and France, in self-imposed exile.

While in Europe, Lindbergh was intrigued by what he was learning about German accomplishments in military aviation and wanted to learn more. He was invited twice as the guest of *Reichsmarschall* Hermann Goering to tour *Luftwaffe* facilities and inspect the secret new *Messerschmitt Bf-109* fighter plane. In 1938, after returning to the United States, Lindbergh was invited for a third time to Germany. During this last visit, Lindbergh was permitted to study the new *Junkers Ju-88* twin-engine bomber and fly the still-under-wraps *Bf-109*.

Lindbergh also was the guest of honor at U.S. Ambassador Hugh R. Wilson's infamous stag dinner at the American Embassy in Berlin. It was a gathering of important diplomatic figures and luminaries in the field of aeronautics. Goering, in a glittering uniform festooned with medals, arrived fashionably late. Wilson introduced the *Reichsmarschall* to his guests and Goering shook hands with each in turn. When he reached Lindbergh he stopped and casually slipped into his hand a small red box. Inside was the *Verdienstkreuz Deutscher Adler*, Service Cross of the Order of German Eagle with Star. Lindbergh smilingly accepted the medal, firmly shook Goering's hand, everyone applauded, and all sat down to dinner and small talk.

"A month after Wilson's dinner, Secretary of the Interior Harold L. Ickes, a Germanophobe of colossal passion, berated Lindbergh for accepting 'a decoration at the hands of a brutal dictator who with that same hand is robbing and torturing thousands of fellow human beings.'"[111]

Ickes, who was Franklin Roosevelt's chief attack-dog, had found a chink in Lindberg's tough mantle and exploited it at every opportunity. The *Deutscher Adler* became, as his wife had predicted in Berlin the night he received the gold medal, his "albatross."

DURING THE LATE 1930s, the U.S. was divided politically between the interventionists, who supported England and France in their growing confrontation with Nazi Germany; and the noninterventionists or isolationists, opposed to their country's involvement in a European war. A Gallup poll in 1939 showed:

"Three percent of the American people in favor of entering such a war and ninety-seven percent in favor of keeping out."[112]

Later polls showed opposition was reduced to eighty-five percent, where it remained right up to the attack on Pearl Harbor.

As war clouds gathered in Europe, a national voice for Americans opposed to intervention was formed, the *American First Committee*. It grew rapidly: at the height of its appeal it numbered 800,000 members with chapters coast to coast. *America First* had an impressive governing body including Hugh Johnson, head of the NRA; prominent economist, Stuart Chase; Great War ace and president of Eastern Airlines, Eddie Rickenbacker; Henry Ford; and Senators Burton K. Wheeler of Montana and Gerald P. Nye of North Dakota. Retired General Robert E. Wood—CEO of Sears, Roebuck—was chairman. A leading member was World War I revisionist historian Harry Elmer Barnes.

On September 15, 1939, Lindbergh delivered his first radio address to the nation, covered nationally by the three major networks. His diary entry for that date recorded that the newspaper editorials he read were about ninety percent favorable. A month later, in another speech to a nationwide radio audience, which he titled "Neutrality and War," Lindbergh emphasized that the new war brewing was not a struggle for democracy or freedom, but it was over the balance of power in Europe. As the election neared, still a private citizen, he again took to the airwaves, calling for the election of leaders whose promises could be trusted, who understood where they were taking America.

America First finally invited him to deliver his anti-war message on their behalf; for the first time he would speak directly to an audience. It would be in great Woolsey Hall on the campus of liberal Yale University in New Haven, Connecticut, before about 3,000 listeners: students, faculty, and invited guests.

> Lindbergh expected to be booed and hissed as he went along. But instead his audience sat spellbound, then erupted in a mammoth standing ovation as he finished. Emotionally affected, he decided then and there that he must speak out publicly and he would do so under the banner of *America First*.[114]

Lindbergh's first address as a member of *America First* was on April 17, 1941. It was a proselytizing message, highlighting his views and those of the Committee's. Lindbergh soon became its principal spokesman. In subsequent speeches, he focused on favorite isolationist topics and slashed away at FDR's foreign-policy initiatives. Then on September 11, he delivered an address at a huge outdoor rally in Des Moines, Iowa that seriously and permanently wounded him. He charged that "The three most important groups which have been pressing this country toward war are the British, the Jewish, and the Roosevelt Administration."[115]

He declared that these groups and other "war agitators" had organized a step-by-step campaign to draw America into the conflict. He pointed out that if it were not England's hope that she could make the United States financially and militarily responsible for the war, England would have months ago negotiated a peace in Europe and would be better off for it.

If Lindbergh had stopped there and moved on, the public's reaction would have been severe enough. But his candor—or was it his anti-Semitism?—pulled him into treacherous waters. He said he understood why American Jews desired the overthrow of the Nazi regime. Instead of agitating for war, however, he advised: "They should be opposing it in every possible way, for they will be among the first to feel its consequences. Their greatest danger to this country lies in their ownership and influence in our motion pictures, our press, our radio, and our government."[116]

Charles Lindbergh had taken on American Jewry and an avalanche of vituperative criticism descended on his head. *America First* managed to roll with the punches and it suffered no membership loss, indicating perhaps that there were many Judeophobes in America at that time. But Lindbergh's reputation had been mortally wounded; he was condemned as an anti-Semite and an ally of Hitler.

> *"Imagine, in just fifteen years, he had gone from Jesus to Judas."*
>
> —Sister-in-law Constance regarding Charles Lindbergh's reputation.[113]

Following the Pearl Harbor attack, *America First* shut its doors and released a statement urging its members to support the nation's war effort and the president. Where did this leave Charles Lindbergh?

His diary entry of December 12 records that his first inclination was to write directly to FDR, offering his services, and telling him,

> "While I had opposed him in the past and had not changed my convictions, I was ready in time of war to submerge my personal viewpoint in the general welfare and unity of the country."[117]

He then wrote in his diary the reasons why, in fact, he would not and could not follow the FDR route, at the same time flaying the president.

> I do not know a single man who has known Roosevelt, friend or enemy, who trusts what he says from one week to the next. And the president has the reputation, even among his friends, for being a vindictive man. If I wrote to him at this time, he would probably make what use he could of my offer... and assign me to some position where I would be completely ineffective and out of the way.[118]

Lindbergh then decided he should turn to the aviation industry, which he knew well, and make his contributions to the war effort through it. Henry Ford, a well-known anti-Semite, was converting his gigantic Willow Run automobile assembly plant into one that would build thousands of Consolidated B-24 bombers. He hired Lindbergh as a jack-of-all-trades aircraft consultant.

Starting in 1944, Lindbergh, in addition to his activities with the Ford Motor Company, entered a consulting relationship with United Aircraft Corporation and its Chance Vought affiliate. In this capacity, he devoted his energies to improving the Navy/Marine *Corsair F4-U* fighter-bomber. His subsequent trip to the Pacific was mainly to study the *Corsair* under combat conditions.

On April 3, the day before he hitched an airplane ride to Pearl Harbor for the start of his tour, he wrote in his diary:

> To Brooks Brothers to buy uniforms and equipment for the trip. Uniforms must be worn in combat areas. I go on a 'technician status.' Therefore, on leaving the country, I must wear a naval officer's uniform without insignia or rank.[119]

While in the Pacific, he typically messed every night with the Army and Air Corps officers on the islands. He was, of course, a well-known and respected figure among flyers. During these informal get-togethers, Lindbergh not only discussed technical matters but he also talked with the officers about the war that was all around them. Frequently, Lindbergh recalled, the discussions turned to atrocities. The following are selected diary entries.

> June 21, New Guinea: "General's account of killing a Japanese soldier. A technical sergeant in an advanced area some weeks ago complained that he had been with combat forces in the Pacific for over two years and never had a chance to do any fighting himself—that he would like the chance to kill at least one Jap before he went home. He was invited to go out on a patrol into enemy territory. The sergeant saw no Jap to shoot, but members of the patrol took a prisoner. The Jap prisoner was brought to the sergeant with the statement that here was his opportunity to kill a Jap. 'But I can't kill that man. He's a prisoner. He's defenseless.' 'Hell, this is war. We'll show you how to kill the son of a bitch.' One of the patrol members offered the Jap a cigarette and a light, and as he started to smoke an arm was thrown around his head and his throat 'slit from ear to ear.' The entire procedure was thoroughly approved by the general giving the account."[120]

> June 26, Hollandia: "The talk drifted to prisoners of war and the small percentage of Japanese soldiers taken prisoner. 'Oh, we could take more if we wanted to,' one of the officers replied. 'But our boys don't like to take prisoners.' 'We had a couple of thousand down at _____, but

only a hundred or so were turned in. They had an accident with the rest. It doesn't encourage the rest to surrender when they hear of their buddies being marched out on the flying field and machine guns turned loose on them.'"[121]

June 28, New Guinea: "Supper and evening with 475th officers. Talk again turned to war, prisoners and souvenirs. I am shocked at the attitude of our American troops. They have no respect for death, the courage of an enemy soldier.... They think nothing whatever of robbing the body of a dead Jap and call him a 'son of a bitch' while doing so. I said during a discussion that regardless of what the Japs did, I did not see how we could gain anything or claim that we represented a civilized state if we killed them by torture. 'Well, some of our boys do kick their teeth in, but they usually kill them first,' one of the officers said in half apology."[122]

July 21, Biak: "This afternoon, I stood outside our quarters and watched the shells bursting on the ridge. For weeks a handful of Japanese soldiers, variously estimated at between 250 and 700 men, has been holding out against overwhelming odds and the heaviest bombardment our well-supplied guns can give them. If positions were reversed and our troops held out so courageously and well, their defense would be recorded as one of the most glorious examples of tenacity, bravery, and sacrifice in the history of our nation.... What is courage for us is fanaticism for him. We hold his examples of atrocity screamingly to the heavens while we cover up our own and condone them as just retribution for his acts. Over to the 35th Fighter Squadron to give a half hour's talk on fuel economy and the P-38."[123]

July 24, Biak: "We had to cross a road and climb another hill to get to the caves. At the side of the road we passed the edge of a bomb crater. In its bottom were lying the bodies of five or six Jap soldiers, partly covered with a truckload of garbage our troops had dumped on top of them. I have never felt more ashamed of my people. To kill, I understand; that it an essential part of war... But for our people to kill by torture and to descend to throwing the bodies of our enemies into a bomb crater and dumping garbage on top of them nauseates me."[124]

August 11, Biak: "Sitting on boxes and the edge of bunks in the rather poorly lighted tent, we discussed the question of Japanese prisoners. 'Take the 41st; they just don't take prisoners. The men boast about it.' 'The officers wanted some prisoners to question but couldn't get any until they offered two weeks in Sydney for each one turned in. Then they got more than they could handle.' 'The Aussies are still worse. You remember the time they had to take those prisoners south by plane? One of the pilots told me later they just pushed them out over the mountains and reported the Japs committed hara-kiri on the way.' 'Well, you remember when our troops captured that Jap hospital? There wasn't anyone alive in it when we got through. You can't blame the Aussies too much. They found some of their men castrated; and they found some with steaks cut out of them. They captured one place where the Japs were actually cooking the meat.' But barbaric as our men are at times, the Orientals appear to be worse."[125]

September 1, Roi Island: "Some of the Marines had a little sack in which they collected teeth with gold fillings. The officer said he had seen a number of Japanese bodies from which an ear or nose had been cut off. 'We found one Marine with a Japanese head. He was trying to get the ants to clean the flesh off the skull, but the odor got so bad we had to take it away from him.' It is the same story everywhere I go."[126]

September 14, Oahu: "Cleared customs as we drove out to the base. The customs officer asked me if I had any bones in my baggage. He said they had to ask everyone that question because they had found a large number of men taking Japanese bones home for souvenirs. He said he had found one man with two 'green' Jap skulls in his baggage."[127]

Notes

[1] James Rusbridger & Eric Nave, *Betrayal at Pearl Harbor: How Churchill Lured Roosevelt Into WWII* (Summit Books, New York, 1991), p. 88.

[2] Thomas E. Mahl, *Desperate Deception: British Covert Operations in the United States, 1939-44* (Brassey's, Washington, 1998), p. Vii.

[3] One of the persistent myths of Franklin Roosevelt's pre-war administrations was that his New Deal had raised America from its Depression. Not so! The year 1937 was a recession year and more than ten million remained unemployed in 1938. In 1939, there were still nine million unemployed and nearly as many in 1940. It was World War II that bailed out the nation—and tarnished Roosevelt's legacy as an economic wizard for those Americans who had not already been bamboozled by FDR's lies.

[4] FDR, under relentless pressure from Churchill, agreed to transfer 50 Great War-vintage U.S. destroyers to Britain. To make the transfer palatable to the still-isolationist American public, Churchill agreed in exchange to give the U.S. 99-year leases for eight naval and air bases inside British colonial holdings in the Western Hemisphere: in Newfoundland, British Guiana, Antigua, Bermuda, Jamaica, St. Lucia, and Trinidad. Article 6 of Convention XIII of the Hague Conference of 1907 was clear that such a transaction was contrary to international law: "The supply in any manner, directly or indirectly, by a neutral Power to a belligerent Power or warships, ammunition, or war materiel of any kind whatsoever, is forbidden." Philip Goodhart, *Fifty Ships That Saved the World—The Foundation of the Anglo-American Alliance* (Doubleday & Company, New York, 1965), p. 236-237.

[5] Winston S. Churchill, *Blood, Sweat, and Tears* (G.P. Putnam's Sons, New York, 1941), p. 453. As a correspondent of the *Morning Post* during the Boer War, Churchill showed his warrior streak: "There is only one way to break the resistance of the Boers: the most severe suppression. In other words, we must kill the parents to teach the children respect for us." He also reported details of a punitive military expedition to the Mamund Valley: "We went systematically from village to village, destroying the houses, ruining the wells, breaking the towers, felling the larger shade-giving trees, burning the harvest and destroying the water reservoirs.... After fourteen days the valley was a desert and our honor was satisfied." Churchill also introduced the phrase "terminological inexactitude," a discreet synonym for the crude word "lie." Cited in Joseph Goebbels, "Aus Churchills Lügenfabrik," *Die Zeit ohne Beispiel*, Munich, February 2, 1941, p. 380-384.

[6] Gore Vidal, *The Last Empire: Essays 1992-2000* (Doubleday, New York, 2001), p. 36.

[7] The tons, literally, of Third Reich documents reviewed postwar unearthed not a single reference to a German plan for attacking the United States. However, there was the *Amerika* bomber being developed that ostensibly was to be used to bomb New York City, refueling on one of the legs at the Azores in mid-Atlantic.

[8] Robert E. Sherwood, *Roosevelt and Hopkins: An Intimate History* (Harper & Brothers, New York, 1948), p. 101.

[9] Robert B. Stinnett, *Day of Deceit: The Truth About FDR and Pearl Harbor* (Simon & Schuster, New York, 2000), p. 273.

[10] Ibid., p. 275. Stinnett prefaced McCollum's proposed eight actions, designed to provoke Japan into an overt act of war, by writing he had discovered them in Box 6 of a special U.S. Navy collection in RG38, January 24, 1995,

[11] Kemp Tolley, *Cruise of the Lanakai—Incitement to War* (Naval Institute Press, Annapolis MD, 1973).

[12] Vidal, p. 101.

[13] John Denson, *The Costs of War: America's Pyrrhic Victories* (Transaction Publishers, New Brunswick NJ, 197), p. 274.

[14] Clive Ponting, *Churchill* (Sinclair-Stevenson, London, 1994), p. 32.

[15] Ibid., p. 44.

[16] Rusbridger and Nave, p. 96.

[17] Ibid., p. 100.

[18] Ibid., p. 103.

[19] Nicholas John Cull, *Selling War: The British Propaganda Campaign Against American Neutrality in World War II* (Oxford University Press, New York, 1995), p. 187.

[20] Ibid., p. 241.

[21] Mahr, p. 3.

[22] C. Cannizzo, *The Gun Merchants* (Pergamon Press, New York, 1980), p. 68.

[23] Gerard Colby Zilg, *Du Pont: Behind the Nylon Curtain* (Prentice-Hall, Inc., Englewood Cliffs NJ, 1974), p. 2.

[24] Ibid., p. 4.

[25] The British Empire of WWII covered one-quarter of the surface of the globe and consisted of about 500 million people: the Commonwealth or self-governing dominions, including Canada, Australia, New Zealand, and South Africa; the mandated territories of Tanganyika, Cameroon, Togoland, and Palestine; the independent protected states of Tonga, Sarawak, Brunei, and Malaya; colonies and territories including Bermuda, Jamaica, British Guiana, the Falkland Islands, British Solomon Islands, North Borneo, Hong Kong, Kenya, Nigeria, Uganda, Somaliland, Malta, and Gibraltar; and the Indian Empire and Burma. Brewer, *To Win the Peace: British Propaganda in the United States During World War II* (Cornell University Press, Ithica NY, 1997).

[26] Churchill, Randolph S. with Martin Gilbert, *Road to Victory, 1941-1945, Vol. VII* (Houghton Mifflin, New York, 1986), p. 236.

[27] Hadley Cantril, *The Invasion from Mars: A Study in the Psychology of Panic* (Harper & Row, Publishers, New York, 1940), p. 47.

[28] Adolf Hitler, *Mein Kampf* (Houghton Mifflin Company, New York, 1925), p. 143.

[29] Ibid., p. 180.

[30] Sidney Rogerson, *Propaganda in the Next War* (Garland Publishing, Inc., New York, 1938), p. 10.

[31] Ibid.

[32] Ibid., p. 11.

[33] Eric Alterman, *When Presidents Lie: A History of Official Deception and Its Consequences* (Viking, New York, 2004), p. 26.

[34] Susan A. Brewer, *To Win the Peace: British Propaganda in the United States During World War II* (Cornell University Press, Ithaca NY, 1997), p. 4.

[35] Mahr, p. 208.

[36] Cull, p. 81.

[37] With much pomp and circumstance, his ashes were returned to Great Britain on December 12, 1945 on the USS *Augusta,* the warship on which the Atlantic Charter had been signed. *The American Speeches of Lord Lothian* (Oxford University Press, New York, 1941), p. 1.

[38] Ibid., p. 20.

[39] Ibid., p. 37.

[40] Ibid., p. 41.

[41] Ibid., p. 47.

[42] Ibid., p. 52.

[43] Ibid., p. 62.

[44] Cull, p. 144.

[45] Ibid., p. 79

[46] Ibid., p. 87.

[47] Cull, p. 90

[48] Ibid., p. 155-156.

[49] Gore Vidal, *Screening History* (Harvard University Press, Cambridge MA, 1992), p. 47.

[50] Rogerson, p. 10-11.

[51] Stinnett, p. 273

[52] John Costello, *Days of Infamy: MacArthur, Roosevelt, Churchill: The Shocking Truth Revealed* (Pocket Books, New York, 1994), p. 202.

[53] In a Secret cable of December 7, 1941, 19:30 GCT, SECNAV [Secretary of the Navy] directed that the Navy EXECUTE WPL [War Plan] FORTY SIX AGAINST JAPAN. AT 22:52 the same day a cable from OPNAV [Chief of Naval Operations] to CINCPAC [Commander in Chief Pacific Fleet] & CINCAF [Commander in Chief Asiatic Fleet], directed that the Pacific and Asian Fleets EXECUTE UNRESTRICTED AIR AND SUBMARINE WARFARE AGAINST JAPAN. INFORM ARMY. CINCAF INFORM BRITISH AND DUTCH. The next day a cable at 04:50 from CINCAF [Admiral Kimmel] to OPNAV outlined what had occurred on December 7. "Despite security measures in effect surprise attack by Japanese bombing planes damaged all battleships except Maryland x Moderate damage to Tennessee and Pennsylvania x Arizona a total wreck West Virginia resting on bottom still burning Oklahoma capsized California resting on bottom Nevada moderate damage beached x Utah and Oglala capsized x Honolulu Helena and Raleigh damaged and unfit for sea x Vestal damaged and beached x Curtis moderate damage x Destroyers Shaw Cassin Downes in drydock complete wrecks x As a result of attack Army airplane losses severe x There remain 13 B17 nine B18 and about 30 pursuit planes x Approximately 10 patrol planes remain available Oahu x 1 Patrol plane squadron at Midway x Recommend all available Army bombers be sent to Oahu x Fire opened promptly by all ships and a number of enemy aircraft destroyed x 1 enemy submarine sunk possibly 2 more x 2 carriers 7 heavy cruisers 3 squadrons of destroyers and all available planes searching for enemy x Personnel behavior magnificent in face of furious surprise attack x Personnel casualties believed to be heavy in Oklahoma and Arizona. WAR PLANS, CINCPAC FILES SECRET Captain Steele's "RUNNING ESTIMATE and SUMMARY," covering the period 7 December 1941 to 31 August 1942. DECLASSIFIED IAW DOD MEMO OF 3 MAY, 1972.

[54] John Toland, *Infamy: Pearl Harbor and Its Aftermath* (Doubleday & Company, Inc., Garden City NY, 1982), p. 321.

[55] *The New York Times*, December 10, 1941.

[56] Thomas Fleming, *The New Dealers' War: F.D.R. and The War Within World War II* (Basic Books, New York, 2001), p. 36.

[57] Churchill, p. 77.

[58] "On wheeling north, [Heinz] Guderian's *Panzer* units headed for Calais, while Reinhardt's swept west of Arras toward St. Omer and Dunkirk. On the 22nd Boulogne was isolated by Guderians's advance, and the next day Calais. That same day [Hubert Lans] Reinhardt reached the Aire-St. Omer Canal, less than twenty miles from Dunkirk—the only escape port left to the BEF." At that moment [Gerd von] Rundstedt told me [Liddell Hart], a sudden telephone call came from Colonel [Hans von] Grieffenberg at OKH, saying that [Ewald von] Kleist's forces were to hold on the line of the canal. It was the Fuhrer's direct order. I questioned it in a message of protest, but received a curt telegram in reply: "The armoured divisions are to remain at medium artillery range from Dunkirk [a distance of eight or nine miles]." B.H. Liddell Hart, *The German Generals Talk* (William Morrow & Co., New York, 1948), p. 134.

[59] Ibid., p. 135.

[60] Ibid.

[61] Ibid., p. 136.

[62] Heinz Guderian, *Panzer Leader* (Dutton, New York, 1952), p. 117.

[63] Churchill, p. 297.

[64] *The New York Times*, June 18, 1941.

[65] J.F.C. Fuller, *The Second World War, 1939-1945* (Duell, Sloan, Pierce, New York, 1948), p. 355.

[66] Fleming, p. 175.

[67] Albert Wedemeyer, *Wedemeyer Reports* (Holt, New York, 1958), 96, p. 169.

[68] Fleming, p. 175.

[69] John Slessor, *The Central Blue* (Praeger, New York, 1957), p. 434.

[70] Lord Hankey, *Politics, Trials and Errors* (Henry Regnery, Chicago, 1950), p. 29, 35-36.

[71] Ibid., p. 46-47.

[72] Fleming, p. 176.

[73] Anne Armstrong, *Unconditional Surrender: The Impact of the Casablanca Policy Upon World War II* (Rutgers University Press, New Brunswick NJ, 1961), p. 43-44.

[74] *The Franco-Prussian War:* Had Prussia been the instigator? No, if the views of the Americans and British *at that time* are assessed. In 1870, Americans considered the war a defensive one on the part of Prussia, and it was well known that France had declared war first. Furthermore, the cause of German national unification was regarded sympathetically by all the great powers.

The Great War: At the end of the war, the victors pointed the finger of sole guilt—*Kriegsschuldfrage*—at Germans and Germany for starting the war. Since then, many objective analyses by diplomatic historians apportion guilt differently. Revisionist historian Sidney Bradshaw Fay has written that as a result of the accumulation of credible documentary evidence by the mid-1920s "no serious historians any longer accept the dictum of the Allied victors of 1919 that Germany and her allies were solely responsible."

World War II: In September of 1939, England declared war on Germany the same day *Wehrmacht's Panzers* crossed the Polish borders. At the same time the Red Army marched into eastern Poland and the Baltic states. Yet, Great Britain did not declare war on the Soviet Union for violating the sanctity of small states—only on Germany. This indicates that Britain's entry into the war was not intended to be a response to aggression. Rather, it was aimed at the restoration of the balance-of-power equilibrium in Europe at the expense of German hegemony.

[75] John Morton Blum, *From the Morgenthau Diaries: Years of War 1941-1945* (Houghton, Mifflin, Boston, 1967), p. 109.

[76] Henry Morgenthau, Sr. had been an important financial contributor to Woodrow Wilson's two presidential campaigns. As compensation for his support Wilson rewarded him with the "Jewish" diplomatic post, the Turkish ambassadorship. He arrived in Constantinople in November 1913 and returned to the U.S. in 1916, resigning his ambassadorship, hoping to work for Wilson's reelection and perhaps be rewarded with the cabinet post he coveted, Secretary of the Treasury. With Germanophobic journalist, Burton J. Hendrick, as his ghostwriter, the two jointly produced *Ambassador Morgenthau's Story*, a staunchly anti-German book filled with lies. Featured in it was the infamous legend of the Potsdam Crown Conference of July 5, 1915, a happening and a date that American and Allied propagandists fixed as the ultimate proof that Germany had started the Great War. In fact, the German war-planning conference never took place, postwar evidence clearly showed. Stewart Halsey Ross, *Propaganda for War: How the United States Was Conditioned to Fight the Great War of 1914-1918* (McFarland & Company, Inc., Publishers, Jefferson NC, 1996), 254-258.

[77] Blum, p. 260.

[78] Morgenthau Jr.'s ties to FDR ran deep and long. In 1915, Morgenthau had bought a tract of land in Duchess Country, New York, close to Roosevelt's estate in Hyde Park. In 1920, when FDR was the Democratic Party's vice presidential candidate, Morgenthau, always the opportunist, helped in the campaign. The following August, infantile paralysis crippled FDR, temporarily forcing him out of politics. Subsequently, Roosevelt spent more time in Hyde Park bringing him into closer relations with his neighbor. In 1928, when FDR ran for governor of New York State, Morgenthau served as his "advance man," seeing dividends down the road. When Roosevelt was elected president in 1932, Morgenthau confidently expected to be named Secretary of Agriculture, but farm leaders in the South and Midwest opposed the idea of a Jew in the Cabinet. Instead he reluctantly accepted a lesser post, Chairman of the Farm Credit Administration. A year later, William Woodin, FDR's first Treasury Secretary, died suddenly, and there was a vacancy to be filled. Morgenthau, never a shrinking violet, went directly to the president to lobby for the job. Because of his proven loyalty—a trait which Franklin Roosevelt valued above all else—FDR named him to the more prestigious position. An important Republican suggested that FDR had managed to appoint "the only Jew in the world who doesn't know a thing about money." *Fortune* joined the chorus of nay-sayers by questioning the appointment of the "son of a philanthropist" who had "spent most of his life farming."

[79] Michael Beschloss, *The Conquerors: Roosevelt, Truman and the Destruction of Hitler's Germany, 1941-1945* (Simon & Schuster, New York, 2002), p. 95-96.

[80] Ibid., p. 103.

[81] Frank Knox, who had been appointed by FDR to be the moderator of the committee, absented himself from the first day's discussions and never again showed up.

[82] Henry L. Stimson, *On Active Service in Peace and War* (Harper, New York, 1948), p. 173. The Morgenthau Plan represented a major retreat from the Atlantic Charter solemnly signed by Roosevelt and Churchill three years earlier. That document had stated publicly—and ostentatiously—that the U.S. and the U.K. would "endeavor... to further the enjoyment by all States, great or small, victor or vanquished, or access, on equal terms, to the trade and to the raw materials of the world which are needed for their economic prosperity."

[83] Ibid., p. 571-572. Stimson might also have mentioned that the in the late 1880s and into the next century, during the great railroad-building boom in Canada and the United States, both countries were major importers of products from Krupp, Germany's giant steelmaker. Krupp's proprietary crucible steelmaking process for seamless railway wheels was superior to everything on the market. In the U.S. nine major railroads were equipping their cars with Krupp wheels and were also using Krupp rails. In 1880, E. H. Harriman placed an order for 25,000 tons of 80-pound rails for the Southern Pacific, a year's supply.

[84] Blum, p. 103.

[85] The USAAF's mean wartime strength was one-fourth of the total army, and aircrew ran almost the same risks as others in the army of being killed, suffering 52,173 of the 291,557 battle deaths inflicted on all Americans during the war. Airmen were more likely to be captured by the enemy and they ran a much greater chance of going missing in action (MIA) and later declared dead (KIA). Moreover, 35,946 airmen died in noncombat situations, about 43 percent of all such deaths in the army. In 1943 alone, for example, 850 airmen died in 298 B-24 training accidents in the U.S., leaving the survivors "scared to death of their airplanes." In fact, the B-24 was more difficult to fly than the more docile B-17. Medical statisticians studied the fate of 2,051 Eighth Air Force (European theater) personnel. Only 559 (26.8 percent) completed twenty-five missions. On average, nearly 4 percent of the forces were KIA or MIA on each mission. Michael S. Sherry, *The Rise of American Air Power: The Creation of Armageddon* (Yale University Press, New Haven CT, 1987), p. 204-205.

[86] World War II's USSBS was the second U.S. post-war study to sum up the results of bombing. At the end of The Great War, Colonel Edgar S. Gorrell, Assistant Chief of Staff of the U.S. Air Service, developed a series of "lessons learned" from American flyers and then expanded the survey to include the results of British and French bombing of Germany. That survey team, consisting of only twelve Army personnel, analyzed the "material and morale effects" of bombing of German cities and factories as well as estimates of German costs of defensive efforts. Among the team's superficial conclusions: "It is certain that air raids had a tremendous effect on the morale of the entire people.... The enormous expense of maintaining balloon barrages, home defense flights, and anti-aircraft artillery must be an indication that the material was needed and that the popular clamor for protection was great."

[87] Galbraith, at six feet, six inches, was too tall to be drafted into the military.

[88] *United States Strategic Bombing Survey,* vol. 31 (Washington, Government Printing Office, 1945-1947) p. 2.

[89] Ibid., Overall Report, p. 107.

[90] Ibid., Overall Report, p. 108.

[91] Ibid., Overall Report, p. 95.

[92] John Kenneth Galbraith, *A Life in Our Times* (Houghton Mifflin Company, Boston, 1981), p. 76.

[93] Guido R. Perera, *Leaves From My Book of Life, Vol. II* (Privately Printed, Boston, 1975), p. 135.

[94] The Police President of Hamburg, *S.S.-Generalmajor* Kehrl, wrote a secret report to Adolf Hitler to describe [with understandable difficulty] what had taken place in his city. "As the result of the confluence of a number of fires, the air is heated to such an extent that in consequence of its reduced

specific gravity a violent updraft occurs which causes great suction of the surrounding air radiating from the center of the fire.... The suction of the fire storm in the larger of these area fire zones had the effect of attracting the already overheated air in smaller area fire zones.... One effect of this phenomenon was that the fires in smaller fire zones was fanned as by a bellows as the central suction of the biggest and fiercest fire causes increased and accelerated attraction of the surrounding masses of fresh air. In this way all the area fires became united in one vast fire."

[95] Perera, p. 111.

[96] David MacIsaac, *Strategic Bombing in World War II—The Story of the United States Strategic Bombing Survey* (Garland Publishing Company, New York, 1976), p. 141-142.

[97] John W. Dower, *War Without Mercy: Race & Power in the Pacific War* (Pantheon Books, New York, 1986), p. 132-134.

[98] Kai Bird and Lawrence Lifschultz, editors, *Hiroshima's* Shadow (The Pamphleteer's Press, Stony Creek CT, 1998), p. 126-127.

[99] Galbraith, p. 232.

[100] *USSBS*, Vol. 31, p. 61.

[101] Ibid., p. 72.

[102] Galbraith, p. 80.

[103] Ibid., p. 232.

[104] Ibid., p. 233.

[105] Sledge, E. B., *With The Old Breed at Peleliu and Okinawa* (Presidio Press, Novato CA, 1981), p. 116-117.

[106] Ibid., p. 260.

[107] Ibid., p. 253.

[108] Excerpt from the press statement by General H.H. Arnold regarding the second attack on Schweinfurt, October 14, 1943. *The New York Times*, October 16, 1943.

[109] Stephen L. McFarland, *America's Pursuit of Precision Bombing, 1919-1945* (Smithsonian Institution Press, Washington).

[110] Stewart Halsey Ross, *How Roosevelt Failed America in World War II* (McFarland & Company, Inc. Publishers, Jefferson NC, 2006), p. 39.

[111] Ibid., p. 44.

[112] Ibid., p. 45.

[113] Ibid., p. 38.

[114] Ibid., p. 49.

[115] Ibid., p. 51.

[116] Charles A. Lindbergh, *The Wartime Journals of Charles A. Lindbergh* (Harcourt Brace Jovanovich, Inc., New York, 1970), p. 567.

[117] Ibid.

[118] Ibid., p. 568.

[119] Ibid., p. 775.

[120] Ibid., p. 853.

[121] Ibid., p. 856.

[122] Ibid., p. 859.

[123] Ibid., p. 879-880.

[124] Ibid., p. 882-883.

[125] Ibid., p. 902-903.

[126] Ibid., p. 919.

[127] Ibid., p. 923 The author was a teenager in 1945 when his brother-in-law-to-be returned from the Pacific. "He had been stationed on Tinian as a medical technician at a Base Hospital and had access to an autoclave. He said he had a souvenir for me as he upended his barracks bag. Out rolled a Japanese skull."

Chapter VII:

The Korean War

"If World War II provided a testing ground for massive area bombing, for widespread use of incendiary devices including napalm, and for nuclear weapons, the Korean War offered new opportunities for refinement: aerial terrorism was pushed to new levels. In three months of 1951 alone, the USAF used B-52s to systematically destroy every significant North Korean city and town, not only slaughtering hundreds of thousands of defenseless civilians but creating widespread homelessness, starvation, disease, and other miseries... By the end of the war the Korean death toll (North and South) reached nearly three million, mostly from U.S. aerial bombardments."[1]

WILLIAM MANCHESTER WROTE in his magisterial biography of Douglas MacArthur that while America's leaders,

"...had long been aware of the [Korean] peninsula, neither they nor their allies knew quite what to do with it."[2]

At Cairo in 1943 the Big Four (U.S., Great Britain, Soviet Union, and Nationalist China) pledged Korea's independence "in due course." At the two subsequent high-level meetings of the Allies, Yalta and Potsdam, only vague declarations were made regarding steps leading to Korea's autonomy. That's where matters stood in August 1945. Until then, the U.S. military regarded the Japanese armies in their colony of Manchuria as tough adversaries. Why not leave the problem—and the casualties—to the Red Army? Besides, the State Department had adopted the stance that Korea was of no long-term strategic interest to the United States.

Then came the two atomic bombs on Japan, on August 6 and 9, ending the war abruptly. The Red Army just as suddenly swept through Manchuria and struck south across the Yalu River, marching right into Korea proper. Literally overnight Washington changed its mind about the desirability of denying at least a part of Korea to the Soviets. The United States decided it should participate in the occupation of Korea. Two members of what was called the State-War-Navy Coordinating Committee, after poring over a large-scale wall map of the Far East, concluded that the 38th Parallel running east/west, pretty much divided the country in half. The line made no intrinsic sense, of course. It sundered the interdependent halves of the Korean economy, the more industrial north, with its 10 million residents, from the more agricultural south, population 20 million.

To the likely relief of the committee, the Soviets accepted the 38th Parallel as the southern limit of their advance. Almost a month before the first U.S. troops landed in South Korea, the Red Army reached the border of the new divide—and stopped, honoring their agreement. The Chinese Communists were in the last stages of pushing Chiang Kai-shek's army off the mainland and onto the offshore island of Formosa. The fates and geographical boundaries of more significant nations also were being decided, and Korea counted for little in the scheme of things.

The hastily-drawn line immediately took on all the characteristics of a political divide, angering the two populations. The two sides quickly drew apart and have remained so ever since. Only two weeks after his troops landed in Korea on September 8, 1945, Lieutenant General John R. Hodge sent a message to the Supreme Commander Allied Powers Douglas MacArthur in Tokyo:

"Dissatisfaction with the division of the country grows."[3]

In the North, the Russians established the Democratic People's Republic of Korea with its capital in Pyongyang, and installed Kim Il-sung as premier. In the South, Syngman Rhee, who had already become a U.S. client, announced the formation of the Republic of Korea. The third player in the tragic drama soon to unfold was Douglas MacArthur.

Kim Il-sung, from his youth, was active in Marxist organizations, joining various anti-Japanese guerrilla groups in northern China. In 1931 he joined the Communist Party of China. In September 1945, when he returned to Korea with Soviet forces, he was installed as head of the Provisional People's Committee. He was not yet head of the Communist Party, whose headquarters were in Seoul, in the U.S.-occupied south. A principal accomplishment of Kim as premier was his creation of a professional army, the North Korean People's Army, formed from guerrillas and former soldiers who had gained combat experience in battles against the Japanese and later the Nationalist Chinese. Using Soviet advisers and equipment, Kim built a large army skilled in infiltration tactics and guerrilla warfare. Before the start of the Korean War, Stalin equipped the NKPA with modern tanks, artillery, trucks, and small arms. Kim also formed a small air force, at first equipped with ex-Soviet propeller-driven fighter and attack aircraft. Later, North Korean pilot candidates went to secret bases in the Soviet Union and China to train in MiG-15 turbojets. At the Sixth Party Congress in 1980, Kim publicly designated his son, Kim Jong-il as his successor.

Syngman Rhee was 70 years old when Americans in Seoul were casting around for a prominent exile to head a new government in the South. Rhee had impeccable credentials for the role planned for him by the United States. He was a veteran anti-government troublemaker and had been jailed for his political activities at the turn of the century. When released in 1904 he went to the United States where he earned an M.A. at Harvard and a Ph.D. at Princeton. He returned to Korea in 1910, which by then had been annexed by Japan. Again Rhee was driven out of the country for his political meddling. He left for China in 1912 and in 1919 was elected president of the Provisional Government in Shanghai. He held this post until 1925 when he was impeached for his misuse of his authority. Rhee once again settled in the United States. He remained there for the next 35 years, ceaselessly lobbying for American support for Korean independence. After Korea was liberated from Japan, Rhee quickly returned to Seoul, ahead of other independence leaders, and was named by U.S. occupation authorities to head the new Korean Government. In 1948, he was formally elected the first president of the Republic of Korea.

Like Rhee, Douglas MacArthur had his best years behind him—he was also 70 years old when President Harry Truman named him Supreme Commander Allied Powers at the outbreak of the war. MacArthur was then living in palatial splendor in a penthouse atop Tokyo's fanciest hotel as *shogun* of the defeated Japanese. MacArthur's biography glittered with accomplishments, his peregrinations matching almost stride-by-stride American military adventures during his lifetime. He graduated first in his class from the U.S. Military Academy in 1903. Over the next fourteen years, he served in the Philippines and Panama, and participated in the U.S. occupation of Veracruz, Mexico. During the Great War he commanded the Rainbow Division in France and then became Superintendent of West Point. By 1930, MacArthur was Chief of Staff of the U.S. Army. In 1935 he was back in the Philippines, charged with building an army for that multi-island nation. MacArthur then retired from the U.S. Army in 1937 to accept an appointment as Field Marshall of the tiny Philippine Army from President Manuel Quezon. His command consisted of 4,000 Filipino regulars, for which he received $33,000 a year in salary and expenses. With his U.S. Army pension, MacArthur was then the highest-paid military officer in the world. Among his assistants was Colonel Dwight D. Eisenhower. Years later, when he was asked if he had known MacArthur, Eisenhower replied, only half-jokingly:

> "Know him? I studied dramatics under him for five years in Washington and four in Manila."[4]

In July 1941, President Roosevelt recalled him to active duty as a major general and Commander of U.S. Army Forces in the Far East. He was in Manila when World War II broke out. In March 1942, as the Japanese advanced down the Bataan Peninsula, he was evacuated to Australia, supposedly at the order of the president.[5] Soon after he left, U.S. and Filipino troops were overrun by the Japanese. General "Vinegar" Joe Stillwell, who was MacArthur's replacement, surrendered.

Promoted to five-star rank in 1944 by Truman, MacArthur directed the liberation of the Philippines and served as a joint commander in the Pacific with Admiral Chester Nimitz. In August 1945, aboard the battleship *Missouri* in Tokyo harbor, it was MacArthur who presided over the formal surrender ceremonies with Japan. During the next five years, headquartered in Tokyo, he oversaw the demilitarization of Japan and successfully reformed its political and economic life. In June 1950, MacArthur was put in charge of United Nations' forces to repel North Korean and Chinese invaders. His new title, added to Supreme Commander of the Allied Powers (SCAP), was Commander in Chief Far East. Eleven months later, his anti-administration views coupled with his dangerous go-it-alone military decisions, often at odds with the president's policies, led to Truman's relieving him of his two commands.[6] He returned to the United States a hero. After an abortive run for the presidency in 1951-1952, he spent the remainder of his life as an elder statesman and a supporter of far-right causes, again in a penthouse, this time in Manhattan's prestigious Waldorf Astoria.

> *"We went into Korea with a very poor army, and came out with a pretty good one*
> *We went into Vietnam with a pretty good army, and came out with a terrible one."*[7]

WITHOUT WARNING, THE KOREAN WAR ERUPTED at first light on June 25, 1950, when the North Korean People's Army (NKPA) attacked south across the 38th Parallel. It was no ordinary incursion at a single point by a company-size group of infantrymen that had been commonplace until then; it was a powerful invasion force of some 90,000 foot-soldiers across a broad front supported by 150 Russian-made T-34 tanks. It remains dictum in nearly every U.S. history book that the North invaded the South without provocation and was aided and abetted by an imperialistic Soviet Union.[8]

In June 1950, John Foster Dulles met with Syngman Rhee and told the South Korean president "if he was ready to attack the communist North, the U.S. would lend help, through the UN.... He advised Rhee... to persuade the world that the ROK was attacked first." A few days later, ROK troops launched an attack into North Korea. When the North counterattacked, this was called an invasion and "the first step in Soviet plans for world domination" ... Resulting civilian death toll: three million. (http://coat.ncf.ca/articles/links/how_to_start_a_war.htm)

How good were the NKPA soldiers? By 1950, the North Korean leadership had molded and organized its army into a formidable offensive war machine modeled on a Soviet mechanized force. It was strengthened by an influx of Korean veterans who had served with Mao Tse Tung's People's Liberation Army (PLA) in China since the 1930s.

How good were the ROK soldiers? They were neither skillfully led nor well-trained nor particularly well-armed despite their patron's training cadres and weapons. On first contact with the enemy in early infantry actions, many promptly deserted to the North or shed their uniforms and became instant civilians. Many more simply dropped their weapons and fled to the rear in disorganized panic.

More importantly, how good were the American infantrymen, who would bear the brunt of the fighting on the ground for 37 months? At the start, they were hastily thrown together from the four Army divisions on garrison duty in Japan and reconstituted in Korea as the U.S. Eighth Army. These GIs had long forgotten the basic infantry skills that had been drilled into them back in the States. Many had not even fired their M-1s with live ammunition during their tours of duty in Japan. They had grown fat and sloppy, and were more familiar with the brothels that lined their bases than with fundamental soldiering. Significantly, of the enlisted men who first fought in Korea, almost half were ranked within the army's two lowest intelligence classifications, and tested below what the army normally considered acceptable. Their officers, too, were deficient, right up to their commanding general.

By most measures the U.S. Eighth was a rotten army. In a few months, this army would be engaged in life-and-death struggles with highly motivated, seasoned Chinese divisions who were fighting to protect their homeland. These *Chicoms*, as MacArthur would disdainfully call them, with no air support, little artillery, and entirely on foot, except for some few horse-mounted riflemen, would engage the soldiers and Marines of the country that boasted the most expensive military in world history—and hold them to a draw.

Before the Chinese engaged the Americans, a patriotic pamphlet was distributed to the troops of the Ninth Army Group, written by one of General Sung's propaganda officers.

> Soon we will meet the American Marines in battle. We will destroy them. When they are defeated, the enemy will collapse and our country will be free from the threat of aggression. Kill these Marines as you would snakes in your homes![9]

In another pamphlet distributed on November 20, *Primary Conclusions of Battle Experience at Unsan*, the Chinese 66th Army had nothing good to say about the U.S. 8th Cavalry Regiment. This indictment of American soldiers makes interesting reading to a layman; one wonders how the top brass reacted to it.

> American soldiers, when cut off from the rear, abandon all their heavy weapons, leaving them all over the place, and play opossum. Their infantrymen are weak, afraid to die, and haven't the courage to attack or defend. They depend on their planes, tanks, and artillery. At the same time, they are afraid of our firepower. They must have proper terrain and good weather to transport their great amount of equipment. They can operate rapidly along good highways and flat country; not in hill country. They specialize in day fighting. They are not familiar with night fighting or hand-to-hand combat. They are afraid of our big knives and grenades; also of our courageous attacks, regular combat, and infiltration. If defeated, they have no orderly formations. Without the use of their mortars, they become completely lost... and become dazed and demoralized. They are afraid when the rear is cut off. When transportation comes to a standstill, the infantry loses the will to fight.[10]

It wasn't only the enemy who scorned American troops. After the winter battles in 1950, British General Leslie Mansergh visited Korea and sent a detailed, secret and altogether devastating appraisal to his Chiefs of Staff in London about the Americans.

> I doubt whether any British think that the war in Korea will be brought to a successful conclusion. The reason for this is primarily because of the American lack of determination and their inability, up to the time of my visit, to stand and fight. Most Americans sooner or later bring the conversation around to an expression of the view that the United Nations ought to quit Korea.... I would judge the American morale as low, and in some units thoroughly bad.[11]

He pointed out [what the Army leadership already knew, but couldn't do much about] that many Americans in uniform had joined in peacetime to get a low-cost education [the GI Bill] and had never expected to get shot at. Mansergh was unrelenting in his pummeling of the U.S. Army and the Pentagon.

> Their training is quite unsuited to that type of country or war and, in spite of lessons learnt, they will not get clear of their vehicles.... Their rations, supplies, and welfare stores are on such a scale as to be comic if they were not such a serious handicap to battle. They have never studied or been taught defense. They do not like holding defensive positions. They have been trained for very rapid withdrawals. Americans do not understand infiltration and feel naked when anybody threatens their flank or rear.[12]

Mansergh had good words for American artillery and expressed respect for the performance of the Marines, but he was acidly critical of the Eighth Army's staff work. They did not understand the importance of reconnoitering ground and invariably overestimated the number of enemy facing them. He wrote, laughingly to readers back in London:

> "At night, main headquarters blazed like gin palaces. Roadblocks, car parks, dumps, etc. were as crowded as Hampstead Heath on bank holiday."[13]

That December the military assistant to the British Ambassador recorded that U.S. Army officers told him quite openly that it was sometimes useless ordering their troops to attack, because they simply wouldn't go. In sum, their British counterparts' attitude toward the American infantry, according to Brigadier Basil Coad, Commander of the British 27th Brigade, was largely one of contempt.

Max Hastings, the well-respected English historian, tried to be fair, commenting that it was desirable to discount somewhat skepticism of one nation towards another's methods of making war. He wrote that throughout the 20th century, there was jealousy in the British Army of the enormous resources available to the Americans.

> A problem that was already familiar from World War II reasserted itself in Korea, as it would again in Vietnam: the disproportionately low percentage of the nation's best manhood that served the infantry regiments of the United States.[14]

> "Stanley Weintraub [author of MacArthur's War] shattered the graven image of MacArthur as the great American warrior of his era. The man Harry Truman lampooned as 'God's right-hand man' emerges as a supreme windbag well past his prime, a myopic commander whose strategic priority was public relations and who never spent so much as one night in Korea." James Tobin, author of Ernie Pyle's War.

THE FIRST CONTACT between NKPA and U.S. troops took place early in the morning of July 5, 1950, when Lieutenant Colonel Charles Smith and his 24th Infantry Division—two infantry companies and an artillery battery, comprised of 540-men—spotted eight T-34 tanks clanking down a main road from the north toward their dug-in position atop a hill. Smith's artillery took them under fire but they had no armor-piercing rounds and their ordinary high-explosive rounds were useless against such armor. Equally ineffectual were their obsolete 2.36-inch bazookas: the rockets merely bouncing off the armor. The North Korean tankers responded with their 85mm cannons and machine guns, literally blowing Smith's men out of their path and inflicting the war's first casualties on the out-gunned Americans.

These first tanks were followed by an attack by NKPA infantry that skillfully fanned out from the road. Smith ordered a pullback which turned into a rout, as men dropped their rifles, helmets and cartridge belts, abandoned the howitzers and fled cross-country through the muck of rice paddies and over hills.

In Japan, one officer remembered distinctly being told that the North Koreans would run as soon as they saw the Americans. A U.S. Army historian, chauvinistic as nearly all of his ilk and obviously far behind the front lines, later referred to the North Koreans as "trained monkeys." Hanson Baldwin, veteran *New York Times* military reporter, who should have known better, called them "an army of barbarians," and the "most primitive of peoples." MacArthur's chief of intelligence, Major General Charles Willoughby foolishly called them "half-men with blank faces."[15] One is tempted to ask how it was possible to so acutely differentiate Koreans living north of a just-drawn boundary from Koreans south of the same line?

These statements were a mix of propaganda clap-trap and misplaced American arrogance, always in plentiful supply within U.S. ranks. GIs would find out soon enough for themselves that these so-called anthropoids with vacant faces were part of a formidable army, well trained and well led. It was U.S. soldiers who had the blank faces, the vacant-eyed survivors from the first weeks' battles, in which as many as 3,000 GIs were left dead, wounded, captured, or missing.

ON THE MORNING OF JULY 26, the 2nd Battalion, 7th Cavalry Regiment of the U.S. Eighth Army had hiked to within a mile or so of the village of Hwangan. Nearby was a double-arched concrete railroad bridge, built by the Japanese during their occupation, which carried the main line over a shallow stream. A path through the archway led to a cluster of mud huts a few hundred yards away. This was the tiny hamlet of No Gun Ri, a name that signified "forest" and "deer," both of which had long since disappeared.

The 7th Cavalry was Lieutenant Colonel George Armstrong Custer's cavalry that was massacred in the famous Battle of the Little Bighorn by a Lakota-Cheyenne combined force in June 1876. The present-day 7th Calvary was known as the *Garryowens,* from the quick-march song that Custer liked so well.

> He first had it played in 1868 to launch the regiment's attack on a Cheyenne Indian encampment on the Washita River in Oklahoma. President Theodore Roosevelt [far more a militarist than a champion of conservation!] later called it 'the finest military march in the world.' But to the natives of the American Plains it was 'devil's music.'[16]

As part of their indoctrination some 80 years later, green recruits in the 7th Division in Japan, most of them teenagers, were sent to the movies to watch swashbuckler Errol Flynn as Custer, famously cut down in *They Died with Their Boots On*. The newcomers were treated to a more formal dose of homegrown propaganda in a pamphlet—for those who could read—that recounted the regiment's history, including exploits as "Indian fighters" in the Philippines. These pseudo-infantrymen in Tokyo had been guards and manned mostly trivial posts throughout the city. Their most important post was the ornate entrance of the Dai-Ichi insurance company headquarters building. That was where General MacArthur was chauffeured every morning in his black Cadillac, and where he ruled Japan from a sixth-floor office.

For the conquerors in occupied Japan, officers and enlisted men alike, life bordered on the aristocratic. At a time when millions of Japanese were homeless, the U.S. occupiers requisitioned hundreds of the best homes in Tokyo for officers and high-ranking enlisted men. Servants of every kind were cheap and readily available. Train travel was free. The PX's were full of American goods at bargain prices and GIs bought these products and resold them profitably in a flourishing black market. GIs could pick out a pretty Japanese concubine who would double as housekeeper and cook—and move together into a rental unit for four or five cartons of sought-after American cigarettes a month.

THE OUT-OF-SHAPE, green-as-grass *Garryowens* that morning in late July 1950—less than 48 hours at the front—were exhausted, hungry, and also unsure of what to do next. At 10AM, their officers received a radio message from division headquarters. The order dealt with refugees and how they should be gathered together for organized movement south. But it was the first fourteen words that counted the most:

> "No —repeat no—refugees will be permitted to cross battle lines at any time."

At midday, over their M-1 and BAR gunsights, the *Garryowens* could make out a large group of people, women and children mostly, all clad in white, making their way toward them. Machine-gunners and mortar crews readied their weapons. These ill-prepared teenagers weren't ready for such a kind of war, in a strange land, among alien people. But they did know enough to obey orders, and orders were given to open fire.

Author Charles J. Hanley selected one GI as an example, PFC Buddy Wenzel, who recalled:

> "Word came through the line, open fire on them. They were running toward us and we opened fire. We understood that we were fighting for these people, but we had orders to fire on them and we did."[17]

For another *Garryowen*, what stuck in his memory was:

> "...the distant sight of a "fountain" of white clothing, of refugees' bodies splashing into the air with the impact of shells. 'Seeing that mortar fire coming in on that mass of people was very hard to take.' Our orders were not to let any refugees through any line."[18]

Not every member of the 660-man 2nd Battalion saw—or chose to remember—the "fountain". Selective memories, the disappearance of records, most of all the reluctance of veterans to talk about the gruesome happenings that day, all contributed to the inconsistencies of the American version of the killings at No Gun Ri.

> "In the end, however, the soldiers' memories at No Gun Ri fit neatly with those of the Korean survivors into a mosaic of wholesale death whose backdrop, whose official design, none forgot."[19]

The U.S. Air Force got its licks in, too. Their F-80 *Starfire* jets flew low, in groups of three, strafing and bombing and then strafing again. They had been called in to attack North Korean artillery and tanks some miles from the No Gun Ri trestle. The GIs who observed the attacks said there was nothing that looked like cannons or armored vehicles among the refugees; others saw the attacks on the refugees as purposeful. In fact, the attacks dovetailed precisely with Air Force policy, which was to strafe all civilian refugee parties that were approaching U.S. positions. This policy also fit in neatly with instructions that were given to fighter pilots flying off the Navy carrier *Valley Forge*. In an Action Summary for July 25, pilots reported strafing a group of

> "...people dressed in white... in accordance with information received from the Army that groups of more than eight to ten people were troops, and were to be attacked."[20]

The butchery carried over to the next day. Survivors and the wounded of the previous day's shootings and strafing, had either made their own way to what appeared to be a safe haven, the two tunnels beneath the trestle—or were driven there by the *Garryowens*. Inside, it was stifling hot and the wounded were desperate for water. Anyone who ventured out to bring back water, however, became the target of concentrated gunfire. There were some 300 villagers inside by their own estimate, huddled together—the dead, the dying, those still alive. U.S. soldiers sprayed unaimed gunfire into both ends of the underpasses. Mortar and artillery rounds pounded the entrances.

> "Precise numbers would never be determined, but decades later survivors compiled a list of the names of some 200 dead or missing. They estimated that actually up to 400 were killed—100 in the strafing and 300 under and around the trestle. Possibly 200 escaped during the initial chaos."[21]

What became known as the massacre at "The Bridge on No Gun Ri" was 7th Cavalry's first confrontation with "gooks." In that encounter, none had fought back and no Americans were killed. In the weeks and months ahead well-armed North Koreans and their Chinese allies—"gooks" all—would not only fight back, they would skillfully take the fight to the Americans.

> *"What had been at stake in the Korean War, and it was to hang over subsequent wars in Asia, was the ability to bear a cost in human life, the ability of an Asian nation to match the technological superiority of the West with the ability to pay the cost in manpower."*[22]

BY THE END OF JULY, all Eighth Army and ROK units were "haulin' ass", a new euphemism less negative than "buggin' out", in the face of concerted North Korean attacks. The Marines would use another synonym in December when they retreated from the Chosin Reservoir, in keeping with their zealously guarded image of heroism—"breakout". All U.S. troops were pulling back for the safety of a new defensive line in the far southeastern quadrant of the peninsula, centered on the port city of Pusan, some 200 miles south of the 38th Parallel. These troops were joined by hundreds of thousands of refugees fleeing to the same refuge. The GIs blew up all the bridges behind them, often filled with refugees, and burned to the ground every dwelling they came across, leaving a scorched-earth swath of destruction behind them. The defensive line became known as the Pusan Perimeter.

The six-week siege of Pusan began officially on July 31, when the last remnants of the Eighth Army crossed the Nakong River. The order of the day to his troops from General Walton Walker was a ringing call to stand fast.

> There will be no more retreating, withdrawal, readjustment of lines or whatever you call it. There are no lines behind which we can retreat. This is not going to be a Dunkirk or Bataan. We must fight to the end. We must fight as a team. If some of us die, we will die fighting together.[23]

American troops dug in on the Pusan Perimeter hung on as best they could amid the continuous nighttime onslaughts of bugle-blowing Communist troops. The suicidal recklessness of the NKPA soldiers gave the defenders the sense they were facing an Asian horde with limitless reserves of manpower. It was a measure of the psychological success the Communists had achieved at that time, that most Americans would have been disbelieving had they been told that the UN forces by then outnumbered the North Koreans significantly, and outgunned them overwhelmingly.

By September, the North Koreans were beginning to run out of steam. In ten weeks of offensive war, they had lost thousands of men. Their supply lines, never stout, were then stretched thin as their armies deployed so far south of the 38th Parallel. On every sector of the front, the aggressiveness that had been the hallmark of the NKPA until that time was in noticeable decline. Their big attacks had become instead probing thrusts seeking weak points in the defensive line. Kim Il-sung's regiments could only muster 70,000 men, against a total of about twice as many in Walker's command inside the Pusan Perimeter, which resembled a 4,000-square-mile beachhead.

EUSAK, the Eighth United States Army in Korea, was hurting too, licking its wounds behind a defensive line of questionable strength. U.S. casualties up to that time were 4,280 killed in action, 12,337 wounded, and 2,508 missing or known to have been captured. But the Allies still maintained absolute command of the air and tremendous superiority in artillery. Historian Hastings gave unqualified credit to General Walker for holding the Pusan Perimeter. He wrote that Walker was

> ...The fiercely energetic little Texan who had made their survival possible...would be remembered for bringing to the battle of the Pusan Perimeter the qualities that made its survival possible: ruthless dynamism, speed of response, dogged determination. He was leading one of the least professional, least motivated armies America had ever put into the field.[24]

ON SEPTEMBER 15, the whole complexion of the war changed. That day marked MacArthur's long-planned amphibious landing at the port city of Inchon, on the west coast some 50 miles south of the 38th Parallel and 25 miles from Seoul. It would become the "end run" that would free up the Eighth Army in the east. The landing force consisted of a newly formed joint Marine-Army X Corps, with a new commander, Army General Edward L. Almond. The landing surprised the enemy and there were few U.S. casualties: 21 dead, 174 wounded. The port of Inchon was again in U.S. hands. By the next morning, 18,000 American troops were ashore, along with supplies and tanks. The powerful invasion force then struck out for its second objective, the capture of Seoul. The plan then called for X Corps to then drive east across the Korean peninsula, trapping the NKPA to the south and linking up with EUSAK.

Seoul was recaptured either on September 25, according to Douglas MacArthur who issued a press statement from Tokyo to that effect that day—or three days later when the house-to-house fighting ceased. An Associated Press correspondent wrote that if the city had been liberated, the remaining North Koreans in the city did not know it. Douglas MacArthur never let reality deter him from public posturing. The "truth" to him was always what he said it was!

General Walker's planned breakout at Pusan, to coincide with X Corps' invasion, called for a thrust up the same central axis the North Koreans had used in their drive south. EUSAK had been revitalized by an influx by fresh troops from the United States and new equipment. Delayed initially by bad weather that grounded the Air Force, once underway the reenergized Eighth Army was surprised to find a new enemy, one that was abandoning its equipment and fleeing—so fast, they left behind their wet laundry hanging on bushes to dry and hot food in mess halls. Many discarded their uniforms to blend in with the local population or hiked north to disappear into the North Korean countryside to form guerrilla bands. In one notable dash, the 1st Cavalry Division advanced 55 miles in three days.[25]

The NKPA was clearly on the run. Should U.S. forces pursue the North Koreans across the 38th Parallel? In this instance, Secretary of State Dean Acheson and Douglas MacArthur agreed; to require commanders in the field to break contact with a retreating enemy and assume a defensive stance once they reached the frontier was considered ridiculous. Ominously, the headlong rush north resulted in a dangerous two-pronged offensive through the trackless Taebaek Mountains. MacArthur had carelessly—or was it arrogantly—laid the foundation for a military catastrophe by splitting his forces.

VII. The Korean War

On the 30th, Chou En-lai, China's multi-lingual foreign minister, broadcast a warning that the Peking regime would not "supinely tolerate" a crossing of the parallel by American troops. The next day, at Acheson's suggestion, MacArthur replied in kind, demanding the surrender of the NKPA.

In response, Chou upped the ante, telling the Indian ambassador to Peking who served as an intermediary to Washington, that China would send its troops to the border to defend North Korea if U.S. troops crossed the parallel. Truman concluded that Chou's message was a bluff, and called it an attempt to blackmail the United Nations.

Five days later, as U.S. Army and Marine troops were approaching the 38th Parallel, MacArthur again appealed to Kim Il sung to capitulate. Chou's reply was that while

> "the Chinese people loved peace, his nation could not stand idly by."

That night Mao's divisions began to cross the Yalu River into North Korea. The following morning, the first ROK troops entered Wonsan; X Corps was water-lifted to reinforce them, and the Eighth Army was about to capture Pyongyang, the North Korean capital. Chou continued to express his concern through every communication channel available, as did Vyacheslav Molotov, the Soviet foreign minister. He had been provoked: on October 9, when two F-80s strafed a Soviet air base near Vladivostok, more than 60 miles inside Russia.

Wonsan — before and after

HARRY TRUMAN MET WITH DOUGLAS MACARTHUR at Wake Island [See Appendix] on October 15 at the same time as American troops rumbled across the 38th Parallel. It was the first time the two had met. Manchester wrote that Truman's motive in

> "...flying two-thirds of the way around the world for less than two hours with MacArthur was mysterious and is still puzzling."[26]

Chinese troops were about to engage U.S. soldiers for the first time, but the two principal conferees on Wake did not know this. Truman wrote in his memoirs that he just wanted to talk to the general. If that's all Truman wanted to do, there were state-of-the-art communications in the White House and the Dai Ichi in Tokyo that could allow the two to talk confidentially. The SCAP's staff was certain the purpose was strictly political: to dramatize a summit meeting in the press. Truman's popularity was dropping and the Congressional elections were just three weeks away. A photo-op of a beaming Truman standing next to a resolute MacArthur would play well among the electorate.

As Supreme Commander Allied Powers, MacArthur arrived in his shiny new SCAP aircraft (a Lockheed *Constellation*) several hours before Truman, and was on the tarmac at 6AM, waiting for the *Independence* (a Douglas *DC-6*) to touch down. Truman was nattily attired as always—he was, it should be remembered, a former haberdasher—with his trademark broad-brimmed fedora on his head. In stark contrast, MacArthur wore a battered campaign cap rakishly cocked; some would call the cap purposefully smudged. What bothered Truman's entourage more, he wore no tie and his khaki shirt was open at the neck. Worse, the general did not salute his commander-in-chief as protocol demanded; instead he firmly grabbed Truman's upper right arm with his left, pulled him forward, and vigorously pumped his hand. That was what MacArthur called his "number-one handshake" his gigantic egotism required him always to be top-dog even when matched against the President of the United States.

While their aides readied a conference room in the island's cinder-block main building for the meeting of all attendees, the two leaders were driven to a Quonset hut, where they spent about an hour alone. Neither took notes but one subject that was discussed was the question of the likelihood of China entering the war. The CIA had previously told the president that Chinese involvement was unlikely. MacArthur acknowledged to the president that the Chinese had some 300,000 troops in Manchuria, with about 125,000 men camped out north of the Yalu River. But the Chinese had no air force, MacArthur reminded Truman. If the Chinese tried to cross the border and move south, MacArthur overconfidently told Truman his Far East Air Force (FEAF) would destroy them.

The two then adjourned to the conference room. Truman and MacArthur sat next to one another at a long table, with MacArthur's staff to Truman's right and the president's advisers to MacArthur's left. This general conference lasted about two hours and covered such subjects as Korean rehabilitation, new elections in Korea; and the chances of Chinese and Soviet intervention—"remote," all agreed. It was decided that both parties would leave before lunch, Truman for a stopover at Pearl Harbor and MacArthur back to Tokyo. Truman was all smiles as he boarded *Independence*, which was airborne at 11:35AM. MacArthur left for Tokyo soon after, seething for all to see. He considered himself and his command diminished by the vigorous questioning by a group of newspapermen for whom he had only contempt.

Biographer Manchester was scathingly critical of the place, the time, and of the principal conferees, pulling no punches in his summary.

> The chief problem at Wake was the very concept of the conference. It was absurd. Here were two exhausted, elderly [call them *old!*] men meeting briefly on a remote island in the middle of the world's largest ocean. Neither was in shape to deal with momentous issues. The General was three time zones away from the Dai Ichi; the President seven time zones away from the White House. They had never met before, and in their fatigue their social antennae were understandably blunted.[27]

Manchester went further, castigating Truman that he should have looked to advisers in the CIA and State Department, not to a field commander, for guidance in what was a political matter.

> "It never occurred to them that the Chinese would not permit an alien army 'to seize the hilt of the Korean dagger'.... The meeting had been a dreadful idea. Many men would pay for it with their lives."[28]

CHINA'S ENTRY INTO THE WAR has been called:

> …an extraordinary achievement of modern warfare. Between October 13 and 25, the intelligence staffs of MacArthur's armies failed to discern the slightest evidence of the movement of 130,000 soldiers and porters. A combination of superb fieldcraft and camouflage by the Chinese, and their lack of use of wireless traffic, mechanized activity, supply dumps, blinded the UN Command to what was taking place on its front. Above all, the generals were not looking for anything of this sort. They had persuaded themselves that the war was all but over.[29]

On the evening of November 1, the troops of G Company, 8th Cavalry, wondered what was happening to a patrol of F Company which had reported by radio it was under attack "by unidentified troops." As darkness closed in, men of G Company began to hear in the distance bugles, drums, cymbals, shouting, and finally shooting—a cacophony of frightening noises drawing close. Accompanying ROK troops couldn't understand the language; it had to be Chinese that they heard—and Chinese soldiers. Then came a wave of screaming enemy troops, firing their submachine guns and grenading as they closed in, overrunning the G Company and ROK foxholes. Those not quick enough to disentangle themselves from their sleeping bags and get to their feet were bayoneted inside them. Neither the Americans nor the South Koreans offered organized resistance.

> "There was just mass hysteria on the position. It was every man for himself… I didn't know which way to go. In the end, I just ran with the crowd. We ran and ran until the bugles grew fainter."[30]

A week later, after the 8th Cavalry's fiasco and the disintegration of many ROK units, the UN Command briefly considered a major withdrawal. Surprisingly, when the sun rose on November 6, it was discovered that the Chinese had pulled back. What were Peking's intentions?

Military sources in China today declare:

> There were problems of supply and coordination, that having warned the Americans of their will and capability to intervene, the Chinese were prepared to linger for a time, to discover whether their messages were heeded.[31]

In Tokyo, MacArthur mistakenly interpreted the Chinese departure as a sign of their weakness; in his view, they had shot their bolt. The Eighth Army and X Corp resumed their separate drives to the Yalu River forthwith.

> *"The Chinese entrance into the war had a profound and long-lasting effect on how Americans looked upon the issue of national security. It gave the ultimate push forward to the vision embodied in NSC-68. It greatly increased the Pentagon's influence and helped convert the country toward more of a national security state than it had previously been."*[32]

How good were these Chinese "volunteers"—who would shortly force upon the U.S. Army and the U.S. Marine Corps what has been called by some military authorities the most humiliating military retreat in the country's history? After 20 years of continuous war, these Chinese were battle-hardened veterans. They had trained to march fast, mile after mile, and even trot. They carried on their persons everything they needed to subsist in the field and engage the enemy: a personal weapon, bayonet, grenades, 80 rounds of ammunition, extra foot rags, sewing kit, chopsticks, and a week's rations—tea, rice, sugar, and a tin of fish or meat.

The Chinese soldier needed less than 10 pounds of supplies per day, compared to 60 for his American counterpart. To sustain 50 divisions in combat, Peking had to move 2,500 tons of supplies south across the Yalu. A single U.S. Army division required 600 tons and the even more profligate Marine

Corps needed 700 tons per division. Each of the tens of thousands of porters supplying the Chinese carried up to 100 pounds on a shoulder pole or A-frame and they carried these loads swiftly up and down the steep hills and mountains of northern Korea.[33]

The Chinese armies' "march-and bivouac" discipline was crucial in minimizing detection, particularly from the air. In a well-documented example, a Chinese army marched on foot from Antung in Manchuria 286 miles to its assembly area in North Korea in 16 days. One division of this army, marching at night over steep mountain trails, averaged 18 miles a day for 18 straight days.

For Chinese infantrymen, the day's march began as soon as it got dark and ended at 3AM the next morning. Defense measures against USAF reconnaissance planes were completed before 5:30AM; by first light every man, animal, and piece of equipment was concealed and expertly camouflaged. During daylight hours, small scouting parties moved ahead surreptitiously to pick out the next day's bivouac area. When Chinese troops were compelled to march by day, every man was under standing orders to stop in his tracks and remain motionless if an aircraft appeared overhead. Officers were empowered to shoot any man who violated this order.

Too often, in their haste to survive, U.S. Army troops cruelly abandoned their wounded on the battlefield, to bleed or freeze to death or be shot in the head by the enemy as they scoured the battlegrounds after the American troops departed.

Survivors of the US Army 7th Division retreat from Chosin Reservoir

To the east, in what was called the Battle of Chosin Reservoir, a 30,000 man unit from the 7th Infantry Division was also unable to hold off determined enemy attacks and was quickly surrounded. These troops managed to escape encirclement, albeit with over 15,000 casualties. The 1st Marine Division was also defeated at Chosin—"frozen Chosin"—and forced to retreat with heavy losses.

In January 1951, the Chinese and North Korean forces struck again in what they called their Winter Offensive. Again, they overran U.N. troops. Seoul was abandoned and recaptured by communist forces.

"Retreat, hell, we're simply attacking in another direction."

—Marine General Oliver Smith's response to a journalist's question about the Marines' "breakout" from Chosin Reservoir.[34]

LIEUTENANT GENERAL MATTHEW BUNKER RIDGWAY, Deputy Chief of Staff, and the Army's rising star, was part of a high-level, three-member team that the Pentagon had dispatched on August 5 to meet with MacArthur amid Washington's growing concern with his too-cozy relationship with Chiang Kai-shek. Ridgway was also charged with inspecting Lieutenant General Walton Walker's Eighth Army, including evaluating the general himself.

Nearly everything in Ridgway's frank report was damning, echoing almost word-for-word the opinion of British critics.

> The troops all too often lacked infantry fundamentals and were not aggressive. They had become prisoners of their machinery, most particularly their vehicles, and this on Korea's poor and limited system of roads. They did not counterattack; they did not dig in properly; attempts at camouflage were careless; fields of fire were poorly drawn up; communication between units weak.[35]

As for Walton Walker, Ridgway considered him way over his head and his staff weak and disorganized. His regimental commanders were too old and lacked World War II combat know-how. On the flight home discussing what they had just learned, Averell Harriman and Air Force General Lauris Norstead, Ridgway's companions, agreed that Walker had to go.

In the event, fate intervened to simplify the problem of his relief. On the morning of December 23, Walker, his driver, his aide, and his bodyguard were recklessly speeding along a crowded road when the inevitable happened. Walker and his driver regularly drove too fast on the narrow, icy, beat-up roads. This time their luck ran out; their jeep flipped over to avoid a truck swinging out into their lane, and all four men were hurled into a roadside ditch. The other three men lived. Walker was killed. Ridgway was appointed his replacement.

> *"What had been at stake in the Korean War, and it was to hang over subsequent wars in Asia, was the ability of an Asian nation to match the technological superiority of the West with the ability to pay the cost in manpower."*[36]

IF A SINGLE DAY could be selected when the Eighth Army showed unmistakable signs of disintegration, it was November 26. The war for the Americans had turned into a series of company-sized mini-battles. Individual companies fought alone with no hope of reinforcement, flanked on every side, it seemed, by onrushing Chinese. Nor could the besieged EUSAK stabilize its lines long enough to call in air strikes and its powerful artillery. Joseph C. Goulden wrote that T. R. Fehrenback, who commanded a unit in the Second Division and also compiled a major study of the war, had this to say about the battles of late November in the bleak, frozen mountains of the north.

> "Unable to maneuver where its wheels could not go, unable to see or communicate in those hills, the U.S. Army was being bitten to death rather than smashed down by numbers."[37]

The magnitude of the impending defeat became apparent that day when the commander of an infantry regiment, who was doing his best to hold the division's right flank in coordination with ROK units, was appalled to see an entire ROK regiment in full flight running through American lines. Walker's goal of reaching the Yalu was not to be realized. He would settle for saving the Eighth Army from annihilation.

At the same time, the first Marine Division in the X Corps area continued its careful climb around the western shores of the Chosin Reservoir. Their mission was to attack through the west to Mupyong, 55 miles away. The Chinese IX Field Army had secretly moved twelve divisions into the Chosin area. Its commander, General Sung Shin-lun, had been commanding troops since he was 17; he had headed a full regiment during the famous Long March of 1934-1945.

Sung's plan was simple: he would move his fresh troops into the gap between EUSAK and X Corps, and then turn east toward the coast, isolating the 100,000 Americans and ROKs of X Corps. He would first overrun the 7th Infantry Division on the east side of the reservoir, then turn his attention to the detached 1st Marine Division, recognized by the Chinese as their most dangerous foe. To build up hatred of the Marines among his soldiers for the forthcoming battles, Sung ordered distribution of thousands of copies of *The Bloody Path*, a propaganda pamphlet that was stark in its candor, as the following excerpt illustrates:

> When in the summer of 1950 the American imperialist marauders provoked the bloody holocaust in Korea, the Wall Street house-dog General MacArthur demanded that the American so-called "Marines" be immediately placed at his disposal. This professional murderer and inveterate war criminal intended to throw them into battle as quickly as possible for the purpose of inflicting, as it seemed to him then, a final blow on the Korean people. In putting forward such a demand, MacArthur proceeded from the fact that U.S. 'Marine' units have been trained more than any other type of American forces for the waging of the unprecedentedly brutal and inhuman, predatory war against the freedom-loving heroic Korean people.
>
> It was precisely to U.S. Marines that the Ober-bandit MacArthur addressed the words: 'A rich city lies ahead of you, it has much wine [the author of the diatribe should have known that Marines don't drink *wine!*] and tasty morsels. Take Seoul and all the girls will be yours, the property of the inhabitants belongs to the conquerors and you will be able to send parcels home.'[38]

A MAJOR PROBLEM CONFRONTING AMERICAN TROOPS in the northern mountains during the bitterly cold winter of 1950, in addition to their rugged enemies, was that they were neither trained for nor properly outfitted to handle the cold—20, 30, even 40 degrees below zero at night. The frozen ground was too hard to dig deep foxholes, weapons would not fire, hand grenades failed to detonate, vehicles would not start. Metal parts could only be touched with gloves; if bare skin touched metal, the skin would peel off, leaving painful, disabling wounds. At night, GIs slept with their rifles, grenades, and canteens of water next to their bodies inside their sleeping bags to keep them warm.

> Everyone knew how important it was to avoid sweating—which was not always possible in the heat of a firefight—because the sweat freezes into a film of ice between your foot and the innersole of the rubberized shoe pac; and if you didn't remove the shoe pacs occasionally, rub your feet, and change your socks, you were a good bet to become a cold-weather casualty.[39]

Avoiding frostbite became an almost obsessive occupation in the freezing cold. Historian Stanley Weintraub related one such incident told to him by a GI:

> My feet are numb and I took off my boots to massage them and try to get some circulation going, but I cannot get the left boot back on. The foot is too swollen, so Clyde McElroy and Doyle Smith of my squad, take me to where we've got all the bodies lined up in the snow. We pick out the bodies with the biggest pair of feet and the three of us spent twenty minutes trying to get their boots off.... We finally tied a C-ration box around the three socks I've got on, and let it go at that. It lasts a couple of days.[40]

U.S. troops not only had to look after their fingers and toes, but their individual weapons needed close attention as well, especially the .30 caliber carbine. The carbine was a popular firearm because it was compact and light, about seven pounds, compared to the cumbersome, nine-pound plus .30

caliber M-1 Garand, standard issue for the U.S. infantry. But the gasses generated in the carbine's small cartridge were too feeble in the cold to eject a spent cartridge and reload a fresh one. One Marine commented that he had learned early on that you could loosen up the action by peeing on it—but how much warm water did you carry around?

> Thus the level to which the United States Marine Corps was forced for its own protection—freezing men crouched in shallow holes on windswept Asian hills—their technology dependent on the amount of urine in a private's bladder.[41]

Medical personnel had an especially difficult time dealing with the cold.

> Plasma froze and the bottles broke. We couldn't use plasma because it wouldn't go into solution and the plastic tubes would clog up with particles. We couldn't change dressings because we had to work with gloves to keep our hands from freezing. We couldn't cut a man's clothes off to get at a wound because he would freeze to death. Actually, a man was better off if we left him alone. Did you ever try to stuff a wounded man into a sleeping bag?[42]

As a consequence, many U.S. wounded died because of the cold, even those with superficial wounds. Those men died quickly, mercifully. A Marine recalled, dispassionately, that he was grateful for what the cold had done to dead bodies.

> You were looking at a chunk of frozen meat, rather than a messy, stinking corpse. A six-by-six truck, full of frozen bodies, was waiting to move out. It looked like a load of meat going to market. I saw a Marine strapped over the barrel of a howitzer covered with a tarp, only his frozen feet sticking out. It reminded me of a deer carcass tied to the top of a car.[43]

In what proved to be a saver of GI extremities, called an "extraordinary improvisation" by a British admirer, was the introduction of "warming tents" several hundreds yards behind the front. Gasoline-fired space heaters were kept running day and night. Eager GIs happily kept the heaters' fuel tanks topped up. Every two or three hours, men withdrew from the front lines to these tents to thaw out and restore circulation to their icy limbs.

The winter was neutral and the Chinese were far less well-equipped than their enemy. While U.S. forces griped about their waterproof and insulated shoe pacs, the Chinese typically had only canvas shoes and lacked such amenities as sleeping bags. Casualties from frostbite, it was learned later, dwarfed those of the Americans: some 90 percent suffered some degree of frostbite. GIs were astonished when they took prisoners with entire limbs blackened and useless. To compound their miseries, the Chinese transportation system broke down.

A captured document painted a dire picture for the Communist troops.

> As a result, our soldiers frequently starve.... They ate cold food, and some had only a few potatoes in two days. They were unable to maintain their physical strength for combat; the wounded could not be evacuated.... The firepower of our entire army was basically inadequate. When we used our guns, there were often no shells, or the shells were duds.[44]

Remarkably, despite these factors, in the months of November and December, Peking's armies managed to achieve psychological dominance over the American forces they faced.

> The flimsiest rumor of men in quilted jackets behind the front was generally enough to generate fears of encirclement, and often outright panic.[45]

As hard as it must have been to accept, U.S. Army officers had to face the harsh reality that, man for man, most of the GIs were nowhere as tough, as skillful, and as determined as the *Chicoms* they fought.

The Marines did better. Their far more demanding enlistment requirements (no draftees until the end of the war), stiffer training, and challenging traditions compared to the run-of-the-mill dogfaces certainly better prepared them to handle the enemy. But the Marines' enviable propaganda apparatus during the war and the plethora of one-sided books written postwar by former leathernecks make it difficult even for a dedicated researcher to separate fact from fiction.

THE FIRST CHINESE JET FIGHTERS, Russian-made MiG-15s,[46] with large red stars painted on their swept wings and distinctive vertical tail, appeared in the skies over Korea in November 1950, sending a shockwave through the USAF comparable to that of the Mitsubishi *Zero* at Pearl Harbor. At the start, only about 50 of these advanced planes were deployed, piloted by Chinese and Soviet pilots. Within six months, however, there were over 400 and by the end of the war, there were 850, piloted mostly by the Chinese.

Initially, only the Lockheed F-80s and Republic F-84Es were available to counter the MiGs, and both these straight-wing airplanes were outclassed. In December, the first North American F-86 *Sabrejets* arrived; these bigger, heavier, more powerful swept-wing planes were less maneuverable and had a lower ceiling than the MiG-15, but were otherwise superior to the Soviet-built jet. During the war, American propagandists touted an exaggerated 10:1 kill ratio as evidence of U.S. aircraft-and-pilot superiority. After the war, the ratio was sharply downgraded.

By the fall of 1951, the B-29 crews found themselves under increasing pressure from the MiGs whose pilots had improved their tactics. In October, five of the lumbering bombers were shot down, despite close escort by F-86s.[47] It was a wake-up call for FEAF and daylight operations were abruptly canceled. Henceforth, the big bombers attacked by night.

On April 11, 1951, eleven months into the war, the president relieved MacArthur of his two commands with the following announcement.

> With deep regret I have concluded that General of the Army Douglas MacArthur is unable to give his wholehearted support of the policies of the United States Government and of the United Nations in matters pertaining to his official duties. In view of the specific responsibilities imposed upon me by the Constitution of the United States and the added responsibilities entrusted to me by the United Nations, I have decided that I must make a change of command in the Far East. I have, therefore, relieved General MacArthur of his commands and have designated Lieutenant General Matthew Ridgway as his successor.[48]

The rest of the war involved little territory change, continuous bombing of the north and its civilian population, and interminable peace negotiations which began in July of 1951. Combat, although on a much reduced level, continued. For South Korean forces, the goal was to recapture all of the territory south of the 38th parallel before a final agreement was reached.

These negotiations went on for two years, first at Kaesong and later at Panmunjom. The final stumbling block was the issue of repatriation of POWs. The Communists agreed to voluntary repatriation but only if the majority would return to North Korea or China. Since many POWs refused repatriation to those countries, the war continued until the Communists dropped the issue.

> *Ever since the U.S. occupied the Southern half of the Korean peninsula in 1945 and created the Republic of Korea, it has maintained a strong military presence there. During 2002, DoD listed among its properties and personnel: 101 separate military installations manned by 37,000 American troops, nearly 3,000 U.S. civilians working for the military, and 7,000 resident American dependents.*

VII. The Korean War

THE KOREAN WAR LASTED just over three years, a war that U.S. military historian S.L.A. Marshall called "the century's nastiest little war". He was only half right. By most standards it was nasty, but it was not a little war. Nearly 34,000 Americans were killed in action and over 103,000 were wounded. Nor was it a "police action" to counter a "bunch of bandits", as President Harry Truman had too-casually dismissed it at the start. It has its own monument on Washington's Mall, stainless-steel sculptures of 19 individual larger-than-life-size statues of GIs on patrol.

Later, American historians belittled it, calling it "the forgotten war" or "the war before Vietnam," although it was the first full-blown conflict between Communism and Capitalism. There had been too little time for the Pentagon's awesome propaganda apparatus to crank up to full speed, and no time at all to demonize North Korea's premier, Kim Il-sung. That would come later.

Unlike the Vietnam War and the two U.S. preemptive wars in Iraq, the Korean War took place before television became the dominant news medium. It was still mainly a war in print, reported in newspapers and magazines, and nearly all in black-and-white. As a result, what violence and brutality escaped government censorship never penetrated the American psyche. Civilians at home decided early that nothing particularly good was going to come out of it. And nothing good did. The war ended in a "no decision" verdict for the first time in American history—and Americans promptly forgot about the war.

Americans didn't care to learn about the destruction of North Korea's cities and villages, the obliteration of dams and dikes to cripple the country's irrigation systems, and the wiping out of the rice crop; the North Koreans saw devastation wherever they looked. The 1951 yearbook of *Brassey's Annual*, the trusted British military guide, wrote:

> "It is no exaggeration to state that North Korea no longer exists as a country. Its towns have been destroyed, much of its means of livelihood eradicated..."[49]

For those Americans who fought in the war in that faraway land, the conflict had none of the glory and legitimacy of the World War II, so recently ended. This war was grim killing, much of it fought in the below-zero temperatures of the mountainous north. Victory always seemed just beyond reach, one bare mountain at a time. Once the Chinese entered the war, the derisive phrase for a stalemate—"die for a tie"—became a popular refrain among GIs.

On November 29, 1952, President-elect Dwight D. Eisenhower fulfilled a campaign promise by going to Korea to hasten the end of the conflict. It took until July 27, 1953, before a cease-fire was established, essentially on the original 38th Parallel. A Demilitarized Zone was configured around it, defended by North Korean soldiers on the north and ROK and American troops on the south side. The United States signed the final Armistice Agreement but Syngman Rhee, stubborn as always, refused. A concluding peace treaty has never been signed and troops on both side of the heavily fortified DMZ continue to patrol.

A RELIC OF THE WAR remains, one unanswered question: did U.S. forces engage in Biological Warfare, the B in CBW (chemical-biological warfare). The Chinese, even more than the North Vietnamese, devoted considerable effort to publicizing their claims that the United States, particularly during January to March 1952, had dropped quantities of bacteria and bacteria-laden insects over Korea and northeast China. They trotted out their POWs to newsmen, all USAF airmen, who had flown the planes purportedly with the deadly cargoes. Many of these POWs gave details of the kinds of germ bombs dropped, the types of insects, and the diseases carried. Could the flyers have been privy to such highly technical biological information? Not likely! Had the airmen been "brainwashed" or subjected to torture? Likely!

Most of the world's microbes are ineffective weapons. They are highly perishable and are destroyed by heat, cold, and even by sunlight. Delivery systems that place germs inside artillery shells, for example, almost guarantee that the microbes will be dead on arrival. While bacteria can be spread as an aerosol by an airplane or helicopter, much like a crop duster sprays insecticide over cropland, the effect is local.

Of all the biological agents known to be extremely toxic to humans, one pathogen stands out as the ideal military germ: anthrax. *Bacillus anthracis* is a spore-forming microbe. When the bacillus is introduced into an unfavorable environment, it coils itself into a tiny sphere and extrudes a tough protein capsule around its outer surface. Such spores are surprisingly stable and resist the destructive influences of heat, light, radiation, even some caustic chemicals. These spores can remain virulent inside their cocoon for years, ready to germinate and kill when conditions improve.

The New York Times reported in a front-page story on March 13, 1949, that Secretary of State James Forestall had broken an official three-year silence by the military on the use or discussion of the term "biological warfare." He advised:

> 'It would be folly to underestimate the potentialities of biological warfare' and 'Germs or their poisonous products could be used effectively as weapons of war'. The government's censorship had been imposed in 1946 following the issuance and then hasty withdrawal of a report by George W. Merck that told of the successful efforts by the Allies during the war to prepare the public for possible use of such weapons by the Axis. General Eisenhower, Chief of Staff at the time and concerned about fear generated among the civilian population, withdrew the report and clamped down on its further distribution.

General Alden H. Waitt, head of the Army's Chemical Corps, told newsmen following Merck's short-lived announcement that the United States was "as far advanced as any nation in the world" in the study of germ-warfare and probably "ahead".

He then proceeded to dish out hyperbole and misinformation that would assure the readers of the next day's newspapers that there was nothing—or practically nothing—about biological warfare they should fear. He used as one example of the agents that had been studied was botulism, the food poison that was the most poisonous agent known to man. Under controlled, ideal conditions, the general said,

> "One ounce of botulinius toxin could probably kill 150 million people."

He quickly backtracked, saying that these baccilli were exceedingly fragile and could be destroyed by heat, shock, and probably by "extended exposure to air".

General Waitt opined that Biological Warfare,

> "…has great potentiality, but it is a weapon of the future."

One wonders why no one among the reporters asked an obvious question:

> "General, with due respect, could you tell us what you mean by 'the future?' Is that this year, next year, or ten years down the road?"

In August 1949 an "International Scientific Committee" was convened, consisting of scientists from the Soviet Union, Great Britain, France, Sweden, and Brazil. Following a two-month investigation in China, the committee concluded in its 600-page report:

> The peoples of Korea and China have indeed been the objectives [sic] of bacteriological weapons. These have been employed by units of the U.S.A. armed forces, using a great variety of different methods for the purpose, some of which seem to be developments of those applied by the Japanese during the second world war.[50]

After World War II, U.S. interrogators learned that the Germans had never planned to engage inbiological warfare. German scientists, among the best in the world, had explored biological weapons only perfunctorily. Instead, they, along with their fellow engineers, devoted their energies to other weapons such as V-1 pulse-jet and the V-2 rocket and advanced manned aircraft to counter the British and American heavy bombers that were pulverizing German cities. They were also far along in the development of a new generation of "all-electric" submarines capable of bursts of high underwater speeds to outrun destroyers.

As for the C for chemistry in CBW, it must be remembered that Adolf Hitler had been gassed by mustard in the Great War, never forgot its terrible effects, and decreed Germany would never be the first to use poison gas. The Fuhrer kept his word. Nevertheless, whatever scraps of scientific or engineering data could be gleaned from the Germans were looked upon by the Americans as useful. The Russians and the British, too, sought the same data. All three raced around Germany after the war to round up top Nazi researchers and bring them and their families to their respective countries. The United States got the choicest plum, Werner von Braun, who had headed up Germany's V-2 rocket program and would play a similar role in America's subsequent rocket developments.

"NAPALM CARRIER... One hundred and fifty gallons of flaming death, seventy five gallons of napalm in each of the dark colored wing tanks, speeds on its way toward enemy lines in Korea through courtesy of an F-80 jet fighter of the U.S. Far East Air Forces, ca. 01/02/1951"

FOR AMERICA AND AMERICANS, WAS THE KOREAN WAR worthwhile? Most people are likely to tell you they don't remember the war. *It was the war between the two big ones.* For the war planners in the Pentagon and the rich and powerful arms makers intent on building a global hegemony for the United States, however, the Korean War had been an opportunity to wring out new weapons for coming conflicts, such as turbojet fighter-bombers, napalm in its many hideous forms, turbine-drive helicopters, and cluster bombs of every conceivable type.

Max Hastings ended his book, *The Korean War,* by quoting the ungrammatical, misspelled, and what he called the "eloquently confused" view of a soldier who served in the U.S. 7th Cavalry.

> A lot of us feels [*sic*] that Truman made a big mistake by not letting MacArthur bomb the bridges on the Yalu river, also not letting him bomb the Chinese that were mass in China. Another big mistake was in 1951, the Chinese made there last big offensive against us and we stop them cold, right after that we could have went north and set up a good line 20 miles north of Pyongyang. My family did not understand the war, except that they knew the communists wanted South Korea. They support our government in the war. The war set the Chinese back 10 to 20 years where in the United States the big companies get richer. Don't get me wrong. I am not sorry I went and fought it was an honor to fight the communists because it had to be done, however I would not do it again for a million dollars.[51]

In February 1946, George Frost Kennan, *charge d'affaires* at the U.S. Embassy in Moscow, had drafted what famously became known as his "long telegram" in response to an urgent request by the State Department for an update on Soviet conduct. While Kennan's cable had been useful and its mature analyses served as a foreign-policy blueprint of sorts well into the 1950s, it was filled with generalities. Truman wanted specifics upon which the Joint Chiefs of Staff could base military strategy particularly in light of America's loss of its nuclear-weapon monopoly.

The result: 151-page NSC-68 "United States Objectives and Programs for National Security". The document was completed in April 1950, formally approved as national policy that September, and kept classified Secret until 1975 [unaccountably!]. War hawk Paul Nitze was its author and it reflected the near-hysterical views of the Soviet Union and Communism that he inherited from the wild-eyed former Defense Department Secretary James Forrestal. In stark language, belying its mild title, it projected a perilous future for the American people. The world, according to Nitze, was irrevocably divided between two antagonistic systems of politics and beliefs. There could be no compromises, no negotiations, only armed resistance and war-readiness: two scorpions in a bottle.

> Nitze added up the balance of power between the United States and the Soviet Union in the winter of 1950 and arrived at a terrifying conclusion. In four years the United States would be looking down the barrel of an awesome weapon, a gigantic Soviet military machine. The nation was in mortal danger. Americans had to realize that Moscow aimed to destroy them.[52]

Further, NSC-68 predicted that, as soon as they were able to do so, the Soviets would launch a preemptive nuclear assault on the United States.

Paul Nitze had done his homework, if his purposeful walk through the ruins of Hiroshima, taking notes on the destruction, was any measure of his thoroughness. He claimed he wanted to measure the immeasurable, as he put it, "to put calipers on it". He came away with the conviction that American policy had to be based on nuclear-weapon dominance, which he defined simply as the United States having more nuclear weapons on hand at the end of the coming World War III than the Soviets. Time was running out, according to Nitze's lights.

Were there any choices for America? Nitze listed three courses of action. One: capitulation. Let the Red Army run up the hammer-and-sickle above the White House? Not conceivable! Two: surprise nuclear-weapon attack on every city in the Soviet Union? Doable, but a tough sell for many Americans and most of the world. Three: a rapid and overwhelming buildup of diversified weaponry that would serve less as a deterrent than as a start for a new arms race that the U.S. would win.

VII. The Korean War

According to Nitze, America had "no alternative" but to build and stockpile thousands of thermonuclear weapons along with a variety of delivery systems—manned bombers and missiles, both ground- and submarine-launched. The government's military budget—a.k.a. *defense* budget—for fiscal 1950 was $13 billion. Nitze's estimated costs for NCS-68's recommended program was breathtaking: between $40 and $50 billion *a year and every year thereafter*. These figures were more than the entire federal budget for 1950 and some 20 percent of the national product. Secretary of State Acheson, apparently flabbergasted by the numbers, told Nitze to keep any mention of costs out of his document. To debate costs, Acheson reasoned, would make implementing the program difficult if not impossible. Rather, the task was:

> "To bludgeon the mass mind of 'top government' with language that was clearer than truth."[53]

What NSC-68 outlined was clear, all right—but patently false.

> It stated that the Soviets would soon match the United States in nuclear firepower Nuclear parity was, in fact, some thirty years away. It spoke of 175 Soviet divisions primed for war. The 175 combat-ready divisions were a mirage, Nitze later conceded. The man who would measure the immeasurable, destruction of nuclear bombs, had tripled the true number of Soviet troops.[54]

The blunt truncheon Acheson had described nevertheless had a positive impact on U.S. military spending: the defense budget leapfrogged to $52.8 billion in 1953. The Korean War devoured less than one-tenth of the increase. Most of the money went to pay for a surge in weapons production and for the construction of new military bases that ringed the Soviet Union and China.

In fact, NSC-68 marked the start of the Cold War—and the first gargantuan strides toward a *Pax Americana* that would reap the rewards—questionable ones, some would say sadly—of military and commercial control of land, sea, air, and space. Growing alongside in scope and influence was the military-industrial complex which was about to be defined and highlighted by outgoing President Dwight D. Eisenhower in his farewell address in 1961.

Two intriguing questions linger. If NSC-68 had not been classified Secret, thereby making transparent American foreign policy, would the North Koreans have dared to strike south? Would the Chinese have sent their "volunteers" across the Yalu River?

A RELIC OF THE WAR remained the unanswered question: did U.S. forces engage in Biological Warfare, the B in CBW? (See Appendix). The Chinese, even more than the North Vietnamese, devoted considerable effort to publicizing their claims that the United States, particularly during January to March 1952, had dropped quantities of bacteria and bacteria-laden insects over Korea and northeast China. They trotted out their POWs to newsmen, all USAF airmen, who had purportedly flown the planes with the deadly cargoes. Many of these POWs gave details of the kinds of germ bombs dropped, the types of insects, and the diseases carried. Could the flyers have been privy to such highly technical biological information? Not likely! Had the airmen been "brainwashed" or subjected to torture? Likely!

In August 1952 an "International Scientific Committee" was convened consisting of scientists from the Soviet Union, Great Britain, France, Sweden, and Brazil. They were tasked to investigate whether U.S. Armed Forces had used germs in Korea and China. Following a two-month investigation in China, the committee concluded in its 600-page report:

> The peoples of Korea and China have indeed been the objectives of bacteriological weapons. These have been employed by units of the U.S.A. armed forces, using a great variety of different

methods for the purpose, some of which seem to be developments of those applied by the Japanese during the second world war.[56]

ON JANUARY 17, 1961, President Eisenhower delivered his Farewell Address to Congress and the American people by radio. He had asked his principal speechwriter Malcolm Moos a year before to write a memorable speech. Indeed he had, and it became known as the "military-industrial complex" speech. [See Appendix] Its key paragraph, below, added luster to his otherwise bland presidency and continues to define Eisenhower a half-century later:

> This conjunction of an immense military establishment and a large arms industry is new to the American experience.... In the councils of government, we must guard against the acquisition of unwarranted influence, whether sought or unsought, by the military-industrial complex. The potential for the disastrous rise of misplaced power exists and will persist. We must never let the weight of this combination endanger our liberties or democratic processes. We should take nothing for granted.

An early draft by Moos had referred to a "military-industrial-*congressional* complex," which targeted the nation's Senators and Representatives as complicit in war-making, because it was they who ratified the legislation for the president to make war—and voted the funds the president requested to conduct the war. However, Eisenhower vetoed Moos's inclusion of Congress as part of the complex because he felt the Executive Branch of government should not arbitrarily rule on another Branch's responsibilities.

THAT KOREANS HAVE NOT FORGOTTEN the war was highlighted in an article from the *New York Times* of August 3, 2008. Datelined Wolmi Island, South Korea, the news story takes the reader back to September 10, 1950, five days before the Inchon amphibious landing that beatified General Douglas MacArthur to the South Koreans.

North Korean forces were thought to be garrisoned in a tiny village on Wolmi, and U.S. military planners decided to neutralize Wolmi, which overlooked the channel that approached the harbor. According to declassified U.S. military documents, 43 *F4-U* Marine fighter-bombers swarmed over Wolmi, dropping 93 napalm canisters. The intent was to burn out the eastern slope of the tiny island to clear the landing area for U.S. troops. Marine pilots reported that they observed no troops on the ground but did see flashes. The reports described strafing on the beaches but did not mention civilian casualties.

Aging South Korean survivors gave their side of the happenings that day, a story of carnage not mentioned in their own country's official histories.

> "When the napalm hit our village, many people were still sleeping in their homes. Those who survived the flames ran into the tidal flats. We were trying to show the American pilots that we were civilians. But they strafed us, women and children."

Lee Beom-ki, age 76, said that dozens of the villagers were killed.

The Wolmi victims' demand for recognition taps into complicated emotions underlying South Korea's alliance with the United States. According to the chairwoman of a Wolmi advocacy group:

> "We thank the Americans for saving our country from Communism, for the peace and prosperity we have today. Does that mean we have to shut up about what happened to our families?"

In 2005, left-leaning civic groups tried to topple MacArthur's bronze statue that appears to gaze down across the narrow channel that separates Wolmi from the beaches of Inchon. Wolmi survivors did not join the protest for fear they would be branded anti-American. According to an Inchon taxi driver whose father was killed by American flyers at Wolmi:

> "We consider MacArthur a hero, but no one can know our family's suffering. Both governments emphasize the alliance, but they never care about people like us who were sacrificed in the name of the alliance."

On November 1, 1952, the U.S. conducted its first test of a full-scale thermonuclear device, or hydrogen bomb. The site was Elugelab Island, a low-lying projection of the Eniwitok Atoll in the Marshall Islands in the Pacific. The apparatus, code-named Mike, exploded with a power the equal of 12 million tons of TNT—and a new word, megaton, was added to man's vocabulary of war. The detonation was estimated to have equaled the TNT that could be packed in a line of standard-size railroad boxcars stretching from Chicago to San Francisco, about 2000 miles. On October 30, 1961, the Soviet Union exploded a hydrogen bomb developing an estimated 58 megatons. [See Appendix]

Notes

[1] Carl Boggs, Ed., *Masters of War: Militarism and Blowback in the Era of American Empire* (Routledge, New York, 2003), p. 205.

[2] William Manchester, *American Caesar: Douglas MacArthur 1880-1964* (Little, Brown and Company, Boston, 1978), p. 538.

[3] Charles J. Hanley, Sang-Hun Choe, and Martha Mendoza, *The Bridge at No Gun Ri: A Hidden Nightmare from the Korean War* (Henry Holt and Company, New York, 2001), p. 49.

[4] Manchester, p. 166. Following the outbreak of war with Japan, MacArthur was offered and did not hesitate to accept a gift of $500,000—an enormous sum at the time—from corrupt President Quezon as payment for pre-war service. Accepting such "gifts" was contrary to U.S. government policy, but MacArthur always considered himself "above the law."

[5] Did MacArthur scuttle away to safety in Australia on his own initiative, as it became clear he would be captured? Some MacArthur-hating historians think so. But what is incontrovertible is that MacArthur ordered a haphazard, pell-mell retreat on Bataan, carelessly leaving equipment and vital foodstuffs behind. When U.S. troops finally surrendered to the Japanese, they were already half-starved. MacArthur, as was his wont in such situations, later denied he was complicit.

[6] Ibid., p. 539. One glaring example of MacArthur's contempt for civilian control, and "the straw that broke the camel's back," was his correspondence with warhawk Joseph Martin, Republican House Minority Leader. On February 12, Martin had delivered an inflammatory speech in New York charging that the president was purposefully preventing hundreds of thousands of veteran Chinese Nationalist troops on Formosa from opening a second front in Asia. He ended his peroration by throwing a gauntlet to the ground. "If we are not in Korea to win, then this Truman administration should be indicted for the murder of thousands of American boys." Martin followed up on March 8 by sending a copy of his comments to MacArthur, inviting him to respond "on a confidential basis or otherwise." MacArthur's answer was dated March 20. First, he flattered Martin by writing that he was pleased to see that he had not lost any of his old-time punch. He then got around to Martin's views on using the Chinese Nationalists. These views, wrote MacArthur, were not in conflict either with "logic" or the tradition of "meeting force with maximum counterforce." He closed with what Harry Truman later called "the real clincher," a calculated slap in his face. "It seems strangely difficult for some to realize that here in Asia is where the Communist conspirators have elected to make their play for global conquest, and that we

have joined the issue thus raised on the battlefield, that here we fight Europe's war with arms while the diplomats there still fight it with words: that if we lose the war to Communism in Asia the fall of Europe is inevitable; win it and Europe most probably would avoid war and yet preserve freedom... There is no substitute for victory." The letter was vintage MacArthur, filled with plenty of hot air!

[7] Max Hastings, *The Korean War* (Simon & Schuster, New York, 1987), p. 333. Comments of a U.S. Army officer who had fought in World War II and the Korean War.

[8] Lloyd C. Gardner, *The Korean War* (Quadrangle Books, New York, 1972), p. 18. The left-wing journalist I.F. Stone was alone in 1952 when he argued in his *The Hidden History of the Korean War: America's First Vietnam*, that Syngman Rhee "had deliberately provoked the attack as the only way to save his tottering regime by bringing America into the war." Stone also painted a sinister portrait of General MacArthur and his "desire to make the Korean War into a Far Eastern 'Sarajevo' for war against China." Gardner wrote, "Stone's book remains an impressive critique of American policy in the first eighteen months of the war."

[9] Martin Russ, *Breakout—Korea 1950: The Chosin Reservoir Campaign* (Penguin Books, New York, 1999), p. 81.

[10] Joseph C. Goulden, *Korea: The Untold Story of the War* (Times Books, New York, 1982), p. 296.

[11] Max Hastings, *The Korean War* (Simon & Schuster, New York, 1987), p. 173.

[12] Ibid., p. 174.

[13] Ibid.

[14] Ibid.

[15] Ibid., p. 175.

[16] Hanley, p. 70.

[17] Ibid., p. 90.

[18] Ibid., p. 127.

[19] Ibid.,

[20] Ibid., p. 75.

[21] Ibid., p. 145.

[22] David Halbertsam, *The Coldest War: America and the Korean War* (Hyperion, New York, 2007), p. 633.

[23] Hastings, p. 84.

[24] Ibid. p. 98.

[25] Hanley, p. 166.

[26] Manchester, p. 588.

[27] Ibid., p. 593.

[28] Ibid., p. 596.

[29] Goulden, p. 94.

[30] Hastings, p. 128.

[31] Ibid., p. 137.

[32] Ibid., p. 128.

[33] Ibid., p. 138.

[34] Halbertsam, p. 470.

[35] Ibid., p. 151-152.

[36] Goulden, p. 342

[37] Ibid., p. 633.

[38] Stephen Endicott and Edward Hagerman, *The United States and Biological Warfare: Secrets from the Early Cold War and Korea* (University of Indiana Press, Bloomington IN, 1998), p. 88.

[39] Goulden, p. 224-225.

[40] Stanley Weintraub, *MacArthur's War: Korea and the Undoing of an American Hero* (The Free Press, New York, 2000), p. 273.

[41] Ibid.

[42] Ibid., p. 268.
[43] Ibid.
[44] Hastings, p. 170-171.
[45] Ibid., p. 172.
[46] The MiG-15 was powered by a copy of the late-WWII Rolls-Royce Nene engine that was used in the Gloster Meteor, Britain's first operational turbojet aircraft. The Meteor saw limited combat in World War II. The Nene used an obsolete-design centrifugal compressor and so did the engine in the MiG-15. For that reason British aircraft designers were astonished when they learned about the MiG's outstanding performance.
[47] The original B-29 that was used over Japan was a flawed, unreliable, and dangerous airplane for its aircrews. B-29s had been hurriedly built and even more quickly inspected during WWII. The airplane had Wright Aeronautical engines that were prone to overheat when heavily loaded. The plane's central fire-control system rarely worked, among lesser deficiencies. Postwar, the Boeing Company fitted new Pratt & Whitney Aircraft engines of higher power and modified the vertical tail to compensate for the increased thrust. The new model was designated B-50, and several hundred were built and served with Strategic Air Command until the jet-powered B-47 became available in the late 1940s.
[48] Goulden, p. 339.
[49] William Blum, *Killing Hope: U.S. Military and CIA Interventions Since World War II* (Common Courage Press, Monroe ME, 1995), p. 54.
[50] Ibid., p. 26.
[51] Hastings, p. 336.
[52] Tim Weiner, *Blank Check: The Pentagon's Black Budget* (Warner Books, Inc., New York, 1990), p. 29.
[53] Ibid., p. 30.
[54] Ibid., p. 34-35.
[55] I.F. Stone, *The Hidden History of the Korean War* (Monthly Review Press, New York, 1952), p. 2.
[56] Weiner, p. 37-38.

Chapter VIII:
The Vietnam War

"Our nation is the greatest force for good in history,"

—President George W. Bush told assembled newsmen in Crawford, Texas, August 31, 2003, when he took time off clearing shrubbery on his property.

IF THE KOREAN WAR WAS DOUGLAS MACARTHUR'S, as many biographers have written, the Vietnam War was certainly Ho Chi Minh's (He Who Enlightens). Ho,[1] who had been born in Vietnam, first appeared on the international political scene in 1919 in Paris, albeit almost surreptitiously, during the Versailles Peace Treaty deliberations that ended the Great War. He was there to petition Woodrow Wilson, whose Fourteen Points included one that Ho considered appropriate for his people in Vietnam.

It was point V:

> A free, open-minded, and absolutely impartial adjustment of all colonial claims, based upon a strict observance of the principle that in determining all such questions of sovereignty the interests of the populations concerned must have equal weight with the equitable claims of the government whose title is to be determined.

Receiving no response from Wilson, Ho then wrote a letter to Secretary of State Robert Lansing (uncle to John Foster Dulles and Allen Welsh Dulles), who was also in Paris as part of the U.S. delegation. Again he was snubbed. It would be twenty-four years before Ho tried again. This time, Harry Truman was president and he, too, gave Ho the cold shoulder. However, an incident had occurred in 1944 that gave Ho Chi Minh hope that the U.S. might support the restoration of independence for the colonies in Indochina. Roosevelt was opposed to European colonialism, in particular the French in Indochina. On one occasion, FDR had remarked:

> "France has milked it for one hundred years. The people of Indochina are entitled to something better than that."[2]

A year earlier, in November 1944, a U.S. reconnaisssance plane flying over the mountainous terrain along the Sino-Vietnamese border experienced engine trouble. Its pilot, Lieutenant Rudolph Shaw, parachuted to safety. Members of a local Vietminh unit were the first to reach Shaw, and they agreed to deliver him to Ho in the town of Pac Bo some 40 miles away. For the next month, the Vietminh troops guided their American guest over trackless mountains and narrow jungle trails, walking at night and resting during the day to avoid Japanese patrols. Enroute, Shaw and his escorts were unable to communicate with one another. The best they could do was to respond "America! Roosevelt!" whenever Shaw shouted "Vietminh, Vietminh!"[3] When Shaw finally arrived in Pac Bo, Ho Chi Minh greeted him in English, much to his astonishment.

If U.S. support for the Vietminh cause "was the ultimate prize," as Ho Chi Minh's biographer wrote:

> Then Lieutenant Shaw's appearance on Ho Chi Minh's doorstep in 1944 was his ticket to take part in the raffle. When Shaw asked for Ho's assistance in reaching the Chinese border, Ho agreed, remarking that he had also intended to go to China on business. Shaw then invited Ho to join him in going to Kunming, then the headquarters of the U.S. Fourteenth Air Force.[4]

DURING WORLD WAR II the Japanese had displaced the French as occupiers in Indochina. When Japan surrendered in 1945, the Vietminh assumed power in the north of Vietnam. The British occupied the south initially, but other overseas commitments were a higher priority to a nation sorting out how it could hold together the pieces of its former empire, and the decision was made to turn the territory back to France. French General Jean Leclerc underscored his nation's plans by publicly declaring in September:

> "I did not come back to Indochina to give Indochina back to the Indochinese."[5]

The French needed help rebuilding their army and they turned to the United States. It was a snug fit for both parties. President Harry Truman was anxious to enlist a reluctant France into America's new anti-Soviet coalition with an imposing name, North Atlantic Treaty Organization, which included former enemy Germany. After all, France had fought Germany in three major wars, in 1879, 1914, and 1939, and mutual distrust and hatreds ran deep. Moreover, the U.S. was dead set against the French negotiating with Ho Chi Minh's Communist movement. There were also powerful colonial supporters among American oil and rubber interests.

For their part, the French, in seeking military aid from the U.S., knew precisely which buttons to push. The most efffective one was their claim that French soldiers would be in the vanguard of the "free world's" fight against Communism. The Pentagon was happy to have a surrogate in Southeast Asia and starting in 1950, U.S. military aid to France averaged about one billion dollars a year. By 1954, when the French were driven out of Indochina, this aid constituted seventy-eight percent of the total French budget for their war.[6]

Photo: "A French Foreign Legionnaire goes to war along the dry rib of a rice paddy, during a recent sweep through communist-held areas in the Red River Delta, between Haiphong and Hanoi. Behind the Legionnaire is a U.S. gifted tank." Circa 1954.

TROUBLE BEGAN for the French occupiers soon after they returned to Vietnam. In March 1946, France reluctantly agreed that the Vietminh were a legitimate part of the French Union, but refused to surrender authority over important elements of the government. To the Vietminh rebels seeking independence, France had double-crossed them and festering popular anger turned into fury in the cities. On November 26, 1946, following anti-French demonstrations in Saigon, the French cruiser *Suffern* stood off the southern capitol and shelled the Vietnamese quarter, killing more than 6,000 civilians. The battle was joined.

To keep a lid on the growing rebel movement, the French installed as head of govenment a hated former emperor, Bao Dai, who earlier had been Japan's puppet. The Vietminh insurgents reacted by intensifying their war with the French. In turn, the French escalated their intervention. By 1953, the war had become a political issue in France and the French military command was looking for a big military victory—or an honorable way out. By then the guerrillas, some 70,000 strong, had been molded into a powerful army, supplied with modern arms by both the Soviets and the Chinese.

THE BIG BATTLE that French forces intended to win, that would quiet the growing antiwar faction in France, took place in a tiny, remote village in southwestern Vietnam. Dien Bien Phu was adjacent to the border with Laos—also a French protectorate—in a bowl-shaped river valley some ten miles long and five miles wide at its broadest. It lay astride an important supply route for the Vietminh into and out of Laos. It was about 200 air-miles to Haiphong, the closest big city. The village had been connected to Haiphong by a main road, but the rebels had made the road unusable. The French planned to build a fortress on the site, lengthen and strengthen the single runway, garrison it with elite troops, lure their enemy into a killing field, and destroy them with their vaunted artillery. Lined up in Haiphong and Saigon were dozens of American C-47 cargo planes and bigger C-119 "Flying Boxcars" in the colors of the French Air Force to supply the isolated fortress.

On March 13, the siege began with a tremendous artillery barrage by the PVA. For three months, the world's attention would be riveted on the battle between Vietminh and French forces at tiny Dien Bien Phu.

Bernard Fall, the French scholar, journalist, and author, chronicled the French buildup and the battle in *Hell in a Very Small Place*. Hindsight is always clearer than foresight, and Fall was critical of the integrity of the French fortifications. He wrote that the French defenders made no attempts at concealment or camouflage, both of which deficiencies would cost them dearly. The narrowest slit trench and the smallest bunker entrance clearly outlined themselves against the brown earth of the valley floor. The firing slots of dug-in automatic weapons were painted black by the Foreign Legionnaires who prided themselves on the detailed execution of their fortifications; these also stood out against the surrounding earth and sand. Another careless visual aid that helped the attackers register their artillery were the tall radio whip antennas "gently swaying in the wind" over every command post and battery position.

More significant was the reality that the attackers occupied the strategically vital "high ground" surrounding the defenders. Thousands of Vietnamese porters had lugged in big cannons, piece by piece, over narrow mountain roads and rickety bridges—from the Chinese border 200 miles away—and up the steep hills surrounding the fortress. There, carefully camouflaged, these guns were reassembled and rolled into tunnels cut into the hills, only their muzzles visible to observers down in the valley. To make it even more difficult for the French to register their counterfire and for fighter-bombers to find targets, the indefatigable Vietminh regularly moved their heavy artillery from place to place.

The French had known for a year that General Vo Nguyen Giap's insurgent forces had acquired heavy guns. What surprised them was that they had been able to transport them to Dien Bien Phu—and to keep the gunners supplied with shells during the siege. Once the artillery duel began, the French estimated that the Vietminh fielded four dozen each of 105 mm howitzers, 120 mm heavy mortars, 75 mm recoilless rifles, and heavy antiaircraft guns. As the battle reached its climax, Soviet Katyusha multiple-barrel rocket launchers arrived, along with a plentiful supply of rockets.

On the French side, equivalent-size cannons totaled 60 and dropped to less than 40 a week after the siege began. Going as far back as Napoleon, the French had looked to artillery as the keystone of its armies. During the Great War, the French 75-mm cannon was recognized by all the armies as the most accurate, fast-firing artillery piece of the war. American doughboys relied on the "75" from their first days in the front lines.

After the battle, the French estimated that the Vietminh had fired some 30,000 shells of 105-mm size and 100,000 shells of smaller caliber. This translated into some 1,500 tons of munitions delivered by porters between December 1953 and May 1954, plus 20,000 tons of rice.

> The fortress of DBP began to take shape during the last weeks of February 1954, behind its thousands of tons of barbed wire, around its unprotected gun emplacements bristling with artillery and heavy mortars, and under the cover of its shoddily built bunkers and foxholes, animated with the hope that its ten light tanks and its handful of fighter-bombers would keep the enemy at arm's length.[7]

Among the surprising aspects of the Dien Bien Phu fortress, noted by critic Fall, were the many faults and make-do elements in the construction of its strongpoints. These apparently escaped the supposedly prying eyes of the stream of French and foreign military officers who inspected it prior to the start of the battle. Colonel Christian de Castries, promoted at the start of the battle to Brigadier General, had refined his reception of visitors to a well-rehearsed scenario:

> Reception at the airfield by an honor guard of Moroccan rifleman in gleaming white turbans and webbings; a visit to the outlying strongpoints in de Castries' own jeep driven by himself; lunch at de Castries' own command mess on an impeccably gleaming table service; a thirty-minute briefing at his headquarters; and, usually a brief glimpse of 'Dien Bien Pfu at war'—either a brief artillery demonstration by the African cannoneers of one of the batteries of [strongpoint] Claudine or a combat reconaissance combining Capt. Hervouet's new *Chaffee* tanks and Col. Langlais' lithe paratroopers.[8]

These public relations gambits proved to be counterproductive as soon as enemy artillery barrages enveloped the fortifications, accurately targeting the French big guns. One-armed Artillery Colonel Charles Piroth, who had boasted of the invulnerability of his artillery, apologized to de Castries and then withdrew to his bunker. He lay down on his bed, and with difficulty managed to pull the pin on a hand grenade and killed himself. He knew that the battle which had just begun was already lost. This—45 days before the end of the siege!

By the end of March, Vietminh artillery had chewed up the runway, beyond restoration by the two small bulldozers that had been airlifted in. Furthermore, the bulldozer operators took their lives in their hands whenever they exposed themselves on the airfield. The last C-47 to take off was on March 27. The remaining F-8F *Bearcat* fighter-bombers that had been based at the airstrip flew back to Haiphong. The only way replacement troops and supplies could then get inside the fortress was by parachute. The growing numbers of wounded were out of luck.

The intense and accurate Communist antiaircraft fire forced daytime parachute deliveries that originally had begun at 2,500 feet, to go to 6,500 feet, and then to 8,500 feet. Many of the supplies were falling outside the fort's perimeter and into enemy hands. This was made clear to the defenders in mid-April when particularly effective 105-mm fire turned out to be shells with American short-delay fuses. Dien Bien Phu had become an isolated island in the jungle, its only lifeline unreliable parachute supply.

At the start, General Giap used "human wave" tactics to overwhelm the defenders, but by the end of January, casualties were so great he switched to a more cautious approach. His hard-working troops dug a network of shallow trenches and tunnels to enable them to advance toward the outlying French defense works without being exposed to French artillery and machine gun fire.

As the situation spiraled down, the French turned to the United States for help. In mid-March, Paris sent General Paul Ely to Washington to ask for U.S. air strikes to relieve the pressure on the French garrison. There was support for the French request from Admiral Arthur Radford, chairman of the Joint Chiefs, and from Vice President Richard Nixon, but not from President Eisenhower:

> Whose appetite for engaging in land wars in Asia had been diminished by the inconclusive engagement on the Korean peninsula, was reluctant to introduce U.S. combat forces into Indochina without guarantees that the battle would henceforth be waged on a multinational basis, and on condition that the French would promise ultimately to grant full independence to all three states of Indochina.[9]

The French refused to agree to the U.S. conditions. Eisenhower, for his part, set his sights on achieving a satisfactory settlement at the peace table.

The final assault by the Vietminh took place on May 6. The end came the next day.

> As Nicolas [Major Jean] looked out over the battlefield from a slit trench near his command post, a small white flag, probably a handkerchief, appeared on top of a rifle hardly fifty feet away, followed by the flat-helmeted head of a Vietminh soldier.
>
> "You're not going to shoot anymore?" asked the Vietminh in French.
>
> "No, I am not going to shoot anymore," said Nicolas.
>
> "C'est fini?" said the Vietminh.
>
> "Oui, c'est fini," said the French major.[10]

All around them, as on some gruesome Judgment Day, mud-covered soldiers, French and Vietnamese alike, crawled out of their sandbagged trenches, breathed in deeply, and stood erect as firing ceased everywhere.

"The silence was deafening."[11]

Fall called that instant a defining moment in the history of Southeast Asia. The battle of Dien Bien Phu presaged what was in store for the next invader and occupier, but American observers took little note of the war-fighting skills and tenacity of Vietnamese infantrymen. This was Western chauvinisin writ large, and would impact the United States heavily in blood and treasure. In fact, the battle was the first in which a non-European colony had evolved from guerrilla bands to a full-fledged army able to defeat the army of a modern Western power. The French defeat was total: more than 1,500 defenders had been killed, 4,000 wounded, and the remainder taken prisoner. Vietminh losses were considerably heavier: over 25,000 casualties, of whom nearly 10,000 were killed in action.

Photo: Surrender of the French at Dien Bien Phu

The French departed Indochina with a solemn ceremony on October 9, 1954. A small detachment of French soldiers in dress uniforms stood at attention around a flagpole in Mangin Athletic Stadium in Saigon. As a bugler sounded mournful notes, the Tricolor was slowly lowered. In eight years of violent war, France had lost nearly 45,000 men killed in action, and close to 80,000 wounded.[12] Few Vietnamese attended the French ceremony; most were far more interested in welcoming the 30,000 Vietminh troops marching in triumphantly as victors.

French and Vietnamese negotiators, along with delegates from the United States, the Soviet Union, China, and Great Britain, then met in Geneva to iron out the details of the peace. Wild-eyed anti-Communist John Foster Dulles, U.S. Secretary of State, was there to stall or better yet prevent a peace agreement. He was unable to do either and left before the final accord was signed. The treaty called for a temporary division of Vietnam at the seventeenth parallel. The Communists would control the north, its capital Hanoi. Former Vietnamese allies of the French would temporarily set up a separate government in the south, in the capital of Saigon. The treaty specified that in two years there would be free elections in the north and south, reuniting the two sides.

"Tank from 1st Battalion, 69th Armor, 25th Infantry Division, moves through Saigon shortly after disembarking from LST at Saigon Harbor., 03/12/1966"

BACK IN WASHINGTON, Dulles was more than ever determined to sabotage the Geneva accord. He picked Colonel Edward Lansdale, considered by many to be the premier U.S. counter-insurgency expert, as point man for America's coming military intervention. Lansdale's first job was to bring aboard a Vietnamese puppet to do his bidding, one nominally acceptable to the people of the South but, more importantly, a compliant individual with confirmed anti-Communist credentials. The obvious candidate was Ngo Dinh Diem. He was a devout Catholic, an important plus, and had been

Interior Minister in one of Bao Dai's cabinets. Diem had recently spent two years living an ascetic life in Maryknoll seminaries in the United States and with the help of fervent anti-Communist Francis Cardinal Spellman had been introduced to State Department officials and key members of Congress. Spellman made sure Diem met Catholic Senator John Fitzgerald Kennedy, a likely candidate for the presidency. To the war planners in the Pentagon, Diem was almost too good to be true.

As the date for nationwide elections drew closer in Vietnam, Lansdale and Diem in Vietnam and Dulles and President Eisenhower in Washington realized that Ho was certain to be elected president of a united Vietnam.[13] With no election, there would not be Communist Ho Chi Minh as president—and no reunification. For the quiet conspirators, it was an easy call.

Stephen Kinzer wrote that as:

> Ho ruled North Vietnam in traditional Communist fashion through a politburo made up of trusted comrades; Diem shaped a politburo of his own, made up of close relatives. They ruled the country as a family.[14]

In the interim, Diem deposed Bao Dai after a rigged referendum that gave him 98.2 percent of the vote and made him Chief of State.

By 1960, it was apparent to Ho and his minions that the United States was intent on replacing France as hated occupier. To crystallize Ho's program, heads of dissident political groups formed a coalition they called the National Liberation Front. It would confront Diem and his corrupt family on the political front in the cities at the same time their guerrillas, newly named Vietcong, would fight Diem's troops, Army of the Republic of Vietnam—ARVN—and the American military in the rice paddies and the jungles of South Vietnam in what some called "the thousand-day war."

Dulles died in 1958 but there was no shortage of virulent anti-Communists in high places in Washington to step into his shoes. President Eisenhower was one. "If we lose Indochina," he declared awkwardly in August 1960, injecting an economic reason to conquer the territory:

> Several things will immediately occur... The tin and tungsten we so much need will stop coming in from that region; thus when the United States votes 400 million dollars in support of the war... we are voting for the least costly method of stopping something which would be disastrous for the United States, for our security, for our strength, and for our ability to draw upon the riches of Indochina for certain things we need.[15]

JOHN F. KENNEDY was also a fervent war-hawk. Soon after he took office as president in 1961 he began the build-up of American troops in Vietnam. It was his successor, Lyndon Baines Johnson, however, who would expand the intervention into a full-blown war. Emulating the devious example set by Franklin Roosevelt in leading the United States into World War II, Johnson took the country into war in Vietnam by sham. He was supported by the Pentagon's awesome propaganda machine. Over and over Americans were lectured:

> "If we don't fight them [the Communists] over there, we'll have to fight them here."

That was the same mantra used in the Great War in France, when "them" were Kaiser Wilhelm II's grenadiers. It was employed in World War II against the Germans again and would be used off and on in other U.S. wars to come. Propaganda must instill fear if it is to be successful!

> *During the Vietnam War, White House news correspondents devised what they called the LBJ Credibility Test. It went like this: "You don't have to worry about the Credibility Gap when the*

president smooths down the hair on the back of his head; you don't have to worry about it when he strokes the side of his nose; you don't have to worry about it when he rubs his hands; but when he starts moving his lips, look out."

By mid-1964, there were 16,000 U.S. "advisers" in Vietnam, the war was costing U.S. taxpayers over one million dollars a day, and "progress" was hard to measure. Johnson ordered the Joint Chiefs to develop an aggressive but still "plausibly deniable" operation that would put sufficiently heavy pressure on Ho so he would abandon his war for unification. OPLAN 34-A was the result, a clandestine scheme for provocative sabotage and hit-and-run attacks by ARVN commandos along the coast of North Vietnam. The CIA contributed eight fast and heavily armed gunboats so the commandos could extend their range and give them shore-bombardment capabilities. The United States was as yet still tip-toeing into the quagmire of Vietnam; Americans were told next to nothing about what was going on there.

Tough, persistent Ho Chi Minh, whose Vietminh troops had pushed the French army all the way back to Paris, was not intimidated by OPLAN 34-A. Years later, Defense Secretary Robert S. McNamara wrote in his retrospective that in May 1964, a CIA intelligence report concluded its bleak assessment and warned:

"If the tide of deterioration was not arrested by the end of the year, the anti-Communist position in South Vietnam is likely to become untenable."[16]

One hundred-and-one pages later, McNamara conceded that the secret project made little sense:

"Most of the South Vietnamese agents sent into North Vietnam were either captured or killed, and the seaborne attacks amounted to little more than pinpricks."[17]

THEN CAME THE INCIDENT that opened a new phase of the still clandestine war against Ho. On August 2, 1964, the U.S. Navy destroyer *Maddox*, cruising close to shore in the Tonkin Gulf (the waters between North Vietnam and Hainan Island)[18] was attacked by two North Korean torpedo boats. Each launched a single torpedo. It was daylight and visibility was excellent. Lookouts on *Maddox* tracked the wakes of the incoming torpedoes and the helmsman skillfully swung his ship out of their paths. Captain John J. Herrick then took *Maddox* to flank speed and outdistanced the small gunboats.

Washington announced to the world next morning that *Maddox* had been in international waters on a routine patrol when it was wantonly attacked. As later revealed in Pentagon documents, the American destroyer had not been in international waters when intercepted and her patrol was anything but "routine". In fact, *Maddox* had been on De Soto patrol, the code name for an ongoing hush-hush mission to collect intelligence on naval and shoreline activities of the North Vietnamese that would be useful to area naval commanders. "De Soto" stood for Hernando De Soto, the 16th century *conquistador* who, while looking for gold, stumbled on the Mississippi River.

The De Soto cruises were rotated among destroyers of the Seventh Fleet. On her way to the Tonkin Gulf, *Maddox* stopped at Taiwan and took aboard an extra crew detachment along with a large "black box" known as a COMVAN. The ship would function as a floating *provocateur*, to snoop close to shore and regularly lob five-inch shells from its main guns at any worthwhile targets ashore and thus give coastal batteries a reason to "illuminate" their defense radars, fire-control systems, and radio communications. In turn, *Maddox's* special eavesdropping equipment would then intercept and record such electronic signals for further processing ashore. At the same time, *Maddox* gathered hydrographic data such as water temperatures at different depths, cataloged junk traffic along the coast, and photographed shore installations. *Maddox's* mission was purposefully made more provocative by being timed to coincide with OPLAN 34-A raids that put North Vietnamese defenses on a razor's edge.

After the attack, Herrick radioed Washington suggesting that his ship's close-inshore mission be moved further offshore, out into international waters. But the Pentagon considered such an action would send the wrong signal that the United States Navy had retreated in the face of attack. Instead, to bolster the operation, a second destroyer, *Turner Joy*, was dispatched immediately to cruise in tandem with *Maddox*.

Two nights later, August 4, the two ships were back in the same area, *Maddox* continuing its surveillance activities. According to the ships' logs, the night was moonless and starless; wind speeds averaged 17 knots, with wind-blown spray from the tops of waves sharply reducing visibility, wave heights five to six feet.

At 8:40PM, *Maddox* suddenly radioed that it had acquired radar signals from three unidentified ships—closing fast. For the next two hours, *Maddox* and *Turner Joy* were in continuous radio communication with U.S. Navy ships in the vicinity. According to these radio messsages, both *Maddox* and *Turner Joy* were under attack. From these messages, called "frantic" by radio operators during the investigation that followed, there was a picture of ferocious fire-fights with an unknown number of enemy torpedo boats. The two destroyers wildly zig-zagged to dodge torpedoes and responded with their 5-inch main batteries and 3-inch deck guns. *Turner Joy* dropped depth charges, set for detonation at shallow depths, standard Navy practice for defense against torpedo attacks.

Could aircraft carrier *Ticonderoga* be of assistance? one message asked. *Ticonderoga* responded by launching fighter-bombers to support the supposedly beleagured destroyers. All returned to report they had observed no torpedo boats, no torpedo tracks, no sparks from hits being scored on enemy ships. There were, however, bursts of frantic commands and shouted reports from both ships as they desperately gave ranges, courses, and torpedo bearings. One pilot reported that he had been startled to hear over his radio so much bedlam and confusion.

A particularly credible eyewitness was *Ticonderoga* pilot James Bond Stockdale, who later spent eight years as a POW in a Hanoi prison and became H. Ross Perot's vice presidential running mate in 1992. Stockdale wrote in his memoir, *In Love and War*, as he overflew the scene "low and slow," he saw no torpedo boats. He also declared that he did not believe any attacks had occurred. Stockdale gave a running commentary of the action from what he called "the best seat in the house." He recalled:

> I leveled off my F-8U *Crusader* after I took off from carrier *Ticonderoga* at about 25,000 feet. Further up the gulf things were looking more and more spooky... I maneuvered close in, very low, darting like a waterbug. I was just going to have to try to see what the destroyers were shooting at. For the next hour and a half I hovered around those two ships at a thousand feet maximum and usually below that altitude, always within two or three miles of the destroyers and never outside the range at which I could keep their vivid, highly luminescent wakes in sight. There's something wrong out there. Those destroyers are talking about hits, but where are the metal-to-metal sparks? And the boat wakes—where are they? And boat gun flashes? The day before yesterday, I saw all of those signs of small-boat combat in broad daylight. Now the *Turner Joy's* guns were firing astern as she took an evasive course. When *Joy* ceased firing, I took a couple of minutes to shoot my other *Zuni* rockets and the dregs of my 20 mm magazines

into the general area astern of her, then added full throttle, picked up the nose, and started climbing out to the southwest toward *Ticonderoga*.[20]

IT WAS ABOUT MIDNIGHT when the U.S. Navy came perilously close to a catastrophe: "friendly fire" was about to blow *Turner Joy* out of the water with all hands. *Maddox's* gun director was given a range and course reading for what he later called:

> "The finest target we had all night. It was a damned big one, right on us. No doubt about this one."[21]

Just as he was about to squeeze the firing key for *Maddox's* main battery of five-inch cannons, the gun director sensed something was not right. Where was *Turner Joy?*

> "There was a lot of yelling of 'God damn' back and forth, with the bridge telling me to fire before we lose contact. I finally told them I'm not firing until I know where *Turner Joy* is."[22]

The bridge then radioed *Turner Joy* to turn on its lights.

> "Sure enough, there she was—right in the cross-hairs. I had six five-inch guns trained on the *Turner Joy*."[23]

The next morning when he was awakened by the junior officer of the deck, Stockdale was told that the *Ticonderoga's* sister carrier *Constellation* in the gulf would fly-off a six-plane strike against a torpedo-boat base. His "Tico's" planes would hit hit oil storage tanks in the city of Vinh.

> "What's the idea of the strikes? Reprisal, sir. Reprisal for what? For last night's attack on the destroyers, sir."[24]

Lieutenant Stockdale went on with his sensitive analysis.

> The fact that a war was being conceived out here in the humid muck of the Tonkin Gulf didn't bother me so much. It seemed obvious that a tinderbox situation prevailed here and that there would be a war in due course anyway. But for the long pull it seemed to me important that the grounds for entering war be legitimate. I felt it was a bad portent that we seemed to be under the conrol of a mindless Washington bureaucracy.[25]

MANY QUESTIONS remained unanswered. Had there been, in fact, a small-scale naval engagement? Were the visual sightings—generally considered reliable sources of information—from frightened or disoriented sailors? Were the radar and sonar instrument readouts influenced by unusual eenvironmental conditions? Nervous radarmen could easily have mistaken "ghosts" on their scopes for real ships, and inexperienced sonarmen, in the confusion of "the battle," might have interpreted the noises from their ships's screws and movements of rudders, for example, as incoming torpedoes.

North Korean sailors who were later captured and interrogated were unanimous in declaring that there had been no torpedo-boat attacks on August 4.

As for Captain Herrick,

> He eventually concluded that it was unlikely that any torpedoes were fired at any time on the night of August 4, 1964, unlikely that the radar image marking the first torpedo run was genuine, unlikely, in fact, that any vessel came within 10,000 yards of the Maddox that night.[26]

On August 5, at first light, *Ticonderoga* and *Constellation* in well-practiced cadences of U.S. Navy efficiency, fueled, armed, and "bombed up" their fighter-bombers, turned smartly into the wind, and accelerated to flank speed. They successively catapult-launched 64 sorties which struck torpedo-boat bases and the oil-tank farm at Vinh. According to MacNamara, in his testimony before the Senate Foreign Relations Committee on February 20, 1968,

> "It was considered a successful mission, a limited but we thought appropriate, reply to at least one and very probably two attacks on U.S. vessels."[27]

MacNamara insisted he had unequivocal proof of the attack, based on Secret NSA reports he clamed had been sent to *Maddox* that night warning of a likely confrontation. He also energetically and long-windedly denied that any skullduggery had occurred in the Tonkin Gulf:

> I must address the suggestion that, in some way, the government of the United States induced the incident on August 4 with the intent of providing an excuse to take the retaliatory action which, in fact, we took. I find it inconceivable that anyone even remotely familiar with our society and our system of government could suspect the existence of a conspiracy which would include almost, if not all, the entire chain of command in the Pacific, the Chairman of the Joint Chiefs of Staff, the Secretary of Defense and his chief assistants, the Secretary of State, and the President of the United States.[28]

Historian James Bamford vigorously countered the defense secretary's "unambiguous" proof of the attack.

McNamara knew full well how disengenous this was. The Joint Chiefs of Staff had become a sewer of deceit. Only two years before... they had presented him with a plan to launch a conspiracy far more grave than 'inducing' the attack on the destroyers. This plan was *Operation Northwoods*, a secret campaign of terrorism inside the United States to blame Fidel Castro's Cuba. Three years later was another Joint Chiefs' scheme that would serve as a pretext for an American attack on North Korea. This idea called for sending the intelligence-gathering ship *Banner*, with a skeleton crew, close to the coast to act as a sacrificial cow of sorts, intended to provoke a violent response by the understandably trigger-happy North Koreans.[29]

McNamara's claims of certainty disarmed those few in the Congress who were likely to challenge his integrity. In the event, Lyndon Johnson went on national television that night to tell Americans that two U.S. Navy destroyers had been attacked by North Vietnames torpedo boats, that it was the second such "unprovoked" attack in two days, and that, in consultation with the Joint Chiefs, he had ordered "limited" retaliatory air strikes.

The next day, August 7, Congress passed the fateful Tonkin Gulf Resolution which gave Johnson, as President and Commander-in-Chief, discretion "to take all necessary measures, including the use of armed forces" against North Vietnam. The Resolution had been prepared months before in anticipation of such an event. It was Johnson's blank check for war in Indochina.

> *A year later President Johnson admitted, during an off-the-record monologue with reporters on the Tonkin Gulf incident, that for all he knew the U.S Navy was "shooting at whales out there."*[19]

The initial media coverage and the man-in-the-street's responses were universally supportive of the president's action. Whenever the U.S. military unleashes its dogs of war—and at the same time the Pentagon unlimbers its awesome propaganda apparatus—inevitably there is overwhelming backing for the newest American adventure. Public opinion polls this time around showed eighty-five percent approvals for the president's "limited" response.

Historian Edwin E. Moise wrote that his research turned up,

> "no exceptions; nobody in the mainstream press appeared to have the slightest doubt about the competence or the moral correctness of any action that U.S. military had taken."[30]

The Resolution passed by a 416-0 vote in the House and 88-2 in the Senate, only Wayne Morse of Oregon and Ernest Gruening of Alaska voting against the measure.

LYNDON JOHNSON FINALLY GOT HIS WAR. He had no inkling that the war that blossomed on his watch would destroy his presidency, take the lives of almost 60,000 young Americans, send untold thousands to hospitals for months and years of treatment, and drive millions of antiwar protesters into the streets to face off against lined-up National Guard troops with fixed bayonets. The Vietnam War would divide the nation like never before in its history. The vicious guerrilla war would also turn a part of the United States Army into torturers and indiscriminate murderers—and nearly shatter it.

> *"If you want to, go ahead and fight in the jungles of Vietnam. The French fought there for seven years and still had to quit in the end. Perhaps the Americans will be able to stick it out for a little longer, but eventually they will have to quit, too."*
>
> —Nikita Khrushchev, Soviet Premier, to a U.S. official, 1963.

Nearly every piece of equipment in America's mighty military arsenal was used in Vietnam. The skies over Vietnam, day and night, were filled with helicopters, fighter-bombers, and high-altitude B-52s. So dense was the air traffic that South Vietnam's airports were recorded as the world's busiest.

Planes not only flew into combat from airports inside the country but from aircraft carriers in the South China Sea and from bases in Guam and Thailand. The waters around Vietnam swarmed with U.S. Navy men-of-war, tankers, hospital ships, and shallow-draft patrol boats that could penetrate the estuaries and canals that harbored the guerrillas.

From 1965 through 1971 the Indochina region of Vietnam, Laos, and Cambodia, somewhat larger than Texas, was pounded by a tonnage of munitions double the total used by the United States in all of the theaters of World War II—an estimated 26 billion pounds, half from the air and half from artillery on the ground. This enormous barrage pitted the landscape with an estimated 26 million craters, making some regions look like the surface of the moon from an arial viewpoint.

Every type of bomb in the Pentagon's vast inventory was used: cluster bombs, many with diabolical time-delay fuses; white-phosphorous bombs that seared the flesh and maimed terribly; fuel-air bombs for wide-area indiscriminate destruction; bombs that spread poisonous chemicals, an array of different-size demolition bombs, and most fearsome of all—napalm. In the interval between the Korean War and the Vietnam War, American chemical companies had developed "improved" napalm formulations that stuck better to the skin, burned at higher temperature, and dug deeper into the flesh. In Korea, 32,000 tons of napalm had been used. In Vietnam, from 1963 to 1971, the total was an astounding 373,000 tons.[31]

The NVA and the Vietcong responded to the heavy USAF bombing by beefing up their anti-aircraft defenses. By war's end, about 2,000 U.S. helicopters had been shot down over South Vietnam. Another 2,500 were lost due to pilot error, mechanical failure, and accidents unrelated to combat.

> "Helicopter pilots and crewmen suffered the highest casualty rates of any contingent of U.S. forces in Vietnam. More than 3,500 were killed."[32]

FIRE AS A WEAPON OF WAR goes back to antiquity, with the Chinese generally being credited as the first users. Their catapults propelled vessels filled with flaming oil over castle ramparts. Archeologists have also unearthed primitive flamethrowers which, when reconstructed, astonished their rebuilders with their ability to project flames over surprisingly long distances. Modern flamethrowers owe their origins, however, to a German engineer, Richard Fiedler, who designed a workable one in 1900, which was tested the following year in secret by the Imperial German Army. By 1912, a *Flammenwerfer* regiment had been formed, as events would show, just in time for deployment in the Great War. These flamethrowers were man-portable consisting of a two-compartment steel tank carried on the back of the operator, attached to a hose and nozzle. The flammable liquid used was oil and the compressed inert propellant was nitrogen. The flame could be projected for up to twenty yards.

The Germans first used the weapon against the French at Verdun in February 1915 and against British trenches in July. All sides used flamethrowers during World War II. U.S. Marines were the biggest users, employing them extensively on the Japanese-held Pacific Islands to flush out enemy troops in caves and in dug-in emplacements. Tank-mounted flamethrowers were also used.

Napalm, the name originally given to a great number of flammable liquids, typically jellied gasoline, revolutionized the use of fire in warfare. Napalm is actually the thickener in such liquids which, when mixed with gasoline, makes a sticky incendiary gel. It was developed during World War II by Harvard University chemists to improve the range and effectiveness of flamethrowers. Its name is a combination of the designation of its original ingredients: aluminum salts of *nap*thenic and *palm*itic acids. Modern napalm is composed primarily of benzene and polystyrene, and is known as Napalm-B, an improved substance that is stickier, burns hotter, is harder to extinguish, and digs deeper into the flesh than the original formulation.

NAPALM IS A HIDEOUS WEAPON. Immolation, its principal impact on living creatures, produces rapid loss of blood pressure, unconsciousness, and quick, merciful death. Napalm also has devastating side effects combining shock, absorption of oxygen from the air, smoke, and, most important, production of the deadly gas carbon monoxide; the latter results from the incomplete combustion of the compound.

The lethality of carbon monoxide is well known. The Nazis were the first to try it on a large scale, as a poisonous gas for the mass execution of Jews in concentration camps during World War II. During the Pacific War, American troops found Japanese tunnels whose entrances had been bathed by flamethrowers in which all the occupants were dead without signs of burning. These Japanese soldiers had died, apparently without pain if their benign visages were accurate indicators, having been poisoned quickly by carbon monoxide.

U.S. Air Force and Navy fighter-bomber pilots, who dropped napalm on the Vietnamese, had no concept of the horrors on the ground following the bursting of the cannisters. All they saw, if they glanced back on their climb-out, was a huge plume of orange fire and an angry, billowing dark grey cloud that obscured the immediate area. It took an explosion and fire aboard an aircraft carrier, U.S.S. *Forrestal*, to bring home to some of these men, a Navy pilot in particular, what was happening beneath the cloud.

"Now that I've seen what the bombs and napalm did to the people on our ship, I'm not so sure I want to drop any more of that stuff on North Vietnam."[33]

RARELY DID NEWS CORRESPONDENTS write about the ecological destruction that was wrought by U.S. bombing and shelling despite its ubiquity. For example, the typical crater left by a 500-pound demolition bomb is about 30 feet in diameter and 15 feet deep in the center, displacing about 130 cubic yards of earth, resembling an inverted cone. Researchers have calculated that such craters in Vietnam covered a total of 423,000 acres, representing a total displacement of about 3.4 billion cubic yards of earth. Ecological damage included the ground adjacent to the crater which was contaminated by steel weapon fragments.

Evidence points to the certainty that these ecological impacts will be long-lasting. Ten years after the end of World War II, for example, craters on heavily shelled areas of Okinawa were still devoid of vegetation and reddened by rusting shell and bomb fragments. In France's Verdun area, the scene of protracted trench warfare during the Great War almost a century ago, many artillery craters remain clearly visible, some even barren of vegetation. The tearing up and scattering of topsoil also results in harmful physical consequences. In hilly terrain, the disturbances promoted undesirable erosion that leads to laterization, the permanent modification of soil to a brick-like consistency that cannot be returned to its original state.

An additional impact is that deep craters close to roads made many areas impassable for travel. Without bulldozers, the Vietnamese peasants are unable to efficiently fill-in the craters. As a result many roads have remained only partly usable for decades. Millions of craters, particularly those in coastal regions, penetrated the shallow water table and remain filled with water most of the year, becoming breeding grounds for mosquitoes that spread malaria and dengue fever.

Most significant of all, cratering affects agriculture, both short- and long-term. Peasant farmers are understandably reluctant to reclaim rice paddies pocked with craters and unexploded munitions buried unseen just below the surface. Steel bomb shards and artillery-shell fragments scattered over the landscape cut the hooves of water buffalo used to pull the plows. Trees not destroyed outright were riddled with steel fragments, discouraging their use as lumber.

Another method of deforestation begun in the mid-1960s by U.S. and ARVN troops was the use of special 20-ton Caterpillar tractors fitted with 11-foot-wide blades known as Rome Plows, armored with 14 tons of steel plates to protect the operators against mines and booby-traps. These mechanical monsters operated in groups and in some areas replaced herbicides for land-clearing. As might be imagined, the behemoths left utter devastation in their wakes. If ever the term "raping the land" was appropriate, the rapers were these massively destructive machines.

To casually dispose of Indochina's tropical forests as merely jungles, a supposedly useless catacomb of densely intertwined trees, vines, and shrubbery, is to belittle their value to their inhabitants. To the contrary, Vietnamese peasants regarded these areas as cornucopias of useful materals. They were sources of timber for charcoal and for building houses and boats. The leaves of the Nipa palm, for example, were dried and stitched together to form lightweight thatch that formed roofs, sides, and inside partitions of houses. These versatile leaves also functioned as umbrellas, sunhats, mats, and bags. The jungles were also the habitat of animals that were part of the villagers' regular food supply.

VIII. The Vietnam War

THE AERIAL SPRAYING of poisonous defoliants and herbicides had a terrible ecological impact on Vietnam, much of it long term. But the effects on both the Vietnamese people and American GIs who handled the poisons proved to be far more devastating. Those who came in contact with its droplets, who breathed its fumes, who drank water contaminated by it suffered permanent damage to their health. Their offspring were crippled by birth defects that would show up years later. Pregnant women exposed to these poisons had a high rate of miscarriages.

America was not the first nation to use such dangerous chemicals in war. It was the British who inaugurated their use on a large scale in the little known "Malayan Emergency," 1948 to 1960, during which they were used as crop-killers against Communist guerrillas. The British at first used sodium arsenite, but gave it up because the danger posed by this chemical to the indigenous population was looked upon as politically unacceptable. A less risky yet still potent crop killer was a mixture of trioxene and diesolene, which both killed crops and rendered the soil sterile for a short time.[34] The British sprayed mostly from helicopters and on small garden plots, supposedly tended by the insurgents when they weren't laying minefields. By most measures, the aerial spraying worked satisfactorily since the rebels retreated from populated areas to the deep jungle to grow their food.

The program of aerial defoliation and crop killing planned and executed by the United States in Vietnam was many magnitudes greater. And when the U.S. was ready to kill foliage and food crops in Vietnam, it had a proven defoliant and herbicide that government officials declared over and over was harmless to humans. It was 2, 4,-D (dichlorophenoxyacetic acid) enhanced by another jaw-breaking chemical, 2, 4, 5-T (trichlorophenoxyacetic acid.). This formulation worked much faster. It was named Agent Orange for the orange bands painted on its drums to identify it. Orange became the most-used herbicide in Vietnam and became the paradigm for American chemical warfare in Vietnam. It was, however, only one of a "rainbow" of different chemical formulations: Purple, Pink, Green, White, and Blue plus eight more that were used as foliage and plant killers.[35]

Agent Orange had its origins as a defoliant in a military laboratory at the University of Chicago during World War II. The researchers found the growth of plants could be regulated through the infusion of hormones. It was learned further that certain broadleaf vegetation could be killed by causing the plants to experience rapid, uncontrolled growth. In particular, 2, 4,-D was effective in inducing such growth spurts. The U.S. Army tested it but found no use for it—at the time.

What the Army scientists didn't know at first—or chose purposefully to ignore or, more likely, to cover-up—was that 2, 4, 5-T contained dioxin, a chemical the EPA would later call potentially one of the most dangerous to man. Tests showed that less than two millionths of an ounce would kill a mouse. It was also learned, but carefully suppressed by all involved, particularly by the big chemical companies—Dow, Monsanto, Hooker, Diamond Alkali, and Hercules—which were enjoying a bonanza of Army orders, that dioxin's toxicity was enhanced by its ability to pass into the body through all entry routes.

The Pentagon insisted from the get-go that use of such poisons was not chemical warfare and that these chemicals were harmless to humans. Such spraying, the military said, had two simple objectives: defoliation, to remove the foliage cover in jungles, alongside roads, and base perimeters that afforded concealment to the enemy; and crop destruction, mainly rice, intended to deny food to the Vietcong.

"Dioxin is the most toxic small man-made molecule we know of. It is less toxic on a per-gram basis than some biological toxins like Botulin, but that's a very large molecule. So molecule for molecule, dioxin is probably the leader of the pack."[36]

AS FOR CROP DESTRUCTION AIMED at the Vietcong, there is plenty of evidence that adult males suffer far less from food shortages than young children. A statement in January 1966 by twenty-nine scientists and physicians from Harvard and MIT condemned U.S. crop destruction in Vietnam. It quoted a letter by Jean Mayer, of Harvard's School of Public Health, to *Science*, April 1966.

> As a nutritionist who has seen famines on three continents... and as a historian of public health with an interest in famines, I can say flatly that there has never been a famine or food shortage... that has not first and overwhelmingly affected the small children. Bands of armed men do not starve and—particularly if not indigenous to the population and therefore unhampered by direct ties with their victims—find themselves entirely justified in seizing what little food is available so as to be able to continue to fight. During World War I, the blockade [by the Royal Navy] had no effect on the nutrition and fighting performance of the German and Austrian armies, but—for the first since the 18th century—starvation, Vitamin-A deficiency, and protein deficiency destroyed the health, the sight, and even the lives of children [nearly all German] in Western Europe.

At the end of World War II, effective and cheap 2, 4-D and was used in large-scale defoliation programs in the United States. According to government officials, no health problems associated with their use were reported. These officials specifically pointed to the state of Montana, where tens of thousands of acres of desert had been sprayed safely with 2, 4-D to kill unwanted sagebrush. No one pointed out that the U.S. Forest Service saw to it that livestock was kept off treated areas for ten days to allow time for the herbicide to completely decompose, nor that spraying was carefully supervised to avoid contaminating surface water and streams.

The same defoliant also was used successfully for thinning saplings that regenerated in forest areas damaged by fires and to suppress the growth of unwanted plant species. Railroads used it to control weeds that damaged ties. Highway maintenance crews sprayed it alongside roads to clear tall vegetation that reduced driver visibility around curves. Consumers bought millions of cans of it, all carefully labeled as to its potential toxicity if improperly used, to keep gardens and lawns tidy.

In 1967, a Department of Defense Report, in its ongoing white-washing campaign, summed up the available data on the effects of herbicides Orange, White, and Blue, with emphasis on their non-toxicity.

> 1. The direct toxicity hazards to people and animals on the ground is nearly nonexistent. 2. Destruction of wildlife, food, and wildlife habitats [due to other efforts to defoliate] will probably affect wildlife survival more than the direct toxic effects of the herbicides. 3. The application of Orange and White alongside rivers and canals, or even the spraying of the water itself at the levels used for defoliation, is not likely to kill the fish in the water. 4. Food produced from land treated with herbicides will not be poisonous or significantly altered in nutritional quality. If residues of a more persisten herbicide such as picloram [Agent White] should carry over to the next growing season it would retard plant growth rather than concentrate some toxic residue in the crop. 5. Toxic residues of these herbicides will not accumulate in the fish and meat animals to the point where man will be poisoned by them.[37]

There was one major difference, however, between the 2, 4-D and 2, 4, 5-T used in the United States and Orange used in Vietnam: concentration. In America it was used in dilute concentrations; in Vietnam, it was highly concentrated to serve not only as a leaf-remover but as a plant killer. In the case of Agent Orange, the rate of application was up to twenty-five times the rate recommended for the use in the United States.

In 1963, it was learned that Orange in heavy doses could cause cancer, birth defects, and other debilitating diseases to humans exposed to it. Despite the warning signals, the U.S. used Orange for eight more years in Indochina, dosing Vietnam with 12 million gallons of the poison. Forty years later, jungles that were heavily saturated with Orange still hadn't recovered. A grass species, cogon, had taken over. Although burned off constantly, cogon stubbornly grew back, overwhelming attempts to supplant it with useful crops such as bamboo and teak.

Scientists Gordon Orians and E.W. Pfeiffer completed a comprehensive overview of the military uses of herbicides in Vietnam by quoting a disingenuous 1966 letter by Dr. John S. Foster, Jr., President Nixon's science advisor, to New York Senator Jacob Javits whose committee was studying CBW in Vietnam:

> Let me state unequivocally that there is no chemical or biological warfare being conducted in Vietnam. While riot control agents and herbicides are chemical substances as are many other items and articles in common use throughout the world, they are not CBW agents.[38]

Later, as Director of Research for the Defense Department, Foster continued to defend the use of crop-killing chemicals.

> Qualified scientists, both inside and outside our government, and in the governments of other nations, have judged that serious adverse ecological consequences will not occur [from use of herbicides and defoliants in Vietnam]. Unless we had confidence in these judgments, we would not continue to employ these materials.[39]

Nevertheless, objective (*non-government*) scientists Orians and Pfeiffer weren't buying what Foster was trying to sell. They wrote:

> "Since the publication of these reassuring statements about the lack of toxic effects on animals, new evidence has been obtained suggesting that animals may indeed be sensitive to herbicides."[40]

The New York Times finally threw its acknowledged political weight and research capabilities on the side of skeptics of the government's continuous sugar-coated statements. On March 15, 1970, it published a story that gave strong evidence that not only plants but animals were directly affected by the poisons masquerading as innocent herbicides. The article was based on its three weeks' survey of South Vietnamese scientists, physicians, health officials, and the villagers themselves. The article pointed out that the South Vietnamese Government,

> Regards the entire subject as taboo. Vietnamese newspapers have been suspended for publishing articles about birth defects allegedly attributed to the defoliant. The Agriculture Ministry, too, chose to stay at arm's length from the controversy.

The Times wrote that the United States command also covered up embarrassing incidents. On December 1, 1968, for example, a *Ranch Hand* sprayer developed engine trouble during climb-out after takeoff. The pilot, to lighten his faltering plane's load and to be able to come around and land safely, dumped the aircraft's entire load of 1,000 gallons of Agent Orange in thirty seconds instead of the normal four minutes and thirty seconds. The village of Tanheip was drenched with the entire overdose.

> "No physicians visited Tanheip to examine the people after their exposure, which like eight similar emergency dumpings since 1968... was not made public by the United States command."

The Times interviewed a Mrs. Tran Thi Tien of Tanheip, who said that she had four normal children and one who still looked like a newborn at 14 months of age. She traced her disfigured, crippled youngest child to the December 1 dousing by Agent Orange.

The article also noted that in the previous October, Dr. Lee A. DuBridge, President Nixon's science adviser, announced:

> As a result of a study showing that... 2, 4, 5-T had caused an unexpectedly high incidence of fetal abnormalities in mice and rats, the compound would henceforth be restricted to areas remote from population.

The rigid defensive stance by the U.S. government was later rejected by a one-sided majority of the UN which voted 80 to 3 to expand the prohibitions of the Geneva Protocol of June 17, 1925 to include herbicides—as well as riot-control gases—as CBW agents. The United States patently rejected this ruling.

> *"... The trends of history are such that crop-killing chemicals were accepted by most Americans as perfectly normal and permissible to use. Distressing as this might seem, it is the natural result of American foreign policy. After all, if it is better to be dead than Red, it is presumably better to be poisoned or deformed than Red. Under this view environmental destruction and human illness are part of the price we must pay to defend ourselves."[41]*

WELL BEFORE THE AIR FORCE'S DEFOLIATION Project, codenamed *Ranch Hand* began in October 1962, the ARVN was already destroying crops they considered food for the Vietcong, laboriously pulling, cutting, and burning the plants with napalm dropped by helicopters. The Kennedy administration and the president himself, however, saw large-scale crop destruction by herbicides as a significant step beyond using these chemicals for clearing jungle. It was a step much deeper into the political risky area of chemical warfare.

There was further evidence that the defoliants and herbicides sprayed over Vietnam in fact bordered on chemical warfare, regardless of how the term was defined. The medical diary of a Dr. Cao Quang Nguyen that was used as evidence at the Russell War Crimes Tribunal in Copenhagen in 1967 described such a chemical attack, perhaps exaggerated but nevertheless more than marginally credible.

> In the beginning of 1964 four single-engine planes bombed and strafed the area where I lived in Lam Dong province. Then came one helicopter and two Dakotas. The smell of chemicals was unbearable. After five minutes leaves of sweet potatoes, rice plants, and trees became completely dessicated. Domestic animals would not eat and almost all died. Only fifteen minutes later Dakota planes returned and sprayed chemicals a second time... no one was able to eat that day, everyone was unable to sleep, the effects on the nervous system were very unusual. The next day all of our poultry was dead, the fish in streams and lakes were floating on the water, discoloured. The grass was poisoned. All the women who were pregnant had miscarried on the spot... Ten days later a squadron of U.S. airplanes came and spread chemicals a third time. I vomited all the time. Fifteen days later I could not read. One month later I could not see. Everytime they spray chemicals they threaten us with loudspeakers, broadcasting from airplanes, telling people to go to areas controlled by Saigon or they will suffer death.[42]

A sober sidebar impact to the forced relocation of villagers, either into refugee camps or cities, was the destruction of what had been a flourishing civilization in Indochina. In 1960, for example, only about twenty percent of South Vietnam's population lived in urban areas; by 1971, mainly for safety reasons and dire economic necessity, this share had more than doubled, to forty-three percent. At the same time, daughters became the unbiquitous prostitutes who served the GIs and sons became the pimps who organized them.

A MEASURE OF THE BROAD SCOPE of Project *Ranch Hand* was the decision that helicopters wouldn't be able to do the job: they couldn't carry the heavy loads planned for the spraying operations and their low speeds made them easy targets for VC gunners. Big fixed-wing aircraft were needed. The Air Force first turned to two of its largest planes then in inventory—the four-engine B-29 bomber and the twin-engine C-119 cargo carrier. In tests, both proved to be clumsy giants during the low-level spraying phase and the climb-out, again ripe targets for enemy anti-aircraft gunners.

A smaller, more nimble aircraft was finally selected, the twin-engine Fairchild C-123 *Provider*. It was the optimum compromise between load-carrying capability and low-level maneuverability and it became *Ranch Hand's* standard sprayer. Two small turbojet engines were hung in pylons under the wing to give the plane improved acceleration as it climbed away after spraying or in the event one of its reciprocating engines were hit by antiaircraft fire. The small fleet of C-123s flew more than 19,000 spraying sorties.

"To read the Pentagon Papers in their vast detail is to step through the looking glass into a new and different world... Clandestine warfare against North Vietnam, for example, is not seen, either in the written words of the senior decision-makers in the Executive Branch or by the anonymous authors of the study, as violating the Geneva Accords of 1954, which ended the French Indochina War, or as conflicting with the public announcements of the various administrations. Clandestine warfare, because it is covert, does not exist as far as treaties and public posture is concerned."—Neil Sheehan, Introduction, The Pentagon Papers.

"Only We Can Prevent Forests."

—Motto over the door to Headquarters, Operation Ranch Hand, Saigon.[43]

Question: "We know you had Gas Blau [nerve gas] which would have stopped the Normandy invasion. Why didn't you use it?" Answer: "The horses." Question: "What have horses to do with it?" Answer: "Everything. A horse lies down in the shafts or between the thills as soon as his breathing is restricted. We never had a gas mask a horse would tolerate." Question: "What has that to do with Normandy?" Answer: "We did not have enough gasoline to adequately supply the German Air Force and the Panzer Divisions, so we used horse transport in all operations. You must know that the first thing we did in Poland, France, everywhere, was to seize the horses. All our material was horse-drawn. Had we used gas you would have retaliated and you would have instantly immobilized us."

—Nuremberg War Crimes Trial, Hermann Goering to his inquisitors.

On October 2, President Kennedy signed on to *Ranch Hand*. All in his Administration involved agreed that it would be a good idea to inform Edward R. Murrow [Director of the U.S. Information Agency] so he could prepare a propaganda defense.[44]

DID THE U.S. MILITARY IN VIETNAM use poison gas? The answer depends on what is meant by "poison." No, the Great War's poison gases, Chlorine, Phosgene, Mustard, and Lewisite were not used. Nor were the newer nerve gases used: Tabun, Sarin, Soman, and Cyclosarin. What were used were "combat gases," three arguably nonlethal "tear gases."[45] The toxicity of these incapacitating gases depended on their concentrations—and who the victims were. It is generally accepted that the very young, the very old, and those with heart and lung ailments exposed to these "ordinary tear gases" would choke to death even at low concentrations.

When asked if cyanides and arsenic compounds were being used in Vietnam, Cyrus R. Vance, U.S. Undersecretary of State for Defense, said at a Washington conference on foreign policy on October 30, 1965, that we are "using them in a limited way" in South Vietnam, but not yet in the North.

Vance's careless statement unleashed a storm of indignation throughout the world. The Pentagon reacted promptly and promised to forbid the use of "toxic" gases, but the high-level prohibition apparently never trickled down to Marines in the field. On September 5, a Marine battalion in the course of an attack on the village of Vinh Quang flooded the civilians taking refuge in air raid shelters with heavy doses of an undesignated gas. Thirty-five were killed and 19 wounded.

> *"In the State Department we used to discuss how much time the mythical 'average American citizen' puts in each day listening, reading, and arguing about the world outside his country. Assuming a man or woman with a fair education, a family, and job in or out of the house, it seemed to us that ten minutes a day would be a high average."—Dean Acheson, Secretary of State, 1969*

BY 1967, THE WAR was not going well for American forces, despite more than 550,000 troops on the ground supported by the greatest aerial armada ever assembled. The Vietcong had no trouble recruiting volunteer replacements anxious to defend their homeland—and kill the despised invaders. Men who had returned to villages that had been "cleared" by bloody "search, kill, and destroy" operations saw clear evidence of American and ARVN atrocities, and eagerly joined the rebels.

When American troops came into a village, they often came in with guns blazing, accompanied by terrifying helicopter gunships roaring low overhead. If there was meaningful opposition, the troops backed out and either radioed for artillery support or fighter-bombers which would blanket the village with napalm. Prisoners were rarely taken; those few that were, generally officers, were savagely tortured during perfunctory interrogations before being murdered.

If troops on the ground were merciless killers and destroyers, those in the air did this work more efficiently. They did their ugly killing in helicopters, in specially configured C-47 "Spooky" gunships with rotating-barrel mini-cannons, and in fighter-bombers with their loads of napalm and white phosphorous canisters and cluster bombs. After they released their bombs, the pilots returned to strafe still-standing huts, if fuel allowed.

> *"Planes are designed to fly much faster than they will ever have to fly in battle and vast sums are eaten up to make them fly that fast. Of the 100,000 flights in planes capable of exceeding Mach 2 [in level flight] during the Vietnam War, only one reached as high as Mach 1.6 for a few seconds, and it ran out of fuel. Its crew was forced to bail out and were captured."*[46]

The most devastating of all aerial weapons was the giant eight-engine B-52 jet bomber. It generally flew at night, hauling up to 27 tons of bombs at 30,000 feet, unseen and unheard on the ground. The crew of six, in a cloistered, almost antiseptic environment, had no concept of what was happening on the ground below as they moved above it at near-supersonic speed. With bomb bay doors open, the B-52s resembled fictional dragons spewing fire from eight orifices. They bombed by reference to map coordinates, essentially inaccurate dead reckoning. On typical sorties, the big bombers released with their intervalometers strings of one hundred 750-pound bombs within 30 seconds, cutting a swath of total destruction a mile long and a quarter-mile wide. This was indiscriminate "carpet bombing" brought to a new level of random inhumanity.

> *In the Vietnam Historical Museum in Hanoi there is a huge mural stretched across a long wall that is both a timeline and a map of Vietnam's unhappy history dating back well over 1,000 years. There are thick red arrows from the north, depicting invasions and occupations by China, some lasting hundreds of years before Vietnamese patriots drove them out, again and again. The Chinese section of the time-line stretches out for about 50 feet. The section devoted to the French and their 150 years of colonial occupation takes up about 12 inches. The part that depicts the war with the United States is only a few inches wide.*[47]

THEN CAME THE MY LAI 4 MASSACRE on March 16, 1968. The horrors exposed fueled the growing antiwar sentiment in the country, and changed the way many Americans viewed the war. Every war has its turning point; and for the Vietnam War it was My Lai 4 and the war crimes of Company "C" or Charlie Company ("A" for Alpha, "B" for Bravo, "D" for Dog, "E" for Easy were part of the GI's lexicon, to make communications more foolproof in combat`.)

That morning, infantrymen from Charlie Company, 1st Battalion, 20th Infantry, 11th Light Infantry Brigade of the 23rd Americal Division brutally slaughtered about five hundred Vietnamese civilians—women, children, infants, and old men—in the tiny hamlet of My Lai 4 in Quang Ngai Province. The killings were not spontaneous reactions to hostile actions; in fact, Charlie's troopers had not received a single round of enemy fire as they entered the village. Rather, the focused butchery was something of a laid-back affair that lasted several hours, during which time many of the GIs who did the shooting took breaks in "the action" to eat their C-rations and smoke leisurely.

The U.S. Army initially covered up the massacre, and Charlie Company's fabricated victory against a Vietcong detachment in the village might well have remained just a statistic. In April 1969, however, a former GI wrote a letter to the White House, the Pentagon, and other government offices including twenty-four Congressmen giving details of the murders. The letter triggered a high-level response and Army attorneys of the Army's Criminal Investigations Division subsequently assigned to investigate the atrocities learned even more. In September, First Lieutenant William L. Calley, Jr. was charged with the murder of 109 Vietnamese civilians.

Still the Army held back making public details of the My Lai 4 killings. Instead, the Army released a deceitful statement that gave no hint of the number of murders and under what circumstances they were committed. But the story was a blockbuster and the facts began to emerge. In November, newspaper articles began to appear that told enough about the massacre to create not only anguished outcries in the United States but world-wide as well. This publicity pushed the Army to dig deeper into the happenings in My Lai 4 and a special panel was created with the forgettable title, "The Department of the Army Review of the Preliminary Investigations into the My Lai Incident." It became known as the Peers Commission, after its director, Lieutenant General William R. Peers.

By the middle of March 1970 the Peers Commission had collected enough evidence to recommend that fifteen officers be charged, including Major General Samuel W. Koster, who had been commanding general of the Americal Division on March 16, 1968, and was then Superintendent of West Point. All would be exonerated.

CHARLIE COMPANY had arrived in Vietnam—"the country"—in December 1967. For a year, Charlie had been in Hawaii, training for combat in Vietnam. Its men looked upon themselves as one of the best and toughest outfits in the newly formed 11th Brigade. When orders were cut for deployment to Vietnam, Charlie led the advance party.

Charlie's commanding officer was Captain Ernest L. Medina, a 33-year-old former enlisted man. He was gung-ho about "wasting" Vietcong even in mock battles in Hawaii, and was eager to get to Vietnam to help win a war he genuinely believed in. Another reason for his anxiety was his Army career. In 1966 he had been promoted to Captain, but making the next step to Major was harder; a successful tour in Vietnam was needed. Assembling a first-rate rifle company that was necessary for him to win him the necessary recognition was a tough job. In 1966 the men who were assigned to infantry units were those who performed poorest on the various Army qualification and aptitude tests. GIs scoring average or above were generally assigned to training or support outfits.

Most of Charlie Company's 130 soldiers were draftees. Nearly half were African-Americans and most were about 20 years of age. Their favorite "reading" matter was comic books, for many could scarcely read with comprehension. Ten percent of the company had not done well enough in the basic intelligence tests to qualify for military service, but the Army was hard up. It had instituted a new program to allow such men to enlist; Project 100,000 was intended to provide remedial education for those otherwise ineligible. Charlie Company's troops were the rotting apples at the bottom of a bushel of bruised ones.

Although ranking officers would almost certainly deny it, they themselves had little respect for the average combat soldier. One colonel in the newly formed Americal Division had this to say about its GIs:

> "When you talk to a bunch of task-force nothings—you're talking about a bunch of guys who don't know anything. They're dumb dogfaces."[48]

The Army's efforts to educate GIs on proper conduct, particularly in regard to the treatment of prisoners, consisted of a meager two hours of lectures a year. GIs assigned to Vietnam got several additional hours of instruction on arrival. They were also issued two wallet-sized cards, both of which were supposed to be carried on their persons at all times. One listed 'Nine Rules" for their behavior. Among these rules, American soldiers were enjoined to remember they were guests in Vietnam, to make friends with the inhabitants, to treat women respectfully, and to avoid "loud, rude or unusual behavior." The second card, "The Enemy in Your Hands," stated explicitly that

> "Mistreatment of any captive is a criminal offense. All persons in your hands, whether suspects, civilians, or combat captives, must be protected against violence, insults, curiosity, and reprisals of any kind."[49]

One wonders how many of Charlie Company's nearly illiterate comic-book aficionados made sense out of the two cards. The Peers Commission, which later investigated the atrocities at My Lai 4, judged the men of Charlie as representative of the cross-section of American youth serving in Vietnam.

LIFE WAS CHEAP in Quang Ngai Province from which Charlie operated. The outfit, when it was still new to Vietnam, had been shocked when a troop carrier passed with

> "about twenty human ears tied to the antenna."[50]

One battalion commander named his helicopter the *Gookmobile* and had his "kills," in the form of conical hats, painted on the side almost if he was a fighter pilot with his tally of enemy planes painted on the fuselage of his jet.[51]

> Many officers stalked Vietnamese in the free-fire zones from the air, shooting at anyone who moved below. Many battalions staged contests among their rifle companies for the highest score in enemy kills, with the winning unit getting additional time for passes.[52]

William L. Calley, Jr. was then a 24-year-old Second Lieutenant serving as Platoon Leader of Third Platoon of Company C. He was boyish-looking, unprepossessing at only five feet, three inches tall. Calley had flunked out of Palm Beach Junior College in his first semester, having earned four F's. Unsure of what to do next, he bought a car and headed west. His friends heard nothing from him for three years. Finally, like many young men searching for their identity, Calley enlisted in the Army. In spite of his abysmal college record, the Army decided he was good-enough officer material. The Army then was just as short of officer candidates as it was of enlisted men without criminal records.

Calley's platoon quickly saw through him and his inadequacies as a leader, some wondering how he had managed to graduate from OCS, others amazed that he was unable to read a compass. Medina, too, had low regard for Calley and often addressed him as "Lieutenant Shithead" in front of his own men—which gave an indication of Medina's own lack of qualifications to be a leader.

> "What if My Lai had come out the day it happened?... The war would have been over two years earlier; not a bad goal for the United States Army; not a bad result for the world or the good guys. My Lai had a terrible effect [once it was made public] because everyone knew they were covering it up."[53]

HERE IS PART OF WHAT HAPPENED THAT DAY at My Lai 4. As Medina later described the March 16th operation, he had begun planning it the day before. He and his battalion commander, Lieutenant Colonel Frank Barker, flew over the target for a quick look. Charlie Company would attack My Lai 4, a tiny hamlet that was said to be home to Vietcong cadre or their sympathizers. Army maps showed that it and the neighboring hamlets of My Lai 1, My Lai 2, and My Lai 3 were part of the larger village of Son My, a heavily populated area embracing dozens of hamlets. The area was known to the GIs as Pinkville because its population density was colored light red on maps. Medina recalled giving a pep talk to the company following a brief funeral service the night before for one soldier who had been killed that day after stepping on a mine. During the later investigation, Medina claimed his orders were to burn dwellings, blow up bunkers and tunnels, and kill the livestock. What about the women and children in the village? Medina said he had not given any instructions to his company how to handle them.

My Lai 4 had a population of about 700, nearly all living in flimsy thatch-covered huts—hootches as the GIs dismissively called them. After being helicoptered into the hamlet about 8AM two of the three platoons of Charlie Company lined up to begin what started out to be an orderly advance into the tiny village. Everything was quiet and peaceful. Most of the residents had moved inside their huts when they heard the noise of the helicopters. No one was running; the villagers understood that to run was to automatically draw the fire of GIs. There was no sniper fire and no other signs of the Vietcong lurking close by. Without a direct order from Platoon Leader Calley, Third Platoon began rounding up the villagers. Then spontaneously the killings began, randomly and without any provocation. Corporal Herbert Carter testified that soon after he moved into the village a lone woman was sighted.

> Somebody knocked her to the ground and Medina shot her with his M16 rifle. The men continued on, making sure no one escaped. We came to where the soldiers had collected fifteen or more Vietnamese men, women, and children in a group. Medina said 'Kill every one. Leave no one standing.'[54]

Carter also recalled that some GIs were yelping in delight as they rampaged around and through the huts, spraying bullets as they went.

> The boys enjoyed it. When someone laughs and jokes about what they're doing, they have to be enjoying it. Even Captain Medina was having a good time. You can tell when someone enjoys their work."[55]

By 9AM, all of Charlie Company had arrived in the hamlet.

> Most families were being shot inside their homes or just outside the doorways. Those who had tried to flee were crammed by GIs into the many bunkers built throughout the hamlet for protection—once the bunkers were filled, hand grenades were lobbed in.[56]

Those Vietnamese not gunned down next to their huts were shepherded to a drainage ditch at one end of the hamlet. The ditch was about seven feet wide and five feet deep. It was there where Calley held court, lining up people, pushing them into the ditch, and shooting into the huddled groups of frantic women and children. He also loudly ordered GIs standing around to do the same. When Calley apparently thought the killings weren't moving along fast enough, he gave a direct order to PFC Robert Maples to load his BAR and "shoot these people." Maples later told the Criminal Investigations Division (C.I.D.) he had refused. He remembered that others who were firing into the ditch kept reloading their magazines. Hand grenades were also tossed into the ditch. Private Dennis Conti noticed that many women had thrown themselves on top of their children to try to protect them and at first some children were alive. Those children old enough to walk then began to climb out of the ditch. Calley methodically shot them to death.

Private Paul Meadlo, one of those standing alongside the ditch, recalled:

> So we pushed our seven or eight people in with the big bunch of them. And so I began shooting them all. So did Mitchell [PFC] and Calley. I guess I shot maybe 25 or 20 people in the ditch... men, women, and children. And babies.[57]

Carter watched from the side of the trench as the screaming mothers grabbed their children at the same time as the weeping, frightened children tried to hide themselves in their mothers' garments. He admitted in testimony later that at first he didn't know what to do. Later that morning, Carter apparently found out what to do: he fired a round from his M-16 into his foot, almost certainly in order to disassociate himself from the butchery. For him, there had been a feeling of bewilderment at the savagery exhibited by his fellow soldiers.

> I still wonder why human beings claim to be human but still conduct themselves as barbarians. The guys didn't know why they were shooting them. The United States is supposed to be a peace-loving country; yet they tell them to do something and then want to hang them for it. The people didn't know what they were dying for and the guys didn't know why they were shooting them.[58]

Meadlo, who lost a foot to a Vietcong land mine the next day, responded later in prompted testimony during the hearings to his killing role at the ditch.

> "I held my M-16 on them." *Question*: "Why?" *Answer*: "Because they might attack." *Question:* "They were children and babies?" *Answer:* "Yes. *Question*: "And they might attack? Children and babies?" *Answer:* "They might've had a fully loaded grenade on them. The mothers might have throwed (sic) them at us." *Question:* "Babies?" *Answer:* "Yes." *Question:* "Were the babies in their mothers' arms? "*Answer:* "I guess so." *Question*: "And the babies moved to attack?" *Answer*: "I expected at any moment they were about to make a counterbalance (sic)."[59]

PFC Harry Stanley told the investigators what Calley did next.

> There was an old lady in a bed and there was a priest in white praying over her. Calley told me to ask about the VC and the NVA and where the weapons were. The priest denied being a VC or NVA. Calley dragged the old man outside and said a few words to the monk. It looked like he was pleading for his life. Lieutenant Calley then took his rifle and pushed the monk into a rice paddy and shot him point-blank.[60]

There was one final incident at the ditch that ended the grisly butchery—that forever painted William Calley, Jr. a ruthless baby-killer, and his platoon that stood by as unthinking accomplices to murder. A bloodied but otherwise uninjured tyke had miraculously avoided the gunfire and managed to crawl out of the ditch, crying for his mother. He then began toddling toward the hamlet. Someone shouted, "There's a kid." There was a long pause, as if every GI was waiting for someone else to deal with the situation. It was Calley who reacted first. He caught up with the child, grabbed his arm, threw him back in the ditch, and shot him.[61]

> ""Before you leave here, Sir, you're going to learn that one of the most brutal things in the world is your average nineteen-year-old American boy."[62]

Charlie's "most notorious rapists," as described by Corporal Kenneth Hodges, a squad leader from the Second Platoon, were busy plying their depraved trade all morning. He told Seymour Hersh, the investigative reporter who broke the story:

> Several members of Charlie became 'double veterans,' GI slang for raping a woman and then shooting her. One female died when someone penetrated her with the muzzle of his rifle, then pulled the trigger. Many women were raped and sodomized, mutilated, and had their vaginas ripped open with knives or bayonets.[63]

Most of the shooting and raping was over shortly after 11AM, when Medina called a break for lunch. The men of Charlie Company were then ordered to mop up and make sure all the huts and useful goods in My Lai 4 were destroyed. The three platoons then formed up and marched through the nearly deserted hamlets of My Lai 5 and My Lai 6, pillaging and burning as they went.

MANY CHARLIE COMPANY GIs were totally unmoved, even in hindsight, by what they and their fellow soldiers had done in My Lai 4. Private John Smail was one, a member of Calley's Third Platoon; he told investigators he appeared at the hamlet some time after most of the shooting had ended. Smail was insistent:

> "I haven't let it bother me. I never wanted to go there in the first place. I hated those people. You know what I thought? Good! I didn't care nothing (sic) about the Vietnamese."[64]

Smail was also one of the few from Charlie Company willing to talk frankly about rape. Nearly everybody knew there had been rapes that morning, but they were reluctant to tell what they knew.

> "That's an everyday happening. You can nail just about everybody on that—at least once. The guys are human, man."[65]

Medina promoted Calley to First Lieutenant soon after My Lai 4, a surprising move considering Medina had often openly belittled him. In April, Calley was relieved as a platoon leader, following his careless order calling in artillery fire dangerously close to his platoon during a field operation. Calley then requested and was given a transfer out of Charlie.

U.S. military officials initially covered up the ghastly murders by summing up the event in a deceitful "after-action report" as a successful infantry engagement in which 128 Vietcong were killed.[66] *The New York Times* next day reported on the front page that American troops had caught a North Vietnamese force in a pincers movement on the central coastal plain, killing 128 enemy soldiers in day-long fighting.

> *"Once one believes colonial people to be untermenschen—gooks is the American term—one has destroyed the basis of all civilized codes of conduct."*[67]

A WEEK AFTER THE ATROCITIES at My Lai 4, PFC Ronald L. Ridenhour, then a helicopter door gunner in the 11th Brigade, happened to fly over My Lai 4. He noted that there were no people and no signs of life anywhere. As the pilot hovered the helicopter close to the ground, Ridenhour noticed the corpse of a woman, spread-eagled as if on display, with an 11th Brigade patch between her legs. He had heard vague accounts of a massacre there and decided to dig deeper. He gathered more details from eyewitnesses of the massacre whom he knew well and trusted.

He wanted to do something about My Lai 4, but wasn't sure what. He knew he would have to wait until he became a civilian before he acted. Cautiously, Ridenhour began to accumulate information, as if he was a criminal investigator. He didn't make written notes, for fear of his own safety if the notes were discovered; he realized he was one man going up against the entire United States Army. He had done nothing during his tour in Vietnam to mark him as an antiwar protester. He kept his anger to himself and bided his time.

It took nearly two years for Americans back home to learn of the horrors perpetrated by Charlie Company in a single morning at My Lai 4. How the deliberate murders and butchery remained a secret so long is hard to understand, in light of so many who knew about it and so many who had been participants. For example, within days the 250 men in two sister companies of Task Force Barker knew many details; so did some 60 men in a dozen helicopter gunships assigned to help Charlie Company fight the expected battle with the VC.

In December 1968, 22-year-old Ronald Ridenhour got an Honorable Discharge from the United States Army and returned home to Phoenix, Arizona.

> "My God, when I first came home, I would tell my friends about this and cry—literally cry. As far as I was concerned, it was a reflection on me, on every American, on the ideals that we supposedly represent. It completely castrated the whole picture of America."[68]

Those friends he spoke to, urged him to forget it—not to report it, not to turn in his buddies, not to help the enemy. But My Lai 4 had burned deeply into his psyche. He first thought of writing an article and selling it to a magazine. Ridenhour had always wanted to be a writer, and he figured he'd never find a better story with which to launch his career. He spoke with one of his former college instructors who had taught a writing course he had taken at a local college before being drafted. He suggested that Ridenhour should instead give the information to the government agencies that investigated such matters. Perhaps a detailed letter would do the trick.

IT WAS APRIL 1969 BEFORE Ridenhour finally wrote the letter. He sent it to the White House, with copies to the Pentagon, the State Department, and to leaders of the Senate and the House. The letter described what Ridenhour had learned about My Lai 4. He cautioned he was reporting what *he heard* and *not what he saw*. His letter turned out to be dynamite! On April 12, Ridenhour got a reply from the Army's Chief of Staff's office which said in part:

> "Because the circumstances related to your letter concern events of a year or so ago, a proper investigation will take some time. This investigation is underway now."[69]

Investigative journalist Seymour H. Hersh had written a number of newspaper articles about My Lai 4 that were published in November, but none attracted much attention. It wasn't until Hersh dug deeper, flying all over the country to interview nearly 50 former members of Charlie Company ex-GI's in person or by phone, that the whole story was unveiled. It was Ridenhour's letter, however—five pages, single-spaced—that provided important credibility for the hard-to-believe details of the atrocities.

Once the TV networks got their hooks into the story, Americans—and people all over the world—finally grasped the full extent of the atrocities. On November 14, CBS broadcast an interview with crippled Paul Meadlo, the former Private in Charlie Company. The widely respected Walter Cronkite moderated the interview. Mike Wallace, part of the panel, asked Meadlo to tell viewers what he had done at My Lai 4.

> "I went in a village and killed everybody."[70]

That wasn't exactly what the inarticulate Meadlo meant, of course: he hadn't killed *everybody*. However, he admitted to shooting babies.

THE GEARS OF MILITARY JUSTICE, with all their interlocking bureaucracies, grind slowly. The Army wanted to find out what happened at My Lai 4 and what role then Second Lieutenant William L. Calley, Jr. and his Third Platoon played in the as yet unproved massacre. But the Army *did not* want the public to learn too many of the details.

On June 9, 1969, more than a year after Charlie Company had run amok in My Lai 4, First Lieutenant Calley was seated before Colonel Norman T. Stansfield in the offices of the U.S. Army Inspector General in Washington. Stansfield told Calley that an investigation was underway that would "possibly charge him with murder." Calley was flabbergasted. He had been pulled out of Vietnam a week earlier and sent to Fort Benning, Georgia, with special orders to proceed to Washington. Calley knew that something was up when his request to extend his duty in Vietnam had been rejected. But charged with murder?

Four days later the IG set up a police-line-up of Army officers, including Calley. Was he the officer in charge of Third Platoon, Charlie Company, on the morning of March 16, 1968 in the hamlet of My Lai 4? Had he been the one who issued direct orders to members of his platoon to kill Vietnamese civilians, including women and children? Was he the one who had also personally killed Vietnamese civilians, including babies? "Yes, Yes, and Yes," answered the former Third Platoon members who were ordered by the IG to report to Washington to view the line-up.

On March 29, 1971, a jury that had deliberated for nearly 80 hours returned their verdict. They found Calley guilty of premeditated murder of 22 villagers of My Lai 4. It took seven more hours for the jury to hand down its sentence: life imprisonment at hard labor. In the end, he served only a few days in the stockade in Fort Benning before being placed under house arrest there. His sentence was repeatedly reduced. Finally, President Richard Nixon commuted his sentence to time served. He was paroled in November 1974.

DURING THE INVESTIGATION OF MY LAI 4, the Peers Committee learned that it had not been the only massacre that day in Quang Ngai Province. There was also one at My Lai 1, about one-and-a-half miles from My Lai 4. Captain Earl R. Michles, CO of Bravo Company, had orders to hit My Lai 1 and then move on to My Lai 2 and My Lai 3. Just as Medina had left Charlie with the impression that everyone they would encounter that morning would be VC, Michles left little ambiguity as to what Bravo should expect when they advanced into My Lai 1. There would be a major battle with veteran VC units. In the event, as at My Lai 4, there would be no Vietcong soldiers, only Vietnamese old men and women, children—and babies.

Hersh wrote that one of the GIs later told him details that, he said, he hadn't given to the Peers Committee during his testimony.

> "We were out there... having a good time. It was sort of like being in a shooting gallery."[71]

He then related to Hersh another shocking incident of depravity in Vietnam that apparently had become endemic among those whom the war had made sadists.

> He told of a tiny infant, barely of crawling age, who became the object of a marksmanship contest. A rifleman had taken careful aim at the infant with a .45-caliber pistol [notoriously inaccurate]. "I remember that the baby was about from here to the tape recorder [a distance of about 10 feet in the ex-GI's living room], and he fired at it. He missed. We all laughed. He got up three or four feet closer and missed again. We laughed. Then he got right on top him and plugged him." Retelling the story prompted the ex-soldier to begin laughing again 'By this point', the ex-soldier said, "the word was out. You know, like you more or less can do anything you like."[72]

The Blade in Toledo, Ohio, published a thorough expose in October 2003, for which the newspaper was awarded the Pulitzer Prize, revealing that the My Lai 1 and My Lai 4 massacres were hardly unique.

> In 1967 an elite Army unit, *Tiger Force,* went on a seven-month rampage, torturing and butchering hundreds of civilians, mutilating bodies, beating elderly farmers to death with shovels, and cutting off ears to wear on necklaces. The savagery visited by American GIs upon an innocent civilian population is breathtaking, and it was conducted with full knowledge of their superiors. In fact, there were hundreds if not thousands of such events; archival research now reveals that My Lai and the Tiger Force atrocities were but the tip of the iceberg of what was basically daily fare. "Vietnam was an atrocity from the get-go," said David Hackworth, the retired colonel who created the Tiger Force: "There were hundreds of My Lais."[73]

My Lai 4 led to a wider scrutiny of the war by heretofore disinterested Americans. They learned of the "free-fire" zones in South Vietnam, in which "anything that moved" was VC and a legitimate target for attack. They learned of the uprooting of the inhabitants from the "free-fire" areas to teeming refugee camps where the culture of farmer-peasant families was destroyed. They learned that GIs came to respect the skills and commitment of their enemies more than their Vietnamese allies; years later it was not unusual to hear veterans recall they wished they had "Mr. Charles" (the VC, or Viet Cong guerrillas) on their side. They learned about the "tiger cages" into which the ARVN routinely threw political prisoners who were tortured, often to death.

Americans were also given a window into the secret CIA-operated *Phoenix* program begun in 1967, a computerized torture and assassination project aimed specifically at Vietnamese civilians. Under *Phoenix* due process was discarded. Individuals whose names turned up on blacklists were kidnapped, tortured, detained for two years without trial, or murdered, simply on the word of an anonymous informer. Defenders of *Phoenix* called it a "scalpel" rather than the "bludgeon" of search-and-destroy operations, air strikes, and artillery barrages that wiped out whole villages.

BY 1967, despite more than 550,000 U.S. soldiers and Marines supported by the greatest aerial armada in world history, the war in Vietnam was not going well for the United States. *Rolling Thunder*, the strategic bombing campaign begun in March 1965, was systematically destroying such targets as bridges, roads, and factories. A principal target was the Ho Chi Minh Trail, but the fighter-bombers never were able to close it. *Thunder's* objective, at the beginning, was to gradually increase the scope and intensity of the bombing until the North stopped their support of the Vietcong. It never worked out that way. Rather, the intense bombing produced mainly awesome statistics: 350,000 missions flown, 655,000 tons of bombs dropped, 928 USAF and U.S. Navy aircraft lost, 818 American airmen killed.[74]

The Vietcong were having no trouble recruiting volunteer replacements anxious to defend their homeland—and to kill the despised invaders. Men who had returned to villages that had been "cleared" by bloody "search-kill-destroy" operations saw clear evidence of American and ARVN atrocities and eagerly joined the rebels

The North Vietnamese speedily built up their air defenses with aid from Russia and China. Their radar systems were up-to-the-minute. These included both long-range search radars for early warning and short-range tracking units for vectoring airborne aircraft.

The excellent MiG-15 of the Korean War gave way to the even better MiG-17, MiG-19, and MiG-21. The North Vietnamese fighter-jets were used to disrupt bombing raids by forcing USAF aircraft to drop their bombs before they reached their targets. The MiGs would typically make a single high-speed attack on the U.S. formations and then break off for home at supersonic speed. Those that loitered to fight were piloted by the most experienced Vietnamese and generally gave as well as they took. Pentagon propagandists intent on promoting USAF "kills" in dog fights, came up with highly exaggerated ratios, as in Korea, all of which were dispelled in the dispassionate months after the war.

It wasn't only enemy jets that challenged the U.S. fighter-bombers. By the time *Rolling Thunder* was underway, the North Vietnamese had one of world's best anti-aircraft defenses and it would continue to improve throughout the war. By the end of 1968, the North had some 8,000 guns, including radar-guided 85-mm cannons—effective to 25,000 feet—and 100 mm guns—good up to 40,000 feet. There were also deadly Soviet SAMs. Anti-aircraft guns caused most of the U.S. aircraft losses during Rolling Thunder, even after the introduction of the MiG-21 with heat-seeking missiles.[75]

Like the Germans in World War II, the Vietnamese became fast and skillful repairers of bomb damaged structures. News correspondent Wilfred Burchett reported how bombed-out bridges on the Ho Chi Minh Trail were replaced by better ones. The new bridges were made of bamboo and were lowered into the water at dawn to make them invisible from the air and winched above the surface at night to coincide with the truck convoys. The Vietnamese were also creative: in the cities, simple but effective air-raid shelters were made. Every few feet on every street, large-diameter concrete pipe sections were dug in, wide enough and deep enough for a single adult. These makeshift shelters had concrete covers which were slid over the top by the occupant.

Michael McClear, a correspondent for the Canadian Broadcasting Corporation, was commissioned to produce a film documentary on the devastation wrought by U.S. bombing. He began his filming through what he called a "wasteland" running down Highway 1 to the border. What he wrote of his observations along the way make stunning reading.

> On the map the distance was 250 miles, once a journey of only four or five hours. Travel time was logged at four days. The awesome bomb craters along the 'highway' interlocked almost end to end... Three weeks were spent covering 1,000 miles of five of the worst hit provinces... Often it was a case of searching for places which on the old maps had once existed... urban civilization had been erased in a region containing one-third or about six million of the North's population. Whatever the French had built in eighty years of occupation, and whatever the North had achieved in fifteen years of independence had been wiped out... Across the whole landscape not a single habitable brick edifice could be seen; the schools, hospitals, and administrative buildings that had certainly once existed were now, like the factories, just so many heaps of rubble. At Ha Tinh, a provincial capital 250 miles from Hanoi, the local mayor-without-a-city produced files citing that between 1965 and 1968 his province of 800,000 people had been bombed 25,529 times. This would equal one air strike every ninety minutes for some 1,500 days (author's emphasis).[76]

In 1971, a leading public-opinion poll recorded that 71 percent of respondents told pollsters that they considered U.S. intervention in Vietnam "a mistake; 58 percent called the war "immoral;" and a majority felt that all U.S. troops should be withdrawn by year's end.[77]

During the talks in 1968 to end the Vietnam War… "the Vietnamese wanted to know what President Johnson had meant in one of his speeches when he told American troops that he wanted them to 'bring the coonskin back and nail it on the wall.'"[78]

ON JANUARY 27, 1973, in Paris, the United States signed the "Agreement on Ending the War and Restoring Peace in Vietnam." At 7:45AM, fifteen minutes before the cease-fire took effect, Turner Joy, cruising off the coast of Vietnam, punctuated the war's end by senselessly firing into Vietnam the last naval salvo of the war.

Article 21 of the Agreement stated:

> In pursuance of its traditional policy, the United States will contribute to healing the wounds of war and to postwar reconstruction of the Democratic Republic of Vietnam and throughout Indochina.

That was another U.S. government lie. In the event, America's signature would be valueless: the United States reneged on the $4.75 million in aid promised. Instead, the U.S. enforced a crushing embargo on trade, which remained in effect until 1994.

At dawn on April 29, 1975, Saigon's residents were awakened by the close-by sounds of heavy explosions. Fast-moving Vietcong sappers were blowing up the runways at Tan Son Hut Air Base. Any hope of an orderly departure by the U.S. Embassy staff, remaining Americans, and "loyal" Vietnamese was shattered. The only option was Operation *Frequent Wind,* emergency evacuation by helicopters. It was not a pretty scene at the U.S. Embassy, the point of departure. Hordes of Vietnamese, particularly those who had collaborated with the Americans and had been assured of evacuation, stormed the Embassy gates. One after another, a train of helicopters took turns landing on the heliport atop the Embassy, filling up immediately and clattering away to a naval flotilla in the South China Sea. As the last choppers took off, hundreds of Vietnamese were still milling around waiting for rides to safety that never came.

The fall of Saigon brought back on the front pages the war that Americans had wanted to forget. With its own land carrying no physical scars of the war, few Americans chose to reflect on the enormous destruction their military forces had wrought in a faraway land—to a peasant people who had never been a threat to the United States or any of its inhabitants. By stark contrast, in Indochina the wreckage and destruction were everywhere.

> Nearly two-thirds of the southern hamlets were in ruins and twelve million acres of forests had been destroyed, much of it by nineteen million gallons of chemical defoliants sprayed by the United States. There were more than two million widows, orphans, and disabled people. Tons of unexploded ordnance and land mines still littered the land.[79]

How did the Pentagon's hallowed Domino Theory fare? Eisenhower argued that if South Vietnam fell to the Communists, all the other countries in the region—Laos, Cambodia, and Thailand as well as Burma, Malaysia, and even Indonesia—were sure to follow. Now more than 30 years since American troops were driven out of Vietnam, the expected wave of Communist expansion in the region has failed to materialize. Americans are yet to fight Communists in Hawaii.

> *To call what we live with today simply a 'military-industrial complex' is to limit it incorrectly... It is, in fact, a coalition of the military services, the service associations, the Pentagon bureaucracy, the giant aerospace industry, trade associations and public relations firms, the employees of the weapons makers and the trade unions that organize them, a vast proportion of the scientific and engineering talent in the country, universities whose departments have become dependent on Pentagon largesse, government-sponsored and privately owned research organizations, local business and civic groups whose communities grow and prosper on Pentagon contracts, and the local and national politicians whose survival hinges on their active representation of these forces in their states or districts."*[80]

ON JANUARY 27, 1973, in Paris, the United States signed the "Agreement on Ending the War and Restoring Peace in Vietnam." At 7:45AM, fifteen minutes before the cease-fire took effect, *Turner Joy*, cruising off the coast of Vietnam, punctuated the war's end by senselessly firing into Vietnam the last naval salvo of the war.

Article 21 of the Agreement stated:

> "In pursuance of its traditional policy, the United States will contribute to healing the wounds of war and to postwar reconstruction of the Democratic Republic of Vietnam and throughout Indochina."

That was another government lie. In the event, America's signature would be valueless: the United States reneged on the $4.75 million in aid promised. Instead, the U.S. enforced a crushing embargo on trade, which remained in effect until 1994.

By war's end, the United States Army in Vietnam was a thin shadow of the self it had been at the start in 1965. The antiwar movement stateside had spread to Vietnam, and some GIs defiantly wore large peace symbols on chains dangling from their necks. In some rifle companies, black soldiers refused to go out on patrol, willingly risking being imprisoned in South Vietnam's infamous Long Binh jail. Few were.

Desertion rates between 1966 and 1971 jumped to more than seven percent, several times greater than during the Korean War. Hard drugs were plentiful and cheap. For example, GIs could buy pure heroin for as little as two dollars per vial; marijuana laced with opium was also popular. The Pentagon acknowledged after the war that about one-third of troops in Vietnam used heroin regularly.

Indicative of the low morale of Army troops was a tactic resurrected from the Pacific War that found its way into the lexicon of GIs in Vietnam, "fragging." The term referred to the use of fragmentation grenades, ordinary issue to troops in the field, by angry enlisted men to kill outright, maim, or otherwise intimidate officers who demanded overly aggressive missions. The practice was a stealthy nighttime one: discreetly roll a grenade, retaining clip withdrawn, under the edges of tent flaps and beneath the cots of a sleeping officer. Sometimes, as a warning, a non-lethal smoke grenade would be used.

> The Army reported 126 fraggings in 1969, 271 in 1970, and 333 in 1971, especially steep increases given the drop in troop levels during those years... the number of actual fraggings surely exceeded the reported incidents, in part those occurring out in the field could, in many instances, be attributed to accidental 'friendly fire' or combat.[81]

How could a drugged-up, undisciplined, and demoralized army manage to successfully fight a war? The answer: it could not and it did not!

Towards war's end, Ho Chi Minh, architect-engineer of his country's "long war" strategy that ultimately proved superior to massive American firepower, would find victory in his grasp and freedom for his people. The remarkable Communist leader with the wispy white beard and rubber sandals died in September 1969, too soon for him to enjoy the fruits of the peace he had so diligently sought and for so long striven. In 1976, Ho's embalmed body was entombed in a masoleum that sits on a prominent hill in the middle of Hanoi.

What is Vietnam like today? The Communists are still in control and the growing number of American tourists report the Vietnamese people appear to be content. The tunnels dug by the Vietcong so many years ago to protect themselves from B-52 bombs have been widened to accommodate larger-size Western tourists. Sections of the Ho Chi Minh Trail have likewise been refurbished and motor scooters are available for rent. Despite calling itself a Communist nation, the DRV has pursued a Capitalist economy. Since the end of the war, when 85 percent of the population lived in poverty, today that figure is down to about 15 percent. Most Vietnamese are too young to remember the bad old days.

THE FOLLOWING IS A SELECTION of "letters home," not unlike those mailed by American soldiers during the Philippines War. Most are newspaper reports interspersed with transparently preposterous lies by high-level U.S. government officials. All are excerpted from Michael Parenti's *The Vietnam Antiwar Movement in America.*[82]

> "I don't like to hit a village. You know you're hitting women and children, too. But you've got to decide that your cause is noble and that the work has to be done"—USAF pilot after 100 missions. *The New York Times*, July 7, 1965.

"We usually kill more women and kids than we do Vietcong but the government troops just aren't available to clean out the villages so this is the only answer"—USAF officer. *Cleveland Plain Dealer*, July 19, 1965.

"As the communists withdrew from Quangnai last Monday, U.S. jet bombers pounded the hills into which they were headed. Many Vietnamese civilians—one estimate was as high as 500—were killed by the strikes. The American contention is that they were Vietcong soldiers. But three out of four patients seeking treatment in a Vietnamese hospital afterwards for burns from napalm were village women." *The New York Times*, June 6, 1965.

"Surely you don't believe that our 'pilots fly to bomb children,' that we send bombs and heavy equipment against innocent civilians? ... You know as well as I do, Geyna, that we are bombing oil storage, transport and the heavy and sophisticated weapons they carry to kill our sons." John Steinbeck, letter to Yevgeny Yevtushenko, *Philadelphia Inquirer*, July 12, 1966.

"The dominant figures of the air war in the Delta were the forward air controllers (FACs)... They cruise over the Delta like a vigilante posse, holding the power of life and death over the Vietnamese villagers living beneath their daily patrol... A FAC can kill a lot of innocent people if he makes a mistake, which sometimes happens. I met a FAC who had been directing gunfire from Navy destroyers against hooches and VC concentrations for several months. The destroyers were many miles offshore in a rolling ocean. This young man had been relieved of duty because he had openly declared himself guilty of assisting in the killing of many civilians because the long-range guns had fired wildly so often. It was impossible not to feel the agony this boy was suffering. I just want to go home and forget it forever," he said. Frank Harvey, *Flying Magazine*, November 1966.

"We and the South Vietnamese use artillery to shell villages; we don't see what happens at the other end... The Vietcong do not use napalm; we do... I have been an orthopedic surgeon for a good number of years... but nothing could have prepared me for my encounters with Vietnamese women and children burned by napalm. It was sickening, even for a physician, to see and smell the blackened flesh. And one never forgets the bewildered eyes of the silent, suffering napalm-burned child." Richard E. Perry, M.D., *Redbook*, January 1967.

"Napalm and its more horrible companion, white phosphorous, liquidize young flesh and carve it into grotesque forms. The little figures are afterwards often scarcely human in appearance, and one cannot be confronted with the monstrous effect of the burning without being totally shaken... The initial urge to reach out and soothe the hurt was restrained by the fear that the ash-like skin would crumble in my fingers. American soldiers in Vietnam who accidentally suffer serious burns from napalm are rushed aboard special hospital planes—equipped to give immediate first aid treatment—and flown directly to Brook Army Hospital in Texas, one of the world's leading centers for burn treatment and for the extensive plastic surgery that must follow. Burnt Vietnamese children must fare for themselves." William F. Pepper, *Ramparts,* January 1967.

"We should be proud of what we are doing out there for the people of South Vietnam."

–Robert S. McNamara, Secretary of Defense, 1967.

"The Pentagon released a letter from Assistant Secretary of Defense John T. McNaughton to Chairman Fulbright claiming that only 109 civilians had been killed and 170 injured in the seven months from last August 1, 1965 to March 1, 1966. One wonders how any American, even the staunchest 'patriot,' could accept such preposterous propaganda." *I.F. Stone's Weekly*, March 28, 1966.

"... Last night two dark-colored delta-wing jets, unidentified but believed to be American or South Vietnamese, killed an estimated 105 people and wounded 175 in a 15-minute bombing and strafing attack. The villagers scrambled into bunkers underneath their homes but many died, some suffocated." London *Times*, March 4, 1967.

"There were sometimes two in a bed, now and then, three. They were peasants of all ages, badly battered. A Vietnamese hospital doctor told me, 'Those you see here are those who were able to come. For everyone who can reach a town, there [are] 10 who die in the village or the fields or wherever they are struck. This is true above all of the badly burned." Robert Guillian, *Le Monde*, March 12, 1966.

"... What years of terror have done to South Vietnam's one-rich wildlife... Wild elephants, which once roamed in herds through the now bomb-pitted jungles of Central Vietnam have altered their breeding habits. 'It appears in many cases that they have stopped mating,' said Dr. Vu Ngoc Tan, director of Saigon's zoo. 'They have been terrorized by the bombing and the artillery attacks and armored vehicles crashing through the forests.' Recently Tan spotted three injured young elephants. 'They had very bad wounds, probably the result of shelling, and there was nothing I could do for them. They had obviously been abandoned by the herd and had come to that spot to die. Tigers and panthers also have suffered. Chemical sprays have played havoc with bird life, destroying vegetation and the insects on which the birds feed. Monkey and deer have also been affected. The one breed of animal that has thrived on the war is rats. Rats the size of cats can be seen any night in the more squalid street of Saigon. These rodents carry a flea which transmits the bubonic plague, the 'black death' that scourged Europe in the Middle Ages." *The Baltimore Sun*, January 15, 1967.

"The French didn't kill enough. If you kill enough you win the war."

–A U.S. Army general in Saigon. The New York Times, May 15, 1966.

"Dear Senator Fulbright: Much has been written about the terror tactics used by the Vietcong. The real terrorists are the Americans and their allies. I don't deny that some of the accusations against the VC are true but from my own experience the terror and havoc we spread make the VC look like a Girl Scout picnic. Can you imagine what an isolated village looks like after it has been hit by over 500 750-pound bombs in a matter of seconds? Women, children, old men, cattle, and every living thing is struck down without ever knowing from where their destruction originated. This particular village ceased to exist because it was in a VC-dominated area. We have not found any dead soldiers but as it is the custom in VC-controlled areas all the dead were listed as VC killed in action. I also saw thousands of pounds of rice dumped in rivers and otherwise destroyed because some small unit commander decided there was too much rice in this particular village for the number of people living there and therefore the surplus must be going to the VC. These people had worked for months to bring in the rice harvest and their 'defenders' had come along and destroyed it in a matter of minutes. This scene was repeated dozens of times during my tour." Letter to Senator J. William Fulbright from a Marine Second Lieutenant in Vietnam.

"We will continue as best we can to help the good people of South Vietnam enrich the condition of their lives."

—President Lyndon B. Johnson, July 28, 1965.

"After the announcement in Saigon of the scorched earth operation a broadcast dispatch from Hanoi accused the United States of carrying out policy of 'burn all, destroy all, kill all.' Col. Marvin Fuller, commander of a brigade in the operation, said anyone living in the operational area is presumed to be an enemy. Fuller said water buffalo, ducks, chickens, and pigs were being slaughtered to deny fresh meat to the enemy battalions. Dogs were also killed because in a pinch the guerrillas slaughter them for food, he said. Hundreds of tons of rice have been destroyed or removed. Some GIs snatched up ducks for their own meals." *Gazette and Daily*, York, PA, March 14, 1967.

"Dompe was asked about the VC who had been shot the previous afternoon. 'It wasn't a VC,' he said. 'It was an old man. He had a stick with a bundle tied to one end over his shoulder. It looked like a rifle. We shouted at him to halt and he began running." Tom Buckley, *New York Times Magazine*, November 1967.

"Today we went on a mission and I'm not proud of myself, my friends, or my country. We burned every hut in sight. It was a small rural network of villages and the people were incredibly poor. We burn these huts and take all men old enough to carry a weapon and the 'choppers' come and get them (they take them to a collection point a few miles away for interrogation)." Everyone is crying, begging and praying we don't separate them. The women wail and moan. Then they watch in terror as we burn their homes, personal possessions and food. Yes, we burn all rice and shoot all livestock. A buddy of mine called 'La dai' (come here) into a hut and an old man came out. My buddy told the old man to get away from the hut... and just threw a hand grenade. As he pulled the pin the old man got excited and started jabbering and running toward my buddy and the hut. A GI, not understanding, stopped the old man with a football tackle just as my buddy threw the grenade into the shelter. We all heard a baby crying from inside the shelter. After the explosion we found the mother, two children, and a baby. That is what the old man was trying to tell us. It was horrible! My last look was an old man in ragged torn dirty clothes on his knees outside the burning hut, praying to Buddha. His white hair was blowing in the wind and tears were rollin' down." A soldier's letter to his father. *Beacon Journal*, Akron OH, March 27, 1967.

"We are going to meet our commitments in South Vietnam and if there are those who don't like it, it's too bad."

—Secretary of State Dean Rusk, July 17, 1966.

"It's one tawdry incident followed by another followed by another. We medivacced a woman yesterday who had been burned by a white phosphorous grenade maybe five days earlier. She could not move because grenade frags were imbedded in her body from head to toe along her left side. She was about three months pregnant and we were able to find the clearing by listening for the sounds of her mother weeping over here. A 27-year-old Buck Sergeant who loves to read Dennis the Menace comic books (after pistol whipping an elderly man, breaking his neck and leaving him to die): 'If that fucking interpreter hadn't come along, I could have finished the mother fucker off with my 45.' Our platoon medic: 'I don't want to treat any gooks for wounds—everybody understand?' Our fire team leader: 'Remember back in November when we raided that village at night and found that family with that Schwinn bicycle? They looked so goddamned funny crying after we kicked the spokes in, I liked to bust a gut laughing.' A GI's letter published in the Contra Costa, California, Newsletter, *Citizens Against the War in Vietnam*, February 1967.

"A new breed of Americans... the 18 and 19-year-olds, fashionably referred to as high school dropouts, have... maybe too much of what prize-fighters call killer instinct. They have killed a lot of Vietnamese, all of their victims listed as Vietcong, of course, whether they are women and children or not. These kids seemed to enjoy killing." Warren Rogers, *New York Journal-American*, September 16, 1965.

"One American helicopter crewman returned to his base... last week without a fierce young prisoner entrusted to him. He told friends that he had become infuriated by the youth and had pushed him out of the helicopter at about 1,000 feet." *The New York Times,* July 7, 1965.

> *"The dissenting minority has the right to speak without penalty. But they are unwittingly—I hope unwittingly—destroying that privilege. They have a right to object, but we deplore their ignorance and their violence."*

—President Lyndon B. Johnson, May 30, 1967.

"The only violence I saw was that practiced against the demonstrators by Federal Marshals and soldiers. Some persons—frequently young women—were kicked and clubbed repeatedly and very severely." Allan Brick, eyewitness testimony on the October 21 (1967) Peace Demonstrations in Washington.

"There are a lot of nice buildings in Haiphong. What their contributions are to the war effort I don't know, but the desire to bomb a virgin building is terrific." U.S. Navy pilot, *The New York Times*, January 20, 1968.

> *"We've never bombed the North Vietnamese embassies. We have never bombed their population. Sure, we try to hit a military target, a petroleum target, or an electric plant."*

—President Lyndon B. Johnson, July 4, 1966.

Notes

[1] Ho Chi Minh's background was as extraordinary as his leadership of the guerrilla army that defeated, one after the other, both the French Army and the United States Army in the jungles and rice paddies of Indochina. Ho was born in Vietnam in 1890, traveled the world as a merchant seaman, spent time in Brooklyn, New York, and spoke seven languages. He was in Paris during the Versailles Peace Conference in 1919, petitioning the U.S. delegation for support for an independent Vietnam. After a self-imposed exile of thirty years, he quietly returned to his native land in 1941 disguised as a Chinese journalist. He formed the Vietnam Independence League—the Vietminh—during the wartime occupation by the Japanese. By 1950, U.S. propaganda had labeled Ho a tool of "International Communism" rather than the bonafide nationalist he was. Ho was a long-time admirer of the United States and its institutions and reportedly had a framed picture of George Washington and a copy of the American Declaration of Independence propped up on his desk. He died in 1969 at the age of 79, not living long enough to see his country finally free of colonial oppression.

[2] William J. Duiker, *Ho Chi Minh* (Hyperion, New York, 2000), p. 283.

[3] Vietminh also spelled Viet Minh or Viet-Minh, short for the League for the Independence of Vietnam.

[4] Duiker, p. 288.

[5] William Blum, *Killing Hope: U.S. Military and CIA Interventions Since World War II*) Common Courage Press, Monroe ME, 1995), p. 122-123.

[6] The New York Times, March 21, p. 1954.

[7] Bernard Fall, *Hell in a Very Small Place*: *The Siege of Dien Bien Phu* (Da Capo Press, New York, 2002), p. 105.

[8] Ibid., p. 107-108.

[9] Duiker, p. 455.

[10] Fall, p. 411.

[11] Ibid.
[12] Stephen Kinzer, *Overthrow: America's Century of Regime Change From Hawaii to Iraq* (Henry Holt and Company, New York, 2006), p. 151.
[13] Ibid., 153. Eisenhower estimated that "possibly eighty percent of the population" would vote for Ho Chi Minh for President.
[14] Ibid.
[15] John Duffett, Ed., *Against the Crime of Silence: Proceedings of the International War Crimes Tribunal* (O'Hare Books, New York, 1968), p. 71.
[16] Robert S. McNamara, *In Retrospect: The Tragedy and Lessons of Vietnam* (Vintage Books, New York, 1995), p. 119.
[17] Ibid., p. 292.
[18] On a smaller scale, *Maddox* took on the sort of surveillance work that the unarmed *U.S.S. Liberty* would perform off the coast of Sinai in 1967, when she was attacked by Israeli Air Force aircraft (their insignia painted out); and the unarmed *U.S.S. Pueblo* in 1968 when she was captured by the North Vietnamese. All of these ships were part of the comprehensive electronic surveillance operations conducted continuously throughout the world by the NSA. *Ticonderoga* and *Constellation*, with their own destroyer escorts, were within radar range of *Maddox* that night, and within radar range of *Turner Joy* as well the next night. This task force was not cruising aimlessly, awaiting distress calls from *De Soto* destroyers; it had its own mission and was busy launching and retrieving its fighter-bombers which were attacking Communist-led Pathet Lao guerrillas inside Laos.
[19] Joseph C. Goulden, *Truth is the First Casualty: The Gulf of Tonkin Affair—Illusion and Reality* (Rand McNally, New York, 1969), p. 160.
[20] Jim and Sybil Stockdale, *In Love and War: The Story of a Family's Ordeal and Sacrifice During the Vietnam Years* (Harper & Row, New York, 1984), p. 18.
[21] Ibid., p. 19
[22] Ibid.
[23] Ibid.
[24] Ibid., p. 24-25.
[25] Ibid.
[26] Edwin E. Moise, *Tonkin Gulf and the Escalation of the Vietnam War* (University of North Carolina Press, Chapel Hill NC, 1996), p. 141.
[27] McNamara, p. 136.
[28] Ibid.
[29] James Bamford, *Body of Secrets: Anatomy of the Ultra-Secret National Security Agency From the Cold War Through the Dawn of a New Century* (Doubleday, New York, 2001), p. 301.
[30] Moise, p. 234.
[31] Sven Lindqvist, *A History of Bombing* (New Press, New York, 2000), p. 162.
[32] Christian G. Appy, *Patriots: The Vietnam War Remembered From All Sides* (Viking, New York, 2003), p. 202.
[33] *The New York Times*, October 28, p. 1967
[34] Gordon Oriens and E.W. Pfeiffer, "Ecological Effects of the War in Vietnam," *Science*, May 1, 1970, p. 149.
[35] 2, 4-D and 2,4,5-T; used between January 1965 and April 1970; Agent Orange II (Super Orange): 2,4-D and 2,4,5-T; used in 1968 and 1969. Used between 1962 and 1964: Agent Purple: 2,4-D and 2,4,5-T; Agent Pink: 2,4,5-T; Agent Green: 2,4,5-T; Agent White: Picloram and 2,4-D; Agent Blue, containing cacodylic acid (arsenic); Dinoxol: 2,4-D and 2,4,5-T; Trinoxol: 2,4,5-T; Diquat; Bromacil; Tandex; Monuron; Diuron and Dalapon.
[36] Gordon Oriens and E.W. Pfeiffer, "Ecological Effects of the War in Vietnam," *Science*, May 1, 1970, p. 148.

[37] J. B. Nielands, Gordon Oriens and E.W. Pfeiffer, *Harvest of Death: Chemical Warfare in Vietnam and Cambodia* (Free Press, New York, 1971), p. 168-169.
[38] Ibid.
[39] Ibid.
[40] Ibid.
[41] Nielands, p. 141.
[42] Duffet, p. 467-468.
[43] The exhortation, "Remember, Only You Can Prevent Forest Fires" is the slogan of conservationists in the United States. The mythical forest ranger, Smokey the Bear, repeats these words on posters and TV, and is widely known to American children. *Ranch Hand* planes flying out of Tan Son Nhut airport perverted this slogan.
[44] Nielands, p. 141.
[45] *DM* (diphenylaminochlorarsin) causes in progressive order: irritation of the eyes and mucous membranes, viscous discharge from the nose, sneezing, coughing, severe headache, acute pains and tightness of chest, nausea, and vomiting. *CN* (choroacetophenone), lachrymatory. Also irritates upper respiratory passages. In high concentrations, irritates the skin, especially on moist parts of the body. *CS* (chlorobenzalmalononitrile) causes extreme burning of the eyes and a profuse flow of tears; constricts respiratory tract; burns moist skin; induces nausea. Incapacitates at 1 to 6 mg per cubic meter; at 20 mg per cubic meter, causes irreparable lesions.
[46] Sidney Lens, *The Military-Industrial Complex* (Pilgrim Press, Philadelphia, 1970).
[47] Harold G. Moore and Joseph Galloway, *We Are Soldiers Still: A Journey Back to the Battlefields of Vietnam* (Harper, New York, 2008), p. 25.
[48] Seymour M. Hersh, *My Lai 4: A Report on the Massacre and Its Aftermath* (Random House, New York, 1970), p. 7.
[49] Ibid.
[50] Michael R. Belknap, *The Vietnam War on Trial: The My Lai Massacre and the Court Martial of Lieutenant Calley* (University Press of Kansas, Lawrence KS, 2002), p. 167.
[51] Hersh, *My Lai 4*, p. 8-9.
[52] Ibid., p. 9.
[53] Michael MacClear, *The Ten-Thousand Day War* (St. Martin's Press, New York, 1981), p. 150.
[54] Hersh, *My Lai 4*, p. 53.
[55] Ibid. p. 56.
[56] Ibid., p. 55-56.
[57] Ibid., p. 63.
[58] Seymour M. Hersh, *Cover-Up: The Army Secret Investigation of the Massacre at My Lai 4* (Random House, New York, 1972), p. 186-187.
[59] Ibid.
[60] Hersh, *Cover-Up,* p. 62.
[61] Ibid., p. 63-64.
[62] Marine Lieutenant Philip Caputo recalled what a veteran NCO had told him: *A Rumor of War* (Holt, Rinehart and Winston, New York, 1977), p. 49.
[63] Hersh, *Cover-Up,* p. 68-69
[64] Hersh, *My Lai 4*, p. 183.
[65] Ibid., p. 185.
[66] Appy, p. 343.
[67] Duffett, p. 5.
[68] Hersh, *Cover Up,* p. 105.
[69] Ibid., p. 112.
[70] Ibid., p. 120-121.
[71] Ibid., p. 15.

[72] Ibid., p. 15, 16.
[73] Morris Berman, *Dark Ages America: The Final Phase of Empire* (W.W. Norton & Company, New York, 2006), p. 123.
[74] MacClear, p. 240-241.
[75] John T. Smith, *Rolling Thunder: The Strategic Bombing Campaign Against North Vietnam 1964-68* (Air Research Publications, Surrey, Great Britain, 1994), p. 65-66.
[76] MacClear, p. 247.
[77] Appy, p. 393.
[78] Gabriel Kolko, *Century of War: Politics, Conflicts, and Society Since 1914* (The New Press, New York, 1994), p. 430.
[79] James Carroll, *House of War: The Pentagon and the Disastrous Rise of American Power* (Houghton Mifflin Company, New York, 2006), 326.
[80] William Proxmire, *Report From Wasteland: America's Military-Industrial Complex* (Praeger, New York, 1970), p. 8.
[81] Appy, p. 394-395.
[82] Michael Parenti, *The Vietnam Antiwar Movement in America* ((Random House, New York, 1996), p. 274-286.

Chapter IX:
The First Iraqi War

General Barry McCaffrey recalled that his assistant commander, then Brigadier General Terry Scott, said as the war began, "I hope we don't fuck this up like we did Vietnam—I'd rather die than go through twenty years of that again."[1]

"While many nations have a terrible record in modern times of dealing out great suffering face-to-face with their victims, Americans have made it a point to keep at a distance while inflicting some of the greatest horrors of the age: atomic bombs on the people of Japan; carpet-bombing Korea back to the stone age; engulfing the Vietnamese in napalm and pesticides; providing three decades of Latin Americans with the tools and methods of torture, then turning their eyes away, closing their ears to the screams, and denying everything... and now, dropping 177 million pounds of bombs on the people of Iraq in the most concentrated aerial onslaught in the history of the world."[2]

FOR EVEN A TOKEN UNDERSTANDING of America's first war with Iraq in 1991, the Gulf War, it is necessary to return to the Middle East region in 1908. That year, a prospecting British oil company struck a gusher in what was then known as Persia. The world's navies were converting their fleets from coal to oil, and the strategic significance of the find was immediately apparent to Great Britain's Royal Navy Admirals.

Just before the outbreak of the Great War six years later, a prescient First Lord of the Admiralty, Winston Churchill, persuaded his government to become a major stockholder in the new Anglo-Persian Oil Company. From then on, the interests of the then greatest imperial power in history and the oil consortium were joined at the hip. An agreement in 1919 strengthened the bond; England took charge of Persia's army, treasury, and transportation and communications network. Martial law ruled. Ordinary Persian citizens lived in poverty while Britain extracted uncounted billions of dollars of oil from the profitable arrangement.

In 1933, under the autocratic rule of Reza Shah Pahlavi, the giant petroleum enterprise was renamed the Anglo-Iranian Oil Company. Persia became Iran two years later. AIOC paid no taxes to Iran, delivered the bulk of its profits to the British government, and sold oil to the Royal Navy at a fraction of the market price. In 1947, as popular discontent grew over AIOC's cozy ties with Britain, the Iranian parliament stiffened its back and passed a law directing the government to renegotiate the arrangements. The man who wrote the law was Mohammed Mossadegh, a wealthy Iranian who nevertheless spoke for Iran's poor. According to one historian, Mossadegh's

> "reputation for decency and integrity was legendary, and his Commitment to democracy and self-determination absolute—which made him the obvious foe of the AIOC. He was, in fact, the country's first genuinely popular leader, and is revered in Iran to this day [2009]."[3]

AS WITH IRAN, the Iraqi story had its origins within the British Empire. Formerly a part of the Ottoman Empire, Iraq was occupied by Britain during the Great War. At the end of the war and the breakup of the Ottoman Empire, Iraq was declared a League of Nations mandate under UK administration. Iraq gained its independence as a kingdom in 1932. A year earlier, the Iraq Petroleum

Company had been established, with principal shares held by British, French, Dutch, Portuguese, and American companies. In 1958, a popular, nationalist revolution overthrew the Hashemite monarchy, which had been installed by the British in 1921.

The new government, headed by Abdel Karim Kassem, helped found OPEC which challenged the stranglehold Western oil companies then held on the marketing of Arab oil. In 1963, in a CIA-organized rebellion, Kassem and thousands of his supporters were massacred. This followed soon after the CIA formed what it mockingly called internally a "health alterations committee" to plot Kassem's assassination.

Saddam Hussein appeared on the scene in 1968 as a leading member of the revolutionary Ba'ath Party which championed secular pan-Arabism, economic modernization, and Arab socialism. He played a key role in the 1968 coup that brought the party to long-term power. As vice president under the ailing General Ahmed Hassan al-Bakr, he successfully controlled the conflict between the government and the armed forces. In the early 1970s Saddam spearheaded Iraq's nationalization of the Western-owned Iraq Petroleum Company, which had long held a monopoly on the nation's oil. In July 1979 Saddam was elected president and maintained power during the Iraq-Iran War, 1980-1988, and the first war with the Americans, 1991-1992. Kuwait was a close ally of Iraq during its eight-year war with Iran, and functioned as the country's major port once Basra was shut down by the fighting. Kuwait had also loaned $40 billion to Iraq to help finance the war. After the war ended the friendly relations between the two countries soured, mainly because Iraq was not in a financial position to repay its loan and Kuwait was reluctant to pardon the debt.

Iraq tried to become financially solvent by cutting oil production, thus raising the price of oil. Kuwait responded by increasing its own production, thus lowering the price and—as seen by Iraqis—preventing the recovery of the war-weakened Iraqi economy. The Iraqi government described Kuwait's action as a form of economic warfare. Further exacerbating relations between the two countries was Iraq's claim that Kuwait was slant-drilling along a portion of the Iraq-Kuwait border.

By seizing Kuwait, the Iraqi government reasoned, it would be able to solve its financial problems and consolidate its regional authority. Further, Kuwait was seen by Baghdad as a historically integral part of present-day Iraq that had been sundered by British imperialism. Kuwait would also be easy pickings for Iraq's large army.

Many Arabs looked upon Saddam as a hero for his strong stance against foreign intervention and for his support of the Palestinians. Other Iraqis and western leaders vilified him for his cruel treatment of the Kurds and for his invasion of Kuwait. During the U.S. invasion of Iraq in 2003, he was deposed and a price was put on his head

Saddam was captured by U.S. forces in December 2003 and brought to trial by the Iraqi interim government, a puppet of the United States. Three years later, he was convicted of charges related to the executions of 148 Iraqi Shi'ites suspected of planning to assassinate him. He was sentenced to death by hanging and was executed on December 30, 2006.

A benchmark in the role of oil in the Middle East had been the San Remo agreement in 1920, in which Great Britain and France agreed to divide the oil between them. Britain, still the principal global empire but fading more quickly than it let on, had earlier set the standard for colonial control of oil, which was simply to put economic pressure on weak, corrupt governments to grant oil concessions. These concessions enabled western corporations to acquire the right to all the oil that lay underground in the area covered by the concession. In turn, these companies paid only token royalties to the governments of the countries. As a result of the first half-century of this brazen exploitation, Western oil companies and a tiny ruling elite in the Arab nations grew enormously wealthy.

U.S. oil companies were unhappy, having been excluded from the bonanza. In 1928, through the intervention of President Herbert Hoover, the San Remo pact was superseded by what was referred to as the Red-Line agreement; this gave American oil corporations a 23.5 percent share of all oil concessions in the defunct Ottoman Empire. Later, this agreement was modified and applied only to Iraq. In 1933, Texaco and Chevron negotiated the biggest plum of all, a 60-year concession from Saudi Arabia, which was soon shared with Exxon and Mobil in the creation of oil colossus ARAMCO. Gulf Oil, not to be excluded, obtained 50 percent of the Kuwaiti concession.

Kuwait was also a child of the British Colonial Office, born after the Great War to buffer Iraq's great oil fields. To create this new country, Britain arbitrarily redrew the maps of the region, establishing new borders between Kuwait, Iraq, and Saudi Arabia. These borders purposefully limited Iraq's access to the Persian Gulf, leaving only a tiny sliver of coastline to Iraq. This latter move by the British disregarded Iraq's historic control of this strategic territory. Oil was discovered in Iraq and Kuwait in the 1930s. In 1961 Kuwait was granted its independence from the UK.

Following Libya's revolution in 1969 and its nationalization of its oil fields, the Iraq Petroleum Company was nationalized in 1972. With the trauma of the Arab oil embargo a year later, oil-producing countries were emboldened to take greater shares of revenues. By 1975, even Western-leaning Saudi Arabia and Kuwait had nationalized their oil operations. In 1977, the U.S. Senate's Energy and Natural Resources Committee put the issue in stark terms:

> A U.S. commitment to the defense of oil resources of the Gulf and to political stability in the region constitutes one of the most vital and enduring interests of the United States.[5]

At that time there were no credible pretexts for direct intervention by the United States, and two factors mitigated against armed aggression. First, there was the high-risk scenario of war with the Soviet Union. Second, strong anti-war sentiments remained in the aftermath of the Vietnam War. The decline of the Soviet Union removed the first obstacle and heavy doses of propaganda took care of the second. As the Soviet economy collapsed, it withdrew its forces from Afghanistan and dismantled the Warsaw Pact. It was time for a new strategy, one even bolder than U.S. overt and covert wars to protect its "vital interests." It would be based on permanent bases filled with U.S. military forces and their advanced weaponry to achieve domination over whole regions and their resources.

> *"Our enemies are innovative and resourceful and so are we. They never stop thinking about new ways to harm our country and our people, and neither do we [sic]."*

—George W. Bush, August 5, 2004.

THE UNITED STATES had been eyeing the Persian Gulf region, Iraq in particular, since World War II. Political analyst and left-leaning author Noam Chomsky assessed America's long-standing policy in that area:

> It's been a leading, driving doctrine of U.S. foreign policy since the 1940s that the vast and unparalleled energy resources of the Gulf region will be effectively dominated by the United States and its clients, and, crucially, that no independents, indigenous force will be permitted to have a substantial influence on the administration of oil production and price.[6]

U.S. Navy admirals and Air Force and Army generals knew what Royal Navy Admirals had learned decades before: oil was critical to fight and win wars. In the intervening years, oil also became the indispensable mineral for America both in wartime and peacetime. It is the fuel to power cars and trucks and airplanes and to heat homes, and a feedstock for the hundreds of different plastics to make the countless products that are the hallmark of modern society. While the U.S. had been until then a net exporter of oil, it was understood that the day would soon come when imports would be needed to make up for the inevitable shortfall. It would not be sufficient just to buy oil from nations willing to sell, *but necessary to control foreign oil supplies.* Iraq, with the world's third largest oil reserves, was up for grabs.

The Pentagon's mission was straightforward: provoke the Iraqis into an overt anti-American action that could be used to justify to the world American military intervention. The CIA stood by, as always, to contribute its clandestine operatives and its effectively bottomless "black budget."

In July 1990, the U.S. ambassador to Iraq, April Glaspie, learned that Iraqi troops were massing near the Iraq-Kuwait border. She carelessly told Saddam that Washington "had no opinion on Arab-Arab conflicts," and that the United States did not intend "to start an economic war against Iraq." These statements led Saddam to believe he had received a diplomatic green light to invade Kuwait. In fact, Glaspie's comments were her own and did not represent American foreign policy in the Gulf region.

Before the Pentagon's program of incitement to war could get underway, on August 2, 1990, Iraq launched its own unprovoked invasion of Kuwait. George H. W. Bush had his window of opportunity. The White House the next day condemned Iraq's action and demanded that all Iraqi forces be withdrawn "immediately and unconditionally." It was a diplomatic hoax. Iraq ignored the U.S. demand.

Within days of the border crossing, an American naval task force, its carrier decks covered with strapped down fighter-bombers and the holds of its fast freighters filled with bombs, was on its way to the Persian Gulf. At the same time, the president sounded out UN members to join a coalition to put down Iraq's violation of its charter. That would take longer. In the meantime, the United States embargoed all trade with Iraq and froze all Iraqi and Kuwaiti assets. The Senate, which had been debating the nation's need for the astronomically expensive B-2 Stealth Bomber [7], decisively defeated efforts to end or freeze the plane's production. Senators also voted to stave off the mothballing of two World War II-vintage battleships.

The few Americans who knew anything about Kuwait, an almost-medieval Sheikdom ruled despotically by a single family, were well aware that it was far from a democracy, but that it certainly pumped plenty of oil. Those who were better informed knew that Kuwait had not been much of a U.S. ally, either. Kuwait had voted with the United States in the UN only nineteen times, three times less often than the Soviet Union. Kuwait's civil rights record was particularly unsavory, treating citizens disdainfully and non-citizens cruelly. Women did not have the right to vote nor could they drive. In 1986 Kuwait closed down its parliament and no longer had political parties.

But these shortcomings of Kuwait society were easily remedied by the overnight dissemination of creative lies, exaggerations, and obfuscations of a gigantic PR program that created a new, benign "image" of Kuwait and Kuwaitis for Americans. George H. W. Bush contributed this warped intelligence in the run-up to the war:

> "Our jobs, our way of life, our own freedom, and the freedom of friendly countries around the world will suffer if control of the world's great oil reserves fell into the hands of that one man Saddam Hussein."[8]

General Norman Schwarzkopf, who would lead the troops, wildly told Congress:

Mideast oil is the West's lifeblood. It fuels us today, and being seventy-seven percent of the Free World's proven oil reserves, is going to fuel us when the rest of the world has run dry... It is estimated that within 20 to 40 years the U.S. will have virtually depleted its economically available oil reserve, while the Persian Gulf will still have at least 100 years of proven oil reserves.[9]

THE FIRST MOVE by the large, well-financed Kuwaiti lobbying delegations in Washington and New York after the Iraqi invasion was to retain the services of Hill & Knowlton, a large, politically savvy, and well-connected advertising and public relations firm. H&K immediately created a "Citizens for a Free Kuwait" cover organization for its new client, to lend credibility to the flood of hyped disinformation that began spewing out of its offices. Every PR firm worth its salt understands that while it should fill its news conduits with almost-daily information releases, it must develop a theme and work it to death. The theme that came out of the sleazy offices of CFK was Iraqi atrocities, the crueler the better, easy to come up with if they are lies!

THE MOST effective tale of Iraqi atrocities—indeed, the most effective propaganda ploy of the entire war—was the sensational and wholly manufactured tale of Iraqi soldiers cruelly killing helpless infants. On October 10, 1990, in a Congressional hearing room, Nayirah, a petite and tearful 15-year-old Kuwaiti girl, was introduced to a gathering of reporters and Congressmen. The program was sponsored by the "Congressional Human Rights Foundation" the brainchild of Congressmen Tom Lantos and John Edward Porter, the sleazy directors of CFK.

With scarcely any prompting, between her nearly continuous sobbing, she related a shocking story. She told the audience she had witnessed Iraqi soldiers remove fifteen infants from their incubators in Al-Adan Hospital in Baghdad and put them on the cold floor to die. That was all she said; no questions were asked and she was quickly whisked out of the room. To those who wanted to find out more about Nayirah, Lantos and Porter said that her identity was being kept secret to protect her family from reprisals in occupied Kuwait.

It was a blockbuster story and media outlets all over the world picked it up. CFK had hit the jackpot. Nearly everyone believed the heart-wrenching story from a distraught teenager including Amnesty International. Its corroboration of the charges undoubtedly influenced the votes of the seven Senators who mentioned the "incubator atrocity" in speeches supporting the January 12 resolution authorizing the war.

> *The Emirate of Kuwait has been portrayed by The New York Times as "less a country than a family-owned company with a flag."*[4]

It turned out later, after the war when it no longer mattered, that there was a far better reason for Nayirah to remain *persona non grata* than to protect her next of kin. Nayirah, her real name, just happened to be the daughter of Saud Nasir al-Sabah, the Kuwaiti ambassador to the United States. John R. MacArthur, publisher of *Harper's Magazine* and author of *Second Front: Censorship and Propaganda in the Gulf War*, had done a little reportorial investigation and uncovered a large can of worms.

Congressmen Lantos and Porter were found to have close financial ties to H&K. The well planned propaganda effort to convince Americans that Iraqis were evil people included a vice president of H&K, Gary Hymel, whose idea it was to use Nayirah as a key witness. According to MacArthur,

Hymel told him he knew her true identity from the start. The Lantos-Porter team arranged for CHRF to be housed in H&K's spacious Washington headquarters. It was also learned that CFK had donated $50,000 to the CHRF.

> According to reports, the Kuwaiti account was one of the most expensive PR campaigns in history, costing $5.6 million from the period from August 20 to November 10; eventually, it was estimated that the local account was $11 million. Hill & Knowlton organized a photo exhibit of Iraqi atrocities [spurious!] displayed at the UN and the U.S. Congress and widely shown on TV; assisted [coached!] Kuwaiti refugees in telling stories of torture; lobbied Congress; and prepared video and print material for the media. There were reported to be six other U.S. PR firms working for the Kuwaitis at the same time.[10]

THE "COALITION" BOMBARDMENT of Iraq began on January 17, 1991, and went on continuously, day and night, for 42 days.

> "It was awful to see a city [Baghdad] being bombed that way. In less than 24 hours, we saw hundreds of buildings, whole blocks in 10 separate residential areas, hospitals, mosques, and churches damaged and destroyed. The center of the city was not completely incinerated, as happened to Dresden and Hiroshima. But every service essential to modern life was severed.
>
> It was months before we realized how much damage the United States had done. Before the assault was over U.S. planes flew more than 109,000 sorties, raining 88,000 tons of bombs, the equivalent of seven Hiroshimas, and killing indiscriminately across the country.
>
> What was visible was a nation with thousands of civilians dead; without water, hospitals, or health care; with no electricity, communications, or public transportation; without gasoline, road and bridge repair capacity, or parts for essential equipment; and with a growing food crisis. The bombing, as could be seen from the ground, was hardly surgical, but was clearly designed to break a whole country and its population for a long time to come."[11]

Those were the words of Ramsey Clark, former U.S. Attorney General and an indefatigable peace advocate. He and four others—John Alpert, independent documentary film-maker; Maryann DeLeo, free-lance photographer; Mohammad al-Kaysi, translator and guide; and an unnamed Jordanian driver—had rented a Toyota sedan in Amman, Jordan and bravely drove into Baghdad after dark on February 2, 1991. This was still during the period of the 'round-the-clock bombing of Baghdad.

They spent the next seven days covering 2,000 miles from Baghdad to Basra and beyond, seeing close-up civilian casualties and destruction. When they returned to Jordan seven days later, they had with them over six hours of uncensored videotape, hundreds of still photos, and vivid impressions of the crushing American air war. *NBC Nightly News* reviewed parts of the tape and knew they had a scoop. But NBC News President Michael Gartner summarily rejected the tape without even viewing it.

> They had in their hands uncensored film from inside Iraq showing civilian damage from U.S. bombing and they refused to show it. Instead they projected the Pentagon myth of surgical accuracy and repeatedly headlined *Scud* missiles striking Israel and Saudi Arabia... Much was made of the *Patriot* missile which was presented by the media and a miraculous defender against the *Scuds*. A year later the *Patriot* was authoritatively branded an "almost total failure" by MIT expert Theodore A. Postol.[12]

Clark also pointed to the wildly overdone patriotic comments of the U.S. TV networks' principal talking heads. For example, on the first day of the bombing, Charles Osgood called it "a marvel." Jim Stewart the next day gushed that there had been "two days of almost picture perfect bombing"—as if he could observe bombing accuracy from some 7,000 miles away. Ted Koppel assured his millions of viewers that great effort was taken, sometimes at great personal cost to American pilots, "that civilian targets are not hit."

That statement was a bare-faced lie. It was soon learned that civilian infrastructure along with civilians were principal targets. Even the well-respected guru of news gatherers, Walter Cronkite, got into the act. He lost his objectivity—and his integrity—when he told his viewers: "*We* knocked out one of *their* Scuds." Finally, Dan Rather, acting the role of a TV news patriarch, summed it up for his fellow news gatherers when he commented on the U.S. assault on Iraq:

> "Congratulations on a job *wonderfully done*." [author's emphasis][13]

Later on, Clark shifted his attention to the conduct of the submissive U.S. media.

> Military censorship, self-censorship, uncritical acceptance of Pentagon stories, suppression of dissenting voices, perpetuation of false stories, each present and inexcusable in and of itself, were minor offenses. Instead, there was a massive media campaign to persuade the public of the righteousness of the American cause and conduct, including an intense promotion of U.S. military actions.[14]

In fact, the U.S. media, as solicitous of the Pentagon's propagandists as Shakespeare's Polonius was of Hamlet, happily used every handout it got.

> *Hamlet:* Do you see yonder cloud that's almost in the shape of a camel?
>
> *Polonius:* By the mass, and 'tis like a camel, indeed.
>
> *Hamlet:* Me thinks it is like a weasel.
>
> *Polonius:* It is backed like a weasel.
>
> *Hamlet:* Or like a whale?
>
> *Polonius:* Very like a whale.[15]

What the media had failed to report was arguably more harmful to an honest assessment of the situation by their readers than the active propaganda it had dutifully carried for the Pentagon.

> A peaceful resolution of the dispute would have been virtually assured if the American people had known how effective the sanctions against Iraq were, and how Saddam Hussein was offering, indeed urging, a negotiated settlement. Twenty-four of the 25 largest newspapers in the U.S. editorially supported the use of force as opposed to economic sanctions in the months before the bombing began.[16]

Lastly, there was no media recognition that Iraq had been rendered defenseless by the six weeks of continuous bombing: for example, not a single Abrams tank nor B-52 bomber had been damaged by enemy fire and not a single significant military engagement had taken place, although U.S. military propagandists promoted the lie that Saddam Hussein's army had been a tough adversary.

The real military story from the Gulf campaign—never told by U.S. media—was that U.S. technology permitted the U.S. to destroy most countries on earth with little risk to U.S. soldiers and airmen. General Colin Powell's ghastly statement that the number of Iraqi casualties was a number he "was not terribly interested in" managed to escape the press condemnation it merited.

Something else that was scarcely touched on was America's use of a remarkable new weapon: Depleted Uranium in ammunition and armor-plating. The performance of DU in both applications was no less than a military revolution. Thousands of Iraq tanks and other vehicles were destroyed or damaged beyond repair by DU munitions fired from U.S. tanks, armored fighting vehicles, and aircraft. DU is an extremely dense material, about 1.7 times the density of lead. When used as a nose cone of an artillery round, it "self-sharpens" as it penetrates; unlike lead and even tungsten, DU does not "mushroom" as it penetrates. DU is also pyrophoric: as the penetrator self-sharpens, small particles flake off and ignite spontaneously.

When DU plates are sandwiched between inner and outer layers of steel armor, the laminate that results protects against most existing non-DU munitions. However, DU comes with a penalty. It is a slightly radioactive (about 40 percent less than U-238) heavy metal, primarily an alpha emitter but also a tiny emitter of more penetrating beta rays. This means that U.S. tank crews were being subjected to radiation whenever they were inside their tanks. And like all heavy metals, DU is toxic. Ingesting DU residue into the body by breathing it into the lungs or swallowing it into the digestive tract are principal hazards. However, DU rounds can penetrate DU-plated tanks, as happened in "friendly-fire" incidents in the Gulf War.

The USAF was responsible for most of the DU expended in the Gulf War. The A-10 *Warthog* used Gatling guns loaded with 30 mm API armor-piercing incendiary) rounds. The Pentagon has estimated that these 30 mm rounds accounted for 259 tons of the overall 320 tons of DU munitions expended in the Gulf region. The 1994-1995 conflict in Bosnia and the 1999 war in Kosovo were two more instances in which the United States used DU munitions.

Some Americans thought that oil was behind the war— was the U.S. seeking to gain a permanent foothold in the region, not only to gain access to oil, but to control its distribution? Yes and yes, again! In fact, in January 2009, the United States officially unveiled its new embassy in Iraq, a three-quarter billion-dollar structure, said to be the largest of its kind in the world. While professing a willingness to get all its troops out of Iraq as soon as the Iraqi government could survive without close U.S. military support, the United States was unquestionably staying, their remaining many thousands of troops inconspicuous inside numerous air force bases and other military infrastructure in the desert.

These same Americans wondered what it was that triggered such a prolonged aerial attack against one of the most advanced and enlightened nations in the Middle East with its ancient yet modern capital city? They were not buying what George H. W. Bush was trying to sell: that Saddam was worse than Hitler, that he was on the verge of building an arsenal of nuclear weapons and the long-range rockets to carry them. By extension, Bush reiterated over and over that Saddam was *a threat to American security.* By destroying Saddam Hussein's so-called WMDs, the United States self-proclaimed as the world's policeman was doing a good turn for all mankind. In the event, UN investigating teams spread out all over Iraq seeking, but never finding, traces of nuclear weapons or poison-gas production.

Douglas Kellner, no war hawk, wrote cogently:

> The Gulf war was not solely a war for oil, for the greater glory of George Bush and the Pentagon, or for the promotion of U.S. geopolitical supremacy to bolster a faltering economy, although all of these factors played a role in producing the war.[17]

Yet, there was arguably an amazing coincidence of interests within the Bush administration, the Pentagon, and influential economic forces. This convergence is itself no accident. George H. W. Bush was the first president in recent years who was himself part of both the corporate economic establishment and the National Security State. Bush was an oil man and his family continues to have important oil interests.[18] He was also a former director of the CIA and consistently supported use of covert operations and military force to bulwark U.S. foreign policy.

IT HAD ALSO BECOME TIME for another U.S. war. The invasions of tiny Grenada in 1983 and Panama in 1989 were good—but insufficient—warm-ups for the U.S. military.

> "The war in the Gulf is not a war we wanted. We worked hard to avoid war... But time and again, Saddam Hussein flatly rejected the path of diplomacy and peace."

Those were President George H. W. Bush's words in his State of the Union Address on August 2, 1989, delivered without even traces of a smirk.[19] The truth was that the Gulf War *was a war wanted* by the U.S. and it wasn't President Saddam Hussein who rejected diplomacy. Bush claimed he wanted to be remembered fondly by future generations of Americans as a peace-seeking president who had been reluctantly drawn into war. But craggy-faced Bush, Sr., with his beak-shaped nose and protruding chin, just didn't look like a peace-maker. In fact, he was sometimes caricatured in political cartoons as a vulture.

"Saddam Hussein, of course, is not unique as a monster. He is as monstrous as General Augusto Pinochet, who, having been brought to power by U.S. Intervention against an elected democratic government, victimized his own people for seventeen years. And Iraq's aggression against Kuwait is as monstrous as the aggressions of the United States against Nicaragua and Panama, against Grenada and Vietnam, as monstrous as the Soviet invasions of Czechoslovakia and Afghanistan. And Saddam Hussein's lobbing of missiles at civilians in Israel is as monstrous as the Israeli's bombing of refugee camps in Lebanon."

—Ariel Dorfman, *Los Angeles Times*, February 1, 1991.

"Very few, even among the neoconservatives, believe that regime change in Iran by military force will be easy... But with Iraq taken, the U.S. military has now almost completely surrounded Iran. There are U.S. forces in Turkey, Iraq, Pakistan, Afghanistan, and Turkmenistan, every state that abuts Iran except for Russia. The United States also exercises effective military control over the Straits of Hormuz, through which most of Iran's oil must travel before it is exported to the world."[20]

The first example of America's ruthless interventions in the Islamic world was the CIA-arranged coup in Iran in 1953, *Operation Ajax*, which toppled Mohammed Mossadegh. *Ajax* set into motion a train of events that reverberated for decades to come and influenced the thinking of millions of Muslims.

Then there are the festering wounds of the Israelis and Palestinians which remained at the top of the list of deep-seated Muslim grievances against the United States. While the story is a long and complicated one, Arab hatreds boil down to America's unequivocal support of the Jewish state and every boldly anti-Muslim move the Israelis make. After all, Israel is America's coddled surrogate in the Middle East. While Israel is the beneficiary of some $3 billion a year in aid, perhaps much more hidden in the CIA's black budget, including the most advanced military hardware, there is a lack of interest in the plight of the Palestinians. Until Americans can grasp that the horrible events of September 11 were retaliation—not simply "evil" or "insane"—for their nation's skein of ill-advised misdeeds, Americans will be unable to end the threat of terrorist attacks—and an end to the unwinnable "war on terror."

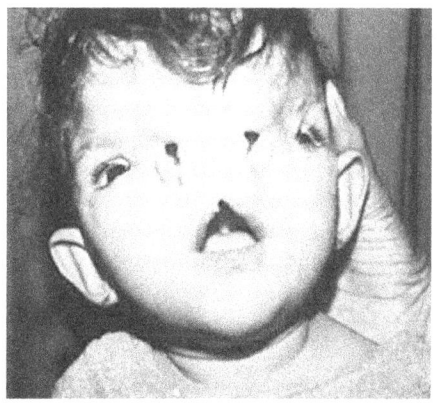

"It is doubtful if there has been a higher percentage of death, destruction, and long-term incapacitation inflicted on a whole country of Iraq's size or larger in a comparable period of time in the history of warfare."[21]

Birth Defect from "Depleted" Uranium-238, which has a radioactive half-life of 5 billion years—Iraq has been contaminated forever. "In September 2009, Fallujah General Hospital, Iraq, had 170 new born babies, 24% of whom were dead within the first seven days, a staggering 75% of the dead babies were classified as deformed."

BY JANUARY 1991, the coalition force of American, British, French, Arabic and twenty-four other nations sanctioned by the UN, totaling some 700,000 troops, were ready to strike. These overwhelming numbers compared to the 156,000 Allied troops that landed in Normandy on D-day in

June 1944, then the largest amphibious invasion in history. The bombing campaign was followed by a one-sided 'hundred-hours' ground war and Baghdad's surrender on February 28, 1992.

But first came the "manufactured demon," Iraqi President Saddam Hussein. U.S. propaganda vilified him as demented, a beast, and a monster. The sensationalist *New York Post* called him "a bloodthirsty megalomaniac," tough to pronounce without biting your tongue. *The New Republic* went to the trouble of retouching a *Time* magazine cover to make Hussein look more like Hitler by narrowing his moustache. A Gannett Foundation study found no less than 1,170 examples in the print media and on TV linking Saddam Hussein with good old reliable fiend Adolf Hitler.

> *"What happens in our system is that the services see one of their management duties as placing their retired officers, just like a good University will place its graduates. And the placed the services had the most influence is with its contractors. If you're a good clean-living officer and you don't get drunk at lunch or get caught messing around with the opposite sex in the office, and you don't raise too much of a fuss about horror stories you come across—when you retired, a nice man will come calling. Typically he'll be another retired officer. And he'll be driving a fancy car, and wearing a $2,000 suit and Gucci shoes and a Rolex watch. He will offer to make a comfortable life for you by getting you a comfortable job at one of the contractors. Now, if you go around kicking people in the shins, raising hell about the outrages committed by the big contractors, no nice man comes calling. It's that simple."*[22]

Next round was the wave of Pentagon propaganda about the Air Force's and the Army's two highly touted new missiles, *Tomahawks* [cruise missiles] and *Patriots* [anti-missile missiles]. At the end of January 1991, Lt. General Thomas Kelly announced that over two hundred *Tomahawks* "had been fired successfully." To further define the claim, the Pentagon later declared "a 98 percent launch success rate." That sounded pretty good to patriotic American journalists looking for success stories. Skeptical British correspondent Phillip Knightley begged to disagree.

No journalist thought to ask what this meant, actually. They wished that they had when an article entitled 'Awestruck Press Does Tomahawk PR' appeared in The Bulletin of Atomic Scientists in April 1991.[23]

Knightley's probing article pointed out that the so-called "launch success rate" was completely unrelated to the missile's accuracy. It meant simply that the *Tomahawks* had managed to get out of their launchers without getting stuck or blowing up just after they left the launcher, maiming or killing the launching crew.

If the *Tomahawk* was imperfect, not so the *Patriot*—the imaginary *Scud* killer—according to General Norman Schwarzkopf, the American commander. He told correspondents, managing a straight face, that everyone knew about the *Patriot:* it was a one-hundred-percent success. It was not until several years later that the truth finally emerged. A Senate Armed Services Committee in August 1993 declared:

> "A postwar review of photographs cannot produce even a single confirmed kill [by a *Patriot*] of a Scud missile."[24]

It wasn't only the high-tech—and high-priced—*Tomahawks* and *Patriots* that came under scrutiny. At an earlier hearing of the House Armed Service Committee, Pierre Sprey, a former Pentagon official [and a self-proclaimed weapons expert] accused the Defense Department of "shamelessly doctoring statistics" to provide a totally misleading image of even "moderate-tech" weapon systems. Sprey pointed out that it had taken an average of 24 laser-guided "smart bombs" to strike each bridge targeted in the first two weeks of the war. As for the highly touted F-117A *Stealth* fighter-bombers, he claimed they were "not so stealthy," and had been tracked "by British-, French-, and Chinese-made radars." Indeed, they had been closely escorted by conventional fighter planes on all their bombing missions, not to shoot down attacking airplanes [there were none] but to confuse radar signals from the ground, not unlike the chaff-dispensing aircraft of World War II.

Other disturbing stories came to light: the *Apache* helicopter, while achieving a high "mission capable rate," required extraordinary maintenance to keep it flying; crews of the more than 2,000 Bradley fighting vehicles, according to a *Times* article of April 11, 1992, complained that its exhaust "tended to blow in the vehicle commander's face," and poor gun sights impaired accuracy. Furthermore, British sources noted that the gas-guzzling U.S. *Abrams* A1M1 tank used four times as much fuel as the *Challenger*, its British counterpart.

There were also serious environmental impacts from the heavy bombings, largely suppressed by both the Pentagon and the compliant media. On January 18, during a military briefing in Saudi Arabia, reporters asked General Schwarzkopf if oil refineries and pipelines were targets. Schwarzkopf sternly replied without missing a beat:

> "We have made it a point to not hit targets that are not of a military nature."[25]

Later that afternoon other military briefers contradicted their boss, openly admitting that U.S. fighter-bombers were hitting oil targets, claiming they were "militarily significant." U.S. bombers also hit two Iraqi oil tankers in the Persian Gulf, resulting in huge oil spills that the Pentagon could hardly deny.

The censorship extended to the Public Affairs Officers who "supervised" the journalists. In fact, the intent was to gag the troops and to muzzle the TV and newspaper reporters. As for unrehearsed interviews, the PAOs left little to chance. TV producer Lucy Spiegel wrote:

> They [the PAOs] would have already called ahead and everything was set up. You never really surprised anybody... You'd watch them take off and you'd watch them come down. You'd interview the crew and you'd go and watch them eat a meal and you'd talk to the CO... There were no great investigative stories. There couldn't be. You were too controlled.[26]

The result, as Spiegel related, was a handful of basic stories reworked over and over by the correspondents trying to create fresh stories.

> Arrival of troops, not enough mail; the weather: it's too hot, it's too cold; the helicopter doesn't work, the gun won't fire, too much sand, too much dirt, too much whatever; women are going to war; should women be going to war?[27]

This First Iraqi War was the first American war organized from the get-go for television. *Tomahawk* cruise missiles and fighter-bombers were over Baghdad precisely in "prime time" for TV viewers on the U.S. east coast, 6:35PM eastern standard time—3:35AM Baghdad time. That night, network TV cameras showed streams of red and white tracers crisscrossing the black sky. There were sounds of explosions in the background accompanied by large plumes of smoke. Good stuff for live TV! No close-up scenes of the wounded and dead Iraqis, no collapsed buildings; just plain-vanilla pyrotechnics, like fireworks, and "suitable for viewing by all ages."

BAGHDAD RADIO announced at 5:35PM (Eastern Standard Time), on February 26, 1991, that their Foreign Minister had accepted the Soviet cease-fire proposal and had issued the order for all Iraqi troops to withdraw to positions held before August 2, 1990, in compliance with UN Resolution 660.

That was the end of the war. But it was not the end of the killing as far as USAF commanders—and one U.S Army general in particular—were concerned.

The next day, in Kuwait and Iraq, roads were clogged with Iraqi vehicles, pulling out as fast as they could, going back home, under direct orders to do so from their commanders in Baghdad. American troops were not driving Iraqi troops out of Kuwait, "heroically" as the Bush administration claimed. Nor were the Iraqis retreating in order to regroup and fight again.

Iraqi tanks were riding on their flat-bed trailers, their cannons swiveled backwards, clear indicators of their peaceful intentions. White surrender flags flew from every vehicle antenna. No weapons were fired at low-flying U.S. reconnaissance helicopters. Despite these obvious signs of peaceful intentions, as far as Air Force commanders and General Barry McCaffrey were concerned, these Iraqis were still enemies and the war was still "on." Or was it an opportunity for live-fire bombing and strafing practice, a jaundiced observer asked rhetorically? Shooting fish in a barrel?

The Highway of Death

Some 2,000 vehicles including hundreds of civilian cars, taxis, and buses piled high with luggage and household furnishings were ruthlessly attacked by the USAF. Fighter-bombers methodically struck front and rear vehicles in the columns, then bombed, rocketed, and strafed the stalled traffic in between, again and again. On the main road into and out of Baghdad every vehicle for miles was destroyed, their burned-out skeletons lining the road, with charred corpses strewn everywhere. This was called the Highway of Death. One GI described what he saw.

> I actually went up close and examined two vehicles that basically looked like refugees maybe trying to get out of the area. You know, you had like a little Toyota pick-up truck that was

loaded down with the furniture and the suitcases and rugs and the pet cat... and those trucks were taken out just like the military vehicles.[28]

The Pentagon first attempted to silence reporting about the Highway of Death, but it was too big a story for reporters to ignore. The White House, however, justified the slaughter by declaring:

"These were the torturers, the looters, the rapists."[29]

Ten days after the cease fire, the results of a second aerial massacre were discovered, this time inside Kuwait. A correspondent from the *Los Angeles Times* reported what he saw—and it was not a pretty sight. This time apparently all the dead were Iraqi soldiers.

> For 60 miles, hundreds of Iraqi tanks and armored cars, howitzers and anti-aircraft guns, ammunition trucks and ambulances are strafed, smashed, and burned beyond belief. Scores of soldiers lie in and around the vehicles, mangled and bloated in the drifting desert sands... Largely unnoticed by the media so far, the tableau stretches for miles. Every vehicle was strafed or bombed. Every windshield is shattered. Every tank is burned. Every truck is riddled with shell fragments. No survivors are known or likely.[30]

American pilots gleefully referred to the butchery as a "turkey shoot." Some carrier pilots were so eager to return to the "battle," they sometimes had their aircraft "bombed up" with unsuitable but immediately available ordnance on the flight deck. On the *USS Ranger* aircraft carrier, loudspeakers blared the theme music from the *Lone Ranger* radio program of the 1930s and 1940s, the stirring and gung-ho Rossini William Tell overture.

General Barry McCaffrey's 24th Infantry Division also contributed to the carnage visited on the Iraqis. Had the 24th come under fire from the "retreating/attacking" Iraqis? That is what McCaffrey testified in three Army investigations, and it remains controversy to this day. After the announcement of the cease-fire, McCaffrey ordered his troops into an aggressive blocking position—a maneuver intended to make contact with the Iraqi troops. Why had he done so, unless he planned to attack them? When the 24th took enemy fire, as McCaffrey insisted, it returned fire under the doctrine of self-defense. The Iraqi forces engaged were destroyed, according to McCaffrey. One suspects that McCaffrey was looking for more medals to cover his chest, to add to his credibility as a prominent authority on the Iraq war in years to come, and a "talking head" on TV programs that paid so well for "experts" who could read from Teleprompters without stumbling.

Journalist Seymour Hersh, in an article published in *The New Yorker* of May 22, 2000, found otherwise. He had interviewed senior officers who decried the "lack of discipline and proportionality" in McCaffrey's "counter-attack." One colonel told Hersh that it made no sense for a defeated Army to invite their own death as the Iraqis supposedly did. It was like shooting fish in a barrel, he said. He was sure no one believed the story.

Hersh described his interview with Corporal Charles Sheehan-Miles from the 24th Infantry that shed more light on the slaughter.

> When I asked Sheehan-Miles why he fired, he replied, "At that point we were shooting everything. Guys in the company told me later that there were some civilians. It wasn't like they came at us with a gun. It was that they were there—'in the wrong place at the wrong time.' We took some incoming once, but it was friendly fire. The folks we fought there never had a chance.' He came away from Iraq convinced that he and his fellow soldiers were, as another tanker put it, part of 'the biggest firing squad in history.'"[31]

ONE EXAMPLE of the deep-seated American fascination with war in general and their nation's wars in particular was given by popular TV personality Andy Rooney and his ludicrous celebration of the Gulf War. As seen by the nineteen million viewers of *60 Minutes*, he nearly toppled off his stool with patriotic pride.

> The war is over everywhere and we feel together. There are some good things about war, sometimes. Everyone accomplishes more in times of war. Our hearts beat faster. Our senses are sharper... This war in the Gulf has been, by all odds, the best war in modern history, not only for America, but for the whole world, including Iraq, probably. [34]

"C'mon Andy," a cynic with a chip or two on his or her shoulder, might ask, "have you forgotten World War II, the 'really good war'?"

While the U.S. military never provided a post-mortem breakdown of the weapons used, an Air Force spokesman admitted that the full complement of tactical munitions was employed throughout the bombardment of Iraq. And this "full complement" included the most terrible anti-personnel weapons yet contrived by American weapons designers and manufacturers. One of the most common was the Cluster Bomb Unit or CBU, that killed and maimed indiscriminately over wide areas. Instead of producing a single large explosion, CBUs contained hundreds to thousands of small to tiny individual bomblets called BLUs. A typical CBU was filled with 1,800 one-pound BLUs such as the BLU-26 *Sadeye*, a cast steel shell with aerodynamic vanes to stabilize flight and a 0.7 pound charge of TNT in which some 600 razor-sharp steel shards were imbedded. The *Sadeye* was fused to explode on impact, some yards above ground, or—even more terribly—a fixed time after impact, days and weeks later. A CBU-75, a canister of 1,800 *Sadeyes*, dispersed its deadly cargo far more broadly than the standard 2,000-pound Mk-84 demolition bomb. This bomb of the 1950s created a crater some 50 feet across and about 35 feet deep in ordinary soil. If fused to explode before it hit the ground, it dispersed shrapnel to a lethal radius of some 400 yards. The *Rockeye* was a 750-pound bomb that carried over 700 anti-tank bomblets.

What all of the CBUs shared was their enormously wide area coverage: the CBU-75, for example, covered an area equal to 22 football fields. The 950-pound CBU-87 was described as the bomb of choice in the Middle East. This "combined-effects munition" carried two-hundred 3.4-pound BLU-97 bomblets. Each of these bomblets, arguably, was the handiwork of a fiend. It carried a triple punch: a prefragmented anti-personnel casing, a hollow-charge antitank warhead, and a disc of incendiary zirconium for a fiery finishing touch. A single B-52 carried 40 CBU-87s with a total of 8,080 BLU-97s. Assuming a danger radius of 250 feet, one B-52 could carpet bomb an astounding 176 million square yards. The twenty-eight B-52s, which reportedly dropped 470 tons of explosives on Iraqi troops in one day, could have obliterated unprotected human life in an area 1,600 square miles, an area one-third the size of Connecticut!

Fuel-air explosives—MADFAE—were also used, supposedly to clear minefields in Kuwait according to the U.S. Central Command. These hideous weapons form gaseous mixtures which, when ignited, produce far more blast than fire. For their size and weight, they achieve more blast than any other weapon except for nuclear bombs. MADFAE consists of 12 containers of ethylene oxide or propylene oxide trailed behind helicopters. The containers release a cloud of highly volatile vapors which, when mixed with air and detonated, cover an area over 1,000 feet long x 1,000 feet wide with blast over-pressures five times that of TNT.

One bombing program—little-publicized, for good reason—was based on a Defense Intelligence Agency Secret document titled "Iraqi Water Treatment Vulnerabilities." The document analyzed the Iraqi water treatment system, the effects of post-war sanctions on a heavily bombed system, and the impact on the Iraqi population forced to drink untreated water. The U.S. program to deny potable water to the citizens of Iraq was carried out with the full knowledge of its effects on the health of Iraqis, a deliberate violation of Geneva protocols.

Another government document, "Medical Problems in Iraq", dated March 15, 1991, stated that there were no longer any operational water treatment and sewage treatment plants in all of Iraq, that there was a fourfold increase in the incidence of debilitating diarrhea above pre-war levels, and that cholera and measles had emerged at refugee camps.

THE POST-WAR SANCTIONS imposed on a supine Iraq, fostered by the still-vengeful United States and its lackey Great Britain, cut even deeper. Within months after the end of the war, reports pointed to an Iraqi calamity in the making. In April 1991 a Harvard Study Team, a group of doctors and social scientists, predicted that unless something was done, "at least 170,000 children under five years of age will die in the coming year from the delayed effects of the Gulf Crisis."

The most authoritative study of child deaths from the sanctions was completed in 1999 by UNICEF. It based its survey of over 20,000 households, and concluded that the under-age-five mortality rate averaged 56 out of 1,000 in the period 1984-89 and 131 out of 1,000 from 1994-99—an increase of over 130 percent.[35]

Another UNICEF report in 2003 recorded that Iraq's regression over the past decade is by far the most severe of the 193 countries surveyed. The child death rate, the best single indicator of child welfare, increased from 50 to 133 per 1,000 live births, placing Iraq below every country outside Africa except Cambodia and Afghanistan.[36]

> To maintain a crushing post-war pressure on Iraq, the United States and the United Kingdom established "no-fly" zones across parts of the seriously wounded country. USAF and RAF aircraft jointly patrolled a northern zone above the 36th parallel and a southern zone below the 33rd. France elected to pull out its aircraft in 1996. These "no-fly' zones were often contested by ground fire from Iraqi anti-aircraft batteries and American and British fighter-bombers responded with bombs. According to a former UN humanitarian coordinator for Iraq, these bombings killed hundreds of Iraqi civilians, most of them from the groups, Kurds and Shias, that the no-fly zones supposedly protected.[37]

On February 29, 1992, an International U.S. War Crimes Tribunal to look into War Crimes by the United States during the Gulf War—organized like the Nuremberg Tribunal in 1945 that had tried high-level Nazis—was convened in New York City. Ramsey Clark was the driving force behind the new Tribunal. Earlier its Commission of Inquiry had held more than thirty hearings in the United States and sponsored similar meetings in over twenty other countries. The Tribunal was presided over by an international panel of important human rights leaders, judges, and political figures. They found nineteen violations of International Law.

The New York Times, one of whose reporters sat in on the meetings, printed nary a word about it. An eminent columnist responded to an invitation to attend by replying he would "lose his job" if he wrote about the Tribunal. While ignored by the media in the United States, the event nevertheless received significant coverage overseas. The purposeful news blackout ensured that as far as nearly every American was concerned, the Tribunal had never taken place—and no large-scale atrocities had occurred! Yet for the Iraqis, their country had been pulverized and tens of thousands of civilians had been killed or maimed.

Astonishingly, but also scarcely mentioned in the media and hence unknown to Americans, the United States, through its control of the UN Security Council, successfully prevented humanitarian aid from entering Iraq for the next decade. Compounding this heinous record, the U.S. blocked purchases of equipment to repair damaged infrastructure. In 2000, the U.S. blocked the importation of flour-milling machinery, yogurt-making equipment, and a billion dollars of medical equipment, heart and lung machines, even vaccines for children (until the *Washington Post* exposed the story in March 2001). On May 12, 1996, CBS ran a *60 Minutes* piece titled "Punishing Saddam." during which Madeleine Albright, former Secretary of State and America's ambassador to the UN, was challenged by the data of a half-million dead Iraqi children. Her flippant response, grammatically incorrect:

> "We think the price is worth it."

Clark reported three instances of news commentators who were castigated or worse for voicing opinions of the war contrary to "conventional wisdom." Warren Hincle of the *San Francisco Examiner* was given a three-month "vacation;" Orlando Garcia, a talk-show host on New York City's Spanish-language station WADO, was fired for his "unbalanced view of the war;" Editor Joe Reedy of the Kutztown *Patriot* was dismissed for writing an editorial "How About a Little Peace?"[38]

Veteran news correspondent Malcolm Browne summed up the suffocating Pentagon control of the media when he told *Newsday* on January 23, 1991, that he had never seen anything that could compare to the degree of surveillance and control the military had over the correspondents.

> "When the entire environment is managed, a journalist ceases to be a reporter in the American or Anglo-Saxon tradition."[39]

IN THE LONG HISTORY of warfare, documented perhaps more thoroughly than other aspects of man's journey:

> It is doubtful if there has been a higher percentage of death, destruction, and long-term incapacitation inflicted on a whole country of Iraq's size or larger in a comparable period. For a nation of 16 million to have 250,000-350,000 of its people killed, suffer a multiple of that figure injured and handicapped, and have water, sanitation, power, communication, transportation, and food production and distribution damaged in six weeks of violence is unprecedented.[40]

Presidential popularity soared and some Americans expected a prompt U.S. attack on another demonized country to help reelect George H. W. Bush. Ramsey Clark singled out two prominent *New York Times* columnists—William Safire and A. M. Rosenthal—for particular condemnation as warmongers. In a column on February 17, 1992, Safire asked rhetorically, referring to Saddam Hussein, Muammar Qaddafi, and Kim Il Sung: "Does it strain credulity that one of these three dictators is going to get zapped?" adding, "I think not."

The next day, Rosenthal had the temerity—the colossal *chutzpah*—to write that Saddam Hussein

> ...alone is responsible for any shortage of food and medicine in Iraq... One day the U.S. will try to separate his head from his shoulders. Not just for his crimes—they sat well enough with the West before the Kuwait invasion. But his refusal to reveal the size and location of his nuclear, chemical, and germ-war capacity [he had none of these weapons] on his throne of skulls.

Sensible Americans, if they had learned of the killing and devastation exacted upon Iraq by their nation's bombers, should have responded to a second preemptive war in 2003 as lunacy. But that is exactly what was about to be foisted on the Iraqi people by incoming President George W. Bush.

Notes

[1] Thomas E. Ricks, *Fiasco: The American Military Adventure in* Iraq (The Penguin Press, New York, 2006), p. 129.

[2] William Blum, *Killing Hope* (Common Courage Press, Monroe ME, 1995), p. 320.

[3] Morris Berman, *Dark Ages America: The Final Phase of Empire* (W.W. Norton & Company, New York, 2006), p. 162.

[4] *The New York Times*, News of the Week in Review, September 23, 1990. At present, Kuwait has the world's fifth largest proven oil reserves and is the ninth richest country in the world.

[5] Ramsey Clark, *The Fire This Time: U.S. War Crimes in the Gulf* (Thunder's Mouth Press, New York, 1992), p. 8.

[6] Noam Chomsky, speaking on the MacNeil/Lehrer Newshour, September 11, 1990.

[7] Author Tim Weiner wrote in 2000 that he "guessed" that "nowadays" that each B-2 Stealth would cost no less than $820 million.

[8] Blum, p. 329.

[9] Theodore Draper, *"The True History of the Gulf War"* (The New York Times Review of Books, January 30, 1992), p. 41.

[10] John R. MacArthur, *Second Front: Censorship and Propaganda in the Gulf War* (Hill and Wang, New York, 1992).

[11] Clark, p. XVI.

[12] Douglas Kellner, *The Persian Gulf TV War* (Westview Press, San Francisco, 1992), p. 37.

[13] Clark, p. 130.

[14] Ibid., p. 129.

[15] Ibid., p. 142-143.

[16] Ibid., p. 142.

[17] Kellner, p. 37.

[18] Ibid.

[19] George H. W.'s son, George W., President No. 43, to those millions of Americans who despised him, frequently wore a smirk during his speeches, which further enraged his haters.

[20] Rahul Mahajan, *The New Crusade: America's War on Terrorism* (Monthly Review Press, New York, 2002), p. 20.

[21] Clark, p. 230.

[22] Ken Silverstein, *Private Warriors* (Verso, New York, 2000), p. 25.

[23] Phillip Knightley, The First Casualty: From the Crimea to Vietnam: The War Correspondent as Hero, Propagandist, and Myth Maker (Harcourt Brace Jovanovich, New York, 1975), p. 495.

[24] Ibid., p. 496.

[25] MacArthur, p. 156-157.

[26] Ibid., p. 158.

[27] Ibid., p. 213.

[28] Clark, p. 53.

[29] Ibid.

[30] Ibid., p. 54.

[31] Ibid., p. 55-56.
[32] Knightley, p. 180.
[33] Kellner, p. 209.
[34] MacArthur, p. 158.
[35] MacArthur, p. 213
[36] Ibid., p. 105
[37] Mahajan, p. 92.
[38] Ibid., p. 139.
[39] Ibid.
[40] Clark, p. 230.

Chapter X:
The Second Iraqi War

The invasion of Iraq was a bandit act, an act of blatant state terrorism, demonstrating absolute contempt for the concept of international law. The invasion was an arbitrary military action inspired by a series of lies upon lies and gross manipulation of the media and therefore of the public; an act intended to consolidate American military and economic control of the Middle East masquerading—as a last resort—all other justifications having failed to justify themselves—as liberation... We have brought torture, cluster bombs, depleted uranium, innumerable acts of random murder, misery, degradation and death to the Iraqi people and call it "bringing freedom and democracy" to the Middle East.

—Harold Pinter, the 2005 Nobel Prize Lecture in Literature, *Guardian*, December 7, 2005.

"It was all lies. It always had been all lies—and not just the specific lies, for example, about the weapons of mass destruction. The lie was the entire false construct spun and spun again with such expertise—that invading Iraq was, if not absolutely essential to America's self-defense, then certainly a plausible and desirable thing to do."[1]

ON MARCH 19, 2003, WITH THE AUTHORIZATION of the House and Senate, President George W. Bush ordered—as Commander-in-Chief—a preemptive attack of Iraq for the second time in twelve years. It was a war of aggression, a bully picking a fight with someone much smaller. This time American GI's would stay, as hated occupiers.

Many Americans were opposed to the very idea of such a war, and eight years later, the country remains polarized on the issue of the U.S. presence in Iraq—or "cutting and running" as the opposition's mantra goes.

"W", the least articulate chief executive in American history, was unable to convince nay-sayers there was any justification for the war or any merit in it. As the simpleton he is, he gave the American people a simple choice: you were either with him or you were not. It was supposedly a war that would bring greater security to Americans, decreed over and over by the Bush administration. Critics, in fact, questioned from the get-go that Americans could be made safer by a war 7,000 miles away.

All these years later, no one is quite sure how and when The Second Iraqi War will end. Almost certainly, it will not end in a clear-cut "victory" for the United States, although that outcome could be proclaimed by a president. Nor will it end when the warring factions—Kurds, Shiites, and Sunnis—stop killing each other. Regardless of which faction finally declares itself the victor, American troops will be garrisoned in Iraq for a long time. There is a growing opinion, even among the wars early supporters, that the Second Iraqi War is regarded as likely the greatest strategic blunder in the nation's history.

Consider the legacy to date: over 4,300 U.S. soldiers killed in action; over 30,000 wounded, many grievously; over half a trillion dollars blown away, and counting; uncounted tens of thousands of Iraqi civilians killed and dismembered; some four million homeless refugees; a once-thriving nation, the Middle East's most advanced, blasted into rubble, its museums of irreplaceable artifacts looted;

the unleashing and intensification of horrific rivalries among its Sunni, Shiite, and Kurdish factions. It seems to be a war without end.

> *The war that Bush-the-younger blundered into was the same imperial war in the same land that had ground down every superpower that dared run up its pennants in sight of Baghdad. Alexander the Great, Genghis Khan, the Ottomans, the French, and the British: all had come to conquer, all had been conquered.*

> *"The reasons why Bush invaded Iraq... will be debated by historians for years to come. Part of it... may well have been the president's gut instincts and a powerful—if not personal—antipathy toward Saddam Husssein... a tyrant who had been accused of plotting to kill Bush's father..."*[2]

The 9/11 attacks on the World Trade Center and the Pentagon had given reigning W. a splendid mandate to expand and intensify his phony war on terrorism. In fact, "terrorism" has become a national obsession due in no small part to pervasive government propaganda. Bush's handlers took advantage of this issue to pose the utterly tongue-tied president as the undoubted champion of national security. Journalist Thomas A. Bailey wrote more than fifty years ago in The Man in the Street: The Impact of American Public Opinion on Foreign Policy, that the issue of security resonates more strongly among Americans than any other personal issue.

Not many of the present occupiers of the Pentagon remembered the Vietnam War. It was, after all, more than a full generation in the past. But for those long-in-tooth whose memories are still sharp, one issue stands out, painfully. Over coffee it is agreed: "it was the God-damned reporters who lost the war for us. And it will never happen again!"

And it has not happened since. In 1983 the U.S. Army kept reporters off the tiny island of Grenada for the first three days while they systematically destroyed the handful of defenders. In the case of Panama in 1989, the intervention was not announced beforehand and the U.S. attacked in the middle of the night. In both instances there was next to no press coverage. As a result, Americans still have only a sketchy understanding of what happened during those quick "wars".

The First Iraqi War in 1992 was "apple pie;" there had been no need to restrict access by the media to what was strictly an aerial war. Reporters could write about the buildings that were no longer standing and show TV images of the destruction, but not too much destruction. They brought their TV cameras to the airstrips and recorded take-offs and landings, scarcely newsworthy. They spoke with the aircrews who were enjoined to tell them little of importance.

This latest war would be a full-blown conflict, not six weeks of bombing. How would the news correspondents be handled? Assign them to front-line troops who would act as guardians, and control them.

During the Great War with its thousands of casualties daily, candid reports by news correspondents from the battlefronts were unacceptable. Nevertheless it was deemed necessary to report on the war. But the hundreds of news correspondents from all the combatants couldn't just be loosed on the battlefronts. They needed "supervision" to ensure not only their safety but their patriotism.

The British Expeditionary Force (BEF) selected six veteran war correspondents, who were given the honorary rank of Captain, wore military uniforms, and were assigned, as officer perks, orderlies, automobiles, and chauffeurs. These experienced hands could be trusted to slant the news properly. Most of all, they were certain never to give a careless hint of the enormous casualties being suffered by Great Britain's sons. For example, on *the first day* of the Battle of Verdun, on July 1, 1916, the BEF suffered 60,000 casualties, including 19,000 dead. Never before in the history of the British

Empire had so many perished in a single day. The people at home couldn't be told this. And they were not.

Rather, the reports from the front always carried the implication that officers and men enjoyed nothing better than clambering out of their trenches and going over the top; that every battle was just a rough, jovial picnic; that a fight never went on long enough for the men; and that their only concern was that the war should end before they had a chance to kill some Huns.

At the end of the war, all were knighted for their services by a grateful nation. One of them, Sir Phillip Gibbs, had the integrity to write in 1923:

> "We identified ourselves absolutely with the armies in the field. There was no need of censorship of our despatches. We were our own censors."[3]

AN EVEN BETTER IDEA for handling TV and press correspondents in the Second Iraqi War was to "embed" them with front-line troops. They were encouraged to identify with their units, to eat and drink together and share the same dangers. There was an obvious sidebar benefit: morale. GIs had plenty of female pals to share their sacks.

The embed system was hailed by most reporters and their organizations as a huge success. What about objectivity? The pronoun "we" that found its way into one story after another, echoed whose side the embeds were on.

> *"What's the difference," goes the journalists' joke, "between the Iraqi army and the American army? Answer: the Americans shoot at you." In the three weeks following the U.S./British invasion of Iraq, seventeen journalists and other media workers were killed, seven of them directly by coalition fire."*[4]

> *"With their Orwellian-sounding Office of Homeland Security, the short-lived Office of Strategic Influence, shadow government, and the USA Patriot Act, the Bush Administration has in place the institutions and apparatus of a totalitarian government. Since Election 2000, the Bush clique has practiced a form of Orwellian "Bushspeak" that endlessly repeats the Big Lie of the moment.*[5]

What about the hardy correspondents who on principle refused to compromise their ideals and elected to go out into the field on their own? The figures in Iraq tell a dreadful story: fifteen media people killed, with two missing and presumed dead.[6] Iraq will almost certainly be the most dangerous war, ever, for journalists. As Phillip Knightley, wrote:

> This is bad enough. But—and here we tread on delicate ground—it is a fact that the largest single group of them appear to have been killed by the American military. We know that the Americans do not target journalists. Brigadier General Vince Brooks, deputy director of operations, told us so.

> But some war correspondents do not believe him, and Spanish journalists have demonstrated outside the US embassy in Madrid shouting 'murderers.' What is going on? I believe that the traditional relationship between the military and the media—one of restrained hostility—has broken down, and that the US administration, in keeping with its new foreign policy, has decided that its attitude to war correspondents is the same as that set out by President Bush when declaring war on terrorists: "You're either with us or you're against us."[7]

Knightley further pointed out that:

> Journalists prepared to get on side—and that means 100 percent on side, become embeds. Those who try to follow an independent path will be on their own. Those who report from the enemy side risk being killed. Just about every returning journalist had remarked about the trigger-

happiness of U.S. troops. "They just don't wait that extra second to see that the car had TV markings."[8]

THE ORDER OF BATTLE was labeled "shock and awe," the concept being that U.S. forces would strike with such speed and overwhelming power that the Iraqi military would be paralyzed. On the eve of battle, the media were reporting that "the United States has assembled a force with more firepower than ever seen before in a single battle."[9]

The war lasted just five weeks. Initial Iraqi estimates for civilians killed in the overwhelming onslaught numbered about 7,000. A study released by a John Hopkins research team in 2005 put the civilian death toll at 10,000.[10]

Liberal Morris Berman wrote that it was not easy to locate alternative voices in the United States concerning media coverage of the "quickie" war. He called the notion of "the liberal media pretty much a joke." What to think of NBC, which fired Phil Donahue (in addition to veteran war reporter Peter Arnett)? Or CNN, which attacked Scott Ritter, who had headed the U.N. weapons inspections teams from 1991 to 1998, as "an apologist for and defender of Saddam Hussein," because he claimed that the case for Hussein as "a threat to the U.S. worthy of war" had yet to be made? Handsome blonde Paula Zahn, with her own prime-time news show, smoothly read from her CNN teleprompter that Ritter had "drunk Saddam Hussein's Kool-Aid."[11]

In fact, the American press corps in Iraq did not distinguish itself. Some reporters themselves later admitted that:

> If they wrote anything too negative, they'd be kicked out of the White House press pool, lose access to the centers of power, and thus damage their careers. Thus they felt obliged or pressured to cooperate with Bush Jr.'s 'scripted' press conference of 6 March 2003, in which they politely submitted to pre-approved questions and even pretended to be spontaneous... The obsequiousness of all this is terrifying, because what exactly *is* the role of the press in a democracy? Surely not ass kissing as we go off to an unjustified war. Surely not kowtowing to transparent government propaganda.[12]

For all the blather about weapons of mass destruction and human rights violations by Saddam Hussein, these were in no way the fundamental issues driving U.S. policy. Rather it was "free access" to Iraqi oil and the ultimate control over that oil that would ensure American global dominance. When American forces entered Baghdad,

> They headed straight for the Oil Ministry building and threw up a protective shield around it. While other government buildings, ranging from the Ministry of Religious Affairs to the National Museum of Antiquities, were looted and pillaged, while hospitals were stripped of medicine and basic equipment, Iraq's oil records were safe and secure, guarded by the US military.[13]

Better proof of America's intentions was hardly needed.

Despite the Pentagon's careful censorship of bad news from the warfront from Day 1, some of it seeped out. On March 23, the fourth day of the war, there was an insurgent ambush in Nasariya with purposefully sketchy reports of a dozen U.S. casualties. March 27 brought superficial news of seriously wounded GIs being flown—off-camera—to the big hospital in Landstuhl, Germany and of Iraqi soldiers in civilian clothes waylaying Americans. In days to come, there were reports of coalition forces inadvertently shooting a van full of women and children, an *Apache* helicopter shot down, and of four U.S. Marines blown to pieces in a suicide bombing at a checkpoint near Najaf.[14]

Pentagon propagandists were looking for a feel-good happening to exploit, to counter the gloomy news. On April 2, such a happy story surfaced: the to-be exquisitely orchestrated human-interest mini-saga of Private First Class Jessica Lynch. PFC Lynch was a 19-year-old army clerk who was captured by the Iraqis on March 26, 2003, when her outfit took a wrong turn outside Nassiriya and was ambushed. Nine of her fellow soldiers were killed and she, wounded, was taken to the local hospital. Back at U.S. headquarters, as details of the ambush filtered in, it was agreed that her incarceration was a splendid propaganda opportunity and one not to be missed.

> *"One single center of power. One single center of force. One single center of decision making. This is the world of one master, one sovereign... Today we are witnessing an almost uncontained hyper use of force in international relations— military force... Primarily the United States has overstepped its national borders."* American military actions, *"unilateral and illegitimate have not been able to resolve any matters at all... They bring us to the abyss of one conflict after another. Political solutions are becoming impossible."*[15]

—Vladimir V. Putin, President of Russia, at 43rd International Security Conference, February 11, 2007, Munich.

Then came the pliant, all too-accommodating, all-too-naive American reporters with their military overseers at their sides. *The New York Times* in its first story wrote that Lynch "had been shot multiple times" according to an unnamed Army official. The *Washington Post* came up with a creative front-page story headlined "She Was Fighting to the Death." Another unnamed U.S. official told the *Post* that "she did not want to be taken alive," which was why she had so many gunshot and knife wounds.

Some days later the fabricated story began to unravel. The American commander of the Landstuhl hospital in Germany where Lynch had been evacuated for treatment told news correspondents curtly that she had been neither shot nor stabbed.

Newsweek of April 14 put Lynch on the cover, at the same introducing a new element in the burgeoning saga. Lynch's wounds were consistent "with low-velocity small arms," suggesting she might have been shot—and stabbed—after her capture and thus was the victim of criminal abuse by Iraqi hospital personnel. In the same story, by then embellished to a fare-thee-well, "the possibility of mistreatment had been very much on the mind of President Bush," an unnamed White House official told *Newsweek*.[16] Eight days later, a Special Forces Army team stormed the hospital in the middle of the night, plucked Lynch from her bed, secured her to a stretcher, gently carried her outside, and airlifted her to safety by helicopter. This action pumped adrenalin back into the story. A Pentagon photographic unit using night-vision equipment captured on video the dramatic rescue, complete with sounds of explosions and plenty of GI shouting (but no audible cursing). It was play-acting of a high order, a Hollywood scenario for the whole world to watch on TV. The videotapes from inside the hospital were green and fuzzy, contributing to the impression that what the viewers were seeing was the "real thing." According to the Pentagon, Lynch had multiple stab and bullet wounds when she arrived back at a U.S. hospital in Baghdad.

The Pentagon's spinmeisters milked dry the story, heaping on the hyperbole for all it was worth. President Bush declared, in his inimitable fractured English, he was "full of joy for Jessica Lynch." Her rescue showed not only American courage and derring-do but also loyalty to a creed. Whose creed? The Marines,' not the U.S. Army's! In the battles in the mountains of Korea in 1950, Army troops routinely left wounded buddies behind to the tender mercies of the Chinese as they "bugged out" to the rear, some even discarding their M-1 rifles in their haste to withdraw.

Regardless, America had its first heroine of the war. Practically overnight: "America Loves Jessica" refrigerator magnets, T-shirts, coffee mugs, a made-for-TV movie, and a big sign outside her hometown announcing "Home of Jessica Lynch, ex-POW." The Iraqi who had revealed her whereabouts was flown to the United States, granted asylum, and then signed a $500,000 contract for a book, *Rescue in Nassiriya*.[17]

The rescue was also a fabric of audacious lies. Lynch *had been* captured, she *had been* in the hospital in Nassiriya, and she *had been* rescued from there by U.S. Special Forces. Everything else was fiction, news management of the highest order, befitting the nation that produces propaganda like no other. The tall tale was exposed as a fraud by a BBC documentary on May 18 entitled "War Spin." The documentary contradicted practically everything that had originated in the Pentagon.

> "There was no [sign of] shooting, no bullet inside her body, no stab wound—only road traffic accident. We gave her three bottles of blood, two of them taken from the medical staff because there was not enough at this time."[18]

None of the BBC's contradictions were ever aired in the United States. The probing media was kept at bay by a far-fetched explanation by her handlers that she remembered nothing of her week-long hospital stay behind enemy lines "and probably never would." That was also baloney.

Where was Jessica Lynch during all the hubbub? The U.S. Army had kept her out of sight—and quiet; in effect she was a bystander in the production of her own action-packed thriller. When she finally was allowed to speak publicly a year later, she acknowledged in an interview with NBC's Diane Sawyer that she had been "showcased" by the U.S. military.

> *President George W. Bush to journalists, casually, January 2, 2003: "You said we're headed to war in Iraq. I don't know why you say that. I'm the person who gets to decide, not you."*

ON APRIL 9, 2003, another feel-good image burst on the scene to take the place of the Lynch extravaganza that had run its course. This time it was the carefully organized toppling of a larger-than-life statue of Saddam Hussein in Baghdad's Firdos Square on live television. Close-up shots, the only kind shown on American TV, conjured up an excited popular uprising in keeping with the administration's prewar projection that liberated Iraqis would celebrate in the streets.

Watching the statue come down on TV, Donald Rumsfeld said he could not help but think of the Berlin Wall and the Iron Curtain. Tim Russert of MSNBC, normally a ramrod-straight reporter and interviewer, climbed on the fast-moving bandwagon, also invoked the Berlin Wall. At the time only Tom Shales of *The Washington Post* registered a different interpretation, commenting that:

> Of all the statues of Saddam Hussein... the crowds had conveniently picked one location across from the hotel where most of the media were headquartered. This was either splendid luck or brilliant planning on the part of the military.[19]

OP-ED columnist Frank Rich wrote that in late 2005, *The Journal of Broadcasting & Electronic Media* found that "wide-angle shots show clearly that the Square was never close to being a quarter full" and "never had more than a few hundred people in it." Furthermore, close analysis of the spectacle, rather than displaying a spontaneous uprising of Iraqis against the Baath regime, established there were few people on the scene, most of whom were supporters Ahmed Chalabi (the exiled crook who helped sell the war in hopes of becoming the new ruler, or at least, a top kleptocrat). Furthermore, they were not the ones who pulled it down. It took some GIs to slip a cable on the statue and connect it to a tank to tip it over. The media purposefully failed to show a long shot of the entire square, which was surrounded by U.S. armored vehicles and practically empty of Iraqi celebrants.

Five days after Saddam Hussein's statue was pulled down, one of television's big-gun anchors, Dan Rather—in the late winter of his career—appeared on CNN's *Larry King Live*, the talk show that serves the Pentagon so well, so often. He babbled:

> Look, I'm an American, I never tried to kid anybody that I'm some internationalist or something. And when my country is at war, I want my country to win, whatever the definition of 'win' may be. Now, I can't and don't argue that that is coverage without a prejudice. About that I am prejudiced.[20]

Bob Herbert, *New York Times* columnist, spoke for those many Americans who were opposed to this latest U.S. preemptive war. On April 17 he wrote perceptively:

> It is time for the American people to wise up. From the very beginning, the so-called war on terror was viewed by the Bush crowd as a magical smoke screen, a political gift from the gods that could be endlessly manipulated to justify all kinds of policies and behavior—including the senseless war in Iraq—that otherwise would never have been tolerated by the American people…. The fear of terrorist attacks inside the U.S., and the patriotism felt by so many millions of Americans, has been systematically exploited by the administration. The invasion of Iraq was not about terror. It was about oil and schoolboy fantasies of empire and whatever oedipal dynamics were at work in the Bush family.

Herbert concluded his powerful polemic with this warning,

> "All of this should be kept in mind as we consider the fact that the administration that once had its hostile eye on Iraq now has it trained like a laser on Iran."

> *"The official title of the bill originally was the 'Uniting and Strengthening America by Providing Appropriate Tools Required to Intercept and Obstruct Terrorism Act'—USA PATRIOT ACT. The name was reminiscent of Hitler's 1933 legislation passed hurriedly following the burning of the Reichstag in 1933 which evolved into the Third Reich. It was called 'The Law to Remove the Distress of the People and State.'"*[21]

THE REPUBLICAN PARTY'S NEOCONSERVATIVE "Project for a New American Century" compiled a report in 2000, titled, "Rebuilding American Defense: Strategies, Forces and Resources for a New American Century." PNAC was built around the right wing of the party and was headed by Cheney, Rumsfeld and Assistant Defense Secretary Paul Wolfowitz. The goals of the Republican Party were a *Pax Americana* based on U.S. global dominance during the coming millennium. It envisioned U.S. control of the Gulf region and its oil "as far into the future as possible." A "core mission" as defined in the report called for America to "fight and decisively win multiple, simultaneous major-theater wars." The report, harking back to the genocidal Indian wars of the late 19th century, referred to the U.S. military as "the cavalry on the new American frontier." Iran should be invaded as soon as U.S. troops could be safely withdrawn from Iraq. A spotlight was trained on China for "regime change." As for outer space, "U.S. Space Forces" would also patrol and control this "newest frontier." This was big-time warmongering.

"No grievances or policies will justify resort to aggressive war. It is utterly renounced and condemned as an instrument of policy."

–Robert I. Jackson, U.S. representative to the International Conference on Military Trials at the end of World War II.

Until the 9/11 attacks, [Attorney General] Ashcroft had been most noticeable to the American public when he ordered an exposed breast covered on the statue called The Spirit of Justice that stands in the Justice Department's Hall of Justice.[22]

FINALLY, ABU GHRAIB prison—the filthy, contemptible hallmark of American occupation of Iraq. The suburb of Abu Ghraib lies some 20 miles west of Baghdad. During Saddam Hussein's harsh regime, the small city's prison had grown into a giant penal complex, housing under deplorable conditions up to 50,000 inmates at one time. The prisoners were a mix of "political" captives and ordinary criminals, both men and women. They were crammed into tiny cells, treated brutally, tortured as a matter of routine, and executed for infractions of prison rules. Following the U.S. invasion and the collapse of Saddam's administration, looters stripped the deserted and empty complex of everything that was movable. Coalition authorities had the floors tiled, cells repaired and painted, and new toilets and showers installed. An up-to-date medical facility was added. Abu Ghraib had become a U.S. military prison.

By the fall of 2004 there were several thousand new inmates in the jail. Most of them were civilians who had been picked up in military sweeps and at highway checkpoints. They were common criminals, detainees for "security" reasons, or individuals suspected of being leaders of the new insurgency.

Earlier, in June 2003, Army Reserve Brigadier General Janis Karpinski was named commander of the 800th Military Police Brigade and given responsibility for all military prisons in Iraq. She was nominally an experienced intelligence officer, but had never run a prison system. Karpinski, the highest-ranking woman officer in Iraq, was in charge of three large jails and 3,400 reservists. Most of these members of a military reserve force, like Karpinski, had no training in dealing with prisoners. It was reported that she was rarely seen in the jails she was responsible for overseeing.

In January 2004, a major investigation of the prison system in Iraq, in particular Abu Ghraib prison the largest, was conducted. There were allegations of systematic and illegal abuse of prisoners, including torture to death of at least two inmates. The evidence, which included dozens of ghastly photographs, stunned the world, including Americans. The U.S. Army again, like post-My Lai 4 in the 1970s, had a lot of explaining to do. Karpinski was formally reprimanded, suspended, and reduced in rank to Colonel.

The investigation was authorized by Lieutenant General Ricardo S. Sanchez, senior commander in Iraq. The chief investigator was Major General Antonio M. Taguba, whose 53-page report included damning specifics:

> Breaking chemical lights and pouring the phosphoric liquid on detainees; pouring cold water on naked detainees; beating detainees with a broom handle and a chair; threatening male detainees with rape; allowing a military police guard to stitch the wound of a detainee who was injured after being slammed against the wall in his cell; sodomizing a detainee with a chemical light and perhaps a broom stick; using military working dogs to frighten and intimidate detainees with threats of attack, and in one instance actually biting a detainee. [23]

General Taguba had sworn testimony as well as plenty of photographs and video tape to support his allegations. He said the photographs and videos taken by the soldiers as the abuses were taking place were omitted from his report because of their "extremely sensitive nature." Indeed, the photographs were "sensitive." "Depraved" and "degenerate" also fit. In one photograph, Private Lyndie England, out of uniform, a cigarette dangling casually from her mouth, gives a thumbs-up sign to the photographer as she points to the genitals of a naked and hooded Iraqi prisoner, who is being forced to masturbate.[24]

Three other hooded and naked Iraqis are standing in line and covering their genitals with their hands as if waiting their turn. Another photograph shows a pyramid of naked prisoners. Nearby stands Specialist Charles A. Graner, smiling; a woman soldier stands in front, also grinning. Yet another photograph shows a kneeling, naked, unhooded male prisoner, head turned away from the camera, posed to make it appear that he was performing oral sex on another male prisoner, who is naked and hooded.[25]

Abu Ghraib table, from "America's Gift Shop," by Phillip Toledano

When U.S. Army Specialist Sabrina Harman, one of the accused MPs, was questioned by the C.I.D. about the photograph of a black hooded and draped prisoner who was standing on a box with electric wires coming from inside the drape—in an image made famous throughout the world—she admitted the wires were attached to his fingers, toes, and penis. Her job was to keep detainees awake.

"MI wanted to get them to talk."[26]

Sergeant Javal Davis, another of the accused, told Tagabu that he heard MI (Military Intelligence) suggest to the guards that they should abuse the prisoners.

"Loosen this guy up for us. Make sure he has a bad night. Make sure he gets the treatment."[27]

There was also good-old-reliable "water-boarding," perhaps the most heinous of all tortures short of burning or dismemberment. The U.S. Army practiced this torture technique as far back as the Philippines War. This time around, U.S. interrogators water-boarded Khalid Shaikh Mohammed, a high-level detainee who was believed implicated in the attacks of September 11. Mark Danner described the "procedure" based on an account from an Algerian prisoner in 1958.

> Then they laid me on a bench, flat on my stomach [naked and blindfolded] head extending into the air, and tied my arms against my body with cords. Again the same question, which I refused to answer. By tilting the bench very slowly, they dipped my head into a basin filled with stinking liquid—dirty water and urine, probably. I was aware of the gurgling liquid reaching my mouth,

then of a dull rumbling in my ears and a tingling sensation in my nose. From time to time one of them would sit on my back and bear down on my thighs. I could hear the water I threw up fall back into the basin. Then the torture would continue.[28]

Such dehumanization as revealed in sworn testimony, photographs, and video tapes is unacceptable in any culture, but is especially so in the Muslim world. Islamic law specifically prohibits homosexual acts and it is particularly humiliating for men to be naked in front of other men. Being piled one on top of another naked and forced to masturbate is a terrible form of torture.

Representatives of the Red Cross, who visited Abu Ghraib nearly thirty times in late 2003, cataloged graphically what U.S. military authorities acknowledged as "methods of physical and psychological coercion."

> Hooding, used to prevent people from seeing and to disorient them, and also to prevent them from breathing freely. One or sometimes two bags, sometimes with an elastic blindfold over the eyes which, when slipped down, further impeded proper breathing. Hooding was sometimes used in conjunction with beatings thus increasing anxiety as to when blows would come. The practice of hooding also allowed the interrogators to remain anonymous and thus to act with impunity. Hooding could last for periods from a few hours up too two to four consecutive days.
>
> Handcuffing with flexi-cuffs, which were sometimes made so tight and used for such extended periods that they caused skin lesions and long-term after-effects on the hands (nerve damage).
>
> Beatings with hard objects (including pistols and rifles), slapping, punching, kicking with knees or feet on various parts of the body (legs, sides, lower back, groin).
>
> Being paraded naked outside cells in front of other persons deprived of their liberty, and guards, sometimes hooded or with women's underwear over the head.
>
> Being attacked repeatedly over several days... with handcuffs to the bars of their cell in humiliating (naked or in underwear) and/or uncomfortable position causing physical pain.
>
> Exposure while hooded to loud noise or music, prolonged exposure while hooded to the sun over several hours, including during the hottest time of day when temperatures could reach 122 degrees Fahrenheit.
>
> Being forced to remain for prolonged periods in stress positions such as squatting or standing with or without the arms lifted.[29]

TODAY is April 1, 2009, April Fool's Day in the United States. The day is generally observed by playing a practical joke on a "victim" who becomes known as an *April Fool*. This custom is thought to have started in France during the 16th century, but the British are credited with bringing it to the United States.

It is also an appropriate day to finish this chapter on the Second Iraqi War, although it ends abruptly. The war continues undiminished in intensity. "Militants Show a New Boldness in Cities of Iraq" was today's *New York Times* lead story. New weapons to kill GIs and increasingly more lethal roadside bombs are being introduced. The latest is the Russian-made RKG-3 grenade. They weigh just five pounds and, attached to small parachutes, can be lobbed by teenagers. They can penetrate the armor of the Army's new, expensive [over half-a-million dollars per copy] and highly touted MRAP (mine-resistant ambush protected) vehicle.

In Washington, a Military Information officer, who was not authorized to be quoted by name, said:

> "In most places there isn't an insurgency in Iraq anymore. What we have now is a terrorism problem, and there is going to be a terrorism problem for a long time."

Elsewhere in the *Times* today was a story dealing with "America's staunchest ally in the Iraq war"—some would say "chief toady"—handing over command of Basra Province to U.S. forces which marked the first step in the withdrawal of most of Britain's 4,100 remaining troops. To punctuate the transfer, a suicide truck bomber killed 7 and wounded 38 in the northern city of Mosul. In the previous week, "despite numerous American and Iraqi military operations in Mosul, at least 29 people have been killed and 85 wounded."

There was one final story headlined "In a Desolate Village, War Is Far From Over" which relates that since joint U.S.-Iraqi operations to clear out insurgents began eight weeks ago, their roadside bombs have struck more than 30 vehicles, killing "a dozen Iraqi troops and seriously wounding three American soldiers." In a corner of Diyala Province the war is still being fought much as it was two years ago when the "surge" began. Here violence remains high, according to the *Times* article. American GIs are still sweeping villages, raiding homes, and countering mortar attacks.

There is no end in sight.

> *"Did you tell her [Helen Thomas, reporter for Hearst News Service] I don't like motherfuckers who gas their own people? Did you tell her I don't like assholes who lie to the world? Did you tell her I'm going to kick his sorry motherfucking ass all over the Mideast?"*[30]

—President George W. Bush to Press Secretary Ari Fleischer, May 1, 2002

Notes

[1] T.D. Allman, *Rogue State: America at War With The World* (Nation Books, New York, 2004), p. 23.
[2] Michael Isikoff and David Corn, *Hubris: The Inside Story of Spin, Scandal, and the Selling of the Iraq War* (Crown Publishers, New York, 2006), p. 16.
[3] David Miller, *Tell Me Lies: Propaganda and Media Distortion in the Attack on **Iraq*** (Pluto Press, London, 2004), p. 251.
[4] Douglas Kellner, *From 9/11 To Terror War: The Dangers of the Bush Legacy* (Rowman & Littlefield Publishers, Inc., New York, 2003), p. 19.
[5] Knightley, p. 100.
[6] Ibid.
[7] Ibid.
[8] Morris Berman, *Dark Ages America: The Final Phase of Empire* (W.W. Norton & Company, New York, 2006), p. 213.
[9] Ibid., p. 214.
[10] Ibid., p. 221.
[11] Ibid., p. 222.
[12] Knightley, p. 122.
[13] Frank Rich, *The Greatest Story Ever Sold: The Decline and Fall of Truth From 9/11 to Katrina* (The Penguin Press, New York, 2006), p. 80.
[14] *The New York Times*, February 11, 2007.
[15] Rich, p. 81-82.
[16] Knightley, p. 545.
[17] Ibid., p. 545-546.
[18] Rich, p. 83.

[19] Ibid., p. 157.
[20] Jim Marrs, *The Terror Conspiracy: Deception, 9/11, and the Loss of Liberty* (Disinformation Company Ltd., New York, 2006), p. 301.
[21] Marrs, p. 315.
[22] Seymour M Hersh, *Chain of Command: The Road From 9/11 to Abu Ghraib* (Harper Collins Publishers, New York, 2004), p. 22
[23] Ibid., p. 23.
[24] Ibid.
[25] Ibid., p. 29-30.
[26] Ibid.
[27] Ibid.
[28] Mark Danner, *Torture and Truth: America, Abu Ghraib, and the War on Terror* (The New York Review of Books, New York, 2004), p. 35.
[29] Ibid., p. 36.
[30] Neil Hanson, *Unknown Soldiers: The Story of the Missing of the First World War* (Alfred A. Knopf, New York, 2005), p. 126.

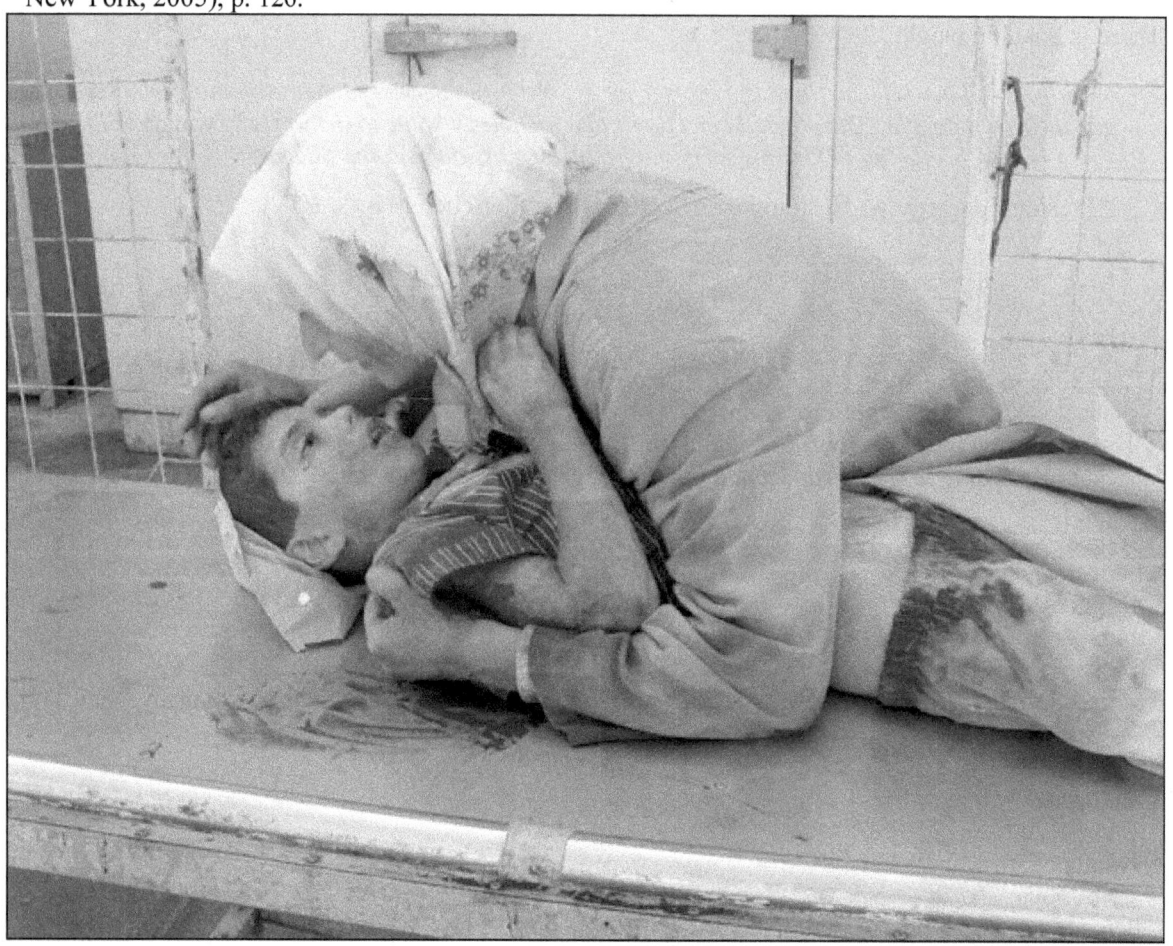

Chapter XI:

9/11

"We believe that senior government officials have covered up crucial facts about what really happened on 9/11. We believe these events may have been orchestrated by the administration in order to manipulate the American people into supporting policies at home and abroad."

—Scholars for 9/11 Truth," 2006.

The "Authorized Edition" of the 9/11 Commission Report, its front cover appropriately red-white-and-blue with an official seal newly designed for the occasion, runs a hefty 576 pages in a small type face. At $10 a copy (paperback), it was a bargain—and was so priced by its patriotic publisher, W.W. Norton & Company, to achieve widespread readership.

On the back cover this summary appears:

NEARLY THREE THOUSAND PEOPLE DIED in the terrorist attacks of September 11, 2001. In Lower Manhattan, on a field in Pennsylvania, and along the banks of the Potomac, the United States suffered the single largest loss of life from an enemy attack on its soil.

IN NOVEMBER [27th] 2002, the United States Congress and President George W. Bush established by law the National Commission on Terrorist Attacks Upon the United States, also known as the 9/11 Commission. This independent, bipartisan panel was directed to examine the facts and circumstances surrounding the September 11 attacks, identify lessons learned, and provide recommendations to safeguard against future acts of terrorism.

In the Preface, Thomas H. Kean, Chair [Republican] and Lee H. Hamilton, Vice Chair [Democrat] signed off on what they called the pursuit of their mandate.[1] They wrote that the Commission had reviewed more than 2.5 million pages of documents; interviewed more than 1,200 individuals in ten countries, held 19 days of hearings, and took public testimony from 160 witnesses. Importantly, they also wrote:

"We have sought to be independent, impartial, thorough, and nonpartisan."

A staff of 81 supported the huge project behind the scenes. It was those staff members—not the Commissioners seen on television—who did the investigative work upon which the Commissioners carried out their discussions and interviews.

For all of its bulk, much of it minutiae, the Report nevertheless managed to avoid confronting important questions. The Commission chose to call no hostile witnesses nor any architects or engineers originally involved in the Twin Towers (and WTC-7's) design and construction to get alternative views on their strange collapses. The Commission also ignored the growing number of critical studies concerning the failure of the Towers that had been published by credible authors and publishers in England, Germany, France, and Italy, as well as in the United States.

Strangely, the author's copy has no date of publication.[2] Something else is bizarre. There is no Index to help the researcher find his or her way through the jungle of details, as exemplified by 2,096 Endnotes, these set in tiny 8-point typeface (8-point typeface), further discouraging cross-referencing. Why? Indeed, there is so much else to question about the government's depiction of the tragic events of 9/11—larger, far more significant issues that bear directly on the integrity of the Commissioners and George W. Bush and his cohorts.

There was a rush to buy the *9/11 Commission Report* as soon as it became available. Buyers were sure it would tell the whole story—a complete history that would stand forever more as the definitive account of a dreadful day in American history. In fact, 9/11 investigator Griffin published a book in 2005, *The 9/11 Commission Report: Omissions and Distortions*, in which he wrote:

> The purpose of the 9/11 Commission... was not to provide "the fullest possible account of the events surrounding 9/11." The purpose was to argue, implicitly, that the U.S. government was not itself complicit in the attacks of 9/11... The Commission could make this argument only by distorting, or completely omitting, dozens of facts.[3]

Under Griffin's magnifying glass, the heavily promoted *Report* is a shabby fraud. In an article published in *Serendipity,* Griffin listed 115 lies that he selected to illustrate the utter unreliability of the contents. The *Report* "simply cannot be trusted," he wrote. Griffin offered two versions of an "alternate conspiracy theory": that the Bush administration "deliberately" failed to prevent the attacks or, more disturbingly, "was actively involved in the planning and follow-through of the attacks."

> Why? To provide justification for the bombing of Afghanistan, the takeover of Iraq's oil fields, and to coalesce the American public in support of further aggressive wars. Embracing the complicity theory, Griffin further claimed the Kean-Zelikow Report emphasized the White House's allegiances of its Republican Chairman and Director.

Griffin concluded his justifiable polemic by writing:

> As this book was going to press, I learned that the *9/11 Commission Report* had been included among the finalists for the National Book Awards. I would not have been shocked by this news except for the fact that the nomination was in the nonfiction category.[4]

Since the Report supposedly presented a factual accounting of the events of the day, what was the "character" of the Commission?

> *"September 11 was the 'open sesame' to the path to world empire. It doesn't matter if things turn out well or badly in Iraq. If they turn out well, they can start to think of the next step. If they turn out badly, that's good for him because of American patriotism. Who's going to be against George W. Bush when he's mourning the deaths of our boys?"*

—Norman Mailer, *New York Times* Interview, January 22, 2003.

WAS THE COMMISSION "NONPARTISAN"? No. While the Commission's ten members were equally divided among Republicans and Democrats, its chair was a Republican. The vice-chair was a Democrat, not a co-chair—splitting hairs, perhaps. Of far more consequence were the political leanings of the Commission's executive director, Philip Zelikow. Zelikow was a rabid reactionary with a long track-record of involvement in far-right causes. His background included extremely close ties to the White House starting with George H. W.'s term. Zelikow had been on the National Security Council as an aide along with Condoleezza Rice to National Security Advisor Brent Scowcroft. In 1995, Zelikow and Rice had been co-authors of *Germany Unified and Europe Transformed: A Study in Statecraft*. Zelikow then served on the NSC's team during the transition between the Bill Clinton and the G. W. Bush administrations. He was also director of the Aspen Strategy Group, a think tank that numbered among its members the likes of Scowcroft, Rice, Cheney, and Wolfowitz. Zelikow was also the principal author of the *National Security Strategy* statement of

2002 that introduced the concept of preemptive warfare. Soon after 9/11, Zelikow was named to Bush's Foreign Intelligence Advisory Board before becoming executive director of the 9/11 Commission in 2003.

Further downstream, and more importantly, Zelikow was in charge of editing the final Commission Report from which he could simply delete anything that he considered inimical to George W. Bush and his agenda, and the Commission members would likely be none the wiser. Talk about a hungry fox in the hen house!

Paul Sperry, author of the polemical web article "*Is Fix In At 9/11 Commission?*" wrote that Zelikow "arguably has more sway than any other member, including the chairman. Zelikow picks the areas of investigation, the briefing materials, the topics for hearings, the witnesses, and the lines of questioning for witnesses. In effect, he sets the agenda and runs the investigations."

> *If a builder build a house for a man and do not make its construction firm and the house he has built collapse and cause the death of the owner of the house—that builder shall be put to death.*
>
> *If it cause the death of the son of the owner of the house—they shall put to death a son of that builder.*
>
> *If it cause the death of a slave of the owner of the house—he shall give to the owner of the house a slave of equal value.*
>
> *If it destroy property, he shall restore whatever it destroyed, and because he did not make the house which he built firm and it collapsed, he shall rebuild the house which collapsed at his own expense.*
>
> *If a builder build a house for a man and do not make its construction meet the requirements and a wall fall in, that builder shall strengthen the wall as his own expense."*

—Code of Hammurabi, 2,200 B.C.[5]

WAS THE COMMISION "INDEPENDENT"? No—not so long as its key player behind the scenes was bound so closely to the White House. The Family Steering Committee, the group of close relatives of those killed in the attacks, repeatedly insisted on Zelikow's removal, who in their view mocked the idea of the Commission's independence. He stayed to the end. Furthermore, any legitimate investigation would have asked questions about complicity or negligence by the administration. None were asked. The conflict of interest was obvious.

WAS THE COMMISSION "IMPARTIAL"? No. In his analysis of impartiality relating to the attacks, thorough investigator, critic, and 9/11 Author Griffin, has suggested that the investigation should have begun its work:

> Like any good crime investigation, collecting evidence and testimonies under oath from all those who might have something to contribute. It would have tried to investigate equally the two basic conspiracy theories about the attacks: that they were planned and carried out by followers of Osama bin Laden—the Administration's theory—or that the attacks were able to succeed only because of the complicity of the Bush administration itself—the revisionists' theory. This was not the Commission's approach. Zelikow himself temporarily emerged from his cocoon by publicly dismissing the discussion of alternate theories to "whacking moles."[6]

WAS THE COMMISSION "THOROUGH"? No. By whatever criteria one chooses to apply, the Commission's report was characterized by a lack of thoroughness. The collapse of 7-WTC, the 47-floor skyscraper adjacent to the two towers, some eight hours after the plane crashes—and never struck by the airplanes, *was not even mentioned!*

> Omission is one of the major flaws in the Commission's report. We are aware of significant issues and cases that were duly reported to the Commission by those of us with direct knowledge, but somehow escaped attention. Serious problems and shortcomings within government agencies likewise were reported to the Commission but were not included in the report.[7]

The United States has for decades sought to gain a sturdy foothold in the Gulf region to ensure a steady supply of oil. Saudi Arabia's enormous reserves obviously were insufficient to the war planners in the Pentagon. Paul O'Neill, a Bush administration Secretary of the Treasury, wrote that plans to attack Iraq were based principally to gain access to its oil.[8] Why wasn't there *even a single brief reference* to the obvious subject of oil in the Report?

The Commission was thorough in some particulars, but only those that were consistent with the official "19-hijackers-directed-by-Osama-bin-Laden" theory put forth by the Bush administration and those theories in which the information was incontrovertible. The responses of the FDNY (Fire Department New York) and the NYPD (New York Police Department) in New York City were covered in excruciating detail. So, too, were the activities of the alleged hijackers in the months preceding the attacks and up to the morning of September 11. The *Report* includes photographs of the Saudi Arabian exile, Osama bin Laden, and a particularly unflattering one of Khalid Sheikh Mohammed, "mastermind of the 9/11 plot." There are also mug shots of the 19 hijackers, divided into groups by airline Flight Numbers, and further subdivided into "pilots" and "hijackers."

The Commission methodically defended the White House, the FBI, CIA, FAA and NORAD by omitting or attempting to explain away anything pointing to complicity—or conspiracy—by these Federal agencies. While it is known that the government's emergency response systems suffered consistent—and inexplicable—breakdowns on September 11, suggesting that such failures were possible only through purposeful obstruction by key U.S. government and military officials—the Report assiduously sidestepped the important issue of possible collusion.

> *I immediately concluded that the events of that day [September 11, 2001], because of their scope, complexity, and technical precision could not have been possible without the massive complicity of a faction of the US political and military command structure... It was also clear to me that the goal of this operation was a new world war on a vast scale—something along the lines of the Thirty Years' War of 1618-1648, which killed about a third of the population of central Europe. In the intentions of its planners, this new conflict was to be a population war, designed to exterminate large parts of the population of the developing sector, including the Arab and Muslim countries, and eventually China. It was the desperate bid of a bankrupt and declining power to re-assert world domination based on blackmail. It was a world-historical turn towards disaster.*[9]

What about the chairman and vice-chairman of the Commission? Seventy-nine-year-old Henry Kissinger was the first appointed by President Bush to head the Commission. That had been an arrogant move by the president that illustrated his back-of-the-hand treatment of the Commission. After all, he had stalled the investigation for two years. Even a cursory Google search of Kissinger's background pointed to his controversial past and his unsuitability to chair the Commission. He had many enemies for justifiable reasons and some even sought to try him for war crimes during his earlier stint as Secretary of State.

In the 1970s in his years of power in Washington he had been involved in the secret bombing of Cambodia and the Watergate cover-up. Kissinger was so paranoid about keeping secrets in the White House that he had some of his colleagues' phones wiretapped. How could he be expected to be eager to expose the truth about anything, 9/11 in particular?

When his appointment was announced, four of the self-named "Jersey girls," widows of the 9/11 crashes from New Jersey, wanted to see for themselves Kissinger Associates' client list. They arranged for a meeting at Kissinger's Manhattan office.

> Kissinger did not flinch at the widows' questions, at least not at first. He explained—slowly, patiently—that clients retained Kissinger Associates with the understanding their identities would never be made public... The widows' questions about the client list kept coming, and they grew more insistent.[10]

Kissinger was growing exasperated. Finally one of the "girls" asked the direct question:

> "With all due respect, Dr. Kissinger, I have to ask you: Do you have any Saudi clients? Do you have any clients named bin Laden?"[11]

Kissinger, who had been pouring himself a cup of coffee, was clearly startled... He fumbled with the pot, spilling coffee on the table. He seemed to lose his balance, nearly falling to the floor. He explained that it was his bad eye and it affected his depth perception.

Another of the widows attempted to put the question more tactfully.

> "Dr. Kissinger, we would certainly hope that no one like that is on your client list. Can you understand our concern?"[12]

Kissinger smirked and looked at his watch. It was obvious he would answer no further questions—and he would not budge on the client list. He drew the meeting to a close, saying he had another appointment.

The next morning, Kissinger phoned the White House announcing he was resigning from the 9/11 Commission. In a long letter to President Bush faxed the same day, he lamely claimed that he had never put his personal interests ahead of the country. Further, to liquidate Kissinger Associates could not be accomplished without "significantly delaying the beginning" of the investigation.

Karl Rove, Bush's principal political advisor, moved fast for a replacement; the media was certain to hammer the White House for indecisiveness. He was also concerned that the "independent" federal commission investigating the 9/11 attacks headed by the wrong person could easily cost Bush a second term. The next day, a Saturday, Rove phoned Tom Kean to offer him the job as chairman. Kean, a former popular governor of New Jersey, was president of small Drew University, lived quietly in rural Bedminster and happy to be out of politics, particularly what he called the "snake pit" of Washington. His duties as chair would only be part-time, he could continue his duties at Drew, and he could get home most nights on Amtrak, Rove told him. Kean accepted the job because of his obligation to so many dead friends. For months after 9/11, his calendar had been filled with funerals and, more often, memorial services for those missing in the rubble.

Rove had Kissinger's replacement. As chairman, Kean was the only member of the Commission named directly by the White House. Under the law creating the panel, the other four Republican commissioners were selected by the party's congressional leaders.

Senate Majority Leader Tom Daschle was besieged by Democrats eager for appointment to the panel. The ideal choice for vice chairman was Daschle's predecessor, George Mitchell of Maine. Mitchell had the right credentials: after leaving the Senate, he had been nominated for the Nobel Peace Prize, had been a federal prosecutor, and knew all about subpoenas and document searches. He was, most of all, a stridently partisan Democrat.

Mitchell joined the Commission somewhat reluctantly, understanding that the work would be part-time, permitting him to continue his law practice. He quickly saw the post of vice chairman was no part-time job and on December 11 he wrote to Daschle that he could not afford to go without his regular income, and was herewith resigning. Like Rove, Daschle was in a bind. Mitchell's sudden departure had probably poisoned the well in finding a replacement of equal stature. His best choice, he figured, was [Lee] Hamilton, who had already accepted a position on the Commission, had the background in national security, and appeared eager for the work.

The Commission was formally titled the Kean-Hamilton, although it quickly was renamed the Kean-Zelikow Commission by those in the know. Cynics titled it the Zelikow-Kean Commission.

UNDERSTANDABLY, the Report's main focus was on the two airliner crashes into the Twin Towers, the signature structures of the World Trade Center in lower Manhattan, and their subsequent collapses which took so many lives. The WTC complex consisted of seven buildings, including one hotel, spread across 16 acres and interconnected by an underground mall. The Twin Towers (1-WTC, or the North Tower, and 2- WTC, or the South Tower) contained 10.4 million square feet of office space. Both towers had 110 stories, were about 1,350 feet high, and were square; each wall 208 feet long. On a typical workday, about 50,000 workers occupied the towers, and about 40,000 visitors passed through the center.

It was obvious to the reader of the Report that as far as the researchers, writers, and editors of the Report were concerned, there never was any question that the Towers collapsed as a direct result of the fires started by burning jet fuel. Yet, it is common knowledge in the professional fire-fighting community the world over that *fires had never before in history caused a steel-frame high-rise building to collapse*, even when the fire was a very energetic, all-consuming one, such as the 1991 fire at One Meridian Plaza in Philadelphia.[13]

FDNY chiefs supported this view. At a meeting with Mayor Rudolph Guiliani at the command center that morning, "none of the chiefs present [before the collapses] believed a total collapse of either tower was possible."[14]

Deputy Chief Peter Hayden later told the Commission that such a happening "was not in our realm of thought." Buttressing this view was Hayden's Battalion Chief, "who reached the seat of the fire in the South Tower—and deemed it easily controllable."[11] So were the courageous FDNY fire-fighters themselves, 345 of whom died in the wreckage of the Twin Towers—the most in a single fire in the nation's history—and who had unhesitatingly charged into the burning skyscraper, some dragging heavy water hoses up the steps behind them, intent on doing what they had been trained to do.

A LOOK AT KEY FACTS about the Towers' design is useful before some of the widely accepted—and erroneous—explanations of their collapses are dismissed. The design of the Twin Towers represented the acme of modern high-rise engineering and architecture. It could not have been otherwise, in light of their location in the heart of New York City's financial district and among other office buildings with tens of thousands of daily occupants. Their steel construction employed extensive cross-bracing, to share the loads from one floor sector to another. The brawny core steel columns that supported the enormous weights were driven down 70 feet into the bedrock underlying the island of Manhattan. Perimeter columns were connected to the core by means of steel bar-joist trusses embedded in the concrete floors. There were criticisms of these "flimsy trusses" which supposedly contributed to the collapses. "Not so," said structural engineer Robert McNamara, president of McNamara and Salvia, a leading New York consulting engineering firm.

> "Nowadays, they just don't build them as tough as the World Trade Center."

The FEMA report agreed:

> "The floor framing system for the two towers was complex and substantially more redundant that typical bar joist floor systems."[15]

The buildings were purposefully designed as elastic structures for safety; swaying nearly imperceptibly in the wind was sometimes noticeable to occupants of the upper stories on windy days. Specifications called for the buildings to withstand 140 mph winds—and, of particular significance, were constructed to resist a crash by the biggest passenger airliner then in service, a four-engine Boeing 707 fully loaded with passengers and fuel. By a remarkable coincidence, the 707's gross weight was nearly the same as the twin-engine Boeing 767s that crashed into the Towers. Finally, following conventional engineering practice for high-rise buildings, a factor of safety of five was incorporated into the structures to take into account possible construction flaws and other unforeseen anomalies. High-speed photography showed that the South Tower shuddered momentarily at impact but recovered almost instantaneously, as it was designed to do. Not a single window was broken except at the immediate crash site and nothing fell off the structure. Given these facts, a second widely disseminated theory that the impact of the airplanes materially weakened the two structures must be rejected as incorrect.

If it was not careless or inadequate design, nor slovenly construction, and it was not the forces of heavy airplanes thundering into the buildings at high speed and supposedly weakening the steel-and-concrete latticework, what caused the Towers' spectacular collapses? *There remained only one obvious remaining culprit to the uninitiated: the fires.*

As observed from the outside, the fires were considered small. The huge fireball that immediately enveloped the South Tower after it was hit had been judged by experts as misleading. This fireball did not indicate a raging inferno inside, however, but quite the opposite. The aircraft in this second crash struck the building near a corner and did not penetrate all the way into the building which meant that much of the jet fuel burned up outside. Photographs clearly support this view: not a single floor beyond the fire's beginning was sufficiently hot to ignite paper or even break windows.

Even assuming the exceedingly remote possibility that the Towers had been brought down by a combination of the heat of their fires and the forces exerted at impact of the crashes, the North Tower could be expected to have collapsed first. *It had been hit 17 minutes before the South Tower and had larger fires, yet the South Tower fell down 29 minutes before the North Tower.* Why? The rational conclusion: some factor other than fire had caused the buildings' collapses. The Commission elected not to address this obvious and significant enigma.

Nor did the Commission mention the two seismic shocks registered by seismographs at Columbia University's Lamont-Doherty Earth Observatory in Palisades, New York, 21 miles north of the WTC. These "spikes" were recorded just before each of the Towers collapsed. The seismographs recorded a 2.1-magnitude ground shock during the 10-second collapse of the South Tower and a 2.3-magnitude quake during the 8-second collapse of the North Tower. The strongest shocks recorded occurred at the start of the collapses, well before falling building walls, floors, and major steel structural members hit the ground. One Columbia seismologist said that the 1993 truck bomb at the WTC did not even register on [their] seismographs.[16] These shocks are further solid evidence that *explosions inside the Towers were the cause of the collapses, not fires that weakened steel structural members to failure.*

The fire temperatures in the Towers and structural steel's capacity to resist elevated temperatures before bending and twisting to failure were issues that became contentious from the beginning of the post-mortem analyses. From an engineering standpoint, steel does not have to melt, i.e., to become fluid, to lose its load-bearing properties. The melting point of a particular alloy-steel formulation is, however, an excellent measure of its resistance to extreme temperatures. The melting point of the structural steel used in the Towers was about 2,700 degrees Fahrenheit, some 1,000 degrees higher than ordinary hydrocarbon fires, such as combustion based on JP-4 jet fuel (basically kerosene). Further, Underwriters Laboratories had certified the steel in the buildings up to 2,000 degrees Fahrenheit for four hours before it would significantly weaken. However, the Tower fires burned at too low a temperature, at an estimated average temperature of around 500 degrees Fahrenheit, and too briefly, about one hour in the South Tower and one-and-a-half hours in the North Tower, to have affected the steel's integrity. If the steel had weakened during these periods, the affected floors would have displayed completely different behavior. There would have been obvious asymmetrical sagging and tilting, which would have been gradual and slow—not the complete, abrupt, and total "pancaking" that occurred.

FOR REASONS THAT CAN ONLY BE GUESSED AT, the 9/11 Commission Report managed to avoid the very real issue of the multiple explosions heard by numerous "ear-witnesses" inside the South Tower prior to the airplane's impact, some of whom managed to survive the collapse. One who did not escape was the head of WTC Security,[17] John O'Neil. He stated over radio shortly before he became a victim himself that he had helped dig out survivors from the rubble on the 27th floor [of 2-WTC] before it collapsed. Flight 175 had smashed into the 80th floor. Whatever had heavily damaged the 27th floor was not Flight 175!

Louie Cacchioli recalled that Engine 47 in Harlem to which he had been assigned "were the first ones in the second tower that was struck. I was taking firefighters up in the elevator to the twenty-fourth floor to get in position to evacuate workers. On the last trip a bomb went off. We think there were bombs set in the building."

Auxiliary First Lieutenant Paul Isaac also talked about explosions and said that New York firemen were very upset by what they considered a cover-up in the WTC destruction.

> "Many... know there were bombs in the buildings but they were afraid for their jobs to admit it because the higher-ups forbid discussion of this fact."[18]

Engineer Mike Pecoraro was also convinced that the explosions he heard were bomb blasts. He told *The Chief Engineer* magazine he had been working with another maintenance worker in the 6th sub-basement of the North Tower when the lights suddenly flickered, then came an explosion. He reported that they were told to "sit tight" and await further orders. When their room began to fill with white smoke, however, the two men decided to get out of the building. On their way up and out, they passed through a machine-shop. According to Pecoraro:

> "There was nothing there but rubble... We're talking about a 50-ton hydraulic press [not its weight, but the force it could exert between its jaws]... gone!"

As the two men climbed the stairs to the parking-garage level they encountered more destruction. One floor above, the B level, the men reported that they were astonished to see a concrete and steel fire door that they judged weighed about 300 pounds, wrinkled up "like a piece of aluminum foil" lying on the floor.[19] By then, both were convinced that a bomb or bombs had gone off in the building. When they reached the lobby, Pecoraro recalled:

> "The whole lobby was soot and black, elevator doors were missing... 20 by 10 foot sections of marble, gone from the walls. The west windows were all gone. They were missing. These are tremendous windows... Broken glass everywhere, the revolving doors were all gone."[20]

To many people streaming down the stairs, the lobby of the North Tower was so unrecognizable that many bypassed it and had to be directed back up the stairs. The official explanation was that jet fuel in the form of a fireball had spilled down elevator shafts, blowing off elevator doors on the way down and rolling through the lobby. Pecoraro had been through the 1993 bombing and recalled seeing similar damage. He was not called to testify, although he was, indeed, an expert witness. Did Pecoraro know too much?

William Rodriguez, the senior custodian in the North Tower and the last man to leave that building, added details to Pecararo's account. Rodriguez had worked for the New York and New Jersey Port Authority for some 20 years. He reported hearing massive explosions in the sub-basements; these explosions could not have come from fires in upper stories that resulted in extensive destruction hundreds of feet below. Rodriguez was certain that the explosions occurred prior to the airplane's impact, a claim that has been substantiated in a study by Craig T. Furlong and Gordon Ross, "Seismic Proof—9/11 Was an Inside Job," which established that these explosions took place as much as 14 to 17 seconds prior to the airplane's impacts. Rodriguez was hailed at the time as a hero by the president for guiding rescue workers and "single-handedly" saving a number of lives.

According to Furlong and Ross, Rodriguez was in the maintenance office of the North Tower sometime around 8:30 that morning. His office was located in the first sublevel, one of six sub-basements beneath ground level. There were thirteen other people in the office, including Anthony Saltamachia, Rodriguez's supervisor for the American Building Maintenance Company, when they heard a powerful explosion that seemed to emanate from between sub-basements B2 and B3. There were 22 people in sub-basement B2 who also heard and felt the same explosion.

At first, Rodriguez thought it was a generator that had failed catastrophically.

> "When I heard the sound of the explosion, the floor beneath my feet vibrated, the walls started cracking and everything started shaking."

Seconds later another explosion "way above" made the building shake momentarily. This, he was told later, was a plane hitting the 90th floor.

When asked about these two explosions, Rodriguez was emphatic:

> "I would know if an explosion was from the bottom or the top of the building." He reiterated hearing separate explosions before and just after the plane struck the tower.[21]

FIREFIGHTERS FROM NEW YORK CITY UNIT SIX began arriving shortly after. In addition to their normal protective clothing, each carried about 70 pounds of equipment. Rodriguez led them up stairwell B. When they reached the 27th floor, they took a quick break, temporarily exhausted from the climb. The Unit Six firemen and Rodriguez heard explosions all around them and chunks of ceilings and walls were falling. They continued their ascent. Rodriguez accompanied the firefighters to the 39th floor where he was instructed by radio to turn back. On his way down he heard the blast of the plane hitting the South Tower. Rodriguez gave a closed-door testimony before the 9/11 Commission, yet there is no mention of his testimony in the Report. He certainly knew too much!

Rodriguez claimed he tried to tell his story to investigators for NIST, the National Institute of Standards and Technology, but was rebuffed.

> "Finally, [at a public hearing] I asked them before they came up with their conclusion... if they ever considered my statements or the statements of any of the other survivors who heard the explosions. They just stared at me with blank faces."[22]

An audiotape of New York City firefighters at the scene, not made public until mid-2002, indicates clearly that fire officials managed to reach the 78th floor of the South Tower, just below the main crash site at the 80th floor. All those there seemed convinced that the fire was controllable. Two of the officials mentioned by name in the tape were Battalion Chief Orio J. Palmer and Fire Marshall Ronald P. Bucca, both of whom perished when the skyscraper collapsed. The *New York Times* reported that the audiotape's transcript:

> "showed no panic, no sense that events were racing beyond their control... At that point, the building would be standing for just a few more minutes... Even so Chief Palmer could see only two pockets of fire and called for a pair of engine companies to fight them."

By the middle of 2005, more accounts of multiple explosions at the WTC were being aired. Investigator Marrs wrote:[23]

> "Perhaps the most significant were 503 oral histories recorded near the end of 2001 by the NYFD [sic]... Although some were edited, the tapes became public on August 12, 2005."

Cumulatively, these tapes are further substantiation of controlled demolition of the Twin Towers. Among them are the following from FDNY officers:

Fire Captain Dennis Tardio:

> "I hear an explosion and I look up [at the South Tower]. It is as if the building is being imploded from the top floor down, one after another, boom, boom, boom."

Fire Battalion Chief John Sudik:

> "We heard a loud explosion... and looked up and saw Tower Two start coming down."

Assistant Fire Commissioner Stephen Gregory:

> "I thought... before... [Tower] No. 2 came down that I saw low-level flashes... You know, like when they demolish a building, how when they blow up a building, when it falls down? That is what I thought I saw."

Captain Karin Deshore:

"Somewhere around the middle of the World Trade Center, there was this orange and red flash coming out. Initially it was just one flash. Then this flash just kept popping all the way around the building and that building had started to explode."

Deputy Fire Commissioner Thomas Fitzpatrick:

'We looked up [at the South Tower]... All we saw was a puff of smoke coming from around two-thirds of the way up... My initial reaction was that this was exactly the way it looks when they show you those [building] implosions on TV.

There is more proof that explosives caused the collapses. Nearly all the concrete floors and the gypsum walls were pulverized, so finely that these materials blanketed parts of lower Manhattan with inches of material as fine as flour. This can only be attributed to explosives. Furthermore, parts of the Towers were thrown up to 500 feet laterally. The energy to "explode" the buildings as they fell can only be explained by explosives. In fact, explosions were clearly visible by observers on the ground as the floors pancaked one on top of another as the buildings came down. As each of the Twin Towers began to fall, the upper floors mushroomed into thick dust clouds much larger than the original volumes of the buildings; this mushrooming could only be produced by explosives.

LASTLY IS THE INCONTROVERTIBLE EVIDENCE that pre-placed explosives had been used because of the speed with which the buildings collapsed—10 seconds for the South Tower and 8 seconds for the North Tower. They fell at *nearly the speed of free fall*, obviously not inhibited by the nearly 100 concrete floors and their steel supports as they "pancaked" on their way to the ground. How was this possible? In fact, *it was not possible*! The phenomenon is only explainable if the lower stories were destroyed in sequence some seconds beforehand by explosives. Furthermore, steel-frame structures like the Twin Towers and 7-WTC were not capable of pancake collapses. These types of failures normally occur only during intentional demolition of steel-reinforced concrete structures of "lift-slab" construction.

Hardened pools of metal and even some small still-molten puddles were found at the sub-basement levels five weeks later, an effect that could not have been produced by the plane-impact/jet-fuel-fire/pancake-collapse scenario. Steven E. Jones, a physics professor at Brigham Young University and a co-founder of Scholars for 9/11 Truth,[24] gave a logical answer based on his investigation. He told a *New York Times* staff writer that he had found traces of fluorine and zinc in metal debris and dust from near the trade center site. He argued that "those elements should not have been found in the building compounds" and that he was studying "the possibility of thermite-based arson and demolition, "using "super-thermite."

Jones described "super-thermite" as compounds that, under controlled circumstances, can quickly cut through steel beams. Another credible voice in the controversy was Morgan Reynolds, an official in George H. W. Bush's administration and a former director of the Criminal Justice Center at the National Center for Policy Analysis and a Texas A & M Professor Emeritus of Economics. Reynolds wrote regarding the collapse, and also speculated on why 7-WTC was brought down:

> Only professional demolition appears to account for the full range of facts associated with the collapses of 1-WTC, 2-WTC and the much-overlooked collapse of 7-WTC.... Why would the killers destroy 7-WTC, especially since a collapse would arouse suspicion in some quarters? A logical if unproven theory is that the perpetrators used Mayor Giuliani's sealed OEM "bunker" on the 23rd floor of 7-WTC to conduct the twin tower implosions, and then destroyed the building and evidence to cover up their crimes, just as a murderer might set his victim's dwelling ablaze to cover up the crime.

Reynolds reflected further that Giuliani's "undisclosed secret location" was perfect because it had been evacuated by 9:45AM on 9/11, enabling unmolested work, provided a ring-side seat, was bullet and bomb-resistant, had its own secure air and water supply, and could withstand winds of 160 mph, necessary protection from the wind blasts generated by collapsing skyscrapers.

Reynolds also joined the growing chorus of criticism directed at FEMA for the hurried destruction of WTC debris. Remarkably, New York City officials tracked every debris truck leaving the ground zero site on GPS

> "and had one truck driver who took an unauthorized 1-1/2 hour lunch fired." [25]

EDITOR BILL MANNING of the venerable publication *Fire Engineering* asked these rhetorical questions: Did they throw away the locked doors from the Triangle Shirtwaist Fire? Did they throw away the gas can used at the Happyland Social Club Fire? Did they cast aside the pressure-regulating valves at the Meridian Plaza Fire?

No, "they" did not! The public—and forensic investigators—might have learned what *really happened to the WTC* if the NYPD and the FDNY had been allowed to do their jobs. The FBI immediately took charge of the criminal investigation and FEMA took responsibility for establishing the cause or causes of the collapses. FEMA was determined to haul away the evidence before forensic engineers had a chance to study the rubble. Bystanders were even arrested and their cameras and film confiscated for taking pictures of the rubble at ground zero. The government's massive cover-up had begun.

Then there was the suspicious "discovery" of one of the hijacker's passports. There are four versions of this almost-impossible-to-believe story. Barry Mawn, New York City's FBI director, told CNN on September 18 that "a grid search of streets surrounding the WTC had come up with several clues. Last week, a passport belonging to one of the hijackers was found in the vicinity of Vesey Street, near the WTC. It was a significant piece of evidence for us.[26]

Indeed, it would be—if true!

Another version (Associated Press, January 27, 2003) was from CBS which reported that the passport had been found "minutes after" the attack, while ABC News reported its discovery "in the rubble" on September 12. Susan Ginzburg, senior counsel to the Commission, testified that the passport of hijacker Suqami [Satan al] came from:

"A passerby who picked it up and gave it to a NYPD detective shortly before the World Trade Center Towers collapsed."[27]

9/11 skeptics who suspect the passport was planted pointed out that Flight 11 went directly into the center of the building and no part of the plane emerged. How could a paper passport survive the flames?

If the investigators considered themselves fortunate to have found a paper passport, where are the "black boxes?" All large commercial airliners are required to carry these, typically bright orange or red to stand out in rubble. One is a cockpit voice recorder and the other a flight data recorder. These recorders are housed in the plane's tail where they are most likely to survive a crash. They are exceedingly resistant to destruction: impact tolerance is 3,400 Gs for 6.5 milliseconds and fire resistant to 1,832 degrees Fahrenheit for 30 minutes. More than 20,000 fragments of human remains were screened out of the ruins, *but the screeners maintained they were unable to find any of the four shoebox-size instruments, even pieces.*

Not only had the investigators failed to recover the four recorders in their meticulous salvage operation, they never found—or purposefully "lost" after they were found—the remains of four six-ton turbojet engines. These nearly indestructible parts of the airplanes had serial numbers on major components that were readily traceable to the aircraft in which they were installed.[28] Big turbojet engine parts would almost certainly have been obvious at the WTC site. A FEMA photograph on page 109 of *911 Revealed* shows what appears to be a turbine housing in the Staten Island landfill in mid-October 2001. Did anyone look for serial numbers?[29] If not, why not?

SEVEN-WTC,[30] a 47-story structure across the street from the Towers, merited separate treatment—although its collapse, as far as Commission members were concerned, had never happened; it warranted not a single word in the Report. This office building, also of steel-frame construction with an all-glass facade, had not been hit by any large pieces of debris investigators all agreed. No windows were broken. There were only minor fires observed on the seventh and twelfth floors observed from the ground. Nevertheless, 7-WTC imploded, crashing to the ground without warning at 5:20PM.

From all outward appearances 7-WTC was a conventional high-rise office building. Inside, it was far different. It housed two huge electrical substations that had been in place prior to its construction. These substations consisted of ten transformers, each 35 feet high and 40 feet wide. Mayor Rudolph

Giuliani's huge Office of Emergency Management "bunker" was also located in the building, along with three 500 KW generators for emergency power and tanks that could hold 42,000 gallons of diesel fuel.

Unlike the Twin Towers, which collapsed from the top down, 7-WTC collapsed from the bottom up, in the characteristic form of a preplanned building demolition: a complete, abrupt and total collapse into its own footprint, where the floors all fall at the same time. In September 2002, during a PBS documentary "America Rebuilds," Larry Silverstein, principal leaseholder of the building, said:

> I remember getting a call from the fire department commander, telling me they were not sure they were going to be able to contain the fire, and I said, "We've had such terrible loss of life, maybe the smartest thing to do is 'pull it.'" And they made that decision to "pull it" and we watched the building collapse.[31]

Is Silverstein to be believed? Why would he be impelled to lie? Why is there no mention of this significant first-person testimony in the Report?

Demolition experts say "pulling" a building means attaching long cables to a weakened structure and literally pulling it down with bulldozers and other powerful machinery—not using explosives. This interpretation was not leaseholder Silverstein's, who claimed, after the "pull" order that he watched the building collapse. Neither Silverstein nor anyone else at ground zero observed cables tied to bulldozers!

Furthermore, why had FEMA been so eager to destroy the debris from the 7-WTC collapse? Building 7 was one of the most important building collapses in the history of high-rise building engineering. FEMA concluded amazingly in May 2002, just after the last debris had been scraped from ground zero, that:

> The specifics of the fires in 7-WTC and how they caused the building to collapse remain unknown at this time.[32]

Authors Morgan and Henshall suggest that in addition to the destruction of structural evidence, there seemed to have been:

> Suppression of aircraft debris at the site that was of interest to plane crash investigators such as the NTSB [National Traffic Safety Board]. There was [also] a singular lack of official zeal in establishing that the aircraft that hit the Twin Towers were... the same jetliners as those that had taken off from Boston.[33]

If explosives had been preplaced in the Twin Towers and 7-WTC, who planted them and who detonated them in the precise sequence to achieve their rapid collapse? Because there is little forensic evidence remaining—the gypsum interior walls and the concrete floor slabs were crushed into powder, inflammables reduced to ash were blown over lower Manhattan, and steel structural members were cut up carted away and shipped to Asian recyclers—the conspirators will likely never be brought to justice. The co-authors of the technical paper *9/11 Was An Inside Job*, members of Scholars for 9/11 Truth, offer no clues as to the identity of those responsible for "the greatest crime and conspiracy of modern times." Rather, they concluded their analysis by demanding:

> A new independent, quasi-private/public, non-political investigation (a real one this time, one with teeth) to be formed immediately... All Americans, especially the NYPD, the Attorney General for the State of New York, Congress, and the Bush Administration need to work in answering this question: Who are the ones responsible for the explosions before the planes hit the buildings?[34]

LET US RETURN TO THE PERIOD between the takeoffs and crashes of Flights 11 and 175. Flight 11 left Boston's Logan International Airport at 7:59AM, destination Los Angeles. At 8:14, besides failing to respond to an order from an FAA ground controller, its radio and transponder went off the air,[35] suggesting a *possible hijacking*. Six minutes later, with FAA ground control monitoring its flight path on radar, the plane deviated sharply off course, a firm indicator that Flight 11 *probably had been hijacked*. At 8:21, flight attendants on the airliner reported by telephone that, in fact, their airplane had been hijacked, and that several people had already been killed by the hijackers. At 8:28, the plane turned on a course heading that would take it over New York City. A minute later, Flight 11 flew directly over what some have called "the number one terrorist target" in the United States, the Indian Point nuclear power station some 30 miles north of midtown Manhattan. Why didn't the pilot dive his plane into the easily recognized reactor containment dome sitting between two cooling towers? Such an attack almost certainly would have ruptured the dome allowing the release of a radioactive cloud that, borne on winds, could poison tens of thousands of Americans and create a wasteland in the heavily populated metropolitan New York City area that would be uninhabitable for decades to come. At 8:46, AA Flight 11 crashed into 1-WTC. The crash followed 32 minutes after it was evident that the plane had *possibly been hijacked* and 25 minutes after it was established that a hijacking had *definitely taken place*.

The principal charge by critics of the government's account is that if standard operating procedures for responding to hijacked airliners had been followed on 9/11, USAF jet fighters should have intercepted Flights 11, 175, and 77 before they struck their targets and intercepted Flight 93 before it crashed in a field in rural Pennsylvania. Standard operating procedure calls for the FAA to contact the National Military Command Center any time it suspects that an airplane has been hijacked. There are three main indicators that an aircraft may have been hijacked: if it deviates considerably from its flight path in the judgment of the FAA controller, if radio contact is lost, or if its transponder goes off the air. If any of these signs occur, the flight controller is enjoined to immediately try to make radio contact with the pilot. If the pilot does not respond appropriately, again in the judgment of the flight controller, or if radio contact cannot be quickly restored, the FAA must contact the NMCC. Further, FAA traffic controllers are instructed to treat all "possible" hijackings as "actual" hijackings. These are the FAA's instructions to their flight controllers in this regard:

> Consider that an aircraft emergency exists... when: There is unexpected loss of radar contact and radio communications with any... aircraft... If you are in doubt that a situation constitutes an emergency or potential emergency, handle it as though it were an emergency.[36]

On the military side, its regulations state:

> In the event of a hijacking, the NMCC will be notified by the most expeditious means by the FAA. The NMCC then tells NORAD (North American Aerospace Defense Command) to 'scramble' jets from the nearest Air Force base that maintains jets on alert.

Generally two jet fighters will take off one after the other to intercept "the bandit."

Interceptions also take place rapidly, as they should be if they are to be a functional deterrent. General Ralph Eberhart, the head of NORAD, reported that from the time the FAA senses something is wrong, "it takes about one minute" for it to contact NORAD, after which NORAD can scramble fighter jets "within minutes to anywhere in the United States." Part of the reason for the quick reaction time is that an F-15 *Eagle* typically "goes from scramble order to 29,000 feet in only 2.5

minutes," after which it can fly over 2,000 miles per hour, tracking its target with its own air-to-air radar.[37]

When planes are intercepted, what follows is a graduated response. The approaching fighter [from the rear and slowly sliding into view of the aircrew in the cockpit] rocks its wings to attract the pilot's attention, or makes a pass directly in front of the offender. If there is no response from the cockpit, the next step is to fire tracer rounds in the airplane's path to clearly indicate that the interceptor "means business."[38] The final step is a serious matter and an Air Force pilot must get Pentagon authorization to shoot down a civilian airplane. According to a spokesman for NORAD headquarters in Colorado Springs, however, interceptions are "routine"—not shoot-downs—and occur about 100 times a year over the continental United States.

CRITICS OF THE LAGGARD RESPONSE TIMES of the FAA and the U.S. military during the hijackings point to the interception of golfer Payne Stewart's Learjet on October 25, 1999. Pilot Stewart and four passengers left Orlando, Florida at 9:20AM. The NTSB reported that there was a regular radio transmission at 9:27. Stewart's plane was given an instruction at 9:34, to which it did not respond. [Everybody in the Learjet had apparently lost consciousness because of insufficient oxygen in the cabin.] The FAA air traffic controller tried for 4-1/2 minutes to reestablish contact, then called NORAD. According to the Air Force, "a series of military planes provided an emergency escort to the stricken Lear, beginning with a pair of F-16 *Falcons* from the Air National Guard at Tyndall Air Force Base, Florida, about 20 minutes after ground controllers lost contact."[39]

In the event, at 8:14, when radio contact was lost with Flight 11, the FAA ground controller should have begun emergency procedures. The loss of the transponder signal was a confirming sign that all was not well aboard the airplane. The ground controller should then have immediately contacted both the NMCC in the Pentagon and NORAD. In turn, NORAD would have lost no time in scrambling fighter jets from the nearest military base. Flight 11 would have been intercepted as early as 8:24 and no later than 8:33, well before it struck the WTC. Why wasn't Flight 11 intercepted?

NEXT OUT OF LOGAN, at 8:14, was United Airlines Flight 175. UAL 175's destination was also Los Angeles, and like AA 11 its fuel tanks were brimming. It was airborne at the same time that the FAA learned that Flight 11 may have been hijacked. At 8:42, Flight 175's radio and transponder went off the air as the plane turned sharply off course. Knowing by then that Flight 11 had been hijacked, the FAA controller responded appropriately and notified NORAD at 8:43. If NORAD's interceptors had reacted as expected, fighter-jets should have been positioned to shoot down the second hijacked airliner if it did not follow orders—well before it crashed into 2-WTC at 9:03. It is known that F-15s were in the air and "in full-blower all the way,"[40] according to Lt. Colonel Timothy Duffy, who flew one of the fighter-jets. Amazingly, and never explained, was NORAD's order to launch its jets from Otis Air National Guard Base in Cape Cod, over 180 miles from Manhattan—rather than McGuire Air Force Base in New Jersey, only 70 miles from the city. When Flight 175 struck the South Tower, the Otis Jets were still 70 miles away.

AMERICAN AIRLINES FLIGHT 77 was the third suicide attack of the morning, which purportedly hit the Pentagon. It left Dulles Airport in Washington, D.C. at 8:20AM, destination Los Angeles nonstop. At 8:46, it deviated significantly from its programmed course and the local cable news channel interrupted its regular newscasts describing an imminent aerial threat to its viewers in the Washington, D.C. area. By that time, Flight 77 was considered a bonafide hijacking and all the gears of the FAA, the NMCC, and NORAD had meshed—or had they?

The final minutes—or moments—of the flying object were strange. Why would the hypothetical pilot in the hypothetical 757 have aimed at one of the facades, only 80 feet high, when he could have more effectively struck the building, which covered 20 acres, from above in a near-vertical dive-bombing attack, a far simpler and more destructive maneuver? CBS reported on September 12:

> "Radar shows that Flight 77 did a downward spiral, turning almost a complete circle and dropping the last 7,000 feet in two and a half minutes."

This last maneuver exposed the aircraft to fighter interception for an additional two minutes or so. It is difficult to imagine that the hijackers would have stayed aloft longer than necessary in the most sensitive and supposedly well-guarded air space in the world. Finally, in performing the most difficult maneuver negotiated by any of the *kamikaze* planes, it would be expected that its pilot, Hani Hanjour, would have been the cream of the hijacker pilots. Not so! He had been considered incapable of flying solo in a Cessna trainer despite the 600 hours listed in his log book, this according to managers at an Arizona flying school where he had been enrolled.

Author Nafeez Mosaddeq Ahmed quotes military expert Stan Goff who gives further details on Hanjour's incompetency:

> A pilot they want us to believe was trained at a Florida puddle-jumper school for Piper Cubs and Cessnas, conducts a well-controlled downward spiral... brings the plane in so low and flat that that it clips the electrical wires across the street from the Pentagon, and flies it with pinpoint accuracy into the side of the building at 460 nauts... When the theory about learning to fly this well... began to lose ground; it was added that they received further training on a flight simulator. This is like saying you prepared your teenager for her first drive on I-40 at rush hour by buying her a video driving game."[41]

Furthermore, if the pilot of Flight 77 had as his destination the Pentagon, whatever his level of skills, why did he meander around the northeast for about a half-hour during which time he was subject to interception by Air Force fighter jets? Why did he make a long circuit near the Pentagon's defensive missile system and the Secret Service's missile launchers at the White House? Why did he aim his plane at the only unoccupied wedge of the Pentagon at its most fortified point if he was planning to kill as many people as possible?

ANDREWS AIR FORCE BASE, with two ready-for-combat fighter wings, is eleven miles from the Pentagon, less than a minute's flying time from afterburner takeoff to visual contact with a "bogey" being tracked by the base's radar and the F-16's own radar.

> Nevertheless, the Air Force proved incapable of getting their assets airborne in time to prevent what could easily have been a decapitation attack on the national capital. It was a record of indescribable ineptitude, *which was itself a cover for active complicity by some key officers in the attack and its geostrategic goals.*[42]

The Report devoted only a skimpy paragraph, below, to this attack, that hewed to Vice-Chair Hamilton's line that

> The focus of the Commission will be on the future. We're not interested in trying to assess blame; we do not consider that part of the Commission's responsibility.[43]

At 9:37, the west wall of the Pentagon was hit by hijacked American Airlines Flight 77, a Boeing 757—or was it? All 64 people aboard the airliner were killed, or were they? One-hundred-twenty-five people inside the Pentagon (70 civilians and 55 military service members) were also killed. One-hundred-six people were seriously injured and transported to area hospitals.

The aftermath of the Pentagon crash saw a potpouri of conflicting evidence, preposterous scenarios, contradictory eyewitness accounts, and much nonsense. Author/Investigator Michael C. Ruppert properly called Flight 77 "the miracle plane":

> The one that nobody actually *saw* hit the Pentagon; the one that left no recognizable debris matching an airliner; the one French author and investigator Thierry Meyssan did a pretty convincing job of proving it never hit the Pentagon because the hole [entry] was way too small and the damage pattern was totally inconsistent with a mid-sized passenger jet like a 757; the one where the engines melted, disappeared or evaporated, or were transported into space by the Starship Enterprise and never found; the one that flew like a fighter plane or a cruise missile.[44]

Ruppert also wrote that French investigative reporter Meyssan had been "crucified in the American press, despite his book, *L'Effroyable Imposture* or *The Horrifying Fraud,* becoming what he called a runaway bestseller in Europe."

The Report, on the other hand, did not bother to vilify Meyssan; instead it printed only a photograph of the collapsed front facade of the Pentagon showing sheared-off offices, with a caption written for simpletons, by a simpleton:

> "The Pentagon, after being struck by American Airlines Flight 77"

Where was the debris? There were no wing or tail panels, no fuselage parts, no seats, no body parts, no luggage, no landing-gear components, and no turbojet-engine parts, the most indestructible components of all. The Pentagon's own videotape does not show a Boeing 757 hitting the building, as even fanatical Bush-lover and Liberal-hater Bill O'Reilly admitted when it was shown on his TV show *The O'Reilly Factor*.

The newspaper and TV accounts created ridiculous scenarios to account for the total absence of aircraft parts on the still-manicured lawn around the Pentagon. Some "experts" explained that the aircraft had broken into tiny pieces on impact and these had melted in the inferno inside the Pentagon. One such soothsayer—Merlin himself, perhaps?—went further, claiming that the aluminum parts of the airplane and all its contents had undergone *not one but two phase shifts*—from solid to liquid to gas. To put that particular magical hypothesis to rest, if the plane did evaporate (at the required temperature of 5,400 degrees Fahrenheit) inside the building at the levels of the ground and first floors, how are we to believe that the upper floors resisted such an inferno? The photograph of the Pentagon in the Report clearly shows unburned office furnishings. The FBI announcement sometime later that one passenger "had been identified thanks to her fingerprints," is impossible to square with the supposed temperatures inside the Pentagon.

> *"The so-called terrorist attack [sic] was in fact a superbly executed military operation carried out against the USA, requiring the utmost professional military skill in command, communications and control. It was flawless in timing, in the choice of selected aircraft to be used as guided missiles and in the coordinated delivery of those missiles to their pre-selected targets."*[45]

—Seminar report of a private group of U.S. military and civilian pilots.

POPULAR MECHANICS magazine attempting to posture itself as a bonafide engineering publication but instead coming off as a sensationalist pseudo-scientific tabloid that it is, featured in the March 2005 issue an article titled "The World Trade Center (9/11 Myths Debunked)". Among other wholly nonscientific claims, the article maintained outrageously and preposterously: "What was left of the plane [after it struck the load-bearing columns of the steel-reinforced building] *flowed into the structure in a state closer to liquid than a solid mass* [author's emphasis]." Such a statement must be considered either pure fantasy or plain idiocy.

There was one piece of supposed airframe wreckage which was "found" on what became known as the Penta-lawn, offered up by the FBI—an aluminum-alloy skin section that matched the color scheme of American Airlines. A consensus of experts agreed that this piece was indeed a part of the starboard forward section of the fuselage of a Boeing 757. It was pristine, with no indication of fire damage, and no soot. Investigator Webster Griffin Tarpley explained:

> This lonely piece of evidence that turned up in such utter isolation increases the natural suspicion that it was simply planted by FBI investigators as part of an effort to shore up the credibility of the Pentagon's claim that a commercial airliner had hit the building.[46]

Author Meyssan concluded, based on his evaluation of the testimonies of eyewitnesses:

> The attack did indeed involve a flying vehicle with propulsion engine or engines. It thus allows us to discard the hypothesis of a booby-trapped vehicle or a helicopter. The nature of the aircraft... remains, however, very problematical.[47]

On the day after the attack, *The New York Times* reported that the aircraft "crashed into the outer edge of the building between the first and second floors, at full power. It penetrated three of the five concentric rings of the building." From a study of the photographs handed out to the press, the vehicle—Flight 77, another airplane, or otherwise—punched a hole several yards wide in the facade. It miraculously entered the building without touching the exterior lawn. The vehicle that passed through the entry hole *could* correspond to the fuselage of a 757 aircraft which is eleven-and-a-half feet in diameter. But what about the two wings, with a total width of 125 feet? What of the 40-foot-tall vertical stabilizer? It is expected that the two underslung turbojet engines, far sturdier than any other part of a commercial airliner, would have dug their way into the lawn or left their outlines in the wall. In fact, they made no marks on the lawn.

The nose section of the fuselage of the 757, which supposedly acted as an auger of sorts in these wild-eyed scenarios, is a thin shell of relatively fragile carbon-fiber construction, not intended to serve as the tip of a battering-ram. It stretches credulity to suggest that the easily crushed nose would have gone through the third ring of a steel-reinforced concrete building sufficiently intact to produce a circular hole where it exited as shown in photographs.

While *there had to have been eyewitnesses*, few came forward. Of these, many thought they had observed a fast-flying object much smaller than a 757. If it had been a 757 on its final approach, its deafening noise level—it was at full power, according to the *Times*—would have been sufficient to have startled and frightened hundreds of people on its long, necessarily flat tree-top trajectory. Why didn't such eye- and ear-witnesses come forward? Had they been muzzled? The few eyewitnesses brought forward by the Pentagon were those more favorably inclined to go along with the conventional wisdom that it had been a commercial jet plane on its final suicide run into the Pentagon.

In the absence of clear evidence that the crash into the Pentagon was an "airplane crash," a logical alternative conclusion that can be reached is that it was a "missile penetration." Many air-to-air and air-to-ground missiles are designed as armor-penetrators using DU warheads. [See Appendix.] The most effective of these warheads would be a hollow-charge warhead used to destroy hardened structures, such as the steel-reinforced-concrete Pentagon.

If it wasn't Flight 77 that hit the Pentagon, an intriguing question remains: what happened to the airplane and its passengers? The author can advance only what he acknowledges to be are far-fetched theories. Was Flight 77 one of two identical airplanes that mimicked the Joint Chiefs' *Operation Northwoods* in 1963,[48] planned—but never implemented—against Fidel Castro's Cuba? Flight 77 *was* inexplicably "lost" to FAA ground controllers for 29 minutes, sufficient time for a well-rehearsed airplane swap. Had the purposefully small number of passengers and aircrew aboard been well-compensated government accomplices sworn to secrecy? Or was Flight 77 skillfully ditched in the Atlantic Ocean at a prescribed rendezvous for safe pick-up of a skeleton-crew aboard? Or had the skeleton crew bailed out over land and the 757, on autopilot, been shot down over the Atlantic Ocean?

The FBI's ham-handed attempt to cover up evidence in and around the Pentagon that might be embarrassing was transparently obvious. To begin with, all available video tapes from local surveillance cameras (not part of classified Pentagon installations) were confiscated as quickly as possible. These included tapes from a gas station directly under the flight path of the intruder and from a second gas station about a hundred yards to the west. Also included was a video tape from a camera at the Sheraton Washington Hotel and from every business in the area that used exterior surveillance cameras. The FBI has never released these tapes, and they were never made public by the Commission. All that were released are five frames from a single surveillance camera, perhaps creatively modified to remove the frame or frames which might have shown the actual flying object. The contents of the flight data recorder and the cockpit voice recorder have never been released [if they had ever existed!] because, according to the FBI, they were destroyed by the fire, an extremely unlikely eventuality as already discussed.

> *"Planes have flown at full speed into mountains, been exploded with bombs in the air, and occasionally fallen out of the sky but this [the Pentagon crash] was the first time in forty years of flight recorder history that cockpit voice tapes had yielded no information."*[49]

THE 9/11 COMMISSION DISPOSED of the fourth suicide-crash of the morning, United Airlines Flight 93 in Shanksville, Pennsylvania, with a single muddy photograph of the "crash site," page 313 of the Report. There is not a word in the Report about the miles-long debris field indicating the certainty of an in-air explosion. There is mention of "only 37 passengers... well below the norm for Tuesday mornings during the summer of 2001."

If it was worth including the one sentence, why didn't the Commission investigators explore further? At that time, airlines were overbooking and canceling unfilled flights in their efforts to save money. The three other hijacked airliners had also been flying nearly empty: United 175 and American 11 and 77 took off with 81, 78, and 74 percent of their passenger seats unoccupied, respectively, a coincidence that demanded an explanation. None was forthcoming. There is, however, much detail concerning "the battle for United 93," which may or may not have been fictitious, but which struck the needed patriotic chord on a day that America was beleaguered as never before.

Flight 93 departed Newark Airport at 8:42AM, 41 minutes late, bound for Los Angeles. At 9:27, passenger Tom Burnett phoned his wife, telling her his plane had been hijacked and that she should inform the FBI, which she did. At 9:34, Burnett again called his wife. This time she told him about the attacks on the WTC, which convinced him his own plane was a *kamikaze*. At 9:36, the plane turned to a new heading, toward Washington, D.C. Between then and 9:57, when one of the hijackers was overheard saying there was fighting outside the cockpit, there were other phone conversations between other passengers and their kin. At 9:58, another passenger, Todd Beamer, told his wife that a group of passengers planned to overpower the hijacker in the back of the plane. Beamer supposedly closed his conversation with these immortal words:

> "Are you ready, guys? Let's roll."

Moments later, a female passenger talking to her husband, said in agitated voice:

> "They're forcing their way into the cockpit. They're doing it. They're doing it."

Her husband then remembers hearing screaming in the background at the same time he heard a "whooshing sound, a sound like wind," then silence as he lost contact. In the restroom, another passenger on the phone, was reported to have said he heard "some sort of explosion" and observed "white smoke coming from the plane."[50] The FBI, months later, denied that the recording of this last call included any mention of an explosion or white smoke—but the person receiving the call was forbidden to speak to the media.[51] One newspaper report later claimed that the last thing heard on the cockpit voice recorder was the sound of wind.

Had the plane's fuselage been holed by an air-to-air missile from a USAF fighter jet to destroy any evidence that it had been Flight 93?

On October 16, the Pentagon made public the flight control transcripts of Flights 11, 175, and 77, *but not Flight 93*.

WHILE THE ABOVE ALLEGED telephone conversations were taking place, Flight 93 was flying at an altitude of about 34,000 feet, its normal cruising altitude. Morgan and Henshall point to a simple experiment conducted by A.K. Dewdney, "a Canadian academic and long-time *Scientific American* contributor," that showed that successful cellular connections were "unlikely" from an airliner at cruising altitude. He had run his air-to-ground tests at 8,000 feet altitude in his own airplane and had gotten only intermittent connections. At 34,000 feet, the signal is only one-sixteenth as strong.[52]

> Skeptics are resigned to never seeing the cellular phone billing evidence that could put this troubling matter to rest. Without such evidence, they feel forced to conclude that much of the telephone evidence that supports the storming legend could be just that: pure patriotic propaganda.[53]

Lending credence to the shoot-down theory were CBS television reports that

> Two F-16 fighter-jets were tailing the flight. And a flight controller, ignoring an order to controllers not to talk to the media, reportedly said that 'an F-16 fighter closely pursued Flight 93.' The existence of a fighter plane in the area is supported, furthermore, by many eyewitnesses on the ground.[54]

Further, evidence from "ear-witnesses" on the ground in the vicinity of the crash buttress the theory that Flight 93 was shot down. One said she heard the plane's engines, then "a loud thump," and two more "loud thumps," and then she didn't hear the plane's engines any longer. Another heard "a loud bang," and watched the plane's right wing dip before the plane rolled and disappeared from view. Another witness heard a noise that "wasn't quite right" after which the plane "dropped all of a sudden, like a stone." The mayor of Shanksville offered additional evidence: he said he knew of two people who heard a missile, and that one of them "served in Vietnam and says he knew what they sounded like."

These conclusions—a strike by one or two air-to-air missiles—were supported by the location of debris. The largest remnant was a thousand-pound component of one of the plane's engines found over a mile away in the direction of the flight. Other witnesses described seeing burning wreckage fall as far as eight miles away, including what appeared to have been human remains. Workers at nearby Indian Lake Marina recalled seeing "a cloud of confetti-like debris" fall on the lake "minutes" after hearing a powerful explosion.

> *On January 22, 2002, the Senate voted unanimously to confirm Tom Ridge as Secretary of the nation's new Department of Homeland Security. The super-sized agency merged 22 existing agencies and included 170,000 employees to start. The budget for Homeland Security was about $40 billion in 2003. Senator Robert C. Byrd of West Virginia, one of eight Democrats who voted against creation of the new department, reminded Ridge that "he was charged with protecting the American people not only from terrorists, but also with protecting the civil liberties of the American people from an overzealous new bureaucracy."*

MUCH LATER, IN 2003, the FBI changed its story: the hijackers had decided to crash the plane just as passengers were about to smash their way into the cockpit.[55] Why would the hijackers have done that? The FBI has never made the transcript of the cockpit voice recorder available to the public, although it supposedly played the tape to Flight 93 victims' families after swearing them to secrecy. The 9/11 Commission also was privy to selected portions of the tape.

Further contributing to the theory that Flight 93 blew up in the air, was the grisly issue of missing body parts. Human remains were collected in and around the crash site, but their combined weight was not commensurate with the number of passengers on the plane. According to the coroner,

> "The collective weight of the forty-four people aboard the plane (37 passengers and a crew of 7) was seven thousand five hundred pounds. Only six hundred pounds of remains were discovered ..."[56]

The former strip-mine at the crash site consisted of soft soil, with much of the wreckage supposedly buried up to 25 feet below the impact crater. The government's version of the crash was that an intact 757 had struck the ground and exploded. How could debris rain down on a lake unless it came from above? A heat-seeking, air-to-air missile like the *Sidewinder* carried by F-16s that exploded inside one engine nacelle of the 757, for example, and throwing pieces into the fuselage, would account for such in-air destruction.

The FBI, which took over control of the investigation from the NTSB refused to release the tapes from either of the plane's two black boxes, which were found at the crash site. The NTSB by that time had embraced the nation's latest war, the terror war, and had a ready pretext to be uncooperative. Before the FBI investigators left Shanksville, the crater was filled in, and then covered with topsoil. The scorched trees around the clearing were chain-sawed and shredded into mulch. Was that done as a good-will gesture to the local community, or was it to destroy any vestiges of evidence contrary to the government's scenario?

> *Most Americans have assumed that regardless of the obvious benefits accruing to the Bush administration from this "new Pearl Harbor," the nation's political and military leaders would not have colluded to allow, much less stage, the attacks. Americans are expected to know a priori that all such conspiracy theories are false, because "Americans do not eat their own children."*

THEN THERE IS THE OVERARCHING QUESTION—the forensic principle of *"who benefits most from the crime"*—*Cui bono*? This approach has been used since the days of the Roman Empire to unravel conspiracies and prosecute assassins. Certainly George W. Bush, the Pentagon, the CIA, the FBI, and the minions of the nation's military-industrial complex benefited enormously from the attacks. The happenings on 9/11 gave the president what amounted to a free-ride on the scandals that surfaced in the weeks after the attacks: the voter frauds in Florida that awarded him the presidency and the unraveling of Enron whose managers had been among the top Bush campaign contributors. Is it reasonable to ask whether those who profited so significantly contributed to the tragedy? *Cui bono!*

More of a stretch was the instantly rejuvenated career of the mayor of New York City, Rudolph Giuliani. He was then completing his second term of office and the city, which had earlier admired his feistiness in dealing with cop killers and drug dealers, was getting tired of his endless political skirmishes and run-ins with school chancellors and African-American-neighborhood leaders. Seeking a new career, Giuliani floated the idea of a U.S. Senate race with successful carpetbagger Hillary Clinton, a contest the whole country would be watching. Then, on April 27, 2000, the mayor suddenly announced he had prostate cancer. While there was an initial burst of sympathy, it was also the start of Giuliani's slide as an unpopular lame-duck city mayor.

A week later, the *New York Post* ran a photograph of Giuliani with "very good friend" Judith Nathan. His long-troubled first marriage—there would be three—was disintegrating in full view of the electorate. There were juicy leaks of his infidelities and the tabloids had a field day. On May 19, a somewhat crestfallen Giuliani told a press conference that he had decided to drop out of the Senate race that he had never formally entered. He used as his excuse his cancerous prostate. The political career of 57-year-old Rudy Giuliani appeared at an end.

Then came 9/11 and an opportunity for political reincarnation. And what a rebirth it was! As New York City's leader and comforter, he united the city at the same time helping it look to a brighter, stronger future. *Time* named him "Person of the Year: Mayor of the World," depicting him:

> A near-miracle of competence in the wake of the attacks... He had to lock down parts of the city and break open others... find a million pairs of gloves and dust masks and respirators... and somehow persuade the city that it had not been fatally shot through the heart... When all levels of government proved humiliatingly inept when dealing with Hurricane Katrina, people said over and over again what New Orleans needed was a Rudy Giuliani.[57]

As of the end of January 2008, announced Republican candidate for president of the United States, Guiliani was running ahead of the field. His campaign faltered soon after and he disappeared from view except for a few cameo TV appearances on behalf of the real candidate, John McCain.

ON THE NIGHT OF THE ATTACKS presidential adviser Condeleeza Rice told a meeting of the NSC that the members should think about how to capitalize on these opportunities, this after Bush himself exulted in the "great opportunity." Rumsfeld followed up on October 12 by telling *The New York Times* unabashedly that 9/11 created:

"the kind of opportunities that World War II offered, to refashion the world."

Political commentators in the U.S. and abroad were in agreement that 9/11 had turned George W. Bush into the most powerful American president in recent times. That power was soon squandered—fortunately for the United States and the world, many Americans would say—by Bush's dissembling, incompetence, intransigence, and appearance as a tongue-tied "boy emperor" by much of the world. His inability to speak coherently unless he was stumbling through his Teleprompters made him a target of the millions of Bush-haters throughout the world.

The attacks of 9/11 led directly to greatly increased funding for the Air Force's already enormously expensive missile defense system, until then only championed—quietly—by Rumsfeld. For him and other "space hawks" in the Pentagon and among contractors who stood to benefit from multi-billion-dollar contracts, the new support for "space wars" was perhaps the most important benefit to come out of 9/ll.

A Department of "Defense" (DoD) document titled "Vision for 2020" began with this ominous mission statement:

> U.S. Space Command—dominating the space dimension of military operations to protect U.S. interests and investment... to dominate space... over $1 trillion will be required from American taxpayers.[58]

The public also obediently climbed aboard DoD's new bandwagon after the 9/11 attacks:

> Whereas in July 2001, a Gallup Poll showed that only 53 percent of the population supported this system, a poll released on October 21"—a sufficiently long interval for government propaganda to work its magic—"showed that support had jumped to 70 percent.[59]

Another positive fallout for the Bush administration was the clear field that 9/11 opened up for the passage of the USA Patriot Act. This restrictive legislation was introduced to the Congress soon after 9/11, indicating that this legislation had been prepared well in advance. The House of Representatives, acting like it was still in shock over the attacks, swiftly voted the Act into law by a vote of 339-79. President Bush lost no time in signing it into law on October 26—five weeks after the Twin Towers fell.

THE USA PATRIOT ACT was 342 pages long, making changes to more than fifteen different U.S. statutes, most of them enacted after previous misuse of surveillance powers by the FBI and CIA.[60] One Congressman recalled that he understood that the bill hadn't been printed before the vote:

> "At least I couldn't get it... They played all kinds of games, kept the House in session all night... Maybe a handful of staffers actually read it, but the bill definitely was not available to members before the vote."[61]

Representative Dennis Kucinich, liberal Democrat from Ohio and ultra-long-shot candidate for president in 2008, described the atmosphere in the House this way:

> "There was great fear in our great Capitol... The great fear began when we had to evacuate the Capitol on September 11. It continued when we had to leave the Capitol again when a bomb scare occurred as members were pressing the CIA during a secret briefing."[62]

The USA Patriot Act harked back eerily to Hitler's dictatorship:

Germans soon saw national identity cards, racial profiling, the equivalent of a national homeland security chief (SS Commander Heinrich Himmler), gun confiscation and later, mass murders and incarcerations in concentration camps.

Shortly thereafter:

> A man's home was no longer his castle. He could be seized by private individuals, could claim no protection from the police, could be indefinitely detained without preferment of charges, his property could be seized, his verbal and written communications overheard and perused; he no longer had the right to foregather with his fellow countrymen, and his newspaper might no longer freely express their opinions.[63]

What were the lessons learned from Adolf Hitler's acquisition of dictatorial powers that George W. Bush and his handlers could adopt? They were several. Take advantage of a crisis—or create one. Call for sweeping powers to "protect" the population against a ruthless enemy, increasingly labeled as Islamic "terrorists." Lace every pronouncement of the president, over and over again, that is the hallmark of effective propaganda, with his signature declaration—that everything he did was to keep Americans safe!

Another new Federal organization that sprang up on the coattails of 9/11 was the Office of Strategic Intelligence, a euphemism if there ever was one, intended to present a favorable view of the United States to overseas news outlets. Its establishment provoked an immediate outcry when it was learned that the OSI would plant phony news stories in foreign media. Critics were concerned that such bogus "information" might find its way back to domestic media. As Jim Marrs wrote:

> "This, of course, was nothing new. The CIA had done the same thing for decades but this was too blatant. Even the major media, including the *New York Times*, were stirred to action."[64]

Early in 2002, in an unusual step backward, the government announced that OSI would be shut down. The Secretary of Defense, intractable as always, admitted that the condemnation of the office "so damaged it that... it cannot function." Later in the year, during a press briefing, Rumsfeld brought up the subject of the defunct OSI. In his inimitable arrogance, glinting steely-eyed through his rimless glasses across the band of reporters facing him, Rumsfeld spewed stern-faced defiance:

> And then there was the Office of Strategic Influence. You may recall that. And "oh, my goodness gracious, isn't that terrible, Henny Penny, the sky is going to fall." I went down the next day and said fine, if you want to savage this thing I'll give you the corpse... You can have the name, but I'm gonna keep doing every single thing that needs to be done and I have.[65]

In 2001, an organization calling itself the Project for the New American Century published a document titled *Rebuilding America's Defenses*. Among those contributing to the document were Richard Armitage, John Bolton, Dick Cheney, "Scooter" Libby, Richard Perle, Paul Wolfowitz, and Donald Rumsfeld, all of whom went on to be key figures in the George W. Bush administration. John Lehman, a member of the 9/11 Commission, had been a contributor to *Rebuilding*. The PNAC document argued that U.S. defense spending had to be sharply increased if the "American peace is to be maintained and expanded," because this *Pax Americana* "must have a secure foundation on unquestioned U.S. military preeminence."[66] It followed that such a transformation of U.S. military forces would be a slow process because of its high costs. *Rebuilding America's Defenses* pointed out, however, that the process could be speeded up if America suffered,

> "some catastrophe and catalyzing event—like a new Pearl Harbor."[67]

> "We must speak the truth about terror. Let us never tolerate outrageous conspiracy theories concerning the attacks of September the 11th, malicious lies that attempt to shift the blame away from the terrorists themselves, away from the guilty."

—George W. Bush before the United Nations General Assembly, November 10, 2001.

A SENSIBLE ANALYSIS OF THE DAY'S TRAGEDIES must begin with the astonishing behavior of the president just outside and inside the Emma E. Booker Elementary School in Sarasota, Florida, on the morning of 9/11. Bush was there for a pre-planned "photo-op" in which he was to be shown reading along with a class of first-graders. In the principal's office, before he went into the classroom, Bush reportedly told the principal nonchalantly that:

> "A commercial plane has hit the World Trade Center and we're going ahead and do the reading thing anyway."

Bush then entered the classroom at about the same time as the second plane struck the South Tower. The children were beginning to read aloud from a storybook, *The Pet Goat*, when Andrew Card came into the room and whispered quietly to Bush that another plane had struck the World Trade Center. Bush then picked up a copy of the book and began to read along with them. He mostly listened, but occasionally asked the class questions to encourage them. Michael Moore's film, *Fahrenheit 9/11*, captured the scene memorably, the president sitting like a dunce on a stool at the head of the class, a vacant expression of incomprehension on his face. At one point, he said:

> "Really good readers, whew!... These must be six-graders."

Bush remained in the classroom for some twenty minutes. Even after he left the classroom, he lingered in an adjacent room, phoning Cheney and Rice. Only then did his Secret Service detail hustle him out of the school, into his armored black Chevrolet Suburban, to the airport and into *Air Force One* for a steep takeoff. Why did Bush's Secret Service detail allow him to dawdle? Why did the motorcade return to the airport following the same route as the originally planned one even after officials were alerted that White House security codes had been compromised? At the same time, in the White House, Cheney had been bundled immediately into the underground shelter.

Puzzling, too, were Bush's later comments, when he claimed he saw the first plane strike the North Tower:

> "I was sitting outside the classroom waiting to go in and I saw an airplane hit the tower—the TV was obviously on, and I used to fly myself and I said, 'There's one terrible pilot.'"

In fact, that claim was patently impossible. There was no video, live or otherwise, of the strike on the North Tower until that night when a French camera crew revealed they had accidentally filmed the crash during their shooting of an unrelated documentary. *How could George W. Bush have known unless he was party to the two crashes?*

WHILE THE REPORT PRESENTED much factual information about the nineteen men it identified as the hijackers, with their mug shots on pages 238 and 239 of the Report, it never touched on the major incongruity that six of them turned up very much alive and well after 9/11. Waleed al-Shehri, for example, said to have been on Flight 11, was interviewed by a reporter from the London-based Arab Al-Quids al-Arabi some days later. Additionally, according to an Associated Press report, al-

Shehri "spoke on September 22 to the US embassy in Morocco, explaining that he lived in Casablanca, working as a pilot for Royal Air Maroc."[68]

Ahmed al-Nami and Saeed al-Ghamdi, alleged to have been on Flight 93, told a London Telegraph reporter that they had been surprised "to hear that they had died in this crash."

Al-Nami added: "I had never even heard of Pennsylvania." Al-Ghamdi claimed "he had been in Tunis the previous ten months learning to fly an Airbus."

The Saudi Arabian embassy in Washington stated that three other supposed hijackers—Mohand al-Shehri, Salem al-Hazmi, and Abdulaziz al-Omari—also were alive and living in that country. Al-Hazmi, who was accused of being one of the hijackers of Flight 77, "had just returned to work at a petrochemical complex... in Yanbou after a holiday... when the hijackers struck."

Al-Omari, who was a pilot for Saudi Airlines, "visited the US consulate in Jeddah to demand an explanation why he had been declared a hijacker. [69]

As for Mohamed Atta, the ostensible ringleader of the band of 19 and pilot of Flight 11, the Report portrayed him as appearing religious, "but not fanatically so. This would change, especially as his tendency to assert leadership became increasingly pronounced."[70]

Griffin pointed out that Atta had gambled, drunk alcohol, and engaged the services of lap dancers in bars. Daniel Hopsicker reported further deviations in Atta's supposed life style as a devout Muslim on the verge of meeting his Maker, "while he was living in Florida; he lived with a prostitute, was a heavy drinker, snorted cocaine, and ate pork chops."[71]

Did the Report present any evidence that any of the 19 hijackers named in it even boarded any of the four planes that day? No, it did not! Nor did the passenger manifests that were eventually released of the four airplanes have any Arab names on them.

"Now, I'm not into conspiracy theories, except the ones that are true."[72]

IN THE DAYS AND WEEKS FOLLOWING 9/11 there was a nationwide orgy of patriotism and a flood of government propaganda not experienced in the United States since the Japanese First Air Fleet bombed Pearl Harbor in 1941. Print media, radio's disc jockeys becoming news analysts overnight, and TV's influential talking heads with their famous guests helped inflame the population. The mouthpieces of the military-industrial complex, including retired generals and colonels on the talk shows who soberly looked viewers in their eyes as they pontificated on the happenings, did their parts by beating the war drums. One critic wrote sarcastically that this period of government-sponsored hysteria was not an especially proud moment for American television.[73] CBS anchor Dan Rather, in one of the most embarrassing media performances of his life, blubbered on the Dave Letterman Show that "George W. Bush is my president" and that he would do whatever he was told—a pathetic collapse of a once-critical and respected journalist.[74]

The two principal "court" TV networks, particularly Fox but NBC as well,[75] ran the White House and Pentagon propaganda handouts as dished to them. Shockingly to perceptive viewers, CNN for the first time joined Fox and ABC, becoming:

> Almost totally propagandistic, in a stunning collapse of a respectable news organization into a vehicle of conservative ideology."[76]

Overnight George W. Bush was catapulted from being represented in some of the media as an inarticulate boob and a stooge for far-right causes, to now being viewed as a resolute leader. Bush's popularity had been on the wane before September 11, but suddenly the media couldn't praise him enough for his seeming decisive leadership and grit. The media at the same time gave legitimacy to a chief executive that many considered wholly illegitimate. Bush had lost the popular vote in 2000 by over 500,000 but had won Florida's electoral votes and the election primarily because the U.S. Supreme Court intervened and stopped the recount. His shirt-sleeved blather through a bull-horn from atop the still-smoldering rubble of the WTC, with a FDNY chief standing at his side, was a photo-op of enormous value to a president whose handlers had studiously kept him away from extemporaneous speech-making. The White House press corps was particularly fawning in praise of how "the new" Bush was handling the crisis, praising his every utterance, no matter how incomprehensible, grammatically twisted, and incoherent to his legions of detractors.

NOT EVERYONE bought into the idea that a bearded Saudi-Arabian exile sitting cross-legged in a dark cave in Afghanistan with a wireless PC on his lap had masterminded the whole operation. Or that the only weapons the alleged hijackers had were box-cutters. Or that four of the hijackers designated as pilots in the Report were able to fly the "heavies" into small targets on the first pass.

> *Within hours of the 9/11 attacks Defense Secretary Rumsfeld directed his aides to find some way to blame Iraq— "best info fast. Judge whether good enough hit S.H. [Saddam Hussein] at same time. Not only UBL [Usama bin Laden]. Go massive... sweep it all up... Things related and not."*

In an impromptu CNN interview four days after the attacks, Egyptian President Hosni Mubarek gave his views on the Pentagon attack. His brief interpretation was credible not only because of his political stature but because he was an experienced fighter pilot. In less-than-grammatically precise English, Mubarek said that the U.S. government's version, then taking shape, was "technically implausible." He noted that the Pentagon:

> "is not very high [about 40 feet high], a pilot could come straight to the Pentagon like this to hit, he should have flown a lot in this area to know the obstacles which he could meet when he is flying very low with a big commercial plane to hit the Pentagon in a special place." [77]

The CNN reporter:

> "Are you suggesting it was an inside operation? If I may ask, who do you think was behind this?"

Mubarek, realizing he was on diplomatic thin ice, backed off:

> "Frankly speaking, I don't want to jump to conclusions... I am speaking as a former pilot... I flew very heavy planes, I flew fighters... I think we should not jump to conclusions for now."[78]

CIVIL AND STRUCTURAL ENGINEERS in the weeks following the WTC collapses convened in symposia to compare notes and attempted to arrive at a consensus. One such technical meeting was held on the campus of Massachusetts Institute of Technology in Cambridge a month after the disaster. *Scientific American* sent a staffer there to observe and report on the engineers' postmortem on the Twin Towers' collapses. As reported in the Web of the highly respected magazine, there was no agreement, only a variety of technically sophisticated theories. One audience attendee, a consulting engineer from a firm on the West Coast who did not give his name when he arose during the open discussion period, created a provocative stir among those seated when he compared high-rise building costs to the value of human lives:

> The Towers would [have] cost about 10 percent more to install floor-joint reinforcements for greater redundancy... which could have added several more hours to the evacuation period. If each Tower cost about $1 billion to build, an extra hundred million dollars could have saved most of the occupants. Though it's horrible to contemplate, a human life is valued for insurance purposes at about a million dollars apiece, so this helps put the extra investment into perspective.[79]

In summer 2002, nine months after 9/11 and a year and a half before the official *Report* became available, Eric Hufschmid was first out of the lists with his pioneering *Painful Questions: An Analysis of the September 11th Attack*. With an abundance of full color photographs, his book compiled a raft of scientific, engineering and psychological evidence for the scenario of controlled demolition of the WTC.[80]

Another among the emerging critics of the government's scenario was Stanley G. Hilton who claimed in 2004 he had documentation that al Qaeda was, in fact, a CIA creation and that Bush "personally authorized the attacks." Hilton, an attorney and a Republican who had been chief of staff to Senator Robert Dole, filed a $7 billion suit in 2004 in behalf of some 400 family members of the victims of 9/11 against President Bush and his top officials. The suit left nothing to the imagination, charging;

> That all conspired with the government of Saudi Arabia prior to 9/11/01 to knowingly finance, encourage, recruit, permit, and aid and abet, certain individuals to carry out the 9/11/01 attacks on the World Trade Center and Pentagon, in order to orchestrate a contrived, stylized and artificial second Pearl Harbor event for the purpose of galvanizing public support for their military adventure agenda in the Middle East, and in order to persuade the Congress to enact their repressive Patriot Acts I and II for the purpose of suppressing political dissent inside the US.

A collective paper by Scholars for 9/11 Truth asked questions of its own: whether:

> "the Bush administration knew in advance about the impending attacks that occurred on 9/11, and allowed these to happen, to provoke pre-planned wars against Afghanistan and Iraq?"

The paper declared that its authors were surprised to learn that the government had brought only one indictment against an alleged hijacker and had not even reprimanded a single individual in a position of responsibility for incompetence or dereliction of duty on 9/11—and there were many. The authors also concluded that the government's theory was unsupportable—that nineteen scruffy Arabs under the control of a Saudi-Arabian exile in far-away Afghanistan had masterminded the whole business on his wireless laptop computer. They indicated that there were also sound reasons to suspect that the video tapes attributed to Osama bin Laden by the government were bogus.

Bush's 2002 State of the Union address was a fleshed-out outline of a new aggressive imperialism that simplistically drew lines between light and darkness—and civilization and barbarism. Bush's team of speechwriters almost certainly had George Kennan's famous *Long Telegram* of 1946 and Paul Nitze's Top Secret NSC-68 document of 1950 at their elbows when they were creating a plan like those documents that had set the ground-rules for the 40-year-long Cold War with the Soviet Union. It was a crusade the president was talking about: the "civilized world" versus the "axis of evil," Iran, Iraq, North Korea and their unnamed terrorist allies.

It was also a bellicose threat of what was to come: preemptive war at the whim of a gun-slinging cowboy president with no oversight by the Congress as the Constitution requires. Dovetailing seamlessly in the address was a call for higher military budgets in order to "defend" an inadequately armed United States. Finally came a jingo appeal to misplaced patriotism:

> "... and as government works to better secure our homeland, America will continue to depend on the eyes and ears of alert citizens."[81]

By this author's count as of mid-2007 there were twenty-six American-published books that offered sober challenges to the official conventional wisdom.[82] Among them was Author Tarpley who wrote in 2005 that "the insuperable problems" posed by the notion that four untrained pilots were somehow skillful enough to fly the big heavies "by the seats of their pants"—without preprogrammed flight data—into small targets, could be explained by the *Global Hawk's* guidance system. He pointed out that *Global Hawk's* guidance system was a more advanced version of that used in the *Predator* drone, and became widely known as a result of its successful trans-Pacific flight in April 2001.

> The existence of this technology in a fully operational form raises the possibility that it might have been installed in commercial airliners, and further that it may have been such airliners under the control of a *Global Hawk* or equivalent system which crashed into the WTC and the Pentagon.[83]

Tarpley concluded his book by summarizing his well-informed rebuttals of what he referred to as "the government's assertions":

> 1. The government's assertion that the so-called hijackers operated without being detected by official surveillance is untenable. 2. The government's assertion that the four supposedly hijacked airliners were taken over and piloted by the four accused hijackers identified by the FBI is at or beyond the limits of physical and technical reality. The planes were in all probability guided to their targets by some form of remote access or remote control. 3. The government's assertion that the failures of air defense were caused by the fog of war is lame and absurd. 4. The government's assertion that a Boeing 757-200 hit the Pentagon is physically impossible. 5. The government's assertion that the Twin Towers of the World Trade Center collapsed as a result of the impact of aircraft and of the subsequent fire is physically impossible. 6. The government's assertion that World Trade Center 7 collapsed at 5:20PM EDT on September 11 purely as a result of fire is physically impossible. 7. The government's assertion that United Flight 93 crashed because of actions by the hijackers or because of a struggle in the cockpit is physically impossible, given the pattern in which the wreckage was distributed. All evidence points towards the hypothesis that United 93 was shot down by U.S. military aircraft.

Tarpley was also ready to suggest specific suspects:

> My thesis that the 9/11 events were organized and directed by a rogue network of high government and military officials of the United States, with a certain participation by the intelligence agencies of Britain and Israel, and with a more general backup from the intelligence agencies of the other Echelon states (Australia, New Zealand, Canada). This US network represents the current form of the Dulles Brothers-Lemnitzer-Lansdale network of the early 1960s, of the Bay of Pigs-Kennedy assassination, Gulf of Tonkin networks, and of the invisible government/secret government/parallel government/shadow government that was widely understood to have been the prime mover of the Iran-Contra affair.[84]

Then there is the simple question, one that many Americans have obviously been asking family members and friends since 9/11: Why haven't there been any terrorist attacks since then? New

Yorkers knew that it would be a simple matter for a terrorist to board a New York City subway train at rush hour carrying a small, flat parcel easily concealed inside his or her morning *Times* containing perhaps a quarter-pound of plastic explosives and time-fused to detonate in 30 seconds. In such a logical scenario, as the train rumbled into the next station, the "bomber" presses a tiny switch that starts the time-fuse, leaves his folded paper behind on his seat as many New Yorkers typically do. Our terrorist exits by the nearest door, merges with the crowd on the platform heading to an exit, and is above ground and perhaps a block away when the blast occurs. It's not necessary for the explosion to be a massive one. Even a tiny explosion would create chaos in New York's public transportation system that would paralyze the entire city and echo from coast to coast. Many such "terrorist attacks" in cities all over the country could bring the nation to its knees.

"Letters Home" From Afghanistan

In Jalalabad, the Sultanpur Mosque was hit by a bomb during prayers, with 17 people caught inside. Neighbors rushed into the rubble to help out the injured, but as the rescue effort got underway, another bomb fell, killing at least 120 people.

In the village of Darunts near Jalalabad, a U.S. bomb fell on another mosque. Two people were killed and dozens—perhaps as many as 150 people—were injured. Many of those injured are languishing without medical care in the Sehat-e-Ama hospital in Jalalabad, which lacks resource to treat the wounded.

In Argandab, north of Kandahar, 10 civilians have died from the bombing and several houses have been destroyed. The same has happened in Karaga, north of Kabul.

On Oct. 7, the first night of the bombing, at least one private residence in Kabul suffered a direct hit and others were damaged. The U.S. also destroyed the Hotel Continental in the city's center. On the same night, bombs were dropped on the houses of the Taliban leaders in Kandahar. Two civilian relatives of Mullah Muhammad Omar were killed; his aged stepfather and his 10-year-old son.

On Oct. 11, a bomb aimed at the Kabul airport went astray and hit Qala-e-Chaman, a village one mile away, destroying several houses and killing a 12-yer-old child. On the same night, another missile hit a house near the Kabul customs building, killing 10 civilians.

As of Oct. 12, the U.N. has independently reported at least 20 civilian deaths in Mazar-i-Sharif and 10 civilian deaths in Kandahar.

On Oct. 13, Khushkam Bhat, a residential district between Jalalabad airport and a nearby military area, was accidentally bombed by U.S. planes trying to down a Taliban helicopter. More than 100 houses were flattened. At least 160 people were pulled from the rubble and taken to hospitals. In Kabul, witnesses described a huge fireball over the Kabul airport, indicating either the possible use of fuel-air bombs, which can cause destruction over a wide area, or the bombing of an enormous fuel storage facility, which can have the same effect. Casualties are not yet known.

On Oct. 17, a bomb scored a 'direct hit' on a boys' school in Kabul, but fortunately didn't explode. A U.S. plane, however, dropped a bomb at Mudad Chowk, a residential area of Kandahar, which did explode, destroying two houses and several shops, and killing at least 7 people. In Kabul, four bombs fell near the city center; casualties are still unknown.

The U.N. reported that Kandahar had fallen into a state of 'pre-Taliban lawlessness,' with gangs taking over homes and looting shops. By the next day, according to the U.N., at least 80 percent of Kandahar's residents had fled the city to escape the bombing. They are swamping the surrounding villages, where there are no resources to care for them. Some have moved on to the border and crossed into Pakistan. One refugee said that there are bodies littering the streets of Kandahar and people are dying in the hospitals for lack of drugs. 'We know we will lead a miserable life in Pakistan, in tents,' he said. 'We have come here just to save our children.'[85]

IN AN UNUSUALLY LONG (32 column inches) front-page article on September 1, 2006, headed "U.S. Counters 9/11 Theories of Conspiracy," *The New York Times* carried rebuttals by the State Department and a federal science agency. They insisted the September 11 attacks were caused by hijackers who used commercial airliners as weapons—not "a shadowy and sprawling plot run by Americans." The article pointed out that the official narrative of the attacks had been condemned as little more than a cover story by radio hosts, academics, amateur filmmakers and others "who have spread their arguments on the Internet and cable television in America and abroad."

The motive given by these sources, according to the *Times*, was the Bush administration's pretext to use the attacks to justify military action in the Middle East.

Most elaborately, they propose that the collapse of the World Trade Center was actually caused by explosive charges secretly planted in the buildings, rather than by the destructive force of the airliners that thundered into the towers and set them ablaze.

If *The New York Times'* Editorial Board remained convinced that the destruction in 2001 was wrought by a small band of suicidal Arabs and an Al Qaeda mastermind, many Americans who otherwise respected the editorials weren't going along with that conviction. A nationwide poll taken earlier that summer by the Scripps Survey Research Center found that more than one-third of the 1,010 adult respondees said that the federal government either took part in the attacks or allowed them to happen. Even more significantly: sixteen percent said the destruction of the WTC was aided by hidden explosives in the buildings.

Vice President Dick Cheney weighed in, pontificating that the war "may never end. At least, not in our lifetime."[86]

By 2007, nearly all of the support for the government's scenarios of 9/11 had faded away. Even President Bush was finally forced finally to acknowledge that Saddam Hussein had nothing to do with the attacks on 9/11, although the president refused to let go of his favorite whipping boy, invoking Saddam's involvement in the attacks whenever he thought it was expedient. This was after the Senate Intelligence Committee announced that Saddam had not been in league with al Qaeda or Osama bin Laden. Even the FBI came around: it admitted that it had "no hard evidence" to tie Osama to 9/11. If Saddam did not do it and Osama did not do it, then who was the mastermind or the masterminds of the attacks? Was it George W. Bush and Dick Cheney—*the two who ate America's children?*

ON AUGUST 22, 2008, *The New York Times* carried an article titled "Fire, Not Explosives, Felled 3rd Tower on 9/11, Report Says." *About time,* some would say: nearly seven years to the month that 7-WTC collapsed "mysteriously." The NIST which prepared the report and presented it to a conference on the subject, claimed that debris from the falling twin towers had damaged structural columns and ignited fires "on at least 10 floors." The NIST report acknowledged, however, that it wasn't structural damage that brought the building down, it was the fires.

Fires in the 47-story office tower at the edge of the World Trade Center site undermined floor beams and a critical structural column, federal investigators concluded... as they attempted to curb still-rampant speculation that explosives caused the building's collapse on September 11, 2001... But the collapse of 7 World Trade Center—home at the time to branch offices of the Central Intelligence Agency, the Secret Service and the Giuliani administration's emergency operations center—is cited in hundreds of Web sites and books as perhaps the most compelling evidence that an insider secretly planted explosives, intentionally destroying the tower.

One of the most preposterous findings of the NIST was that the fires in the building were "fed mainly by office paper and furnishings." Fact: Such materials do not burn at temperatures nearly high enough to weaken steel members. Another finding was equally absurd: that the investigators ruled out the possibility that explosives were used, because:

> "The noise associated with such an explosion would have been 10 times louder than being in front of the speakers at a rock concert and detectable from as far as a half mile away."

Interviews with eyewitnesses and a review of a video taken that day provided no evidence of a sound that loud just before the collapse. The incendiary material used to take down the Trade Center Towers would not necessarily create an explosive boom.

Members from Architects and Engineers for 9/11 Truth held their own press conference following the NIST presentation. Richard Gage, a California architect and the leader of the group, dismissed the government investigation as flawed. A *New York Times* reporter who attended wrote:

> "Five armed police officers and a bomb-sniffing dog stood guard near the rear of the room."

It is legitimate to ask: What in the world were armed guards and a bomb-sniffing dog doing at the press conference?

The Almost-Certain Political Assassination of Senator Paul David Wellstone

MID-MORNING on October 25, 2002, Minnesota Senator Paul David Wellstone was killed in a fiery private-airplane crash, along with his wife, daughter, three staff members, and their pilot and co-pilot, during the plane's final approach to the Eveleth-Virginia airport near Duluth. The airplane was a Beechcraft *King Air A-100* twin-turboprop. Both the pilot and co-pilot were thoroughly experienced. Debris recovered from the crash site included both engines, which suffered severe blade damage, certain evidence that the engines were running when the plane crashed. Significantly, the plane was equipped with a loud and unmistakable stall-warning horn. According to an article in *The New York Times* three days later, during the pilot's last transmission to the airport, some two minutes before the crash,

> "There was no evidence... from the pilot's voice that there was any difficulty, no reported problems, no expressed concern."

Putting an official imprimatur on this last radio transmission, the FAA spokeswoman on the case said that no indications of distress came from the plane's crew during the last minutes on its final approach.[87]

The mainstream media quickly blamed bad weather as the cause of the accident. Icing on the wing surfaces, which reduces lift, was pointed to as the likely culprit. However, the *King Air* had de-icing boots on its wings and tail surfaces and electrical de-icing on the blades of its propellers. Had the controls for those de-icers suddenly failed? Over the next several days, news reports described sharply reduced visibility in freezing rain, snow, and fog at the time of the crash. What was not reported was that other planes had landed safely that morning. Gary Ulman, co-owner of Taconit Aviation based out of the Eveleth airport, stated that icing had not been at a dangerous level the morning of the crash.

What was also not reported was the weather coverage from an FAA radar station at nearby Nashwauk. Automated instruments at that location, only minutes before the crash, indicated that the wind was calm, visibility was three miles in light snow, with scattered clouds at 400 feet and overcast at 700. According to air traffic control records, the flight had proceeded normally until its final minutes. Wellstone's plane took off at 9:37AM from Minneapolis-St. Paul, received permission to climb to 13,000 feet at 9:48, and received clearance to descend toward Eveleth at 10:01 at which time the pilot was told there was icing at the 9,000-11,000 foot level. The *King Air* began its descent at 10:10, passed through the icing band without apparent difficulty, and at 10:18 was cleared for final approach. A minute later, at 3,500 feet, the plane began to drift away from its approach to the runway. [88]

The final NTSB report, issued on November 18, concluded it was not the weather, after all, nor the airplane: the crash was due to pilot error. According to the NTSB, the flight crew had stalled the plane by flying too slowly. The *King Air* had rapidly lost altitude, veered sharply off course, and crashed two-and-a-half miles short of the runway. The NTSB's Director of Traffic Safety postulated that the plane was flying too high and too fast as it began its final approach and the aircrew carelessly allowed the plane to slow down too much to compensate for their mistake. The plane went from 190 mph to 87 mph, the stall speed, in the final 90 seconds of the flight.[89] Had the stall-warning horn malfunctioned?

The NTSB report overlooked several eyewitness reports from the Eveleth area. These accounts indicated that both engines cut out just as the plane began to nosedive into the trees, clearly not how an airplane reacts to a stall. Several people observed two strange happenings at the same time as the engines stopped: triggering of automatic garage-door openers and unusual cell-phone activity. Both are traceable to small electromagnetic pulses. If such a pulse occurred aboard the plane, every instrument-panel indicator would go haywire. Sophisticated ground-based equipment could produce electromagnetic pulses, precisely the CIA's cup-of-tea.

A second item in the news stories was mention of the ultra-rapid arrival on the scene of an FBI rapid-response team. The FBI was at the crash site no later than 1PM. These investigators immediately ruled out sabotage. How could they possibly come to that conclusion so soon when the wreckage, still smoldering, was spread out over a wide area in a swamp? Why was the FBI on the scene before the NTSB and why was the FBI permitted to investigate? A cover-up, perhaps? The protocol for investigations of fatalities in airplane accidents is straightforward: the NTSB has primacy. Until their investigators arrive, other government agencies may only protect the site and do what is necessary to save lives.

The first report that Wellstone's plane had crashed was at 11:15AM. Official confirmation of his death came at 12:10. The NTSB arrived on the scene at 8:15PM, *eight to nine hours later*. NSTB investigators are on call 24-7. Why did it take so long? It is well known that the FBI and the NTSB partner up on aviation accidents. Critics suggest this partnership is useful when the government chooses to cover-up details of a plane crash.

Acting Chair of the NTSB, Carol Carmody, was in charge of the investigation. A look into her background shows her selection was suspect. A former CIA operative, she had chaired the hearing on the crash of American Airlines Flight 587 on November 12, 2001 and the subsequent controversial findings. The official NSTB report stated at that time that the cause AA Flight 587 crash was the pilot's overuse of the A300-600 Airbus's rudder to counter wake turbulence—i.e., pilot error, always a convenient scapegoat; the smoke and fire resulted from fuel leakage as the engines separated from the wings due to engine compressor surges.[90]

More importantly, Carmody was also on the scene of the aircraft "accident" that killed liberal Democrat Mel Carnahan, Governor of Missouri, on October 16, 2000. Carnahan, like Wellstone, was a leader of the progressive branch of the Democratic Party. He was one of the most popular governors in that state's history and his background of liberal leadership marked him as a strong opponent of the Republican Party on the national stage.

Carnahan was aboard a twin piston-engine Cessna 335, along with his son, Roger, who was the pilot, and an aide. It was a rainy night and the pilot chose to fly under instrument flight rules for extra safety. During the flight, the pilot told the air traffic controller he was experiencing minor problems with his attitude indicator. At 7:32PM, the pilot lost all contact with the ground controller and shortly thereafter the plane disappeared from the radar at Jefferson City, Missouri, the plane's destination. The plane descended 6,500 feet in 77 seconds—a steep dive—between last contact and impact.

The NTSB concluded that the probable cause of this accident was the pilot's failure to control the airplane while maneuvering due to spatial disorientation—pilot error!—and that failure of the plane's attitude indicator and weather-related turbulence were contributory causes. Excluded from the report were eyewitness accounts of a "bright flash" in the vicinity of the Cessna at the time of the crash. This "flash" was attributed to lightning—but the National Weather Service reported that a lightning strike was extremely unlikely at the time and place of the crash.

WHY ALL THE HULLABALOO? Fatal airplane crashes occur every day. What was so special about Paul Wellstone's "accidental" death is that it was *political assassination!* In every criminal investigation, the prosecutor seeks out the individual or individuals who had the most to gain by the victim's death—*Cui bono*? That person was almost certainly W. He had his own personal army, the CIA, to carry out his orders. At the time of the crash, 69% of Minnesotans polled said they believed a "GOP Conspiracy" was guilty of Wellstone's death.

Wellstone was at the top of the White House's enemies list, for a long list of reasons. Among them: he was the Senate's most outspoken critic of the repressive USA PATRIOT ACT; he was skeptical of the intelligence supporting the 9/11 attacks; he had voted against the Iraqi war resolution; he was chairman of the new Securities Reform Committee; he was attempting to block the nomination of William Webster, a "best friend" of big business and big accounting firms, to be the new chairman of the SEC's Accounting Oversight Commission; he was outspokenly critical of U.S. involvement in Colombia. More broadly, with the Senate controlled by the Democrats by a margin of 50-49, the loss of even a single seat could shift control to the Republicans.

A last reason to do away with him: Wellstone was in the midst of a hotly contested reelection campaign and the latest polls showed he was finally pulling ahead of the Republican nominee. Government conspirators would soon arrange to destroy two skyscrapers, shoot down a commercial airliner, and launch a missile at the Pentagon, and kill over 3,000 American civilians in a single day. Why should they hesitate to destroy three little airplanes and their thirteen occupants?

Notes [B33]

[1] In addition to Kean and Hamilton there were eight other Commission Members: Richard Ben-Veniste, Fred F. Fielding, James S. Gorelick, Slade Gordon, Bob Kerry, John F. Lehman, Timothy J. Roemer, and James R. Thompson.

[2] The Report was available in bookstores the third week of July 2004 and was nominated for a Pulitzer Prize in Literature.

[3] David Ray Griffin, *The 9/11 Commission Report: Omissions and Distortions*, (Olive Branch Press, Northhampton MA, 2005), p. 277.

[4] Ibid., p. 291.

[5] Jacob Feld, *Construction Failure* (John Wiley & Sons, Inc., New York, 1968), p. 5.

[6] Griffin, p. 8.

[7] Paul Sperry, "Is Fix in at 911 Commission?"

[8] Griffin, p. 7.

[9] Ibid., p. 10.

[10] Philip Shenon, *The Commission: The Uncensored History of the 9/11 Investigation* (Twelve, New York, 2008), p. 12.

[11] Ibid., p. 13.

[12] Ibid.

[13] Investigator Jim Marrs lists other steel-framed high-rise office buildings that experienced large fires—that did not collapse: "In 1988, a fire in the First Interstate Bank Building in Los Angeles raged for 3.5 hours and gutted 5 of the building's 62 floors, but there was no significant structural damage. In 1991, a huge fire in Philadelphia's One Meridian Plaza last for 18 hours and gutted 8 of the building's 38 floors, but, said the FEMA report, although 'beams and girders sagged and twisted... the columns continued to support their loads without obvious damage.' In Caracas, Venezuela in 2004, a fire in a 50-story building raged for 17 hours, completely gutting the building's top 20 floors, and yet it did not collapse... Unlike the fires in the towers, moreover, the fires in Los Angeles, Philadelphia, and Caracas were hot enough to break windows." Jim Marrs, *The Terror Conspiracy: Deception, 9/11, and the Loss of Liberty* (Disinformation Company, Ltd., 2006,) p. 58-59.

[14] Rowland Morgan and Ian Henshall, *9/11 Revealed: The Unanswered Questions* (Carroll & Graf Publishers, New York, 2005), p. 94.

[15] Ibid.

[16] David Ray Griffin, *The New Pearl Harbor: Disturbing Questions about the Bush Administration and 9/11* (Olive Branch Press, Northhampton MA, 2004), p. 13.

[17] Marvin P. Bush, the president's younger brother, was a principal in Securacom, the company that furnished security for the entire World Trade Center complex. Wirt D. Walker III, a cousin of Marvin P. and George W. Bush, was also a principal in the company, which later was renamed Stratesec. Walker had been the CEO of the company from 1999 to January 2002.

[18] Marrs, *The Terror Conspiracy*, p. 48.

[19] Ibid., p. 43.

[20] Ibid.

[21] Carl T. Furlong and Gordon Ross, "Seismic Proof—9/11 Was an Inside Job." Technical paper.

[22] Marrs, *The Terror Conspiracy*, p. 46.

[23] Ibid., p. 46-47.

[24] In 2006, Jones teamed with James H. Fetzer, Distinguished McKnight University Professor of Philosophy at the University of Minnesota, to found "Scholars for 9/11 Truth." These renowned co-

[25] Marrs, p. 69-70.
[26] Morgan and Henshall, p. 68.
[27] Ibid.
[28] While a modern airliner is mostly aluminum alloy for weight-saving, parts of the heavily-stressed landing gear are steel for strength, and the "hot" parts of the turbojet engines—from the combustion chamber aft to the exhaust nozzle—are by necessity high-temperature steels. These "hot" parts include the turbine discs and their "buckets" that are directly in line with the super-hot gases from the combustion chamber. It is inconceivable that these components would be destroyed in a fire that they were designed to resist during operation.
[29] Griffin, *The 9/11 Commission*, p. 117.
[30] 5-WTC and 6-WTC, low-rise buildings, also suffered explosions and severe fires which were not addressed by the Commission.
[31] Marrs, p. 61.
[32] Morgan and Henshall, p. 105.
[33] Ibid., p. 106.
[34] Furlong and Ross, p. 12.
[35] The transponder is a combination radio transmitter and receiver which sends out signals announcing each flight's airline name and flight number, and thus indicates the plane's position. For flight controllers on the ground in busy aviation corridors, these transponder signals are an important supplement to radar.
[36] Griffin, *The New Pearl Harbor*, p. 4.
[37] Griffin, *The 9/11 Commission*, p. 140.
[38] Ibid.
[39] Ibid., p. 168.
[40] "Full blower" is the USAF slang term for maximum power—and maximum speed—to be coaxed from the engines through use of the engines' afterburners.
[41] Stan Goff, "The So-Called Evidence is a Farce," Narco News #14: October 10, 2001.
[42] Griffin, The 9/11 Commission, p. 157.
[43] Ibid., p. 158.
[44] Michael C. Ruppert, *Crossing the Rubicon: 9/11 and the Decline of the American Empire at the End of the Age of Oil* (New Society Publishers, Gabriola Island, BC, Canada, 2004), p. 351.
[45] Webster Griffin Tarpley, *9/11: Synthetic Terror Made in USA* (Progressive Press, Joshua Tree CA, 2005), p. 253.
[46] Ibid., p. 91.
[47] Thierry Meyssan, *Pentagate* (Carnot Publishing Ltd., London, 2002), p. 52.
[48] *Operation Northwoods*: "An aircraft at Eglin AFB would be painted and numbered as an exact duplication of a civil registered aircraft belonging to a CIA proprietary organization in the Miami area. At a designated time the duplication would be substituted for the actual civil aircraft and would be loaded with the selected passengers, all board under carefully aliases. The actual registered aircraft would be converted to a drone. Take-off times of the drone aircraft and the actual aircraft will be scheduled to allow a rendezvous south of Florida. From the rendezvous point the passenger-carrying aircraft will descend to a minimum altitude [to slip under civil ground-based radar] and go directly to an auxiliary field at Eglin AFB where arrangements will have been made to evacuate the passengers and return the aircraft to its original status. The drone aircraft [empty except for explosives wired to go off by remote signal] meanwhile will continue to fly the filed flight plan. When over Cuba the drone will be transmitting on the international distress frequency a "MAY DAY' message stating he is under attack by Cuban MiG aircraft. The transmission will be interrupted by destruction of the aircraft which will be triggered by radio signal." Griffin, *The New Pearl* Harbor, p. 102-103.

[49] Morgan and Henshall, p. 146.
[50] Griffin, *The New Pearl Harbor*, p. 49-50.
[51] Ibid., p. 50.
[52] Morgan and Henshall, p. 152
[53] Ibid.
[54] Griffin, *The New Pearl Harbor*, p. 51.
[55] Tarpley, p. 263.
[56] Ibid., p. 270.
[57] Griffin, *The New Pearl Harbor*, p. 53.
[58] Tarpley, p. 263.
[59] October 7, 2001 marked the first *public* operational deployment of *Global Hawk*, a high-altitude, long endurance, unmanned air vehicle (UAV)—a pilotless drone that can take off, perform missions such as battlefield reconnaissance, return to its base and land, all the while under remote electronic control. One version of *Global Hawk* is powered by a turbojet engine, has a wingspan of a Boeing 737 airliner, has a publicly announced range of 14,000 nautical miles, and can fly at altitudes of up to 65,000 feet for about 40 hours. According to Australia's Defence Science and Technology Organisation, "*Global Hawk* flew nonstop from Edwards AFB, California, to Edinburgh AFB, South Australia, becoming the first unmanned aircraft to fly nonstop across the Pacific Ocean (in 23 hours and 20 minutes). Jim Marrs, *Inside Job: Unmasking the 9/11 Conspiracies* (Origin Press, San Raphael CA) 2004, 108. In an interview with former German secretary of defense Andreas von Buelow in January 2002, the newspaper *Tagesspiegel* noted: "There is also the theory... that the steering of the planes was perhaps taken out of the pilots' hand from the outside." The Americans had developed a method in the 1970s whereby they could rescue hijacked planes by intervening into the computer piloting [the electronic flight system]. Several researchers have gone on record as stating that *Lufthansa*, Germany's national airline, had been aware of "electronic capture," and quietly stripped the flight control systems of American-built jetliners delivered to Germany. The *Global Hawk* hypothesis can also be used to explain one of the anomalies of the 9/11 hijackings. None of the transponders in the planes ever broadcast the coded message telling ground controllers that the aircraft had been hijacked. This could have meant that *Global Hawk* operated by taking over the transponder channel and monopolizing it for the purpose of controlling the plane.
[60] Tarpley, p. 109.
[61] Wayne Barrett and Dan Collins, *Grand Illusion: The Untold Story of Rudy Giuliani and 9/11* (Harper Collins Publishers, New York, 2006), p. 24-25.
[62] Griffin, *The New Pearl*, p. 128.
[63] Ibid.
[64] Ibid.
[65] Marrs, *The Terror Conspiracy*, p. 299.
[66] Ibid., p. 300.
[67] Ibid., p. 299.
[68] Griffin, *The 9/11 Commission Report: Omissions*, p. 117.
[69] Ibid., p. 118.
[70] *The 9/11 Commission Report: Final Report of the National Commission on Terrorist Attacks Upon the United States* (W.W. Norton & Company, New York), p. 160.
[71] Daniel Hopsicker, *Welcome to Terrorland: Mohammed Atta and the 9/11 Coverup in Florida* (Common Courage Press, Monroe ME, 2003), p. 8.
[72] Michael Moore, *Dude, Where's My Country* (Seven Stories Press, New York, 2003), p. 2.
[73] Douglas Kellner, *From 9/11 to Terror War: The Dangers of the Bush Legacy* (Rowman & Littlefield Publishers, Inc., New York, 2003), p. 67.
[74] Fox is owned by Australian ultra-conservative Rupert Murdoch, run by Republican spinmeister Roger Ailes, and features far-right Bill O'Reilly as anchor five nights a week on his "No Spin Zone" TV show. O'Reilly himself and guests—"bellicose, barely literate military 'analysts' who parrot the Pentagon's

line of the day, and antiterrorist 'experts' who outdo each other with belligerence and hostililty" are a parody of 'no spin.' Ibid., p. 167.
[75] Ibid.
[76] Rahul Mahajan, *The New Crusade: America's War on Terrorism* (Monthly Review Press, New York, 2002), p. 108.
[77] Ibid.
[78] *Scientific American*, October 9, 2001.
[79] "When the Twin Towers Fell: One month after the attack on the World Trade Center, M.I.T. structural engineers offer their take on how and why the towers came down," *Scientific American*, October 9, 2001.
[80] Eric Hufschmid, *Painful Questions: An Analysis of the September 11th Attack* (Endpoint Software, Goleta CA, 2002).
[81] Robert B Stinnett, *Day of Deceit: The Truth About FDR and Pearl Harbor* (Simon & Schuster, New York, 2000) and Stewart Halsey Ross, *How Roosevelt Failed America in World War II* (McFarland Publishing Company, Inc, Jefferson NC, 2006).
[82] See "9/11 and Terrorism" in Bibliography
[83] Tarpley, p. 193-195.
[84] Ibid., p. 322.
[85] *New York Times* Magazine, January 28, 2007, p. 16.
[86] Recorded in October 2001 by American journalist and peace advocate Geov Parrish, based on refugee testimony and reports from Western and Pakistani journalists. Cited in *The War on Freedom*, p. 252-253.
[87] Morgan and Henshall, p. 231.
[88] Rahul Mahajan, *Full Spectrum Dominance: U.S. Power in Iraq and Beyond* (Seven Stories Press, New York, 2006), p. 42.
[89] Ibid., p. 42-43.
[90] Four Arrows and James H. Fetzer, *American Assassination: The Strange Death of Senator Paul Wellstone* (Vox Pop, Brooklyn, New York, 2004), p. 6
[91] Ibid., p. 7.
[92] Washington DC, Associated Press, November 18, 2003.
[93] The crash of AA Flight 587, just after takeoff from Kennedy Airport, was witnessed by hundreds of people, who gave conflicting accounts of what they observed. Many reported seeing a fire or explosion before the plane hit the ground. On April 8, 2005, Rockaway, New York's local newspaper, *The Wave*, wrote an editorial titled "Getting Harder to Maintain the Fiction on AA 587." The editorial reminded its readers that, according to the NTSB, First Officer Sten Molin, who was flying departure from JFK the day of the disaster, "unnecessarily and aggressively" over-controlled the rudder of the aircraft as he encountered turbulence from the airplane in front. According to *The Wave*, "even many pilots scoffed at the report." At the time, an official of the Airline Pilot's Association said, 'Building a plane where the tail falls off if you over-control the rudder is like building a car where the wheels fall off every time you hit the brakes too hard.'

Chapter XII:
Epilogue

"One wonders how the decisions made in the past sixty years in the office of the secretary of defense... would have been altered if, before issuing their orders, the leaders of the nation's military establishment had been required to adjourn for the few moments it would have taken to mount the ridge of Arlington, to look across the hillsides salted with headstones... Operation Pointblank, Los Alamos, the Truman decision, the Truman Doctrine, the atomic bomb, NSC-68, Korea, the hydrogen bomb, the Gaither Report, the missile gap, Berlin, Cuba, mutual assured destruction, Vietnam, the antiballistic missile, the Dominican Republic, the Mayaguez, the Iran hostage rescue attempt, the Carter Doctrine, Lebanon, El Salvador, Grenada, Star Wars, Reykjavik, Panama, the first Gulf War, gays in the military, Somalia, the Nuclear Posture Review, the Balkan Wars, NATO expansion, Afghanistan, the Global War on Terror; preventive war, Iraq, Abu Gharab, Guantanamo, the high frontier, nuclear resumption, force projection, mission accomplished."[1]

"ON SUCH A GOLDEN DAY as this, there should have been beach umbrellas and barefoot children, building sand castles with tunnels and moats to catch the tide, and mothers reading and gossiping, but now there was no audience for the dancing of the waves or the clowning of the wind. Now there was only the earth itself and the sunlight and the wind that had never ceased to blow since the bombs fell. What a dear world it had been! Had I been an exception to think so? Had most people hated life, with or without cause. They must have hated it or they could not have endured the prospect of ending it with eyes open as to what was coming for years before it came. Why was the nation with the highest standard of material comfort for every citizen the one that hated life the most, and so dropped the first atomic bomb ...?"[2]

"A really great people, proud and high-spirited, would face all the disasters of war rather than purchase that base prosperity which is bought at the price of national honor. All the great masterful races have been fighting races, and the minute a race loses the hard-fighting virtues... it has lost its proud right to stand as the equal of the best... No triumph of peace is quite so great as the supreme triumphs of war."[3]

"MAY I COME WITH YOU, in the submarine?" She paused, and then she said, "I don't believe that I'll have anything at home to come back to..." "I've been asked the same thing by four men this morning," he said. "I've run this vessel in the Navy way right through, and I'm running her that way up till the end. I can't take you honey..." He took her in his arms and kissed her, and she clung to him for a minute.

"What time are you leaving? "Very soon, "he said. "We'll be casting off in about five minutes." "What time will you be sinking her?" she asked. "Thirty miles down the bay and then twelve miles out, Forty-two sea miles..." She nodded slowly... "Go now, Dwight. Maybe I'll see you in Connecticut one day."

She watched as Dwight appeared on the bridge from the interior of the submarine and took the con, watched as the lower end of the gangway was released, as the mooring lines were singled up. She saw the stern line and the spring cast off, watched as Dwight spoke into the voice pipe giving orders for the crew below, watched the water churn beneath her stern as the propellers ran slow ahead and the stern swung out. The bow line and spring were cast off and the crew coiled them down and slammed the steel hatch of the superstructure shut as the submarine went slow astern in a great arc away from the carrier. Then they all vanished down below, and only Dwight and another officer remained on the bridge. He lifted his hand in salutation to her, and she lifted hers to him, her eyes blurred with tears, and the low hull of the vessel swung away around Point Gellibrand and vanished in the murk...

The sea lay before her, grey and rough with great rollers coming in from the south on to the rocky beach below... She parked across the road in full view of the sea, got out of her car, took another drink from her bottle, and scanned the horizon for the submarine. Then as she turned toward the lighthouse on Point Lonsdale and the entrance to Port Phillip Bay she saw the low grey shape appear, barely five miles away and heading southwards from the Heads.

She could not see detail but she knew that Dwight was there on the bridge, taking his ship out on her last cruise. She knew he could not see her and he could not know she was watching, but she waved to him. Then she got back into the car because the wind was raw and chilly from south polar regions, and she was feeling very ill, and she could watch him just as well when sitting down in shelter.

This was the very end of it, the very, very end... Then she put the tablets in her mouth and swallowed them down with a mouthful of brandy, sitting behind the wheel of her big car."[4]

"An unprejudiced observer from another planet, looking upon man as he is today, in his hand the atomic bomb, the product of his intelligence, in his heart the aggressive drive inherited from his anthropoid ancestors, which this same intelligence cannot control, would not prophesy long life for the species."[5]

THE AFTERMATH OF A NUCLEAR WAR, immediate and short-term, will not be nearly as romantic as the exchange between Gregory Peck and Ava Gardner,[6] nor quite so antiseptic. Five authoritative American scientists, including well-known Carl Sagan, collaborated on an article that concluded that the long-term climatic effects in the aftermath of a major nuclear war would likely to be much more severe and farther-reaching than had been supposed. Following such a war vast areas of the earth would be subjected to prolonged darkness, abnormally low temperatures, violent windstorms, toxic smog and persistent radioactive fallout—in short, the combination of conditions that has come to be known as "nuclear winter." Insofar as the effects of a nuclear war originating in the Northern Hemisphere extending into the Southern Hemisphere, the authors postulated grimly:

"Even in regions far from the conflict the survivors would be imperiled by starvation, hypothermia, radiation sickness, weakening of the immune system, epidemics and other dire consequences. Under some circumstances, a number of biologists and ecologists contend, the extinction of many species or organisms—including the human species—is a real possibility."[7]

"In October 1962, President John Kennedy chose a path of action that in his judgment, entailed a one-in-three chance of nuclear war... Given the potential consequences, how could he have possibly chosen this course?"[8]

The scenario is likely to be this for Americans: Nuclear warheads (if launched from silos inside Russia or China, for example) will explode over U.S. cities about thirty minutes later. If they are submarine-launched they will reach their targets sooner. During this brief interval, U.S. early-warning satellites will trigger signals of the attack to a command center inside a mountain in Colorado and to the president. He has to decide immediately whether to launch a counterattack. He does so—and outward bound U.S. ballistic missiles pass incoming missiles in near-space.

The nuclear weapons arrive over U.S. cities at hypersonic speed; those asleep will die merciful deaths. The most powerful of the bombs will churn up craters 200 feet deep and 1,000 feet in diameter if fused to detonate on impact. However, most will be purposefully fused to explode above ground, creating far more destruction. From the epicenter of each explosion reaching out miles in all directions all ordinary wood-frame structures will be incinerated along with their occupants. Those not instantly killed will be burned so severely they will die in agony in hours. Fifty miles away, those unfortunate enough to have glanced at the gigantic flash will be blinded at once.

Enormous firestorms will envelop all of the suburbs of even the largest cities, fanned by mega-hurricane winds spawned by the explosion. Those in basements or other protective shelters will be mercifully asphyxiated as the gigantic fires inhale the oxygen from inside their pitifully inadequate shelters.

The giant mushroom clouds, cauldrons of radioactive particulates, will boil up thousands of feet. The area of immediate lethal fallout from these clouds will cover thousands of square miles. People not burned terribly or crushed in their collapsing homes, office buildings, or factories will receive killing doses of radiation. With most hospitals destroyed and few physicians left to provide even rudimentary palliative medical care, burn victims by the hundreds of thousands, in intractable pain, will envy the dead.

Medium-term, diseases are certain to claim those still alive.

> Millions of decaying bodies—human and animal alike—will rot, infected with viruses and bacteria that will mutate in the radioactive environment to become more lethal. Trillions of insects, naturally resistant to radiation—flies, fleas, cockroaches, and lice—will transmit diseases from the dead to the living.... Epidemics of diseases now controlled by immunization and good hygiene will reappear: measles, polio, typhoid, cholera, whooping cough, diphtheria, smallpox, plague, tuberculosis, meningitis, malaria, and hepatitis.[9]

Lastly, the destruction of the environment of the planet earth, the dread culmination of a nuclear-weapons exchange: nuclear winter. The firestorms will consume all burnable materials and blanket the globe with a thick, black mantle of radioactive smoke and dust, sharply reducing the sunlight that falls on the earth. Worst-case scenarios point to one year or more before sunlight returns to normal. During this period of darkness, subfreezing temperatures will almost certainly destroy humankind's biological support system.[10]

> *On November 1, 1952, the U.S. conducted its first test of a full-scale thermonuclear device, or hydrogen bomb. The site was Elugelab Island, a low-lying projection of the Eniwetok Atoll in the Marshall Islands in the Pacific. The apparatus, code-named Mike, exploded with a power the equal of 12 million tons of TNT—and a new word megaton, was added to man's war vocabulary The detonation was estimated to have equaled the explosive power equivalent of TNT that could be packed in a line of standard-size railroad boxcars stretching from Chicago to San Francisco, about 2000 miles. Not to be outdone and relegated to the "dust-bin of history" as Soviet Premier Nikita Khruschev famously said, on October 30, 1961 the Soviet Union exploded a hydrogen bomb developing an estimated 58 megatons of explosive power.*

> *"After ages during which the earth produced harmless trilobites and butterflies, evolution progressed to the point at which it has generated Neros, Genghis Khans, and Hitlers. This, however, I believe is a passing nightmare; in time the earth will become again incapable of supporting life, and peace will return."*[11]

Notes

[1] James Carroll, *House of War: The Pentagon and the Disastrous Rise of American Power* (Houghton Mifflin Company, New York, 2006).

[2] Helen Clarkson, *The Last Day: A Novel of the Day After Tomorrow* (Dodd, Mead & Company, New York, 1959), p. 178-179. Fiction.

[3] Theodore Roosevelt, *"A Navy Second to None"* Speech to Navy League, 1904.

[4] Neville Shute, *On the Beach* (Heinemann, London) 1957, p. 308-312. The novel is a poignant interpretation of the end of mankind. Dwight, the U.S. Navy nuclear-powered submarine captain from Connecticut and the woman from Australia who has come to love him, have been awaiting the "arrival" of radiation-filled clouds from the north that will extinguish all remaining life on earth. The two decide not to wait. Finis!

[5] Konrad Lorenz, *On Aggression* (MJF Books, New York, 1997).

[6] In the motion picture *On the Beach*, Gregory Peck was the U.S. submarine captain and Ava Gardner was his Australian lover.

[7] Scientific American, August 1984, p. 33-43.

[8] Robert F. Kennedy, *Thirteen Days: A Memoir of the Cuban Missile Crisis* (W.W. Norton & Company, New York, 1971).

[9] Helen Caldicott, *The New Nuclear Danger: George W. Bush's Military-Industrial Complex* (The New Press, New York), p. 10.

[10] Ibid., p. 11.

[11] Cited by Judith Toth, *Bertrand Russell Quarterly*, February 2003.

Appendices

1. A History of Interventions by U.S. Armed Forces in the Western Hemisphere, 1806-1933

Prepared by the Foreign Affairs Division, Congressional Research Service, Library of Congress, U.S. Government Printing Office, Washington DC, 1975. As reprinted in William Blum, *Killing Hope: U.S. Military and CIA Interventions Since World War II*, p. 444-452.

1806 Mexico (Spanish territory): Captain Z. M. Pike invaded Spanish territory at the headwaters of the Rio Grande. He was made a prisoner without resistance at a fort he constructed in present-day Colorado, taken to Mexico, and later released.

1806-1810 Gulf of Mexico: American gunboats operated from New Orleans against Spanish and French privateers off the Mississippi Delta.

1810 West Florida (Spanish territory): Gov. Clairborne of Louisiana occupied territory in dispute east of Mississippi as far as Pearl River, later the eastern boundary of Louisiana. No armed clash.

1812 Amelia Island and other parts of east Florida then under Spain: Temporary possession was authorized to prevent occupation by any other power.

1812-1815 Great Britain: War of 1812 was formally declared.

1813 West Florida (Spanish territory): General Wilkinson seized Mobile Bay in April, a small Spanish garrison giving way. Thus the U.S. advanced into disputed territory to the Perdido River. No fighting.

1814 Spanish Florida: General Andrew Jackson took Pensacola and drove out the British with whom the U.S. was at war.

1814-1825 Caribbean: Engagements between pirates and American ships took place repeatedly ashore and offshore about Cuba, Puerto Rico, Santo Domingo, and Yucatan. Three thousand pirate attacks on merchantmn were reported between 1815 and 1823.

1816 Spanish Florida: U.S. forces destroyed Nicholls Fort which has harbored raiders into U.S. territory.

1816-1823 Spanish Florida-First Seminole War: The Seminole Indians, who territory was a haven for escaped slaves, were attacked by troops under Generals Jackson and Gaines. Spanish posts were attacked and occupied and British citizens executed.

1817 Amelia Island: U.S. forces landed and expelled a group of smugglers and freebooters.

1818 Oregon: The U.S.S. *Ontario* landed at the Columbia River and in August took possession. Britain had conceded sovereignty but Russia and Spain asserted claims to the area.

1822 Cuba: U.S. naval force suppressing piracy landed on the northwest coast of Cuba and burned a pirate station.

1823 Cuba: Brief landings in pursuit of pirates on April 8 near Escondido; April 16 near Cayo Blanco; July 11 at Siquapa Bay; July 21 at Cape Cruz; and October 23 at Camrioca.

Appendices

1824 Cuba: In October the U.S.S. *Porpoise* landed sailors near Matanzas in pursuit of pirates.

1824 Puerto Rico (Spanish Territory): Commodore David Porter with a landing party attacked the town of Fajardo which had sheltered pirates and insulted U.S. naval officers. In November, Porter landed with 200 men and forced an apology.

1825 Cuba: In March with cooperating U.S. and British forces landed at Sagua La Grande to capture pirates.

1833 Argentina: October 31 to November 15: A force was sent ashore at Buenos Aires to protect the interests of the U.S. and others during an insurrection.

1835-1836 Peru: December 10, 1835, to January 24, 1836; and August 21, 1836 to December 7, 1836: Marines protected American interests in Callao and Lima during an attempted revolution.

1836 Mexico: General Gaines occupied Nacogdoches, Texas, disputed territory from July to December during the Texas war for independence.

1842 Mexico: Commodore T.A.C. Jones, in command of a squadron cruising off California, occupied Monterey on October 19 believing war had come. He discovered peace, saluted and withdrew.

1844 Mexico: President Tyler deployed U.S. forces to protect Texas against Mexico, pending Senate approval of a treaty of annexation. (Later rejected.)

1846-1848 Mexico: The Mexican War. President Polk's occupation of disputed territory precipitated the war. War formally declared.

1852-1853 Argentina: February 3 to 12, 1852; September 17, 1852 to April, 1853: Marines were landed and occupied Buenos Aires to protect U.S. interests during a revolution.

1853 Nicaragua: March 11 to 13: To protect U.S. lives and interests during a political disturbance.

1854 Nicaragua: July 9 to 15: San Juan del Norte was destroyed to avenge an insult to the U.S. minister to Nicaragua.

1855 Uruguay: November 25 to 30: U.S. and European naval forces landed to protect U.S. interests during an attempted revolution in Montevideo.

1856 Panama: September 19 to 22: To protect U.S. interests during an insurrection.

1857 Nicaragua: April to May, November to December: To oppose William Walker's attempt to gain control of the country.

1858 Uruguay: January 2 to 27: Forces from two U.S. warships landed to protect American property during a revolution in Montevideo.

1859 Paraguay: Congress authorized a naval squadron to seek redress for an attack on a U.S. warship in the Parana River during 1855.

1859 Mexico: Two hundred U.S. soldiers crossed the Rio Grande in pursuit of the Mexican bandit Cortina.

1860 Colombia: September 27 to October 8: To protect U.S. interests during a revolution.

1865 Panama: March 9 and 10: To protect the lives and properties of U.S. residents during a revolution.

1866 Mexico: To protect American residents, General Sedgwick and 100 men in November obtained surrender of Matamoras. After three days, he was ordered to withdraw, his act repudiated by the president.

1867 Nicaragua: Marines occupied Managua and Leon.

1868 Uruguay: February 7 and 8, 19 to 26: To protect foreign residents and the customhouse during an insurrection in Montevideo.

1868 Colombia: April 7 at Aspinwall: To protect passengers and treasure in transit on the occasion of the death of the president of Colombia.

1870 Mexico: June 17 and 18: To destroy the pirate ship *Forward*, which had been run aground up the Rio Tecapan.

1873 Colombia: May 7 to 22, September 23 to October 9: To protect American interests during hostilities over possession of the government of the State of Panama.

1873 Mexico: U.S. troops crossed the Mexican border repeatedly in pursuit of cattle thieves. Agreements between Mexico and the U.S., the first in 1882, finally legitimized such raids. They continued, with minor disputes, until 1896.

1876 Mexico: February 12 to 20: To police the town of Matamoros temporarily while it was without other government.

1885 Panama: January 18 and 19: To guard the valuables in transit over the Panama Railroad and its safes and vaults during revolutionary activity.

1888 Haiti: December 20: To persuade the Haitian government to surrender an American steamer, which had been seized on the charge of "breach of blockade".

1890 Argentina: A naval party was landed to protect U.S. consulate and legation in Buenos Aires.

1891 Haiti: To protect U.S. lives and property on Navasaa Island.

1891 Chile: August 28 to 30: To protect the U.S. consulate and the women and children who had taken refuge in it during a revolution in Valparaiso.

1894 Brazil: January: To protect American commerce and shipping at Rio de Janeiro during a civil war. No landing was attempted but there was a display of naval force.

1894 Nicaragua: July 6 to August 7: To protect U.S. interests at Bluefields following a revolution.

1895 Colombia: March 8 and 9: To protect American interests during an attack on the town of Bocas del Toro by a bandit chieftain.

1896 Nicaragua: May 2 to 4: To safeguard U.S. interests in Corinto during political unrest.

1898 Nicaragua: February 7 and 8: To protect American lives and property at San Juan del Sur.

1898 The Spanish War: Fully declared.

1899 Nicaragua: To protect American interests at San Juan del Norte, February 22 to March 5, and at Bluefields a few weeks later in connection with the insurrection of General Juan P. Reyes.

1901 Colombia (State of Panama): November 20 to December 4: To protect American property on the Isthmus and to keep transit lines open during serious revolutionary disturbances.

Appendices

1902 Colombia: April 16 to 23: To protect American lives and property at Bocas del Toro during a civil war.

1902 Colombia: September 17 to November 18: To place armed guards on all trains crossing the Isthmus and to keep the railroad line open.

1903 Honduras: March 23 to 31: To protect the American consulate and the steamship wharf at Puerto Cortez during a period of revolutionary activity.

1903 Dominican Republic: March 30 to April 21: To protect American interests in the city of Santo Domingo during a revolutionary outbreak.

1903-1914 Panama: To protect American interest and lives during the revolution for independence from Colombia over the construction of the Isthmian Canal. With brief intermissions, Marines were stationed on the Isthmus from November 4, 1903 to January 21, 1914 to guard American interests.

1904 Dominican Republic: January 2 to February 11: To protect American interests in Puerto Plata and Sosua and Santo Domingo City during revolutionary fighting.

1904 Panama: November 17 to 24: To protect American lives and property at Ancon at the time of a threatened insurrection.

1906-1909 Cuba: September 1906 to January 23, 1909: Intervention to restore order, protect foreigners, and establish a stable government after serious revolutionary activity.

1907 Honduras: March 18 to June 8: To protect American interests during a war between Honduras and Nicaragua. Troops were stationed for a few days or weeks in Trujillo, Ceiba, Puerto Cortez, San Pedro, Laguna and Choloma.

1910 Nicaragua: February 22: During a civil war, to get information on conditions at Corinto. May 19 to September 4, to protect American interest at Bluefields.

1911 Honduras: January 26 and some weeks thereafter: To protect American lives and interests during a civil war in Honduras.

1912 Honduras: Small force landed to prevent seizure by the Government of an American-owned railroad at Puerto Cortez. Forces withdrawn after the United States disapproved of the action.

1912 Panama: Troops, on request of both political parties, supervised elections outside the Canal Zone.

1912 Cuba: June 5 to August 5: To protect American interests in the Province of Oriente, and in Habana.

1912-1925 Nicaragua: August to November 1912: To protect American interests during an attempted revolution. A small force, serving as a legation guard and as a promoter of peace and governmental stability, remained until August 5, 1925.

1913 Mexico: September 5 to 7: A few Marines landed at Ciaris Estero to aid in evacuating American citizens from the Yaqui Valley, made dangerous for foreigners by civil strife.

1914 Haiti: January 29 to February 9, February 20 to 21, October 19: To protect American nationals in a time of dangerous unrest.

1914 Dominican Republic: June and July: During a revolutionary movement, United States naval by gunfire stopped the bombardment of Puerto Plata, and by threat of force maintained Santo Domingo City as a neutral zone.

1914-1917 Mexico: The undeclared Mexican-American hostilities following the *Dolphin* affair and Villa's raids included capture of Vera Cruz and later Pershing's expedition into northern Mexico.

1915-1934 Haiti: July 28, 1934, to August 15, 1934: To maintain order during a period of chronic and threatened insurrection.

1916-1924 Dominican Republic: May 1916 to September 1924: To maintain order during a period of chronic and threatened insurrection.

1917-1922 Cuba: To protect American interests during an insurrection and subsequent unsettled conditions. Most of the U.S. armed forces left Cuba by August 1919, but two companies remained at Camaguey until February 1922.

1918-1919 Mexico: After the withdrawal of the Pershing expedition, U.S. troops entered Mexico in pursuit of bandits at least three times in 1918 and six in 1919. In August 1918, American and Mexican troops fought at Nogales.

1918-1920 Panama: For police duty according to treaty stipulations, at Chiriqui, during election disturbances and subsequent unrest.

1919 Honduras: September 8 to 12: A landing force was sent ashore to maintain order in a neutral zone during an attempted revolution.

1920 Guatemala: April 9 to 27: To protect the American Legation and other American interests, such as the cable station, during a period of fighting between Unionists and the Government of Guatemala.

Appendices

1921 Panama-Costa Rica: American naval squadrons demonstrated in April on both sides of the Isthmus to prevent war between the two countries over a boundary dispute.

1924 Honduras: February 28 to March 31, September 10 to 15: To protect American lives and interests during election hostilities.

1925 Honduras: April 19 to 21: To protect foreigners at La Ceiba during a political upheaval.

1925 Panama: October 12 to 23: Strikes and rent riots led to the landing of about 600 American troops to keep order and protect American interests.

Prisoners in Nicaragua, Nov. 1928. Records of the U.S. Marine Corps, 1775 - 9999

1926-1933 Nicaragua: May 7 to June 5, 1926; August 27, 1926, to January 3, 1933: The *coup d'etat* of General Chamorro aroused revolutionary activities leading to the landing of American Marines to protect the interests of the U.S. U.S. forces came and went, but did not leave the country entirely until January 3, 1933. Their work included activity against the outlaw leader Sandino in 1928.

"One of our speed cars mounted with Heavy Browning Machine Gun to offset any possibility of rioting during the 1932 Presidential Elections in Nicaragua., 1927."
Records of the U.S. Marine Corps, 1775 - 9999.

1933 Cuba: During a revolution against President Gerardo Machado naval forces demonstrated but no landing was made.

2. America's First Red Scare, 1917-1921

On June 15, 1917, three months after Woodrow Wilson delivered his war message to Congress, Postmaster General Albert Sydney Burleson, the nation's chief censor, had the weapon he needed in his vendetta against those he perceived to be radicals, pacifists, and German-Americans—"hyphenates"—troublemakers in America's virtuous quest to build a new world order. It was the harsh Espionage Act and it called for fines of up to $10,000 and imprisonment for up to 20 years for a variety of broadly interpreted offenses: for example, "willful interference with the operation of the nation's military and naval forces; willful attempt to cause insubordination, disloyalty, mutiny, or refusal of duty."

Only once before in the nation's history had the Congress dated enact such a repressive law. That law was the 1798 Alien and Sedition Act, which gave the president the power to deport aliens he considered dangerous to the nation's "peace and safety." "False, scandalous, and malicious writings" directed at the president or the Congress were also subject under that act. When Thomas Jefferson took office as president in 1801, he pardoned all those imprisoned by the act and the Congress eventually repaid all fines. The 1917 law, reflecting a national phobia against "enemies from within," dealt more severe penalties, yet a unanimous Supreme Court decision upheld the Espionage Act as constitutional. Increasingly restrictive federal legislation followed that same year. On October 6, the

Appendices

Congress passed the Trading-with-the-Enemy Act, which authorized censorship of messages between the United States and foreign countries. One of its sections gave the federal government the aurthority to control all of the foreign-language press in the country.

Using as a subterfuge several gruesome examples of mob violence against anti-war agitators, the Senate Judiciary Committee on May 16, 1918, amended the Espionage Act by adding nine additional offenses. These amendments created what became known as the Sedition Act. It prohibited: disloyal, profane, scurrilous, or abusive language about the form of government of the United States, or the Constitution... or the military or naval forces... or the uniform of the army or navy... or any language intended to bring the form of government of the United States... into contempt, scorn, contumely, or disrepute."

Burleson wielded his power of censorship capriciously and ruthlessly. He cracked down on left-wing publications, although he "didn't know socialism from rheumatism" according to Socialist Norman Thomas. He cut off mailing privileges from a single issue of *The Masses* because it contained what he considered anti-government cartoons—and then refused to reinstate the publication's second-class mailing permit because it had missed an issue and was thus not a bonafide periodical

Woodrow Wilson gave free rein to his postmaster general. In the fall of 1917, the president asked Burleson if he did not agree "that we must act with the utmost caution and liberality in all our censorship." The president prefaced an inquiry about suppression of the Socialist *Milwaukee Leader* by timidly writing, "I am afraid you will be shocked, but I must say that I do not find this hearing very convincing." Only once did Wilson overrule a Burleson decision. That was when the postmaster general cut off the mailing privileges to the liberal *Nation* because of its criticism of the reactionary labor leader Samuel Gompers. Burleson maintained his choke-hold on the nation's media for two-and-a-half years after the Armistice, although Wilson had formally ended censorship on November 27, 1918. Like most Americans, he made a smooth transition from hatred of Germans, the former enemy, to hatred of Bolsheviks, the new enemy.

Senator Lee Slater Overman's Judiciary Subcommittee, "Brewing and Liquor Interests and German Propaganda," also made a seamless changeover. On February 4, 1919, the Senate unanimously passed a resolution extending the committee's investigation to focus on the new menace to the nation. At the same time, it pinned an expanded title on the upcoming hearings: "Brewing and Liquor Interests and German and Bolshevik Propaganda." What triggered the Senate action was the general strike called the day before in Seattle and the perceived threat of a Communist revolution on the west coast that could envelop the entire country.

Starting a week later, on the same day the Seattle strike collapsed—and running through March 10—the panel heard testimonies from 26 witnesses. Most of those who testified were fervent anti-Communists who told astonishing fables to the appropriately stern-faced Senators. There was near unanimity that Lenin and Trotsky were German agents financed by Germany; that the Red Army was mostly made up of criminals; that the Soviet government sponsored "free-love" clinics; and that those who opposed the new regime were summarily shot or hanged. A Russian émigré soberly testified that in the first year of Soviet rule the number of Russians killed, women and children included, by the Bolsheviks was twice that of all the Russian soldiers who had died on the war fronts from 1914 through 1917. Most sinister of all, the witnesses told the Senators that Bolshevism was anti-Christ. The panel saved the best witness for last, former ambassador to Russia, David R. Francis. Francis's anti-Soviet testimony did not disappoint the Senators.

Almost overnight, American patriots in and outside of government had manufactured a new bogeyman to fit the nation's imperial destiny—the godless Bolshevik, out to subvert everything the United States stood for. It was time for America to embark on a new propaganda crusade, which the nation would wage in earnest for most of the remainder of the twentieth century.

3. Woodrow Wilson's *Aide-Memoire* to Allied Ambassadors Regarding U.S. Intervention in Russia, July 17, 1918

"The whole hearts of the people of the United States is in the winning of this war. The controlling purpose of the Government of the United States is to do everything that is necessary and effective to win it. It wishes to cooperate in every practicable way with the Allied Governments, and to cooperate ungrudgingly; for it has no ends of its own to serve and believes that the war can be won only by common counsel and intimate concert of action. It has sought to study every proposed policy or action in which its cooperation has been asked in this spirit, and states the following conclusions in the confidence that, if it finds itself obliged to decline participation in any undertaking of course of action, it will be understood that it does so only because it deemed itself precluded from participating by imperative considerations either of policy or of fact.

"In full agreement with the Allied Governments and upon the unanimous advice of the Supreme War Council, the Government of the United States adopted, upon its entrance into the war, a plan for taking part in the fighting on the western front into which all its resources of men and material were to be put, and put as rapidly as possible, and it has carried out that plan with energy and success, pressing its execution more and more rapidly forward and literally putting into it the entire energy and executive force of the nation. This was its response, its very willing and hearty response, to what was the unhesitating judgment alike of its own military advisers and of the advisers of the Allied Governments. It is now considering, at the suggestion of the Supreme War Council, the possibility of making very considerable additions even to this immense program which, if they should prove feasible at all, will tax the industrial processes of the United States and the shipping facilities of the whole group of associated nations to the utmost. It has thus concentrated all its plans and all its resources upon this single absolutely necessary object.

"In such circumstances it feel it to be its duty to say that it cannot, so long as the military situation on the western front remains critical, consent to break or slacken the force of its present effort by diverting any part of its military force to other points or objectives. The United States is at a great distance from the field of action on the western front; it is at a much greater distance from any other field of action. The instrumentalities by which it is to handle its armies and its stores have at great cost and with great difficulty been created in France. They do not exist elsewhere. It is practicable for her to do a great deal in France; it is not practicable for her to do anything of importance or on a large scale upon any other field. The American Government, therefore, very respectfully requests its associates to accept its deliberate judgment that it should not dissipate its force by attempting important operations elsewhere.

"In regards to the Italian front as closely coordinated with the western front, however, and is willing to divert a portion of its military forces from France to Italy if it is the judgment and wish of the Supreme Command that it should do so. It wishes to defer to the decision of the Commander in Chief in this matter, as it would wish to defer in all others, particularly because it considers these two fronts so closely related as to be practically but separate parts of a single line and because it would be necessary that any American troops sent to Italy should be subtracted from the number used in France and be actually transported across French territory from the ports now used by the armies of the United States.

"It is the clear and fixed judgment of the Government of the United States, arrived at after repeated and very searching reconsiderations of the whole situation in Russia, that military intervention there would add to the present sad confusion in Russia rather than cure it, injure her rather than help her, and that it would be of no advantage in the prosecution of our main design, to win the war against Germany. It can not, therefore, take part in such intervention or sanction it in principle. Military intervention would, in its judgment, even supposing it to be efficacious in its immediate avowed object of delivering an attack upon Germany from the east, be merely a method of making use of Russia, not a method of serving her. Her people could not profit by it, if they profited by it at all, in time to save them from their present distresses, and their substances would be used to maintain foreign armies, not to reconstitute their own. Military action is admissible in Russia, as the Government of the United States sees the circumstances, only to help the Czecho-Slovaks consolidate their forces and get into successful cooperation with their Slavic kinsmen and to steady any efforts at self-government or self-defense in which the Russians themselves may be willing to accept assistance. *Whether from Vladivostok or from Murmansk and Archangel, the only legitimate object for which American or Allied troops can be employed, it submits, is to guard military stores which may subsequently by needed by Russian forces and to render such aid as may be acceptable to the Russians in the organization of their own self-defense*. For helping the Czecho-Slovaks there is immediate necessity and sufficient justification. Recent developments have made it evident that that is in the interests of what the Russian people themselves desire, and the Government of the United States is glad to contribute the small force at its disposal for that purpose. *It yields, also, to the judgment of the Supreme Command in the matter of establishing a small force at Murmansk, to guard the military stores at Kola, and to make it safe for Russian forces to come together in organized bodies in the north*. But it owes it to frank counsel to say that it can go no further than these modest and experimental plans. *It is not in a position, and has no expectation of being in a position, to take part in organized intervention in adequate force from either Vladivostok or Murmansk and Archangel*. It feels that it ought to add, also, that it will feel at liberty to use the few troops it can spare only for the purposes here stated and shall feel obliged to withdraw those forces, in order to add them to the forces at the western front, if the plans in whose execution it is now intended that they should cooperate should develop into other inconsistent with the policy the Government of the United States feels constrained to restrict itself *[author's emphases]*.

"At the same time the Government of the United States wishes to say with the utmost cordiality and good will that none of the conclusions here stated is meant to wear the least color of criticism of what the other governments associated against Germany may think it wise to undertake. It wishes in no way to embarrass their choices of policy. All that is intended here is a perfectly frank and definite statement of the policy which the United States feel obliged to adopt for herself and in the use of her own military forces. The Government of the United States does not wish it to be understood that in so restricting its own activities it is seeking, even by implication, to set limits to the action or to define the policies of its associates.

"It hopes to carry out the plans for safeguarding the rear of the Czecho-Slovaks operating from Vladivostok in a way that will place it and keep it in close cooperation with a small military force of its own from Japan, and if necessary from the other Allies, and that it will assure it of the cordial accord of all the Allied powers; and it proposes to ask all associated in this course of action to unite in assuring the people of Russia in the most public and solemn manner that none of the governments uniting in action either in Siberia or in northern Russia contemplates any interference in her internal affairs, or any impairment of her territorial integrity either now or hereafter, but that each of the associated powers has the single object of affording such aid as shall be acceptable, and only such aid as shall be acceptable, to the Russian people in their endeavor to regain control of their own affairs, their own territory, and their own destiny.

"It is the hope and purpose of the Government of the United States to take advantage of the earliest opportunity to send to Siberia a commission of merchants, agricultural experts, labor advisers, Red Cross representatives, and agents of the Young Men's Christian Association accustomed to organizing the best methods of spreading useful information and rendering educational help of a modest sort, in order in some systematic manner to relieve the immediate economic necessities of the people there in every way for which opportunities may open. The execution of this plan will follow and will not be permitted to embarrass the military assistance rendered in the rear of the westward-moving forces of the Czecho-Slovaks."

4. Wake Island, 1895-1945

Wake Island is a V-shaped group of three tiny coral atolls enclosing a central lagoon midway between the Hawaiian Islands and Tokyo. Each slender arm stretches about five miles with total land area of about three square miles. Wake remained an unspoken-for dot in the Pacific until 1898 when it was casually claimed for the United States by the commanding officer of a contingent of U.S. troops heading for the Philippines during the Philippines War. The United States formally annexed Wake Island the next year. The tiny atoll remained barren and uninhabited until 1935, when Pan American Airways constructed a small village there, nicknamed "PAAville," to service flights on its U.S.-China flying-boat route.

By December 1941, it was occupied by 449 Marines, 1,145 civilian workers in the employ of Morrison-Knudsen, and 72 Pan Am employees. In the second week of November, Marine Major James P.S. Devereux, who headed the Marine forces, hosted special Japanese envoy Saburo Kurusu on his way to Washington to meet with Secretary of State Cordell Hull. In an attempt to bolster his tiny garrison against what he perceived was an imminent Japanese attack, Devereux turned to the civilian construction workers for volunteers. Barely 20 percent came forward and contributed to the defense of Wake. Some feared—rightfully—that the Japanese would summarily execute these "guerrilla" fighters clad in civilian clothes if captured. Most, however, refused to fight, whether out of fear or principle. They were angry because Morrison-Knudsen had failed to evacuate them. In the event, the surviving civilians were captured and imprisoned and treated as POWs when Wake fell. In post-war reviews that glorified the Marines' gallant stand against overwhelming odds—it was likened to a 20th century Alamo—little was said about the uncooperative American civilians. On December 8 the same day as the attack on Pearl Harbor—Wake being on the opposite side of the International Date Line—Japanese *Nell* bombers flown from bases on Truk attacked Wake Island. The bombers caught all of the twelve F4F *Wildcat* fighter aircraft on the ground, destroying them.

Wake also figured in the Navy's cover-up of Vice Admiral William S. Pye's decision to abandon the island's defenders. Admiral Jack Fletcher commanded *Saratoga*'s Task Force 14 which was at sea intended to relieve Wake but Pye recalled TF 14 in fear of losing an aircraft carrier. News of the recall was totally censored by the Navy, the nation hardly needed to learn of another U.S. Navy failure. After the war when Americans learned details of the Navy's unwillingness to engage the enemy, it was treated as old news. Pye managed to hang on to his job in the Pacific for ten months after the debacle before being reassigned to oblivion in stateside desk jobs.

Appendices

5. The Military-Industrial Complex, January 17, 1961

"If any merchant, selling spears or shields, would fain have battles to improve his trade, may he be seized by thieves and eat raw barley."

—c. 350 B.C., Aristophanes, *Peace.*

Stepping down after eight years in office, President Dwight D. Eisenhower delivered a remarkable farewell address on January 17, 1961, that even after the passage of years has lost none of its pertinence. The former five-star general first pointed to "the noble goals" of America: "to keep the peace, to foster progress in human achievement, and to enhance liberty, dignity and integrity among peoples and among nations." Standing in the way of these worthy aims, however, was what he called a "hostile ideology global in scope, atheistic in character, ruthless in purpose, and insidious in method." It was Soviet Communism, a dangerous adversary, and only by bearing "burdens of a prolonged and complex struggle," he warned, could the nation hold true to its charted course toward "permanent peace and human betterment."

The nation's military establishment, he continued, was the key to keeping the peace, and "our arms must be mighty, ready for instant action." Until the recent Korean War, America had no armaments industry, but "now we can no longer risk emergency improvisation of national defense." As a result, "we have been compelled to create a permanent armaments industry of vast proportions." The country annually spends on military equipment, Eisenhower said, more than the net income of all U.S. corporations. "This conjunction of an immense military establishment and a large arms industry is new in the American experience."

Then came a sentence and the brief phrase within it that has resonated so profoundly in America's psyche ever since. Eisenhower's chief speechwriter, Malcolm C. Moos continued, elegantly, that "we must guard against the acquisition of unwarranted influence... *by the military-industrial complex*" – and that there was "potential for the disastrous rise of misplaced power" by this alliance. "Only an alert and knowledgeable citizenry," he warned, "can compel the proper meshing of the huge industrial and military machinery of defense with our peaceful methods and goals."

With the passage of time, Eisenhower's straightforward caveat—watch out for the military-industrial complex—has become his most memorable and lasting statement as president, and the most quoted line he ever delivered. Indeed, long after he left office, he recalled them with pride.

Before coming to the White House, Moos had been a political scientist and historian at Johns Hopkins University in Baltimore. Early in what became an intimate relationship, Moos recalled giving the president a book on noteworthy presidential decision-making and speeches. The book included George Washington's famous Farewell Address, and Moos remembered that Eisenhower was intrigued to learn that many historians believed that Alexander Hamilton was Washington's ghost-writer. According to Moos, the president told him that he hoped when he was leaving office that he could say something memorable to the American people. Moos then set up a file of ideas for Eisenhower's Farewell Address to be delivered two years hence. During that period, Moos encouraged a doctoral candidate at Hopkins to write his dissertation about high-ranking military officers who took early retirement to become well-paid officials at corporations doing business with the Pentagon. That "revolving door" was one of the key elements that made up the military-industrial complex.

Moos recalled that his office at the White House was always flooded with copies of glossy, full-color magazines and brochures from major defense contractors and their associations. He was observing up close the powerful clout these arms makers and the organizations they indirectly sponsored engendered. Moos, who continued to lecture at Hopkins at the same time he was writing the president's speeches, also saw first-hand the growing influence of Pentagon research contracts and grants to universities. What educators feared then was that such financial support would give the government untoward influence on campuses, in turn threatening educational freedom. Moos was homing in on his thesis for the president's address.

As for the origin of the phrase, military-industrial complex, Moos later said that he could not remember how he hit upon it. He believed he may have read it somewhere, but years later when the term became famous, he said Library of Congress researchers were unable to find any previous reference to it. When he handed the president an early draft of the speech, he recalled that Ike had liked it.: "I think you have got something here, Malcolm." In an earlier version Moos had included a third caveat, "congressional," that properly included elected officials. Eisenhower was reluctant to have his speech be divisive, and considered the role of the executive branch was not to dominate the legislative. Eisenhower cut it out of his address.

It is the size—and consequent clout—of the MIC that is frightening to well-informed Americans. It is the nation's largest single activity, employing one in ten working Americans, either within the military or its 120,000 suppliers. The money flows in an unending flood into every state and into "at least 363 of the nation's 435 Congressional districts." There are whole towns that are totally dependent on the MIC. The number of military and naval bases, in the United States and in 39 foreign countries, is mind-boggling: over 400 major bases and nearly 2,300 smaller ones that DoD maintains at a cost of about $8 billion annually.

To illustrate the clout of the MIC, there is the stunning example of Charleston, South Carolina and its warmonger representative L. Mendel Rivers, also chairman of the House Armed Services Committee. In Charleston there is: an Air Force Base, an Army Depot, a Naval shipyard, a Marine air station, the Parris Island Marine boot camp, two Naval hospitals, a Naval station, a Naval supply center, a Naval weapons station, a fleet ballistic-missile submarine training center, a Polaris missile facility, an Avco plant, a Lockheed plant, a General Electric plant, and an 800-acre plot of land purchased by Sikorsky Aircraft. The military payroll alone was $2 billion a year. Another warhawk Senator Barry Goldwater of Arizona, one of Congress' staunchest defenders of the MIC, is on record as stating: "Thank heavens for the military-industrial complex. Its ultimate aim is peace in our time, regardless of the aggressive, militaristic image that the left wing is attempting to give it."

When it comes to propaganda the Pentagon boasts (quietly) a vast force of over 6,000 public-relations practitioners around the world. In 1969, the military also had 339 well-paid "legislative liaison" lobbyists, with a budget of $4.1 million, to promote its agenda in the Congress. Add to these numbers are the myriad PR people working for the military contractors

6. The U-2 Incident, May 1, 1960

On May 1, 1960, two weeks before a scheduled summit meeting in Washington between President Dwight D. Eisenhower and Russian Premier Nikita Khrushchev, the Soviets shot down an American spy plane over the Soviet Union. Historian Michael R. Beschloss in his Preface to *Mayday: Eisenhower, Khruschchev and the U-2 Affair*, wrote that the downing of the U-2 was the CIA's first massive public failure, the first time that many Americans discovered that their government practiced espionage. May 1, 1960, was also the first time many learned that their leaders did not always tell them the truth... just as most Americans decades later naively viewed NASA's well-publicized

Appendices

Shuttle flights and space-walks as peaceful scientific explorations—rather than adjuncts to the nation's military programs to fight wars in space.

When word got back to Washington that a U.S. "weather-research" plane had crashed in Russian territory on May 1, a joint U.S. State Department/NASA statement aimed to assuage the Russians was hurriedly drafted in a crude attempt to cover-up the incident. The formal statement acknowledged that an Air Force plane was missing. During the flight of this plane, the pilot reported difficulty with his oxygen equipment. It also included the following: "Soviet Premier Khrushchev announced that a U.S. plane has been shot down over the U.S.S.R. on that date. It may be that this was the missing plane. It is entirely possible that, having a failure in the oxygen equipment which could result in the pilot losing consciousness, the plane continued on automatic pilot for a considerable distance and accidentally violated Soviet airspace."

No one in the United States, including the president, yet knew that the Soviets had captured the American pilot, Gary Powers, who was alive and well—and talking. Eisenhower had egg on his face. The big lie was more than an embarrassment. The upcoming U.S.-Soviet summit meeting was cancelled by the angry Russians and what had been improving relations between the two super powers soured.

The history of aerial reconnaissance goes back some 300 years when the French army first flew tethered balloons over the battle of Fleuries in 1794. Later, during the Great War, although the public was enamored of the glamorous pursuit-plane aces with their scarves stiff in the slipstream as they battled each other, one warrior against another, like knights of long ago, the more important functions of the new flying machines were as observers, scouts, and artillery spotters. Aerial observers in their slow-flying planes, for example, were able to discern with the naked eye individual soldiers from altitudes of three or four thousand feet and larger groups on the move at perhaps twice that altitude. Cameras with telephoto lenses were also introduced that provided close-up details of enemy trenches and precise locations of artillery batteries and munitions dumps.

In the late 1940s, at the start of the cold war, the U.S. Navy and Air Force floated balloons from Western Europe fitted with automatic cameras. These aerial snoopers were designed to be carried along by the prevailing winds from Russia to Japan (America's new ally) where a radio signal would detach the instrument package which would parachute to the ground. Many of these balloons never made it to Japan and fell into the hands of the Russians who gleefully put them on display in Moscow as examples of American duplicity. These U.S. balloons were similar to the Japanese balloons fitted with incendiary packages that had been launched against the west coasts of the U.S., Canada, and Alaska during World War II.

A far better way was to overfly the Soviet Union at high altitude and high speed in a manned aircraft. The RF-86 *Sabrejet* was the first specially configured long range reconnaissance plane. It was trucked close to the Soviet border, its big auxiliary tanks filled with fuel, and strapped beneath the fuselage of a B-50 bomber. The B-50 was a modified B-29 Superfortress fitted with more powerful—and more reliable—Pratt & Whitney R-4360 engines. The pilot climbed down into the cockpit through the bomb bay, slid up the canopy, fired up his engine, carefully synchronized its power to the speed of the mother plane, and then dropped away, accelerating to near-supersonic speed as he climbed to the plane's 40,000-foot-plus ceiling. The F-86 darted across the border, completed its mission, and streaked back to safety. But these missions were limited by the short range of the F-86 and the single-place fighter's limited room for cameras and other eavesdropping equipment.

A second try that might do the trick used the twin-jet RB-57, the reconnaissance version of the British *Canberra* with broadened wings, special engines, and other modifications that extended its ceiling. However, its first flight was almost fatal to its two-man crew; it landed in Iran full of shrapnel holes; that was the last time the RB-57 overflew the Soviet Union. This single mission demonstrated that a special ultra-high-altitude aircraft was needed.

The program to develop and fly what became the U-2 was given to the CIA. The project was completed in a remarkably short time. The first prototype was successfully flown only eight months after start-up, on August 15, 1955. Less than one year later, on July 4, 1956, the first U-2 mission was flown into Soviet airspace.

The final design of the hush-hush Lockheed plane looked more like a glider than a conventional jet, its wingspan twice the length of its fuselage. On the ground it needed out-rigger landing gear to support its droopy wings, which were dropped off as soon as the plane was airborne. To conserve fuel and extend its range, its single engine would be operated intermittently in the stratosphere. As a result, the U-2, originally named *Angel* by its innovating designers, could stay aloft for an amazing eleven hours, during which time it would cover over 4,700 miles. Its operational altitude ceiling was a remarkable 85,000 feet; its cruising speed was an equally unremarkable 460 miles per hour, but speed did not count. The plane was equipped with a specially designed aerial camera that was able to record a 2,600-mile-long strip of land on a single piece of film, resolving details so accurately that golf balls could be identified on a green from an altitude of 55,000 feet. The U-2's instrument package also included sensors for intercepting and recording radio and radar signals emanating from the ground.

The U-2 program operated under the cover of NACA, a supposedly civilian agency. The pilots were USAF personnel who had been "sheep-dipped," i.e., false Defense Department records were created to indicate that they had either resigned or had been discharged from the Air Force. The program ended on May 1, 1960, when Francis Gary Powers and his U-2 were shot down.

Secretary of State Christian Herter, in a NATO meeting in Athens when he learned of the downed U-2, was disturbed by the misinformation coming out of Washington on May 3 and 5. The Soviets had the espionage equipment in their hands as well as the American pilot [in civilian clothes]. "Were we going to keep lying about this or were we going to tell the truth?" After a well-publicized trial in Moscow and twenty months in a USSR prison, Powers was released.

7. The Potsdam Declaration, July 26, 1945

(1) We, the President of the United States, the President of the National Government of the Republic of China and the Prime Minister of Great Britain, representing the hundreds of millions of our countrymen, have conferred and agree that Japan shall be given an opportunity to end this war.

(2) The prodigious land, sea and air forces of the United States, the British Empire and of China, many times reinforced by their armies and air fleets from the west are poised to strike the final blows upon Japan. This military power is sustained and inspired by the determination of all the Allied nations to prosecute the war against Japan until she ceases to resist.

(3) The result of the futile and senseless German resistance to the might of the aroused free peoples of the world stands forth in awful clarity as an example to the people of Japan. The might that now converges on Japan is immeasurably greater than that which, when applied to the resisting Nazis, necessarily laid waste to the lands, the industry and the method of life of the whole German people.

The full application of our military power, backed by our resolve, will mean the inevitable and complete destruction of the Japanese armed forces and just as inevitably the utter devastation of the Japanese homeland.

(4) The time has come for Japan to decide whether she will continue to be controlled by those self-willed militaristic advisers whose unintelligent calculations have brought the Empire of Japan to the threshold of annihilation, or whether she will follow the path of reason.

(5) Following are our terms. We will not deviate from them. There are no alternatives. We shall brook no delay.

(6) There must be eliminated for all time the authority and influence of those who have deceived and misled the people of Japan into embarking on world conquest - for we insist that a new order of peace, security and justice will be impossible until irresponsible militarism is driven from the world.

(7) Until such a new order is established and until there is convincing proof that Japan's war-making power is destroyed, points in Japanese territory to be designated by the Allies shall be occupied to secure the achievement of the basic objectives we are here setting forth.

(8) The terms of the Cairo Declaration shall be carried out and Japanese sovereignty shall be limited to the islands of Honshu, Hokkaido, Kyushu, Shikoku and such minor islands as we determine.

(9) The Japanese military forces, after being completely disarmed, shall be permitted to return to their homes with the opportunity to lead peaceful and productive lives.

(10) We do not intend that the Japanese shall be enslaved as a race or destroyed as a nation, but stern justice shall be meted out to all war criminals, including those who have visited cruelties upon our prisoners. The Japanese government shall remove all obstacles to the revival and strengthening of democratic tendencies among the Japanese people. Freedom of speech, of religion, and of thought, as well as respect for the fundamental human rights shall be established.

(11) Japan shall be permitted to maintain such industries as will sustain her economy and permit the exaction of just reparations in war. To this end, access to, as distinguished from control of raw materials shall be permitted. Eventual Japanese participation in world trade relations shall be permitted.

(12) The occupying forces of the Allies shall be withdrawn from Japan as soon as these objectives have been accomplished and there has been established in accordance with the freely expressed will of the Japanese people a peacefully inclined and responsible government.

(13) We call upon the Government of Japan to proclaim now the unconditional surrender of all the Japanese armed forces, and to provide proper and adequate assurances of their good faith in such action. The alternative for Japan is prompt and utter destruction.

8. U.S. Germ Warfare, 1930s to May 14, 1988

At the start of the World War II, the United States had no active programs for the study of germs for use as weapons, nor laboratories staffed and equipped to do such research. When it became apparent that both Germany and Japan were likely to be looking at such programs, the War Department decided that the U.S. must embark on such research too, if only for defense.

In November 1941, Secretary of War Henry L. Stimson called together a blue-ribbon committee of twelve civilian scientists and charged them with the task of determining the feasibility of biological warfare. The WBC Committee, as it was called, responded that not only was BW practicable but that other countries were already at development work to produce BW weapons and it behooved the United States to catch up and gain leadership in the field.

In March 1943, the Army's Chemical Warfare Service took over the former airfield of the Maryland National Guard outside the city of Fredrick, a country town midway between Washington, D.C. and New York City. It had been named Detrick Field after the unit's flight surgeon; it was renamed Camp Detrick.

By the end of 1943, Camp Detrick, Maryland, had become the hub of activity for such research and home of the nation's first biological warfare laboratory. By the start of the following year, the facility's biologists and scientists had perfected pilot plans for the mass production of anthrax and botulinus toxin. The team was also studying a wide range of other diseases: glanders, brucellosis, cholera, dysentery, plague, typhus, foot and mouth, rinderpest, and fowl plague. Parallel work was also underway on means of airborne delivery of the virulent germs. Research was later conducted on psittacosis, encephalitis, Rift Valley fever, typhoid, and yellow fever.

Detrick's research was not limited to anti-personnel biological agents. Animal diseases and plant-killing agents were also studied. A plot of rice fields was reserved in Florida where Detrick scientists tested rice diseases which might be used to destroy Japan's critically important rice crop. Florida had been chosen not only because its climate was similar to that of Japan but because the state had no domestic rice industry that could be accidentally infected.

At the end of the war, there was no let up in American research work on biological weapons. When reports surfaced that the Japanese had tested their biological weapons on humans, they were greeted with skepticism.

In occupied China, in the remote countryside close to Mukden in the small city of Ping Fan, unknown to the Allies, an enormous Japanese facility had been built and its hundreds of biologists were studying bacteriological weapons, their mass production, and delivery systems and had been doing so since the early 1930s. They were well ahead of the Americans. This main facility was known as Unit 731 and there were satellites in Dairen, Hailar, Linkow, and Sunyu, China.

U.S. Historians Peter Williams and David Wallace wrote; "From small beginnings Ishii [Ishii Shiro] built, in little more than a decade, a mighty research empire... He had given Japan a weapon which in theory had the power to rival the Manhattan Project." Ishii had based Unit 731 in remote northern Manchuria for a good reason: he planned to use humans in his experiments. He was confident that, as a result, no other country would match his capabilities in the development of biological weapons. The Manchurian Incident in 1931 was the start of Ishii's use of human guinea pigs, at first performed only on prisoners sentenced to death. It was estimated that three thousand people were sacrificed over the 14 years of Ping Fan's existence, mostly Chinese.

The entire operation was headed by General Shiro. His main facility in Ping Fan included some 150 buildings, with accommodations for thousands of workers, a railroad siding, an incinerator and powerhouse with tall cooling towers, an animal house, an airfield, and an insectarium. At the peak of Unit 731's production, the single facility could create sufficient deadly pathogens to kill everyone on earth several times over.

Should the BW agents have lethal or just temporary incapacitating effects? Did the agents lend themselves to mass production such as would be required in wartime? How could these living organisms be kept alive and remain virulent through storage and shipment? What kind of vehicle was needed to deliver the agents to the target? And what method used to disperse the agents would not, in turn, kill the organisms? These were some of the questions addressed.

Various delivery systems were tested: air-dropped feathers were laced with bacteria; bacteria were sprayed from airplanes; packages of infected fleas were parachuted which were dispersed with a small demolition charge upon impact with the ground; for assassinations, infected-flea sprayers in the form of fountain pens and bacteria-filled chocolates were developed. Special self-destructing paper containers were used and helium-filled "free" balloons were used to deliver plague-infected fleas and rats to the target.

In the fall of 1945 when General MacArthur's Far East Headquarters staff first questioned Ishii, he had given them the standard response of military scientists everywhere, that their work was strictly defensive in nature. Later, in 1947, Ishii, fearing that he would be handed over to the Russians, changed his story. He admitted that he had conducted what he called "field trials" with anthrax on humans. He then made an offer the Pentagon could not—and did not refuse. If he and his subordinates were guaranteed immunity from war crimes trials, Ishii said, he would describe the program in detail.

Following up Ishii's proposal, the Pentagon sent two biologists from Camp Detrick to Tokyo. They learned that the Japanese had studied a broad group of diseases, including anthrax, plague, tuberculosis, small pox, typhoid and cholera. More significantly, several of those interrogated admitted they had tested such germs on humans. Those experiments were as ghastly as any that had been conducted by the Nazis, yet the Detrick report impassively concluded that the potential benefits to the U.S. germ warfare program outweighed the demands of justice. In fact, the full extent of U.S. knowledge of Japanese testing on humans was kept secret for thirty years.

On August 9, 1945, following the nuclear bomb attacks on Hiroshima and Nagasaki and the Red Army's drive across the border in Manchuria and Korea, orders came to destroy Unit 731. All buildings, equipment, and documents, in particular, were destroyed and all personnel were evacuated. The Japanese intended to cover-up the crimes of Unit 731.

At Dugway, Utah, a U.S. Army CBW Base extends over 840,000 acres of the barren desert of western Utah. Hidden away in the base's technical library is an unmarked box containing more than twenty reports compiled by American scientists from their postwar interviews with Ishii... and other surviving Unit 731 authorities. This box also contains three extraordinary autopsy reports that covered glanders, plague, and anthrax. Each autopsy report contains hundreds of pastel-colored artist drawings of human organs in various states of disintegration.

> "As far as I know, it was true that a deal was made. But it was the U.S. side which approached my father, not the other way around... What I would like to emphatically say... is: Isn't it important that not a single man under my father's command was ever tried as a war criminal? I am really sorry for those who had to live in seclusion to evade possible prosecution but were it not for my father's courage in making a deal with the occupation authorities... you know what I mean."

—Ishii Harumi in the *Japan Times*, August 29, 1982.

9. The Saga of the Banana, United Fruit Company, and U.S. Interventions in Latin America, 1890-1970

The not-so-humble banana played an altogether remarkable role in the evolution of American imperialism in Latin America from the 1880s on. Before that time few if any Americans had even seen a banana much less try to "open" one. Ten years later, due mainly to the effective marketing efforts of the United Fruit Company, they were beginning to be sold in principal U.S. cities as luxury foods, individually wrapped in tinfoil. As banana prices dropped after the turn of the century, they gradually became part of the basic diet of Americans and were no longer looked upon as an exotic fruit. By the 1930s, bananas were found in grocery stores across the country twelve months of the year.

United Fruit Company, or *La Frutera* as it came to be known throughout Latin America, has a long history in Latin America. In 1871, Minor C. Keith, who came from an entreprenurial Brooklyn family, pooled resources with his two brothers for a foreign endeavor that would make him rich and famous. He assembled a hard-bitten construction crew from New Orleans, took them down to Costa Rica, and started to build a railroad in that country. To advance his railroad interests he married the daughter of the Costa Rican president and at the same time began to sell bananas. By 1883 Keith owned three banana companies and was convinced that bananas could be profitably exported to the United States. Along with a sailor from New England and a Boston businessman, Keith formed the Boston Fruit Company which was merged into the United Fruit Company in 1899.

United Fruit quickly became the world's largest banana grower and exporter. Land holdings were expanded from Costa Rica to Nicaragua, Panama, Colombia, Santo Domingo, Cuba, Jamaica, and in particular Guatemala. The company's "Great White Fleet" of steamships which it owned and others which it chartered allowed it to deliver the perishable fruit to U.S. markets with minimum spoilage.

Appendices

In 1901, the company negotiated with Guatemalan dictator Manuel Estrada Cabrera an exclusive concession for carrying the nation's mail between Puerto Barrios and the United States. This contract marked the beginning of more than a half-century of uninterrupted profit-making for UFCO—all based on the humble banana. The Guatemalan Railroad Company tied Guatemala City, the nation's capital, to Puerto Barrios, the only port on the Caribbean coast, which became virtually a United Fruit city.

The ever-increasing demand for bananas, driven by relentless advertising and marketing, became a growing incentive for UFCO not only to expand its production but also to drive out its weaker competitors. Among the creative ways United Fruit expanded the demand was to introduce new ways to eat bananas. In 1924, for example, United Fruit distributed a recipe book promoting the consumption of bananas with corn flakes and milk for breakfast. This was such a success that in the years following, the company made deals with cereal companies in order to mutually promote their products.

In 1927, the company funded publication of a book, *The Banana: Its History, Cultivation, and Place Among Staple Foods*, that proved that the banana, in addition to being a tasty treat, was a health food; containing most of the vitamins and proteins individuals needed.

UFCO, while exploiting the labors of its employees, was nevertheless both benevolent and paternal. United Fruit workers enjoyed better conditions than most agricultural workers. For those workers and their families who lived on the banana plantations, adequate housing was provided as well as medical care and schooling for the children.

United Fruit selected Guatemala as the principal nation for growing its banana not only because it contained excellent banana land but also because Guatemala's government was the region's weakest and most corrupt. United Fruit's profits there flourished for fifty years. Then, in 1951, Jacobo Arbenz was elected president.

Arbenz introduced an agrarian reform law that required expropriation of a large tract of the company's uncultivated land. In October 1951, a half-year after Arbenz took office, United Fruit sent one of its top executives to meet with the new president. His mission was to reaffirm the company's dominant position in the country. He insisted that United Fruit's labor contract be extended for three more years without change and demanded that Arbenz agree not to increase the trivial taxes then being paid by the company. Arbenz's negative response was a shock to UFCO'S emissary. For the contract to be extended, the company would have to abide by the laws of Guatemala and accept the government as the final arbiter. Arbenz also had a list of proposals of his own: the docks on the Pacific coast be upgraded, rail freight rates be reduced, the company start paying export duties and consider compensating Guatemala for the "exhaustion" of banana lands.

In March 1953, United Fruit was hit hard when over 200,000 acres of uncultivated land was expropriated. The company had always left large acreage uncultivated, claiming it needed fallow lands as insurance against plant diseases. In October 1953 and again in February 1954, the government expropriated additional UFCO lands, this time on the Atlantic coast, bringing the total to some 387,000 acres

At the same time, back in Washington, the company was working quietly to build a strong case of Communist influence as driving the Arbenz regime. Its theme: government was a threat to freedom and its actions could trigger similar uprisings in neighboring states. Arbenz and his left-wing cronies had to go. As early as 1950, the company had hired lobbyists and public relations people to shape the views of both U.S. lawmakers and the general public toward Guatemala. The company also enlisted the support of Massachusetts Senator Henry Cabot Lodge, a stockholder, who denounced the Guatemalan government's land reforms. In 1954, Lodge, as U.S. ambassador to the United Nations, continued his drum-beat of criticism against the Arbenz regime.

United Fruit could count on a phalanx of high-level U.S. government officials for support. Heading the list was Secretary of State John Foster Dulles who had been a senior partner in the Sullivan and Cromwell law firm, which did legal work for the J. Henry Schroder Banking Corporation, an important financial adviser to the International Railways of Central America, which owned most of the train lines in Guatemala. Allen Welsh Dulles also did legal work for Sullivan and Cromwell and became a member of the board of the bank. Other influential figures included John Moors Cabot, Assistant Secretary of State for Inter-American Affairs, whose family were United Fruit stockholders. His brother Thomas was a former president of United Fruit. UN Ambassador Henry Cabot Lodge was also a stockholder. The wife of Edmund Whitman, United Fruit's director of public relations, was Eisenhower's personal secretary.

With covert help from the CIA, and backed by President Harry Truman, Arbenz was ousted from power and Castillo Armas was installed as president. One of Armas' first moves was to overturn all of Arbenz's social reforms and to return the expropriated land to United Fruit.

Francis Cardinal Spellman of New York, a bitter anti-communist, fearing social change more than he feared God, according to his critics, was enlisted by the CIA in another of its nefarious plots. On April 9, the right-wing prelate's pastoral letter, signed by the Archbishop of Guatemala, was read in Guatemalan Catholic churches. It called attention to the "devil called communism" and demanded that the people "rise as a single man against this enemy of God and country." Since the peasant class by and large was illiterate—and extremely religious—this was an effective way to "receive the Lord's word." For those who could read, thousands of pamphlets carrying the Archbishop's were air-dropped around the country.

In the next two years the U.S. pumped ninety-million dollars into Guatemala to prop up the new Armas government. Armas quickly returned United Fruit's expropriated lands and did away with the tax on interest and dividends to foreign investors, saving the Fruit Company about eleven million dollars. He launched a vindictive campaign again Communists, jailing over five-thousand individuals. He also eliminated the secret ballot and purposefully disenfranchised some seventy percent of the country's citizens. This enabled him to win what Eisenhower later called a "thundering majority" in a single-candidate election.

Armas was assassinated three years later, one of the numerous coups in the next decade. But throughout the comings and goings of one "strongman" after another, American influence in the country remained secure.

A 25-year-old Argentinian, Ernesto Guevara—later known as "*El Che*"—was a witness to the coup. Earlier he had applied for a position with United Fruit as a physician. He had been living in Guatemala as a doctor. He saw the coup for what it was and organized rebel guerrillas to fight Armas's army. Unsuccessful, he fled to Mexico where he met another political refugee, Fidel Castro, who became a close friend. These two revolutionaries later played important roles in Cuba's revolution.

Appendices

10. Nuclear Weapons, 1945 On

In 1945's technology, ton for ton, nuclear explosives were about 4,000 times as powerful as TNT. During the next decade, atomic bombs grew more powerful but their gradual improvement was dwarfed by the hydrogen-bomb breakthrough. This meant that the newly developed B-52 jet bomber, which first flew in 1954, could carry two 20-megaton bombs—about 2,000 times the lethality of the B-29. Put another way, twenty-five B-52s could deliver nuclear explosives equal to a billion tons of TNT. As scientist Ralph Lapp wrote dramatically, the lithium-uranium superbomb provided "firepower beyond the imagination of all but a demented militarist" and placed it into the hands of Air Force generals.

The Strategic Air Command was the darling of the Congress during the 1950s and 1960s. A total of 1,800 B-47 and 850 B-52 bombers were built plus 383 B-36 piston/turbojet engine hybrids to close the mythical bomber "gap" with the Soviet Union. When wiser heads prevailed, it was learned that the Soviets deployed only 120 *Bison* turbojet bombers and 70 *Bear* turboprop bombers. The turboprop engine harnessed a propeller to the turbine shaft of the jet engine, which combined power and light weight and provided somewhat better fuel economy compared to the "pure" turbojet.

On at least seven occasions following the Hiroshima and Nagasaki bombings, U.S. leaders seriously contemplated using nuclear weapons. The first, in 1950, was by President Harry Truman who threatened their use during a press conference on November 30 on the Korean War. He declared "we will take whatever steps are necessary to meet the military situation." Did those steps include use of atomic bombs? Truman's response: "That includes every weapon we have" and "there has always been active consideration of its [atomic bomb's] use." The next, in 1953, was intended to force China to end its military support of North Korea. One year later, Secretary of State John Foster Dulles offered three nuclear bombs to France [which soon after exploded one of its own], one to be used against China and two against the Vietminh at Dien Bien Phu. In 1958, the Joint Chiefs advised President Eisenhower that the Chinese coastal islands of Quemoy and Matsu could not be held for Chiang Kai-shek's nationalist troops unless nuclear weapons were used. That same year, Eisenhower ordered secret preparations for nuclear-weapon use during the so-called "Lebanon crisis."

In 1961, President John F. Kennedy considered using nuclear weapons over Laos to force the communist Pathet Lao to join a tripartite government. That same year, to break the Soviet blockade of Berlin, Kennedy again weighed use of atomic bombs. In 1968, President Lyndon B. Johnson asked his Joint Chiefs about the use of nuclear weapons to prevent the North Vietnamese from overrunning the U.S. Marine base at Khe Sanh. President Richard Nixon, in 1968 and 1969, sent word to the North Vietnamese government in Hanoi that he was prepared to use nuclear weapons to end the war in Vietnam.

There also were three instances of confrontation with the Soviet Union that might have escalated into a disastrous exchange of nuclear weapons. The first was the 1946 U.S. ultimatum to the Soviets to withdraw their troops from Iran or face nuclear attack. The second, in 1962, was the well-publicized confrontation over the stationing of nuclear-tipped missiles in Cuba. The third was the DefCon alerts during the 1973 Yom Kippur War. This last incident was hidden from the American public because it touched a sensitive political nerve: U.S. unconditional support of Israel's aggressive foreign policy based on its well-stocked nuclear arsenal, in turn based on American know-how and bomb-grade raw materials.

One can speculate on a U.S. Navy Trident-missile submarine rising to periscope depth off a foreign shore some days after launching its complement of MIRV missiles. It is a barren landscape, day after day, as the ship cruises just below the surface to avoid radioactive contamination, the submarine representing the apogee of man's technological progress—nuclear power, remarkable electronics, super-strength steels, life-sustaining environmental systems. Just like Gregory Peck, the captain of an earlier-generation nuclear submarine, this naval officer and his crew, too, is doomed. [See Epilogue].

11. The B-2 Stealth Bomber, 1990 to Present

One example of the Pentagon's secret weapons systems, initially funded through the CIA's black budget, is the B-2 Stealth bomber, *Spirit*. Tim Weiner wrote in 2000 that the B-2 was the perfect symbol for the black budget: a staggeringly costly weapon with hard-to-pin down advantages over existing weapons, i.e., the venerable B-52 *Stratofortress*.

> The Air Force says the B-2's radar-absorbing skin and its sleek boomerang shape will make it nearly undetectable to any enemy. Its mission is unique: to dodge Russian air defenses, drop nuclear bombs on the Russian's mobile missile systems, and destroy the Russian leadership in their hardened bunkers.

In fact, wrote Weiner, the B-2 is the most expensive airplane ever built, rivaling the costs of development of *Little Boy* and *Fat Man*. He guessed that "nowadays"—1990—each one would cost no less than $820 million. This figure is only slightly less than if the 70-ton plane was constructed of *solid gold*. The Pentagon at that time planned to build a fleet of 75 at a total cost of $61.5 billion. Weiner equated the cost with the annual budget of California, the sixth largest economy in the world.

Such an expensive airplane would supposedly never be used unless a full-blown nuclear war erupted. And that is precisely its purpose; to win World War III, sometime after the nation's cities and populations were destroyed. Few Americans dwell on the reality that their own government considers them cannon fodder. Or that their taxes are spent on such doomsday weapons. In 1999, the Air Force couldn't wait for World War III to break out to showcase its new B-2.

Today, if someone curious goes on-line to *Google* to learn about the B-2, he or she is treated to a first-class dog-and-pony show: exquisite in-flight photography of the airplane from every angle, smoothly accelerating down the runway, coming in for an equally silky landing. Special music was composed for this special airplane, including one segment with an all-male chorus as appropriate background glorifying the masculine machine. How much did that Internet propaganda segment cost, all chargeable to the taxpayer?

What do the Department of Defense, the U.S. Air Force, and the American people get for these enormous costs? Stealth technology is supposed to make airplanes invisible or nearly so to radar, hence all but immune to ground-to-air missiles. Has the B-2's stealthy performance vindicated the Pentagon's confidence in the new technology, the Air Force's Holy Grail for nearly three decades? One report indicates that the B-2 is as visible to the naked eye as a Boeing 747, one reason that it and the F-117 fly combat missions only at night. The Air Force also went to great pains to avoid press leaks that both these aircraft went into action over Yugoslavia accompanied by the same radar-jamming escorts that flew in support of conventional bombers in World War II.

Nevertheless, the USAF remains committed to stealthy aircraft. The earliest was the F-117 fighter which saw action over Yugoslavia, whose anti-aircraft gunners shot one down with a Soviet-made SA-3 ground-to-air missile, a 35-year-old model. A second F-117 limped home after being hit by another SA-3. That happening stayed secret for years. Meanwhile, the Pentagon, unfazed and undeterred, has spent hundreds of millions to produce two additional stealth fighters, the F-22 and the Joint Strike Fighter.

Paradoxically, stealthy design produces an aerodynamically inefficient warbird. Because surface irregularities must be minimized to help achieve even marginal stealthiness, the B-2 must carry all "accessories" internally, such as bombs, cruise missiles, and auxiliary fuel tanks.

Exposure to rain or hail can create small nicks in the outercoat that dramatically affect the plane's radar "signature," hence its stealthiness. After every flight a special maintenance team must go to work inspecting every square inch of the skin, recoating where necessary. The outercoats also add considerable weight, which means more powerful engines that burn more fuel which, in turn, means reduced range. The B-2s that bombed Kosovo had to be refueled twice going in and twice coming home. Lastly, these planes need to be stored, between flights, in special air conditioned hangars.

Boeing engineers are alleged to have designed the B-52 over the course of a long weekend, using data from their earlier and successful B-47. Even after more than 50 years and counting, the B-52 remains a highly effective warbird. Compared to the B-2, it flies as fast and almost as high, flies 1,500 miles farther without refueling, and carries nearly double the bomb load.

Bibliography

This Bibliography consists of works that the author has cited and/or that have contributed to his understanding of the issues and events described in the book.

Adams, Gordon. *The Iron Triangle: The Politics of Defense Contracting* (The Council of Economic Priorities, New York, 1981).

Agee, Philip. *Inside the Company: CIA Diary* (Harmondsworth, Middlesex, England, 1975).

Ahmed, Nafeez Mosaddeq. *The War on Freedom: How and Why America Was Attacked September 11, 2001* (Tree of Life Publications, Joshua Tree CA, 2002).

Allman, T.D. *Rogue State: America at War With the World* (Nation Books, New York, 2004).

Alterman, Eric. *When Presidents Lie: A History of Official Deception and Its Consequences* (Viking, New York, 2004).

_____. Unmanifest *Destiny: Mayhem and Illusion in American Foreign Policy—From the Monroe Doctrine to Reagan's War in El Salvador* (The Dial Press, Garden City NY, 1984).

Anderson, David L., Ed. *Facing My Lai: Moving Beyond the Massacre* (University Press of Kansas, Lawrence KS, 1998).

Andreas, Joel. *Addicted to War: Why the U.S. Can't Kick Militarism* (AK Press, Oakland CA, 2002).

Appleman, Roy. *Disaster in Korea: The Chinese Confront MacArthur* (Texas A & M University Press, College Station TX, 1989).

Appy, Christian G. *Patriots: The Vietnam War Remembered From All Sides* (Viking, New York, 2003).

Armstrong, Anne. *Unconditional Surrender: The Impact of the Casablanca Policy Upon World War II* (Rutgers University Press, New Brunswick NJ, 1961).

"Arms and the Men", *Fortune,* March 1934.

Ashley, Steven. "When the Twin Towers Fell," *Scientific American,* October 9, 2001.

Atkinson, Rick. *An Army at Dawn: The War in North Africa, 1942-1943* (Henry Holt and Company, New York, 2002).

_____. *The Day of Battle: The War in Sicily and Italy, 1943-1944* (Henry Holt and Company, New York, 2007).

Austin, Anthony. *The President's War: The Story of the Tonkin Gulf Resolution and How the Nation Was Trapped in Vietnam* (J.B. Lippincott Company, Philadelphia, 1971).

Bacevich, Andrew J. "Dewey and the Germans at Manila Bay,"*American History Review,* Vol. XLV.

_____. *American Empire: The Realities & Consequences of U.S. Diplomacy* (Harvard University Press, Cambridge MA, 2002).

Bailey, Thomas A. *The Man in the Street: The Impact of American Public Opinion on Foreign Policy* (Peter Smith, Gloucester MA, 1964).

Bailey, Thomas A. and Paul B. Ryan. *Hitler vs. Roosevelt: The Undeclared Naval War* (The Free Press, New York, 1979).

Baldwin, Hanson. *Great Mistakes of the War* (Harper and Brothers, New York, 1950).

Bamford, James. *Body of Secrets: Anatomy of the Ultra-Secret National Security Agency From the Cold War Through the Dawn of a New Century* (Doubleday, New York, 2001).

_____. *A Pretext for War: 9/11, Iraq, And The Abuse of America's Intelligence Agencies* (Doubleday, New York, 2004).

Barnes, Harry Elmer. *The Genesis of The World War: An Introduction to The Problem of War Guilt* (Alfred A. Knopf, New York, 1926).

_____. *In Quest of Truth and Justice: De-bunking the War Guilt Myth* (National Historical Society, Chicago, 1928).

_____. *Perpetual War for Perpetual Peace: A Critical Examination of the Foreign Policy of Franklin Delano Roosevelt and its Aftermath* (The Caxton Printers, Ltd., Caldwell ID, 1953).

_____. "Why America Entered the War," *The Christian Century,* November 1925.

Barnet, Richard J. *The Economy of Death* (Atheneum, New York, 1969).

_____. *Roots of War* (Atheneum, New York, 1972).

_____. *Intervention and Revolution: The United States in the Third World* (The World Publishing Company, New York, 1968).

Barrett, Wayne and Dan Collins. *Grand Illusion: The Untold Story of Rudy Giuliani and 9/11* (Harper Collins Publishers, New York, 2006).

Barry, John M. *The Great Influenza: The Epic Story of the Deadliest Plague in History* (Viking, New York, 2004).

Bartlett, Bruce. *Cover-Up: The Politics of Pearl Harbor, 1941-1946* (Arlington House Publishers, New Rochelle NY, 1978).

Bauer, K. Jack. *The Mexican War: 1846-1848* (Macmillan Publishing Co., Inc., New York, 1974).

Baumgartner, John Stanley. *The Lonely Warriors: Case for the Military-Industrial Complex* (Nash Publications, Los Angeles, 1970).

Beach, Edward L. *Scapegoats: A Defense of Kimmel and Short at Pearl Harbor* (Naval Institute Press, Annapolis MD, 1995).

_____. *The Navy: Defense or Portent* (Harper & Brothers, Publishers, New York, 1932).

Beard, Charles Austin. *President Roosevelt and the Coming of the War 1941* (Yale University Press, New Haven CT, 1948).

Beck, Earl R. *Under the Bombs: The German Home Front, 1942-1945* (The University Press of Kentucky, Lexington KY, 1986).

Beisner, Robert. *Twelve Against Empire: The Anti-Imperialists 1898-1900—How Twelve Men Opposed the Acquisition of Empire in the Spanish-American War* (McGraw-Hill Book Company, New York, 1968).

Belgion, Montgomery. *Victors' Justice* (Henry Regnery Company, Hinsdale IL, 1949).

Belknap, Michael R. *The Vietnam War on Trial: The My Lai Massacre and the Court Martial of Lieutenant Calley* (University Press of Kansas, Lawrence KS, 2002).

Bemis, Samuel Flagg. *First Gun of a Revisionist Historiography For The Second World War* (The Journal of Modern History) March 1947.

Berman, Morris. *Dark Ages America: The Final Phase of Empire* (W.W. Norton & Company, New York, 2006).

Bernstein, Barton J. "America's Biological Warfare Program in the Second World War," *Journal of Strategic Studies*, September 3, 1988.

_____. "A postwar myth: 500,00 U.S. lives saved," *Bulletin of the Atomic Scientists*, June/July 1986.

Beschloss, Michael. *The Conquerors: Roosevelt, Truman and the Destruction of Hitler's Germany, 1941-1945* (Simon & Schuster, New York, 2002).

Beyden, John. *Deadly Allies: Canada's Secret War 1937-1947* (McCelland & Stewart Inc., Toronto, 1989).

Bill, Alfred Hoyt. *Rehearsal for Conflict: The War with Mexico 1846-1848* (Alfred A. Knopf, New York, 1947).

Bird, Kai and Lawrence Lifschultz. Editors, *Hiroshima's Shadow* (The Pamphleteer's Press, Stony Creek CT, 1998).

Black, George. *The Good Neighbor: How the United States Wrote the History of Central America and the Caribbean* (Pantheon Books, New York, 1988).

Blackett, P.M.S. *Fear, War and the Bomb: Military and Political Consequences of Atomic Energy* (McGraw-Hill Book Company, Inc., New York, 1948).

Blair, Clay. *The Forgotten War: America in Korea 1950-1953* (Times Books, New York, 1987).

_____. *Silent Victory: The U.S. Submarine War Against Japan* (Naval Institute Press, Annapolis MD, 1975).

Blum, John Morton. *V Was for Victory: Politics and American Culture During World War II* (Harcourt Brace Jovanovich, 1976).

_____. *From the Morgenthau Diaries: Years of War 1941-1945* (Houghton, Mifflin, Boston, 1967).

Blum, William. *Rogue State: A Guide to the World's Only Superpower* (Common Courage Press, Monroe ME, 2000).

_____. *Killing Hope: U.S. Military and CIA Interventions Since World War II* (Common Courage Press, Monroe ME, 1995).

Boerneke, Manfred Franz. *The Treaty of Versailles: A Reassessment After 75 Years* (German Historical Institute, Washington, 1998)

Boggs, Carl, Ed. *Masters of War: Militarism and Blowback in the Era of American Empire* (Routledge, New York, 2003).

Bohning, Don. *The Castro Obsession: U.S. Covert Operations Against Cuba 1959-1965* (Potomac Books, Inc., Washington, 2005).

Bongaretz, Ray. "*Muckuppery Along the Potomac*", Esquire, June 1970.

Bonner, Raymond. *Weakness and Deceit: U.S. Policy and El Salvador* (Times Books, New York, 1984).

Boot, Max. *The Savage Wars of Peace: Small Wars and the Rise of American Power* (Basic Books, New York, 2002).

Borosage, Robert. "The Making of the National Security State," in Leonard S. Rodberg and Derek Shearer, Editors, *The Pentagon Watchers* (Doubleday, Garden City NY, 1970).

Brackman, Arnold. *The Other Nuremberg: The Untold Story of the Tokyo War Crimes Trials* (William Morrow & Co., New York, 1988).

Bradbury, Ray. *Fahrenheit 451—The Temperature at Which Book Paper Catches Fire and Burns* (Simon & Schuster, New York, 1951).

Brewer, Susan A. *To Win the Peace: British Propaganda in the United States During World War II* (Cornell University Press, Ithaca NY, 1997).

Brock, H.I. "Wartime Propaganda," *The Journal of American History*, p. 55, 1968.

Broeckers, Mathias. *Conspiracies, Conspiracy Theories and the Secrets of 9/11* (Progressive Press, Joshua Tree CA).

Brown, Charles H. *The Correspondent's War: Journalists in the Spanish-American War* (Charles Scribner's Sons, New York, 1967).

Brown, Frederic. *Chemical Warfare, A Study in Restraints* (Princeton University Press, Princeton NJ, 1968).

Browne, Malcolm W. *The New Face of War* (Bantam Books, New York, 1963).

Brownlow, Donald Grey. *The Accused: The Ordeal of Rear Admiral Husband Edward Kimmel, U.S.N.* (Vantage Press, New York, 1968).

Bruning, John R. Jr. *Crimson Sky: The Air Battle for Korea* (Brassey's, Dulles VA, 1999).

Bruntz, George S. *Allied Propaganda and the Collapse of the German Empire in 1918* (Arno Press, Hoover Institute, Palo Alto CA, 1938).

Bryden, John. Deadly Allies: *Canada's Secret War, 1937-1947* (McClelland & Stewart, 1989).

Brzezinski, Matthew. *Fortress America: On The Front Lines of Homeland Security, An Inside Look at the Coming Surveillance State* (Bantam Doubleday Dell, New York, 2004).

Bucheli, Marcelo. *Bananas and Business: The United Fruit Company in Colombia, 1899-2000* (New York University Press, New York, 2005).

Buckingham, William A. Jr. *Operation Ranch Hand: The Air Force and Herbicides in Southeast Asia* (U.S. Government Printing Office, Washington, 1982).

Buchanan, Patrick J. *State of Emergency: The Third World Invasion and Conquest of America* (Thomas Dunne Books, New York) 2006.

_____. *Day of Reckoning: How Hubris, Ideology, and Greed Are Tearing America Apart* (St. Martin's Press, New York, 2007).

Burlingame, Roger. *Don't Let Them Scare You: The Life and Times of Elmer Davis* (J.P. Lippincott Company, New York, 1961).

Buitenhaus, Peter. *The Great War of Words: British, American, and Canadian Propaganda and Fiction, 1914-1933* (University of British Columbia Press, Vancouver, 1987).

Calder, Bruce J. *The Impact of Intervention: The Dominican Republic During the U.S. Occupation of 1916-1924* (University of Texas Press, Austin TX, 1984).

Calder, Nigel. *Unless Peace Comes: A Scientific Forecast of New Weapons* (The Viking Press, New York, 1968).

Caldicott, Helen. *The New Nuclear Danger: George W. Bush's Military-Industrial Complex* (The New Press, New York, 2002).

Cannizzo, C. *The Gun Merchants* (Pergammon Press, New York, 1980).

Cantor, Mackinlay and Curtis LeMay. *Mission with LeMay* (Doubleday, New York, 1965).

Cantril, Hadley. *The Invasion from Mars: A Study in the Psychology of Panic* (Harper & Row, Publishers, New York, 1940).

Caputo, Philip. *A Rumor of War* (Holt, Rinehart and Winston, New York, 1977).

Carey, Omer L. Ed. *The Military-Industrial Complex and United States Foreign Policy* (Washington State University Press, Pullman WA, 1969).

Carroll, James. *House of War: The Pentagon and the Disastrous Rise of American Power* (Houghton Mifflin Company, New York, 2006).

Carroll, Wallace. *Persuade or Perish* (Houghton Mifflin Company, Boston, 1948).

Carson, Rachel. *Silent Spring* (Mariner Books, New York, 2002).

Catalinotto, John and Sara Flounders, Editors. *Depleted Uranium: Metal of Dishonor—How the Pentagon Radiates Soldiers & Civilians with DU Weapons* (International Action Center, New York, 1997).

Catton, Bruce. *The Warlords of Washington* (Harcourt, Brace and Company, New York, 1948).

Chamberlain, William. *America's Second Crusade* (Henry Regnery Company, Chicago, 1950).

Chandrasekaran, Rajiv. *Imperial Life in the Emerald City: Inside Iraq's Green Zone* (Alfred A. Knopf, New York, 2006).

Chidsey, Donald Barr. *The War With Mexico* (Crown Publishers, Inc., New York, 1968).

Chomsky, Noam. *Rogue States: The Rule of Force in World Affairs* (South End Press, Boston, 2000).

_____. "Cambodia," *New York Review of Books*, June 4, 1970.

_____. *Turning the Tide: The U.S. and Latin America* (Black Rose Books, New York, 1987).

_____. *Hegemony or Survival: America's Quest for Global Dominance* (Henry Holt and Company, New York, 2003).

_____. "The Menace of Liberal Scholarship," a review of *No More Vietnams?* in *New York Review of Books*, January 2, 1969.

Choukas, Michael. *Propaganda Comes of Age* (Public Affairs Press, Washington, 1965).

Churchill, Randolph S., with Martin Gilbert. *Road to Victory, 1941-1945, Vol. VII* (Houghton Mifflin, New York, 1986).

Churchill, Winston S. *Blood, Sweat, and Tears* (G.P. Putnam's Sons, New York, 1941).

Clark, Ramsey. *The Fire This Time: U.S. War Crimes in the Gulf* (Thunder's Mouth Press, New York, 1992).

Clarkson, Helen. *The Last Day: A Novel of the Day After Tomorrow* (Dodd, Mead & Company, New York, 1959). Novel.

Coffin, Tristram. *The Passion of the Hawks: Militarism in Modern America* (The Macmillan Company, New York, 1964). Also published as *The Armed Society* (Penguin, Baltimore MD) 1964.

Cohen, Warren I. *The American Revisionists: The Lessons of Intervention in World War I* (The University of Chicago Press, Chicago, 1967).

Cole, Leonard. *Clouds of Secrecy: The Army's Germ Warfare Tests over Populated Areas* (Rowman & Littlefield, Totowa NJ, 1988).

Cole, Wayne, S. *Senator Nye and American Foreign Relations* (University of Minnesota Press, Minneapolis MN, 1962).

Compton, Karl T. "If the Bomb Had Not Been Dropped," *Atlantic Monthly,* December 1946.

Connors, Michael F. *Dealing in Hate: The Development of Anti-German Propaganda* (Institute for Historical Review, New York, 1981). Pamphlet.

Cook, Blanche Wiesen. *The Declassified Eisenhower: A Divided Legacy* (Doubleday & Cook, Fred J., *The Warfare State* (The MacMillan Company, New York, 1962).

Cookson, John and Judith Nottingham. *A Survey of Chemical and Biological Warfare* (Monthly Review Press, New York, 1969).

Cooling, Benjamin Franklin. *Gray Steel and Blue Water: The Formative Years of America's Military-Industrial Complex 1881-1917* (Archon Books, Hamden CT, 1979).

_____. Ed., *War, Business and American Society: Historical Perspectives on the Military-Industrial Complex* (Kennikat, Port Washington NY, 1977).

Costello, John. *Days of Infamy: MacArthur, Roosevelt, Churchill—The Shocking Truth Revealed: How Their Secret Deals and Strategic Blunders Caused Disasters at Pearl Harbor and the Philippines* (Pocket Book, New York, 1994).

_____. *The Pacific War* (Perennial, New York, 1981).

Coulter, Mathew Ware. *The Senate Munitions Inquiry of the 1930s: Beyond the Merchants of Death* (Greenwood Press, Westport CT, 1977).

Creel, George. *How We Advertised America: The First Telling of the Amazing Story of the Committee on Public Information that Carried the Gospel of Americanism to Every Corner of the Globe* (Harper & Brothers Publishers, New York, 1920).

Crispell, Kenneth R. and Carlos P. Gomez. *Hidden Illness in the White House* (Duke University Press, Durham NC, 1988).

Crossman, R.H.S. "Apocalypse at Dresden: The Long Suppressed Story of the Worst Massacre in the History of the World," *Esquire*, November 1963.

Cudahy, John. *Archangel: The American War with Russia* (A.C. McClurg & Co., Chicago, 1924).

Cull, Nicholas John. *Selling War: The British Propaganda Campaign Against American "Neutrality" in World War II* (Oxford University Press, New York, 1995).

Cullather, Nick. *Secret History: The CIA's Classified Account of its Operations in Guatemala, 1952-1954* (Stanford University Press, Stanford CA, 2006).

Dadge, David. *Casualty of War: The Bush Administration's Assault on a Free Press* (Prometheus Books, Amherst NY, 2004).

Dallek, Robert. *An Unfinished Life: John F. Kennedy 1917-1963* (Little Brown and Company, New York, 2003).

Danner, Mark. *Torture and Truth: America, Abu Ghraib, and the War on Terror* (The New York Review of Books, New York, 2004).

Davis, Elmer. *Report to the President* (Journalism Monograph, No. Seven, Association for Education in Journalism, Austin TX, August 1968).

Denson, John. *A Century of War* (Von Mises Institute, New York, 2006).

_____. *The Costs of War: America's Pyrrhic Victories* (Transaction Publishers, New Brunswick NJ, 1997).

"Depleted Uranium—the truth and nothing but the truth," Mike Sheheane (Army Chemical Review, January 2000).

"Depleted Uranium: Scientific Basis for Assessing Risk," (Nuclear Policy Research Institute, Washington, July 2003).

Detzer, David. *The Brink* (J.M. Dent & Sons, Ltd., London, 1980).

Detzer, Dorothy. *Appointment on the Hill* (Holt, Rinehart & Winston, New York, 1948).

DeWeerd, Harvey A. *President Wilson Fights His War: World War I and the American Intervention* (The Macmillan Company, New York, 1968).

Dibble, Vernon K. "The Garrison Society," in Seymour Melman, Ed., *The War Economy of the United States* (St. Martin's Press, New York, 1971).

Dierks, Jack Cameron Dierks. *A Leap to Arms: The Cuban Campaign of 1898* (J.B. Lippincott Company, New York, 1970).

Divine, Robert A. *The Illusion of Neutrality* (The University of Chicago Press, Chicago, 1962).

Dmitrievich, Boris. *The Military-Industrial Complex of the U.S.A.* (Progress Publishers, Moscow, 1997).

Donovan, James A. *Militarism, U.S.A.* (Charles Scribner's Sons, New York, 1970).

Donovan, Robert J. "Moos Recalls Idea for Eisenhower's Militarist Phrase," *Washington Post*, March 31, 1969.

Doob, Leonard W. *Propaganda: Its Psychology and Technique* (Henry Holt and Company, New York, 1935).

Dosal, Paul J. *Doing Business With the Dictators: A Political History of United Fruit in Guatemala, 1899-1944* (Rowman & Littlefield, New York, 1993).

Dower, John W. *War Without Mercy: Race and Power in the Pacific War* (Pantheon Books, New York, 1986).

_____. *Embracing Defeat: Japan in the Wake of World War II* (W.W. Norton & Company, New York, 1999).

Draper, Theodore. *"The True History of the Gulf War,"* The New York Times Review of Books, January 30, 1992.

Duffett, John, Ed. *Against the Crime of Silence: Proceedings of the International War Crimes Tribunal* (O'Hare Books, New York, 1968).

Dufour, Charles L. *The Mexican War: A Compact History, 1846-1848* (Hawthorne Books, Inc., New York, 1968).

Duiker, William J. *Ho Chi Minh* (Hyperion, New York, 2000).

Dunbar, David and Brad Reagan. Editors, *Debunking 9/11 Myths: Why Conspiracy Theories Can't Stand Up To The Facts* (Hearst Books, New York, 2006).

Dupuy, R. Ernest and Trevor N. Dupuy. *The Encyclopedia of Military History* (Harper & Row, Publishers, New York, 1970), p. 908.

Eichelberger, Robert. *Dear Miss Em* (Greenwood Press, Westport CT, 1980).

Eisenhower, John S.D. *So Far From God: The U.S. War With Mexico 1846-1848* (Random House, New York, 1989).

Ellsberg, Daniel. *Secrets—A Memoir of Vietnam and the Pentagon Papers* (Viking, New York, 2001).

_____. *Papers on the War* (Simon and Schuster, New York, 1972).

Endicott, Stephen and Edward Hagerman, *The United States and Biological Warfare: Secrets from the Early Cold War and Korea* (University of Indiana Press, Bloomington IN, 1998).

Engelbrecht, H.C. and F.C. Hanigan. *Merchants of Death: A Study of the International Armament Industry* (George Routledge & Sons, Ltd., London, 1934).

Enthoven, Alain and K. Wayne Smith. *How Much is Enough* (Harper and Row, New York, 1971).

Evans, Richard J. *The Third Reich at War* (The Penguin Press, New York, 2009).

Fall, Bernard. *Hell in a Very Small Place: The Siege of Dien Bien Phu* (Da Capo Press, New York, 2002).

_____. *Street Without Joy: The French Debacle in Indochina* (Stackpole Books, New York, 1994).

Fay, Sidney Bradshaw. *The Origins of the World War*, two vols. (The Macmillan Company, New York, 1928).

Feerick, John D. *From Falling Hands: The Story of Presidential Succession* (Fordham University Press, New York, 1965).

Feifer, George. *The Battle of Okinawa: The Blood and the Bomb* (The Lyons Press, Guilford CT, 1992).

Feldman, Jonathan. *Universities in the Business of Repression: The Academic-Military-Industrial Complex and Central America* (South End Press, Boston, 1989).

Ferguson, Charles H. *No End in Sight: Iraq's Descent Into Chaos* (Public Affairs, New York, 2008).

Ferguson, Niall. *The Pity of War* (Basic Books, New York, 1999).

Ferrell, Robert H. "The Merchants of Death: Then and Now," *Journal of International Affairs*, Vol. 26. No. 1, 1972.

_____. *American Diplomacy: A History* (W.W. Norton & Company, Inc., New York, 1959).

_____. *Ill-Advised: Presidential Health and Public Trust* (University of Misssouri Press, Columbia MO, 1998).

Fetzer, James H. and Don Trent Jacobs. *American Assassination: The Strange Death of Senator Paul Wellstone* (Thomson-Shore, Dexter MI, 2004).

Finkelstein, Sidney, "The Power of the Pentagon," *The Progressive*, June 1969.
Fleming, D.F. *The Cold War and Its Origins, 1917-1960* (Doubleday, Garden City NY, 1995).
Fleming, Thomas. *The New Dealers' War: Franklin D. Roosevelt and The War Within World War II* (Basic Books, New York, 2001), p. 175.

_____. *The Illusion of Victory: America in World War I* (Basic Books, New York, 2003).

Flynn, John T. *The Roosevelt* Myth, The Devin-Adair Company, New York, 1948).

Foner, Phillip S. *Spanish-Cuban-American War and the Birth of American Imperialism 1895-1902* (Monthly Review Press, New York, 1972).

Frank, Richard B. *Downfall: The End of the Imperial Japanese Empire* (Random House, New York, 1999).
Freidel, Frank. *The Splendid Little War* (Little Brown and Company, Boston, 1958).

Fulbright, William. *The Pentagon Propaganda Machine* (Vintage Books. New York, 1971).

_____. *Report From Wasteland: America's Military-Industrial Complex* (Praeger Publishers, New York, 1970).

Fuller, J.F.C. *The Second World War, 1939-1945: A Strategical and Tactical History* (Duell, Sloan, Pierce, New York, 1948).

Furlong, Craig and Gordon Ross. "Seismic Proof:: 9/11 Was an Inside Job." Technical paper.

Galbraith, John Kenneth. "How to Control the Military," *Harpers*, June 1969.

_____. *The New Industrial State* (Signet., New York, 1967).

_____. *A Life in Our Times* (Houghton Mifflin Company, Boston, 1981).

Gallagher, Hugh Gregory. *FDR's Splendid Deception* (Dodd, Mead & Company, New York, 1992).

Gardner, Lloyd C., Ed. *The Korean War* (Quadrangle Books, New York, 1972).

Gerard, James W. *My Four Years in Germany* (George H. Doran Company, New York, 1917).

_____. *Face to Face With Kaiserism* (George H. Doran Company, New York, 1918).

Gerassi, John. *The Great Fear in Latin America* (Collins Books, New York, 1965).

Gibbs, Phillip. *Now It Can Be Told* (Garden City Publishing Co., Inc., Garden City, New York, 1920).

Gibson, James William. *The Perfect War: Technowar in Vietnam* (The Atlantic Monthly Press, New York, 1986).

Gilbert, Robert E. *Mortal Presidency: Illness and Anguish in the White House* (Basic Books, New York, 1992).

Gilderhus, Mark T. *Pan American Visions: Woodrow Wilson in the Western Hemisphere 1913-1921* (The University of Arizona Press, Tucson AZ, 1986).

Ginsberg, Benjamin. *The Captive Public: How Mass Opinion Promotes State Power* (Basic Books, Inc., Publishers, New York, 1986).

Goldhurst, Richard. *The Midnight War: The American Intervention in Russia, 1918-1929* (McGraw-Hill Book Company, New York, 1978).

Goodheart, Philip. *Fifty Ships That Saved the World: The Foundation of the Anglo-American Alliance* (Doubleday & Company, New York, 1965).

Goodman, Amy and David. *Static: Government Liars, Media Cheerleaders, and the People Who Fight Back* (Hyperion, New York, 2006).

Gottleib, Sanford. *Defense Addiction: Can American Kick the Habit* (Westview Press, Boulder CO, 1997).

Goulden, Joseph C. *Truth is the First Casualty: The Gulf of Tonkin Affair—Illusion and Reality* (Rand McNally, New York, 1969).

_____. *Korea: The Untold Story of the War* (Times Books, New York, 1982).

Grant, Ulysses S. *The Personal Memoirs of Ulysses S. Grant* (Charles L. Webster & Company, New York, 1885).

Grattan, C. Hartley. *The Deadly Parallel* (Stackpole Sons, New York, 1939).

_____. *Why We Fought* (The Bobbs-Merrill Company, Inc., New York, 1930).

Greene, David. *The Containment of Latin America: A History of the Myths and Realities of the Good Neighbor Policy* (Quadrangle Books, Chicago, 1971).

Gregg, Charles T. *Tarawa* (Stein and Day, New York, 1984).

Greider, William. *Fortress America: The American Military and the Consequences of Peace* (Public Affairs, New York, 1998).

Grenfell, Russell R.N. *Unconditional Hatred: German War Guilt and the Future of Europe* (The Devin Adair Company, New York, 1959).

Griffin, David Ray. *The New Pearl Harbor: Disturbing Questions About the Bush Administration and 9/11* (Olive Branch Press, Northhampton MA, 2004).

_____. *The 9/11 Commission Report: Omissions and Distortions* (Olive Branch Press, Northhampton MA, 2005).

_____. *Debunking 9/11 Debunking: An Answer to Popular Mechanics and Other Defenders of the Official Conspiracy Theory* (Olive Branch Press, Northhampton MA, 2007).

Griffin, David Ray and Peter Dale Scott. *9/11 and American Empire: Intellectuals Speak Out* (Olive Branch Press, Northampton MA, 2006).

Guderian, Heinz. *Panzer Leader* (Dutton, New York, 1952).

Gunther, John. *The Riddle of MacArthur: Japan, Korea and the Far East* (Harper & Brothers, New York, 1950).

Gurney, Gene. *The Pentagon* (Crown, New York, 1964).

Halbertsam, David. *The Making of a Quagmire* (Ballantine Books, New York, 1964).

_____. *The Best and the Brightest* (Random House, New York, 1969).

_____. *The Coldest War: America and the Korean War* (Hyperion, New York, 2007).

Hamlin, Charles Hunter. *Propaganda and Myth in Time of War* (Garland Publishing, Inc., Norton & Company, New York, 1979).

Hanley, Charles J., Sang-Hun Choe, and Martha Mendoza. *The Bridge at No Gun Ri: A Hidden Nightmare from the Korean War* (Henry Holt and Company, New York, 2001).

Hankey, Lord. *Politics, Trials and Errors* (Henry Regnery, Chicago, 1950).

Hanson, Neil. *Unknown Soldiers: The Story of the Missing of the First World War* (Alfred A. Knopf, New York, 2006).

Hanson, Victor Davis. *Mexifornia: A State of Becoming* (Encounter Books, San Francisco, 2003).

Harper's, "Should the United States Fight Secret Wars?" September 1984.

Harris, Robert and Jeremy Paxman. *A Higher Form of Killing: The Secret Story of Chemical and Biological Warfare* (Hill and Wang, New York, 1982).

Harris, Sheldon H. *Factories of Death; Japanese Biological Warfare 1932-1945 and the American Cover-Up* (Routledge, New York, 1994).

Hart, B.H. Liddell. *The German Generals Talk* (William Morrow & Co., New York, 1948).

Hastings, Max. *The Korean War* (Simon & Schuster, New York, 1987).

Heilbroner, Richard. "Military America," *New York Review of Books,* July 23, 1970.

Heise, Juergen Arthur. *Minimum Disclosure: How the Pentagon Manipulates the News* (Norton, New York, 1979).

Henry, Robert Selph. *The Story of the Mexican War* (The Bobbs-Merrill Company, Inc., New York, 1950).

Herman, Edward. *The Real Terror Network* (Sound End Press, Boston, 1982).

Herr, Michael. *Dispatches* (Vintage Books, New York, 1991).

Herring, George C. *America's Longest War: The United States and Vietnam, 1950-1975* (John Wiley & Sons, New York, 1979).

Hersey, John. *Hiroshima* (Vintage, New York, 1989).

Hersh, Seymour M. *My Lai 4: A Report on the Massacre and Its Aftermath* (Random House, New York, 1970).

_____. *Cover-Up: The Army Secret Investigation of the Massacre at My Lai 4* (Random House, New York, 1972).

_____. "Overwhelming Force: What Happened in the Final Days of the Gulf War?" *The New Yorker*, May 22, 2000.

_____. *The Samson Option: Israel's Nuclear Arsenal and American Foreign Policy* (Random House, New York, 1991).

_____. *Chemical and Biological Warfare: America's Hidden Arsenal* (Bobbs-Merrill, New York, 1968).

_____. *Chain of Command: The Road from 9/11 to Abu Ghraib* (Harper Collins Publishers, New York, 2004).

_____. "Torture at Abu Ghraib," *The New Yorker*, May 10, 2004.

Hertsgaard, Mark. *On Bended Knee* (Farrar Straus, New York, 1988).

Hitler, Adolf. *Mein Kampf* (Houghton Mifflin Company, New York, 1925).

Hoffman, Don Paul and Jim Hoffman. *Waking Up From Our Nightmare: The 9/11/01 Crimes in New York City* (Irresistible/Revolutionary, San Francisco, 2004).

Hooks, Gregory. *Forging the Military-Industrial Complex of the U.S.A.: World War II's Battle of the Potomac* (University of Illinois Press, Chicago, 1991).

Hopsicker, Daniel. *Welcome to Terrorland: Mohammed Atta and the 9/11 Coverup in Florida* (Trine Day, New York, 2004).

Horowitz, Irving Louis. *The War Game* (Ballantine, New York, 1963).

Hough, Stanley B. *Extinction Bomber* (The Broadley Head, London, 1956).

Howe, Quincy. *England Expects Every American To Do His Duty* (Simon and Schuster, New York, 1937).

Hudson, Miles. *Intervention in Russia 1918-1920: A Cautionary Tale* (Leo Cooper, Barnsley, South Yorkshire, England, 2004).

Hufschmid, Eric. *Painful Questions: An Analysis of the September 11th Attack* (Endpoint Software, Goleta CA, 2002).

Hyde, H. Montgomery. *Room 3603: The Story of the British Intelligence Center in New York During World War II* (Farrar, Straus and Company, New York, 1962).

Immerman, Richard H. *The CIA in Guatemala: The Foreign Policy of Intervention* (University of Texas Press, Austin TX, 1983).

Irving, David. *The Mare's Nest* (Little, Brown and Company, Boston, 1965).

_____. *The Destruction of Dresden* (Kimber, London, 1963)

Irwin, Will. *Propaganda and the News* (Greenwood Press, Westport CT, 1970).

Isikoff, Michael and David Corn. *Hubris: The Inside Story of Spin, Scandal, and the Selling of the Iraq War* (Crown Publishers, New York, 2006).

Ivor, Stephen F. *Neutrality* (The Neutrality Press, Chicago, 1916).

Jenkins, Dominick. *The Final Frontier: America, Science and Terror* (Verso, London, 2002).

Johnson, Chalmers. *Blowback: The Costs and Consequences of American Empire* (Henry Holt and Company, New York, 2000).

_____. *The Sorrows of Empire: Militarism, Secrecy, and the End of the Republic* (Henry Holt and Company, New York, 2004).

_____. *Nemesis: The Last Days of the American Republic* (Henry Holt and Company, New York, 2006).

Jones, Neville. *The Beginnings of Strategic Air Power* (Frank Cass, London, 1987).

Kagan, Robert. *Dangerous Nation* (Alfred A. Knopf, New York, 2006).

Karnow, Stanley. *Vietnam, A History* (Penguin, New York, 1997).

_____. *In Our Image: America's Empire in the Philippines* (Ballantine Books, New York, 1990).

Karp, Walter. *The Politics of War: The Story of Two Wars Which Altered Forever the Political Life of the American Republic 1890-1920* (Harper & Row, Publishers, New York, 1979).

"The Kennedy Vendetta, *Harper's*, August 1975, p. 49-63.

Kean, Thomas H. and Lee H. Hamilton. *Without Precedent: The Inside Story of the 9/11 Commission* (Alfred A. Knopf, New York, 2006).

Kellner, Douglas. *From 9/11 to Terror War: The Dangers of the Bush Legacy* (Rowman & Littlefield Publishers, Inc., New York, 2003).

_____. *Media Spectacle and the Crisis of Democracy* (Routledge, New York, 2003).

Kennedy, Paul. *The Rise and Fall of the Great Powers: Economic Change and Military Conflict from 1500 to 2000* (Random House, New York, 1987).

Kennedy, Robert F. *Thirteen Days: A Memoir of the Cuban Missile Crisis* (W.W. Norton & Company, New York, 1968).

Kershaw, Ian. *Fateful Choices: Ten Decisions That Changed the World 1940-1941* (The Penguin Press, New York, 2007).

Kennan, George F. *Russia Leaves the War: Soviet-American Relations 1917-1920* (W.W. Norton & Company, New York, 1958).

Keynes, John Maynard. *The Economic Consequences of the Peace* (Macmillan and Co., Limited, London, 1920).

Kimball, Warren F. *The Most Unsordid Act: Lend-Lease, 1939-1941* (Johns Hopkins Press, Baltimore MD, 1969), p. 48.

King, Benjamin & Timothy Kutta. *Impact: The History of Germany's V-Weapons in World War II* (Sarpedon, Rockville Centre NY, 1998).

Kinzer, Stephen. *Bitter Fruit: The Untold Story of the American Coup in Guatemala* (Doubleday, Garden City NY, 1982).

_____. *Overthrow: America's Century of Regime Change From Hawaii to Iraq* (Henry Holt and Company, LLC, New York, 2006).

Kipp, Robert M. "Counterinsurgency from 30,000 Feet: The B-52 in Vietnam," (*Air University Review*, Maxwell AFB, Alabama) January-February 1968.

Kirk, Donald. *Wider War: The Struggle for Cambodia, Thailand, and Laos* (Praeger, New York, 1971).

Klare, Michael. *War Without End: American Planning for the Next Vietnams* (Vintage, New York, 1972).

_____. *Blood and Oil: The Dangers and Consequences of America's Growing Dependence on Imported Petroleum* (The Johns Hopkins Press, Baltimore MD, 2002).

_____. "The Pursuit of Perpetual Supremacy: Decoding the Administration's Military Budget," *The Nation*, July 15, 2002.

Knebel, Fletcher & Charles W. Bailey II. *Seven Days in May* (Harper & Row, Publishers, New York, 1962). Novel.

Knightley, Philip. *The First Casualty: From the Crimea to Vietnam: The War Correspondent as Hero, Propagandist, and Myth Maker* (Harcourt Brace Jovanovich, New York, 1975).

Kolko, Gabriel. *Century of War: Politics, Conflicts, and Society Since 1914* (The New Press, New York, 1994).

_____. *Anatomy of a War: Vietnam, the United States, and the Modern Historical Experience* (Pantheon, New York, 1986).

Konlechnor, Peter and Peter Kubleka. "The Industrial-Military Complex," *Business History Review* 41, Winter 1967, p. 378-403.

_____. "The Industrial-Military Complex: Inter-War Years," *Journal of American History* vol. 56, March 1970, p. 819-839.

Kornbluh, Peter, Editor. *Bay of Pigs Declassified: The Secret CIA Report on the Invasion of Cuba* (The New Press, New York, 1998).

Kostinen, Paul A.C. *The Military-Industrial Complex: A Historical Perspective* (Praeger Publishers, New York, 1980).

Kurtz, Howard. *Spin Cycle: Inside the Clinton Propaganda Machine* (The Free Press, New York, 1998).

Kwitny, Jonathan. *Endless Enemies: The Making of an Unfriendly World* (Penguin, New York, 1986).

La Feber, Walter. *The New Empire: An Interpretation of American Expansion 1860-1898* (Cornell University Press, Ithica NY, 1963).

Lapp, Ralph E. *The Weapons Culture* (W.W. Norton & Company, Inc., New York).

Lashmar, Paul. *Spy Flights of the Cold War* (Naval Institute Press, Annapolis MD, 1996).

Lasswell, Harold D. *Propaganda Technique in the World War* (Alfred A. Knopf, New York, 1927).

Lavine, Harold. *War Propaganda and the United States* (Garland Publishing, Inc., New York, 1972).

Leahy, William D. *I Was There: The Personal Story of the Chief of Staff of Presidents Roosevelt and Truman, Based on His Notes and Diaries Made at the Time* (Arno Press, New York, 1979).

Leckie, Robert. *The Wars of America* (Harper & Row, Publishers, New York, 1968).

Leigh, Michael. *Permanent War: The Militarization of America* (Scoken Books, New York, 1987).

Lens, Sidney. *The Military-Industrial Complex* (Pilgrim Press, Philadelphia, 1970).

_____. *Permanent War: The Militarization of America* (Scoken Books, New York, 1987).

Lerner, Daniel. *Sykewar* (George W. Stewart, Publishers, New York, 1949).

_____. *Propaganda in War and Crisis* (Arno Press, New York, 1972).

Leslie, Paul, Editor. *The Gulf War as Popular Entertainment* (Columbia University Press, New York, 1985).

Leslie, Stuart W. *The Cold War and American Science: The Military-Industrial Complex at MIT and Stanford* (Columbia University Press, New York, 1993).

Levine, Alan J. *The Strategic Bombing of Germany, 1940-1945* (Praeger, Westport CT, 1992).

Lewin, Leonard C. *Report From Iron Mountain On the Possibility and Desirability of Peace* (Dial Press, New York, 1967).

Lewis, Justin. *Constructing Public Opinion: How Power Elites Do What They Like and Why We Seem to Go Along With It* (Columbia University Press, New York, 2001).

Lewy, Guenter. *America in Vietnam* (Oxford University Press, New York, 1978).

Lifton, Robert Jay. *Destroying the World to Save It: Aum Shinrik, Apocalyptic Violence and the New Global Terrorisim* (Owl Books, New York, 2000).

Lindbergh, Charles A. *The Wartime Journals of Charles A. Lindberg* (Harcourt Brace Jovanovich, Inc., New York, 1970).

Lindqvist, Sven. *A History of Bombing* (The New Press, New York, 2000).

Linenthal, Edward T. and Tom Engelhardt, Editors. *History Wars: The Enola Gay and Other Battles for the American Past* (Henry Holt and Company, New York, 1996).

Linn, Brian McAllister. *The Philippine War 1899-1902* (University Press of Kansas, Lawrence KS, 2000).

Lippman, Walter. *Public Opinion* (Harcourt, Brace, New York, 1922).

Littauer, Raphael and Norman Uphoff, Editors. *The Air War in Indochina* (Beacon Press, Boston, 1972).

Loewen, James W. *Lies My Teacher Told Me: Everything Your American History Textbook Got Wrong* (The New Press, New York, 1995).

Lorenz, Konrad. *On Aggression* (Harcourt Brace Jovanovich, New York, 1963).

Lothian, Lord. *The American Speeches of Lord Lothian: July 1939 to December 1940* (Oxford University Press, New York, 1941).

Lumley, Frederick E. *The Propaganda Menace* (Century, New York, 1933).

Lyle, D. "Plague and War," *Esquire*, September 1966.

MacArthur, John R. *Second Front: Censorship and Propaganda in the Gulf War* (Hill and Wang, New York, 1992).

MacClear, Michael. *The Ten-Thousand Day War* (St. Martin's Press, New York, 1981).

MacDonald, Callum A. *Korea: The War Before Vietnam* (The Free Press, New York, 1986).

MacIsaac, David. *Strategic Bombing in World War II—The Story of the United States Strategic Bombing Survey* (Garland Publishing Company, New York, 1976).

Mahajan, Rahul. *The New Crusade: America's War on Terrorism* (Monthly Review Press, New York, 2002).

_____. *Full Spectrum Dominance: U.S. Power in Iraq and Beyond* (Consortium Book Sales, New York, 2003).

Mahr, Thomas E. *Desperate Deception: British Covert Operations in the United States, 1939-44* (Brassey's, Washington, 1998).

Mahurin, Walker "Bud". *Honest John: The Autobiography of Walker M. Mahurin* (G.P. Putnam's Sons, New York, 1962).

Malcolm, Noel. *Kosovo: A Short History* (New York University Press, New York, 1998).

Manchester, William. *American Caesar: Douglas MacArthur 1880-1964* (Little, Brown and Company, Boston, 1978).

_____. *Goodbye Darkness: A Memoir of the Pacific War* (Little, Brown and Company, Boston, 1979).

_____. *The Arms of Krupp: 1587-1968* (Little Brown and Company, Boston, 1964).

Marrs, Jim, *Inside Job: Unmasking the 9/11 Conspiracies* (Origin Press, San Raphael CA, 2004).

_____. *The Terror Conspiracy: Deception, 9/11, and the Loss of Liberty* (Disinformation Company Ltd., New York, 2006).

Marshall, Logan. *Horrors and Atrocities of the Great War* (Office of Air Force History, Washington, 1978).

Martin, James J. *Revisionist Viewpoints; Essays in a Dissident Historical Tradition* (Ralph Myles Publisher, Inc., Colorado Springs CO, 1971).

Massing, Michael. "Grenada Before and After," *Atlantic Monthly*, February 1984, p. 79-80.

Mast, Gerald, Editor. *The Movies in our Midst* (University of Chicago Press, Chicago, 1982).

McCann, Thomas. *An American Company: The Tragedy of United Fruit* (Crown, New York, 1976).

McCarthy, Richard D. *The Ultimate Folly: War by Pestilence, Asphyxiation and Defoliation* (Alfred A. Knopf, New York, 1969).

McCoy, Alfred W. *A Question of Torture: CIA Interrogation, from the Cold War to the War on Terror* (Henry Holt and Company, New York, 2006).

McCormick, Anita Louise. *The Vietnam Antiwar Movement in America,* (Enslow Publishers, Inc., Berkeley Heights NJ, 2000).

McCullough, David. *The Path Between the Seas: The Creation of the Panama Canal 1870-1914* (Simon and Schuster, New York, 1977).

McDermott, Jeanne. *The Killing Winds: The Menace of Biological Warfare* (Arbor House, New York, 1987).

McFarland, Stephen L. *America's Pursuit of Precision Bombing, 1919-1945* (Smithsonian Institution Press, Washington, 1966).

McGovern, James. *To the Yalu: From the Chinese Invasion of Korea to MacArthur's Dismissal* (William Morrow and & Company, Inc., New York, 1972).

McNamara, Robert S. *In Retrospect: The Tragedy and Lessons of Vietnam* (Vintage Books, New York, 1995).

McNeill, William H. *The Pursuit of Power: Technology, Armed Forces and Society Since A.D. 1000* (The University of Chicago Press, Chicago, 1982).

McQuaig, Linda. *It's the Crude, Dude: War, Business and the Fight for the Planet* (Doubleday Canada, 2004).

Mearsheimer, John J. and Stephen M. Walt. *The Israel Lobby and U.S. Foreign Policy* (Farrar, Straus and Giroux, New York, 2006).

McKeen, Alexander. *Dresden 1945: The Devil's Tinderbox* (E.P. Dutton, Inc., New York, 1982).

Melman, Seymour. *Pentagon Capitalism: The Political Economy of War* (McGraw-Hill, New York, 1970).

Melton, Carol K.W. *Between War and Peace: Woodrow Wilson and The American Expeditionary Force in Siberia, 1918-21* (Mercer University Press, Macon GA, 2001).

Merk, Frederick. *The Monroe Doctrine and American Expansionism: 1843-1849* (Alfred A. Knopf, New York, 1966).

Meserve, Walter J. *Robert E. Sherwood: Reluctant Moralist* (Pegasus, New York, 1970).

Meyssan, Thierry. *9/11: The Big Lie* (Carnote Publishing Ltd., London, 2002).

_____. *Pentagate* (Carnot Publishing Ltd., London, 2002).

Middlebrook, Martin. *The Battle of Hamburg: The Firestorm Raid* (Cassell & Co., London, 1980).

_____. *The Berlin Raids: RAF Bomber Command Winter 1943-44* (Viking, London, 1988).

_____. *The Nuremberg Raid: The Worst Night of the War, March 30-31, 1944* (William Morrow & Company, Inc., New York, 1974).

Miller, David. *Tell Me Lies: Propaganda and Media Distortion in the Attack on Iraq* (Pluto Press, London, 2004).

Miller, John C. *Sam Adams: Pioneer in Propaganda* (Little Brown, Boston, 1936).

Miller, Stuart Creighton. *Benevolent Assimilation: The American Conquest of the Philippines, 1899-1903* (Yale University Press, New Haven CT, 1982).

Millis, Walter. *Road to War: America 1914-1917* (The Riverside Press, Cambridge MA, 1935).

_____. *The Martial Spirit: A Study of Our War With Spain* (The Literary Guild of America, Cambridge MA, 1931).

_____. *Arms and Men: A Study in American Military History* (Rutgers University Press, New Brunswick Press, New Brunswick NJ, 1981).

Mills, C. Wright. *The Power Elite* (Oxford University Press, New York, 1956).
Milton, Joyce. *The Yellow Kids: Foreign Correspondents in the Heyday of Yellow Journalism* (Harper & Row, Publishers, New York, 1989).

Mitchell, Donald W. *A History of the Modern American Navy: From 1883 Through Pearl Harbor* (Alfred A. Knopf, New York, 1946).

Mock, James R. and Cedric Larson. *Words That Won the War: The Story of the Committee on Public Information, 1917-1919* (Princeton University Press, Princeton NJ, 1939).

Moise, Edwin E. *Tonkin Gulf and the Escalation of the Vietnam War* (University of North Carolina Press, Chapel Hill NC, 1996).

Moore, Harold G. and Joseph Galloway. *We Are Soldiers Still: A Journey Back to the Battlefields of Vietnam* (Harper, New York, 2008).

Moore, Michael. *Fahrenheit 911* (Simon and Schuster, New York, 2004).

_____. *Dude, Where's My Country?* (Warner Books, Inc., New York, 2003).

Morgan, H. Wayne. *America's Road to Empire: The War With Spain and Overseas Expansion* (John Wiley and Sons, Inc., New York, 1966).

Morgan, Rowland and Ian Henshall. *9/11 Revealed: The Unanswered Questions* (Carroll & Graf Publishers, New York, 2005).

Morgenthau, Henry. *Ambassador Morgenthau's Story* (Doubleday, Page, New York, 1918).

Morgenthau III, Henry. *Mostly Morgenthaus—A Family History* (Ticknor & Fields, New York, 1991).

Morris, Christopher. *The Day They Lost the H Bomb* (Coward-McAnn, Inc., New York, 1966).

Mosier, John. *The Myth of the Great War: How the Germans Won the Battles and How the Americans Saved the Allies* (Harper Collins Publishers, New York, 2001).

_____. *The Blitzkrieg Myth: How Hitler and the Allies Misread the Strategic Realities of World War II* (Harper Collins Publishers, New York, 2003).

Mueller, John. *Overblown: How Politicians and the Terrorism Industry Inflate National Security Threats and Why We Believe Them* (Free Press, New York, 2006).

Musicant, Ivan. *Empire by Default: The Spanish-American War and the Dawn of the American Century* (Henry Holt and Company, New York, 1998).

Nardo, Don. *The Mexican-American War* (Lucent Books, Inc., San Diego CA, 1999).

Nasaw, David. *The Chief: The Life of William Randolph Hearst* (Houghton Mifflin Company, New York, 2000).

National Commission on Terrorist Attacks, *The 9/11 Commission Report: Final Report of the National Commission on Terrorist Attacks Upon the United States* (W.W. Norton & Company, New York, 2004).

Nelson, Lars-Erik. "Military-Industrial Man," *The New York Review,* December 21, 2000.

Neufeld, Michael J. *The Rocket and the Reich: Peenemunde and the Coming of the Ballistic Missile Era* (The Free Press, New York, 1995).

Nicholson, Harold. *Peacemaking 1919: Being Reminiscences of the Paris Peace Conference* (Houghton Mifflin Company, New York, 1933).

Nielands, J.B., G.H. Orians, E.W. Pfeiffer. A Vennema, and A.H. Westing, *Harvest of Death: Chemical Warfare in Vietnam and Cambodia* (Free Press, New York, 1972).

Noel-Baker, Phillip. *The Private Manufacture of Armaments* (Dover Publications, Inc., New York, 1972).

The New York Times editorial, "The Lie That Wasn't Shot Down," January 18, 1988.

Oberdorfer, Don. *Tet* (Doubleday, New York, 1971).

O'Connor, Raymond G. *Diplomacy for Victory: FDR and Unconditional Surrender* (W.W. Norton & Company, Inc., New York, 1971).

Offner, John L. *An Unwanted War: The Diplomacy of the United States and Spain Over Cuba* (The University of North Carolina Press, Chapel Hill NC, 1992).

Oriens, Gordon and E.W. Pfeiffer. "Ecological Effects of the War in Vietnam," *Science*, May 1, 1970.

Orwell, George. *1984* (New American Library, New York, 1961).

O'Shaughnessy, Hugh. *Grenada: An Eyewitness Account of the U.S. Invasion and the Caribbean History That Provoked It* (Dodd, Mead Company, New York, 1985).

O'Toole, G.J.A. *The Spanish War: An American Epic 1898* (W.W. Norton, New York, 1984).

_____. *Honorable Treachery: A History of U.S. Intelligence, Espionage, and Covert Action From the American Revolution to the CIA* (The Atlantic Monthly Press, New York, 1991).

Palmer, Bruce. *The 25-Year War: America's Military Role in Vietnam* (The University Press of Kentucky, Lexington KY, 1984).

Parenti, Michael. *The Terrorism Trap: September 11 and Beyond* (City Lights Books, San Francisco, 2002).

_____. *Against Empire* (City Lights, San Francisco, 1995).

_____. *To Kill a Nation: The Attack on Yugoslavia* (Verso, London, 2000).

_____. *Inventing Reality* (St. Martin's, New York, 1993).

_____. *The Anti-Communist Impulse* (Random House, New York, 1969).

_____. *The Vietnam Antiwar Movement in America* (Random House, New York, 1996).

Park, Bert Edward, *The Impact of Illness on World Leaders* (University of Pennsylvnia Press, Philadelphia, 1986).

Patti, Archimedes L.A. *Why Vietnam: Prelude To America's Albatross* (University of California Press, Los Angeles, 1980).

Paul, Don and Jim Hoffman. *Waking Up From Our Nightmare: The 9/11 Crimes in New York*.

Pearce, Jenny. *Under the Eagle: U.S. Intervention in Central Amrica and the Caribbean* (South End Press, Cambridge MA, 1983).

Perera, Guido R. *Leaves From My Book of Life,* Vol. II (Privately printed, Boston, 1975).

Perkins, Dexter. *Hands Off: A History of the Monroe Doctrine* (Little Brown and Company, Boston, 1945).

Perlo, Victor. *Militarism and Industry: Arms Profiteering in the Missile Age* (International Publishers, New York, 1963).

Perrucci, Robert and Marc Pilisuk. *The Triple Revolution* (Little Brown, Boston, 1971).

Persico, Joseph E. *Nuremberg* (Penguin Books, New York, 1995).

_____. *11th Month, 11th Day, 11th Hour: Armistice Day, 1918, World War I and its Violent Climax* (Random House, New York, 2004).

Pilger, John. *Heroes* (South End Press, Cambridge MA, 1986).

Ponsonby, Arthur. *Falsehood in War-Time* (E.P. Dutton & Co., Inc., New York, 1928).

Ponting, Clive. *Churchill* (Sinclair-Stevenson, London, 1994).

Prados, John. *The Sky Would Fall—Operation Vulture: The U.S. Bombing Mission in Indochina, 1954* (The Dial Press, New York, 1983).

Pratkanis, Anthony and Elliott Aronson. *Age of Propaganda: The Everyday Use and Abuse of Persuasion* (W.H. Freeman and Company, New York, 1992).

Price, Glenn W. *Origins of the War with Mexico: The Polk-Stockton Intrigue* (University of Texas Press, Austin TX, 1967).

Pringle, Henry F. *Theodore Roosevelt: A Biography* (Harcourt Brace and Company, New York, 1931).

Prestowitz, Clyd. *Rogue Nation: American Unilateralism and the Failure of Good Intentions* (Basic Books, New York, 2003).

Prouty, L. Fletcher. *The Secret Team: The CIA and its Allies in Control of the United States and the World* (Ballantine Books, New York, 1974).

Proxmire, William *Report from Wasteland: America's Military-Industrial Complex* (Praeger Publishers, New York, 1970).

Pursell, Carroll W. Jr., *The Military-Industrial Complex* (Harper & Row, Publishers, New York, 1972).

Pyadyshev, B. *The Military-Industrial Complex of the USA* (Progress Publishers, Moscow, 21, Zobovksy Boulevard, 1977).

Pythian, Mark. *Arming Iraq: How the U.S. and Britain Secretly Built Saddam's War Machine* (Northeastern University Press, Boston, 1997).

Quester, George. *Deterrence Before Hiroshima* (Wiley, New York, 1966).

Quigley, John. *The Ruses for War: American Intervention Since World War II* (Prometheus Books, Buffalo NY, 1992).

Ranelagh, John. *The Agency: The Rise and Decline of the CIA From Wild Bill Donovan to William Casey* (Simon and Schuster, New York, 1986).

Rappaport, Armin. *The Navy League of the United States* (Wayne State University Press, Detroit MI, 1962).

"Ravaging Vietnam," *The Nation*, April 21, 1969.

Ray Robert. *A Certain Tendency of the Hollywood Cinema, 1930-1950* (Princeton University Press, Princeton NJ, 1985).

Regis, Ed. *The Biology of Doom: The History of America's Secret Germ Warfare Project* (Henry Holt and Company, New York, 1999).

Remarque, Erich Maria. *All Quiet on the Western Front,* Novel, Fawcett Publications (1967)

Philip K. Reynolds. *The Banana: Its History, Cultivation, and Place Among Staple Foods* (Houghton Mifflin, Boston, 1927).

Rhodes, Benjamin D. *The Anglo-American Winter War with Russia, 1918-1919: A Diplomatic and Military Tragicomedy* (Greenwood Press, Westport CT, 1988).

Rhodes, Richard. *Arsenals of Folly: The Making of the Nuclear Arms Race* (Alfred A. Knopf, New York, 2007).

Rice, Berkely. *The C-5A Scandal: An Inside Story of the Military-Industrial Complex* (Houghton Mifflin Company, Boston, 1974).

Rich, Frank. *The Greatest Story Ever Sold: The Decline and Fall of Truth From 9/11 to Katrina* (The Penguin Press, New York, 2006).

Rickover, Hyman G. *How the Battleship Maine was Destroyed* (Naval History Div., Dept. of the Navy, Washington, 1976).

_____. *Eminent Americans: Namesakes of the Polaris Submarine Fleet* (H.G. Rickover, Washington, 1972).

Ricks, Thomas E. *Fiasco: The American Military Adventure in Iraq* (The Penguin Press, New York, 2006).

_____. *The Gamble: General David Petraeus and the American Military Adventure in Iraq 2006-2008* (Penguin Group, New York, 2008).

Roberts, Chalmers M. *The Nuclear Years: The Arms Race and Arms Control, 1945-1970* (Praeger, New York, 1970).

Rogerson, Sidney. *Propaganda and the Next War* (Garland Publishing, Inc., New York, 1972).

Rose, Steven. *CBW: Chemical and Biological Warfare* (Beacon Press, New York, 1969).
Roshwald, Mordecai. *Level 7* (Lawrence Hill Books, Chicago, 1959). Fiction.

Ross, Bill D. *Iwo Jima: Legacy of Valor* (The Vanguard Press, New York, 1985).

Ross, Stewart Halsey. *Propaganda for War: How the United States Was Conditioned to Fight the Great War of 1914-1918* (McFarland & Company, Inc., Publishers, Jefferson NC, 1996).

_____. *How Roosevelt Failed America in World War II* (McFarland Publishing Co., Inc., Jefferson NC, 2006).

Rotberg, Robert I. *Haiti: The Politics of Squalor (*Houghton Mifflin Company, Boston, 1971).

Rowland, Morgan and Ian Henshall. *9/11 Revealed: The Unanswered Questions* (Carroll & Graf Publishers, New York, 2005).

Roy, Jules. *The Battle of Dien Bien Phu* (Harper & Row, New York, 1965).

Ruppert, Michael C. *Crossing the Rubicon: 9/11 and the Decline of the American Empire at the End of the Age of Oil* (New Society Publishers, Gabriola Island, BC, Canada, 2004).

Rusbridger, James & Eric Nave. *Betrayal at Pearl Harbor: How Chuchill Lured Roosevelt Into WWII* (Summit Books, New York, 1991).

Russ, Martin. *Breakout—Korea 1950: The Chosin Reservoir Campaign* (Penguin Books, New York, 1999).

Russell, Bertrand. *War Crimes in Vietnam: "Prevent the Crime of Silence"* (Bertrand Russell Peace Foundation, Nottingham, England, 1966)

Russett, Bruce. *No Clear and Present Danger* (Harper & Row, New York, 1972).

_____. *What Price Vigilance? The Burden of National Defense* (Yale University Press, New Haven CT, 1970).

Ryan, Mark. *Chinese Attitudes Toward Nuclear Weapons: China and the US During the Korean War* (Armonk, NY, 1992).

Sanders, M.L. and Philip M. Taylor. *British Propaganda During the First World War, 1914-1918* (Macmillan, London, 1982).

Sarkesian, Sam S., Editor. *The Military-Industrial Complex: A Reassessment* (Sage Publications, Inc., Beverly Hilla CA, 1972).

Saul, Norman E. *War and Revolution: The United States and Russia, 1914-1921* (University Press of Kansad, Lawrence KS, 2001).

Sayers, Michael and Albert E. Kahn. *The Great Conspiracy: The Secret War Against Soviet Russia* (Little, Brown and Company, Boston, 1946).

Scahill, Jeremy. Blackwater: *The Rise of the World's Most Powerful Mercenary Army* (Nation Books, New York, 2007).

Schell, Jonathan. *The Military Half: An Account of Destruction in Quang Ngaia and Quang Tin* (Alfred A. Knopf, New York, 1968).

_____. *The Seventh Decade: The New Shape of Nuclear Danger* (Henry Holt and Company, LLC, New York, 2007).

Schelling, T.C. *Arms and Influence* (Yale University Press, New Haven CT, 1966).

Schlesinger, Arthur M., Jr. *A Thousand Days* (Houghton Mifflin, Boston, 1965).

_____. *The Imperial Presidency* (Houghton Mifflin Company, Boston, 1973).

Schlesinger, Stephen and Stephen Kinzer, *Bitter Fruit: The Untold Story of the American Coup in Guatemala* (AnchorBooks, Garden City NY, 1983).

Schriftgeissee, Karl. *The Lobbyists: The Art and Business of Influencing Lawmakers* (Little Brown and Company, Boston, 1951).

Schroeder, John H. *Mr. Polk's War: American Opposition and Dissent, 1846-1848* (Univ. of Wisconsin Press, Madison)

Schuman, Frederick Lewis. *American Policy Toward Russia Since 1917: A Study of Diplomatic History, International Law & Public Opinion* (International Publishers, New York, 1928).

Scientific American, "When the Twin Towers Fell: One month after the attack on the World Trade Center, M.I.T. structural engineers offer their take on how and why the towers came down," October 9, 2001.

Scott, Bill. *Inside the Stealth Bomber: The B-2 Story* (Tab/Aero Books, New York, 1991).

Seib, Philip. *Broadcasts From the Blitz: How Edward R. Murrow Helped Lead America Into War* (Potomac Books, Inc., Washington, 2007).

Seldes, George. *Iron, Blood, and Profits* (Harper, New York, 1934).

Shawcross, William. *Sideshow: Kissinger, Nixon and the Destruction of Cambodia* (Cooper Square Press, New York, 1979)

Sheehan, Neil. *A Bright Shining Lie: John Paul Vann and America in Vietnam* (Random House, New York, 1988).

Shenon, Philip. *The Commission: The Uncensored History of the 9/11 Investigation* (Twelve, New York, 2008).

Sherrod, Robert. *Tarawa: The Story of a Battle* (Duell, Sloan and Pearce, New York, 1944).

Sherry, Michael S. *The Rise of American Air Power: The Creation of Armageddon* (Yale University Press, New Haven CT, 1987).

Sherwood, Robert E. *Roosevelt and Hopkins: An Intimate History* (Harper & Brothers, New York, 1948).

Shoup, David M. "The New American Militarism," *The Atlantic*, April 1969.

Sifry, Micha L. and Christopher Cerf. *The Gulf War Reader* (Times Books, New York, 1991).

Silverstein, Ken. *Private Warriors* (Verso, New York, 2000).

Silverstein, Ken and Jeff Moag "The Pentagon's 300-Billion-Dollar Bomb," *Mother Jones*, January/February, 2000.

Singletary, Otis. *The Mexican War* (University of Chicago Press, Chicago IL, 1962).

Sisson, Edgar. *One Hundred Red Days: A Personal Chronicle of The Bolshevik Revolution* (Yale University Press, New Haven CT, 1931).

Sledge, E. B. *With The Old Breed at Peleliu and Okinawa* (Presidio Press, Novato CA, 1981).

Slessor, John. *The Central Blue* (Praeger, New York, 1957).

Sloan, Bill. *Brotherhood of Heroes: The Marines at Peleliu—The Bloodiest Battle of the Pacific War* (Simon & Schuster, New York, 2005).

Smith, Daniel M. *The Great Departure: The United States and World War 1914-1920* (John Wiley and Sons, Inc., New York, 1965).

Smith, Howard K. *The State of Europe* (Alfred A. Knopf, New York, 1949).

Smith, John T. *Rolling Thunder: The Strategic Bombing Campaign Against North Vietnam 1964-68* (Air Research Publications, Surrey, England, 1994).

Smith, R. Harris. *OSS: The Secret History of America's First CIA* (University of California Press, Berkeley CA, 1972).

Snepp, Frank. *Decent Interval: An Insider's Account of Saigon's Indecent End Told by the CIA's Chief Strategy Analyst in Vietnam* (University Press of Kansas, Lawrence KS, 1977).

Solow, Herbert. "The Ripe Problems of United Fruit," *Fortune*, March 1959.

Sorenson, Ted. *Kennedy* (Harper & Row, New York, 1965).

Spector, Ronald H. *Eagle Against the Sun: The American War with Japan* (The Free Press, New York, 1985).

Sprout, Harold and Margaret Sprout. *The Rise of American Naval Power 1776-1918* (Princeton University Press, Princeton NJ, 1939).

Stimson, Henry L. *On Active Service in Peace and War* (Harper, New York, 1948).

Stinnett, Robert B. *Day of Deceit: The Truth About FDR and Pearl Harbor* (Simon & Schuster, New York, 2000).

Stockdale, Jim and Sybil Stockdale. *In Love and War: The Story of a Family's Ordeal and Sacrifice During the Vietnam Years* (Harper & Row, New York, 1984).

Stone, I.F. *In a Time of Torment 1961-1967: A Nonconformist History of Our Times* (Little, Brown and Company, New York, 1967).

_____. *The Hidden History of the Korean War* (Monthly Review Press, New York, 1952).

Suid, Lawrence H. *Guts & Glory: The Making of the American Military Image in Film* (University Press of Kentucky, 2002).

Swanberg, W.A. *Citizen Hearst—A Biography of William Randolph Hearst* (Charles Scribners' Sons, New York, 1961).

Swomley, John M., Jr. *The Military Establishment* (Beacon Press, Boston, 1964).

Sylvester, Arthur. "The Government Has the Right to Lie," *The Saturday Evening Post*, November 18, 1967.

Szulc, Tad. *Dominican Diary* (Delacorte Press, New York, 1965).

Takaki, Ronald. *Hiroshima: Why America Dropped the Atomic Bomb* (Little Brown and Company, New York, 1995).

Tancredo, Tom. *In Mortal Danger: The Battle for America's Border and Security* (Cumberland House Publishing, Inc., Nashville TN, 2006).

Tansill, Charles Callan. *America Goes to War* (Little, Brown and Company, Boston, 1938).

_____. *Back Door to War: The Roosevelt Foreign Policy 1933-1941* (Henry Regenry Company, Chicago, 1951).

Tarpley, Webster Griffin. *9/11: Synthetic Terror Made in USA* (Progressive Press, Joshua Tree CA, 2005).

Tashiro, Akira. *Discounted Casualties: The Human Cost of Depleted Uranium* (The Chugoku Shimbun, Hiroshima, 2001).

Taylor, Philip M. *War and the Media: Propaganda and Persuasion in the Gulf War* (Manchester University Press, Manchester, England, 1992).

Taylor, Telford. *Nuremberg and Vietnam: An American Tragedy* (Quadrangle Books, Chicago, 1970).

Thayer, George. *The War Business: The International Trade in Armaments* (Avon, New York, 1969).

Tobias, Fritz. *The Reichstag Fire* (G.P. Putnam's Sons, New York, 1963).

Toland, John. *In Mortal Combat: Korea, 1950-1953* (William Morrow and Company, Inc., New York, 1991).

_____. *Infamy: Pearl Harbor and Its Aftermath* (Doubleday & Company, Inc., Garden City NY, 1982).

Tolley, Kemp. *Cruise of the Lanakai—Incitement to War* (Naval Institute Press, Annapolis MD, 1973).

Toynbee, Arnold J. *Experiences* (Oxford University Press, London, 1985).

Trask, David F. *The AEF and Coalition Warmaking, 1917-1918* (Lawrence, Kansas, 1993).

Tuchman, Barbara W. *The Proud Tower* (The Macmillan Company, New York, 1966).

_____. *The Guns of August* (Presidio Press, New York, 2004).

_____. *The March of Folly: From Troy to Vietnam* (Alfred A. Knopf, New York, 1984).

_____. *The Zimmermann Telegram* (The Viking Press, New York, 1958).

Turco, Richard P. Owen B. Toon, Thomas P. Ackerman, James B. Pollack and Carl Sagan, "The Climatic Effects of Nuclear War," *Scientific American*, August 1984.

Turner, John Kenneth. *Shall It Be Again?* (B.W. Huebsch. Inc., New York, 1922).

Tye, Larry. *The Father of Spin: Edward L. Bernays & the Birth of Public Relations* (Crown Publishers, Inc., New York, 1998).

Tyrell, C. Merton. *Pentagon Partners: The New Mobililty* (Grossman, New York, 1970).

Underwood, Michael. *Anything but the Truth* (St. Martin's Press, New York, 1978).

United States Strategic Bombing Survey, Government Printing Office, Washington.

U.S. Department of State, "The Top September 11 Conspiracy Theories," USINFO.STATE.GOV, September 19, 2006.

Unterberger, Betty Miller. *America's Siberian Expedition, 1918-1920: A Study of National Policy* (Greenwood Press, Publishers, New York, 1956).

Van Alstyne, Richard W. *The Rising American Empire* (Blackwell and Mott, Ltd., New York, 1960).

V*anity Fair,* May 2004, "The Path to War," Bryan Burrough, Evgenia Peretz, David Rose, David Wise.

Vidal, Gore. *Screening History* (Harvard University Press, Cambridge MA, 1992).

_____. *The Last Empire: Essays 1992-2000* (Doubleday, New York, 2001).

von Hippel, Karin. *Democracy by Force: US Military Intervention in the Post-Cold War World* (Cambridge University Press, Cambridge, England, 2002).

Walker, Gregg B., David A. Bella and Stephen J. Sprecher, Eds. *The Military-Industrial Complex: Eisenhower's Warning Three Decades Later* (P. Lang, New York, 1992).

Walker, Paul F. and Eric Stambler. "...And The Dirty Little Weapons: Cluster bombs, fuel-air explosives and 'Daisy Cutters,' not laser-guided weapons, dominated the Gulf War" (The Bulletin of the Atomic Scientists, New York, May 1991).

Walt, Stephen M. *Taming American Power: The Global Response to U.S. Primacy* (W.W. Norton & Company, New York, 2005).

Walworth, Arthur. *Woodrow Wilson* (W.W. Norton & Company, Inc., New York, 1978).

Warner, Roger. *Shooting at the Moon: The Story of America's Clandestine War in Laos* (Steerforth Press, South Royalton VT, 1996).

Wedemeyer, Albert C. *Wedemeyer Reports!* (Holt, New York, 1958).

Weinberg, Albert. *Manifest Destiny* (Quadrangle, New York, 1963).

Wells, Mark K. *Courage and Air Warfare—The Allies' Aircrew Experiences in the Second World War* (Frank Cass, London, 1995).

Weinberger, Caspar and Peter Schweizer. *Chain of Command* (Atria Books, New York, 2005).

Weiner, Tim. *Blank Check* (Grand Central Publishing, New York, 1991).

Weintraub, Stanley. *MacArthur's War: Korea and the Undoing of an American Hero* (The Free Press, New York, 2000).

Weisberg, Barry. *Ecoside in Indochina: The Ecology of War* (Canfield Press, San Francisco, 1970).

Wells, Herbert George. *The War in the Air* (George Bell and Sons, London, 1908).
Wells, Tom. *The War Within: America's Battle Over Vietnam* (University of California Press, Berkeley CA, 1994).
Westing, Arthur H. and E.W. Pfeiffer. "The Cratering of Indochina." *Scientific American,* May 1972.

Wheaton, Philip E. *Panama Invaded* (The Red Sea Press, Trenton NJ, 2001).

Whiteside, Thomas. *Defoliation* (Ballantine Books, New York, 1970).

Wiest, Andrew. *Rolling Thunder in a Gentle Land: The Vietnam War Revisited* (Osprey Publishing, Midland House, Oxford UK, 2006).

Wilcox, Fred. *Waiting for an Army to Die: The Tragedy of Agent Orange* (Random House, New York, 1983).

Wilkerson, Marcus. *Public Opinion and the Spanish-American War: A Study in War Propaganda* (Louisiana State University Press, Baton Rouge LA, 1932).

_____. *Roots of the Modern American Empire* (Random House, New York, 1970).

Williams, William Appleman. *American Russian Relations, 1781-1947* (Rinehart, New York, 1952).

Wiltz, John E. *In Search of Peace: The Senate Munitions Inquiry* (Louisiana State University Press, Baton Rouge LA, 1963).

Windchy, Eugene G. *A Documentary of the Incident in the Tonkin Gulf on August 2 and August 4, 1964 and Their Consequences* (Doubleday & Company, New York, 1971).

Winkler, Allan M. *The Politics of Propaganda: The Office of War Information 1942-1945* (Yale University Press, New Haven CT, 1978).

Wisan, Joseph E. *The Cuban Crisis as Reflected in the New York Press 1895-1898* (Columbia University Press, New York, 1938).

Wise, David. *The Politics of Lying: Government Deception, Secrecy, and Power* (Random House, New York, 1973).

Wolff, Leon. *Little Brown Brother: America's Forgotten Bid for Empire Which Cost 250,000 Lives* (Longmans, New York, 1970).

Wood, Bryce. *The Making of the Good Neighbor Policy* (Columbia University Press, New York, 1961).

Woodward, Bob. *State of Denial: Bush at War Part III* (Simon & Schuster, New York, 2006).

_____. *Bush at War* (Simon & Schuster, New York, 2002).

_____. *Veil: The Secret Wars of the CIA 1981-1987* (Simon & Schuster, New York, 1987).

Wukovits, John. *Pacific Alamo: The Battle for Wake Island* (New American Library, New York, 2003).

Wyden, Peter. *Bay of Pigs: The Untold Story* (Simon and Schuster, New York, 1979).

Yahara, Hiromichi. *The Battle for Okinawa* (John Wiley & Sons, Inc., New York, 1995).

Yarmolinsky, Adam. *The Military Establishment: Its Impacts on American Society* (Harper & Row, Publishers, New York, 1971).

Zilg, Gerard Colby. *DuPont: Behind the Nylon Curtain* (Prentice-Hall, Inc., Englewood Cliffs NJ, 1974).

Zinn, Howard. *The People's History of the United States* (Harper & Rowe, New York, 1980).

_____. *Terrorism and War* (Seven Stories Press, New York, 2002).

Zwicker, Barrie. *Towers of Deception: The Media Cover-Up of 9/11* (New Society Publishers, BC, Canada).

Acronyms and Abbreviations

ACLU: American Civil Liberties Union
AEC: Atomic Energy Commission
AFB: Air Force Base
AIOC: Anglo-Iranian Oil Company
AP: Associated Press
API: Armor Piercing Incendiary
ARAMCO: Arabian American Company
ARVN: Army of the Republic of Vietnam (South Vietnam)

BAR: Browning Automatic Rifle (Light Machine Gun)
BBC: British Broadcasting Corporation
BEF: British Expeditionary Force (Great War and WWII)
BLU: Bomb Live Unit
BMI: British Ministry of Information
BSC: British Security Coordination

CBS: Columbia Broadcasting System
CBU: Cluster Bomb Unit
CCF: Chinese Communist Forces
CENTCOM: U.S. Central Command
C.I.D.: Criminal Investigations Division (U.S. Army)
CINCFE: Commander in Chief of Far Eastern Forces
CNN: Cable News Network
CO: Commanding Officer
CPA: Coalition Provisional Authority
CPI: Committee on Public Information (Great War)

DefCon: Defense Condition
DMZ: Demilitarized Zone (between North and South Korea)
DPRK: Democratic People's Republic of Korea (North Korea)
DRV: Democratic Republic of Vietnam
DU: Depleted Uranium

EUSAK: Eighth United States Army Korea
EPA: Environmental Protection Agency

FAA: Federal Aviation Administration
FEBC: British Far East Combined Bureau
FEMA: Federal Emergency Management Agency
FBI: Federal Bureau of Investigation
FDR: Fraanklin Delano Roosevelt
FDNY: Fire Department of New York City
FEAF: Far Eastern Air Force

GCSS: British Government Code & Cipher School
GOP: Republican Party
GPS: Global Positioning System
GNP: Gross National Product

HCC: Herndon Command Center

IED: Improvised Explosive Device (Roadside Bomb)
IG: Inspector General (U.S. Army)
IRA: Irish Republican Army
IWW: Industrial Workers of the World

JN-25 Japanese Naval Code

KBR: Kellogg, Brown & Root
KGB: Soviet Secret Police

MADFAE: Mass Air Delivery Fuel-Air Explosive
MI: Military Intelligence
MIT: Massachusetts Institute of Technology
MGM: Metro Goldwyn Mayer
MP: Military Police

NASA: National Aeronautics and Space Administration
9/11: September 11, 2001
NATO: North Atlantic Treaty Organization
NBC: National Broadcasting Company
NCO: Non-Commissioned Officer
NEADS: Northeast Air Defense Sector
NIST: National Institute of Standards and Technology
NKPA: North Korean People's Army
NLF: National Liberation Front
NORAD: North American Aerospace Defense Command
NKPA: North Korean People's Army
NSA: National Security Agency
NTSB: National Transportation Safety Board
NVA: North Vietnamese Army
NYPD: New York City Police Department

OCS: Offfcer Candidate School
OPEC: Organization of Petroleum Exporting Countries
OP-ED: The Page opposite the Editorial Page in *The New York Times*
OSI: Office of Strategic Influence

PAVN: People's Army of Vietnam
PBS: Public Broadcasting System
PFC: Private First Class

PLA: People's Liberation Army
PNAC: Project for the New American Century
PAO: Public Affairs Officer
POW: Prisoner of War
PVA: People's Volunteer Army
PX: Post Exchange

RAF: Royal Air Force
RAAF: Royal Australian Air Force
ROK: Republic of Korea (South Korea)

SCAP: Supreme Commander Allied Powers

TNT: Trinitrotoluene

UNICEF: United Nations Children's Fund
UK: United Kingdom
USSBS: United States Strategic Bombing Survey
USAAF: United States Army Air Forces (before 1947)
USAF: United States Air Force (after 1947)
USIA: United States Information Agency (World War II)
USSR: Union of Soviet Socialist Republics

VA: Veteran's Administration
VC: Vietcong
VPA: Vietnam People's Army

WBC: Biological and Chemical Warfare Committee
WMD: Weapons of Mass Destruction
WTC: World Trade Center

Author Biography

Stewart Halsey Ross brought a broad education and diversified background to his works. He earned a B.S. in Mechanical Engineering, M.S. in Technical Writing, and a M.S. in American History. He has been a Vice President with a major New York "Business-to-Business" Advertising and Public Relations Agency; was Associate Editor with Consulting Engineer Magazine; was Project Engineer with Pratt & Whitney's nuclear aircraft engine program; and was responsible for the Air Force's precision bombing range at Edwards Air Force Base. His books reflect this in-depth writing and engineering experience. In Strategic Bombing by the U.S. in World War II, Ross mocks the supposed "pickle-barrel" accuracy of the famed Norden bombsight, recalling an incident at EAFB when a "fat man" missed its target by more than a mile. Ross considered himself a "revisionist" historian, choosing an approach contrary to "conventional wisdom." He was not reluctant to take on icons. Ross read widely to bring to his readers authoritative overviews of his topics. His Bibliographies are useful references on their own, and his comprehensive Notes typically run in the many hundreds. Progressive Press is publishing his Propaganda for War and Global Predator. To our deep regret, Stewart Ross passed away at the age of 81 on October 6, 2010.

Index

9/11 (September 11th false-flag attacks), 2, 5, 6, 143, 227, 235, 238, 244-253, 256-263, 267-287, 316, 317, 319, 323, 325-328, 332-345. *See also* WTC

9/11 Commission, 249-251, 253, 256, 258, 270, 273, 284-286, 326, 328, 334

Abu Ghraib, 244-246, 248, 322, 327

Afghanistan, 5, 6, 56, 65-67, 220, 227, 233, 250, 276, 277, 279, 288

Agent Orange, 193, 195, 196, 215, 342. *See also* chemical warfare

aggression, 23, 27, 31, 64, 76, 107, 124, 128, 149, 155, 220, 227, 237

airplanes, 109, 130, 131, 150, 168, 196, 221, 229, 252, 255, 261, 268, 275, 283, 309, 314

Alaska, 11, 103, 189, 305

Allies, 2, 15, 71, 73, 74, 76-78, 80, 81, 83, 85, 86, 89-91, 93, 95, 97, 102, 106, 109, 118, 120, 126-135, 138, 140, 149, 152-154, 160, 162, 170, 227, 300, 301, 306-308, 318, 319, 334, 336, 342, 346

American interests, 38, 293, 294-297

antiwar, 86, 88, 180, 189, 199, 204, 209

Arab, 219, 220, 221, 227, 252, 274, 275

Arbenz, Jacobo, 311, 312

Archangel, 90, 91, 97, 102, 301, 322

artillery, 21, 22, 76, 77, 80, 134, 139, 148, 150, 153, 155, 156, 158-160, 165, 170, 180-182, 190, 192, 198, 204, 207, 211, 212, 225, 305

ARVN (Army of the Republic of Vietnam - South), 184, 185, 192, 196, 198, 207, 344. *See also* Vietnam

assassination, 13, 60, 61, 82, 96, 207, 219, 278, 281, 283, 287, 309, 324

Atlantic, the, 14, 26, 46, 47, 71, 74, 86, 101, 107, 108, 112, 119, 128, 141, 147, 150, 268, 311

atomic bomb, 128, 136-140, 152, 218, 288, 289, 313. *See also* nuclear weapons

atrocities, 2, 36, 57, 59, 60, 61, 68, 73, 84, 94, 112, 136, 141, 144, 145, 198-200, 205, 206, 207, 222, 223, 233

B-17 Flying Fortress bomber, 131, 132, 140, 141, 150. *See also* bombers

B-2 Stealth bomber, 2, 221, 235, 314, 315, 339

B-24 Liberator bomber, 131, 132, 140, 141, 144, 150

B-29 Superfortress bomber, 67, 131, 132, 136, 168, 177, 197, 305, 313

B-52 Stratofortress bomber, 67, 198, 210, 225, 232, 313-315, 329

bacteria, 169, 170, 173, 290, 309

Baghdad, 219, 222-224, 228-230, 238, 240-242, 244

bananas, 13, 310, 311

Barnes, Harry Elmer, historian, 7, 74, 84, 85, 100, 101, 111, 142, 317

battleships, 36, 39, 41, 42, 46-48, 61, 66, 101, 107, 109, 110, 119, 123, 131, 135, 148, 154, 221. *See also* warships

Berlin, 12, 94, 96, 113, 124, 127, 128, 130, 134, 142, 242, 288, 313, 333

biological warfare, 170, 171, 173, 193, 195, 290, 307, 308. *See also* bacteria, chemical warfare

Bolsheviks, 71, 84, 89-93, 97, 103, 299, 300, 339. *See also* Communism

bombers, 16, 67, 110, 119, 123, 131, 132, 138-142, 144, 146, 148, 168, 171, 173, 197, 198, 211, 225, 229, 234, 247, 279, 302, 305, 313, 314

bombs, bombing, 5, 6, 16, 67, 113, 131-141, 148, 150, 152, 158, 168, 170, 172, 173, 190, 192, 198, 207, 208, 210-212, 218, 221-225, 227, 228, 230, 232, 233, 237, 238, 241, 246, 247, 250, 253, 256, 257, 268, 279, 280, 288, 290, 313-315, 342, 347

Britain, British, 2, 5, 9-14, 16, 19, 20, 22, 26, 28-32, 62, 66, 70, 73-79, 80, 82, 83, 85, 86, 90, 91, 93, 98-102, 105-128, 133, 135, 143, 146, 147, 149, 150, 152, 155, 156, 165, 167, 169, 171, 173, 177-179, 183, 190, 193, 217-220, 227-229, 233, 238-241, 246, 247, 276, 278, 292, 293, 306, 319, 320, 322, 328, 331, 336, 338, 344, 345

British Empire, 14, 75, 93, 107, 117-119, 122, 124, 125, 126, 147, 218, 239, 306

Burleson, General Albert Sydney, 88, 298, 299

Bush dynasty, 5, 6, 9, 17, 69, 178, 220, 221, 226, 230, 234, 237-243, 247, 249-253, 260, 262, 271-277, 280, 284, 286, 291, 320, 322, 326, 328, 343

California, 5, 11, 17, 19-22, 24-28, 39, 57, 121, 123, 148, 213, 281, 286, 293, 314

Calley, Lt. Wm. Jr., 61, 199, 201, 202, 203, 204, 205, 206, 216, 318

Cambodia, 49, 66, 190, 209, 216, 233, 253, 320, 329, 334, 339

Camp Detrick. *See* Fort Detrick

Canada, 9, 10, 12, 119, 147, 150, 278, 285, 305, 318, 319

carriers, 101, 105, 108, 109, 110, 119, 121, 131, 135, 148, 158, 186, 187, 190, 191, 197, 200, 221, 231, 289, 302. *See also* warships

casualties, 12, 25, 48, 49, 50, 56, 57, 77, 78, 79, 80, 89, 90, 97, 102, 130, 136, 148, 152, 156, 160, 164, 174, 182, 224, 225, 238, 240, 279. *See also* killed

cavalry, 21, 22, 31, 39, 49, 70, 122, 155, 157, 159, 160, 163, 172, 243

CBS (Columbia Broadcasting System), 205, 234, 260, 265, 269, 275, 344

CBW (chemical-biological warfare), 169, 171, 173, 195, 196, 309, 337. *See also* chemical warfare, biological warfare, bacteria, poison

censorship, 74, 76, 88, 169, 170, 224, 229, 239, 240, 299

Charlie Company (My Lai), 199, 200, 201, 202, 203, 204, 205

chemical warfare, 5, 76, 78, 79, 100, 170, 190, 193, 195, 196, 209, 212, 216, 234, 244, 308, 319, 321, 322, 326, 327, 334, 337, 346. *See also* Agent Orange, biological warfare, bacteria, chlorine gas, mustard gas, poison

children, 5, 28, 49, 57, 58, 59, 70, 79, 94, 95, 98, 121, 146, 158, 174, 194, 196, 199, 201- 206, 210-214, 216, 233, 234, 241, 271, 274, 280, 288, 294, 299, 311

China, Chinese, 5, 6, 10, 12, 24, 44, 45, 48, 53, 55, 56, 90, 91, 100, 102, 105, 106, 109, 132, 152, 153, 154, 155, 159, 161-173, 175, 176, 178, 180, 183, 190, 199, 207, 209, 214, 242, 243, 252, 289, 306, 308, 313, 316, 332, 338, 344

chlorine gas, 77, 78, 100. *See also* chemical warfare

Churchill, Winston, 90, 93, 99, 105, 108, 109, 112, 119, 124, 125, 126, 128, 140, 146, 147, 148, 150, 218, 321, 336

CIA, 16, 102, 111, 162, 177, 185, 214, 219, 221, 226, 227, 252, 271-273, 277, 282, 283, 285, 292, 304, 306, 312, 314, 316, 318, 322, 328, 330, 332, 335, 336, 339, 343

civilian, 6, 12, 13, 16, 48, 102, 107, 113, 128, 132-135, 138, 141, 152, 154, 158, 168, 170, 174, 175, 179, 198-200, 204-207, 211, 223, 224, 227, 230, 231, 233, 237, 240, 244, 264, 266, 279, 283, 302, 306, 307

cluster bomb (CBU), 5, 132, 157, 172, 190, 198, 232, 237, 344

CNN (Cable News Network), 240, 243, 260, 275, 276, 344

coal, 11, 41, 43, 44, 46, 47, 53, 61, 62, 63, 67, 83, 102, 128, 129, 138, 218

coalition, 90, 93, 97, 179, 184, 209, 221, 227, 239, 241

collapse of WTC Towers, 249, 251, 252, 254-256, 259-262, 275, 276, 280, 281, 284

Colombia, 14, 32, 283, 293, 294, 295, 310, 319

Colonel House, 72, 81, 83, 85, 86

colonies, colonial, 9, 10, 13, 17, 19, 31, 32, 39, 50, 53, 55, 65, 67, 71, 83, 102, 106, 122, 125, 136, 146, 147, 152, 178, 179, 182, 199, 204, 214, 219

Communism, Communists, 6, 16, 55, 152-154, 159, 164, 167-169, 172, 174, 175, 179, 181, 183, 184, 193, 209, 210, 214, 299, 303, 311, 312, 313, 344. *See also* Bolsheviks

Congress, 6, 7, 10, 12, 13, 14, 19, 26, 32, 38, 43, 44, 52, 53, 56, 59, 61, 64, 66, 70, 76, 81, 87, 88, 99, 103, 105-107, 111, 124, 153, 174, 184, 189, 221, 223, 249, 262, 272, 277, 278, 292, 293, 298, 304, 313

conspiracy, 6, 84, 93, 96, 101, 102, 188, 189, 248, 250-252, 262, 271, 274, 275, 280, 283, 284, 286, 319, 323, 326, 332, 338, 341

CPI (Committee on Public Information, WWI), 75, 88, 93, 344

crash, 255, 258, 261-263, 266, 268-270, 274, 275, 281-283, 287

craters, 25, 77, 78, 145, 190, 192, 208, 232, 270, 290

cruisers, 47, 48, 66, 68, 101, 106, 108, 109, 110, 122, 131, 148, 179. *See also* warships

Cuba, 5, 10, 12-14, 17, 30-55, 61-69, 189, 268, 285, 288, 291-293, 295, 296, 298, 310, 312, 313, 319, 322, 329, 330, 335, 343

defoliant, 193-195. *See also* chemical warfare

democracy, 6, 12, 53, 70, 84, 97, 113, 117, 118, 119, 125, 143, 218, 221, 237, 240

demolition, 132, 190, 192, 232, 258-260, 262, 277, 309

Department of "Defense." *See* Pentagon

destroyers, 48, 107, 120, 122, 185, 186, 215. *See also* warships

Dewey, Cmdr./Adm. George, 36, 44, 45, 46, 47, 48, 55, 56, 91, 316

Diem, Ngo Dinh, 183, 184

Dien Bien Phu, 180-182, 214, 313, 324, 337

diplomacy, diplomats, 6, 9, 14, 17, 21, 26, 30, 38, 39, 44, 51, 67, 69, 71, 74, 81, 82, 85, 87, 90, 91, 93, 95, 96, 107, 142, 149, 176, 221, 226, 276, 316, 324, 334, 335

drone aircraft, 278, 285, 286

Du Pont, 24, 111, 147

DU, "depleted" uranium, 225, 268, 320, 344. *See also* uranium

Dulles brothers, 154, 178, 183, 184, 264, 278, 312, 313, 319

Dunkirk, 120, 124, 125, 148, 159

Dutch East Indies, 45, 106, 109

economics, 6, 16, 33, 45, 64, 84, 97, 106, 107, 130, 133, 135, 145, 146, 150, 152, 154, 184, 197, 210, 219-221, 225, 226, 237, 302, 307, 313, 314

Eisenhower, Dwight D., 16, 68, 127, 154, 169, 170, 173, 174, 182, 184, 209, 215, 303-305, 312, 313, 321, 323, 342

embassy, US, 226, 239, 275

enemies, 6, 24, 33, 34, 41, 48, 65, 76, 77, 80, 86, 88, 96, 102, 106, 114, 122, 125, 126, 128, 129, 131, 135, 139, 141, 144, 145, 148, 150, 154, 155, 156, 160, 163, 164, 166-168, 171, 179, 180, 181, 186, 190, 193, 197, 199, 201, 204, 207, 213, 220, 225, 230, 231, 239, 242, 249, 252, 273, 283, 298, 299, 302, 305, 312, 314

England. *See* Britain

Espionage Act, 87, 88, 102, 298, 299

Europe, Europeans, 5, 10, 12, 14-17, 20, 22-24, 26, 29, 32, 38, 53, 64, 70, 71, 76, 80-82, 85, 87, 89, 93, 94, 98, 106, 110, 111, 113, 118, 122, 124, 126, 128-133, 135, 136, 140, 142, 143, 149, 150, 176, 178, 194, 212, 250, 252, 266, 293, 305, 326, 339

FAA (Federal Aviation Administration), 252, 263, 264, 265, 268, 281, 282, 344

Fay, Sidney Bradshaw, historian, 7, 84, 87, 96, 101, 102, 103, 104, 111, 149, 324

FBI (Federal Bureau of Investigation), 122, 252, 260, 266-272, 278, 280, 282, 344

FDNY (Fire Department of New York City), 252, 254, 258, 260, 276, 344

FEMA (Federal Emergency Management Agency), 255, 260, 261, 262, 284, 344

fighter-bombers, 132, 172, 174, 180, 181, 186, 188, 189, 198, 207, 215, 221, 228, 229, 233. *See also* bombers, B-2 etc.

Filipinos. *See* Philippines

fleet, 25, 32, 36, 44-48, 62, 67, 86, 101, 105, 106, 108-110, 118, 119, 121, 123, 138, 148, 185, 197, 275, 304, 310, 314, 337. *See also* Navy

Fleming, Thomas, historian, 84, 87, 90, 100, 101, 102, 148, 149, 324

Flight 11, 261, 263, 264, 274, 275

Flight 77, 265, 266, 267, 268, 275

Flight 93, 263, 268, 269, 270, 275, 278

flight controllers, 263, 264, 269, 283

Florida, 9, 10, 31, 39, 49, 264, 265, 271, 274, 275, 276, 285, 286, 292, 308, 327

Fort Detrick, 308, 309

France, French, 5, 11, 13, 14, 19, 22, 23, 26, 30-32, 48, 56, 62, 67, 73, 74, 76, 78-84, 88, 90, 93, 98, 102, 111, 113, 118, 119, 122, 124-126, 128, 135, 142, 149, 150, 153, 171, 173, 178-185, 189, 190, 192, 197, 199, 208, 212, 214, 219, 227, 229, 233, 238, 246, 249, 266, 274, 292, 300, 305, 313, 324 freedom, 6, 12, 42, 45, 55, 75, 76, 92, 97, 117, 118, 128, 143, 176, 210, 221, 237, 304, 311

Galbraith, John Kenneth, 132, 133, 137, 139, 150, 151, 325

Germany, Germans, 5, 12, 14, 15, 29, 56, 64, 66, 70, 71, 73, 74, 76-80, 83-89, 92-142, 146, 148-150, 171, 179, 184, 190, 194, 197, 207, 240, 241, 249, 250, 273, 286, 299, 301, 306, 307, 316-319, 325, 326, 329, 330, 334

GIs, 155-159, 166, 167, 169, 193, 197, 199-203, 206, 207, 209, 210, 213, 239, 240, 243, 246, 247

Giuliani, Rudy, 260, 262, 271, 281, 286, 317

Global Hawk, 278, 286

Goebbels, Josef, 114, 118, 127, 128, 130, 146

Griffin, David Ray, 250, 251, 275, 284-286, 326

Guam, 52, 53, 57, 67, 131, 190

Guatemala, 296, 310, 311, 312, 322, 323, 328, 329, 338

guerrilla, 31, 33, 56, 57, 153, 160, 180, 182, 184, 189, 190, 193, 207, 213, 214, 215, 302, 312

guilt, war guilt, 70, 74, 84, 95, 96, 149, 206, 211, 274, 283

Gulf of Tonkin affair, 185, 187-189, 215, 278, 316, 325, 333, 343

Gulf War, 65, 218, 222, 225, 226, 232, 233, 235, 288, 323, 327, 330, 331, 339, 340, 342

Haiti, 10, 14, 30, 71, 294, 295, 296, 337

Hanoi, 179, 183, 186, 199, 208, 210, 212, 313

Havana, 31, 33, 36-40, 42, 45, 47, 51, 61

Hawaii, Hawaiians, 5, 10, 11, 17, 33, 39, 46, 56, 67, 68, 105, 106, 123, 200, 209, 215, 329

Hearst, William Randolph, 35-38, 41, 44, 63, 67, 247, 323, 334, 340

helicopters, 170, 172, 189, 190, 193, 196, 197, 198, 201, 202, 204, 209, 214, 229, 230, 232, 241, 267, 279

Henry Cabot Lodge, 12, 32, 53, 64, 312

herbicides, 192-196. *See also* defoliant

Hersh, Seymour M., 8, 203, 205, 206, 216, 231, 248, 327

"hijackers," 252, 260, 263, 265, 269, 270, 274-278, 280

Hiroshima, 137, 138, 140, 141, 151, 172, 223, 309, 313, 318, 327, 336, 340

historians, 11, 15, 16, 63, 64, 66, 74, 75, 81, 82, 84, 86, 87, 90, 91, 96, 97, 99, 111, 112, 116, 118, 122, 123, 126, 128, 130, 142, 149, 156, 157, 169, 175, 194, 218, 238, 303, 347

history, 2, 5, 7, 15, 22, 24, 27, 29, 31, 35, 37, 43, 48, 54, 62, 65, 68, 73, 74, 75, 84, 87, 88, 90-95, 98, 99, 108, 110, 111, 116, 119, 124, 130, 131, 135, 141, 145, 154, 155, 157, 163, 169, 178, 182, 189, 196, 199, 207, 218, 223, 227, 228, 231, 232, 237, 238, 250, 254, 262, 268, 283, 290, 298, 305, 310

Hitler, Adolf, 15, 78, 106, 113-116, 118-120, 122, 124-126, 133, 143, 147, 150, 171, 226, 228, 243, 272, 273, 317, 318, 327, 334

Ho Chi Minh, 178, 179, 184, 185, 207, 210, 214, 215, 323

Honduras, 295, 296, 297

hospital, 29, 36, 76, 78, 145, 151, 189, 190, 208, 211, 212, 222, 223, 227, 240-242, 266, 279, 280, 290, 304

Indians, 9, 13, 31, 48, 53, 60, 157, 243

Indochina, 6, 15, 56, 178, 179, 182-184, 189, 190, 192, 195-197, 208, 209, 214, 324, 331, 336, 342

insurrection, 10, 12, 31, 32, 34, 49, 59, 60, 63, 68, 293-296

intelligence, 105, 106, 110, 113, 121, 133, 155, 157, 163, 185, 200, 221, 244, 278, 283, 289

international law, 6, 69, 103, 104, 106, 146, 233, 237, 338

intervention, 12-14, 16, 38, 42, 44, 48, 64, 65, 70, 71, 84, 86, 90, 91, 97, 102, 125, 142, 162, 180, 183, 184, 208, 219, 220, 221, 227, 238, 301

invasion, 24, 49, 65, 86, 90, 91, 93, 98, 103, 113, 135, 138, 139, 140, 154, 160, 197, 219, 221, 222, 228, 234, 237, 239, 243, 244

investigators, 134, 203, 204, 244, 250, 251, 258, 260-262, 266-268, 270, 281, 282

Iran, 218, 219, 227, 243, 277, 288, 306, 313

Iraq, Iraqis, 2, 6, 13, 16, 17, 66, 67, 97, 169, 215, 218-247, 250, 252, 276, 277, 283, 287, 288, 317, 320, 324, 328-331, 333, 336, 337

Ishii Shiro, 308, 309

Israel, 120, 224, 227, 278, 313, 327, 332

Italy, 73, 76, 85, 90, 102, 105, 107, 111, 113, 124, 126, 127, 135, 136, 249, 300, 316

Japan, Japanese, 5, 10, 14, 44, 53, 67, 90, 91, 97-111, 119, 121, 123, 124, 126, 127, 131, 132, 135-141, 144-146, 148, 151-155, 157, 171, 174, 175, 177-180, 191, 214, 218, 275, 301, 302, 305-309, 318, 323, 324, 326, 340, 345

Jefferson Davis, 24, 66, 120

jet aircraft, 68, 133, 158, 168, 171, 198, 201, 207, 211, 212, 254-257, 263-267, 269, 306, 313

Jews, 29, 95, 103, 143, 149, 191, 227

jingoism, 2, 12, 32, 38, 41, 52, 66, 99, 278

journalists, journalism, 6, 14, 35, 36, 43, 63, 93, 95, 149, 164, 176, 180, 205, 214, 228, 229, 234, 239, 242, 275, 287

Kaiser Wilhelm II, 12, 64, 66, 84, 87, 93, 96, 100, 184

Kean-Hamilton commission, see 9/11 Commission.

Kennan, Geo. F., 92, 93, 103, 122, 172, 277, 329

Kennedy, John F., 184, 196, 197, 287, 289, 291, 313, 322, 328, 329, 340

killed, 6, 12, 14, 17, 21, 30, 34, 36, 40, 43, 46, 48, 53, 54, 58, 59, 60, 76, 77, 78, 80, 81, 89, 100, 102, 113, 128, 136, 139, 140, 145, 150, 157, 159, 160, 165, 167, 169, 170, 174, 175, 179, 181, 182, 183, 185, 190, 191, 193, 196, 198, 201, 204, 205, 207, 211-213, 223, 227, 229, 231-234, 237-241, 247, 250-253, 263, 266, 279, 281, 283, 290, 299. *See also* casualties

Kissinger, Henry, 252, 253, 339

Knightley, Philip, 228, 235, 236, 239, 247, 329

Korea, Koreans (North), 152-161, 164, 168, 169, 173, 174, 185, 187, 189, 277, 313, 344, 345

Korea, Koreans (South), 152, 154, 163, 168, 172, 174, 344, 346

Kuwait, 219-222, 227, 230-235

Laos, 49, 66, 180, 190, 209, 215, 313, 329, 342

Latin America, 2, 10, 12, 16, 30, 48, 53, 54, 218, 310, 320, 325

Lenin, V. I., 85, 89, 91-93, 102, 299

Lindbergh, Chas. A., 48, 141-144, 151, 331

Lothian, Lord, 116-119, 147, 331

Luftwaffe, 125, 128, 131, 133, 135, 142

Lynch, Jessica, 241, 242

MacArthur, Gen Douglas, 123, 131, 148, 152-157, 160-164, 166, 168, 172, 174-176, 222, 235, 236, 309, 316, 321, 326, 331, 332, 342

Manifest Destiny, 2, 13, 17, 33, 39, 55, 64, 342

Manila, Manila Bay, 36, 45, 47, 48, 55-67, 86, 91, 154, 316

Marines, 14, 55, 60, 81, 136, 139, 145, 155, 156, 159, 164, 166, 168, 190, 198, 207, 241, 293-295, 297, 302, 339

massacre, 8, 60, 61, 159, 199, 204-206, 216, 231, 316, 318, 322, 327

McCaffrey, General Barry, 218, 230, 231

McKinley, Pres. Wm., 11, 13, 22, 35, 37, 38, 39, 43, 44, 45, 49-52, 56, 59, 60, 63, 64, 66, 67

McNamara, Robert S., 185, 188, 189, 211, 215, 255, 332

media, 7, 35, 98, 189, 222-225, 228, 229, 231, 233, 234, 237-240, 242, 243, 253, 269, 273, 275, 276, 281, 299. *See also* movies, newspapers, radio, TV

Medina, Capt. Ernest L., 200-204, 206

Mexican, Mexicans, 2, 10, 15, 17, 19-30, 293, 294, 296, 317, 323, 327, 339

Mexico, 2, 5, 8, 9, 10, 13, 14, 19-32, 64, 65, 71, 100, 153, 292-296, 312, 318, 320, 323, 336

Midway Island, 11, 53, 105, 121, 148

military-industrial complex, 2, 7, 15, 63, 173, 174, 209, 216, 217, 271, 275, 291, 303, 304, 317, 320, 321, 323, 324, 327, 330, 336, 337, 338, 342

missiles, 62, 67, 68, 133, 173, 207, 224, 227, 228, 229, 265, 266, 268-270, 272, 279, 283, 288, 289, 304, 313-315

Monroe Doctrine, 10, 12, 13, 17, 19, 26, 316, 333, 335

Moos, Malcolm, 174, 303, 304, 323

morale, 90, 97, 125, 133, 134, 138, 150, 155, 210, 239

Morgenthau, Henry, 95, 96, 97, 101, 103, 127-130, 134, 149, 150, 318, 334

movies, 70, 73, 75, 120, 121, 157, 242

Muslim, 6, 227, 246, 252, 275

mustard gas, 76-79, 100, 171. *See also* chemical warfare

My Lai (massacred Vietnamese village), 8, 61, 199-206, 216, 316, 318, 327

Nagasaki, 44, 137, 140, 141, 309, 313

napalm, 5, 136, 152, 171, 172, 174, 190-192, 196, 198, 211, 218

Navy, naval, 9, 11, 12, 14, 22, 24, 31, 32, 37, 39-49, 53, 55, 61-68, 73, 75, 76, 97, 102, 105-110, 115, 118-124, 131, 132, 135, 138, 144, 146, 148, 158, 185-191, 194, 207-209, 211, 214, 218, 220, 221, 288, 291-299, 302, 304, 305, 313, 317, 333, 336, 337. *See also* fleet

Nazi, 5, 15, 64, 105, 107, 108, 114-116, 124, 128, 133, 135, 142, 143, 171

NBC (National Broadcasting Company), 224, 240, 242, 275, 345

neutral, neutrality, 9, 15, 32, 41, 71, 73, 85, 100, 103, 107, 118, 146, 167, 296

New York Times, 52, 65, 67, 73, 75, 86, 87, 99, 104, 108, 113, 117, 122, 125, 126, 131, 148, 151, 157, 170, 174, 195, 204, 210-215, 222, 233-235, 241, 243, 246, 247, 250, 258, 259, 267, 271, 273, 280, 281, 287, 323, 334, 345

newspapers, 5, 12, 27, 34-37, 41, 43, 44, 46, 48, 57, 62, 63, 73, 74, 84, 105, 111-114, 117, 121, 124, 142, 143, 169, 170, 195, 199, 205, 206, 210, 225, 229, 266, 269, 273, 286, 287

Nicaragua, 14, 32, 33, 65, 227, 293-298, 310

NIST (National Institute of Standards and Technology), 258, 280, 281, 345

Nitze, Paul, 172, 173, 277

NKPA (North Korean People's Army), 153-161, 345

NORAD (North American Aerospace Defense Command), 252, 263-265, 345

Norden bombsight, 131, 140, 347

NSC (National Security Agency), 250, 271

NTSB (National Transportation Safety Board), 262, 264, 270, 282, 283, 287, 345

nuclear weapons, 5, 16, 140, 141, 152, 172, 173, 226, 232, 234, 263, 288, 289, 290, 309, 313, 314, 347. *See also* atomic bomb

oil, 6, 15, 16, 27, 101, 106, 107, 134, 135, 138, 179, 187, 190, 211, 218-222, 226, 227, 229, 235, 240, 243, 250, 252

Osama bin-Laden, 251-253, 276, 277, 280

Pacific, the, 10, 11, 12, 14, 15, 17, 20, 22, 24, 26, 33, 38, 45, 46, 48, 53, 67, 101, 106, 116, 121, 123, 124, 126, 131, 136, 138, 139, 144, 148, 150, 151, 154, 175, 188, 190, 191, 210, 286, 290, 302, 311, 321, 323, 332, 339, 343

Panama, 11-14, 32, 46, 62, 65, 107, 153, 226, 227, 238, 288, 293-296, 297, 310, 332, 342

Paris, 5, 52, 53, 67, 71, 81, 82, 95, 97, 113, 128, 178, 182, 185, 208, 209, 214, 334

Patriot Act, 239, 243, 272, 277, 283

patriotism, 6, 33, 43, 75, 93, 116, 121, 133, 155, 224, 228, 232, 238, 243, 249, 250, 268, 269, 275, 278

peace, 10, 14, 17, 22, 25, 26, 37, 38, 51, 55, 63, 67, 70, 73, 74, 76, 80-89, 94, 95, 97, 100, 107, 116-118, 122, 124, 125, 129, 143, 161, 168, 169, 174, 182, 183, 209, 210, 224, 226, 273, 287, 288, 290, 293, 295, 298, 303, 304, 307

Pearl Harbor, 5-7, 11, 14, 53, 67, 102, 105, 108, 110, 116, 121-124, 131, 132, 142-144, 146, 148, 162, 168, 271, 273, 275, 277, 284-287, 302, 317, 321, 326, 333, 337, 340, 341

Pentagon (Dept. of "Defense"), 6, 65, 135, 156, 163, 164, 168, 169, 171, 177, 179, 184, 185, 186, 189, 190, 193, 197-199, 205, 207, 209, 210, 211, 217, 221, 224-226, 228, 229, 231, 234, 238, 240-243, 252, 264-272, 275-278, 283, 286, 291, 303, 304, 309, 314, 319, 320, 323, 324, 326, 327, 333, 339, 341

Philippines, Filipinos, 2, 5, 12, 13, 31, 44-49, 52, 53, 55-62, 65, 67, 68, 71, 106, 108, 123, 131, 138, 153, 154, 157, 210, 245, 302, 321, 328, 331, 333

phosphorus, 136, 198, 211, 213, 244

pirates, 292, 293

poison, 70, 76-78, 92, 100, 113, 170, 171, 190-195, 197, 263. *See also* chemical warfare

Polk, Pres. James, 10, 19-22, 24, 26, 64, 71, 293, 338

Potsdam, 2, 95, 96, 128, 136, 149, 152, 306

prisoners, 36, 48, 57, 59, 60, 65, 70, 88, 89, 100, 136, 144, 145, 165, 167, 200, 207, 244, 245, 307, 308

propaganda, 6-8, 12, 14, 16, 31, 34, 36, 37, 48, 63, 64, 70, 71, 73, 74, 81, 85, 86, 90-96, 101, 103, 105, 106, 108, 112-121, 126, 128, 130, 131, 138, 149, 155-166, 168, 169, 184, 189, 197, 207, 211, 214, 220, 222, 225, 228, 238, 240-242, 269, 272, 273, 275, 300, 304, 314 public opinion, 10, 103, 104, 106, 189, 208, 238, 317, 330, 331, 338, 342

Puerto Rico, 46, 47, 50-53, 67, 292, 293

Pulitzer, Joseph, 34-36, 63

radar, 16, 186, 187, 207, 215, 229, 263-265, 282, 283, 285, 306, 314, 315

radio, 27, 28, 34, 102, 105, 107, 108, 111-115, 120, 124, 126, 143, 158, 163, 174, 180, 185, 186, 231, 256, 258, 263, 264, 275, 280, 281, 285, 305, 306

rape, 36, 192, 203, 204, 231, 244

Republican Party, 7, 21, 52, 61, 64, 81, 101, 129, 149, 175, 243, 249, 250, 253, 271, 277, 283, 286, 345

research, 62, 94, 96, 98, 132, 138, 171, 189, 193, 195, 206, 209, 240, 254, 286, 304, 307, 308

revolution, 5, 11, 14, 19, 27, 29, 33, 64, 65, 89, 90, 92, 93, 98, 102, 103, 219, 220, 225, 293-299, 312, 317, 335, 338, 339

Rickover, Admiral Hyman, 62, 63, 68, 337

Ridenhour, PFC Ronald L., 204, 205

rifles, 56, 121, 141, 157, 166, 180, 182, 200-203, 209, 213, 242, 246

Rodriguez, Wm., 257, 258

ROK. *See* Korea (South)

Roosevelt, Franklin D, 5, 7, 14, 32, 64, 65, 101, 102, 105-108, 115, 116, 122, 124, 126-129, 134, 142-144, 146, 149, 150, 178, 184, 287, 317, 324, 325, 334, 340, 344

Roosevelt, Theodore, 13, 32, 37, 41, 49, 56, 60, 64, 66, 67, 71, 87, 157, 291, 323, 336

rubble, 6, 128, 136, 141, 208, 237, 253, 256, 257, 260, 261, 276, 279

Rumsfeld, Donald, 9, 242, 243, 271-273, 276

Russia, Russians, 2, 5, 6, 11, 16, 17, 20, 26, 66, 73, 76, 79, 85-94, 97-99, 102-104, 122, 128, 132, 135, 136, 139, 153, 161, 171, 207, 227, 241, 289, 292, 299-301, 304, 305, 309, 314, 322, 325, 327, 329, 337, 338, 342. *See also* Soviet Union

Saddam Hussein, 219, 221, 225-228, 234, 238, 240, 242, 243, 244, 276, 280, 336

Saigon, 179, 180, 183, 196, 197, 208, 209, 212, 339

Saudi Arabia, 220, 224, 229, 252, 253, 275, 277

security, 12, 16, 23, 71, 88, 92, 119, 148, 163, 184, 226, 237-239, 244, 254, 270, 273, 274, 284, 307, 319

Senate, 12, 13, 32, 33, 38, 45, 53, 54, 81, 86, 88, 99, 106, 142, 174, 188, 189, 205, 220-222, 228, 237, 253, 270, 271, 280, 283, 293, 299, 321, 342

senators, 13, 44, 52-55, 111, 184, 195, 212, 270, 277, 281, 287, 299, 304, 312, 321, 324

Siberia, 91, 97, 103, 301, 302, 333

Sigsbee, Capt. Charles D., 39, 40, 42, 62, 63

Sisson, Edgar, 92-94, 103, 339

slavery, 19, 21, 22, 24, 55, 71, 128, 251, 292

soldiers, 5, 14, 20, 21, 23, 24, 26, 30, 34, 38, 48-50, 56-60, 65, 76, 78, 80, 84, 89, 91, 97, 98, 100, 102, 107, 109, 114, 121, 125, 127, 136, 144, 145, 153-155, 157-159, 161, 163, 166, 167, 169, 179, 182, 183, 191, 200, 202, 203, 204, 206, 207, 209-212, 214, 222, 225, 231, 237, 240, 241, 245, 247, 293, 299, 305

Soviet Union, 15, 16, 89-93, 97-99, 102, 106, 122, 124, 130, 135, 136, 149, 152-154, 161, 162, 168, 171-173, 175, 180, 183, 189, 207, 220, 221, 227, 229, 277, 290, 299, 303-306, 313, 338, 345, 346

Spain, Spanish, 2, 5, 9-13, 17, 19, 20, 22, 23, 27, 29-52, 55, 56, 59-69, 71, 239, 292-294, 333-335

Stimson, Henry L., 129, 130, 150, 307, 340

strategic bombing, 130, 132, 133, 150, 151, 207, 217, 330, 331, 339, 341, 346, 347

structural engineering, 61, 255, 256, 262, 280, 281, 284, 287, 338

submarines, 43, 67, 68, 70, 73, 74, 85, 89, 99-101, 106, 107, 112, 123, 128, 135, 138, 148, 171, 288, 289, 291, 304, 313. *See also* warships

Syngman Rhee, 153, 154, 169, 176

Tarpley, Webster Griffin, 267, 278, 285, 286, 287, 340

telegram, 44, 74, 89, 97, 100, 116, 122, 148, 172, 277, 341

television, 5, 27, 28, 111, 115, 169, 189, 205, 216, 223, 224, 228, 229, 231, 232, 235, 238-243, 249, 259, 266, 269, 271, 274, 275, 280, 286 terror, terrorism, 6, 8, 33, 74, 76, 113, 152, 189, 212, 213, 237, 238, 243, 247-249, 270, 274, 284-287, 327, 328, 332-335, 340, 343. *See also* War on Terror

Texas, 8, 9, 10, 17, 19, 20, 21, 26, 27, 28, 29, 62, 65, 100, 178, 190, 211, 260, 293

Third Reich, 78, 114, 115, 120, 146, 243, 323, 334. *See also* Nazi, Germany

threat, 71, 82, 86, 92, 128, 134, 155, 209, 226, 227, 240, 265, 278, 296, 299, 311

TNT (Trinitrotoluene), 175, 232, 290, 313, 346

Tokyo, 105, 110, 131, 132, 152-154, 157, 160-163, 302, 309, 319

torpedoes, 39, 41, 67, 68, 110, 123, 185, 186-189

torture, 13, 65, 71, 95, 145, 170, 173, 189, 198, 207, 218, 223, 231, 237, 244-246

treaties, 10, 11, 13-15, 19, 25, 26, 33, 38, 52, 67, 76, 81-90, 95, 102, 105, 111, 118, 129, 169, 178, 179, 183, 197, 293, 296, 318, 345

troops, 6, 10, 12, 14, 21-25, 36, 38, 49, 51, 56, 57, 59, 60, 73, 76, 77, 80, 83, 90, 91, 94, 97, 99, 100, 107, 120, 124, 130, 133, 135, 145, 152-169, 173-175, 178, 180-185, 189, 190-192, 198, 200, 204, 208-211, 221, 226, 227, 229, 230-232, 237-243, 247, 292, 294, 296, 297, 300-302, 313. *See also* soldiers

Truman, Harry, 22, 136, 140, 150, 153, 154, 156, 161, 162, 169, 172, 175, 178, 179, 288, 312, 313, 318, 330

Turkey, 14, 94, 95, 102, 103, 227

U-2, 2, 304, 306

Unconditional Surrender, 126-129, 134, 139, 149, 307, 316, 334

United Fruit Co., 2, 310-312, 319, 323, 332, 339

uranium, 27, 136, 137, 225, 237, 320, 322, 340, 344. *See also* DU

USAAF (United States Army Air Forces - before 1947), 128, 130, 131, 133, 135, 141, 150, 346

USAF (United States Air Force - after 1947), 16, 152, 164, 168, 169, 173, 190, 207, 210, 211, 225, 230, 233, 263, 269, 285, 306, 314, 346

USS Maddox, 185-188, 215. *See also* Gulf of Tonkin

USS Maine, 36, 39-44, 46, 61-63, 66, 68, 107, 337

USSBS (United States Strategic Bombing Survey), 132-135, 138, 139, 150, 151, 346

Versailles, 15, 81, 83-85, 87, 93, 111, 118, 178, 214, 318

Vietcong, 184, 190, 193, 194, 196-213, 346

Vietminh, 178-183, 185, 214, 313

Vietnam, Vietnamese, 2, 7, 15, 34, 48, 49, 59, 65, 67, 97, 100, 139, 154, 156, 169, 173, 176, 178-186, 189-218, 220, 227, 235, 238, 270, 288, 313, 316, 318, 323, 325, 327-346

villages, 57-60, 78, 146, 157, 159, 169, 174, 180, 192, 195, 196, 198-207, 210-213, 247, 279, 280, 302

violence, 5, 16, 36, 88, 118, 169, 200, 214, 234, 247, 299

Wake Island, 2, 53, 161, 302, 343

War on Terror, 6, 227, 235, 238, 239, 243, 248, 287, 288, 322, 331, 332. *See also* terror

war planners, 45, 86, 109, 110, 115, 130, 133, 140, 171, 174, 184, 252

wars and interventions, lists of, 3, 65, 292

warships, 12, 39, 41, 43, 46, 47, 61, 62, 108, 110, 146, 147, 293. *See also* battleship, carrier, cruiser, destroyer, submarine

Wehrmacht, 102, 125, 127, 128, 135, 136, 149

Wellstone, Sen. Paul, 281-283, 287, 324

Weyler, General Valeriano, 33-36, 38, 43, 60

Wilson, Woodrow, 2, 13, 14, 15, 22, 29, 55, 70-73, 75, 76, 81-93, 95, 97, 101-103, 142, 149, 178, 298-300, 322, 325, 333, 342

WTC (World Trade Center), 249, 254-262, 264, 269, 272, 274, 276-281, 287, 316, 338, 343, 346. *See also* 9/11

Yalu River, 152, 161-163, 165, 172, 173, 332

yellow fever, 12, 24, 308

Zelikow, Philip, 250, 251

PROGRESSIVE PRESS BOOKS
In bookstores, online, or discount priced at ProgressivePress.com

RECENT RELEASES

Fall of the Arab Spring: from Revolution to Destruction. Protests as cover for destabilization. 205 pp, ~~$14.95~~ **$11.95.**

The Globalization of War: America's Long War against Humanity by Michel Chossudovsky, 240 pp, ~~$22.95~~ **$14.**

Target China: How Washington and Wall Street Plan to Cage the Asian Dragon by Engdahl. The secret war on many fronts to thwart the Chinese challenge. 256 pp, ~~$24.95~~ **$19.95**.

Three by Prof. Donald Gibson: *Battling Wall Street: The Kennedy Presidency*, JFK: our martyr who strove mightily for social and economic justice. 208 pp, ~~$14.95~~ **$11.95.** *The Kennedy Assassination Cover-up*: a conspiracy by an upper-class élite, not the FBI or Mafia. ~~$19.95~~ **$15.** *Ecology, Ideology and Power*. Reactionary motives of elite behind population and resource control. 162 pp., ~~$14.95~~ **$13.**

Killing us Softly: the Global Depopulation Policy by Kevin Galalae, 146 pp. Both the Why and How. ~~$15.95~~ **$13.**

The Iraq Lie: How the White House Sold the War, by congressman Joseph M. Hoeffel. Bush Lied about WMD -- and went ahead with war. ~~$14.95~~ **$13**

JFK-911: 50 Years of Deep State. Was an Israeli strategy behind the JFK and 9/11 murders? 238 pp, ~~$15.95~~ **$13.00**.

Subverting Syria: How CIA Contra Gangs and NGO's Manufacture, Mislabel and Market Mass Murder. Syrian "rebels" are US-backed provocateurs. 115 pp, ~~$10.00~~ **$7.50**.

The Money Power: *Empire of the City* and *Pawns in the Game*. The illuminist Three World Wars conspiracy – two geopolitics classics in one volume. 320 pp., ~~$16.95~~ **$13**

Four More by Michel Chossudovsky

Towards a World War III Scenario: The Dangers of Nuclear War. The Pentagon is preparing a first-strike nuclear attack on Iran. 103 pp, ~~$15.95~~ **$10**.

The Global Economic Crisis: The Great Depression of the XXI Century. by Prof. Chossudovsky with a dozen other experts. 416 pp, ~~$25.95~~ **$15**.

The Globalization of Poverty and the New World Order. Corporatism feeds on poverty, pollution, apartheid, racism, sexism, and ethnic strife. 401 pp, ~~$27.95~~ **$17**.

America's "War on Terrorism" Wide-reaching, hard-hitting geopolitical study on 9/11. 387 pp, ~~$22.95~~ **$14**.

Four More by F. Wm. Engdahl

A Century of War: Anglo-American Oil Politics and the New World Order. The empire controls the oil to control the world. 352 pp, ~~$25~~ **$15**.

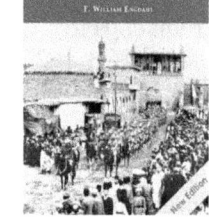

Full Spectrum Dominance: Totalitarian Democracy in the New World Order. They are out for total control: land, sea, air, space, outer space, cyberspace, media, money, movements. 258 pp, ~~$23.95~~ **$19**.

Gods of Money: Wall Street and the Death of the American Century. The banksters stop at nothing to foment chaos and corruption. 390 pp. ~~$24.95~~ **$15**.

Seeds of Destruction: The Hidden Agenda of Genetic Manipulation. A corporate gang is out for complete control of the world by patenting our food. Inside the corporate boardrooms and science labs, a world of greed, intrigue, corruption and coercion. 340 pp. ~~$25.95~~ **$19.95**.

Six by Webster Griffin Tarpley

9/11 Synthetic Terror: Made in USA — by a network of moles, patsies, killers, corrupt politicians and media. The authoritative account of 9/11. "Strongest of the 770+ books I have reviewed" – R. Steele. 5th ed., 569 pp., $19.95 **$14**. In Spanish: ***11-S Falso Terrorismo***. 408 pp, **$15**.

George Bush: The Unauthorized Biography Vivid X-ray of the oligarchy dominating U.S. politics, with a full narrative of GWHB's long list of crimes. How Skull-and-Bonesmen Bush and Brown Bros. Harriman made fortunes building up Hitler's war machine. Bush Sr. linked to Iran-Contra, Watergate, and war crimes like luring Iraq to attack Kuwait. 700 pp, $19.95 **$11**.

Barack H. Obama: the Unauthorized Biography The abject corruption of a Wall Street lackey, with a richly detailed profile of the finance oligarchy. 595 pp, $19.95 **$18**.

Obama – The Postmodern Coup: Making of a Manchurian Candidate. The Obama puppet's advisors are radical reactionaries. This work distills decades of astute political insight and analysis. 320 pp, $15.95 **$6**.

Surviving the Cataclysm, *Your Guide through the Greatest Financial Crisis in Human History*, by W.G. Tarpley. Detailed history of the financier oligarchy who plunder our nation. How to cope with the crisis. 668 pp, $25 **$16**.

Just Too Weird: Bishop Romney and the Mormon Putsch against America; Polygamy, Theocracy, and Subversion, by Webster Tarpley. 284 pp., $14.95 **$10**.

Two by Henry Makow

Illuminati: Cult that Hijacked the World tackles taboos like Zionism, British Empire, Holocaust denial. How international bankers stole a monopoly on government credit, and took over the world. They run it all: wars, schools, media. 249 pp, $19.95 **$13**.

Illuminati 2: Deception & Seduction, more hidden history. 285 pp. $19.95 **$14**.

History

Two by George Seldes: ***1,000 Americans Who Rule the USA*** (1947, 324 pp, $18.95 **$13**) and ***Facts and Fascism*** (1943, 292 pp., $15.95 **$12**) by the great muckraking journalist, whistleblower on the plutocrats who keep the media in lockstep, and finance fascism.

Afghanistan: A Window on the Tragedy. 98 black and white photos, how life goes on amid the ruins. 110 pp, $19.95 **$3.00**.

Enemies by Design: Inventing the War on Terrorism. A century of imperialism in the Middle East. Bio of Osama bin Ladeen; Zionization of America; PNAC, Afghanistan, Palestine, Iraq; 416 pp, $17.95 **$10.00**.

Global Predator: US Wars for Empire. A damning account of the atrocities committed by US armed forces over two centuries. Also by Stewart H. Ross: ***Propaganda for War: How the US was Conditioned to Fight the Great War*** Propaganda by Britain and her agents like Teddy Roosevelt sucked the USA into the war to smash the old world order. 350 pp and $18.95 **$15** each.

Inside the Gestapo: Hitler's Shadow over the World. Intimate, fascinating tale of ruthlessness, intrigue, and geopolitics. 287 pp, $17.95 **$14**.

The Nazi Hydra in America: Suppressed History of a Century. US plutocrats launched Hitler, then recouped Nazi assets to erect today's police state. Fascists won WWII -- they ran both sides. "Shocking and sobering... deserves to be widely read." – Howard Zinn. 700 pp, $19.95 **$12**.

Sunk: The Story of the Japanese Submarine Fleet, 1941-1945. The bravery of doomed men in a lost cause, against impossible odds. 300 pp, $15.95 **$13**.

Terrorism and the Illuminati: A 3000-Year History. "Islamic" terrorists are tentacles of western imperialism— the Illuminati. 332 pp, $16.95 **$13**.

Psychology: Brainwashing

What is brainwashing? What traits help us resist? Self-directedness, sense of purpose, loved ones...

The Rape of the Mind: The Psychology of Thought Control, Menticide and Brainwashing. Tools for self-defense against torture or social pressure; Conditioning in open and closed societies. 320 pp, $16.95 **$12**.

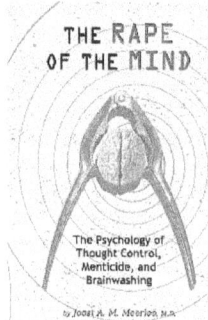

The Telescreen: An Empirical Study of the Destruction of Consciousness, by Prof. Jeffrey Grupp. Mass media brainwash us with consumerism and war propaganda. Fake history, news, issues. 199 pp, $14.95 **$10**. Also by Grupp:

Telementation: Cosmic Feeling and the Law of Attraction. Deep feeling rather than thought or faith is our secret nature and key to self-realization. 124 pp, $12.95 **$8.00**.

Conspiracy, NWO

Corporatism: the Secret Government of the New World Order by Prof. Jeffrey Grupp. Corporations control all world resources, media, information and institutions. Their New World Order is the "prison planet." 408 pp, $16.95. 408 pp, $16.95 **$12**.

Descent into Slavery? How the banksters took over America and the world. Founding Fathers, Rothschilds, the Crown and the City, the world wars, and globalization. 310 pp, $16 **$11**.

Dope Inc.: Britain's Opium War against the United States. "The Book that Drove Kissinger Crazy." Underground Classic, new edition. 320 pp, $19.95 **$15**.

Final Warning: A History of the New World Order. Classic, in-depth research into the Great Conspiracy: the Fed, the CFR, Trilateral Commission, Illuminati. 360 pp, $14.95 **$15**.

In Search of the Truth: an Exposure of the Conspiracy. Spies, Sufism, and the NWO in the USSR and the West. A portrait of our times, society and religion, and the threat we face. 208 pp, $17 **$13**

How the World Really Works by A.B. Jones. Crash course in conspiracy offers digests of 11 classics like *Tragedy and Hope, Creature from Jekyll Island*. 336 pp, $15 **$9.00**.

The Triumph of Consciousness by Chris Clark. The real Global Warming and Greening agenda: more hegemony by the NWO. 347 pp, $19.95 **$15**.

Conspiracy: False Flag Operations

9/11 on Trial: The W T C Collapse. 20 closely argued proofs the World Trade Center was destroyed by controlled demolition. 192 pp, $12.95 **$6.00**.

Conspiracies, Conspiracy Theories and the Secrets of 9/11, German best-seller explores conspiracy in history, before tackling 9/11. 274 pp, $14.95 **$9.00**.

Enigma of Gunpowder Plot 1605: *The Third Solution*. Guy Fawkes was a patsy in a false-flag terror scheme by England's War Party. 528 pp, hardback, sale price: **$55**.

Gladio, NATO's Dagger at the Heart of Europe: *The Pentagon-Mafia-Nazi Terror Axis*. The blood-red thread of terror by NATO death squads across Europe, 1945 to 2012. 488 pp, $29.95 **$17**.

Terror on the Tube: Behind the Veil of 7/7, an Investigation. The only book with the glaring evidence that all four Muslim scapegoats were completely innocent. 322 pp, $17.77 **$15**.

Truth Jihad: *My Epic Struggle Against the 9/11 Big Lie*. Kevin Barrett's seriously funny story. 224 pp, $9.95 **$5.00**.

Coming Soon

ISIS IS US: *The Shocking Truth*.
NWO in Action: Subjugating the Middle East
A Prisoner's Diary.

E-Books:

9/11 Synthetic Terror; Barack Obama Unauthorized Biography; Gladio; Iraq Lie; ISIS IS US, JFK-911; Just Too Weird; Fall of the Arab Spring; Killing us Softly; Nazi Hydra; Rape of the Mind; Subverting Syria; Surviving the Cataclysm; Target: China

~ **PROGRESSIVEPRESS.COM** ~

www.ingramcontent.com/pod-product-compliance
Lightning Source LLC
Chambersburg PA
CBHW081215170426
43198CB00017B/2618